DEADLY SECRETS

DEADLY SECRETS

The CIA-Mafia War Against Castro and the Assassination of J.F.K.

WARREN HINCKLE

WILLIAM W. TURNER

Thunder's Mouth Press

NEW YORK

To Bentley and Marge
and to
the CIA men who wouldn't

Portions of the introduction to the second edition previously appeared in a slightly different form in the San Francisco *Examiner*.

First Thunder's Mouth trade paperback edition.
First printing, 1993.

Published by Thunder's Mouth Press
632 Broadway, 7th Floor
New York, NY 10012

Reprint. Originally published under the title, *The Fish Is Red*, by Harper and Row, ©1981.
Hinckle, Warren
   Deadly secrets: the CIA-Mafia war against Castro and the assassination of JFK/Warren Hinckle and William W. Turner.
      p.   cm.
   Rev. ed. of The Fish is red 1st ed. 1981
   Includes bibliographic references and index.
   ISBN 1-56025-53-4
   1. United States—Foreign relations—Cuba. 2. Cuba—Foreign rela-
tions. 3. Castro, Fidel, 1927-. 4. United States, Central Intelligence
Agency, 5. Subversive Activities—Cuba. 6. Kennedy, John F. (John
Fitzgerald), 1917-1963-Assassination. 7. Mafia—Cuba. 8. Espi-
onage, American—Cuba.
   I. Turner, William W. II. Hinckle, Warren. Fish is red.
III. Title.
E183.8.C9H55   1992
364.15'24'0973-dc20   92-22925
                                                           CIP

Text design by Glen M. Edelstein.

Distributed by Publishers Group West
4065 Hollis Street
Emeryville, CA 94608
(800) 788-3123

"Alert!
Alert!
Look well at the rainbow.
The first will rise very soon.
Chico is in the house.
Visit him.
The sky is blue. . . . The fish is red."

*—from E. Howard Hunt's coded
CIA radio message to Cuba to deceive Castro
about the nature of the Bay of Pigs invasion.
Castro was not deceived.*

CONTENTS

ACKNOWLEDGMENTS

THE Secret War against Fidel Castro and his Cuban regime, which began just prior to the moment of revolutionary victory in 1959, stretched through the 1960s into the ensuing decades and endures, vestigially at least, to this day, is a significant gap in America's modern military and political history. Despite the voluminous literature on the Eisenhower, Kennedy, Johnson, and Nixon administrations, nothing has previously been written that even approaches a book-length chronicle of the Secret War and virtually nothing at all has been written about the Reagan-Bush administration's revival of the Secret War in its most insidious forms. A plethora of books and articles has been written on the Bay of Pigs invasion, the most visible event of the Secret War, but this is like writing the history of the Battle of the Bulge while never addressing the larger issue of World War II. Similarly, the many books about Watergate and the accounts of the Iran-Contra affair published to date are analogous to histories of individual campaigns rather than the overall war. The developing literature of the John F. Kennedy assassination has reinforced and in many areas supplemented the authors' original view when this study was first published in 1981: that the JFK assassination was rooted in the deadly secrets of the clandestine alliances forged to assassinate Fidel Castro and overthrow the Cuban government.

Part of the void can be attributed to the understandable reluctance of those involved in the Secret War to avoid dwelling on their own failures, and in some cases their successes. For many the personal trauma was so painful that it was justifiably a reason to try to forget. Part is due to the fact that the Secret War was compartmentalized, with no one person able to span, if so inclined, its formidable length. We also encountered a reluctance to kick dead horses, and at times ran headlong into the CIA's fabled secrecy oath (Grayston Lynch, for example, said he had been cleared by the agency to talk about events up to and including the Bay of Pigs, but not beyond. Asked what the consequences might be if he breached that clearance, he said that he was on a CIA pension, and the checks might stop.)

Since the late 1960s when we began work on this book, we have personally interviewed over 200 veterans of the Secret War and have had access in our research to the unpublished papers of participant-historians of the anti-Castro movement, research materials at the University of California on the co-mingling of organized crime and American intelligence activities, and internal FBI and CIA documents relating to Secret War activities.

We have extensively consulted and brought into our narrative the Kefauver and McClellan crime hearings and the U.S. Senate hearings on intelligence activities in the United States. Our files have been consulted by staff members of the House Assassinations Committee, and material obtained from that source is incorporated in this book. We have also interviewed Cuban government officials in Cuba.

Additional documentation has come from the National Archives in Washington, D.C., and the files of newspapers in New York, San Francisco, Las Vegas, Miami, and Havana. In the course of our research we have had access to the files of the paramilitary Minutemen, and of former New Orleans District Attorney Jim Garrison, whose own late 1960s investigation of the John F. Kennedy assassination has taken on new significance in light of the work of the House Assassinations Committee, which retreaded much of Garrison's then ridiculed ground.

We have been careful in this narrative to balance the statements of present and former government officials we interviewed and official testimony before Senate bodies with the personal accounts of our paramilitary sources which include organized crime figures, soldiers of fortune, and pro- and anti-Castro Cubans. Extraordinary about the research is the considerable number of times the accounts of the surface world and of the netherworld dovetailed; where they have not, we have so indicated.

Many of the men who provided us with information are not written about in the newspaper; they would sooner play Russian roulette than testify before a Senate committee. They did the flying and the fighting and the killing in the dirtiest, most secret war in American history. Some of them have been murdered since we interviewed them. In the course of researching this book we have come to respect many of these adventurers as individuals and have come to understand them as men who were acting out of principle, while disagreeing with the politics that motivated them. We have eaten stone crabs and gone drinking with some of these characters; some have visited our homes regularly. We consider their stories unique in the annals of American dementia — stories out of a Cold War Catch-22.

Some of these people we can only thank anonymously, for reasons which become obvious in the narrative. We also owe a considerable debt to those we interviewed whose positions in government or the press put them in a unique position to shed light on aspects of the Secret War. Among them:

In Providence, Rhode Island, former CIA inspector general Lyman B. Kirkpatrick commented from the agency's vantage point and graciously instructed us in the art of opening a bottle of wine without a corkscrew. In Miami, a former president of Cuba, since deceased, Dr. Carlos Prío, talked at length about the intrigues in the anti-Castro movement. The enigmatic and dreaded Rolando Masferrer, known as the Darth Vader of pre-Castro Cuba, described his Miami-based fight against his personal enemy Fidel Castro; shortly after we interviewed him Masferrer was killed by a bomb planted in his car. Enrique Ruíz-Williams, an American-educated geologist who was badly injured in the Bay of Pigs invasion, discussed with great fervor his mission as an intermediary between Robert Kennedy and Cuban exile forces being prepared for a possible second invasion as the Kennedys continued the Secret War.

Three of the "Miami four" in the Watergate burglary — Frank Sturgis, Eugenio Martínez, and Virgilio Gonzáles — along with Felipe de Diego, charged (but not convicted) in the burglary of Daniel Ellsberg's psychiatrist's office in Beverly Hills, reminisced about their experiences in CIA-sponsored operations and helped strip some of the mystery from the supersecret Operation 40. A number of American paramilitary advisers and soldiers of fortune were of invaluable assistance. Towering Gerry Patrick Hemming, who helped train exile units, provided a panoramic view of the action-packed madness, including the CIA's mysterious use of Howard Hughes's Caribbean island. Martin X. Casey, a paramilitary historian who participated in air strikes on Haiti, was unstinting in furnishing information and also served as a translator. Pilot Howard K. Davis, who once flew for the rebel forces in Cuba, and former Special Forces Colonel Robert K. Brown, who publishes *Soldier of Fortune* magazine, provided inside paramilitary accounts. Former CIA contract pilots including Robert Plumlee and Carl Davis gave graphic descriptions of their CIA missions into Cuba. Gordon Winslow, a Yankee with a lovely Cuban wife, helped immeasurably in setting up contacts inside the Miami Cuban community.

In Columbus, Ohio, Edward I. Arthur detailed his arms-procuring role with Commandos L, and told about a Mafia bounty of $90,000 he was offered to assassinate Castro. In Powder Springs, Georgia, munitions maker Mitch WerBell was a considerate if devilish host on his tightly guarded estate as he showed us his poison dart collection and discussed over neat Scotches how he supplied weapons and know-how to the anti-Castro irregulars. In New York, Colonel René Leon, a Haitian exile leader, was forthcoming in dealing with the CIA aspects of foiled plots to overthrow "Papa Doc" Duvalier.

Shortly before his death former Ambassador William D. Pawley took time out from his own memoirs to talk to us about his secret attempts to forestall Castro diplomatically and later, in conjunction with the CIA, topple him militarily. Dade County (Miami) district attorney Richard Gerstein helped put in perspective the political and financial chicanery accompanying the campaign against Castro, which led us into the sinuosities of Watergate. Former New Orleans district attorney Jim Garrison allowed us access to his files on the Louisiana phases of the Secret War and the Cuban links to the Kennedy assassination.

Mike McLaney, a tough-talking gambling casino owner dispossessed by Castro, told what he felt he could about free-lance anti-Castro operations he backed. Robert DePugh, founder of the paramilitary right-wing Minutemen, gave many details of the armaments traffic, and his former aide, Jerry Milton Brooks, revealed the who's who of the New Orleans intelligence branch of the Secret War.

Many of our journalist colleagues provided indispensable information. Andrew St. George, who began covering the Cuban revolution when Castro was still in the hills, then became the Lucepress's premier paramilitary journalist, recounted daring exile raids he went on and furnished intimate background information on the face cards of the counterrevolution. Other Lucepress types were also of help: Jay Mallin, once *Time*'s man in Havana, shared his views of exile activities, and Richard Billings, a former *Life* bureau chief in Miami, confirmed the bizarre *Flying Tiger* kidnapping expedition recounted in this book. Jim Savage, the Miami *Herald*'s organized crime specialist, and Haynes Johnson of *The Washington Post*, who authored *The Bay of Pigs*, were most cooperative. Columnists Jack Anderson and Les Whitten generously permitted us access to their files on the CIA–Mafia plots to assassinate Castro.

In Los Angeles, deputy district attorney David Nissen provided early information about Mafioso Johnny Roselli's CIA role. In Washington, D.C., former Kennedy and Johnson White House aides, among them Harry McPherson and John Nolan, were of valuable assistance in providing information on the Secret War.

Ex-CIA official Victor Marchetti and Colonel Fletcher Prouty, an Air Force officer who was CIA liaison, provided otherwise unobtainable insights into the inner workings of the agency. Former CIA employees Elsie and Jim Wilcott discussed with us the internal affairs of the agency's Miami station—during the Secret War the largest CIA station in the world. Attorney Bernard Fensterwald, Jr., opened his counterintelligence files to us, which were packed with documented episodes such as the scheme to sabotage the Cuban economy by counterfeiting pesos.

Among those interviewed who wish to remain unnamed are current FBI agents and Miami detectives, former CIA operatives, a mate on the CIA raider *Rex*, a Cuban exile boat skipper, and some criminals.

We wish to express our gratitude to those who read advance copies of this manuscript and provided helpful critiques: Latin American Specialist Tad Szulc; former banker-turned-novelist and international finance expert Paul Erdman; G. Robert Blakey, former chief counsel and staff director of the House Assassinations Committee; the late distinguished literary critic Maxwell Geismar and his wife, Anne; and Alan Frankovich, director of the excellent documentary film on the CIA, "On Company Business," which was first shown on the PBS network. Sandra Levinson of the Center for Cuban studies in New York was most helpful during the laborious process of updating the original edition of this work.

The following should be acknowledged for their assistance and advice: Emile de Antonio, Jack Blum, Bill Bonanno, Pamela Brunger, Susan Cheever, Harvey Cohen, Peter Collier, Liadian O'Donovan Cook, Bernie Cornfeld, Robert Cowley, Joan Fucillo, Gene Grove, Fredric Hobbs, Joe Ippolitto, Albert Kahn, Mary Kaplan, Ken Kelley, Michael and Eleanora Kennedy, Paul Krassner, Robert Lewis, Marc Libarle, Ester Margolis, John Marks, Terry McDonnell, Marcia Nasatir, Patrick Nolan, Ellen Ray, Ted Rubenstein, Bill Schaap, Peter Dale Scott, Ingvar Tornberg, and Bob Weil.

The authors owe special debts of thanks to the learned Steve Wasserman, who was research director in the manuscript stage of this long project; to our agent, Barbara Lowenstein, a guerrilla fighter on publishing terms; to Andrew St. George, a photojournalist, who is nothing but *sui generis*, who made available his private collection of Secret War photographs for this book; and to Thom Hartmann and Lamar Waldron of Marietta, Georgia, who were generous with their own research and provided a vital publishing link.

CHRONOLOGY

1933 Franklin Roosevelt adopts the Good Neighbor Policy toward Latin America.

1942 Office of Strategic Services formed.

1947 Central Intelligence Agency and National Security Council formed.

1948 While at Yale, George Bush joins Skull and Bones, the secret society that many consider to be a recruiting ground for the CIA.

March 10, 1952 Cuban president Carlos Prío Socarras overthrown in a coup led by Fulgencio Batista.

1954 President Eisenhower forms the Doolittle Commission. Its report recommended that the U.S. "learn to subvert, sabotage, and destroy our enemies by more clever, more sophisticated, and more effective methods than those used against us."

January 1959 Castro takes control of Cuba.

December 1959 Col. J. C. King, chief of the CIA's Western Hemisphere Division, sends a memo to CIA Director Allen Dulles. Calling Castro's regime a "far-left dictatorship" King offers several recommendations, including the "elimination of Fidel Castro." Dulles approves assassination of Castro.

January 1960   Dulles proposes the idea of a "Cuba Project" to the Special Group, a subcommittee of the National Security Council established to consider CIA operational proposals.

March 1960   At a meeting of the NSC's Cuba Task Force, Col. King announces a special policy paper citing evidence that Cuban leaders were considering an attack on the U.S. Naval Base at Guantanamo Bay. President Eisenhower tells Dulles that he will sign a National Security directive, eliminating the need for NSC approval of the CIA's secret operations.

May 1960   CIA unifies several principal Cuban exile groups into the Democratic Revolutionary Front, providing office space, salaries, and funding.

September 1960   CIA operative Robert Maheu recruits mobster Johnny Roselli to assassinate Castro.

November 18, 1960   Richard Bissell and Alan Dulles brief President-elect Kennedy about plans for a CIA-led invasion of Cuba.

1961   In a classified memo, the FBI advises the CIA that mob boss Sam Giancana had boasted to several people that "Fidel Castro was to be done away with very shortly."

January 1961   JFK sworn in as President.

April 1961   Bay of Pigs invasion of Cuba, code named "Operation Zapata," fails. Anti-Castro Cubans and various CIA operatives are infuriated because they believe Kennedy refused to provide military air cover for the operation.

Sept. and Oct. 1961   In Cuba, two separate plots to assassinate Castro are thwarted. The second is materminded by Antonio Veciana, a Cuban accountant specializing in sending embezzled government funds to the exile community in Miami. Veciana went on to found Alpha 66, one of the most militant of the exile groups.

October 1961   JFK orders the Joint Chiefs of Staff to begin planning a second invasion of Cuba.

November 28, 1961   Kennedy fires CIA Director Allen Dulles.

November 30, 1961   Operation Mongoose, a multi-pronged action plan aimed at overthrowing the Castro government, is launched at the directive of JFK.

December 1961   In Operation Fantasma, part of Operation Mongoose, contract pilots drop leaflets over Cuban cities, urging Cubans to form "phantom cells" for sabotage against the Castro regime.

1962   Prescott Bush, Sr. (father of George) and William Casey form the National Strategic Information Center, a right-wing think tank advocating increased covert operations.

1962–63   Angered by CIA incompetence during the Bay of Pigs, JFK establishes several measures limiting the power of the agency.

August 24, 1962   Attempted assassination of Castro by CIA-backed Cuban Student Directorate fails.

October 1962   Cuban Missile Crisis. JFK makes nonaggression pact with Cuba.

Late Fall 1962   JFK suspends diplomatic relations with Haiti in protest over abuses by dictator François "Papa Doc" Duvalier. Six years of covert CIA-backed invasion and assassination plots ensue.

January 11, 1963   Dean Rusk, testifying before the Senate Foreign Relations Committee, admits that the U.S.'s nonaggression pact with Cuba is worthless, since it had been contingent upon on-site inspection of Cuban missiles—a condition that Castro refused.

June 1963   JFK orders escalation of sabotage against Cuban infrastructure.

Summer 1963   Lee Harvey Oswald begins passing out pro-Castro pamphlets in downtown New Orleans, using the office of rabidly anti-Castro Guy Banister as his headquarters.

September 7, 1963   Castro tells Daniel Harker of the Associated Press: "United States leaders should think that if they assist in terrorist plans to eliminate Cuban leaders, they themselves will not be safe."

Late September 1963   JFK authorizes William Attwood, the President's special adviser for African Affairs at the UN, to meet secretly with Cuba's UN envoy to discuss the possibility of negotiations between the two nations.

September 26–October 3, 1963   Dates that the CIA claimed Lee Harvey Oswald visited the Cuban and Soviet Embassies in Mexico City.

October 1963   Jack Ruby and Lee Harvey Oswald reportedly meet in Dallas at Ruby's nightclub, The Carousel.

October 1963   Arthur Krock, in a *New York Times* editorial, quotes a "high U.S. official" stationed in Vietnam as saying the CIA's growth was like "a malignancy" and that "if the United States ever experiences [or attempt a coup to overthrow the government] it will come from the CIA and not the Pentagon."

November 18, 1963   Attwood, on the President's instructions, calls a top Castro aide and suggests preliminary negotiations at the UN.

November 22, 1963   John F. Kennedy assassinated in Dallas.

November 29, 1963   Lyndon Johnson establishes the President's Commission on the Assassination of President Kennedy, chaired by Chief Justice Earl Warren and including recently fired CIA head Allen Dulles.

September 27, 1964   Warren Commission releases its report. It ruled out conspiracy and concluded that Oswald acted alone.

June 5, 1968   Presidential candidate Robert Kennedy assassinated in California.

January 1969   Richard Nixon sworn in as President.

July 1969   Nixon dispatches Nelson Rockefeller to Haiti to normalize relations with the Duvalier government.

March 1970   U.S. intelligence passes swine fever virus to a terrorist group for use in decimating Cuba's pig herds.

October 1971   CIA-backed attempt to assassinate Castro on a state visit to Chile fails.

March 1972   John Mitchell, head of the Committee to Re-elect the President, approves Operation Gemstone, an espionage and dirty tricks campaign against the Democrats.

May–June 1972   Watergate break-ins. Frank Sturgis, E. Howard Hunt, G. Gordon Liddy, and Charles Colson (among others) are implicated.

June 1972   Frank Sturgis, Eugenio Martínez, Virgilio González, James McCord, and Bernard L. Barker arrested in second Watergate break-in.

August 1974   Nixon resigns.

June 19, 1975   Days before he was scheduled to appear before the Senate Intelligence Committee, mob boss Sam Giancana is shot point-blank in his Chicago home.

1976   George Bush appointed director of the CIA.

1976   Orlando Bosch and other right-wing Cuban exiles form CORU (the Command of United Revolutionary Organizations), partly at the instigation of the CIA. The new umbrella group claims seventy-six murders in its first four months of existence.

March 29, 1977   George deMohrenschildt found dead from a shotgun blast—an "apparent suicide"—just before a scheduled interview with the House Select Committee. DeMohrenschildt was a CIA contract agent with ties to Lee Harvey Oswald. DeMohrenschildt's phone book eventually became public, and included the following entry: "Bush, George H.W. (Poppy). 1412 W. Ohio also Zapata Petroleum Midland."

September 1977   During a debate with author Mark Lane, David Atlee Philips admits "there never was a photograph taken of Lee Harvey Oswald in Mexico City."

1978   Maria Lorenz, former CIA operative, testifies before the House Select Committee. In her testimony, she claims to have traveled from a CIA safe house in Miami to Dallas, days before the assassination. The heavily armed caravan also included several other CIA operatives and anti-Castro Cubans. Lorenz, who left Dallas before November 22, would later claim that Frank Sturgis told her, "We killed the President that day. You could have been part of it—you know, part of history."

October 5, 1986 C–123K Contra resupply cargo plane shot down over Nicaragua. Pilot Eugene Hasenfus survives to tell his story, which eventually leads to the discovery of the Iran–Contra network. Members of the Cuban exile community who played a role in the Contra resupply scheme included Felix I. Rodriquez — who had volunteered to assassinate Castro in 1961 — and Operation 40 member Luis Posada Carriles.

September 1987 Castro brings in from the cold twenty-seven double agents. On television, the agents give their accounts of CIA plots, including assassination, against Cuba.

July–August 1988 The *Nation* publishes two articles charging that George Bush's involvement with the CIA goes back to 1960–61, despite Bush's insistence that he was not involved with the Agency before he was appointed its Director in 1976.

AGENTS, ASSETS, AND COVERT OPERATORS

Manuel Artime   Cuban exile leader and the CIA's golden boy who headed the Movement for the Recovery of the Revolution (MRR). Developed Operation Second Naval Guerrilla, a campaign of attacks on Cuban shipping and shore installations.

W. Guy Banister   Private detective in New Orleans who headed the FBI's Chicago office until 1955. Active in facilitating paramilitary attacks on Cuba. Allowed Lee Harvey Oswald to use office space and store pro-Castro literature at his agency in a possible attempt to paint Oswald as a pro-Castro communist.

Dr. Orlando Bosch   Right-wing Cuban exile, organizer of and participant in numerous air raids and acts of sabotage against Cuba. Leader of the far right groups the MIRR (Insurrectional Movement of the Recovery of the Revolution) and Cuban Action. Served four years in a U.S. prison for the attempted sinking of a Polish freighter in Miami Harbor, but later resumed his anti-Castro efforts. Suspected of, although never convicted of, the 1976 bombing of Cubana Airlines Flight 455 that killed seventy-three people.

Allen Dulles   Director of the Central Intelligence Agency from 1953 through 1961. (John Foster Dulles, his brother, was Secretary of State from 1953 to 1959.) Proposed formation of the Special Group, a National Security Council subcommittee, to screen the CIA's operational proposals. Member of the Warren Commission, 1963–64.

David William Ferrie   CIA contract employee, associate of Guy Banister. Briefly commanded Lee Harvey Oswald during Oswald's high school stint in the Civil Air Patrol. Flew firebomb raids against Cuba in 1959, helped train exiles for a land invasion of Cuba, and worked to purge dissidents from the Cuban Revolutionary Council. In February 1967, after New Orleans DA Jim Garrison began investigating Ferrie's CIA past in relation to JFK's assassination, Ferrie was found dead in his apartment of mysterious causes.

Sam Giancana   Chicago Mafia capo and CIA operative who conspired with Johnny Roselli to assassinate Castro. Shot to death in his home on June 19, 1975, just days before he was scheduled to testify on Castro assassination plots before the Senate Intelligence Committee.

William K. Harvey   Headed covert action section of the CIA during the early 1950s, and in the early 1960s developed ZR/RIFLE, the CIA's "Executive Action" (assassination) group. Head of Cuban Task Force W; directly supervised Johnny Roselli's attempts to assassinate Castro.

Richard Helms   Became the CIA's chief of clandestine services in 1962; headed Operation Mongoose, CIA enterprise to infiltrate and overthrow Castro's regime. Deputy director of CIA, 1965–66; Director, 1966–73. In 1977 pleaded no contest to two charges of failing to testify "fully and completely" before Congress.

Gerry Patrick Hemming   Onetime member of Castro's rebel army who soured on the revolution and left Cuba. Leader of the Intercontinental Penetration Force, an anti-Castro paramilitary group independent of the CIA.

E. Howard Hunt   CIA operative active in assassination attempts on Castro and invasions of Cuba. Watergate conspirator and author of dime-store spy novels.

H. L. Hunt   Texas oil millionaire who provided financial backing for bombing raids on Cuba and Orlando Bosch's MIRR.

Edward G. Lansdale Air Force Major General who directed the Philippine government's campaign against the Huk guerrillas and guided the Diem regime in Vietnam. Chosen by JFK to revitalize the CIA's efforts against Cuba.

Maria Lorenz Former mistress of Fidel Castro, she has worked with several U.S. intelligence agencies, most notably the CIA. Lorenz would later claim that she was part of a heavily armed caravan that traveled from Miami to Dallas several days prior to the assassination of JFK. The caravan included Orlando Bosch, Frank Sturgis (the operative who recruited Lorenz into the CIA), Major Pedro Diaz Lanz, Gerry Patrick Hemming, and the Novos brothers. Once in Dallas, Lorenz says, her group met with E. Howard Hunt and Jack Ruby.

Robert Maheu Contract employee for the CIA from the mid-fifties, former FBI agent who managed Howard Hughes's Las Vegas interests. Provided link between Hughes and the CIA; recruited Johnny Roselli to assassinate Castro.

Eugenio "Rolando" Martínez One of the Cuba Project's highest paid and most accomplished operatives, who made more clandestine boat runs to Cuba than anyone else. Member of the Watergate burglary team.

John A. McCone Director of the Central Intelligence Agency, 1961–65.

Guillermo and Ignacio Novo Brothers and anti-Castro Cuban exiles. They, along with American Michael Townley, were convicted of the 1976 assassination of Orland Letelier, the Chilean ambassador to the U.S. At their trial, Guillermo insisted that Townley was a CIA operative and that the Agency was responsible for the murder. According to Maria Lorenz, the Novos brothers were also part of the caravan that traveled to Dallas several days before the Kennedy assassination.

David Atlee Phillips CIA's head of operations for the Western Hemisphere in the 1960s, and covert operative in Havana from 1958 to 1961. He blamed Kennedy for the failure of the Bay of Pigs, and was seen meeting with Lee Harvey Oswald prior to the assassination of JFK. Phillips is believed to have used the alias "Maurice Bishop."

Carlos Prío   Cuban president overthrown in 1952 coup. From exile in Miami plotted with Castro to oust Batista; afterwards plotted to oust Castro. Head of Cuban Americans for Nixon-Agnew. Death in 1974 termed a suicide.

Johnny Roselli   Mobster drafted by the CIA to assassinate Castro. Found dead in Dumbfoundling Bay near Miami in August 1976.

Joaquin Sanjenis   Cuban-born CIA operative and head of Operation 40, a top-secret group formed to eliminate Cuban leftists and middle-of-the-roaders after the unsuccessful Bay of Pigs invasion. When invasion did not succeed, the group was reassigned to eliminate anti-Castro leftists from the exile movement. Retired in 1972, died in 1974 of natural causes.

Frank Sturgis   CIA operative who ran guns to Castro before the revolution and who later helped organize paramilitary operations against him. Recruited Castro's ex-mistress, Maria Lorenz, to assassinate the Cuban leader. Arrested in the Watergate break-in.

Santos Trafficante   Miami Mafia capo, worked with Roselli, Giancana, and Maheu on elimination of Castro; brought former Cuban prime minister in to poison Castro.

Antonio Veciana   Founder of the anti-Castro group Alpha 66, Veciana claims that approximately three months prior to the JFK assassination, he saw a man he knew as "Maurice Bishop" speak to a man who would soon be revealed as Lee Harvey Oswald. Veciana also said that "Bishop" (the CIA alias of David Atlee Phillips) asked him to fabricate a story that Oswald had visited the Cuban embassy in Mexico City.

Mitch WerBell   International arms dealer and weapons developer; OSS man with close ties to the CIA. Did prep work for the 1965 invasion of the Dominican Republic; participant in and initiator of Cuban raids and plots to kill Castro.

Enrique "Harry" Ruiz-Williams   Cuban exile and invader during the Bay of Pigs operation. Chosen by RFK to lead a second expedition force of exiles, later scratched by LBJ.

PUBLISHER'S NOTE

DEADLY Secrets: The CIA-Mafia War Against Castro and the Assassination of JFK was first published in 1981 under the title The Fish Is Red. To date, this ground-breaking work stands as the most accurate and comprehensive account of the secret war against Fidel Castro—a vast, clandestine struggle spanning more than three decades.

Deadly Secrets probes the hidden workings of our foreign and domestic intelligence communities, including collaboration with the Mafia, the obsessive involvement of several presidential administrations, and the zeal of paramilitary forces—particularly Cuban exiles based in Miami and Latin America who were armed and encouraged to "neutralize" Castro and the Cuban leadership. But beyond the Bay of Pigs and the deceptive, internecine struggles within the U.S. government, beyond the silence and complicity of the American press, beyond Watergate and the Mafia, Deadly Secrets reveals the ironic twists by which assassination plots turned and took the life of a president.

This new edition has been updated to incorporate further details and revelations that have emerged since the first publication. In the new introduction, Warren Hinckle and William Turner explore the myriad threads of George Bush's involvement in this covert operation.

It has been said that those who do not learn from the past are doomed to repeat it; *Deadly Secrets* uncovers a hidden chapter of this nation's history that should not be ignored.

INTRODUCTION
George Bush's Deadly Secrets

I

PRESIDENT Bush's father, Prescott Sr., once stole Geronimo's skull. When people asked him if he had it, he said of course not. He lied. It is a fine Eastern-seaboard Wasp tradition to lie for a good cause. Like father, like son.

The late Prescott Bush, Sr., a Republican senator from Connecticut, was a great golfer and a Whiffenpoofer who sang a mean harmony. His cause was Skull and Bones, the secret Yale society with roots somewhere back in the trenches of seventeenth-century Bavaria. When Bush Sr. and another Skull and Bones joker stole Geronimo's skull from his grave in Fort Sill, Oklahoma, they took it to the windowless Skull and Bones building on the Yale campus, and hid it like a dog would a bone. The Apaches were darn mad. Decades later, when they came to Yale to try to get their main man's skull back, a representative of the Apaches claimed that the Bonesmen tried to palm someone else's skull off on them.[1]

George Bush joined Skull and Bones in 1948, along with a bunch of spooks-to-be — the society has more CIA men than the Vatican has cardinals. There he partook of the usual secret initiation rites such as telling his sexual history to the group. (Bonesmen have few secrets from each other, but the rest of the world is for lying to. Like father, like son.)

George Bush matured in a moral atmosphere where lying is an art form — and Bush has had lots of practice. As Director of the Central Intelligence Agency, where prevarication is a competitive lifestyle, he stonewalled the Justice Department to protect Richard Helms, and in doing so kept the CIA's dirty secrets — its illegal domestic operations, the agency's strategic alliances with drug lords and narcoterrorists, and the dealings of the agents it had recruited to assassinate Fidel Castro of Cuba. As Vice President of the United States under the somnolent Reagan, Bush helped arm the Contras at a time when that was against the law — and he lied like a rug about it. By the time he became President in his own right in 1989, George Bush was without compeer the most accomplished liar in American politics.

Participation in the "clandestine services of the United States" (as the Puck of Watergate, E. Howard Hunt, reverentially refers to it) is a Bush family tradition. Prescott Bush, Sr., had served in army intelligence during World War I. In 1962, Prescott Sr. and William J. Casey, an old friend, an old hand from the Office of Strategic Services (the OSS was the CIA's father figure) and Ronald Reagan's CIA director during the Iran-Contra scandal, set up the National Strategic Information Center, a right-wing think tank which has, among other things, advocated increased covert operations. (The NSIC's recommendations have been more than welcome in the Bush administration.) Prescott Jr., George Bush's older brother, is a prominent member of the Americares Foundation, which has been linked to efforts to aid far-right elements in Honduras and Guatemala.[2]

George Bush's Skull-and-Bones networking and his family's intelligence connections have materially shaped his life. Young George was husbanded into the oil business by Henry Neil Mallon, an old family friend and Skull and Bonesman who had done his part for the commonweal by helping Allen Dulles recruit people into the CIA.[3] Whether Mallon actually recruited Bush *fils* into the CIA remains unknown, although Bush has obliquely hinted at his connections with the agency. In his 1988 campaign autobiography, *Looking*

Forward, Bush wrote that when President Gerald Ford appointed him CIA director in 1976, "I'd come to the CIA with some general knowledge of how it operated."[4]

George Bush made his first real money through offshore oil drilling in the Caribbean in the late 1950s, and Castro's revolution could hardly have been construed as anything but bad news for the freebooting oil fraternity—as it was for the CIA. At the time of the Bay of Pigs invasion in 1961, Bush had rigs positioned thirty miles north of Cuba near Cay Sal, coincidentally an island the CIA used as a service station for covert operations.

(The oil business and the intelligence business have long been hand-in-glove. The CIA was doing the bidding of the American oil companies even before the landmark year of 1953, when CIA operative Kermit Roosevelt—grandson of Teddy and cousin to FDR—was dispatched to Iran by Secretary of State John Foster Dulles and his CIA-director brother Allen Dulles to get rid of "that madman Mosadegh." In retrospect the coup was unfortunate for American foreign policy since the reinstated Shah was eventually tossed out, and the Ayatollah and the mullahs took charge of Iran's oil. Even so, a CIA-sympathetic oil man would see a military solution as the best solution when Saddam Hussein's threat to a feudal oil monarchy threatened U.S. access to fossil fuels. For oil, Bush acted like the cow that jumped over the moon. But on two other epochal events of his presidency, the demise of Red Russia and the collapse of the S&Ls, he was as slow to choose as a teenager in a record shop.)

If the young George Bush was not a CIA "asset," he was certainly user-friendly to the agency. He could not have been anything else considering that his family brought him up to revere spooks, and from a tender age he kept their company. Two of his tapmates in the Skull and Bones went on to become top CIA operatives in the 1950s.[5] Another fraternity-mate, William F. Buckley, Jr., was assigned to the CIA station in Mexico City in the 1950s, when E. Howard Hunt was in charge. George Bush's 1980 grab for the presidential gold ring was supported by a virtual army of spies. Retired CIA agents came out of the shadows to do precinct work. *The Washington Post* reported that "no presidential campaign in recent memory—perhaps ever—has attracted as much support from the intelligence community as the campaign of former CIA director George Bush."[6] When Bush had to console himself with the second spot on the ticket—his selection as Veep was engineered by his father's friend, Reagan's all-knowing campaign manager, William Casey—Bush's spook supporters moved en masse into the Reagan-Bush campaign.

During his attempt to wrestle the Republican nomination from Ronald Reagan, Bush received campaign contributions from Skull and Bones members with go-go messages written on the checks in the Yale society's secret code. In 1981 when Bush and his wife, Barbara, hosted a reunion of his Skull and Bones class at the vice presidential mansion in the federal city, twelve aging Bonesmen and their spouses attended (a group photo published in *The Washington Post* memorializes the occasion). The intelligence community had reason to go all the way for George. As DCI—CIA shorthand for Director of Central Intelligence—he had burned bridges to keep President Gerald Ford's barking dogs away from the former DCI Richard Helms, who was being pursued in an unholy manner by the Justice Department for lying to Congress. Helms had been running what LBJ had called "a damned Murder Inc. in the Caribbean" and of course Helms lied about that—along with the lying about the plot to kidnap General Schneider of Chile (which resulted in his death) and the other dirty little arrangements involving the CIA, Henry Kissinger, and officials of that symbol of corporate virtue, ITT, to destabilize and overthrow the democratically elected government of Chile. These "arrangements" resulted in the murder of Chilean President Salvador Allende and the installation of a dictatorship. Bush protected Helms to the hilt, helping to keep him a free man. But in 1977 Helms pleaded no contest to two criminal counts of failing to testify "fully, completely and accurately" before Congress. Helms was so distressed by what he considered irreligious attempts to pry into the agency's secrets—the company's "family jewels"—that he accosted Daniel Schorr, then a correspondent for CBS, in a Capitol Hill hallway, calling him a "cocksucker" loud enough for all within the Beltway to hear.[7]

DCI Bush saved some seventy current and former CIA agents from the dock. He performed the rescue by simply refusing to turn the requisite CIA records over to the Justice Department, which was seeking to prosecute the spies. In the course of his defense Bush did not raise the issue of the national interest (as past CIA directors had in similar circumstances) or the Nixonian concept of national security. Instead he took the admirably stubborn position that because the CIA had told its operatives to do what they had done, it could not be a crime.[8]

In one of life's little ironies, Bush's opponent at Justice was then Assistant Attorney General Dick Thornburgh, who was with the department's criminal division. As President Bush's attorney general in 1989 Thornburgh tried to keep the dirty linen of the Iran-Contragate fandango from becoming public. However, back in 1975 Thornburgh didn't believe in stonewalling but his struggles to get Bush to cough up classified documents met with just that — some papers that Bush finally handed over were so fuzzy Thornburgh couldn't read them.

According to an October 14 memorandum by Robert Keuch of the criminal division of the Justice Department, at a meeting on October 2, 1976, then Attorney General Edward Levi had "strongly recommended that neither Mr. Bush nor any other CIA official contact Mr. Helms" about the grand jury investigation.[9] Yet on October 13, Bush wrote both Helms and former CIA Director John McCone telling them a federal grand jury might call them as witnesses, and offering his apologies and CIA assistance in preparing their testimonies.[10] Bush continued in his reluctance to provide documents throughout the fall even after McCone, in a "Dear George" letter dated November 18, warned Bush flat out that he was "greatly troubled" that a CIA official had perjured himself in testimony before Congress.[11] Also that fall then White House counsel Phillip Buchen wrote a thundering letter to President Ford that was somewhat prophetic in view of the national security controversies of the 1980s. Buchen said that Bush's having his way would:

> abort the pending investigation and lead to no prosecution, with the consequences that otherwise prosecutable persons will be saved from prosecution merely to protect their identities and CIA connections from disclosure . . .

Such an outcome would be interpreted by knowledgeable people as setting a precedent for never investigating or prosecuting a confidential source of information, even though he may have committed perjury; also for not prosecuting anyone for any crime if the evidence to do so would involve disclosing confidential CIA sources or methods.[12]

Ford tried ordering Bush to cooperate with the prosecutors, but Bush remained stubborn and the CIA men in question were never brought to the bar.

More than a few among the grateful spies became volunteers on Bush's 1980 presidential campaign and stayed aboard for the Reagan-Bush effort. This gaggle of former CIA agents practiced their tradecraft to destabilize President Jimmy Carter's re-election in what became known as the "dirty tricks" campaign. They not only stole Carter's briefing book before his television debate with Reagan, they also set up Carter's brother Billy to look like a cheerleader for Libya, planted moles in the National Security Council, and even used the White House situation room to spy on Carter's every move and waking thought.

Stefan Halper was one of George Bush's helpers in that campaign. Halper is instructive because his activities touch on Bush's roles in the anti-drug wars of the seventies and eighties and his part in the Iran-Contra affair. Halper had bonded with the intelligence community when he married the daughter of CIA mano a mano Ray Cline, a former deputy director of the agency and their man in Taiwan for many years. Cline was to the CIA what Knute Rockne was to Notre Dame — coach, good old boy, and role model.

Cline organized an "Agents for Bush" team and piped his son-in-law aboard the primary campaign as Bush's research chief and director of policy development.[13] Halper then rolled over onto the Reagan-Bush team where he worked for William Casey. (Later as Reagan's CIA director Casey would work with Ollie North to develop the "neat idea" that became Iran-Contra.) Casey openly boasted of running an "intelligence operation" against the incumbent President Carter. A Reagan-Bush campaign official told *The New York Times* how the campaign had acquired the Carter administration documents: "There was some CIA stuff coming from Halper, and some agency guys were hired."[14] After the election Halper joined the administration and worked with William Clark, Reagan's first national security adviser, on strategies for Central America. Halper later became deputy director of the State Department's Bureau of Politico-Military Affairs.

Halper also has the distinction of being the last thought on Ollie North's mind as he signed off his White House diary on November 25, 1986, while his secretary, Fawn Hall, was working overtime at the shredder. Next to Halper's name North made the cryptic notation: "Legal Defense Fund."[15] Halper had known North since 1980 when the Lieutenant Colonel was working on the National Security Council (but clearly not pushing for Carter's re-election), and he came through for North, organizing his defense fund and seeing to it that it was plump with bucks. Halper was in a unique position to accomplish this, as, by the mid-eighties he was a bank executive—cofounder of Palmer National Bank in Washington, D.C. Established in 1983, Palmer Bank occupies a modern building three blocks from the White House. It quickly gained a reputation as the favorite bank of the far right, specializing in loaning money to conservative PACs.

In 1990 the Houston *Post* reported that Palmer National Bank, established in 1983, had been capitalized "with seed money from a Louisiana organized crime figure." The *Post* also said that the bank had loaned money to individuals and organizations involved in the Reagan-Bush administration's "off-the-books" aid to the Contras, and had channeled money to a Swiss bank account used by North to purchase arms for the Nicaraguan rebels.[16] This was at the time that the office of the Vice President was overseeing intimate details of the secret Contra resupply operation.

Also at this time, Vice President George Bush was also in charge of the much-ballyhooed "War on Drugs." It is significant to note that Bush is the only figure in public life who has been a key player in the drug wars of three administrations.

In 1971 Bush was first brought into the anti-drug war by Richard Nixon, who appointed him to the White House Cabinet Committee on International Narcotic Control. This "war" proved useful for

Nixon as a cover for the White House plumbers and the other hijinks that ended in Watergate. It was also useful for the CIA, which tucked its agents under deep cover in the Drug Enforcement Agency and thus tasted the forbidden fruit of domestic operations—like assassination plots and wide-scale electronic eavesdropping. And there were the CIA-favored drug traffickers who enjoyed a certain immunity as long as they did the agency's bidding. (There were also clear indications that traffickers who helped finance the right-wing death squads in certain Latin American countries were able to bring drugs into the United States unmolested.)

In the mid-seventies Congress and the Justice Department had begun a crackdown on the CIA covert operatives, or "cowboys," as they were endearingly called. (This was the investigation that Bush, as President Ford's CIA director, had tried to block.)[17] But in 1977 Jimmy Carter's CIA director, Admiral Stansfield Turner, purged the cowboys in the worst bloodletting in agency history—more than 800 covert ops were fired,[18] and even General Noriega was taken off the payroll. (It was after Turner's Great Terror that angry CIA cowboys went in droves to the 1980 Bush-for-president campaign, and then to the Reagan-Bush team.)

Thus began the second phase of George Bush's war on drugs. Once in office President Reagan began his holy war against the Sandinistas. He put Vice President Bush in charge of the War on Drugs *and* the War on Terrorism, and the cowboys enjoyed a magnificent restoration. Under Bush's dual commands the CIA's airlines began to fly again; the Miami station, once the biggest spy post in the world during the anti-Castro plots of the sixties, was retrofitted; Noriega was put back on the payroll; and in the name of helping the Contras the inevitable exceptions to the crackdown on drug traffickers were made. The war on drugs again provided cover for the pursuit of certain foreign policy goals.

The CIA's history of cooperating with drug-dealing nations for Cold War purposes has been described as early as 1972 in Alfred McCoy's classic study, *The Politics of Heroin in Southeast Asia*, which detailed the agency's role in the heroin kingdoms of the Golden Triangle—Laos, Burma, and Thailand. In a more contemporary example, on May 13, 1990, *The Washington Post* front-paged a story detailing the Bush administration's failure to act on persistent reports of drug trafficking among U.S.-backed factions in the Afghan civil war. "The U.S. government has for several years received, but declined to investigate, reports of heroin trafficking by some Afghan guerrillas and Pakistani military officers with whom it cooperates in the war against Soviet influence in Afghanistan,"[19] the *Post* story began.

Flash back to May 15, 1984, when then Veep George Bush was visiting Pakistan, the first ranking U.S. official to come to Islamabad since General Mohammad Zia ul-Haq took power at the barrel of a gun in 1977. General Zia's gratitude knew few bounds and the Vice President was treated like royalty. At a magnificent state banquet George Bush rose to acknowledge the applause of the beribboned Pakistani generals, and speaking as America's head narc praised the Zia government's antinarcotics efforts as a "personal" satisfaction. The general beamed in self-congratulation. When Bush left Pakistan three days later, he announced an extraordinary outpouring from the U.S. treasury — $3.2 billion in new U.S. military aid, and another $2 billion for the Pakistani army, which was the arms pipeline to the CIA-supplied Afghan rebels.[20] (This supply operation was touted as the largest CIA "covert op" since the early days of the Vietnam War.)

At this time Pakistan was providing as much as 70 percent of the high-grade heroin entering the world market. The dope came courtesy of an elite Pakistani military unit which managed the truck convoys carrying the CIA's arms to Afghanistan. (The trucking company, owned by the Pakistani army, was the largest transportation business in the country.) The trucks delivered their cargos of weapons and returned from Afghanistan laden with poppy; fabulous profits were spread throughout the military hierarchy all the way to General Zia himself. (In the summer of 1984 at the instigation of Norwegian police, who had caught a Pakistani smuggler with 3.5 kilos of heroin at the Oslo airport the previous December, an official of the Pakistani state-owned Habib Bank was arrested for being a middleman in a heroin ring. Reportedly among the contents of the banker's briefcase were account statements of General Zia and his wife and daughter.)[21]

Pakistan's role in transporting raw opium gum from Afghanistan and then processing it into heroin was well known in the European intelligence community; it was well known to the American Drug Enforcement Agency and to the CIA. Certainly former CIA Director Bush knew about it — as head of the National Narcotics Border Interdiction System he was privy to worldwide narcotics intelligence.

"I fear I owe you an apology," C. L. Sulzberger of *The New York Times* wrote poet Allen Ginsberg on April 11, 1978. "I have been reading a succession of pieces about CIA involvement in the dope trade in Southeast Asia and I remember when you first suggested I look into this I thought you were full of beans. Indeed you were right."

The CIA has been entangled in the drug trade since World War II when the OSS and its sister agency, the Office of Naval Intelligence (ONI), entered into indiscreet alliances with the Mafia and with Chiang Kai-shek's opium-smuggling secret police. In the postwar years the young CIA enlisted as Cold War "assets" the heroin-smuggling Corsican network and the Sicilian Mafia.

Soon the CIA was knee-deep in the operations level of the heroin, opium, marijuana, and LSD trade — cocaine would come later. In the fifties, fearful that the Soviets were getting a leg up on mind control drugs, the CIA through its notorious MKULTRA and MKDELTA projects unloaded hundreds of millions of tabs of LSD on unaware Americans, many of them university kids. In the sixties during the Vietnam War, the CIA collaborated with the members of Southeast Asia's Golden Triangle; stories of the CIA's Air America planes taking dope to market are legend. After the Bay of Pigs the CIA's paramilitary anti-Castro Cubans drifted from their Miami base into major narcotics smuggling and by the seventies had developed alliances with far right, dope-financed terrorist organizations, which the agency kept at arm's length but occasionally used to its advantage. In the eighties the CIA's Contra resupply network and cooperating Central American military honchos took advantage of the cocaine boom with the agency's knowledge and sometimes under its protection.

As Richard Nixon once put it, "a lot of hanky panky" goes on between the CIA and its underworld assets and allies. The CIA's m.o. was to hold its soiled cards close to its vest, but it would intercede with the law when a drug-dealing asset was caught by the cops. Seventy-six major narcotics cases were dropped at CIA insistence during the 1970s. During the 1980s the agency was so effective at protecting its Contra-resupply narcotraffickers that R. Jerome Stanford and Richard Gregorie, two assistant United States Attorneys in Miami in charge of drug prosecutions, resigned in frustration.[22] Gregorie told a Senate subcommittee that the CIA's lack of cooperation in drug prosecutions amounted to a "constitutional crisis."

When Richard Nixon made the CIA the chief drug intelligence agency in 1971, one result was that within a year more than 100 of the CIA-trained Cuban exiles were working on the White House goon squad. When the DEA was formed out of the Bureau of Narcotics and Dangerous Drugs in 1973, old CIA hand Lucien Conein headed its Special Operations Branch. He created a deep-cover CIA/DEA narcotics operation in Miami, code-named BUNCIN/DEACON, and recruited a staff of nineteen—a dirty dozen of whom were anti-Castro CIA contract agents—to supply drug traffic intelligence.[23]

BUNCIN/DEACON documents released under the Freedom of Information Act to researcher John Hill describe a "gentleman's agreement" between the CIA and the Justice Department "to ask for dismissals rather than expose sensitive sources or techniques."[24] (At least one of these DEA assets, convicted drug smuggler and Bay of Pigs veteran Carlos Hernandez Rumbaut, continued his trafficking activities through 1976.)[25] Justice dumped that agreement in 1976 (forcing DCI Bush's stonewalling), but Conein had worked out a "crossover" arrangement whereby the DEA would claim that any CIA asset busted for narcotics smuggling was on a deep-cover DEA assignment that was part of an ongoing investigation. In the end, none of the CIA's Cubans were prosecuted for drug smuggling. And twenty-seven U.S. prosecutions of Latin America drug cases and two other major cases had to be dropped because of the CIA's domestic involvement. (It would seem that BUNCIN/DEACON, the CIA's major experiment in drug interdiction, actually increased the flow of drugs into the country.)

In 1976 CIA Director George Bush received two reports — one from the DEA, the other from the General Accounting Office — evaluating the CIA's sadsack role in the drug wars. Both concluded that drug enforcement and intelligence were two different worlds, and never the twain would meet; it was folly to throw the CIA, whose covert operations required maintaining unsavory alliances, into the prosecution-oriented drug wars.

However, as Reagan's first anti-drug czar, Bush did just that. In 1983 he announced a major new effort keyed to increased "CIA help in the crackdown" against drugs. The results were, once again, a calamity. DEA officials later testified before Congress that all the CIA did was sandbag them. Kept in the dark, the DEA was sending "attaboy" letters congratulating General Noriega on his anti-drug efforts while the CIA knew that the Medellín cocaine cartel was using Panama as a parking lot. The Senate subcommittee on narcotics (chaired by Democrat John Kerry of Massachusetts) was told that the CIA protected drug smuggling by Contra resuppliers operating on the rebels' southern front in Costa Rica. And the CIA's close relations with the now-defunct Mexican Directorate of Federal Security (a corrupt version of the FBI) obstructed the DEA's investigation into the 1985 torture-murder in Mexico of one of its agents, Kiki Camarena. (There was another factor that hampered the investigation: one of the key suspects, Miguel Angel Félix-Gallardo, was a Contra arms supplier as well as a drug trafficker.)[26] These unsavory relationships were nurtured during Bush's long reign as anti-drug enforcer; the Contra-resupply operation had come to depend heavily on drugs-for-guns financing through CIA-favored Mexican druglords.

George Bush had other Mexican secrets to hide. One was of the relationship that existed between himself and Jorge Díaz Serrano, who was convicted of looting Mexico's national oil monopoly, Pemex.

After learning the oil business from the ground up Bush formed his oil company, Zapata Petroleum Corporation, in 1953. He raised eyebrows throughout the Texas oil industry when he established an unusual relationship with Mexican oil man Serrano. In 1960 Bush and Díaz Serrano entered into a joint venture in a Mexican drilling company called Permargo. (Bush's 50 percent interest in the corporation was hidden because his ownership violated Mexican law. Permargo got government favors as a Mexican-owned company; only 100 percent Mexican-owned companies receive such special consideration.) Permargo had lucrative contracts with Pemex and in 1975 Díaz Serrano became head of Pemex, a post he held for five years. It was during the reign of Bush's ex-partner that the CIA began using Pemex as an operational cover, according to agency sources. (Bush was CIA director in 1976.) Reports later surfaced of Pemex's being bilked of millions during Serrano's tenure. And in 1983 he was convicted of defrauding the Mexican government. Bush's former partner spent five years in prison.[27]

When *Barron's* financial magazine looked into Bush's shadowy Mexican operation, investigative reporter Jonathan Kwitny found that the key Zapata records detailing Bush's business relationship with Díaz Serrano from 1960 to 1966 were gone. They had been "inadvertently destroyed" a few months after Bush was sworn in as Vice President, the SEC admitted.[28]

When Bush took office in 1981 his staff included Admiral Dan Murphy, who had served as his deputy CIA director; ex-CIA man Donald Gregg, who as the Vice President's national security adviser kept contact with the organizers of the illegal Contra resupply operations; and Jennifer Fitzgerald, Bush's secretary at the CIA and longtime aide. (Fitzgerald was the woman in question when, during the 1992 Democratic presidential primaries, Hillary Clinton, furious at press stories about her husband's sleeping around, suggested that the press inquire into rumors of George Bush's extramarital interests.)[29]

Bush had occasion to recruit other ex-CIA employees when he developed a safe harbor for Marine Lt. Col. Oliver North's domestic dirty tricks. In *Looking Forward* George Bush gave the distinct impression that he hardly knew North, but that was another lie. In his public pronouncements on the Iran-Contra affair he also insisted that he was "out of the loop" on North's ill-fated arms-for-hostages dealing with Iran and the *baksheesh* of guns for the Contras.

Bush's bad-relative treatment of North was somewhat ungenerous, since in his testimony before the Iran-Contra committee North hailed Bush's bravery in reading the riot act to the death squads when he and Bush had visited El Salvador together in 1983. The Marine came close to tears in reciting how the Veep was one of the few people in the Reagan administration to console him when his father died. Despite these public suggestions of intimacy, the committee remained uncurious about the Bush-North relationship. It passed up fertile ground.

The Bush-North cup ran over in 1990 with the release of 2,600 uncensored pages of North's White House diaries. The unmistakable picture to be drawn from these copious entries is that Ollie North and Bush were as close as the stamp to the envelope. For example, North was keenly interested in the Vice President's travel schedule. Whenever Bush went abroad North made a note of it, and then devised a plan for hitting up the head of the country Bush was visiting for aid for the Contras. Whether Bush actually made such solicitations himself is not indicated in North's hen-scratchy shorthand, but specific diary entries — even the early pages were either partially blacked out or deleted from the redacted version released by the Iran-Contra committee — show Bush performing a variety of delicate tasks for North.

In September 1985, shortly after the first Israeli-arranged shipment of U.S. TOW missiles to Iran, Israeli spy Amiram Nir emerged as North's contact man and Bush met with Nir in Israel. Nir, who died in a mysterious plane crash in Mexico in 1988, was a key player in the shipment of arms to Iran and the "diversion" of profits from the overpriced arms to the Contras. (The September meeting may have been the embryo of the diversion scheme.) At North's request Bush met with Nir a second time on July 29, 1986, in Jerusalem and Bush's aide Craig Fuller took detailed notes on the briefing Nir gave on the arms-for-hostages progress, or lack thereof. Yet Bush has repeatedly said he knew nothing of the arms schemes until December 1986.[30]

Students of the Iran-Contra affair who have compared the uncensored North diaries with the edited version used by the committee note that many of the deletions were of North's references to Bush.

This is consistent with press reports that the committee, once it had hastened to determine that there were no grounds to recommend the impeachment of Ronald Reagan, wanted to wind up its inquiry as quickly as possible, and was disinclined to open a separate track into the activities of the Vice President.

North's diaries also reveal that the committee was less than independent. On March 4, 1985, then National Security Adviser Robert McFarlane met with four Republican representatives, a meeting at which the idea of seeking contributions from third countries, such as Saudi Arabia, to get around a congressional ban on aiding the Contras was discussed. Two of the congressmen present, Representatives Henry Hyde of Illinois and Bill McCollum of Florida, went on to become North's staunchest defenders on the Iran-Contra committee.[31]

According to the report issued by Kerry's Senate Foreign Relations Subcommittee on Terrorism, Narcotics, and International Operations (called *Drugs, Law Enforcement, and Foreign Policy*) there was "obvious and widespread" drug trafficking by Contra suppliers going on in the war zones of northern Costa Rica. The Kerry subcommittee found that these drugs-for-guns activities were being covered up by CIA operatives and other players in the resupply network.

And there are indications aplenty of Contra drug dealing in North's diaries. For instance, there is this entry on July 12, 1985: "$14M[illion] to finance came from drugs." But North was able to contain reports of Contra drug money because Bush's Task Force on Combating Terrorism gave North the mandate and the equipment to pursue a wide range of domestic intelligence operations against opponents of the administration's Central America policy. Bush's staff brought CIA experts in propaganda and disinformation into his anti-terrorism loop, using them to confuse the American people about the situation in Central America — the line was put out that the Sandinistas were dealing drugs — and to bypass both Congress and the Constitution in the Contra resupply effort. North also coordinated fund-raising efforts to defeat anti-Contra congressmen up for re-election, and even sicced the FBI on disaffected Contra suppliers, such as Jack Terrell, who was attempting to tell about Contra drug trafficking.[32]

In the early 1980s, while working as the National Security Council liaison to the Federal Emergency Management Agency (FEMA), Ollie North helped develop a rash plan to suspend the Constitution and declare martial law. The plan provided for the opening of internment camps for dissenters in the event of "widespread internal dissent, or national opposition to a U.S. military invasion abroad" — presumably an invasion of Nicaragua. When Congressman Jack Brooks attempted during the Iran–Contra hearings to ask about this plot to heist the Constitution, he was cut off by Chairman Daniel Inouye, who declared that discussion of the matter had to be reserved for executive session.[33]

In January 1986 Bush's Task Force recommended that a secret Office to Combat Terrorism be created for North and that its existence be kept from those members of the National Security Council who did not have a need to know. Two key Bush Task Force staff members, Robert Earl and Craig Coy, then moved into North's new office where they worked on matters related to the care, feeding, and arming of the Contra forces. Under the aegis of the Alien Border Control Committee, an offshoot of the Bush Task Force's counter-terrorism program, the FBI cooperated in the surveillance of opponents of the administration's policies in Central America. Although this was not a CIA operation, its existence brings to mind the words of the framers of the CIA's 1947 enabling legislation, who had cautioned against ever using the CIA's awesome powers within the country. The covert services were forbidden by charter and congressional mandate from operating domestically. In the 1980s their black arts were practiced under the vice presidential seal.[34]

Aside from his role as chief combatant of terrorism, Bush's other area of command was to stop the flow of drugs into the country. As head of the Florida Task Force to combat drugs and the National Narcotics Border Interdiction System, Bush made Admiral Murphy his sidekick and once again assigned CIA agents to the war on drugs. Although Bush has stubbornly maintained that his anti-drug efforts have been successful, during his years minding the nation's drug store the metric tonnage of cocaine coming into the United

States *tripled*, its price fell more than 50 percent from what it was in 1982, and the crack wars exploded in the inner cities of America.

Once again, a significant factor in the failure of the war on drugs was the CIA's long-standing policy — at which George Bush excels — of ignoring the drug-dealing of perceived friends. As Berkeley professor Peter Dale Scott, who has made an extensive study of the 'CIA absolution' for certain drug deals, observed in 1988: "Most North Americans know that when the U.S. was involved in covert operations in Southeast Asia in the 1960s and 1970s, we had a heroin epidemic on this continent. Now in the 1980s, when some of the same people are involved in a covert operation in Central America, we have a cocaine epidemic. That's not a coincidence."[35]

If there is one CIA operative who symbolizes the sum of George Bush's deadly secrets it is Luis Posada Carriles, a terrorist with nine lives. Posada was last in the news in February of 1990, when he drove a black Suzuki jeep into an Esso gas station in Guatemala City. He couldn't talk because he had been shot in the jaw and the chest, and he gestured impatiently for a pencil and paper. "Please help me," he scribbled. "I am an adviser to Cerezo." He wrote down a phone number, made the sign of the cross, and then collapsed against the steering wheel.

That blood-stained note indicated that the man had friends in high places (Vinicio Cerezo is the Guatemalan president), and that he had some familiarity with being wounded. "Allergic to penicillin," he had troubled to write in his last moment of consciousness. When the service station owner called the number, a woman answered the telephone; she seemed to know what to do. Fifteen minutes later, according to the Miami *Herald*, two ranking members of President Cerezo's government — Rolando Castro, the director of Guatemala customs, and Francisco Ramirez, chief of the Guatemala telephone company — were at the Esso station with an ambulance.

A Cuban trained in demolition and assassination by the CIA, Posada's assignment for Cerezo had been to set up a super-secret security and surveillance squad, capable of snooping on Guatemala's corrupt military. The injured Posada was taken discreetly to El Pilar sanatorium, a pricey private facility in Guatemala City, and presidential guards and members of the National Police were stationed day and night outside the sickroom door. But a month later the still-recovering Posada slipped silently away from the sanatorium.[36] (Posada has a professional habit of disappearing when things get hot.)

Posada is another instructional figure from George Bush's past. With his long ties to the CIA, he figures in incidents from Bush's careers as DCI and as Ronald Reagan's first drug czar.

According to intelligence sources the CORU (the Commando of United Revolutionary Organizations) was formed in 1976, partly at the CIA's instigation, as an umbrella organization for Cuban exile terrorism. CORU enjoyed support from the mysterious World Finance Corporation. WFC was involved in drug trafficking and money laundering and had on its payroll a gaggle of ex-CIA Cubans and even a known associate of Florida mob boss Santos Trafficante. Orlando Bosch, Miami's favorite terrorist who became a founder of CORU, had received funding from the WFC. In the 1980s it became the subject of the largest federal narcotics investigation in South Florida until the CIA killed the probe (which prompted the later resignations of federal prosecutors Stanford and Gregorie).[37]

Posada received his CIA training at Fort Benning, Georgia. He came to the CORU by way of Operation 40, a clandestine CIA affiliate formed to enter Cuba after the Bay of Pigs invasion and eliminate liberals and Castro sympathizers. When the invasion failed, Operation 40 was kept intact by the CIA both to spy on the Cuban exile movement itself and to launch raids against Cuba from the U.S. mainland. But Operation 40 members soon became involved in drug smuggling. The unit was hastily shut down by the CIA in 1970 when an Operation 40 plane carrying a cargo of heroin and cocaine crashed in Southern California.

After his Operation 40 stint, from 1967 to 1976 Posada was a CIA double agent inside the DISIP, the Venezuelan secret police. While on that assignment in 1971 he arranged cover for the gunmen attempting to assassinate Fidel Castro during his state visit to President Allende of Chile.[38] (Three years later Allende was overthrown and killed during a CIA-backed coup.)

Posada's career was put on ice for eight years when he was arrested and jailed in Venezuela for the 1976 bombing of Cubana

Airlines Flight 455 which killed seventy-three people. Also arrested was his CORU-cohort Orlando Bosch, the fanatically anti-Castro pediatrician-turned-bomber. Neither man was convicted of the crime. (Some years later Bosch found a friend in George Bush's son, Jeb).

On August 16, 1985, Posada escaped from his Venezuelan prison cell and became involved in the 1985–86 Contra resupply operation at Ilopango Air Base in El Salvador, which thirty-year CIA spook Donald Gregg, Bush's national security adviser (now U.S. ambassador to South Korea), was helping to coordinate.

The Ilopango base has been cited in congressional hearings as a nexus for a guns-for-drugs operation in which planes would arrive in El Salvador with guns for the Contras and return to the U.S. with cocaine. Although the Iran-Contra select committee shied away from investigating allegations about Contra drug trafficking, it did reveal that Amalgamated Commercial Enterprises (ACE), a Panamanian front organization, paid part of the salaries of the Contra resupply ground crews. ACE has been linked in court proceedings to Steven Samos, a Panamanian businessman who has admitted to laundering millions of cocaine narcodollars into clean U.S. currency. ACE was also the funding vehicle for the purchase of the C-123K Contra resupply cargo plane which was shot down over Nicaragua on October 5, 1986.[39] Eugene Hasenfus survived the crash and talked, leading to the unraveling of the Iran-Contra affair.

After Posada's escape from jail, he began working at Ilopango with his old friend, the CIA agent and fellow Bay of Pigs veteran, Felix Rodriguez, who had gone to El Salvador with the blessing of Donald Gregg. Since Rodriguez and Posada were on the scene, the Vice President's office received the first word of the crash of the C-123K cargo plane. (Hasenfus later described both Posada and Rodriguez as "U.S. agents" and said they had bragged of being friends of George Bush.)[40]

Posada disappeared from El Salvador shortly after the Hasenfus crash. This saved Bush from being asked embarrassing questions about how an escaped terrorist came to be working hand in glove with the Vice President's point man in El Salvador in an illegal Contra resupply operation.

Details of the CIA's relationship with Mexican druglords enliv-
ened the Los Angeles trial of the four men accused of the 1985 murder of DEA agent Kiki Camarena in Guadalajara, Mexico. Although
not on trial in the U.S., one suspect in the agent's death was Mexican
drug kingpin Rafael Caro Quintero. On July 3, 1990, U.S. District
Judge Edward Rafeedie released a previously classified DEA interview with an informer who said that in the early 1980s the CIA had
used Caro's Mexican ranch to train "Guatemalan guerrillas."[41]
(Caro was later convicted of Camarena's murder in a separate trial
in Mexico.) Earlier the CIA had interfered in the investigation of
the role of another drug trafficker, Miguel Felix Gallardo, in
Camarena's murder. Defense lawyers in the Los Angeles trial said
that Gallardo enjoyed protection from prosecution because of his
large "charitable contributions" to the Contras. Mexico's biggest
smuggler, Felix Galardo boasted to friends that his operations were
safe.[42] Indeed his pilot testified that his boss moved four tons of cocaine into the United States *every* month.

Felix Gallardo's partner, Juan Ramon Matta Ballesteros, also has
extensive CIA ties. He developed SETCO, an air transport firm, to
deliver "humanitarian" supplies to the Contras; SETCO carried
millions of rounds of ammunition and other military supplies between 1983 and 1985. For this "humanitarian effort" drug smuggler
Matta, whose worth is estimated at $2 billion, received $186,000
from the U.S. State Department as well as other funds from the
pocket Contra accounts of Ollie North.[43]

II

Deadly Secrets, which chronicles the United States government's
obsession with destroying Fidel Castro, and the disastrous consequences for America as the Secret War against Cuba turned inward,
was first published in 1981 under the title *The Fish Is Red*. Since then
the political parameters of the world-as-we-knew-it have changed
fundamentally; now the Cold War is over, but one element of its anticommunist zealotry remains hot: the continued attempts by U.S.
policy makers to overthrow the government of Cuba and replace it
with one of their design. Of all the Cold War policy makers, Presi-

dent George Bush is the one most intimately connected with keeping the secrets of the failed attempts to achieve that goal, and forwarding its deadly agenda. By the fall of 1987 the bellicose Ronald Reagan had softened (sufficiently for *The New York Times* to report a "warming trend" in U.S.-Cuba relations), and had even reached an immigration agreement with the Cuban government.[44] But once Bush assumed full control of the White House he quickly decried as "willful speculation" the idea that any element of sanity would enter relations between the two countries.[45] Bush then proceeded to underscore his point by initiating a series of hostile actions against Cuba, which included freeing *el primo* anti-Castro terrorist Orlando Bosch; launching F-4, F-5, and F-16 fighter planes and B-52 bombers from Florida in aggressive military maneuvers near the Cuba coastline; restricting Cuban immigration despite the 1987 agreement; tightening the economic embargo that by the Cuban government's estimate has cost it more than $15 billion since 1961 and made life increasingly difficult for Cuban citizens; creating the propaganda-intensive TV Martí, to follow Radio Martí; and outrageously harassing the Cuban embassy in Panama City during the December 1989 U.S. invasion of Panama.[46] Bush hardened Washington's policy toward Cuba despite the fact — as Wayne Smith, former head of the U.S. Interests Section in Havana (and a critic of U.S. foreign policy) has pointed out — that the conditions of successive Washington administrations for "normalizing" relations with Cuba had already been substantially fulfilled: Cuban troops had left Angola, political prisoners in Cuba had been released in large numbers, and Soviet-Cuban ties had been reduced in a major way. "Cuba has the same effect on American administrations that the full moon used to have on werewolves: they just lose their rationality at the mention of Castro or Cuba," Smith said.[47]

The preservation of the Secret War against Cuba has become for George Bush a crusade. And as that war entered its third decade, Bush sent his own son into the dark corridors of the anti-Castro movement first formed by the alliance between the intelligence agencies and organized crime. The experience has both enriched and degraded Jeb Bush. Like father, like son.

In the mid-1980s the bilingual Jeb Bush became the Republican

Party's unofficial ambassador to Miami's Cuban-American community; he also served as a cheerleader for Miguel Recarey, Jr., a rich anti-Castro Cuban with connections, both peripheral and mainline, to organized crime, and the Contras.

An exile to Miami from a wealthy, politically connected Havana family (his uncle had been Batista's minister of health), Recarey artfully traded on his anti-Castro credentials to build a health-maintenance organization, International Medical Centers (IMC), to become the medical-care czar of Dade County. Recarey maintained both a Dom Perignon lifestyle and a paranoid existence. (He especially feared assassination by poison. The bedroom on his estate outside Miami had bulletproof windows and steel doors, and he was guarded night and day by Uzi-carrying security men who drove cars equipped with mobile telephones with voice scramblers.) Recarey had openly boasted of his close connections with Florida mob boss Santos Trafficante (Meyer Lansky's narcotics syndicate leader) who was an early recruit to the CIA's assassination attempts against Fidel Castro. Trafficante provided short-term financing to IMC which under the beneficial gaze of the Reagan-Bush administration became the largest health maintenance organization in the nation. (The mob connections of the "White Feather"—Recarey's code name to his security team was Pluma Blanca—were well known to South Florida law enforcement officials. "As far back as the 1960s he had ties with reputed racketeers who had operated out of pre-Castro Cuba and who later forged an anti-Castro alliance with the CIA," *The Wall Street Journal* reported in 1988.)[48]

Recarey, a certified public accountant, got a jump start in the HMO business by signing up 10,000 Cuban political prisoners and their families as they stepped off the plane in Miami after Castro released them from jail. A bigtime contributor to both the Democratic and Republican parties, Recarey paid enormous fees to former Reagan-Bush campaign officials to represent him in Washington—$400,000 to Lynn Nofziger, $400,000 to the p.r. firm of Black, Manfort and Stone, and $300,000 to former Reagan campaign manager John Sears.[49]

But despite this high-powered help, Recarey asked the Vice President's son to make a key phone call to the Department of Health and

Human Services when he needed a waiver of Medicare rules to expand his health empire, which was largely dependent on money from the government program for the elderly. After Jeb Bush called a federal regulator in 1985 and (according to later testimony in Congress) said that "America could trust Mike Recarey," the HHS suspended the regulation that no more than 50 percent of an HMO's income could come from Medicare payments.[50] The Miami *Herald* reported that at the time he intervened on Recarey's behalf, Jeb Bush's Florida real estate firm stood to make $250,000 in a deal Bush was negotiating for IMC. Even though the deal did not go through, Recarey in 1986 paid Bush Realty $75,000 for work on the failed project.[51]

Even though CPA Recarey had been jailed briefly for failing to file income tax returns, and had a history of fraud allegations in prior business relationships with Florida hospitals, HHS did relax the rules for him, and IMC's income from Medicare checks grew to more than 80 percent of its receipts. When it collapsed in a billion-dollar Medicare fraud in 1987, it was the largest recipient of Medicare benefits in the nation. Thousands of elderly Floridians never received the medical care for which IMC received their Medicare checks.[52]

IMC was a classic "bust-out" operation where bills weren't paid, services weren't provided, and millions from its Medicare income of $30 million a month were siphoned off to Miguel Recarey's other "business ventures." IMC was tied in to a private network that supported the Contras, and federal investigators suspected that some of the hundreds of millions in Medicare funds that disappeared through the "black hole" of Recarey's accounting went to the Nicaraguan rebels.[53] The construction supervisor at IMC was Jose Basulto, a Bay of Pigs veteran who in the early 1980s was an adviser to Argentine intelligence officers training torture squads in Central America. He later "coordinated" IMC medical aid to the Contras in conjunction with their leader Adolfo Calero and the ubiquitous Felix Rodriguez. The three men held a summit meeting at an IMC facility in Miami to coordinate the free medical treatment.[54] (It turned out that many of the wounded Contras were also involved in drug smuggling.)

One of IMC's suppliers was Calmaquip Engineering Corporation, which was staffed by ex-Bay of Pigs figures who did national security-type business with third world customers — servicing police hospitals in Colombia, shipping merchandise to El Salvador's defense ministry, and arranging for medical care at IMC for Peruvian military officers. IMC was a rarity for Calmaquip — a U.S. client.[55] For investing a mere $1 million in a separate Recarey business venture, Calmaquip got the contract to supply all his hospitals. (That contract contained an unusual clause: the supplier was not to be bound by "the best available prices.") Under the cover of a Florida debt collection business the man whom Jeb Bush had described as trustworthy also ran a bugging operation that employed two dozen people, including secretaries to transcribe recordings of telephone conversations. The FBI described the operation as "massive," but never learned its purpose, and Recarey's client list didn't surface.

Miguel Recarey's mysterious friends in high places served him to the last. Although under indictment for massive fraud and racketeering in the IMC collapse, Recarey was allowed to keep his passport, get passports for his children, sell off assets — including condos, Ferraris, and BMWs — and he received an "expedited" $2.2 million tax refund from the IRS, all before fleeing the country, presumably for Venezuela, in 1988.[56]

In 1989, Jeb Bush was the campaign manager for Ileana Ros-Lehtinen, the first Cuban American elected to Congress. She ran on a platform demanding secular sainthood for the baby doctor-turned-bomber, Orlando Bosch. America's most prolific terrorist, since the 1960s Bosch had been responsible for dozens of bombings in the United States and abroad. (Despite his acquittal by juries in Venezuela on charges of masterminding the 1976 bombing of Cubana Airlines Flight 455, even the doubting Thomases in the Criminal Division of the United States Department of Justice believed Bosch to be the maniac responsible.)

During the campaign, the object of Ms. Ros-Lehtinen's affections was lodged in a federal clink in Miami pending deportation for entering the country illegally. (Bosch had fled to Latin America in

1974, violating parole on his 1967 conviction for firing a bazooka at a Polish freighter in Miami harbor. The freighter had had the gall to unload goods in Havana.) The future congresswoman and the President's son were outraged that the Justice Department, citing an FBI report that said Bosch "repeatedly expressed and demonstrated a willingness to cause indiscriminate injury and death," had ruled that Bosch should be deported.[58]

After the election, Congresswoman Ros-Lehtinen and Jeb Bush continued their campaign to free Dr. Death (as the less-reverent in the Miami Cuban community called the bomb-throwing pediatrician). At one point Jeb Bush visited hunger strikers who were demanding the convicted terrorist's release and fed them encouraging words. On July 17, 1990, the Justice Department succumbed to the entreaties of Congresswoman Ros-Lehtinen and the political weight of the High Right in Miami, heeded the wishes of the Bush *pere* and *fils*, and reversed itself. Upon his release Dr. Bosch immediately called a news conference and unkindly called "ridiculous" the fourteen conditions he had agreed to as the terms of his freedom, including house arrest, electronic monitoring, and the renunciation of terrorism. "They purchased the chain but they don't have the monkey," he said.[59]

The bomb-making baby doctor is symbolic of the anti-Castro cause, but he is a symbol of what his supporters would be least likely to brag about. After the financing he had received in the sixties from right-wing Texans had petered out, Dr. Bosch's terrorist activities were underwritten by the narcodollars that flowed through the Miami financial pipelines. Bosch's benefactor was the World Finance Corporation, the money laundering conglomerate headquartered in Coral Gables. An unpublished report by the House Select Committee on Narcotics Abuse and Control concluded that WFC was a gigantic front for many crimes "including aspects of political corruption, gunrunning as well as narcotics trafficking on an international level."[60] World Finance Corporation was to the South Florida drug trade of the 1970s what the notorious Nugan Hand Bank of Australia was to the Southeast Asian opium money of the 1980s. (Nugan Hand was yet another CIA-connected financial institution used to launder drug money and funds for intelligence operations.

It folded after one of its founders was found dead—an alleged suicide—and the other disappeared.)[61] WFC was openly drug-connected; several times a week large sacks of cash were deposited to its account in another Cuban exile-owned bank which was subsequently shut down by banking regulators.[62] When Bosch helped found the terrorist umbrella organization CORU in 1976, it began to receive funding from WFC, which printed and sold "bonds" to finance Bosch's terrorist work.[63] CORU founders, including Bosch, were implicated in the terrorist horrors of 1976—the Cubana Airlines bombing and the assassination in Washington, D.C., of former Chilean ambassador Orlando Letelier. The deaths of Letelier and his research assistant, Ronni Moffitt, in a car bombing brought to seventy-six the number of people CORU claimed to have killed in North and South America since its founding barely four months earlier.[64]

John Dinges and Saul Landau, in their book on the Letelier case, *Assassination on Embassy Row*, concluded that CORU had the "active support of the CIA" and was "allowed to operate to punish Castro for his Angola policy without directly implicating the United States." At the time of the assassination, not-directly-implicating-the-United-States in the terrorist activities of CIA surrogates was George Bush's job. If CIA dads in their old age tell their sons war stories, George Bush had a good one to relate to Jeb about how back in 1976 he came to save the bacon of Jeb's later-life hero Orlando Bosch and his Cuban exile pals. CIA Director Bush had to work overtime to keep the agency out of the storms when Letelier's murder on Embassy Row brought death squad politics to the nation's capital. Even by the agency's laissez-faire standards of anything-goes-against-Castro, Bosch was considered a loose cannon. In fact, that February the CIA had tipped off the Costa Rican police to detain Bosch when it heard he was plotting to kill Henry Kissinger because Kissinger wanted to improve relations with Cuba.[65] (If federal investigators had learned about the CIA's CORU associations and the WFC financing it had been protecting, there would have been more Senate hearings not only into the CORU linkage, but into the connections of the CIA-trained Cubans with the DINA, Chile's secret police. The DINA had organized a Murder Inc.-type exercise called Operation Condor to coordinate the intelligence services of Paraguay, Argentina, and other bastions of democracy. Condor sent assassins about Latin America—and, in Letelier's execution, into the United States itself—for the purpose of "neutralizing leftists."[66] The CIA-trained assassins in CORU availed themselves of Condor assignments like day laborers taking on a shift.)

As later revealed in court proceedings in the Letelier case, the CIA under Bush knew within a week that the Letelier assassination was an Operation Condor action; one American working with the DINA and several CIA-connected Cuban exiles working with Paraguayan intelligence officers on assignment for the Chilean secret police had been involved.[67] But the CIA artfully leaked a different story to the media. It first sought to divert suspicion from the rightist Chilean government of General Augusto Pinochet—an October 11, 1976, item in *Newsweek*'s "Periscope" column read: "The CIA has concluded that the Chilean secret police was not involved in the death of Orlando Letelier . . . "[68] Then it began a subtle campaign which implied that Letelier, a loyalist to Salvador Allende (slain in the CIA-supported 1973 coup that brought Pinochet to power), might have been assassinated by the Chilean left in the misguided cause of creating a martyr. There were also attempts to paint Letelier as a Castro agent—for example, the December 20 Jack Anderson-Les Whitten column, titled "Letelier's Havana Connection,"[69] was based on papers allegedly found in Letelier's briefcase. But two coworkers of Letelier at the Institute for Policy Studies, a Washington, D.C., liberal think tank, believe that the CIA may have planted the documents in Letelier's briefcase.[70]

It wasn't until years later, after the trials of two Cuban exiles and one American charged with assassination, that it became apparent that Letelier was the DINA's victim, and that the CIA had unexplored relationships with the plotters. The possible nature of those relationships was discussed by Dinges and Landau: "Pinochet turned over to the United States Drug Enforcement Administration a planeload of cocaine dealers rounded up after the coup. Their drug dealing could be blamed on Allende's ousted government. Then Pinochet's right-hand man, Contreras, could set up his own men with DINA protection in the same cocaine factories and shipping points. The anti-Castro Cubans had a piece of the action. The enormous profits went to supplement DINA's clandestine budget. The Cubans' share went into individual pockets and to the anti-Castro cause."[71] And in *Cocaine Politics*, Peter Dale Scott and Jonathan Marshall describe the "dominance of the U.S. cocaine and marijuana trade by intelligence-trained Cuban exiles."[72] (In a footnote to the Letelier-Moffitt murders, in 1990 the new civilian government of Chile agreed to pay compensation for the assassinations, which George Bush had tried to blame on the left. It is also interesting to note that five of the 1976 founders of the terrorist CORU later joined the Contras.)[73]

George Bush is the only former director of the CIA to become President of the United States and he has continued to keep the faith with the agency that spawned him. In the 1980s at the top of the CIA's wish list was the removal of the prohibition against assassination as a means of covert action. (Congress had insisted on the proscription after the mid-seventies revelations of the CIA-Mafia assassination plots against Castro.) But the agency's request for a green light was met with disfavor by congressional intelligence oversight committees during the Reagan-Bush years. However, upon his election President Bush tackled the touchy subject with renewed vigor.

On November 16, 1989, the Los Angeles *Times* reported that the Bush administration and congressional intelligence oversight panels had agreed that the CIA may participate in covert operations that might lead to violence against, or the death of, foreign leaders. Assassination would not be approved overtly, but it would no longer be illegal.[74]

After the Bay of Pigs, John F. Kennedy asked the planners of the Secret War against Cuba to search for means other than direct military invasion to overthrow Castro. The plotters leaned heavily on the assassination option, but that was taken away from them. Now, in the fullness of time, George Bush has restored it.

PROLOGUE
A Swim for Havana

THE Rio Grande as it nears the Gulf of Mexico turns a foaming chocolate brown, a quarter-mile-wide milk shake spilled between the United States and Mexico. The river's steep barren banks are dotted with dun-colored scrub brush. On first glance, it is no place to go swimming. Yet in the noon-hour heat of a September day in 1956 a tall man, wearing the clothes of a Mexican laborer, got out of a jalopy and stumbled down the incline to the river's edge. He stripped off his clothes and dashed into the dirty tan water with the vigor of a vacationer taking the cool blue waves of the Riviera.

He swam frogman style with the strong, certain strokes of an accomplished swimmer. Behind him was the dusty Mexican border town of Reynosa; ahead, through the haze toward the United States side of the river, was the ranching town of McAllen, an oasis of Texas hospitality in the fertile farmlands of the Rio Grande Valley. As he approached the northern bank of the river, the swimmer submerged. For minutes there was no sign of him.

He surfaced in the midst of a motley crew of bathers, oil workers who had not bothered to remove their dungarees, splashing and frolicking in the shallow muddy water. The men surrounded the na-

ked submariner and clasped him around the shoulders. Hand after
calloused hand joyously slapped his dripping back as he waded toward shore. A fresh set of clothes had been secreted for him. The
swim had been carefully prearranged. The oil workers' bathing
party was camouflage. The name of the mysterious wetback was
Fidel Castro.

The man who walked into the lobby of the Hotel Casa de Palmas
in McAllen could hardly have been the wretched creature who had
climbed out of the river scarcely an hour before. The automobile
ride into town had effected a transformation. The wetback had become a bourgeois gentleman of leisure returning from a round of
golf at the country club; from the half smile set in his thick red lips,
and the jaunty angle of the cigar protruding from them, it looked as
though he had broken par. To the careful student of the human anat-
omy, the victorious golfer bore certain resemblances to the soaking-
wet illegal alien: the athlete's poise, balancing broad shoulders on a
slender waist; the long nose, coming straight down from his high
forehead like a ski jump; the hypnotic brown eyes and scraggly
chestnut hair, which, when excited, he shook the way a spirited
thoroughbred horse tosses its head. He was clean-shaven except for
a thin mustache that looked somehow out of place on so large a face
still firm with the unlined flush of youth. A man would have guessed
his age at about thirty, a woman might more admiringly say
twenty-six, but the man would be right. He was tall, very tall, and
seemed higher than his six feet three inches. This hatless olive-
skinned man towered over the hotel lobbyful of Stetson-topped
Texans like an oil derrick in a cotton field. The illusion of size was
generated by a magnetism that commanded attention and, at the
same time, respect.

The desk clerk dropped an octave in the scale of officiousness with
which blazer-clad guardians of the gate usually greet routine re-
quests for information from men in sports clothes. Was Señor the
guest that Señor Prío was expecting? Good. Señor should go right
up. He would call ahead. Fidel Castro walked into the elevator looking for all the world more like a racket and tennis club member than
a revolutionary.

The door to Casa de Palmas's finest suite was opened by a distinguished Cuban gentleman of middle age and imperial bearing. His eyes met those of his visitor with an instant's flash of fire. Then the fire was gone, smothered in the practiced warmth of eyes which had smiled through a thousand state receptions. Dr. Carlos Prío Socarrás, the third president of the Republic of Cuba, a millionaire many times over, a veteran aficionado of the good life, graciously waved his young guest toward an unmacho flowered sofa. Fidel took a seat on a hard-backed chair instead.

Both men wore sport shirts and slacks. Fidel's had the rough look of a Brownsville waterfront war surplus store; Prío's, the sheen of a Miami Beach haberdashery. Each man took his time taking the measure of the other. It was a thorough inspection; they did all but sniff at one another's pants legs. In Cuba the two men were political enemies. Now they both were in exile. For the first time in their lives they had something in common. They shared a hatred. The object of their enmity was the dictator Fulgencio Batista, a Cuban Caligula, the former army sergeant who governed their island paradise by the gun and had made it a chamber of horrors. Both men were sworn to destroy this beast who had deformed the pearl of the Antilles. To this revolutionary end Fidel Castro had pledged his life, and Carlos Prío Socarrás his fortune.

Both were in trouble with the authorities. Prío was under indictment in Miami for violations of the U.S. Neutrality Act; the violations were in the form of bullets, which Prío had smuggled into Cuba with Batista's name on them. Castro's stay in Mexico had all the security of a trapdoor. The Mexicans arrested him and took all his arms when they caught him training a Cuban invasion force in the shadow of the Popocatépetl volcano near Mexico City. Castro was desperate to get his invasion under way before the Mexicans closed in again. It gave him indigestion to ask for it, but he needed Prío's money. He needed it so badly that he had taken the wetback highway across the Rio Grande to get it. The youthful revolutionary could not get a visa to enter the United States, and the ex-president was barred by his indictment from leaving. The meeting in McAllen was a compromise of sorts, although Castro knew full well that he had been the one who had to take the plunge. He had no pride where the revolution was concerned. Still, there were limits to the obeisance that could be paid to a former enemy who, if the revolution were victorious, would doubtless become an enemy again. Castro would not beg, but he would implore. If Paris were worth a mass, Havana was worth a swim.

The difference between the two Cubans was more than skin-deep. For the moment they were thinly fused in exile and adversity. But in the souls of these enemies so warily eyeing each other in the Texas hotel room were the seeds of Cuba's second revolution—a counterrevolution—which was to follow the first revolution as intimately and inevitably as the shadow follows the body. Theirs was the difference of urban from rural, of bureaucrat from peasant, of sophisticated from simple, of mortgages from malnutrition, of law from justice, of satisfaction from hope, of plenty from poverty. Such distinctions, like the poor of Saint John, are always with us, the unsung litany of the obvious. But in Cuba, where the ordinary often takes on airs of the fantastic, these differences were more keen and poignant than on any island on earth.

Fidel Castro was born to privilege and opted out of it. The youthful revolutionary would spend his maturing years trying, and failing, to maintain his own lingering regard for middle-class freedoms and institutions while serving the tapeworm needs of a proletarian revolution, in a country where most of the rural children suffered the ravages of malnutrition and parasitic infection on a rich island whose resources were milked dry by absentee owners.

Prío, like Fidel, was born to savor the sauces of Dives. But he remained consistent in his tastes. Prío became *el presidente de la cordialidad*. He created a Cuban Camelot for those who could afford it. His dream upon overthrowing Batista was to return to his beloved farm, La Chata, a mini Garden of Eden done with the understatement of a Busby Berkeley production. Surrounded by miles of bougainvillea, gardenias, hibiscus, and roses, La Chata had outdoor rainbow fountains, indoor solid marble floors, a shooting range, and a private barbershop with six chairs. An artificial waterfall roared into the deepest swimming pool in Cuba, the sit-down dinner facilities accommodated hundreds, and the daiquiris flowed. Prío raised racehorses and prize-winning chickens, a hobby in which he became so competitive that should a hen or rooster not of his flock capture a blue ribbon, the luckless bird would invariably be found with its neck wrung.

Prío's political party, the Auténticos, had been in power for eight years before Batista picked up all the marbles of government. The Auténticos had become known as the party of privilege, an appellation they barely bothered to disavow. The graft and corruption were astounding. Even the moths disappeared from the public purse. Never in the history of democratic countries had so much been taken from so many for the benefit of so few.[1]

Prío himself had become a fabulously wealthy man by the time his presidential term ended abruptly in Batista's coup of March 10, 1952. Estimates of his worth ranged from $50 million to $100 million. There was considerable speculation about how this loyal son of Cuba had amassed such riches during his public service as a senator and his four years as president of the Republic of Cuba at an annual salary of $25,000. One theory, held dear by his enemies, was that his brothers, Francisco and Antonino, were the funnels through which the Cuban treasury ran off into Prío's pocket. The robust Cuban narcotics trade, supposedly derailed by the 1947 expulsion of Lucky Luciano from Cuba, was helped back on the track by Francisco Prío with a little look-the-other-way assistance from a former Cuban gangster type whom President Prío appointed as chief of the secret police. Antonino Prío, a prominent playboy, was for a time minister of finance in his brother's administration. According to the tale told by indignant Auténtico party members,[2] the Prío brothers were as rapacious as the James brothers and profited scandalously from a scheme in which worn-out pesos turned in to the Finance Ministry for destruction were secretly baled up and the soiled notes deposited by the pound in the brothers' bank accounts.

Prío, who had a great love for the stage, cast himself in the role of reformer. He pledged to cure his nation of the *gangsterismo* that had plagued Cuban politics since the Roaring Twenties days of the three-fingered tyrant Gerardo Machado, a former cattle rustler. Yet the gangsters flourished under Prío; he jailed a few sacrificial underlings while cutting deals with their bosses. Prío outlawed the code duello (the handsome Prío had twice been slashed in duels) and issued an edict permitting the machine wrapping of Cuban cigars; such were his reforms. The cordial president was a happy collaborator with those among his countrymen who shared the harvest of the monopolies and lined up to sup at the public trough; various estimates have from 40 to 60 percent of the Cuban treasury passing into private hands—army officers, police, bureaucrats, educators, student leaders, businessmen small and large, and gangsters professional and amateur—their numbers not in the hundreds, but in the thousands. In the eighteenth century upwards of 10,000 pirates operated in the Caribbean, many of them out of Cuba's Isle of Pines; by the twentieth century they seemed to have moved to Havana, dressed in business suits. Said the former United States ambassador to Cuba, Philip W. Bonsal; "I know of no country among those committed to the Western ethic where the diversion of public treasure for private profit reached the proportions that it attained in the Cuban Republic."[3]

For all this, there seemed always the need for more. Prío was generally reputed[4] to have taken a quarter-million-dollar bribe from Meyer Lansky, the J. P. Morgan of organized crime, to let Lansky's good friend Batista, the former dictator who wore white suits and high-heeled shoes and was addicted to monster movies, return to Cuba from a comfortable exile in his Florida mansion. When Batista arrived in Cuba, Prío provided him with a military guard for his protection. Prío lived to regret this largess when the former sergeant again took over the reins of Cuba by putting the military in the saddle. Batista's means for assuring the loyalty of the army rank and file was simple: He doubled their pay.

President Prío used Miami as a sort of Antillean Switzerland, as had the legion of government officials who preceded him on the grafters' milk run between Havana and the friendly Miami banks which asked no questions. The most notorious of this breed was José Manuel Alemán, the minister of education under Prío's dreary predecessor, President Ramón Grau San Martín, whose aphoristic philosophy of government was: "To govern is to distribute"; when asked how he had managed to take $20 million from the Cuban treasury during just two years on the job, Señor Alemán replied, "In suitcases." Prío, along with Alemán and the other urban pirates of

Havana, invested heavily in Miami real estate. The respect accorded him by the management of the Casa de Palmas in McAllen was that traditionally afforded by one hotel owner to another. On Collins Avenue in Miami, Prío owned the Vendome Hotel, where he lived in the penthouse.

Outside Prío's suite the end–of–summer sun was bleaching the colors from the large Texas afternoon. The two men had been talking for hours. The topic was revolution. Both had some experience. Since his exile to Miami in 1952, Prío had been putting money into anti–Batista plots the way a gambler feeds the slots, hoping one will eventually pay off. He participated in these intrigues from his penthouse; he was one of those revolutionaries that Castro disdained as "heroes from afar," although that opinion went unexpressed by Castro this afternoon.

Castro was impatient. He paced up and down the room. He announced that he and his men were ready to attack Batista. All they needed was money. Prío appraised this rambunctious young Cuban with the skepticism of age. Castro, at thirty, had a history of rushing in where fools feared to tread. At twenty-one he had joined an abortive invasion of the Dominican Republic to oust the tyrant Trujillo, escaping arrest by diving into a shark-infested bay and swimming to shore carrying his submachine gun.[5] His reaction was no less nervy when Batista seized the Cuban government and canceled the 1952 presidential elections. A yearling lawyer in Havana with an impoverished clientele, Castro wrote Batista a personal letter calling down the fires of Hades on him and then sued Batista in the high courts of Cuba, demanding that the nonplussed judges sentence the dictator to no less than 108 years in jail for violating the Cuban Constitution of 1940.

Castro had made good his threats against Batista. "When the worst is enthroned, a pistol at his belt, it is necessary to carry pistols oneself in order to fight for the best," he had said. On July 26, 1953, he led an attack on the Moncada army barracks in Santiago. His men were armed mostly with hunting rifles and outnumbered ten to one. Half of his force of 160 were immediately captured. They were systematically tortured and murdered by Batista's army and his secret police. Newspapers in Batista's control printed photographs of men who had been dressed in clean clothes after being murdered in a clumsy attempt to show that they had been killed in the battle. The facts of the atrocities won for Batista the reputation of a monster. The Moncada assault became the stuff of legend. The Cuban Communist party, which had made its arrangements with Batista, attacked Castro for "putschist" methods.

It was said that Fidel Castro could outfight, outrun, outswim, outride, and outtalk any man in Cuba. Of this last, Prío was that afternoon convinced. The man sitting across the room was the greatest nonstop talker in the world. According to his brother Raúl, Fidel was the kind of man who, when asked if he owned a dog, would go into rhapsodies of detail about the dog's size and color, his pedigree, the tricks he knew, his intelligence, his hunting ability, his housebrokenness; whereas Raúl, if asked the same question, would say, "*Sí*, I have a dog," and that would be the end of it. This was the man who, prisoner in a Batista court, indicted his jailers for their crimes, delivering a five-hour extemporaneous speech, not pleading for mercy but making the case for revolution, reciting the history of the economic exploitation of Cuba and the regime of blood and terror of that *monstrum horrendum* Batista, quoting from memory Thomas Aquinas and Thomas Paine on the right of revolution, and the Spanish Jesuit Mariana on the efficacy of tyrannicide, telling the cowed judges to go ahead and sentence him, he didn't mind. "History will absolve me," he said in a speech that was smuggled out of prison, sentences written on scraps of paper hidden in matchboxes, sentences written in lime juice between the lines of letters to friends, to live as the Gettysburg Address of the Cuban Revolution.[6] Now Fidel was talking to Prío. It was not enough that Prío might agree to give him the money he needed; Fidel would not stop until the former president believed that the unlikely plan he was outlining would succeed.

Castro sat on the couch next to Prío, the better to convince him. As he talked, he jabbed the former president's chest with his finger. His brown eyes blazed inches from Prío's eyes. The words came in deluges, like tropical rain. He talked at full speed, all energy and enthusiasm and concentration. When he finished, it was dark, and Prío had agreed to give him $100,000.[7]

Castro could hardly conceal his excitement. With the money he could buy arms to replace those confiscated, he could bribe the Mexicans to leave him alone while he readied his invasion force, and he could buy a boat to float his revolution.

Castro got up to go. His comrades were waiting to sneak him back across the boarder into Mexico. Prío stopped him at the door. There was one last thing: There must be a united front against Batista. Prío volunteered to be in charge. He used all his considerable charm to put a bridle on the headstrong revolutionary. He extracted from Castro a promise to notify him when he was leaving for Cuba. "We will coordinate our activities," said Prío.[8]

Castro nodded. He had no intention of letting this master of the spoils system look over his shoulder. But he would resist any suggestion that he had lied to Prío; the Jesuits had taught him the term for this in school; it was a "mental reservation."

Prío also had his secrets. He did not tell Castro that he was organizing an invasion of Cuba from the Dominican Republic in league with the tyrant Trujillo; he would align himself with the very devil to get back in power. His hope was to beat his new ally to the revolutionary punch. Prío was businesslike about everything, none the less about revolutions; the money given to Castro, was, to him, a $100,000 insurance policy.

The two Cubans parted smiling with faint lies on their lips.

DEADLY SECRETS

ONE

"Plausibly Deniable"

> *The USA seems destined by Providence*
> *to plague us with all kinds of evils*
> *in the name of liberty.*
>
> SIMÓN BOLÍVAR,
> *the George Washington*
> *of Latin America*

THIS book is the story of the smoking gun held against Cuba by
the United States, and how that gun has been turned inward, most
horrendously in the assassination of John F. Kennedy. The Secret
War against Cuba dates back to the first term of President Franklin
Roosevelt, when Cuba became the first country in the hemisphere
to have its government overthrown by the United States without
direct military force. FDR's renunciation of America's traditional
send-in-the-Marines approach to Latin America relations was
called, perhaps ironically in retrospect, the Good Neighbor Policy.
(FDR was also the first American president, as far as is known, to
employ the Mafia, at devil's bargain prices, in patriotic endeavors,
a leaf the CIA took from his book.) The new type of intervention
pioneered by Roosevelt's policy makers in Cuba in 1933 —
economic blackmail, political intrigue, manipulation of the military,
labor, and student groups to overthrow "unstable" administrations
or those unservile toward Washington — produced the succession of
corrupt Cuban governments that ultimately led to the Castro revolution of the late 1950s.[1] It was also the precursor of later, more covert CIA tactics in Latin America that in the 1960s reached an

---

3

apotheosis in Ecuador, where the CIA owned as so much Tupper-ware government wheels, heads of political parties, leading editors and army officers, labor and student leaders, and even the country's vice-president.

America has come a long way from the time when Secretary of State Henry L. Stimson abolished the Black Chamber, the State Department's post-World War I cryptanalysis division, on the grounds that "Gentlemen do not read each other's mail."[2] Since violence has become as American as apple pie, spying is also as American as Indians; indeed, CIA courses in spycraft give homage to the Indian fieldwise techniques of surveillance. (The CIA's spy professors do not, however, generally trumpet it about that U.S. Cavalry secret agents gave blankets from tuberculosis wards to Indians considered hostile.) There remains at bedrock of the national subconscious that Ben Hecht has called the American schizophrenia the notion that if dark deeds are to be done, they are best done abroad, in the cold with the spies. It is one thing for the CIA to steal King Farouk's urine or run a 35,000-man *armée clandestine* in Laos. It is another thing entirely to foul the home soil with the chamber pot of dirty tricks. In the case of Cuba, this was what happened.

The CIA is forbidden by charter and mandate, and by a peculiarly American sense of Emersonian moralizing, from clandestine operations inside the United States. Nevertheless, it undertakes them. Occasionally it is caught. In the mid-1960s it was revealed that CIA agents had been traveling about the country like commission salesmen, buying intellectuals, co-opting universities, leasing labor unions for cover, and subsidizing students as spies through a billion-dollar network of fronts and foundations which funneled tens of millions of dollars each year to American institutions quick to do the CIA's bidding. In addition to money, the CIA provided domestic fringe benefits; among *Ramparts* magazine's 1967 revelations of the CIA's secret fifteen-year subsidization of the National Student Association was the courtesy draft card that NSA leaders received for cooperating with the agency — Selective Service deferments for an "occupation vital to national interests."[3]

A mid-1970s flurry of CIA exposés showed the agency spying on radlibs and other domestic recusants, including women's liberationists. The resulting Rockefeller Commission and Senate Intelligence Committee investigations established that during the tempest of the 1960s intelligence techniques previously applied to foreign elements were turned inward on a wide range of perfectly legal domestic political activities. The CIA ended up with 1,500,000 names of Americans on one computer, the names of 300,000 on another;[4] the agency kept files on 50,000 members of the California Peace and Freedom party alone during 1969 and 1970.[5] CIA spies hung out on college campuses, and the agency maintained a massive letter-opening campaign (it opened a quarter million letters to and from Americans, including the post of John Steinbeck and former Senator Frank Church). The FBI acted similarly until J. Edgar Hoover, a wise old owl who saw the handwriting on the wall, put the brakes on FBI letter openings and black-bag jobs in 1966.[6] (In fairness to the agency, it did not make confetti of the Constitution all by itself but rather at the insistent urgings of Presidents Johnson and Nixon and others.)

The agency proved itself singularly resilient in the adverse circumstances of such disclosures. It suffered the purgative rhetoric of its critics and even offered to cooperate in its own investigation. In 1975 then CIA Director William Colby, a steely-eyed Boy Scout master who in Vietnam had run the CIA's notorious Phoenix program of wholesale assassinations, flogged himself with a gray-flanneled whip and apologized to the senators for venial sins. Colby bent over so far as to refer to the Department of Justice allegations that former high CIA officials — as high as former CIA Director Richard Helms — had lied to Congress about CIA destabilization operations in Allende's Chile, and about other dark agency secrets. George Bush, who replaced Colby in the CIA director's hot seat, effectively blocked all the investigations Colby had encouraged.

The CIA by curtsying to congressional review avoided a jailhouse massacre of its domestic assets which included proprietary companies, secret paramilitary bases, and countless arm's-length contract operatives through which it had developed a capability for almost-overnight intervention in other people's business. All the while the Senate was investigating the CIA, the CIA was busily "destabilizing" Angola. The 1976 Church Report was frankly pessimistic on

Congress's ever finding its way through the briar patch of CIA domestic fronts: " . . . to the extent that details regarding the organizing of the Central Intelligence Agency remain cloaked in secrecy, the identity of the unofficial affiliates of the CIA will continue to be elusive."[7]

Of all the domestic-based CIA operations that were the agency's bittersweet secrets from the 1960s, the largest remains the least known. The agency called it the Cuba Project.

The Cuba Project was an overreaching program of clandestine warfare, offhanded military adventures, sabotage, and political and economic subversion. It ran the gamut from counterfeiting to biological warfare to assassination. It began in 1959 during the Eisenhower administration, reached its paramilitary heights under the brothers Kennedy, slumbered under Lyndon Johnson, and was reawakened with a vengeance under Richard Nixon. President Carter mothballed the Secret War, but assassination plots against Castro, economic warfare, sabotage, and other aspects of the dormant Cuba Project were again activated during the rebirth of covert action as a primary instrument of foreign policy in the Reagan–Bush administration. George Bush, the first CIA man to become president, has carried the torch of overthrowing Fidel Castro.

The history of the Cuba Project in its primary years of the 1960s is the story of a major American war undeclared by Congress, unacknowledged by Washington, and unreported in the press.

It was the most ambitious undertaking of what E. Howard Hunt liked to call the clandestine services of the United States. It was also the CIA's most expensive failure. The cost in dollars was over a billion, but it cost the country much more than money. The Secret War corrupted American institutions in ways that occasioned the destruction of two presidencies. As the framers of the 1947 legislation creating the CIA had warned, once the pistol of domestic espionage was loaded, one could never be sure in what direction it might point. The best evidence is that during the administration of John F. Kennedy it pointed at the President. Richard M. Nixon pointed the gun at the government itself, and it backfired in his face. The Reagan–Bush administration pointed it at Nicaragua, and shot itself in the foot with the Iran-Contra affair.

The overwhelming concern of the Secret War plotters was that everything they did be, in the words relished by E. Howard Hunt, "plausibly deniable," a phrase dating from the Eisenhower administration. In a curious way such denials became more important than even success. Since everything they attempted was, in one way or another, illegal under international law and the various laws of the United States (the CIA's Cuba Project adventures violated, in addition to the agency's own enabling legislation, the Neutrality Act, the Firearms Act, and the Munitions Act, IRS, FAA, Customs, and Immigration regulations, and laws in a half dozen states), it became an imperative that the domestic operations be carried out in ways that could never be traced back to the prime movers in the federal city.

To hide its Secret War, the CIA generously expended its unvouchered funds establishing a domestic paramilitary operations apparatus. Many of the agency's covers and special operatives enlisted in the Cuba Project included businesses and individuals that also shared rentals with organized crime and fanatical right-wing paramilitarists. In time it became impossible to separate the wheat of intelligence from the chaff of the underworld.

Despite a series of operational blunders of the Katzenjammer Kids genre, the Cuba Project remained one of the agency's best-kept secrets. Compartmentalization was watertight, and many senior CIA employees knew of its existence only by rumor.[8] Within the agency the project was so compartmentalized, and outside the agency so "plausibly deniable" at the end of a purposely twisted chain of command, that the CIA's Special Operations Division often lost effective control of what was going on in the field. The Black Pope of covert action in Langley, Virginia, saw things as going in one direction, while his hired acolytes in armed assembly on Stock Island near Key West would be aiming in another. If this absurd bifurcation made success that much more elusive, there was at least the assurance that it increased the likelihood of covering up a failure.

The Special Operations Division is the skull-and-crossbones section of the CIA. It is looked upon with something approaching contempt by the agency's social engineers, who consider the paramilitaries, or PMs as they are known in the familiar — these range from aging former OSS derring-doers to out-of-work Green Beret demolitionists to on-the-make mercenaries—a regrettably necessary adjunct to the gentlemanly calling that is the intelligence trade. However, the special ops do the CIA's dirty work, which in recent years amounts to most of the work the CIA does. This view of the agency's dirty-tricks workload is supported by Victor Marchetti and John D. Marks, the authors of the famously agency-censored tell-all *The CIA and the Cult of Intelligence*, who say that CIA covert operations consume two-thirds of its public budget of just under $1 billion a year (with an additional $5 billion or so for covert operations hidden in the budgets of other government departments) and account for 11,300 of the 16,500 employees the CIA will admit to (this is exclusive of contract employees and employees of proprietary companies, which number twice again that).

The CIA's paramilitary capabilities took a quantum leap during the Kennedy administration. This seems to have reflected a bureaucratic necessity for the agency to expand with Kennedy's adventurism. The classic methods of espionage—the czar's sort of spy operative—had by the late 1950s given way to the technology of spy planes and the extensive electronic eavesdropping of the National Security Administration. The CIA couldn't do much about modern totalitarian Goliaths, such as the Soviet Union or China, but hide and watch. This left the Davids of the Third World as the turf where the agency could carry out its covert games; luckily for the CIA, this dovetailed with JFK's love affair with unconventional warfare.

The rationale for the CIA's formidable apparatus for mischief was formulated by Richard M. Bissell, Jr., the agency's Ivy League scholar and incurable schemer who was the Clausewitz of the Bay of Pigs. Bissell described the function of the CIA's "clandestine services" as "attempting to influence the internal affairs of other nations—sometimes called 'intervention'—by covert means." It was left for Henry Kissinger to cut out the double-talk. Kissinger was speaking of the Nixon administration's CIA-engineered overthrow of the Allende government in Chile. He said with uncharacteristic succinctness: "I don't see why we need to stand by and watch a country go communist due to the irresponsibility of its own people."[9]

CIA accountants are, of course, practitioners of poltergeist, but the paucity of agency statistics about its clandestine division becomes all the more spooky when it is understood that most CIA special operatives are so-called contract employees who work job by job, often in succession, and are paid in cash without regard to FICA deductions, or work for a CIA wholly owned front, or are paid on the payroll of a legitimate corporation so cooperating—all steps into the shadows of unaccountability.

The Cuba Project was the first time in the agency's history that these hired adventurers were extensively employed inside the United States. They were a splendidly checkered crew who accepted as a risk of doing business with the CIA the disagreeable fact that it would disavow them if they were caught. Other than that, the agency was not too sticky as an employer. Many CIA special ops found their intelligence covers gave them license to steal, usually with an official look-the-other-way attitude; if smuggling guns or dope happened to be integral to their covers, they pocketed the profits.

The clandestine house built by the Special Operations Division was a domestic network of airlines, maritime covers, arms storehouses, and commando training camps. A map of the United States showing the sites of CIA paramilitary installations would be spotted with more than forty dots, stretching from Southern California to Maryland, with the majority in the southeastern part of the country; one CIA arms storage facility was in a bunker on a campus of the University of Miami.

For the Secret War, the Special Operations Division purchased its own ships and planes, registered them under corporate fronts, rigged them for combat, and hired civilian seagoing mercenaries and flyboys to pilot them. The symbiotic relationship between intelligence activities and organized crime that flourished in the hothouse environment of the Cuba Project was nurtured by the restlessness of the thousands of anti-Castro Cuban commandos the CIA kept bivouacked in cheap rooming houses and swampholes from New Orleans to Miami. Their CIA bosses eventually lost control of them and they became involved in profitable intrigue—high-stakes dope smuggling, gunrunning, murder for hire, and other lucrative enterprises on the central exchange of the Caribbean black market.

As it is sometimes said of socialism, the domestic expansion of the CIA came about in a creeping manner. The room number paint was barely dried on the new intelligence agency's doors in 1947 when it acquired a clandestine operations unit by absorbing the grossly misnamed Office of Policy Coordination, a Cold War dirty-tricks outfit set up by President Truman as separate and distinct from the CIA. Truman at first had stubbornly insisted that the CIA be limited only to information gathering, but the intelligence bureaucrats gradually dissuaded him. By the early 1950s the CIA was infiltrating American institutions and setting up fronts in the United States to hide its clandestine programs overseas. In less than ten years, with the advent of the Secret War, the CIA brought the covert-action business home. To hide the fact it had done that which was forbidden it, the agency undertook intelligence dodges and feints, many of them imaginative, that brought the CIA deeper and deeper into the domestic sector; this was the beginning, as far as the intimacies of courtship may be reconstructed, of its marriage of convenience with Howard Hughes; it was also the occasion of the CIA's burrowing into the hedgerows of the "war against drugs" and the infrastructure of the DEA, to hide its domestic activities.

In the beginning the agency's paramilitarists trod lightly on American soil. When the CIA overthrew the Arbenz regime in Guatemala from bases in Honduras and Nicaragua in 1954, the only U.S. facility used was a former naval air base at Opa-Locka, Florida, where the CIA airlifted supplies to its Central American camps and E. Howard Hunt, then a "disinformation" expert, prerecorded doomsday broadcasts to terrorize the Guatemalan people on invasion day.

The Bay of Pigs invasion was a more homegrown product, although the agency, mindful of the Neutrality Act, collected its due bill from the Guatemalan government, establishing the main invasion training camp at Retalhuleu, and launched the actual invasion in April 1961 from ever-cooperative Nicaragua. The covert-action command post for the Bay of Pigs was in suburban Coral Gables. In nearby Coconut Grove, E. Howard Hunt was holed up in an agency-leased tract house drafting the constitution for the New

Cuba; the conservative Hunt bridled at writing a proposed land reform clause, which he considered pink.

Despite a White House dictum that invasion-connected activities were not to take place in the United States, the CIA organized a "diversionary" strike force in New Orleans and screened and trained Cuban exiles for the main invasion brigade in the Florida Everglades and Keys and even in Miami hotels. The agency freely utilized U.S. military air bases — at Florida's Opa-Locka, the Cabinet members of the CIA's handpicked provisional government of Cuba were held under house arrest, while in New York City a public relations man in CIA employ lip-read their lines for them to the press. Throughout the history of the Cuba Project, the agency made its white hired hands the knights and treated the exiled Cubans as pawns.

Once it had begun its involvement in domestic operations, the CIA wanted more. After its public humiliation over the Bay of Pigs, the agency, ignoring its own Dunkirk, merely changed the names of its domestic paramilitary fronts and proceeded in business-as-usual fashion with black operations against Cuba. It did not do this unbridled, but rather under the tight rein of the Kennedy administration.

Although it is a popular liberal belief that the CIA is an "invisible government" answerable to none but its own, the reality is that the agency is a relatively slavish, if twisted, tool of the imperial presidency. Few, if any, major CIA operations have been carried out without White House approval. Contrary to Camelot hagiography, the Bay of Pigs was not the end but the beginning of the Kennedy administration's scorched-earth policies toward Cuba. The Kennedy brothers were Irish don't-get-mad-get-even determined to avenge the macho embarrassment of the Bay of Pigs. They wanted, in the words of General Edward Lansdale — a sort of Dr. Strangelove of clandestine warfare who helped install the Diem regime in Vietnam and became the model for the "Ugly American" — "boom and bang" on the island of Cuba. The Kennedys' zeal for meddling was such that they were willing to listen to the most James Bondish of schemes to knock off Castro. (John Kennedy, as a senator, once solicited Ian Fleming's advice on ways to remove the Cuban revolutionary.) One of the more imaginative suggestions came from

Landsdale himself, who was called to Camelot to contribute his talents to Operation Mongoose, the CIA code name for the Kennedy post–Bay of Pigs war against Castro. According to the testimony of a CIA intimate before the Senate Intelligence Committee, the general had a plan to get rid of Castro by spreading the word that the Second Coming was imminent and the new Christ was anti-Castro.[10] Two bearded leaders would be too much.

Jack Kennedy would stand for no CIA bungling the second time around. He put his brother, Attorney General Robert F. Kennedy, in personal command of the Secret War against Castro. The CIA was sent back to the drawing board. Another full-scale invasion would hardly be "plausibly deniable," so the parameters of CIA conduct were set by logistical standards: If the CIA found it necessary to call on the Pentagon for support, the operation was too large, or "noisy," to use a State Department word of art. This was not the stumbling block it first appeared. In the time-honored tradition of interservice rivalry, the CIA bypassed the Pentagon by assembling its own army, navy, and air force for the undeclared Caribbean war. The Kennedys had no patience for the clauses of the Neutrality Act. This time the center of operations was Miami.

Miami became the largest CIA station in the world. Back at the Pickle Factory, as some insiders called CIA headquarters in Langley, Miami was known as the company town. The CIA set up so many fronts there that the agency deserved a separate category in the Yellow Pages. The cream of local institutions—from banks and department stores to the ever-willing University of Miami—was skimmed to provide cover and auxiliary services. The agency's car pool for the Miami station had more vehicles than the local Hertz, and the sudden influx of CIA personnel contributed to rising costs on the local housing market. The CIA never got the credit for the millions of dollars it pumped into the local economy while making Miami a Cold War Zürich. Most Miamians never suspected that the biggest paramilitary operation ever mounted from American soil was going on in their city. It was generally assumed that the muffled sounds of explosions coming from the Everglades was dynamiting for the construction of the Palmetto Expressway. Nor was it recognized that some expensive cabin cruisers gliding out to the Gulf Stream were disguised CIA warships headed for Cuba.

Modesty forbade, but had the CIA's navy been entered in *Jane's Fighting Ships* it would have ranked as the largest in the Caribbean. They spy fleet consisted of demothballed subchasers, converted patrol craft, hopped-up speedboats, and supercharged pleasure cruisers. CIA ships were equipped with radar and electronic gear and armed with 40 mm naval cannon, recoilless rifles, and .50-caliber machine guns. Normally of foreign registry, usually Nicaraguan, the boats were manned by special ops and Cuban seamen working under commercial covers of marine engineering and oceanic research firms in Miami and West Palm Beach. This spook navy infiltrated saboteurs and commando raiding parties into Cuba. The CIA ships on several occasions engaged in sea battles with Cuban naval and MiG air defenses, creating near-international incidents that the agency made frantic moves to hush up.

The agency's air force consisted largely of reconditioned B-26 bombers flown by pilots of fortune on itinerant raids against such Cuban targets as sugar mills, cane fields, oil storage facilities, and power plants. The choice of the B-26 was dictated by the fact that the World War II propeller-driven sturdy had survived in large numbers on the worldwide war surplus market and could not be automatically traced to the United States. The raiders took off from commercial airports under business covers and from isolated airstrips and mothballed military fields in Florida and, to a lesser extent, Louisiana, as well as from improvised runway strips hacked out of the jungles in Guatemala, Nicaragua, and Costa Rica.

Under the impetus of the Cuba Project, the CIA during the 1960s established one proprietary domestic airline—Intermountain Aviation—and greatly expanded another it already controlled, Southern Air Transport (which it eventually sold in 1973). Although in the heyday of the Cold War United Airlines boasted that it was the "largest airline in the free world," that honor may well have belonged to the agency, the various subsidiaries of which owned more planes than any domestic airline and employed more people than the CIA proper. The head of air operations for the Bay of Pigs, an agent known mysteriously as Mr. G, was assigned in the fall of 1961 to develop the Intermountain line along with the sprawling Marana Air Park complex near Tucson into a paramilitary air-support facility of such self-sufficiency that the agency could launch an invasion strike anywhere in the world without requiring so much as a can of kerosene from the U.S. Air Force.

The CIA's Cuban exile soldiers were equipped from the agency's own arms supply depots in Missouri and Virginia. They received their basic training in a half dozen states: Cuban pilots practiced precision supply drops at the Marana air base in Arizona; officers were schooled at the Farm, a CIA training center located at Camp Peary near Williamsburg, Virginia, and at Fort Benning in Georgia; Cuban frogmen were taught the art of underwater demolition at the CIA's secret Isolation Tropic base on the North Carolina coast; Cuban enlisted men (CIA pay was $175 a month for bachelors, $225 for married men plus a child allowance) trained at Kendall, south of Miami, on the north shore of Lake Pontchartrain in Louisiana, and at other spots where the rule was the more remote, the better. The agency between 1962 and 1965 financed exile contingents in secret military bases in Costa Rica and Nicaragua. As late as 1966 it was still bivouacking Cuban commando units in rural encampments on the Gulf Coast.

The Secret War lords did not rely solely on the paramilitary banderilleros and sea pirates. During the fourteen-year life of the Cuba Project, the CIA was itself involved in at least a dozen attempts on Castro's life. The assassination plots led to the agency's famous *liaisons dangereuses* with the Mafia. In addition to taking a contract out on Castro, the CIA availed itself of the full-service mob banks in Miami in laundering cash for its domestic operations. After a series of abortive Mafia-CIA attempts to assassinate Fidel between 1960 and 1963 the mob, businesslike as usual, cut its losses over Cuba and went on to invest in other islands, notably the Bahamas and Haiti. The CIA continued to initiate and support others' plots on Castro's life. In 1971 when Castro paid a state visit to Allende's Chile there was a plot, a back-up plot, awaiting him. Designs on Castro's life can be tracked into 1987, when Cuban officials the CIA had recruited turned out to be double agents, and blew the whistle.

The agency's flirtations with the underworld were not among its more subtle ploys during the 1960s. Once, in a *Goldfinger* type of plot to undermine the Cuban economy with bogus currency, the CIA allowed a counterfeiting ring to set up shop in a house on Thirty-second Street in Georgetown next door to the home of CIA Director Allen Dulles. The Secret Service eventually raided it.

The Kennedy administration had completed extensive top-secret plans for a second major invasion of Cuba in the spring of 1964 that were scratched by President Johnson after John F. Kennedy's assassination. LBJ's objections to another Cuban invasion seem to have been prompted more by his well-known lack of love for Robert Kennedy—whose pet project it was—than an inordinate concern for the territorial integrity of Cuba.

To mollify Johnson, the Secret War plotters in the mid-1960s turned their sights to Haiti. They formulated a plan to overthrow the dreaded Papa Doc Duvalier, the witch doctor-dictator, with a combination of Haitian and Cuban exiles and then to allow the Cubans to invade their homeland from Haiti across the narrow Windward Passage separating the two islands. The scheme came to an end that was not without irony when Papa Doc beefed up his military defenses by a Faustian lend-lease pact with the Mafia, the long-range planners of which saw Haiti as a potential casino paradise to replace the lost crown jewel of Havana.

Richard M. Nixon, as Vice President, in 1959 helped create the Cuba Project. It was President Nixon, in 1969, who rekindled the Secret War from the dead coals of the Kennedys. He modernized the plotting against Castro with the addition of biological warfare (introducing African swine flu to Cuban cattle) and weather warfare (cloud seeding to precipitate rains out of Noah to ruin Cuba's agricultural economy). Until President George Bush, the most up front of the anti-Castro presidents (plotters) was Nixon, who posed for newspaper photographs personally congratulating anti-Castro raiders. Bush went Nixon one better by assigning his son Jeb to the job of chief cheerleader for Miami's *gusanos*, whom Bush let dictate the administration's Cuba policy.

Throughout this history of the Secret War a recurring theme is how the small triumphs and large tragedies of the faceless men the

CIA sent off to its paramilitary expeditions affected the lives of the great and the near great pledged to keep their deadly secrets. Not the least of the lives so affected was that of Richard Nixon, its procreator. It was the war heroes of the Cuba Project who broke into Watergate. Veterans of the Secret War may have played a role in the theft of President Carter's briefing book during the 1980 presidential campaign, and they started the back-channel negotiations that led to the Iran-Contra affair.

The history of Richard Nixon's creation—the Cuba Project—is the story of a prohibition failed and a warning come true. The prohibition, in the 1947 legislation establishing the CIA, restricted it to foreign intelligence gathering. The warning from the CIA's founders was that domestic undertakings by a secret intelligence agency would take a Frankenstein turn. But no one thought the turn would be toward the Mafia.

While the nation was making light of President Dwight Eisenhower's cautions about the dangers of a military-industrial complex, its more nasty kid brother, the intelligence-industrial complex, was growing up unnoticed. The Cuba Project's concentric circles of domestic intelligence operations, organized crime, and cooperating businessmen whose bottom line was blessed by the CIA are to be delineated in this book, a chain linking, among others, Howard Hughes, Richard Nixon, and Meyer Lansky. An indication of the stakes is that Howard Hughes, whose corporate embrace of the CIA was little less than total, made a paltry $547 million selling Trans World Airlines while racking up some $6 billion in contracts for paramilitary and clandestine warfare hardware.[11]

There are profiteers in every war, none less than in a Secret War. The legacy of the Cuba Project is more frightening. The Secret War compromised the democratic system it deigned to secure. The disease of secrecy spread through the system. One dreadful thing led to another, and to the most dreaded of all: The major figures in the John F. Kennedy assassination were, in one way or another, connected to the Cuba Project—to the CIA, or the mob, or, as was more often the case, to both. The CIA kept the involvement of its operatives and clandestine fronts in the Kennedy assassination from the

Warren Commission. It left the nation a legacy of doubt. The agency lied about Watergate for no less noble motives. It was again protecting its fronts and its people, as when former CIA Director Richard Helms testified before the Watergate Committee that Eugenio "Rolando" Martínez, one of the Watergate burglars, was a third-rate CIA tipster who was occasionally paid a pittance. This was within that special category of lie known within the agency as CYA—for "Cover Your Ass." Martínez was, in fact, one of the Cuba Project's highest paid and most accomplished operatives, who had made more clandestine runs to Cuba than anyone else and was involved with his CIA cronies in secret domestic political activities.

Watergate was nothing but the bringing home to Washington of the Secret War. The CIA lied about that, as it did about the Kennedy assassination, because to do otherwise would have revealed the infrastructure of the war itself—and the clandestine government's questionable ties to men like Lansky, Hughes, and Nixon, and, as Nixon himself put it, "a lot of hanky-panky." This hanky-panky has left a particularly murderous legacy for the 1980s and the 1990s, as Cubans trained by the CIA drifted into an international far-right terrorist network of assassins and bombers that profits in narcotics, operating largely unhampered by the rigors of George Bush's war on drugs.

The demiworld in which the Secret War was fought makes impossible the answering of all questions about its many-layered intrigues. This book does, however, make one thing perfectly clear—namely, what Richard Nixon meant, on the presidential tapes, when he authorized the White House cover-up of the Watergate break-in because ". . . the problem is it tracks back to the Bay of Pigs," and to the nation's Deadly Secrets.

TWO
The Gangster as James Bond

I

THE judge was surprised. It was to be but a routine pleading by a routine gangster. His name was Johnny Roselli, and he was, by reputation, a rather bad fellow. He had run numbers and broken legs and leased wires for the mob in Chicago, Las Vegas, and Los Angeles for the better part of half a century. The latest crime of which he had been found guilty was that of cheating at cards. Roselli's card cheating was not of the garden variety. He had drilled peepholes in the gilded ceiling of the card room in Beverly Hills' exclusive Friars Club and spied down upon the celebrity gin rummy players below, sending electronic signals to his confederates at the card tables, who took unfair advantage — in the aggregate of some $400,000 — of club members of the cut of Phil Silvers and Harry Karl, the millionaire shoe man otherwise known as Mr. Debbie Reynolds.

The judge had given Roselli five years. There were many in the movie colony who considered this permissive treatment for a man caught cheating the pants off Hollywood's finest. Yet Roselli had the effrontery to petition the court to reduce his sentence. This petition was not supported by his former friends Dean Martin and Frank

Sinatra, who had put their countryman up for membership in the Friars Club and were trashed by him.

Roselli had not appreciably improved his manners since he fled Eliot Ness and moved west to become a muscleman in the Hollywood extortion rackets of the forties. It was this unreconstructed past, together with the bizarre nature of Roselli's petition, that contributed to U.S. District Judge William P. Gray's considerable surprise on the afternoon of July 6, 1971.

The mobster's lawyers rose in the brightly lit, antiseptically modern federal courtroom in Los Angeles and dramatically requested that Judge Gray reduce their client's sentence for card cheating on the grounds that this onetime associate of Al Capone was an unsung hero of the Cold War — a secret American patriot who had risked his life attempting to assassinate Fidel Castro for the CIA.

The silver-haired gambler was fashionably dressed for his day in court in a neat dark gray suit and a red turtleneck sweater with a gray stripe. He sat attentively at the defense table, the diamond brightness of his gambler's eyes softened by stock dark glasses. Roselli politely declined to answer the judge's prompt questions about the CIA on the ground that he was sworn to secrecy under a national security oath.

The United States attorney bounded to his feet; to call Mr. Roselli an American hero was to mock the Alamo. He pointed a prosecutor's finger at the dapper, hawk-faced offender — alias Filippo Sacco, as he was born in Esteria, Italy, in 1905, alias Don Giovanni, as he was known to his Mafia cohorts, a man known to keep the company of the likes of Bugsy Siegel, Frank Costello, Meyer Lansky, Little Augie (Pisano) Carfano, and Lucky Luciano, a convicted extortionist of more than $1 million from Loew's and Fox and Warner Brothers studios, the stylish front man overseeing the mob's Los Angeles-Las Vegas gambling axis, a frequent invoker of the Fifth Amendment, whose one brush with respectability was a stormy marriage to actress June Lang. "Your Honor," declared U.S. Attorney David R. Nissen, "this man is a menace to society."

Yet this was the man the clandestine services of the United States had drafted to murder Fidel Castro.

In their haste to establish their client's bona fides as a patriotic assassin, Roselli's lawyers were to put into the public record certain names and facts that they perhaps should not have. The name of William K. Harvey was one. William Harvey was a ruddy-faced giant of an intelligence agent who headed the covert action or dirty-tricks section of the CIA in the early fifties. He was in residence at the Berlin station in 1956 at the time of the fabled Berlin tunnel, which the CIA dug to tap the telephone lines at Soviet military headquarters in East Berlin; the Russians eventually discovered the tunnel, and it became something of a minor tourist attraction.

Harvey, a heavy-drinking, two-gun-toting, womanizing, over-weight secret agent, in the early sixties developed the CIA's "Executive Action" capability — "Executive Action" was the intelligence euphemism for assassination. The CIA called Harvey's Executive Action group ZR/RIFLE. Harvey called it "the magic button."[1] Harvey rode shotgun on Roselli during most of the years the gangster tried to kill Castro. Roselli had graciously refused the usual CIA contract operative's salary, asking only that some expenses be paid by the government. The expenses were never totaled, but they embraced high-speed motor launches, handcrafted Belgian hunting rifles with "sanitized" bullets, poison capsules, and comfortable quarters in far-flung hotel suites. Roselli worked for the CIA from 1960 through 1963, during which time he ramrodded six attempts on the life of the Cuban premier. This was done at some risk to the gambler's life and limb; once his speedboat was sunk from beneath him by the Cuban Navy.

Roselli's lawyers held the courtroom spellbound with fantastic tales of domestic intrigue and Caribbean derring-do that ranged from the Desert Inn in Las Vegas to the Fontainebleau in Miami Beach to the Hilton in Havana and implicated both the Chicago crime syndicate and the Howard Hughes business empire in clandestine United States intelligence operations.

Washington has found it expedient in the past to cooperate with organized crime. Lucky Luciano helped keep the labor peace on the East Coast docks during World War II and was subsequently released from the penitentiary for conduct unbecoming a gangster. Meyer Lansky at the behest of Naval Intelligence in 1944 paid a special visit to his old associate in the businesses of liquor and gambling,

Fulgencio Batista, to deliver the bad news that Franklin Roosevelt desired Batista's retirement from the profession of president-dictator of Cuba. And there have been other accommodations. But the employment of Johnny Roselli was the first known time, even off the record, that the government had attempted to utilize that aspect of the syndicate known in the pulps as Murder Inc.

One is loath to question the patriotic motivation of the syndicate, but it should be pointed out here that if the joint Mafia–CIA venture to murder Castro had been successful, many advantages would have befallen the party of the first part. The return of its Havana gaming tables and ancillary graft would have been true manna from heaven for the mob. It is a fundamental assumption of syndicate theology that the Lord helps those who help themselves first, and the Mafia overlords were fully prepared to take advantage of the miraculous sudden death of the puritan Cuban leader. Roselli's first hit was timed to coincide with the Bay of Pigs, and on the eve of April 17, 1961, waiting in Nassau, in the wings of the theater of the invasion, was Lansky lieutenant Joe Rivers — with a stable of gaming technicians ready to reactivate the casino equipment and a stash of cash to grease the wheels, just in case a miracle came to pass.

Roselli's lawyers had one more stroke to complete this portrait of the gangster as James Bond. The CIA operative who originally recruited Roselli was one Robert Maheu — the right-hand man of Howard Hughes and the boss of the recluse billionaire's Nevada gambling interests.

The patriot from Esteria sat demurely at the defense table as his attorneys extolled his high-blown business relations with Howard Hughes and his patriotic, if murderous, undercover work for the secret government of the United States. Surely here was a man who deserved the mercy of the court.

The surprised judge said he would take the CIA material under submission, although he expressed some judicial misgivings about its relevance to a $400,000 gin rummy swindle in Beverly Hills.

Johnny Roselli was sent back to the McNeil Island federal penitentiary without getting time off for his good behavior in the Caribbean. His unsuccessful attempt to cash in on his CIA connection caused a flurry of cover-up activity that presaged the Watergate tentmaking that would occupy many of the same disinformation artists a year later. As pious as the mafioso had been about keeping his blood oath of silence, he had said enough in open court to imperil the shadow alliance of the underworld, big business, and United States intelligence operations that was the nexus of the Secret War. This alliance did not prosper in the harsh light of day. When Johnny Roselli sang his assassination song as if it were "The Star-Spangled Banner," a good many normally patriotic people did not stand up.

In Robert A. Maheu's office high above the Las Vegas strip, the telephone jangled annoyingly. Maheu answered with a sigh. It was the fifth call in thirty minutes from Los Angeles reporters. Would Mr. Maheu care to comment on the statement made that afternoon in federal court that Mr. Maheu, the manager of the Howard Hughes holdings in Las Vegas, was also a CIA bagman who had hired a notorious mobster to do in Premier Castro of Cuba?

Bob Maheu was a short man with a round face and receding curly hair and the pleasant gaze of a Rotarian Santa Claus. He was a former FBI agent, the former head of an international public relations and private investigation firm that put his Old Boy FBI contacts to profitable use, and a devout Roman Catholic and family man. He was paid $500,000 a year by Howard Hughes.

There were certain matters that Mr. Hughes wanted in the press, and others that he did not, and it was Maheu's charge to see that the press reflected his wishes. When Hughes wanted the world to know that Hughes Aircraft had built Surveyor II, Bob Maheu arranged it, despite a NASA rule prohibiting product identification in the space program. At Cape Kennedy, Maheu hired an RCA employee who played Scrabble with the astronauts, and later, out in space, one of the new American heroes just happened to let the name Hughes Aircraft slip out during a moon walk back to his craft.[2] Maheu was usually successful. His one failure of record was in 1960, when Hughes instructed him to delay a story about a $205,000 loan to Richard Nixon's brother Donald, but Drew Pearson, the feisty Quaker columnist, refused to be reasonable. There was but one other task at which Bob Maheu labored in vain: Johnny Roselli failed to kill Fidel Castro — not that he didn't try.

Robert Maheu had been a contract employee of the CIA from the mid-fifties. Like most CIA operatives, he was loath to talk about even what he had for breakfast while on a CIA expense account. But in 1974 Bob Maheu broke his silence about the Mafia-CIA joint venture to do in Castro in the same forum that Johnny Roselli chose — in court. His motivations were not dissimilar to Roselli's. Maheu had suffered a stunning falling-out with his billionaire boss — Hughes convened a bizarre telephone hookup press conference to depict unkindly his former employee as "a son of a bitch who stole me blind" — and Maheu's lawyers had responded with a $17.5 million slander suit. It was by way of establishing the sterling attributes of Maheu's character that his lawyers questioned him in court about his government service, albeit service in the secret government. Maheu disclosed that in late 1960 or early 1961 he undertook, with Hughes's permission, a "very sensitive assignment" for the CIA.[3] The assignment was the elimination, for reasons of compelling national interest, of the contrary ruler of Cuba. In this high purpose Maheu recruited the gangster and introduced him to his friends in the CIA.

The red flag raised by Johnny Roselli's late-blooming attempt to take refuge in patriotism encompassed substantially more than the controversial politics of assassination. It involved the interlocking of secret intelligence projects with private gain that was the way of life of the Secret War. Howard Hughes was up to his uncut three-inch fingernails in such practices. Even Johnny Roselli got a piece of the action. The mobster, introduced to the Hughes court via the back door of the CIA, came to perform some business functions for the billionaire that were not to be sneezed at. Roselli was even invited to dinner parties for the select Hughes few at Hughes's corporate bastion on Romaine Street in Los Angeles, where access to the inner sanctum was so restricted that employees without top-secret clearances were paid by checks lowered by a fishline from a second-story window.

As Maheu recalled it, Roselli provided the "grease" for Hughes's entry into the starry world of Las Vegas gambling. Said Maheu, delicately: "I told Mr. Hughes that I thought I had found a person fitting the background that he had requested me to seek, to wit, a person who had connections with certain people of perhaps unsavory background as described to me by sources in the United States government agencies . . . the FBI and CIA."[4] The problem was that the hygiene-frantic Hughes wanted to rebuild the entire ninth floor of the Desert Inn as a germproof haven for himself before he would settle down in Las Vegas to play Monopoly. The proprietors of the Desert Inn were the intractable gentlemen of the Cleveland Mayfield Road Gang, who were unenthusiastic about the remodeling because the ninth floor was reserved for private accommodations for the casino's high rollers. Exhibiting the diplomatic skills of a Mafia Kissinger, Roselli was able to intercede on Hughes's behalf with the Cleveland people and convince them to give the bashful billionaire his way. Hughes liked the ninth floor of the Desert Inn so much that he decided to buy all the others, and Roselli helped arranged the sale, pocketing a $50,000 "finder's fee."

There were thus several matters to be covered up on that July afternoon of 1971 when Bob Maheu was being besieged by the newspapers. Howard Hughes, of course, did not desire his business dealings with Johnny Roselli reported on the financial pages, the CIA understandably preferred that its liaison with the syndicate remain an in-house secret, and Maheu could not afford to have himself or his boss linked to the CIA. In the days of the pre-Watergate press, when "national security" was not a phrase of levity and power was still presumed to be practiced by responsible men, the bold lie was a more effective exercise in prevarication that it may be today. So Robert Maheu answered the reporters' preposterous questions about his and Howard Hughes's ties to the likes of Johnny Roselli and to the CIA. He summoned all his soft-spoken authority in reply.

"I will not dignify such a story by even commenting upon it," he said.[5] And it worked.

We only kill each other.
—BUGSY SIEGEL

Robert Maheu and Johnny Roselli were hunched over drinks at the Brown Derby in Beverly Hills. It was September 1960. They were talking business. The price for the star-spangled contract on the life of Fidel Castro was $150,000, plus expenses, but Roselli said he wouldn't do it for money.

Roselli pondered Maheu's offer over another drink. As Maheu later testified, the gangster "was very hesitant about participating in the project." Maheu said he convinced Roselli that assassinating Castro was "a necessary ingredient so as to effectuate a successful invasion. . . . He finally said that he felt an obligation to his government, and he finally agreed to participate."

But first, Roselli wanted to meet someone from the CIA who would verify that it was, in fact, a "patriotic" enterprise.[6]

A week later Maheu introduced Roselli to "Jim Olds," in reality CIA Operations Support Chief James "Big Jim" O'Connell. O'Connell, a lugubrious man with a basset-hound face, had served with Maheu in the FBI during World War II and thereafter had become Maheu's CIA case officer. The meeting was held in the Plaza Hotel in New York, where O'Connell was staying on important business. Uptown in Harlem Fidel Castro was encamped at the Theresa, where he had moved after angrily vacating a midtown hotel that had made "unacceptable cash demands."

The Cuban leader was in town to attend the annual General Assembly of the United Nations. While Castro was bear-hugging Soviet Premier Nikita Khrushchev and pumping the hand of Egypt's Gamal Abdel Nasser at the UN, Jim O'Connell was plotting his death at the Plaza. The CIA had decided to exploit Castro's weakness for cigars. The task of concocting substances with which to impregnate the cigars fell to the Technical Services Division, the laboratories of which had proved irresistible to CIA Director Allen Dulles. According to a Dulles biographer:

> He was interested in the more sinister Agency experiments in mind-bending drugs, portable phials of lethal viruses, and esoteric poisons that killed without trace. Allen's sense of humor was touched when he learned that the unit working on these noxious enterprises was called the Health Alteration Committee (directed by Dr. Sidney Gottleib and Boris Pash), and he added to his collection of CIA curios a noiseless gun which the committee had produced for firing darts

smeared with LSD, germs or venom at enemy agents or foreign per-
sonalities whose existence the CIA was finding embarrassing.[7]

Just how drastically the CIA intended to alter Castro's health in
New York is a matter of debate. Some months earlier Joseph
Scheider, a bioorganic chemist in Technical Services regarded as the
agency's Lucrezia Borgia, had the idea of spraying Castro's broad-
casting studio in Havana with a chemical that produced halluci-
nations. He subsequently proposed that the same chemical be
soaked into a cigar that the premier might smoke before a speech.
These ideas were rejected because the chemical proved unreliable.
But the notion of a trick cigar in Castro's mouth became a CIA
fixation.[8]

The CIA set up a hospitality suite at the Waldorf–Astoria to enter-
tain New York policemen assigned to protect Castro during the
United Nations session. The agency fed them strawberries with
Devonshire sauce. According to David Wise and Thomas B. Ross
in *The Espionage Establishment:*

> New York Chief Inspector Michael J. Murphy (later commis-
> sioner) wandered into the suite and was approached by a CIA man
> with a chilling story. The agency had a plan, the CIA man recounted
> casually, to plant a special box of cigars at a place where Castro would
> smoke one. When he did so, the agent said, the cigar would explode
> and blow his head off. Murphy, who could scarcely believe his ears,
> was appalled, since his responsibility was to protect Castro, not to in-
> ter him. If the CIA man was pulling Murphy's leg, it was a shockingly
> foolish subject to joke about. But, much worse yet, the agent seemed
> completely in earnest. Much to Murphy's relief, however, the CIA
> man explained that the plan would not be carried out.[9]

A variation on the theme: The CIA wouldn't kill Castro — only his
macho image. In place of an explosive device, Castro's cigars were
to be treated with a vicious depilatory that would leave him hairless,
stripped of his title "The Beard." This plan called for a box of depilatory cigars to be available to Castro during an appearance on the
David Susskind television talk show. CIA psychological specialist

David Phillips was consulted on whether the premier's image would suffer as much as was hoped. "I agreed that it would," Phillips said, "and asked how the cigars could be given to the Cuban revolutionary with the assurance that he and not others — perhaps David Susskind — would not actually smoke the stogie. That was the last I heard of the scheme."[10]

The CIA's cigar dream was long dying. After Castro returned to Cuba a box of his favorite brand, Cahiba, was treated with a botulin toxin so deadly that a person would die after putting one in his mouth. The cigars were passed to a double agent who was to offer Castro one, which, apparently, the Cuban declined. The pie-in-the-sky cigar schemes were only the beginning of the CIA's attempts on Castro's life.

"If you needed somebody to carry out murder," former CIA director Richard Helms once said of Johnny Roselli, "I guess you had a man who might be prepared to carry it out." The idea of using the Mafia to carry out "national security" projects can be traced back to the drafting of Lucky Luciano's work for Naval Intelligence during World War II. The CIA and the Mafia subsequently came to be as tight as fraternity brothers. "To understand how it works," said retired Air Force Colonel Fletcher Prouty, the former liaison officer between the Pentagon and the agency, "you have to think of the CIA and organized crime as two huge concentric circles spread all over the world. Inevitably, in some places, the circles overlap."[11] They do more than overlap. CBS correspondent Daniel Schorr reported in 1975 that investigators on Senator Henry Jackson's Permanent Investigations Committee had discovered evidence of a vast CIA-Mafia counterfeiting scheme. Schorr said the CIA shipped actual U.S. Bureau of Printing and Engraving currency plates to Southeast Asia, where, in cooperation with the Mafia, counterfeit U.S. dollars were turned out in the billions. One estimate put the output as high as $20 billion. The CIA used its share of the funny money to finance its covert operations and to purchase opium in Southeast Asia and Turkey to keep it from coming into the United States. Jackson's investigators never found out what the CIA did with the dope it kept off the market. The agency denied that it had done any such thing.[12]

In the fall of 1960 the CIA was murder-minded with regard not only to Castro but to other Third World leaders such as Patrice Lumumba in the Congo. The agency went so far as to contemplate putting together a Mafia hit squad to carry out assignments anywhere in the world. To this end the CIA approached Charles Siragusa, a top official of the federal Bureau of Narcotics who probably knew more about the Mafia than any other lawman in the country. Siragusa, a World War II military intelligence officer, was the Narcotics Bureau's liaison with the CIA. He was incredulous when he heard his CIA opposite number propose that he draw on his knowledge and contacts in the underworld to recruit assassination bounty hunters, who would be paid $1 million drawn from unvouchered funds for each kill. "At first I thought he was joking," Siragusa said. But it was no joke. Siragusa turned the proposal down. "In wartime it's one thing, but in peacetime, it's something different," he said.[13]

The CIA went ahead with the plan anyway, hiring as a talent scout a European gangster given the code designation QJ/WIN. He was to seek out "individuals with criminal and underworld connections in Europe for possible multi-purpose use." According to the Senate Intelligence Committee interim report, Senate probers discovered that one of the men enlisted was a forger and bank robber known as WI/ROGUE. QJ/WIN recruited WI/ROGUE, as the cable to CIA headquarters in Washington breaking the news put it, TO PARTICIPATE IN INTEL NET AND BE MEMBER "EXECUTION SQUAD."[14]

"It is likely that President Eisenhower's expression of strong concern about Lumumba at a meeting of the National Security Council on August 18, 1960, was taken by Allen Dulles as authority to assassinate Lumumba," the Intelligence Committee concluded. Dulles, after the Security Council meeting, cabled the CIA station in the Congo that "in high quarters" the "removal" of Lumumba was "an urgent and prime objective."[15]

The CIA's hired assassins were sicced on Lumumba. However, the effort sputtered because, in the words of the Congo station chief, WI/ROGUE was as controllable as "an unguided missile." Impatient to get on with it, the agency dispatched Joseph Scheider to the scene with a kit containing germs selected to cause fatal disease "indigenous to that area." Although Lumumba was not known to smoke cigars, it was presumed he used a toothbrush. But before access could be gained to his toilet kit, Lumumba was done in by political opponents.

It was, one CIA officer dryly noted, "purely an African event."

CIA headquarters in 1960 was a cluster of makeshift World War II Navy buildings off Ohio Drive in Washington near the Reflecting Pool and Lincoln Memorial. Its nerve center was a former WAVES barracks called Quarters Eye. In July 1960, a cable came into Quarters Eye from the Havana station. One of its Cuban undercover agents had a meeting scheduled with Raúl Castro, the armed forces minister. The Havana station requested any specific intelligence that might be sought. The answering cable caused the case officer to "swallow hard." It stated, "Possible removal top three leaders is receiving serious consideration at HQS," and inquired whether the Cuban agent was sufficiently motivated to risk "arranging an accident" to befall Raúl. In a matter of hours a second cable arrived from Quarters Eye saying, "Would like to drop matter." It was too late. The Cuban had already left for his meeting with Raúl. The Havana station later reported that there had been no opportunity to arrange the "accident."[16]

If the countermanding cable reflected a certain ambiguity over the matter of assassination at Quarters Eye, it soon vanished.

Although E. Howard Hunt in his memoirs claims the honor for himself, it appears that the first man in the CIA to suggest killing Castro was Colonel J. C. King, the chief of the Western Hemisphere Division. King had plotted unsuccessfully the previous year, 1958, with former ambassador to Brazil and Peru William "Flying Tiger" Pawley to head off Castro before he came to power.[17] King was a classic of the Cold War hybrid of doctrinaire anticommunist and buccaneer capitalist. The West Point man proved his mettle in the world of business when, against the prevailing wisdom, he built a condom factory in Brazil, where the overwhelmingly Catholic population was presumed to be a poor market for birth-control software. King knew better. He eventually sold out his thriving business to Johnson & Johnson at a king's profit.

King and Pawley had Eisenhower's ear, and they convinced Ike that Castro was a communist, something about which, at that point, the CIA itself was uncertain. Castro, who in the first year of his regime desperately wanted to get along with the United States—he spent his first few months in office boning up on his English—was a headstrong nationalist determined to keep his promises to Cuba's peasants, but he had his differences with the Communist party, which, after all, had backed Batista. The then cooperative Castro even submitted to an interview by the CIA, set up, according to then Deputy Director Richard M. Bissell, because the agency was in "doubt as to whether Castro was a committed Communist or just leftward leaning."[18] The interview was conducted by Frank Bender, the political action officer for Latin America. Bender, born Frank Droller in Germany, had been a resistance organizer behind Nazi lines during World War II. Slight, balding, a chain smoker, he tended to be politically liberal. "Castro is not only not a Communist," he concluded, "he is a strong anti-Communist fighter."[19]

King, Pawley, and their breed saw any step to correct the prerevolutionary imbalances in Cuban society as a giant leap toward socialism, and their fervent belief was that socialism was but communism by another name. As is often said of revolutionaries, the politics of these capitalists came out of the barrel of a gun. When their point of view—with a healthy assist in the White House from Vice President Nixon—assumed a majority in the Eisenhower administration, the view that Castro was a "communist" became a self-fulfilling prophecy.

On December 11, 1959, King, in a memorandum for Dulles's eyes only, contended that there now existed in Cuba a "far left" dictatorship, which, if permitted to stand, would encourage similar actions against American holdings in other Latin American countries. King had several "Recommended Actions" to solve the problem. One was that "thorough consideration be given to the elimination of Fidel Castro. None of those close to Fidel, such as his brother Raúl or his companion Che Guevara, have the same mesmeric appeal to the masses. Many informed people believe that the disappearance of Fidel would greatly accelerate the fall of the present government."[20]

Dulles took King's suggestion to the crafty Richard M. Bissell, Jr., his trusted deputy director for plans under whom King served in the clandestine services. A Yale man, Bissell possessed the voice of a Milton Cross and the fussy ways of the professor he once had been. He had joined the CIA in 1954 at the invitation of Dulles, and that year he had engineered the overthrow of the leftist regime which had sinned against United Fruit in Guatemala. He had proceeded to oversee the development of the U-2 spy plane; Bissell was a rising star in the CIA firmament. He readily agreed with King's recommendation that Castro be "eliminated." The decision is memorialized by a handwritten note scrawled on the King memorandum indicating that Dulles, with Bissell's concurrence, approved King's recommendations.[21]

The following month Bissell asked Colonel Sheffield Edwards, chief of the Office of Security, to find someone capable of assassinating Fidel Castro. Bissell has said that he discussed the decision with Allen Dulles, who presumably briefed Eisenhower. Bissell did not expect specific authorization from the President because, he said, such matters were always referred to obliquely so that the "chief of state can never be proved to have authorized a particular type of operation." But since there was no red light he took it as approval "to get rid of someone."[22]

Colonel Edwards suggested that syndicate members who had operated casinos in Havana might be willing and able to carry out the assignment. Jim O'Connell, who worked under Edwards, suggested Robert Maheu to make the approach.

Maheu was on a $500-a-month CIA retainer. The agency also covered his office rent so that, as Maheu later told Senate investigators, "I would be available to them as situations arose." Maheu's job description was to deal with situations in which the CIA "didn't want to have an Agency person or a government person get caught."[23] Maheu, for instance, took on the sleazy CIA assignment of producing a porno movie showing Indonesian President Sukarno doing unmentionable things with a woman in Moscow. The twist was that the film was to be produced in such a way that it would appear to be a product of Soviet guile; desired result: turning Sukarno against the Russkis. Maheu had hired an actor resembling Sukarno and was looking for a blue-movie lady when the project was shelved.[24]

When O'Connell tapped him for the Castro job, Maheu was working practically full time for Howard Hughes. Several years before Hughes had hired Maheu to, among other personal tasks, keep an eye on his lady friends. The relationship had expanded to the point where Hughes asked Maheu to drop his other clients and move to Los Angeles at $500,000 a year. This time Maheu's job was, as Maheu discreetly described it, to be "an adviser in the political and government arena."

When Jim O'Connell approached him with the Castro assignment, Maheu was only too glad to accept. But he had to come clean with his boss. Hughes was not difficult to convince. That was his kind of hardball.

In 1951 then Senator Nixon eulogized then movie producer Howard Hughes in the *Congressional Record* for stripping a Hollywood writer of his screen credits for an RKO epic titled *The Las Vegas Story* and ordering every page the unfortunate wretch had written consigned to the wastebasket because he had refused a canary's role with the House Un-American Activities Committee barbershop quartet then touring the country with the popular ditty "Are you now, or have you ever been, a member of the Communist party?"

Hughes had reasons other than ideological for the move. He wished Maheu to increase his empire's collaboration with the CIA in return for government favors. And he had his own designs on Cuba. According to a former aide, Hughes envisioned a Castro-less Cuba as a giant tax dodge for himself. As soon as Castro was gone, the aide said, Hughes intended to rush into Cuba and buy up casinos (as he later did in Las Vegas), develop a series of resort parks on the beachfront, and build his own jumbo airport, thus setting himself up as the new king of Cuban tourism. Because casino accounting was so notoriously sleight-of-handish, he expected to convert the entire venture into a tax dodge. All this would be, of course, contingent on his cutting a deal with the syndicate, something to which the billionaire was not averse. Hughes had long been fascinated with mobsters—in 1931 he filmed Ben Hecht's *Scarface*, about Al Capone, and later he launched the acting career of George Raft, who liked his gangster parts so much that he played host for Meyer Lansky's casino in Havana. "Hughes had a lot of respect for the mob, especially Lansky," a former aide said. "My guess is that he hoped to form some sort of partnership with Lansky."[25] Thus the billionaire joined the Secret War.

Maheu, O'Connell, and Roselli met in Miami to work out details of the operation. It was decided that Roselli would use the name John Ralston; his cover story was that he represented Wall Street interests who owned nickel mines and other properties in Cuba and wanted them back.

Roselli by any spasm of the imagination would have had difficulty being accepted as a Wall Street type. The agency did not expect this cover story to wash, nor did it wish it to. In agency shorthand, the mob had terrific CYA—"Cover Your Ass"—potential. The CIA planned to use the mob's pop-culture pull to draw attention away from itself when one of its assassination plots succeeded. Any American who had seen *The Untouchables* became an armchair expert on how the syndicate boys would be likely to handle someone such as Castro who had cut them out of their territory, and Havana was no numbers route on the Chicago South Side but a money machine that had produced hundreds of millions in profits from gambling, dope, and abortion operations each year. In this measure of the thinking public the CIA's propaganda ministry was onto something solid—in the American heart of hearts, the Godfather is sexier than James Bond, and it would have taken little sweat to pass off Castro's death as a simple act of mob revenge.

Roselli's fifties gambling connections in Havana made him a natural for the assignment. In 1960 he still had excellent contacts within the politically controlled cooks and bartenders union, the pension funds of which, in pre-Castro days, were used in building the Havana Hilton in the same manner as teamster pension millions were invested in gambling-connected edifices in the States. His union cronies could provide couriers to Cuba to make the necessary backup arrangements and seek out some less-than-loyal member of Castro's entourage to do the deed.

The mechanics of how to kill Castro were discussed at another meeting several days later amid the expensive naugahyde of the Fontainebleau Hotel. This time Roselli brought along two friends who he said could help get the job done. He introduced them to O'Connell as "Sam Gold" and "Joe." It wasn't until the weekend, when Maheu sheepishly showed him a Sunday supplement story on the Justice Department's drive against organized crime replete with mug shots of Sam and Joe, that O'Connell realized he had been meeting with Chicago Mafia capo Sam "Momo" Giancana and Santos Trafficante, his Miami counterpart. By that time, O'Connell later recalled, "we were up to our ears in it."[24]

The CIA had assumed that the Mafia would simply blow away Castro, like in the movies, but the Holy Trinity of Roselli, Giancana, and Trafficante was opposed to a standard hit on the grounds that hitting a head of state required a little more ingenuity than hitting, say, Albert Anastasia. Roselli wanted something less noisy and "nice and clean." He suggested slipping Castro a Mickey Finn—if the CIA could make a knockout drop both lethal and slow-acting. That would give the guy who did it a chance to get away.

The CIA loved the idea and called on the considerable talents of Joseph Scheider of the Technical Services Division, who perfected a batch of pills containing botulin toxin; when tested on monkeys, the pills "did the job expected of them." Scheider turned them over to O'Connell in February 1961.

O'Connell delivered the pills to Roselli, who soon reported back that they had been given to "an official close to Castro who may have received kickbacks from gambling interests," according to the 1975 Senate Intelligence Committee report.[27] A few weeks later the official returned the pills with the excuse that he had lost his government position, but Roselli and O'Connell chalked it up to a bad case of "cold feet."[28]

Roselli went looking for someone else to handle the contract.

The cunning enterprise began almost immediately to be bedeviled by complications that can be traced to the fact that, as in a good many other of its business dealings, the mob got greedy. It held some markers of the CIA's, and it began to trade them in for government favors far sooner than the agency might have anticipated. One of these markers proved almost to be the undoing of the agency's limited partnership in Murder Inc. It involved an affair of the heart.

Sam "Momo" Giancana, a trampy little man with hairless legs who wore baggy white socks and generally walked around looking as glum as an unpaid undertaker, had fallen in love. The love object was Phyllis McGuire, the singer late of the McGuire Sisters, but Giancana was fretful and concerned that she had sly eyes for Dan Rowan, the comedian late of Rowan and Martin. The strain was affecting Giancana's work. In an effort to dispel the don's amative anxieties, Maheu had a quiet word with a fellow FBI Old Boy, Edward DuBois, who ran a private detective agency in Miami. What ensued would later be characterized by O'Connell as a "Keystone comedy act." With $5,000 in CIA cash transmitted by Maheu, DuBois dispatched one of his private eyes to Las Vegas to rifle Rowan's room in the Riviera Hotel and tap his phone so the don could hear for himself if Miss McGuire's heart belonged to Momo. But the man was a bit careless, and his tapping equipment was found by a maid. He was arrested by the local sheriff, and a miffed Roselli had to put up the bail. "It was blowing everything, blowing every kind of cover I had tried to arrange to keep quiet," Roselli complained. Giancana didn't share his consternation. "I remember his expression," Roselli said, "smoking a cigar, he almost swallowed it laughing about it."[29]

A tight FBI surveillance of its mobsters, mounted in accordance with Bobby Kennedy's war against organized crime, began to give the CIA men hives. On October 18, 1961, the bureau forwarded an "eyes only" memorandum to Richard Bissell advising that Giancana had boasted to several people that "Fidel Castro was to be done away with very shortly." About the same time FBI agents tried to pressure Roselli into becoming an informer by showing him a snapshot of himself as youthful Filippo Sacco in his native Esteria, Italy; they knew who he was. The gangster had to call upon his new CIA partners to get the bureau off his back in the name of national security.

The Mafia seemed genuinely hurt that other branches of the federal government did not respect the new aura of legitimacy they seemed to feel their CIA duty had cast about them. Chuckie English, a lieutenant to Sam Giancana, once strode indignantly out the door of the Armory Lounge, and syndicate mead hall in Forest Park, Illinois, to assail an FBI surveillance party hanging around in front. "What's wrong? Why don't you guys stop all this? We're all part of the same team."

III

In July 1960, just before the Democratic National Convention in Los Angeles, four Cuban exile leaders were secreted into the Senate Office Building in Washington, D.C., into the anteroom of Camelot.

Shaking hands with Senator John F. Kennedy were Manuel Artime, Tony Varona, Aureliano Sánchez Arango, and José Miró Cardona, who had been the first premier in the Castro government. The four would play key roles in the Bay of Pigs, and two of them would be involved in CIA attempts to assassinate the Cuban leader. The private meeting was arranged by the CIA. It was its way of letting the front-running Democratic candidate know it had plans to overthrow Castro.

The CIA was, of course, hedging its bets. It wanted to insure that it would have its way with Castro no matter who was sitting in the Oval Office. A strong pro-Kennedy faction within the agency was headed by the Ivy League schemer Richard Bissell. After winning the nomination, Kennedy was given the traditional CIA briefing on July 23 by Allen Dulles at the family compound in Hyannisport. Kennedy emerged from the session to comment that Cuba and Africa — for that read Ike's bogeymen Castro and Lumumba — had been discussed "in detail."

The Cuba issue immediately began to play havoc in the 1960 campaign. The Kennedy camp grew paranoid over rumors out of Miami of a CIA-sponsored invasion force. If Castro was toppled before the election, Nixon would get all the credit. Kennedy strategists considered having the candidate give a speech anticipating the event and, it was hoped, neutralizing its political impact. William Attwood, who was writing speeches for JFK, placed several calls to a journalist in Florida preparing a *Life* article on the training of Cuban exiles. Attwood expressed deep concern that an invasion might be launched before election day, but the *Life* man assured him that the exiles were too disorganized for that to happen.[30]

The Nixon brain trust was rooting for the invasion to come before the November voting; Nixon thought "it would have been a cinch to win" if Castro bit the dust before the election. Nixon's press secretary at the time, Herbert G. Klein, later wrote:

> From the start of the 1960 campaign many of us were convinced that Cuba could be the deciding issue in a close election. Certainly, in retrospect, it was one of the decisive factors in what was the closest presidential election of modern history. . . .
>
> Only four of us on the Nixon staff shared the secret that refugees were being trained for an eventual assault on Castro and a return to Cuba. We had stern instructions not to talk about this.
>
> For a long time, as we campaigned across the country, we held the hope that the training would go rapidly enough to permit the beach landing. The defeat of Castro would have been a powerful factor for Richard Nixon. . . .
>
> But the training didn't go rapidly enough for a preelection landing. . . ."

For both Nixon and Kennedy, Cuba was a paradox of special bittersweetness. Richard Nixon, professional hawk, White House action officer for the invasion, had to bite his tongue and bide his time and, on the subject of Cuba, take refuge in statesmanship. John Kennedy, the trendy liberal, carrying the handicap of his Catholicism, adopted the tactic of red-baiting his conservative opponent; already having made a campaign issue of the nonexistent missile gap, he further flexed the wings of his hawkishness and, in a tactic that struck even his opponent, the master of the cheap shot, as foul, he began to beat Nixon over the head with Cuba. On September 23

Kennedy said that the "forces fighting for freedom in exile and in the mountains of Cuba should be sustained and assisted." On October 6 he called for "encouraging those liberty-loving Cubans who are leading the resistance to Castro." He implied negligence on the part of the Eisenhower administration when he referred in classic yahoo phrases to "a Communist menace that has been permitted to arise under our very noses, only ninety miles from our shores."

Nixon could only fuss and fidget; he even worried that if the invasion did come off in time, his adroit opponent would somehow wangle credit for it. As the final television debate between the candidates approached, it was apparent to both sides that any invasion would have to come after the election. On October 20, the eve of the debate in New York, Kennedy staffers handed out a press release that read in part: "We must attempt to strengthen the non-Batista democratic anti-Castro forces in exile, and in Cuba itself, who offer eventual hope of overthrowing Castro."

The statement was tantamount to a charge that the Eisenhower administration had short-sheeted the exiles. Nixon was beside himself. In *Six Crises*, he wrote in a tone of characteristic self-righteousness that the "covert training of Cuban exiles" by the CIA was due "in substantial part at least, to my efforts"—and here was Kennedy making as if he thought of it first! Nixon instructed Interior Secretary Fred Seaton, who was with him in New York, "to call the White House at once on the security line and find out whether or not Dulles had briefed Kennedy on the fact that for months the CIA had not only been supporting and assisting but actually training Cuban exiles for the eventual purpose of supporting an invasion of Cuba itself."

Seaton talked to Brigadier General Andrew J. Goodpaster, Eisenhower's liaison with the CIA. Within a half an hour the answer came: "Kennedy had been briefed on this operation."

Keepers of the Camelot flame, such as Richard Goodwin, insist that the Kennedy campaign had no advance information about an invasion and that their escalatory statements about Cuba were merely gut level. Indeed, in the summer of 1960 the CIA's ambitious paramilitary plotting was just firming up into a full-scale invasion plan. However, given the general hawkish line of Kennedy's campaign and the knowledge, by no means restricted to those among the select briefed by Allen Dulles, that the CIA was up to no good with the Cuban exiles, there is little question that Kennedy knew something was afoot and was deliberately rubbing Nixon's nose in it by upping the ante.

Nixon was left without any alternative. He stood on principle, as he reported in *Six Crises*:

> There was only one thing I could do. The covert operation had to be protected at all costs. I must not even suggest by implication that the United States was rendering aid to rebel forces in and out of Cuba—in fact, I must go to the other extreme; I must attack the Kennedy proposal to provide such aid as wrong and irresponsible because it would violate our treaty commitments.

The next night during the debate he attacked the Kennedy proposal as "dangerously irresponsible" and in subsequent speeches branded it "shockingly reckless" and a "fantastic recommendation." Nixon in his dove feathers even went so far as to accuse JFK of risking World War III by making noises about an invasion of Cuba.

The Cuban exiles, ever chafing at the bit, saw Kennedy as their new hope, and when the election results were in, Little Havana went wild with anticipation.

Bissell and Dulles flew to Palm Beach on November 18 to brief the President-elect about the full-scale invasion on the drawing board. Kennedy gave them a qualified go-ahead.

"Hello, Chico." David Atlee Phillips, a suave man with a long handsome face and the beguiling brashness of a Luke Skywalker, looked up from his desk in the propaganda section of Quarters Eye at the sound of the familiar voice. There was a smiling E. Howard Hunt extending his hand. "Good to be working with you again," he said.

"Welcome aboard," said the other spy.

"Chico" was a name Hunt used for friends. He considered Phillips, a former actor and frustrated playwright turned professional spy, to be his friend. Hunt and Phillips were both veterans of the

CIA's 1954 Guatemala campaign. The Cuba Project was to be a carbon copy. In Guatemala the CIA trained a "patriotic" opposition army, gave it logistical support, and orchestrated an "invasion." The target was landholder and military man Jacobo Arbenz, who upon being elected president unexpectedly began social and economic reforms. He made the unforgivable error of expropriating more than a quarter-million acres of the United Fruit Company, offering what the firm considered inadequate compensation.

United Fruit had powerful friends in Washington. Then CIA Director Allen Dulles was a stockholder. His brother, then Secretary of State John Foster Dulles, also held a large block of shares, and Dulles's New York law firm, Sullivan & Cromwell, was United Fruit's counsel. General Robert Cutler, chairman of the National Security Council, which approved covert operations, sat on the United Fruit board of directors.

Hunt had just arrived from Uruguay, where he had been station chief, his first (and last) command posting. A tall, lean man with the wise eyes of an owl and the disposition sometimes of a fool, Hunt seemed born to the clandestine life with the fated, lazy attraction of the windmill for the breeze. When he wasn't playing spy games, he was writing about them in pulp spy novels that were a pale copy of James Bond. Sometimes he acted with the bravado of his fictional spook heroes; and sometimes, like his heroes, he got in trouble with the brass. It was Hunt's ultimate misfortune that there was no Miss Moneypenny around to cover the daring spy's tracks with the boss.

His reassignment to Quarters Eye was not what you would call a promotion, for Hunt had engaged in a characteristic bit of mugwumpery that had irritated Eisenhower himself. Hunt seems to have spent much of his time in Montevideo riding the cocktail circuit in a CIA Cadillac and cranking out the espionage dime novels that provided him with a sizable supplemental income. Early in 1960 he was notified that he was being routinely transferred back to Washington. Reluctant to give up the good life, he told the incoming Uruguayan president, Benito Nardone, that he, Howard Hunt, was indispensable to equitable relations between the two countries and urged him to urge Eisenhower during a forthcoming state visit to leave Hunt in Montevideo. To Ike's utter surprise,

Nardone did just that. Eisenhower's military mind was affronted by such a deviation from channels. He told the U.S. ambassador that he had no intention of interfering with the CIA's staffing policies, and who was this fellow Hunt anyway?

Many of Hunt's colleagues regarded him as lacking some of his judgment marbles. Phillips recalled that before the 1954 coup Hunt had taken Guatemalan exile leaders whose presence in Miami was supposed to be a secret on a nightclub binge with near-disastrous results. But Hunt retained the confidence of Bissell's deputy, Tracy Barnes, another Ivy League spy who had served with Hunt in the OSS. Barnes sent him off to check out Havana, posing as a tourist. After a whirlwind tour, which included stops at the famous Sloppy Joe's, a sort of Sardi's for spies, Hunt reported back that the CIA should not rely on a popular uprising to back the invasion. He suggested destroying all electronic communications just before the attack so that Cuba's leaders could not rally public support. His main recommendation was the assassination of Fidel Castro coincident with the invasion so that the Cuban armed forces "would collapse in leaderless confusion."[32]

Barnes told Hunt that his report would be considered in the final invasion plans. As time passed and he heard nothing, Hunt nagged Barnes about his assassination suggestion. "It's in the hands of a special group," was all Barnes would say.

The National Security Council was formed by an act of Congress in 1947 to deliberate matters of foreign policy and their implementation. It is composed of the president, vice president, secretary of state, and secretary of defense. The same legislation chartered the CIA, limiting it to intelligence gathering that would enable the NSC to make its decisions. But there was a loophole permitting the agency to perform other functions as the NSC "may from time to time direct." At its very first meeting the NSC issued a highly secret directive authorizing the CIA to engage in covert operations. Almost from the start, nobody played by the agreed rules. The Senate Intelligence Committee report described it this way: "Covert action is activity which is meant to further the sponsoring nation's foreign policy objectives, and to be concealed in order to permit that nation to plausibly deny responsibility."

Its covert authority gave the CIA, literally, license to steal. But Allen Dulles found it intolerably restrictive that each operation had to be approved by the NSC. In the afterglow of the agency's Guatemalan success Dulles made a pitch to the White House. Why not set up a subcommittee of the NSC, a Special Group, that would consider the CIA's operational proposals on a regular basis? It would be chaired by the president's national security adviser, who could judge whether the proposal should go to the NSC for ratification. This would streamline the procedure and not incidentally function as a "circuit breaker," insulating the Oval Office from dirty talk of international skulduggery; plausibly deniable, plus.

The new Special Group was called the 5412/2 Committee, after the original NSC directive licensing the CIA for cloak-and-dagger operations (it has been renamed several times and is currently the 40 Committee). In 1960 it consisted of National Security Adviser Gordon Gray; Admiral Arleigh "21 Knots" Burke, Chief of Naval Operations and a stone-age-cold warrior; Livingston Merchant of the State Department, another friend of the ever-influential Pawley; and Dulles. It was not much of a defensive line to block any CIA end runs.

Dulles, tweedy, pipe-smoking, white-haired, was the master of the subtle; he could sell snake oil to a snake. He first broached the Cuba Project to the Special Group on January 13, 1960. The CIA did not contemplate "a quick elimination of Castro," he said. But it would be nice to have a capacity for "covert contingency planning" in the likely event that it became necessary to remove the wart from the palm of the Caribbean.

The Special Group formed a Cuban Task Force to pursue unspecified actions against Castro. Dulles had what he wanted; a special group within the Special Group, specializing in the plausibly deniable. "It's in the hands of a special group," Tracy Barnes had told Hunt.

Although Castro had taken no aggressive action against the United States, there was always the threat that he might. At the initial meeting of the task force on March 9, Colonel King advised that a special policy paper would be presented to the Special Group citing evidence that Cuban leaders "have been pushing for an attack on the U.S. Navy installation at Guantánamo Bay." This was the stuff of war. Having struck the colors, King warned that "unless Fidel and Raúl Castro and Che Guevara could be eliminated in one package—which is highly unlikely—this operation can be a long-drawn-out affair and the present government will only be overthrown by the use of force."[33]

The quantum leap from contingency planning to undeclared war had been made. The following day the National Security Council held a fateful meeting in the White House. Eisenhower was present, as were Nixon, Dulles, Secretary of State Christian Herter who took over from John Dulles in 1959, and Admiral Burke, who had once accepted a medal from Batista. Burke had been agitating to get Castro almost as long as Nixon had.

Minutes of that NSC meeting released by the Senate Intelligence Committee make it clear that this was a hanging jury:

> Admiral Burke thought we needed a Cuban leader around whom anti-Castro elements could rally. Mr. Dulles said some anti-Castro leaders existed, but they are not in Cuba at present. *The President said we might have another Black Hole of Calcutta in Cuba, and he wondered what we could do about such a situation* [italics added]. . . . Mr. Dulles reported that a plan to effect the situation in Cuba was being worked on. Admiral Burke suggested that any plan for the removal of Cuban leaders should be a package deal, since many of the leaders around Castro were even worse than Castro.[34]

Burke, however, later denied that he intended "package deal" to mean multiple assassinations.

Eisenhower had been pushed along the war road by William Pawley, whom he regarded as an authority in matters of intrigue. Pawley was, by any measure, a doer. He formed the first commercial airline in Cuba, organized the famous Flying Tigers with Claire Chennault in 1940, established Havana's bus system after World War II, and served as Eisenhower's ambassador to Brazil and Peru. His extensive holdings included the Miami Transit Company and the Talisman Sugar Corporation. In addition, he was a real estate developer and, of course, a millionaire many times over. (He was also a man of rather extreme political views. In a publication of the arch-conservative American Security Council, former Ambassador Pawley once advocated unleashing Chinese Nationalist troops from Taiwan to run the reds out of Vietnam—and then letting them go on to an invasion of the Chinese mainland.)

In 1954 Ike formed the Doolittle Committee to forestall a congressional inquiry into CIA covert actions and named Pawley one of the four members. The panel was chaired by General Jimmy Doolittle, like Pawley a famed World War II aviation figure. The Doolittle Report said the United States had to abandon its traditional concepts of fair play in the face of an "implacable enemy" and "learn to subvert, sabotage and destroy our enemies by more clever, more sophisticated, and more effective methods than those used against us." The American people, the report said, might have to be acquainted with "this fundamentally repugnant philosophy."

Ike bought the Doolittle Report. He issued a follow-up National Security directive seeking the destruction of "international communism" and authorizing "all compatible activities" to achieve that goal. The Cuba Project was to stretch the definition of compatible.

"I had several conferences with the President," Ambassador Pawley said, "and finally he was convinced that the anticommunist Cubans in Florida should be armed and given every assistance to overthrow the communist regime." This was, of course, in direct violation of the Neutrality Act, and the Munitions Act to boot. The old Flying Tiger made a pitch to take over command of the project himself; his argument was the highly selective one that the CIA was primarily an intelligence-gathering outfit and should not be simultaneously in charge of operations. "Eisenhower wanted me to assume overall command of the operation, with veto power over the CIA," Pawley told the authors. "But Allen Dulles, joined by Christian Herter who was easily led, prevailed, and it became a CIA operation."[35]

On Saint Patrick's Day the red hot line phone rang on Dulles's desk. It was the President, giving him the green light and promising to issue a blanket National Security directive so that operations did not have to be individually approved by the Special Group or NSC. The Cuba Project was a go.

IV

Although Marilyn Monroe did him one better in the description department by calling L.A. one big varicose vein, Arnold Toynbee, the historian, paired Miami with Los Angeles as places without vision, urban erections that have still to attain even "the rudiments of soul." Miami had one further distinction. It was the perfect swamp to the CIA's crocodile.

At the turn of the century Miami was little more than a rat's nest of shacks on the banks of a tropical river, all of sixty-five miles from the civilization of Palm Beach. A great freeze that had ruined most of Florida's citrus crop stopped short of Miami, and Henry Flagler was convinced to extend his railroad from Palm Beach. The Roaring Twenties brought in a ridiculous land boom with front lots on Flagler Street going for $50,000 a foot. Silver-tongued real estate salesmen such as William Jennings Bryan sold the blazes out of the surrounding countryside, and Miami became a boomtown where ice was rationed and sold by the cube and lumber bootlegged like liquor. There followed the inevitable bust, but the boom returned with a vengeance in the bust-out days after World War II, when "anything goes" rose above cliché to reality. The Golconda which developed the Florida Gold Coast and the former tidal sandbar of Miami Beach into a resort hotel jungle came from the Havana casinos and other mob tributaries and from the hundreds of millions looted from the Cuban treasury by the larcenous Cuban class that opposed Castro's economic reforms. Miami gave the nation the Miss Universe contest. It gave the CIA a politically compatible city populated in the main by red-neck businessmen, blue-collar right-wingers, retired hard hats, the military, and a booming Cuban exile colony made up mainly of the haves whose income in Cuba had been ten times that of the have-nots they left behind. One Cuban-exile bank president described Miami as "the number-one stronghold of radical anticommunism in the United States."

The CIA with Bourbon complacency went ahead in violation of

its charter to build Miami into the largest CIA station in the free world. The agency spent no less than $50 million locally on invasion preparations, and in Miami's Little Havana exiles delightedly called the CIA the Cuban Invasion Authority. The Miami establishment outdid itself in cooperating with the CIA. The University of Miami, previously known for its academic achievements by the epithet "Suntan U" during the fifties, let the CIA use its campus as a school for espionage. When the agency need to camouflage its operations as legitimate businesses, a full-feathered flock of geese of Miami businessmen considered it their patriotic duty to front as corporate officers. One stand-up businessman affording the agency cover was Lindsay Hopkins, Jr., who was also to help Richard Nixon and Bebe Rebozo make a bundle in real estate. Another was the distinguished lawyer Paul L. E. Helliwell, whose career is illustrative of the CIA's sinuous relationships with the bar establishment.

Helliwell's shingle hung on an office building on fashionable Brickell Avenue, but his practice was far from routine. He had been OSS chief of special intelligence in China during World War II, and he retained an affinity for clandestine affairs taking place half a world away. He was listed as counsel to Sea Supply, Inc., a Miami-based trading company, and was general consul of Thailand, posts that were delicately related. Sea Supply was a CIA proprietary operating chiefly out of Bangkok.[36] At the time Thailand was ruled by a right-wing strong man and puppet prince and served as a friendly "host country" for CIA operations in Southeast Asia. One operation was to supply 10,000 renegade Chinese Nationalist troops squatting in Burma in defiance of the government. Although the troops had turned to banditry and opium smuggling, the CIA maintained them as an "asset" which could stage raids into Red China or pose an internal threat if Burma softened its attitude toward Peking.

During the campaign against Cuba Helliwell's office was linked with the allegorically named Red Sunset Enterprises, which reportedly was an employment agency for espionage and sabotage specialists. Like Zenith Technical Enterprises, Red Sunset was listed in the Miami white pages but without an address.

In May 1960 the CIA pulled together several of the principal exile groups under an umbrella called the Democratic Revolutionary

Front and provided a headquarters on Biscayne Boulevard and an office in Coral Gables, close to the agency's own station. It paid the salaries of many of the front's officers and subsidized its publications; when word of the impending invasion spread through Little Havana, volunteers flocked to its doors. Those selected were taken to Useppa Island, a former resort off Fort Myers on the Gulf Coast, leased by the CIA for interrogation and lie detector testing designed to weed out Castro spies.

It was impossible to mask completely war preparations in the midst of a civilian population. Residents of suburban Opa-Locka were frequently awakened at night by low-flying CIA aircraft using a nearby blacked-out air base. Thousands of explosions from exiles practicing guerrilla arts were a familiar sound in the Greater Miami area. In an interview, a former Cuban mercenary for the CIA has described some of the training to the authors:

> The array of outlawed weaponry with which we were familiarized included bullets that explode on impact, silencer-equipped machine guns, homemade explosives, and self-made napalm for stickier and hotter Molotov cocktails. We were taught demolition techniques, practicing on late-model cars, railroad trucks, and gas storage tanks. And we were shown a quick method of saturating a confined area with flour or fertilizer, causing an explosion like in a dustbin or granary.
>
> And then there was a diabolical invention that might be called a minicannon. It was constructed of a concave piece of steel fitted into the top of a number ten can filled with a plastic explosive. When the device was detonated, the tremendous heat of friction of the steel turning inside out made the steel piece a white-hot projectile. There were a number of uses for the minicannon, one of which was demonstrated to us using an old army school bus. It was fastened to the gasoline tank in such a fashion that the incendiary projectile would rupture the tank and fling flaming gasoline the length of the bus interior, incinerating anyone inside. It was my lot to show the rest of the class how easily it could be done. It worked, my God, how it worked. I stood there watching the flames consume the bus.

The CIA's penchant for secrecy was unfortunately not shared by the exiles, who gossiped excitedly about the invasion as if it were the premier event of the social season. The exile government headquarters on touristy Biscayne Boulevard looked more like a convention center than a clandestine recruiting station. The CIA legend that the invasion was being financed by Wall Street interests or, in the alternative, millionaire exiles was the source of much barroom humor.

The CIA barely bothered to disguise the ships of the "Cuban Revolutionary Navy," as the growing exile fleet was called. One boat was moored under the Flagler Street Bridge with a battery of .50-caliber machine guns mounted on her stern, in full view of downtown Miami rush-hour traffic. Sightseeing boats began to point out the warships as part of their tour. The CIA had two electronic eavesdropping boats—the *Dart* and the *Barb*—constantly cruising the Miami River, trying to locate Castro intelligence clandestine radio transmissions.

The only people to whom the invasion preparations seemed to be a secret were the American people.

The CIA over the years had developed a professionally effective method of killing stories it did not wish disseminated to the nation's press. This method was used to a high degree of success in keeping stories of the invasion planning from leaving the Miami area over the leased news wires. The agency planted what it euphemistically called stringers in key wire service bureaus. If an offensive story happened to clatter down the wire, the CIA's ace newsman would scurry to the keyboard and type HOLD FOR MORE. This is wire service lingo for story not complete, more coming. In regional and national bureaus, wire service editors would dutifully put the dispatch aside, awaiting the rest before transmitting it to subscriber newspapers. The MORE never came.

An inquisitive press is the CIA's natural enemy, but in this area Miami posed no special problem. Southern Florida publishers and editors seemed to have an unusually well-developed sense of "national security" and of what was not cricket to publish. In *The Cuban Invasion*, Karl E. Meyer and Tad Szulc disclosed that shortly before the Bay of Pigs "a Philadelphia editor called up a Miami publisher to ask if the rumors about Guatemala training camps were true. He was told by his friend in Florida that there was nothing to the story."

Castro's G-2 was working overtime trying to keep up with the intrigue that was turning Havana into a World War II Lisbon. The Cuban capital was still an open city. The ferries ran to Key West, Pan Am flew between Havana and Miami (although on a reduced schedule because of the shrinking numbers of tourists and businessmen), and phone service was uninterrupted. The American Embassy still functioned, and the busiest part of it was the CIA station.

One of the CIA's most unlikely spies was a shapely Boston Yankee widow named Geraldine Shamma, who had married into a tobacco fortune. For a number of years Shamma had maintained a seaside estate in the swank Miramar section of Havana. After the revolution she frequently entertained government officials. As time went by, the cocktail talk turned to disaffection with the regime; when some of the officials decided to defect, "I hid Castro defectors in my house, in the guesthouse, and in two secret rooms I had built under the swimming pool," Shamma said. Her CIA case officer at the embassy, Major Robert Van Horne, would make arrangements to smuggle the defectors to Miami.[37]

Since Shamma virtually commuted to Miami for social events, she played hostess at that end, too. "We rented a mansion at 1410 Brickell Avenue, a very exclusive section of Miami in those days," she said. "The agency paid for it, and I maintained it. I stayed in an apartment on the top floor of a two-story guesthouse behind the main building." When the invasion brigade began forming, newly arrived recruits were quartered there temporarily. Shamma recalled, "The boys who came over from Cuba to go into the brigade would be sent to the safe house first. They'd stay there a day or two, and then they'd be screened by the CIA and sent somewhere else."

Shamma was also used as a courier to the underground in Havana. She noticed that her mansion was under surveillance but didn't quit. "All I could do openly was walk my dog," she said. "He was a very intelligent black cocker spaniel named Kipper. I would write messages on tiny bits of paper, wrap them in cellophane, and hide them in Kipper's mouth." Shamma deposited and picked up messages in a dead drop—a hole in the base of a tree on a church lawn. But in November 1960 she was arrested by the G-2, which had found a large cache of arms and explosives in an apartment she owned in the fashionable Marianao section. She was convicted of "crimes against the powers of the state" and sentenced to ten years.

A luckier CIA spy was Frank Sturgis, later of Watergate celebrity, a high-flying double agent who ran guns to Castro before the revolution and served for a time as Castro's director of security for the Havana casinos before Fidel pulled the plug on the slots.

On a May night in 1959, Fidel Castro and a flying wedge of bodyguards swept into the lobby of the Riviera Hotel. With them was an attractive nineteen-year-old girl named Maria Lorenz whom, revolutionary gossip had it, Castro was keeping as a mistress. As the premier conferred with his aides, Frank Sturgis sidled up to Lorenz and whispered to her in English.

"I know about you," he said.

"Can you help me? Can you get me out of here?" she responded.

"Yes," Sturgis said. "I'm with the American Embassy. I'll get you out."[38]

Sturgis had become obsessed with the notion that communists dominated the Cuban government, and he was helping out the counterrevolutionary side. One of his principal intelligence sources inside the government was Dr. Juan Orta, Castro's secretary. Now he planned to convert Maria Lorenz into a Mata Hari.

Little is known of Castro's private life, and most of the accounts, such as they are, come from disaffected women, such as Ms. Lorenz. At any rate, her tale is more spy story than love story.

As Lorenz later told it, she met Castro the previous February, when the German cruise liner *Berlin*, captained by her father, called on Havana. A launch flying the revolutionary flag had pulled alongside the ship, and twenty bearded, heavily armed Cubans wearing olive green fatigues with hand grenades dangling from their belts boarded. Women in evening gowns and their dinner-jacketed husbands scurried for cover, thinking it a bandit raid. The leader of the band obviously enjoyed the commotion. He shouted, "I'm a friend. I like Americans."

It was Fidel Castro. "My father spoke Spanish, and he got along well with Castro," Lorenz recalled. "He took Castro and his men on a tour of the ship, then asked them please to leave their guns outside the dining room before they sat down for dinner." Castro sat between the captain and his daughter and, before the meal was over, offered her a job as his secretary. "My father said that I was going back to Germany to finish my education," Lorenz said.

Castro proved persistent. Two weeks later, when the *Berlin* was in New York, two Cuban officers contacted Lorenz with a message from the premier saying that he was desperately in need of a translator. A plane was ready to take her to Havana. "I made a big mistake," she said. "I got on that plane." Castro ensconced her in Suite 2408 of the Havana Hilton, which he used as living quarters as well as an office. There love bloomed. One day, while the premier was gone, his aides drove her to the prison on the Isle of Pines. "They showed me a cell where dictator Batista had imprisoned Fidel and Raúl years before. I went into the cell to look at a bronze plaque on the wall. They shut the door and locked me in the cell." It had been decided to sequester Lorenz since rumors were sweeping Havana that Castro·was keeping a foreign girl in the Hilton. After a week she was brought back to Havana but kept under virtual house arrest. "I was his prisoner, I was trapped," she claims. Frank Sturgis learned of her situation and saw an opportunity to make her an agent in place in return for a promise of future evacuation. She began reporting on Castro's conversations with visitors to Suite 2408 and filching confidential documents. "The suite was full of guns and papers," Lorenz recalled. "Fidel had papers strewn all over. He had one filing cabinet that was never locked. It was full of money, papers, documents, maps. I took papers out and slipped them to Frank. Fidel never missed them."

The headstrong Sturgis was not content to gather intelligence — he wanted to topple the government of the man who had once regarded him as his favorite Yankee. As air force chief of security he had control over a strongly anticommunist cadre of military police. As he envisioned it, he could form a commando squad of volunteers and seize Camp Columbia, the nerve center of the armed forces.

But Sturgis's plans were dashed when his friend, air force chief Pedro Díaz Lanz, fled with his family to Miami on a cabin cruiser. The next day Sturgis hightailed it to Miami, arranging to smuggle Maria Lorenz out in his wake. Sturgis had been forewarned by a confidant, the army intelligence chief Captain Sergio Sanjenís, that "the communists" knew he was an American agent. "Frank, they know who you are," Sanjenís told him. "They'll kill you."

The return of Sturgis and Díaz Lanz to Havana in October 1959 was a grand show. It was the cocktail hour at the convention of the American Society of Travel Agents, which Castro had wooed to Havana in an attempt to bolster the sagging tourist trade. The premier himself was preparing to address the conventioneers, who were at the Havana Hilton watching a grass-skirted Hawaiian type of dancer perform the classic tourist dance.

Suddenly an unmarked B-25 bomber came into sight, flying low over the harbor. At the controls was Pedro Díaz Lanz; in the copilot's seat was his sidekick, Frank Sturgis. A frigate fired at the intruder, and then shore batteries opened up. "Everybody was shooting," Sturgis recalled. "I thought for sure we'd be hit." As the B-25 droned on, untouched by the flak, its bomb bay doors opened. When it reached the center of the city, thousands of leaflets fluttered out. The leaflets branded Castro a tool of the communists.

As the plane disappeared to the north, Fidel Castro dashed over to the CMQ television studios to accuse the United States of at least tacit complicity. Two persons were killed, and forty-five injured — by bombs, Castro charged. Sturgis insists his plane was unarmed. The Cuban government excitedly labeled the incident "Havana's Pearl Harbor," and the newspaper *Revolución* proclaimed: THE AIRPLANES [sic] CAME FROM THE U.S.A.

Sturgis, an almost pathological loner who reacted to bosses the way wild horses do bridles, turned down an offer to go on the CIA payroll, but he developed a spy-happy relationship with the agent who tried to recruit him, Joaquín Sanjenís, known in the vernacular as Sam Jenis, a cousin of the turncoat Castro police official who had warned Sturgis to hightail out of Cuba.[39]

Sanjenís was an opportunistic little man who managed to punch a CIA meal ticket the rest of his life. When he met Sturgis he was filling a bucket of rotten eggs which would become known as Operation 40 — the secret police of the Cuban invasion force. The ultrasecret Operation 40 included some nonpolitical conservative exile businessmen, but its hard core was made up of dice players at the foot of the cross — informers, assassins-for-hire, and mob henchmen whose sworn goal was to make the counterrevolution safe for the comfortable ways of the old Cuba. They were the elite troops of the old guard within the exile movement, who made an effective alliance with CIA right-wingers against CIA liberals in order to exclude from power any Cubans who wanted, albeit without Castro, Castro-type reforms from land redistribution to free milk for rural children. Their hero was Manuel Artime, who became the CIA's Golden Boy; their bogeyman was Ray, a progressive Cuban anticommunist who many observers agreed had the most effective underground in Cuba, but who was tossed aside like an old taco by the invasion planners.

Sanjenís got Sturgis a CIA mail drop and gave him the right phone numbers, and Sturgis agreed to coordinate his own operations with Sanjenís and work on a contract basis on special agency assignments. This working relationship extended for better than the next decade, until Sturgis and several other longtime Sanjenís operatives were caught in the Watergate.

Sturgis soon had use for his new CIA phone numbers. He pulled off an espionage coup of a sordid sort. Castro had left Havana for a few days, and Sturgis talked Maria Lorenz, the mistress-in-exile, into returning to the scene of her lost love affair. Posing as an American tourist, she carried an overnight bag. Inside were her old Castro uniform and the key to Suite 2408 in the Havana Hilton, where she had lived with Fidel. "Nobody recognized me when I came into the hotel," she later remembered. "I just walked right through. Nobody was around. When Fidel left, they all left with him." She tried the key. It still worked.

"I unlocked the door, went inside and double-locked the door behind me. I felt pretty confident because I knew Fidel was at Ciénega de Zapata. When he left the suite, no one was to go in. Those were the orders.

"I took as much as I could and stuffed papers and maps into my uniform pockets and inside the jacket. Then I left the Hilton, went back to the other hotel, changed into a dress, and caught the next flight to Miami."[40]

Lorenz joined Sturgis's new paramilitary group, which he grandly called the International Anti-Communist Brigade. Most of his funding came from dispossessed casino owners and was funneled through Norman "Rough-house" Rothman, a mob gofer who knew Sturgis from his Havana days. "Norm also helped out with his own contributions and by putting me in touch with well-heeled Cuban friends," Sturgis said, referring to the mob's Batista-ite allies. Sturgis began drilling a tatterdemalion band of Cuban and American volunteers at an out-of-the-way site in the Everglades. Some of the Cubans were later tapped by the CIA for an eighty-man sabotage team infiltrated into Cuba shortly before the Bay of Pigs landing.

Sturgis also flew "green light" missions (approved by the CIA) parachuting agents into Cuba and "over the beach" boat sorties infiltrating agents and dropping supplies. He "borrowed" tiny Norman's Cay in the Bahamas from its Canadian industrialist owner as an advance base for fuel and provisions caches and a radio shack to communicate with guerrillas inside Cuba. Sturgis would pilot his boat to the south tip of large Andros Island, only a short distance from Las Villas Province, and wait for nightfall. Then he would dash across the channel, often riding the wake of a freighter to avoid radar detection.

The units that Sturgis was supplying belonged to Victor Manuel Paneque, code name Major Diego, a squat, cigar-chomping tough guy in the Edward G. Robinson mold. On one mission Sturgis and Paneque waited in a designated cove on the Cuban coast, listening to muffled oars in the black night. "As a rowboat with four men pulled alongside," Sturgis said, "Diego and I cocked our tommy guns. But our visitors spoke the right password, which was based upon the Bible." After a brief conference and transfer of arms Sturgis headed back into the channel. A Cuban patrol boat spotted him and gave chase. Sturgis escaped by dodging inside an atoll where the water was too shallow for pursuit.

Sturgis's missions were part of a much larger Cuban underground supply operation mounted by the CIA, an operation that relied chiefly on airdrops. David Phillips recalled that during a Quarters Eye briefing, General Charles Cabell discovered that only one-tenth of the plane's cargo capacity was being utilized. He ordered the remainder of the space filled with sacks of beans and rice. "General," the operations chief objected, "we're dropping specific items requested by the team by radio. Only a few men will be at the DZ. They can't carry many sacks."

"Let's be forward-leaning" said the cliché-leaning general, dropping one of his favorites: "Let 'em know we're behind them all the way." Then he turned to Phillips. "Son, I don't want to have to explain to an appropriations committee why we're flying nearly empty planes over Cuba. Drop the rice and beans!"

That night the pilot managed to hit the drop zone squarely. Back came a radio message from the guerrilla team: YOU SON OF BITCH. WE NEARLY KILLED BY RICE BAGS. YOU CRAZY? Cabell thereafter was known as "Old Rice and Beans."[41]

Meanwhile, in Miami, Howard Hunt was busy as a queen bee. He took an apartment in a Brickell Point highrise, from which he mother-henned his exile charges and oversaw an invasion recruitment station at Dinner Key. He was so busy that he was assigned an assistant named Bernard L. Barker, the future Watergate burglar.

A Cuban-American who had lived in Havana, Bernie Barker had flown in the U.S. Army Air Corps during World War II and had been shot down in Germany. After the war he had joined the Havana police force at the urging of the CIA to provide an inside view of Cuban intelligence. When Mrs. Harry Truman and her daughter, Margaret, visited Havana, Barker had headed the security detail. But someone in the American Embassy noticed that, in obtaining the police job, Barker had signed a form swearing allegiance to Cuba, and when his passport came up for renewal he was coldly informed that he had forfeited his American citizenship. Characteristically the CIA refused to acknowledge its role, and it took Barker years to regain his citizenship status.

But Barker's hatred of Castro far surpassed his pique at the CIA. For a time, he worked out of the American Embassy arranging the exfiltration of important Cubans, then he fled to Miami himself. His task as Hunt's right-hand man was to deliver CIA cash laundered through foreign banks to the exile groups. Some of the young exiles recruited by Hunt and Barker were sent to Frank Sturgis for basic training before being shipped off to Guatemala. Although the normally brusque Sturgis got along famously with Hunt, he loathed his future Watergate companion Barker as a patronizing "confidential clerk."[42]

The traffic at Hunt's Brickell Point aerie soon became so heavy that his landlady concluded he was a bookie. He decided to move, but when he tried to rent a spacious house on the bay in Coral Gables by paying a year's rental in advance, the owner suspected he was a racketeer and notified the police. Hunt finally settled into a house in a secluded part of suburban Coconut Grove, but his privacy was again invaded. As he recalled it, a neighbor named Liz "asked why so many foreign-looking visitors called at my house, and I explained that I owned a piece of a Cuban prize fighter, and that my visitors were partners in the syndicate . . . she seemed to believe the story."

Not quite. Liz later confided that the steady flow of nocturnal male visitors convinced her that Hunt was a homosexual.[43]

V

The American in the wheelchair was bumped up the steps of the Presidential Palace by guards whose tommyguns bounced crazily on their shoulders as they pushed. He was on his way to see Batista. His name was Lyman G. Kirkpatrick, and he was the inspector general of the CIA. He had come to inspect a monster of his own making.

The intelligence Frankenstein the CIA had created in Cuba was the BRAC — Buró para Represión de las Actividades Communistas. It was the bright idea of none other than Secretary of State John Foster Dulles, the Cardinal Richelieu of the Cold War, who suggested it to his brother Allen at the CIA, who in turn entrusted it to Kirkpatrick, who personally, on a visit to Batista in 1956, laid it on the little dictator in white.[44]

It was not that Batista at the time lacked security forces. He had goons in cops' clothing running all over the island; their ranks encompassed the widely hated military intelligence, called the SIM, and a sort of rump FBI known as the Buró de Investigaciones. Some of Batista's security forces were known more familiarly as the *cortacuellos*, the throat cutters; one particularly efficient servant of the master called himself Dracula (after Batista's favorite movie) and bragged about "sucking blood" to get confessions.[45] In the opinion of the Brothers Dulles, these security forces did little good because they terrorized everyone indiscriminately; they wanted a security force that would specialize in terrorizing just communists. Thus the BRAC, which the CIA helped organize; and thus Inspector General Kirkpatrick's unpleasant visit to Cuba, in September of 1958, a few months before Batista fled with his white suits and his collection of American horror films and the loot which represented grand theft of the birthright of future Cuban generations.

Kirkpatrick discovered that the American-trained BRAC was using its methods against all political opposition. Those methods included torture. This is not a word over-used in the CIA vocabulary; Kirkpatrick preferred the phrase "violence in its interrogations."[46] The inspector general was at first skeptical at the reports of brutality and torture; he asked for evidence. He was shown photographs of a young woman, a schoolteacher, who had been arrested on suspicion of plotting against the government. When she was released she was a shambles: "The doctor who treated the woman said he had never seen a human body more mistreated." The CIA man in the wheelchair examined the pictures. "The horrible wounds on the woman's body were convincing, as were the reports of case after case of the sons of prominent Cuban families who had joined either the students' organization or the July 26 movement (of Castro) and had been arrested and killed."

The inspector general summoned the chief of the BRAC, Colonel Mariano Paget, to the American Embassy on the Malecón, the picturesque highway along Havana's waterfront. Colonel Paget was a former policeman who had served for a time in the United States; he was the great white hope of the CIA. "When I told him of my concern over reports of brutality in his organization, he held out his hands in the classical gesture of despair," said Kirkpatrick.[47]

Kirkpatrick told the authors that the agency's protestations to Batista about the beastly conduct of its Cuban stepchildren went unheeded. The atrocities cost Batista "the last of his support among the people of Cuba," he later wrote in his account of his CIA stewardship, *The Real CIA*. Kirkpatrick sounds an almost wishful tone that the agency might have learned something from this experience. If it did it was a lesson soon forgotten, as the CIA went on, in the 1960s and 1970s, in Korea and Vietnam, in Uruguay and in Chile, to assist the bloody-minded secret police of friendly dictatorships and to help train their men in the more sophisticated mechanics of torture.

Kirkpatrick sent a cable from Havana that created a major flap at CIA headquarters. It predicted that Batista probably couldn't last until the end of the year. (The dictator played his last canasta game—he habitually cheated—and ran away from his country on December 31.) The cable heightened an at times acrimonious debate within the CIA that would be months in the resolving. Opinion within the agency—both in the Havana station and in Washington—was divided over whether Castro was not, or was, or might become, a communist. Earl T. Smith, the newly appointed U.S. Ambassador to Cuba, a former stockbroker who believed in free enterprise with the passion that Mae West believed in men, was already complaining to Washington that some elements in the Havana station were too anti-Batista and too close to Castro's July 26 guerrillas; to read some of Smith's cables, you'd think CIA men were up there in the hills helping the revolutionaries clean their rifles.

In March of 1960, shortly after Castro took power, an incident took place which had the result of making up the CIA's mind about Castro—at least the minds of many in the Havana Station. The decision was more personal than political, but it was enough to shift the station's thinking firmly rightward to the position of overthrowing Castro. It had to do with the CIA's attempts to bargain for the life of a Cuban official of its naughty stepchild, the BRAC.

This story was told to the authors by Andrew St. George, a paramilitary journalist who, as is his forte, or fate, became part of the story himself. By profession a journalist, St. George is forever showing up where the paramilitary action is — often as much a participant as a reporter. He was in the Sierra with Fidel Castro and Che Guevara, then later hopped another freight and began covering the anti-Castro Cubans for *Life* in the old picture book's pugnacious days, accompanying, and sometimes sinking with, the CIA-backed Cuban exile sea raiders on their fallow but constant Florida-based raids against their homeland. In 1968, he was in Bolivia, acting as middleman in the frantic media negotiations hosted by greedy Bolivian generals attempting to sell for profit the Bolivian diary of St. George's one-time friend Che Guevara, whom the generals with a little asset from the CIA, had captured and executed in the Andes foothills.

St. George's not infrequent rubbing of elbows with intelligence types led New Left conspiracy theorists to conclude that he worked for the CIA. (The CIA, for its part, has bitterly attacked St. George in U.S. Senate hearings as an agent of the Cubans for his men's magazines stories, indelicately disclosing one CIA operation or another.)

The beleaguered St. George has spent so much time denying that he is a CIA agent that, naturally, a lot of people believe he is. Even his wife of some twenty years, Jean, sometimes thinks so. One day when St. George was suffering all the agonies of Christ because of acutely painful hemorrhoids, his wife suggested that he "go to Walter Reed" (the government hospital). "Those people in Washington must have some sort of medical plan for guys like you," she said.

Born in Hungary of partial royal stock, St. George did a stint in post-WWII Army intelligence, then took up pulp journalism, and eventually got to revolutionary Cuba by the same sort of vague routes that Irish monks first discovered America. He found himself in the Sierra Maestra with the rebels and gained the confidence of Fidel, who asked him in the fall of 1958 to undertake a secret mission to America. Castro wanted a representative of the U.S. government to come to the mountains to maintain communications with the rebels, lest Washington come to a misunderstanding about the revolution's intentions. "Fidel was deeply concerned about American intervention," St. George said. "He wanted channels opened. He really wanted a CIA man up there with him. He offered to provide coded radio facilities."[48] The CIA station in Havana was in favor of the idea, but in Washington State Department hard-liners vetoed it, St. George said. To get Castro's message to the widest possible audience, St. George promised the story to *The New York Times*, which put it on its front page on December 11, 1958 — CASTRO SEEKING U.S. TALKS ON CUBAN POLITICAL ISSUES, the headline read. It was the luck of St. George's journalistic draw that the paper had gone on strike, and the only people who saw that issue were the executives who put it out for the file copy.

When the *barbudos* from the hills marched into Havana the day after New Year's of 1959, the first thing the happy street throngs did was to smash parking meters and slot machines in the casinos, the most immediate symbols of the American presence in their lives. The first thing the rebels did was to seize the BRAC building, the symbol of Batista's oppression and torture of his people. The voluminous BRAC files were carted to the fortress at the entrance to Havana Harbor, there to be joined by BRAC officials who were hapless enough to be caught. Colonel Paget had got away (he later surfaced in the employ of the United States government at the Opa-Locka detention center in Florida, screening Cuban exiles to weed out those of the pink persuasion), but the rebels eventually captured, in March, the BRAC second in command, a captain named José Castaño Quevedo, who had been trained in the United States by the FBI and had functioned as a sort of liaison officer with the Havana CIA station.

St. George got a 6 A.M. phone call from the CIA saying that Quevedo, their house pet, had been arrested the day before and had been promptly sentenced to death by a revolutionary night court. Quevedo after all had studied spycraft in America and it was almost as if a CIA man were being done in. St. George was someone with close ties to the rebel leaders; the CIA asked him to get to Fidel or Che and get them to call this whole unseemly thing off.

"It was a time of incredible tensions," said St. George, "and I thought it would be best for Fidel if he acceded to the CIA's wishes in a manner such as this. After all, just a few months before he had invited them up to the mountains with him."

St. George could not find Fidel. He went to see Che instead, with whom he felt on intimate terms as they had many times shivered together through a muddy night in the hills. The journalist found Che in bed, suffering from one of his asthma attacks.

He suggested to Che that it would be "diplomatic" to grant the CIA its wish about this man Quevedo.

"In the mountains, we learned nothing about diplomacy," Che said.

The two argued all day. When St. George left it was dusk: "I had exhausted my tired liberal semantics," he said. Che gave him departing instructions: "Tell them my answer exactly as I tell you."

A small crowd of CIA men and Embassy officials were waiting for St. George in the Embassy conference room which looked out over the Malecón into the Gulf of Mexico.

"What did he say?" asked Jim Noel, the CIA station chief.

St. George reported glumly that Che didn't seem cooperative.

"Well, what did he say?" Noel demanded.

"Che said to tell you that if he didn't shoot him for a *Batistiano verdugo* (Batista thug) he would shoot him for an American agent," St. George said.

There was a grim silence in the room. "This," Noel said, "this is a declaration of war."

The next morning Quevedo was shot.

From that day on, St. George says, even the formerly more pro-revolution CIA agents "began to plot against Che and Fidel."[49]

The episode was also the end of St. George's relationship with Che, who later, in his *Diary of the Cuban Revolution*, called him an "FBI agent" who had been with them in the hills. Perhaps he meant CIA.

THREE

"The Fish Is Red"

I

IT WAS to be a purely Latin affair. "We were careful," said CIA Deputy Director Richard Bissell, "not to have a white face on the beach, not a modern aircraft in the air." The movie to be presented to the world was that the invasion was a patriotic enterprise carried out by Cuban exiles funded by private contributions. It turned out to be a combination of *The Longest Day* and the *Gong Show*.

The CIA had Miami yacht broker Charles C. Mills arrange the purchase of two wartime LCIs (landing craft infantry) on the surplus market. They were worth about $30,000 each. By the time they were put to sea the agency had expended $240,000 on each. The *Barbara J* and *Blagar* were based at Key West and registered under a dummy front called Mineral Carriers Limited, which supposedly was prospecting for oil in the nearby Marquesas Keys.[1] They loaded weapons, explosives and supplies at a warehouse converted from the Key West-Havana ferry terminal (service had now been discontinued) and circled Cuba making drops to the underground. The deliveries became so routine that Grayston Lynch, a CIA paramilitary in charge of the *Blagar*, described the job in terms of United Parcel.

The ships' crews were originally all Cubans. However the CIA, exhibiting a racist distrust of its Cuban charges that would continue throughout the Bay of Pigs fiasco, soon replaced the Cuban skippers with captains commandeered from the Navy's Military Sea Transportation Service. The MSTS captains were given the standard warning that they would be disavowed by the CIA if the Mineral Carriers' cover was blown.

To provide a sealift to Guatemala, the CIA hopped a ride with its longtime collaborator the United Fruit Company. Former company vice-president Thomas P. McCann wrote in his memoirs:

> We were told of the CIA's plan in detail, including the training of mercenaries in Guatemala and Nicaragua by U.S. personnel. The plan would culminate in a large-scale invasion of Cuba by air and sea. That's where we came in. We dealt directly with Robert Kennedy. The main company contact was J. Arthur Marquette, a crusty New Orleans seafaring man who had worked his way up from the ships to become vice-president in charge of steamships and all Terminal Operations. Marquette told me how much he disliked Kennedy — everything from his arrogant and demanding attitude to his "dirty long hair." But he was the Attorney General and he and the CIA wanted us to supply two of our freighters to convey men, munitions and material during that invasion. The arrangements were made and it was all very cloak-and-dagger: our own board of directors didn't know about it, and certainly only a handful of us within the company were party to the secret.[2]

The CIA mustered an invasion armada from the García Line, a shipping company with offices in New York and Havana. Owned by Alfred García and his five sons, the line's aging freighters hauled rice and sugar between Cuba and Central American ports. It was the only Cuban-owned line still operating from Havana. To avert suspicion, it was agreed that Alfredo García would remain in Cuba until the invasion clock tolled.

The agency already had an air force that required only a bit of sprucing up. In mounting clandestine operations around the globe it had acquired a large variety of planes that were concentrated at Eglin Air Force Base in the Florida panhandle, where the Air Force ran a Special Air Warfare Center developing techniques for aerial support of guerrilla operations. The long-haul transport of this air division was the C-54, the military version of the Douglas DC-4. The C-54s had previously been used on espionage flights along Iron Curtain frontiers, to transport Asian operatives under the cover of Western Enterprises, Inc., on Saipan, and on paradrop missions over Greece and Jordan. The planes were a paramilitary hot-rodder's special: They bore no markings, engine decals, or manufacturer's labels and were fitted with highly advanced electronic gear.

The CIA chose B-26 light bombers as its combat craft because they were sufficiently dated to fit the cover story and could be painted with Cuban insignia since they were also in use in Cuba. The agency's B-26 fleet had been modified for the unsuccessful attempt to oust Sukarno in Indonesia in 1958. The old crates had souped-up engines and eight bridge-busting .50-caliber machine guns packed into the nose. Additional B-26s were hurriedly modified by the Air Force at an Arizona base, while in Washington a front called Falcon Aeronautical, Inc., was set up to procure spare parts and equipment.

To find American pilots experienced in these vintage aircraft, Double-Check, the CIA front which recruited pilots, focused on the Air National Guards of Alabama, Arkansas, and Virginia—the last squadrons to fly B-26s. Albert C. "Buck" Persons of Birmingham, who was flying for a construction company at the time, has provided a rather remarkable account of the cloak-and-dagger recruiting antics of the CIA. He was summoned to the office of Major General George Reid Doster, commander of the 117th Tactical Reconnaissance Wing of the Alabama Air National Guard at the Birmingham airport. "Buck, I've got a job to recruit six experienced pilots for four-engine work, and six B-26 pilots," Doster said. "These have to be pilots with military experience, but with no current military connections. I want you for C-54's. About all I can tell you right now about the job is this. It's outside the continental limits of the United States. It's in this hemisphere. There will be shooting involved. And it's very much in the interest of our government. The job will last about three months."[3]

Persons guessed the target was Cuba. He jumped at the offer even before learning that the pay was $2,800 a month, plus bonuses. He sat in on a briefing by four men from Washington headed by a tough-guy type who called himself Al. As Persons remembered it, "Al said that he and the other three men with him were agents for a group of wealthy Cubans who were financing an operation to remove Castro from power. . . . "

At a subsequent meeting the wealthy-exile story was dropped. "We were told that we were now working for an electronics company located in one of the New England states," Persons said. The pilots picked a city that they knew fairly well, and the CIA prepared documents establishing new identities for them as residents there. To correspond with their families, they used a mail drop care of Joseph Greenland, Box 7924, Main Post Office, Chicago, Illinois (possibly this belonged to Robert P. B. Lohmann, chief of the CIA's Office of Training, who occupied Room 302 in the U.S. Court of Appeals Building in Chicago). The pilots were given a fat roll of $100 bills as an advance; thereafter their pay was deposited to their bank accounts by bank transfer from a St. Louis bank. No checks were ever used. The identity of the payer remained anonymous.

After polygraph screening in Miami, the pilots were driven by night in a closed Hertz rental van to a secluded airport, where they boarded a C-54. Persons was baffled by the crew, who spoke a foreign language that was not Spanish. "They were a group of pilots who, as we later understood it, had come over from somewhere in the Orient. They were in an entirely different category from our group. Their flying activities were apparently confined entirely to flights between Miami and Central America and to the transport of Cuban exiles and supplies to the training bases. There were five or six of these 'contract' pilots. I believe at least one or two were Polish."[4]

Just before takeoff a nervous group of forty Cubans in stiff new fatigues was herded aboard. Their Anglo leader had a pistol dangling from his belt. He took up a position guarding the cockpit — in case there was "trouble."

"For such a person to commandeer a C-54 load of anti-Castro rebels along with a mixed bag of CIA-hired pilots would be a neat trick to pull off," Persons thought as the old plane droned across the Caribbean to the Retalhuleu air base in Guatemala.

One of the American pilots who flew airdrop missions directly out of Florida in violation of the U.S. Neutrality Act was W. Robert Plumlee, who had put himself through flying school by staging high-diving exhibitions at Miami Beach hotels. He had originally flown for the 26th of July Movement supplying Castro's forces. But when the CIA turned against Castro, one of his Cuban contacts, Raúl Martínez, recruited him to fly for the Dodge Corporation, an agency front doing business as "management consultants" on Flagler Street in downtown Miami. "It had the legitimate ring of the auto maker," Plumlee said, "but the name was a dodge."[5] Plumlee was paid $700 a month retainer, plus $300 for each mission.

Near the colonial shrine of Williamsburg, Virginia, is the CIA's West Point, a thinly disguised military base called Camp Peary. Graduates of this institution of higher "black" learning frequently refer to it simply as the Farm. Its curriculum is Tradecraft—dead drops, communications, recruitment of operatives, electronic and physical surveillance, lock-picking, photography, microfilming, and invisible inks. The fledgling agents practice in the nearby "foreign city" of Norfolk.

Cubans earmarked for espionage and underground assignments in support of the invasion were brought to the Farm. Consistent with the almost programmatic racism that the agency displayed throughout the Cuba Project, the Cubans were carefully segregated from the American career agents. (E. Howard Hunt was representative of those who derided Cuban input into the Bay of Pigs planning: "To paraphrase a homily: this was too important to be left to Cuban generals."[6]) Those selected for frogman and demolition duty were sent to a decommissioned navy flying boat base on the wide Pasquolank River near Elizabeth City, North Carolina, that was known as Isolation Tropic. There trainloads of old army jeeps and combat vehicles were brought in to be blown up. UDT (underwater demolition teams) instruction was held in the tepid waters of Vieques Island in Puerto Rico. Advanced leadership training was held at the Army's Jungle Warfare Center at Fort Gulick in the Panama Canal Zone.

Near Phoenix, Arizona, exiles were taught parachuting and air-drop techniques, including packaging arms, ammunition, and radios in shockproof containers and bringing in supplies by STOL (short takeoff and landing) aircraft. According to former CIA official Victor Marchetti, a small Phoenix-based airline then called Intermountain Aviation posed "as a private general-purpose air company. It gets contracts from the Interior Department, ostensibly to train firefighters. Of course, the way you train firefighters is to make parachutists out of them, which is what the CIA uses the airline for."[7]

Meanwhile, the ranks of the combat force, Brigade 2506, were swelling in Guatemala (the designation was in honor of an early recruit, serial number 2506, who had been killed in an accident; the CIA wise men began numbers at 2000 to deceive Castro agents as to the brigade's size). The Guatemala training camp called Base Trax was under the direction of a dour Army lieutenant colonel who used the nom de guerre of Colonel Frank and was intensely disliked by his Cuban trainees, who in turn didn't get along with the elitist Green Berets who instructed them. The men the emotional Cubans took to heart were the CIA's gung-ho contractual specialists under renewable contracts who were variously called "paramilitaries," "PMs," or the more descriptive "cowboys." CIA official Ray S. Cline said, "You've got to have cowboys—the only thing is you don't let them make policy. You keep them in the ranch house when you don't have a specific project for them."[8]

The hardworking candidate for the most legendary of these free-booters was William "Rip" Robertson, who was nearly fifty when he showed up in Guatemala to be one of the boys. A hulking Texan who had played college football, Robertson transferred to the CIA after fighting in the Pacific war as a Marine captain. He never got over the idea of storming beaches. During the 1954 Guatemalan coup he dispatched a pilot to bomb a Soviet ship, but accidentally sent a British merchantman to the bottom instead. The ensuing flap forced the CIA to quietly indemnify Lloyds of London to the tune of $1.5 million. Robertson was benched indefinitely. When the Cuba Project came up the CIA snuck Robertson back onto the team, primarily because he had achieved a good-buddy rapport with the

Somoza family while prospecting for gold in Nicaragua. He had little use for paper work and referred to Quarters Eye desk men as
"feather merchants." His military demeanor was out of a Ken Kesey
novel: He wore his perpetually rumpled clothes with a careless
slouch, he never took off his baseball cap, his glasses were tied behind his head with a string, and a pulp mystery routinely stuck out
of his back pocket. The Cubans loved him. To them he was a real
Yankee. He was one of the few among the hired many who would
stay with his Cuban charges during the Secret War's many campaigns.

Down the Pacific slope at Retalhuleu, the Birmingham pilots and
USAF instructors were training former Cuban airline and air force
pilots in formation flying and gunnery. The Retalhuleu base was
cordoned off, but a railway trunk line bordered one site, and the passengers could almost touch the wingtips of the combat-ready planes
lined row upon row. This led to considerable rumors, which were
denied, although not very effectively, by Guatemalan authorities.

The Cuban government, of course, knew otherwise. For this it
didn't need spies, although Castro had those in sufficient numbers;
by this time, all over Latin America people were talking about the
coming invasion of Cuba with routine familiarity. But what Castro
didn't know was the staging area from which the invasion would be
launched. The site was Puerto Cabezas, on the Caribbean coast of
Nicaragua. The ruling Somoza family had collaborated with the
CIA in the 1954 Guatemalan coup, and they now itched to get further U.S. brownie points by cooperating in the overthrow of Castro. The installation was dubbed Base Tide. The airfield, which had
been built by the U.S. Navy for antisubmarine patrols during World
War II, was called Happy Valley.

Buck Persons recalled the security measures on his flights transporting munitions to Puerto Cabezas: "To insure the security of this
base, we were required to check out charts at the beginning of each
flight—and under no circumstances was a Cuban allowed to get his
hands on a chart that would show courses leading to Puerto
Cabezas." Even when Brigade 2506 was brought down from Base
Trax for the flight to Puerto Cabezas, they were not told where they

were going. And when they got there, they were not told where they were.[9]

The invasion date remained up in the air. Despite his earlier determination to leave office with Castro's head in his lap, Eisenhower backed off because Brigade 2506 had not achieved anything approaching a state of combat readiness. Ike knew a thing or two about D-Days. The invasion decision was to be left to John Kennedy.

On Friday, November 18, 1960, CIA Inspector General Lyman B. Kirkpatrick, Jr., addressed the Commonwealth Club in San Francisco. It is the custom of the club to have members submit written questions to be put to its prestigious guest speakers. One of the questions put to the CIA inspector general that day was: "Professor Hilton of Stanford says there is a CIA-financed base in Guatemala where plans are being made for an attack on Cuba. Professor Hilton says it will be a black day for Latin America and the U.S. if this takes place. Is this true?"

There was a long pause. Finally, Kirkpatrick replied, "It will be a black day if we are found out."[10]

Of the many-splendored wonders of how the disaster of the Bay of Pigs came to be, perhaps the most curious is the role of the American free press. The almost Vichy-type collaboration of the media with the government in suppressing and distorting news of the coming invasion effectively eliminated American public opinion as a factor in one of the United States' most disastrous foreign policy decisions. The role of the press over Cuba was analogous to the Big Sleep of Journalism during the escalation of the U.S. breaking and entering in Vietnam—either stories about the developing disaster were ignored, or the press did the government's propaganda work for it.[11] In the big Bay of Pigs story, where the CIA was Mr. Bumbletoes and its elaborate invasion covers were stripped away like bed sheets in a porn movie, American editors had what you would call ample advance notice.

Said journalist Andrew Tully in his *CIA: The Inside Story*, "Practically everybody in Central America knew about this [Retalhuleu] training base." Finally, somebody wrote about it. On October 20 the story was front-paged by Guatemala's leading daily, *La Hora*. This was read with interest by Professor Ronald Hilton, director of Stanford's Institute of Hispanic American and Luso-Brazilian Studies and editor of the prestigious *Hispanic American Report*.

The *Hispanic American Report* was an independent scholarly publication providing information on developments in Spanish- and Portuguese-speaking countries, without ideological filter. Its back issues remain the best source of information on hemispheric developments in the fifties and sixties.

Hilton published an item that it was "common knowledge" the CIA was training Cuban exiles in Guatemala for an invasion of Cuba. Hilton's report was the basis of a November 19 editorial in *The Nation* which labeled the pending invasion a "dangerous and hare-brained project" and urged "all U.S. news media" to check out the story. Just to make sure it wouldn't be ignored, *The Nation* sent proofs of the editorial along with a press release about the reports of the impending invasion to the AP, the UPI, and all major news media in New York. They sent four copies to *The New York Times*. Nothing much happened.

It is becoming an item of journalistic faith that no one in the major media spotted the small editorial in *The Nation* and hence didn't hop to the way reporters go after hot stories in the movies. This fiction was repeated most recently in Peter Wyden's 1979 book *The Bay of Pigs*. Wyden says the *Times* did not know about the "brief editorial in the little weekly" until considerably later, when a reader sent a clipping of *The Nation* piece to then *Times* assistant managing editor Clifton Daniel asking, if this were true why wasn't it in the *Times*? However, Victor Bernstein, who was then *The Nation*'s managing editor, says that he virtually flooded the *Times* with copies of the invasion report and followed this up with telephone calls to the newspaper requesting it check out the story. Nine days later, on page 32 of its November 20 edition, Bernstein got his answer: The *Times* printed an unsigned dispatch from Guatemala City quoting President Miguel Ydigoras Fuentes branding as "a lot of lies" reports of invasion preparations from Guatemala and calling the new base in the mountains a purely Guatemalan Army facility. Bernstein told his sorry story of trying to alert the press to one of the decade's biggest stories in "The Press and the Bay of Pigs," by Victor Bernstein and Jesse Gordon, in the Fall 1967 issue of the *Columbia University Forum*.

Castro's claims that the United States was preparing to invade his island were dismissed as rantings by the American media. When the United States broke relations with Cuba on January 3, 1961, an article in the Sunday *New York Times* "News of the Week in Review" reported: "What snapped U.S. patience was a new propaganda offensive from Havana charging that the U.S. was plotting an 'imminent invasion' of Cuba."

On January 10, following on the heels of articles in the *St. Louis Post-Dispatch* and the Los Angeles *Times* confirming that American funds had been used in building a mysterious airstrip in the Guatemalan jungle, *The New York Times* printed a front-page story on the Guatemalan base. There was no mention of the CIA, and the overall impression given by the story was that these were Guatemalan military preparations with U.S. assistance to defend against a feared invasion from Cuba. The *Times* correspondent noted a bit wryly that the base seemed to be on the wrong side of Guatemala to defend against a Cuban assault from the Caribbean side. The New York *Daily News* piped in with a series in which the camps were said to be sponsored by "American and Cuban industrial interests"— precisely the agency's cover story. It was left to the Lucepress unexpectedly to state from right field what was happening: *Time* on January 27 said the entire operation was in charge of a CIA agent known only as Mr. B.

Dr. Hilton finally had his story confirmed. You'd never have known it by reading the papers.

The *Hispanic American Report* further angered the CIA by reporting on the questionable South American antics of the CIA-subsidized American Institute for Free Labor Development (AIFLD), supposedly a free creature of the AFL-CIO. Professor Hilton was rewarded for his scholarly independence by having his Ford Foundation funding yanked. The publication eventually ceased. Hilton said that it had been "suggested" to him by university officials that he was "offending powerful fund raisers."[12]

By April, American involvement was such an open secret that the

New York Spanish-language newspaper *El Diario* was printing the addresses of local invasion recruiting stations. On April 6, *The New York Times* received a dispatch from Tad Szulc in Miami that clearly linked the CIA to the invasion and predicted that the attack was "imminent." The *Times*'s Clifton Daniel in a 1966 confessional speech before the World Press Institute told of the journalistic statesmanship that followed. Then *Times* publisher Orvil Dryfoos was "gravely troubled by the security implications of Szulc's story. He could envision failure for the invasion, and he could see *The New York Times* being blamed for a bloody fiasco."[13] In the editorial bullpen the *Times* trimmed Szulc's references to the CIA and the "imminence" of the invasion and moved the story down on page one to a one-column head from its original the-dead-walk, four-column placement. Daniel said he and other *Times* persons present protested this editorial legerdemain as inconsistent with the newspaper's tradition. This was the famous story about which, after the Bay of Pigs, President Kennedy told the managing editor of the *Times*, "If you had printed more about the operation, you would have saved us from a colossal mistake."

This was, however, not the standard Kennedy White House position on freedom of the press. Kennedy leaned on publishers whenever he could to keep news out of the papers. He called it "premature disclosures of security information." The White House convinced the liberal *New Republic* in March 1961 to drop a rather complete account of the invasion preparations in Miami. Arthur Schlesinger, Jr., the Camelot hagiographer, brandished the President's big stick at the little magazine and later allowed that this "patriotic act" left him feeling "slightly uncomfortable."

Alan J. Gould, who was general manager of the Associated Press at the time when that august news agency's wires did not exactly hum with news of the forthcoming invasion fiasco, said upon his retirement: "Occasionally we have withheld stories for a time in the national interest. When the President of the United States calls you in and says this is a matter of vital security, you accept the injunction."[14]

The role of the press as revealed in this history of the Cuba Project shows the overwhelming propensity of the statesmen-executives of the major American media to exhibit the litmus-paper sensitivity toward Washington's wishes that *Pravda* editors had toward the Moscow morning line. In the case of Cuba, the White House did not have to wave much of a stick. The press was often upping the ante on it. In an extraordinary editorial just after the Bay of Pigs, *The Washington Post* said of the "Cuban affair": "It is a fair commentary that some American intelligence activities and covert operations classified under that title have been inept and too much in the public eye. Yet few persons would question their necessity."[15]

The British journalist Henry Fairlie later said, "The *Post* was inciting the Administration to act more secretly, more often; it was abetting the Administration in the very secrecy for which, with the publication of the Pentagon Papers, the *Post* would later blame the Kennedy Administration."[16]

In all its scheming and secrecy and fellow-traveling with the government in its plots against Cuba, the American press was keeping nothing from Fidel Castro.

It was keeping everything from the American people.

II

John Kennedy was strolling in the White House Rose Garden with his good-time buddy, Senator George Smathers of Florida, AKA the senator from Cuba, a sobriquet earned for his unwavering support of Batista. Now the talk concerned Castro. According to Smathers's later testimony, JFK raised the subject of assassination because someone else "had apparently discussed this and other possibilities with respect to Cuba."[17] Smathers suggested that any assassination attempt be coupled with a staged incident at the Guantánamo naval base that would provide a pretext for intervention by American forces.

Shortly thereafter Kennedy "learned enough about Smathers's right-wing associations to make him wary. While still valuing the Senator as an entertaining companion, Kennedy ordered him not to bring up the subject of Cuba again," according to journalist Hank Messick, a Smathers watcher.[18] But Smathers, who was close to Bebe Rebozo, Carlos Prío, and a number of other prominent exiles, persisted. At an *à deux* White House supper the President became so angry at Smathers's assassination table-talk that he cracked his fork against his plate, breaking the plate. After that Smathers gave up.[19]

At that moment of anger, Kennedy perhaps was unwitting of the fact that an indecent time after he took office, the CIA institutionalized assassination by creating the "Executive Action" campaign. Dick Bissell briefly discussed the chilling matter with McGeorge Bundy, Kennedy's national security adviser who had been a student of Bissell's at Yale. Bundy had voiced no objection. But Bundy didn't inform the President because he assumed, as he later testified, that the CIA would first seek specific authorization before "killing the individual."[20]

The CIA was by now up to its electronic ears in assassination scheming. There were two major plots timed to coincide with the invasion—one with the Mafia, the other in collaboration with the Cuban underground. There also seem to have been some direct attempts by the agency. According to author Roy Norton, CIA "assassination squads were trained in the Florida Everglades, under the direction of a graduate of a WW II OSS assassination school. Marine officers, assigned to the CIA, assisted in the training."[21]

Air Force Colonel Fletcher Prouty claimed that the CIA's Air Division "used a special Helio Courier L-28 STOL aircraft to land on a small road near Havana to infiltrate a team trained to attempt to assassinate Fidel Castro. We went to great lengths to support this operation, and the plane returned safely. The pilot informed us that he had left the assassin team exactly as planned. Later we learned that Castro's forces had rounded up the team."[22]

The agency's internal Cuban assassination plot was working in cooperation with an underground umbrella organization called Unidad Revolucionaria, which the CIA provided with weapons, equipment, and money. These were delivered aboard a World War II subchaser named the *Tejana III*, which had been converted into a pleasure craft by a wealthy Texas oilman, then purchased by an even wealthier Cuban expatriate, Alberto Fernández. Fernández, a former sugarcane czar, was the Unidad coordinator in Miami. He registered the *Tejana* under a dummy front called Inter-Key Transportation Company, and she was refitted by the CIA at its Stock Island warehouse. Powered by German pancake engines, she could clip along at more than thirty knots in choppy water. Removable .50- and .30-caliber machine guns were mounted on her decks, which were strewn with crab pots for disguise. With an all-Cuban crew, the *Tejana* shuttled personnel and matériel at night between Key West and secluded spots on Cuba's north coast. "Each shipment was large enough to fill two trucks," a Unidad officer said. "The ship brought in .30 and .50 caliber submachine guns, M-1 Garand rifles, C-3 and C-4 plastic explosives and incendiary materials. Some of the weapons were distributed to the groups. The remainder was hidden for future use."[23]

A number of deserting Castro high officials secretly joined Unidad, among them Aldo Vera, commandant of the Bureau of Investigation, and Humberto Sorí Marín, the wiry, pinch-faced minister of agriculture. They frequently rode the *Tejana* to conferences with CIA officers in Key West. Although aware of the Guatemalan exile base, they were not informed of the impending invasion for the CIA's own reasons. The agency nonetheless counted on Sorí Marín and company's removing Castro before D-Day.

Sorí Marín termed the plan a putsch. Mutinous air force officers would seize the San Antonio de los Baños air base near Havana, and navy ships would raise the flag of rebellion and sail from their ports. The University of Havana would be taken over by the Student Revolutionary Directorate (DRE), the young hotspurs who had backed Carlos Prío in his brief post-revolutionary struggle with Fidel Castro. Also, Vera and his police colleagues would take control of Havana police stations. The underground would seize or sabotage strategic targets, including communications facilities and public utilities.

There was an additional component to the plan, one that only a handful of key conspirators knew about. Fidel and perhaps his brother would be assassinated, plunging the government and military into a leaderless chaos. Sorí Marín, now Unidad's military chief, knew how to do it. He had stood at Fidel's side many times on reviewing stands as parades passed by. What could be simpler, he told his CIA friends, than planting one of the *petacas* ("plastic bombs") smuggled in on the *Tejana* under the stand and blowing the heart of the regime to kingdom come?

On the afternoon of March 18 a climactic meeting was held in a pastel yellow home on sleepy Calle Once in suburban Miramar. Humberto Sorí Marín, Rafael Hanscom, and Roger González hunched over a refectory table with six others. They were buoyed by recent successes; *Petacas* had exploded in theaters and other public places, and incendiary devices had gutted the two major Havana department stores, La Época and El Encanto. Chain-smoking Camels as usual, Sorí Marín pointed his bony finger at targets on spread-out street maps.

Several blocks away a militia unit on routine patrol stopped in front of a house and knocked on the door. The nervous woman occupant bolted out the back door and ran to the yellow house on Calle Once, which was owned by friends. But the patrol spotted her and smashed its way in. Sorí Marín drew his pistol but was chopped down by a militiaman's snub-nosed Czech machine gun and badly wounded. The others raised their hands.[24]

Unidad's back was broken, and the CIA abandoned the underground as a factor in the coming invasion. That left all its assassination eggs in the Mafia's basket.

Miami Beach was mobbed with gangsters for the third heavyweight championship fight between Floyd Patterson and Ingemar Johansson on March 13, 1961. Johnny Roselli and Sam Giancana were there with Bob Maheu. They shared a Fontainebleau suite with Joseph Shimon, a Washington police detective. A Runyonesque character, Joe Shimon had moonlighted for Maheu on confidential assignments and had come to know Roselli and Giancana as "fine fellows—the nicest guys you'd ever want to meet."[25]

The two mafiosi and Maheu had more than a boxing match to occupy them while in town—they were also arranging for a TKO of Fidel Castro. While Shimon whooped it up in the Fontainebleau's Boom Boom Room, they were visited in the suite by Florida Mafia boss Santos Trafficante. With him was an unsmiling Cuban in his fifties with short gray hair and sunglasses. This was the man to whom the Mafia had awarded the contract on Castro.

As Roselli later recalled the scene, Maheu "opened his briefcase and dumped a whole lot of money on his lap . . . and also came up with the [poison] capsules and he explained how they were going to be used. As far as I remember, they couldn't be used in boiling soups and things like that, but they could be used in water or otherwise, but they couldn't last forever."[26]

The Cuban nodded. He quickly counted the money — $10,000 — and stuffed it and the capsules, which were in an envelope, into his pocket. Then he left.

The Cuban was cut of royal cloth. He was Manuel Antonio "Tony" de Varona, prime minister of Cuba under Carlos Prío and now coordinator of the CIA political front group managed by Howard Hunt. Hunt, who had repeatedly braced Dick Bissell with the suggestion that Castro be assassinated coincident with the invasion only to be told that the matter was "in the hands of a special group," had no idea that Varona was involved in the plot. In fact, CIA headquarters was ignorant of the identity of the Cuban the Mafia had enlisted. This would lead to a denouement of Eric Ambler irony.

Tony Varona and Carlos Prío had matriculated together in the Auténtico party in Cuba, and it was only natural that when Prío was elected president in 1950, he should appoint Varona prime minister. Two years later, when Batista sprung his coup, the two fled to Miami together. Varona became Prío's top lieutenant in the struggle to oust Batista, and when the dictator suddenly decamped on New Year's Day of 1959, he returned with Prío to Havana to plot against the victorious Fidel. But while Prío hung on at his La Chata estate until early 1961, Varona hastened back to Miami.

As the counterrevolution formed in Florida, Varona became in effect Prío's stand-in. He assembled a small action group called Rescate that was composed mostly of Prío's Auténticos. Because of his prominence in Cuban politics, Varona was brought into the FRD and was among its leaders who met secretly with John Kennedy in the summer of 1960. But Varona didn't hit it off with Howard Hunt.

He considered the CIA entirely too parsimonious in dispensing money and equipment for his Rescate operations and, to Hunt's chagrin, rooted for the election of Kennedy because of the support promised during the campaign. "Maybe with Kennedy we'll get the help we need," he taunted Hunt. "The help your group ladles out with a teaspoon."[27]

Hunt had given Varona the standard cover story that he represented an international business group eager to recoup its Cuban holdings. Varona had seen through that. When Varona had the brass to propose that the U.S. government simply lend the exiles $10 to $20 million so that they could do it all on their own, Hunt reminded him that there would then be no way of "fixing" the watchdog federal agencies so that planes and boats slinking off to Cuba would not be intercepted. Keeping up the fiction, Hunt said that through "the influence of my backers, these government agencies were already cooperating with us."[28]

The headstrong Varona sought other sources to help finance his operations. He found a prime one in Meyer Lansky.

That an ex-prime minister of Cuba would link up with the syndicate's chairman of the board was not within the realm of the unexpected. Since Prío's corruption-riddled presidency, he had had financial interests which interlocked with those of Lansky through the Ansan Group, which had been buying up southern Florida with money looted from Cuba. In any case, according to congressional investigator Michael Ewing, Varona "was dealing with Lansky, who offered to back him. Lansky turned him over to Trafficante."[29] It was a matter of *quid pro quo*. As a 1975 Senate Intelligence Committee report expressed it—while carefully omitting Varona's name—"Trafficante and other racketeers" supplied funding in the expectation of securing "gambling, prostitution and dope monopolies" in a Cuba rid of Castro.

Varona told Trafficante that he had a contact inside a Havana restaurant frequented by Castro and his top aides. Varona's man should be able to administer the poison capsules. Trafficante informed Roselli, who notified Maheu, who served as a liaison in this instance between the mobsters and the CIA. Maheu made haste to brief his case officer, Jim O'Connell.

To eyeball the situation, O'Connell met briefly in Miami with Roselli and Varona. The CIA man was introduced as Jim Olds, a member of an "industrial group" seeking to recover Cuban properties. Varona had heard that line before—from Howard Hunt. Afterward he remarked to Roselli, "Look, I don't know [sic] like the CIA, and you can't tell me this guy isn't a CIA man."[30] But O'Connell, who had nothing to do with Hunt and his assault group, didn't recognize Varona. He returned to Quarters Eye with the recommendation that Roselli's Cuban be given what he demanded; cash and $1,000 worth of communications equipment. Dick Bissell handed O'Connell $50,000 in untraceable bills and authorized release of the equipment from the agency's Communications Office. The previously authorized $150,000 would be paid once the deed was done.

The money was hardly munificent for a feat of such scope, but Varona may also have had his eye on the $1 million bounty Meyer Lansky had put on Castro's head when the gambling syndicate was evicted from Havana. In any event, the $10,000 that Maheu gave him at the Fontainebleau was an expense advance, and the electronic gear was packed into an automobile that Maheu left at a designated empty lot for Varona to pick up.

A few days later Varona appeared on the doorstep of Howard Hunt's safe house. He was in a frenzy. A Coast Guard patrol had turned back one of his Cuba-bound launches, he said, and Hunt must get it cleared to proceed at once. "You've been playing a double game, Tony," Hunt rebuked him. He was unaware that it was actually a triple game with the Mafia. Hunt wagged his finger. "Heading the Frente [the FRD, Hunt's CIA political front group] and mounting your own private *Rescate* expeditions."

But Varona was desperate. "I have people waiting for supplies," he said. "They depend on me. You've got to—"

"Your radio signals have been intercepted, Tony," Hunt interrupted.

"They're in code," Varona argued.

"A code that was childishly simple to break. If we can read them do you think Castro's Soviet cryptographers aren't doing the same?" Hunt accused Varona of engaging in free-lance heroics "so that later in a free Havana when the question comes up as to what *Rescate* contributed, you'll be able to cite maritime missions."[31]

Nevertheless, Varona succeeded in getting the capsules into the proper hands in Havana. But, as Maheu has pointed out, "the go signal still had to be received before in fact they were administered." The CIA intended that the assassination be synchronized with the invasion. It was part of the "something else" that Dulles would later say the CIA expected to happen. This had been the case even back in November, when it was hoped the invasion could be launched before Eisenhower's term ran out.

It was a plan of some logic. With the Cuban people stricken by the loss of their *caudillo* and the rebel army in leaderless disarray, the brigade's chance of military success was inestimably enhanced. But an invasion date had not yet been set when Varona was given the capsules. All anyone knew was that it had to be soon. Cuban pilots were completing their training in MiGs in Czechoslovakia, and crates of the advanced jet were on board Soviet freighters bound for Cuba. Castro knew that an invasion was in the works. His frantic preparations to repulse it were evidenced by gun emplacements on the Malecón.

Timing was important. The lethal botulism synthesized by the CIA's Dr. Strangeloves would take a day or two to act, but it gave no symptoms of poisoning and left no traces. Death would be attributed to natural causes, and no suspicion would fall on the United States. According to Bob Maheu, Jim O'Connell revealed after the invasion that "the Cubans had an opportunity to administer the pills to Fidel Castro and either Ché Guevara or Raúl Castro, but the 'go signal' never came."[32]

Why the word that might have reversed the outcome of one of recent history's most momentous events was never sent is an explanation out of Eric Ambler. The most plausible explanation lies in the fact that the CIA didn't know that Tony Varona, the secretary of war in its puppet FRD Cabinet, was the Cuban the Mafia was depending upon in the assassination scheme. For in the days leading up to the invasion, the agency took measures that effectively prevented Varona from passing the "go signal." The CIA's "plausibly deniable" superprotections bollixed up its best chance to assassinate Castro.

To his curious glory, it was Howard Hunt who suggested the measures. Despite their differences, Hunt trusted Varona, and he trusted the other FRD leaders he had dealt with as well. But the liberal Manuel Ray had become a fixture in the FRD as a result of the Kennedy administration's nettlesome insistence on including liberal Cubans, which made Hunt paranoid. Hunt viewed Ray as the embodiment of "Fidelism without Fidel" and could envision his "informing the enemy" of the invasion plans. To forestall such treachery, he proposed that at the proper moment all the exile leaders be summoned to New York on a pretext. "Once assembled," Hunt wrote, "they were to be told invasion day was near, and that for both personal and operational security those who wanted to learn the assault plans — and be flown to the beachhead — would have to agree to isolation from that time on." That meant, Hunt said, "there would be no contact with the outside world."[33]

On April 13, four days before D-Day, the six top leaders gathered as instructed at the Lexington Hotel and were briefed by Frank Bender. They were placed under CIA guard. Then, on the eve of the invasion, they were hustled aboard an agency C-46 with taped-over windows and flown to the Opa-Locka airfield outside Miami. When the brigade waded ashore at the Bay of Pigs, the provisional government was being held under house arrest in a clapboard house on the airfield's border.

Tony Varona could only pace back and forth in the house, wondering where he was and what was going on. Meanwhile, a fit-as-a-fiddle Fidel Castro was preparing to crush the invasion.

The CIA never knew, until after the Bay of Pigs, that it had destroyed its own best shot at Castro. Convinced he had his options covered, Allen Dulles had urged JFK to go ahead with the invasion with calm assurances of success. If he didn't invade Cuba, Dulles told Kennedy, he'd have a "disposal problem" with all those armed exiles in Guatemala.[34]

III

The mob was ready to cash in its CIA chips. In the Bahamas on Invasion Eve, Lansky lieutenant Joe Rivers waited with a satchel stuffed with gold for the word to rush in and take charge of the dark casinos. Off the north Cuban coast two gambling pals of Frank Sturgis, Georgie Levine and Sally Burns, along with Pennsylvania Mafia boss Russell Bufalino and henchman James Plumeri, bobbed on the seas in a syndicate-owned boat with a CIA man aboard, ready to land and dig up the $750,000 they had buried in Havana before fleeing.

The overly optimistic gangsters had fed the CIA reports from underworld sources in Cuba that, in the words of investigative reporter Denny Walsh, "many of the people of Havana were unsympathetic to Castro and would almost certainly rise up in support of a counterrevolutionary force once it had established a beachhead."[35] This was wishful thinking, but the mob very dearly wished to be back in business in Havana, where the yearly take from gambling operations had been in the uptown neighborhood of $100 million a year after the skim. The ever-cautious Santos Trafficante, even though the CIA was his silent ally, was taking no chances. By one report, "Trafficante had infiltrated Operation Forty with Syndicate henchmen."[36]

The infiltrator was Richard Cain, a long-strided legman for Sam Giancana. Ex-cop Cain, who was fluent in Spanish, as a Chicago police detective had been the Mafia bagman inside the department. He was kicked off the force in 1960, when he was discovered tapping the phones of Mayor Richard Daley's commissioner of investigations. Then *Time* magazine discovered:

> With the consent of the CIA, intelligence sources say, Detective Cain began recruiting Spanish-speaking toughs on the Windy City's West Side. Some of the hoodlums were sent to Miami and Central America for training in commando tactics. . . . U.S. sources say that the CIA spent more than $100,000 on the operation, while Giancana laid out $90,000 of the Mob's own funds for Cain's expenses. When some Mafia officials objected to the payments, Giancana contended that the funds should be considered as "ice" [protection money].[37]

The CIA did in fact show heart by helping Giancana, Roselli, and Maheu get off the hook on the tapping of comedian Dan Rowan's phone in Las Vegas. Shortly before the invasion, Maheu took the problem to Colonel Sheffield Edwards, saying the FBI probe might jeopardize the assassination operation. The CIA deputy said that if Maheu was "approached by the FBI, he could refer them to me to be briefed that he was engaged in an intelligence operation directed at Cuba." When contacted by the bureau, Edwards declared that the CIA would oppose any prosecution because sensitive information about the invasion might come out. The agency subsequently briefed Attorney General Robert Kennedy, who agreed that the case should be dropped in the "national interest."[38]

As word of the impending invasion spread through the executive suites of American corporations the properties of which had been expropriated by Castro, there was more cautious optimism. The president of the Francisco Sugar Company, B. Rionda Braga, told *The Wall Street Journal* on February 9, 1961, that it was "reasonable to hope that the present Cuban government will fall and American companies will be able to resume operations there."

Francisco Sugar exemplified the interlock between the business world and the netherworld of intelligence. Braga's brother, George A. Braga, a Francisco director, sat on the board of Schroder's Limited, a British merchant bank that long had been the repository of a CIA contingency fund—estimated at $50 million—which was controlled by Allen Dulles. Gerald F. Beal, the president of Schroder's New York branch, where the fund was on deposit, also was a Francisco director. The Schroder's connection dated from 1937, when Dulles, then a member of the prestigious Sullivan & Cromwell law firm that represented Schroder's, was named a bank director. When Dulles joined the CIA, other Sullivan & Cromwell partners sat in his well-warmed seat on the board.

The interests of the CIA and Schroder's had coincided before. The 1953 CIA-engineered coup in Iran benefited the Anglo-Iranian Oil Company, the board of directors of which had been graced by a Schroder's executive for thirty years. And the 1954 overthrow of Arbenz in Guatemala made it possible for the Schroder's-funded International Railways of Central America, of which Gerald Beal was board chairman, to resume profitable business as usual.[39]

When the White House gave the final green light for the Cuban invasion, a number of CIA insiders began buying the stocks of Francisco and other sugar companies the earnings of which had been depressed by the loss of Cuban plantations. Stockbrokers became curious about the sudden influx of orders as friends were cut in on the tip that cheap sugar shares might prove a sweet gamble. One astute broker called the manager of a mutual fund believed to cater to CIA types of investors. The manager revealed that the fund was very bullish on sugar stocks. The broker recommended the stocks to his firm's clients, resulting in a new wave of buying. Prices were climbing sharply when the brigade hit the beach.

On April 3, the State Department issued a White Paper to prepare the American public for the invasion of Cuba. It took familiar refuge in democratic rhetoric. The paper was drafted by Arthur Schlesinger, the former OSS man and JFK's favorite bow-tie professor. After condemning the Batista regime, the paper argued that the Castro government, for all its early promise, had consummated "a betrayal of the Cuban Revolution." The U.S. role in aborting Cuba's struggle for national independence and social and economic equality by making the island a plantation for American corporations rated but one Schlesingerian sentence: "We acknowledge past omissions and errors." The next day John Kennedy, in a summit meeting with advisers, gave the final invasion go-ahead. "Let her rip," said the old New Dealer Adolf Berle.[40]

A week before the invasion a peeling banana boat named the *Santa Ana* flying a Costa Rican flag slipped her moorings at the Algiers naval base on the Mississippi River below New Orleans and steamed into the Gulf of Mexico. On board were Nino Díaz, who had fought with Raúl Castro in the Sierra, a CIA adviser — an American Marine of Portuguese descent named Curly Sanchez — and 168 exile troops. In her hold was a "cargo" of arms and ammunition. Destination: Baracoa, a town on the Oriente coast near the Guantánamo naval base.

The *Santa Ana* had been leased by the CIA for $7,000 a month, plus a guarantee of $100,000 against damage. Díaz and his Movement for the Recovery of the Revolution (MRR) expeditionary force had been trained in a wilderness camp north of Lake Pontchartrain. Their mission, as afterward described in published accounts, was to launch a diversionary strike in the Baracoa vicinity to lure Cuban military units away from the Bay of Pigs.

But Díaz's men were outfitted with the distinctive uniforms of Castro's rebel army, indicating that their real purpose was a deception of some nature and information has surfaced that the CIA did in fact intend to mount a fake attack on Guantánamo that would make Castro look like the aggressor and justify direct American intervention. U.S. Marines were off Cuba ready to land if the ploy worked. This — in addition to the twin assassination plots — was the "something else" the agency hoped for to make the invasion work.

The information did not come out until 1978, when former CIA officer James B. Wilcott testified before a congressional committee. Wilcott, who had served in Tokyo, Washington, and Miami from 1957 to 1966, said the Guantánamo deception was widely discussed by agency personnel at the time. It was conceived, he said, after it became clear that there would be no popular uprising in support of the invasion. "The original invasion plans were then changed to include the creation of an incident that would call for an all-out attack by the U.S. military," he testified. "Kennedy was not to know of this change, and it was not discussed at the November 1960 meeting of the invasion briefing."

According to Wilcott, "one such plan was to somehow get Castro to attack Guantánamo by making him believe that rebels were attacking from there. Another was to interpose a ship in a rebel attack and get it blown up. This was said to have been discarded when ONI [Office of Naval Intelligence] got wind of it and became very angry. . . . Just prior to the Bay of Pigs, and some said even earlier, the military intelligence community had become antagonistic to CIA since they were not let in on the invasion as they thought they should have been."

The ex-CIA man went on: "The theme was always the same: Get something started to overtly call in the military and follow up with complete seizure and installation of a favorable government. Once started, Kennedy would go along with it. . . . . How much Dulles was to be cut in on the full extent of the provocation incident was also debated."[41]

On the night of April 10 a long convoy of trucks carrying Brigade 2506 wound down the mountain roads from Base Trax to Retalhuleu. The troops filed onto C–54s which took off for Nicaragua. The airlift was completed the next night. Albert Persons, who piloted one of the last flights, recalled the scene upon landing at the Happy Valley airfield: "We were guided off the runway onto one of the hardstands. The area was crowded with Company personnel and Cubans in uniforms. They were all milling around in the lights of a half-dozen trucks lined up alongside the ramp. The trucks were quickly filled with the men we had brought in from Retalhuleu. The Company people mounted jeeps and took off down the runway in the direction of the harbor, followed by trucks."

The field fell suddenly silent. "A long row of B–26s squatted in the darkness along the far side of the runway. As we passed we could see clusters of rockets mounted under the wings of many of the aircraft," Persons said.[42]

The following morning John Kennedy held his weekly press conference. Adolf Eichmann was on trial in Jerusalem. Soviet Major Yuri Gagarin had rocketed into space in *Vostok*, becoming the first human to orbit the earth. Guerrillas in Laos were routing the CIA-backed royalists. But the first question put to Kennedy was about intervention in Cuba. The President replied that he would not undertake, "under any condition, an intervention in Cuba by the United States armed forces." Howard Hunt thought that Kennedy's statement was "a superb effort in misdirection."[43]

The CIA hardball artists were convinced that when faced with the realities of the invasion, Kennedy would send in American forces rather than swallow defeat. It wouldn't even be necessary to nuke 'em.

In the final briefing to the brigade commanders, their CIA boss led them to expect American air support. Castro's troops could not get to the Bay of Pigs because, he said, "every five minutes there will be a plane over all the major roads of Cuba." No such plans had in fact been made. After the beachhead was held for seventy-two hours, he declared. "We will be there with you for the next step." He added a last bravado: "But you will be so strong, you will be getting so many people to your side, that you won't want to wait for us.

"You will go straight ahead. You will put your hands out, turn left, and go straight to Havana."[44]

On Thursday, the morning after Kennedy's "no intervention" statement, a Lockheed Super-Constellation touched down at the Happy Valley airfield. Its USAF markings were still visible through a clumsily applied coat of paint. Dick Bissell and McGeorge Bundy, JFK's national security adviser, were among the passengers — some of whom changed from uniforms to civilian clothes before getting off. The group was taken to the recreation hut. The tarpaulin side panels had been lowered despite the heat. Leo Baker, one of the Birmingham pilots, asked what was going on. A CIA man told him the visitors had come from Washington to make a final "accounting."

Meeting the group was Marine Colonel Jack Hawkins, the American commander of the invasion. Bissell had sent him down a few days earlier to appraise the brigade's combat readiness. A lean six-footer with wavy brown hair, Hawkins had participated in the World War II amphibious assault on Iwo Jima. Hawkins had already made one critical decision — the underground in Cuba would not be alerted. "With those dumb bastards over there it'll be all over town," he had explained to James Noel, the former CIA station chief in Havana who had nursed the anti-Castro underground through its early days. "If we tell them it's going to be on a certain day, the whole goddamn island will know about it." When Noel argued to the contrary, Hawkins declared, "Well, I don't trust any goddamn Cuban."

After a four-hour session in the hut, during which the brigade's Cuban officers trooped in and out, the group was taken on an inspection of the combat planes on the line. A flash cable was sent to Quarters Eye that enthusiastically described the brigade as "a truly formidable force." The officers were described as "intelligent and motivated," and the brigade air arm was said to be all it was cracked up to be. It concluded: "The Brigade officers do not expect help from the U.S. armed forces." The cable was signed by Colonel Hawkins. The visitors boarded the big Connie and took off before dark.[45]

Quarters Eye rushed the cable to the White House where President Kennedy was still agonizing over whether to cancel the invasion. He remembered Hawkins as the battle-hardened officer with a precise military mind who had sat in on many of the planning sessions.

Kennedy said later that Hawkins' unqualified endorsement was instrumental in his decision to go ahead.

Fidel Castro had taken to sleeping days and staying up nights, convinced that the exiles would land in the early-morning darkness. Afterward in one of his usual lengthy speeches, he ticked off the signs that an attack was in the wind: "The constitution of the Council of Worms in exile [this was Castro-ese for the Cuban Revolutionary Council; Castro called the exiles *gusanos*, meaning "worms"], the infamous 'white paper' of Mr. Kennedy, plus the things that filtered through the United States press, plus some disagreement among themselves about the strategy to follow, demonstrated that the moment of attack was drawing near. News had come to us that the last embarkment of men and arms from Guatemala had been made, that the enemy was in movement, and it made us increase the vigilance."[46]

The vigilance had been all too apparent in the weeks before the invasion. On March 20, eight of Frank Sturgis's men, including an American, tried to slip ashore in Pinar del Río, but the guerrilla band they were to join had been captured, and the area was under tight security. The men were captured and executed. On April 5, a flotilla of Christian Democratic Movement ships, one skippered by Sturgis's sidekick Pedro Díaz Lanz, tried to discharge a large cargo of arms to guerrillas near Moa Bay but were chased off by patrol boats.

The CIA seemed unperturbed by the Cuban state of readiness.

It was a Broadway show scene on the long pier at Puerto Cabezas as Brigade 2506 marched out to be lightered to the invasion fleet anchored in the harbor. General Luis Somoza, the portly Nicaraguan strong man, stood in the bright sunlight, bidding the men hail and farewell. "He was dressed like a musical comedy potentate, wore powder on his face and was surrounded by gunmen," said Haynes Johnson of *The Washington Post*. "He waved and said, 'Bring me a couple of hairs from Castro's beard'; then he clenched his fist, turned and walked away, followed by his sycophants."[47]

As the brigade's top commander, Pepe San Román, was about to step into a lighter, a CIA man drew him aside and issued curious instructions. If a radio message was sent saying, "Come back, don't go ahead," it meant the opposite. But if the message read, "The quetzal is on the branches of the tree," it meant that Castro was waiting and the invasion was canceled. What the CIA man didn't say was that the President had reserved the option to cancel up to twenty-four hours before D-Day H-Hour, now less than three days away. If the President exercised that option, only the CIA could transmit it.

The night the invasion fleet sailed, the *Santa Ana* arrived off its landing zone near Baracoa after the long trip from New Orleans. Nino Díaz's men donned their Cuban Army uniforms. But a party that was sent ashore to reconnoiter returned with accounts of strange lights, cigarettes glowing in the dark, and unexpected auto traffic. Díaz, never known for his daring, decided against a landing by his troops. The CIA adviser on board, Curly Sanchez, engaged him in heated argument. But Díaz was the captain. He ordered the *Santa Ana* out to sea to await the next night.

At 2:00 A.M. on Saturday, April 15, the brigade's B-26 pilots were summoned to the briefing room at Happy Valley and told that they were to launch attacks on the airfields at San Antonio de los Baños and Camp Columbia, near Havana, and Santiago and Baracoa, in Oriente. U-2 photographs taken the previous day showed Castro's modest air force (the Fuerza Aerea Revolucionaria, or FAR) lined up on the fields; the term "sitting ducks" was used. CIA estimates placed the FAR's strength at about fifteen B-26s, a half dozen ancient British Sea Furies, and three Lockhead T-33 armed jet trainers. The pilots were told that if forced down outside Cuba they were to claim to be defecting FAR pilots.

Al Persons watched the B-26s, carrying 500-pound bombs and rockets under their wings, take off:

> As each pilot got his engines running he pulled out and fell into the line of aircraft taxiing toward the takeoff position. One by one they took position. Red exhaust flames turned to bright blue as full power was applied. The heavily loaded aircraft accelerated slowly. They were far down the runway, only the wing lights and exhaust flames visible when they broke ground. Then wing lights were switched off. We watched each aircraft until the twin pin-pricks of exhaust flames blended and disappeared into the curtain of stars across the night sky.

Persons was puzzled. He had counted only nine B-26s taking off. Thirteen had been available for the crucial task of wiping out the FAR on the ground.[48]

As the B-26s droned toward Cuba, Fidel Castro rushed to Camp Columbia in response to a report that ships had been sighted off Baracoa. Ordering a state of alert, the premier dispatched two battalions to the Baracoa area. At the first light of dawn a B-26 marked with the Cuban flag under its wing and "FAR" on its tail flew low over Camp Columbia. It was a brigade plane under false colors. Castro heard the thud of bombs exploding and the sharp report of antiaircraft fire.

"This is the aggression," he said calmly.

IV

At 7:00 A.M. on April 15, a B-26 bearing Cuban insignia crash-landed at the Key West naval air station. Its pilot disappeared behind closed doors. Minutes later another B-26 radioed a distress call to the Miami International Airport and touched down with the propeller of one engine feathered. Although its pilot was also kept isolated, the press was allowed to inspect and photograph the plane with its FAR markings and bullet holes in an engine nacelle and the fuselage.

At Quarters Eye, David Phillips picked up the phone and called Lem Jones, whose New York public relations firm was paid by the CIA to mouthpiece the Cuban Revolutionary Council. Phillips dictated a press release in the name of CRC president José Miró Cardona. It stated that the two pilots had defected from the FAR and had shot up Cuban airfields before escaping to Florida. "The Council had been in contact with and has encouraged these brave pilots," it said.

The defector scenario had been stage-managed by Phillips, who had ordered the machine gunning of the Miami B-26 before it took off from Happy Valley. On the floor of the United Nations that afternoon, Cuba's Raúl Roa angrily accused the United States of backing a "cowardly, surprise attack" carried out by mercenaries trained by "experts of the Pentagon and Central Intelligence Agency." Roa said that the attacks cost seven dead and many wounded.

Adlai Stevenson rose to the defense. Two days earlier the U.S. Ambassador to the United Nations had been informed by the CIA's Tracy Barnes that exile military preparations were under way and a transmitter was operating on Swan Island, but Barnes insisted that the United States was not involved. In what he would later describe as the most humiliating moment of his career, Stevenson held aloft a wirephoto of the B-26 that had landed in Miami. He pointed to the FAR insignia and said, "These two planes, to the best of our knowledge, were Castro's own air force planes, and according to the pilots, they took off from Castro's own air force fields."

In Florida, some unusually perceptive reporters noted that the B-26s had Plexiglas noses while those of the FAR were opaque, that tape covered the gun muzzles, and that the bomb racks were corroded. But in general the nation's press passed on the CIA's disinformation. The Associated Press chimed in with a dispatch from Havana: "Pilots of Prime Minister Fidel Castro's air force revolted today and attacked three of the Castro regime's key air bases with bombs and rockets."

The Miami *News* won the disinformation derby with a by-lined story by Hal Hendrix, a CIA "asset" who years later, while on the payroll of ITT, was implicated in the overthrow of the Allende government in Chile.[49] "It has been clearly established now," Hendrix wrote on April 15, "that there will be no mass invasion against Cuba by the anti-Castro forces gathered at bases in Central America and this country. The *News* has stated this for several months."

Noon on Sunday was the deadline for the President to call off the invasion. When he allowed it to proceed, Quarters Eye erupted in foot-stamping, backslapping glee, despite a bad omen — U-2 photos taken after the raids of the previous day showed that the FAR had not been completely destroyed. Two B-26s and several Sea Furies were undamaged, and the three T-33 jets, the most dangerous of all, sat combat-ready on the field at Santiago. To finish the job, a second strike was set for the first blush of dawn on Monday. Total air superiority was indispensable to the success of an amphibious operation.

What ensued laid John Kennedy open to charges that he *canceled* this second strike, thereby sabotaging the invasion. These charges would plague him the rest of his life and became the core of the CIA apologia. CIA instructors told new agent classes that Kennedy had "chickened out" at the Bay of Pigs.

But a man at the core of the operation has given an entirely different version. According to Howard Hunt, no Kennedy lover, the requirement for a second strike was raised only after the telltale U-2 photos were examined. As the air operations officer at Quarters Eye was ordering up ordnance for the "cleanup strike," General Cabell dropped by, still in his golfing attire after a round at the Chevy Chase Country Club. "Now it seems to me we were only authorized one strike at the airfields," Cabell said.

"Oh, no sir," the officer objected, "the authorization was to knock out the Cuban air force. There was no restriction on the number of strikes."

Cabell was in charge. Allen Dulles was in Puerto Rico fulfilling a longstanding speaking engagement in order not to arouse suspicion that something big was up. Playing it safe, Cabell ordered the strike to be held up until he could get approval from higher authority.[50]

Cabell went to Dean Rusk, who telephoned JFK at his rural estate, Glen Ora, in Virginia. The Saturday raids had begun to boomerang. Castro, of course, knew that none of his airmen had defected, and he was convincing the world that the United States was behind the deception. Moscow and Peking were making ominous noises, depicting the raids as a threat to peace and implying intervention.

Kennedy apparently realized that a new round of raids could not be covered by the same charade. That evening, as the agonizing continued, *The New York Times* published an article by Tad Szulc poking holes in the defection fiction.

Kennedy said a firm no to the second strike. "There's been a little change in our marching orders," Cabell announced in the War Room at Quarters Eye.

Howard Hunt, who fancied himself a disinformation expert, had been busy composing messages to be broadcast to Cuba from the CIA radio station on Swan Island, a guano heap off Honduras that was overpopulated by lizards. He said later that his model was the BBC wartime broadcasts which confused enemy intelligence. Hunt's favorite ditty would have been suitable stuff for one of the pulp spy novels he cranked out in his spare time. It was beamed to Cuba in Spanish on invasion eve:

> Alert! Alert! Look well at the rainbow. The first will rise very soon. Chico is in the house. Visit him. The sky is blue. Place notice in the tree. The tree is green and brown. The letters arrived well. The letters are white. The fish will not take much time to rise. The fish is red.[51]

Hunt's message was intended to deceive Castro into thinking the underground was about to rise. Castro was not deceived.

Toward dusk Frank Bender phoned Hunt from Opa-Locka, where he had just put the entire CRC command under house arrest. The CIA did not want the leaders of the New Cuba talking unless the correct American words came out of their mouths. "How are things in Honeymoon Hotel?" asked Hunt, who was not known for his humor. The exile leaders were not taking their quarantine well. They had heard reports of the air attacks on a radio. They wanted to know what was going on. They wanted to call their families. They were going stir-crazy. The man most anxious to get out was Tony Varona.

As night fell over Oriente, Nino Díaz again eased the *Santa Ana* toward shore. The previous night a second attempt at landing had been begun and, in the words of the CIA adviser aboard, "aborted primarily because of bad leadership." This time the scouting party returned to the ship with reports of jeeps on the roadways, undoubtedly the soldiers Castro had rushed to the area after hearing of ship sightings on Friday night. Díaz radioed Base Tide that it would be suicidal to land. He was ordered to proceed. He refused. The orders were changed for the *Santa Ana* to head for the Bay of Pigs and wait offshore for landing instructions. The CIA had lost its planned excuse to send in the Marines, who were aboard ship nearby.

Shortly after dark the invasion armada rendezvoused off the south coast of Cuba with the LCIs, *Barbara J* and *Blagar*, which had come from Vieques Island with tanks, heavy equipment, and frogmen. Nearby was a task force of the U.S. Atlantic Fleet, led by the carrier *Boxer*, which had been ordered into position by Admiral Arleigh Burke. On board a destroyer was a battalion of combat-ready Marines.

Burke and his CIA counterparts were convinced that JFK, given the proper excuse, would permit intervention. Howard Hunt, who, true to the CIA need-to-know rule, apparently knew nothing about the plan to fake a Castro attack on Guantánamo, never did understand why the Marines weren't sent in. "If the armada was not charged with ensuring victory," he wrote thunderously in 1973, "why else had it been assembled?"[52]

Around midnight the *Blagar* crept in close to shore, and CIA paramilitary Grayston Lynch, joined by five Cubans, slipped into his wet suit, mask, and flippers, got into a black rubber raft, and paddled toward the beach. Their task was to plant colored lamps to mark the landing zone. Instead of the open approach and smooth beach predicted by CIA hydrographic experts, they encountered sharp coral reefs and rocky terrain. Despite JFK's insistence that Americans stay out of combat, Lynch was the first to land in the invasion. Not a white face on the beach, Dick Bissell had said.

Far down the beach a second American, the very gung-ho William "Rip" Robertson, nicknamed Alligator by the Cubans because of his wizened skin, led a second team of frogmen ashore and planted

a marker painted in luminous yellow: WELCOME LIBERATORS—
COURTESY OF THE BARBARA J. Both teams were spotted by militia
patrols and came under fire.

The element of surprise was gone.

At Happy Valley four B-26s, engines idling, were lined up on the
runway waiting for the signal to take off for Santiago to finish off
the remaining Cuban T-33s. Flash cables from Base Tide to
Quarters Eye brought no response. The men in the War Room still
hoped that the President would change his mind and give the green
light.

The B-26s would have to reach Santiago no later than first light
to catch the T-33s on the ground. That meant take-off could be no
later than 2:30 A.M. The CIA air chief, who used the name Billy Carpenter, kept stalling the anxious pilots, telling them that a final check
of the target photographs was being made. Carpenter hoped that
when he hopped on his bicycle and pedaled off for another check at
the operations tent, the pilots would take off on their own.

They didn't. The deadline passed. The engines were shut down.

At 3:15 A.M. Fidel Castro was awakened in Havana and notified
that two microwave stations in the Bay of Pigs area were reporting
that a landing in force was under way (CIA intelligence had not
learned of the stations). The premier immediately ordered a 900-
man battalion quartered at a nearby sugar mill into action. He also
ordered the FAR to take off at dawn and attack the invasion fleet.

When he received word that the landing was under way, David
Phillips woke up Lem Jones in New York and dictated Cuban
Revolutionary Council War Communiqué No. 1, for Immediate
Release: INVASION OF CUBA REPORTED BEGUN BY A REBEL FORCE; MIRÓ
CARDONA SAYS GROUP OF HUNDREDS HAS LANDED IN ORIENTE
PROVINCE.

The communiqué was intended to focus Castro's attention on the
diversionary landing (to be coupled with the pretext assault) at
Baracoa. In a communications screw-up that would typify the entire operation, no one at Quarters Eye yet knew that the *Santa Ana*

had abandoned her mission and was steaming in the direction of the Bay of Pigs.

In the fretful period during which the War Room was trying to persuade Kennedy to authorize the Santiago strike, no one had thought to order the B-26s at Happy Valley to fly air cover over the beachhead in case the authorization was not given. It was now 4:00 A.M. — far too late for them to get there in time. Cabell and Bissell phoned Dean Rusk, pleading for help from the Navy jets on the *Boxer* standing offshore. Rusk was adamant but finally agreed to get the President on the line. As he listened to Cabell's pleading, Kennedy must have wondered how his original okay to back covertly an exile force had escalated to the point of full-scale armed intervention.

"The President says no deal," Cabell said as he hung up. "I guess we'll just have to be headsy-headsy about this."[53]

At dawn, as the brigade was fanning out from the landing zone and paratroops were securing the swampy approaches to the Bay of Pigs, the depleted FAR arrived. One B-26 was downed by small-arms fire from the *Houston*, but two rocket-equipped T-33s scored direct hits on the ship, and she scraped onto a reef. Then a Sea Fury came in out of the rising sun and sank the *Rio Escondido*, sending the bulk of the supplies to the bottom.

As the morning wore on, B-26s hurriedly dispatched from Happy Valley began arriving in pairs to fight off the FAR and provide strafing support. Vic and Connie, Americans who Albert Persons believed "were permanent employees of the Company," chewed up an approaching Castro column that was trapped on a narrow road flanked by salt marshes, inflicting nearly 900 casualties.

But the long haul from Nicaragua had left the B-26s with too little time over the beachhead, and the absence of tail gunners to save weight rendered them vulnerable to fighter attack. Chirrino Piedra, a brother-in-law of future Watergate figure Felipe de Diego, was jumped from behind by a T-33 and sent spinning into the sea. Four more B-26s were shot down by the FAR. Castro lost only two planes.

At nightfall the situation map showed the brigade holding a perimeter of roughly thirty-six miles. But the FAR owned the skies, and the destruction of the *Houston* and *Rio Escondido* had cut off supplies. Upon seeing the ships sunk, the other supply vessels had scattered. Pepe San Román, practically out of ammunition after only one day of fighting, was furious. When the truant ships did not respond to his blinker signals, he took a small boat six miles to sea, yelling vainly into the darkness.

JFK realized that the news from the front portended disaster unless the FAR was knocked out. He gave the go-ahead for an air-to-ground strike. Intelligence reports indicated that the dangerous T-33s were now based at San Antonio de los Baños, much closer to the front than Santiago. Six B-26s from Happy Valley arrived over San Antonio at dawn on Tuesday. But the field was obscured by a heavy cloud cover and ground haze. The planes did not have enough fuel to circle until the cover broke. They returned to Happy Valley.

At 8:45 A.M. Pepe San Román gathered his staff and told them that the brigade's Dunkirk was at hand unless the situation turned around dramatically. Castro, in personal command, had launched a three-pronged attack, and the beachhead was shrinking.

One of San Román's aides proposed that the brigade march east on the coastal highway and fight its way into the sanctuary of the Escambray Mountains. They stayed instead because no one knew that such an escape plan had been approved by JFK and his advisers. The CIA had withheld the plan from the Cubans for fear it would weaken the brigade's resolve to fight if the going got tough.

At midmorning the *Blagar* reestablished radio contact with San Román, who swore like a Texan at having been abandoned. Grayston Lynch took over the mike, promising that supplies would be landed that night. And, the CIA man announced, "Jets are coming." San Román was buoyed. Around three in the afternoon they came—two Sabrejets, with markings painted over. The planes pranced low over the front, then disappeared. They were only on a reconnaissance mission.

Around noon an urgent CIA request for air cover had reached the White House. As Bobby Kennedy recalled it, "Jack was in favor of giving it. However, Dean Rusk was strongly against it. He said that we had made a commitment that no American forces would be used and that the President shouldn't appear in the light of being a liar." RFK pointed out that information on whether air cover might make any difference in the outcome was lacking, and it was decided to try to determine from the air "if there was any possibility or chance of these men holding out."[54]

The supply situation was desperate. That afternoon C-54s from Happy Valley made airdrops, but inaccuracy and capricious winds caused most of the parachutes to fall into the swamps or the sea. That night the *Blagar* and *Barbara J* rendezvoused some fifty miles at sea and began loading tons of supplies into landing barges for the trip to shore. But the exile crews, terrified of returning to the battle zone, foot-dragged, and progress was slow. The *Blagar* radioed Base Tide that the operation could not be finished before dawn. "If low jet cover is not furnished at first light," the message concluded, "believe we will lose all ships."

At the White House the traditional President's reception for congressmen and their wives was getting under way. As JFK entered with Jacqueline on his arm, the Marine Band swung into "Mr. Wonderful." Around midnight guests noticed that their host was missing, although Jackie still circulated. In his tuxedo, Kennedy was holding an emergency meeting in the Oval Office. Richard Bissell informed him of the *Blagar*'s doomsday message. The CIA official and Admiral Burke reeled off several proposals: Send in a company of Marines; order a Navy destroyer to shell Castro's positions; post a picket line of Sabrejets at the three-mile limit. Kennedy said no. Burke suggested that Sabrejets from the *Essex* fly protective cover with their markings obliterated. Kennedy finally agreed to a compromise: The Sabrejets could cover a dawn strike by B-26s from Nicaragua for only one hour. It would be a "dead cover," meaning they could interpose themselves between the B-26s and FAR craft. But they could not fire unless fired upon.

At Happy Valley the mission to cover the beachhead had already been scheduled, but there was a shortage of exile pilots. Ten had been killed, others were exhausted, and some simply refused to go.

A decision was made to fill the empty seats with seven of the Birmingham instructors. Six B-26s took off in pairs at half hour intervals beginning at 3:00 A.M. After the departure of the first four, a flash cable arrived from Quarters Eye that read: from 0630 TO 0730 THE SKY WILL BE CLEAR. General Doster, who headed the Birmingham contingent, dashed for the airstrip and climbed onto the wing of one of the last two B-26s as it prepared to leave. Doster elatedly told the pilot, Riley W. Shamburger, Jr., a personal friend, that the mission would be given air cover by Navy jets.

As darkness faded over the Bay of Pigs, the first B-26, piloted by Gonzalo Herrera, arrived. Herrera was alone. His copilot had jumped out of the cockpit and vanished into the woods as the plane was taxiing at Happy Valley. A companion plane had been forced back with engine trouble. Herrera picked out a concentration of blue-clad militia and began strafing.

Soon two more B-26s with American crews out of Birmingham were on the scene. Pilots Thomas W. "Pete" Ray and Bill Peterson selected targets and began bombing and strafing runs. They were soon joined by Don Gordon, then Riley Shamburger and Hal McGee.

Herrera was hit but managed to limp home. Pete Ray and his observer, Leo F. Baker, were not as lucky. "We're going in!" Ray yelled just before crashing near the Bay of Pigs airstrip.

Shamburger was becoming alarmed that the Navy jets hadn't shown up. "How about our little friends?" he radioed Gordon. "See anything of them?"

"Little friends?" Don Gordon was perplexed. The message about the Navy jet cover had reached Happy Valley after his departure.

"We're supposed to have some little friends with us at the beach," Shamburger explained. "You know, the good guys."

"I didn't see anybody," Gordon replied. He still wasn't sure what Shamburger was talking about.

Hal McGee saw it happen. Two T-33s jumped on Shamburger's tail as he was making a low strafing pass. Two streams of tracer bullets converged on the B-26, and its right engine burst into flames. It went into a steep right bank, then knifed into the sea in a geyser of spray.

"T-birds!" Hal McGee shouted into his mike. "They got Riley!" Don Gordon heard the transmission. His right engine had been hit by ground fire and was running rough, and he was already fifty miles south on his way back to Happy Valley. He looked at his watch: 6:18. Although Gordon was unaware of it, the Navy jets were due over the beachhead at 6:30. Just then an unmarked Sabrejet pulled into formation on his left wing. The pilot tossed the surprised Gordon a casual salute. Gordon tried to radio the jet, but the frequencies were different. He gestured with his hand for the jet to turn around and head for the beach. The pilot understood and peeled off into a sweeping turn. Gordon saw two more jets flying higher and behind follow.[55]

It was too late. The supply ships could not risk unloading in daylight.

The timing foul-up has never been satisfactorily explained. But there obviously was a monumental breakdown in communication between the CIA and the Navy. The Navy arbitrarily used 6:30 as the hour of dawn, while the CIA had already scheduled the B-26s to begin arriving at the first glimmer of light nearly an hour earlier.

At 8:30 A.M. Havana radio announced that the bodies of two American fliers had been recovered from the wreckage of their B-26 at the Bay of Pigs. One was identified as Leo Francis Bell. "The registered address of the Yankee pilot is 48 Beacon Street, Boston," the broadcast said. Leo Francis Bell was the fictitious identity the CIA had created for Leo Baker.

The brigade pilots listening to the broadcast were grim. They had just been asked to go on a support mission at the beachhead and realized that the situation was deteriorating rapidly. They demanded to know why the mission was so important. "We must hold twenty-four hours more," a CIA adviser told them. "Don't play the bells loud, but something is going to happen."[56]

The allusion was to the seventy-two-hour period that would expire the following morning, after which a government-in-arms could be declared, and outside military assistance requested. Castro was well aware of the deadline. Afterward he told foreign newsmen that "it became an urgent political problem for us to oust them as quickly as possible so that they would not establish a government there."

The brigade had, in fact, captured the Bay of Pigs airfield the first day, and only that same morning a C-46 had landed to drop off supplies and evacuate the wounded. Once the magic hour arrived, the CRC provisional government being held at Opa-Locka would be flown in to proclaim the new government. When that happened, the CIA planners apparently had convinced themselves, John Kennedy would cave in and permit the landing of Marines.

The desperate mission to save the beachhead was to be flown in six P-51 Mustang fighters that belonged to the Nicaraguan Air Force and were lent by General Somoza. As the Nicaraguan pilots who had just ferried them in from Managua lounged about, ground crews were busy painting out the air force markings, attaching extra gas tanks, and installing machine-gun belts and rockets. Buck Persons, who had had combat experience in Mustangs during World War II, was to lead the fuzz-cheeked brigade pilots, none of whom had ever flown one. They planned to land at the Bay of Pigs airfield and refuel from drums that had been dropped off there.

It was early afternoon before the planes and pilots were ready to go. Just then a jeep raced out to the runway. "Forget it, Buck," a CIA man told Persons, "they've lost the field."

News that the beachhead was collapsing reached the White House just before noon. Robert Kennedy recalled:

> The President for the previous three hours was battling hard to make arrangements to evacuate. By the time we received this information, however, the men were in the water. It was too late to send the destroyers in because they could be destroyed by artillery fire. He ordered them, however, to run up and down the beaches as close as they could and try to pick up any survivors.[57]

At Happy Valley a C-54 was being loaded with supplies to drop to the brigade in a last-ditch effort to fend off defeat. When a Cuban crew refused to fly it, Persons and another Birmingham flier volunteered. Finally, about 2:00 P.M., the last bundle was aboard. Persons was kicking the chocks from the wheels of the big plane when a jeep again came racing toward him. This time it was the CIA man called Colonel Frank with the bad news. "They're wiped out," Frank said. "You'd just be dropping this stuff to the bad guys."

"Well, in other words, that's the old ball game then?"

"That's the ball game. No hits, no runs—all errors."

At 4:32 P.M. Pepe San Román called Base Tide on the radio. "I have nothing left to fight with," he said. "Am taking to the swamps. I cannot wait for you." On the *Blagar* Grayston Lynch overheard the transmission and cut in urging San Román to hold on because "we're coming with everything." Told that it would take three or four hours, San Román curtly declared, "That's not enough." He signed off.

At 5:30 the members of the might-have-been provisional government of Cuba, their faces frozen in shock, filed into the Oval Office to shake hands with the President. The ceremony was intended to placate them after the house arrest at Opa-Locka.

A few hours later, at Quarters Eye, Howard Hunt dictated a final deception to Lem Jones in New York. Given out at 9:00 P.M. as Bulletin No. 6 of the CRC, it said:

> The recent landings in Cuba have been constantly although inaccurately described as an invasion. It was, in fact, a landing of supplies and support for our patriots who have been fighting in Cuba for months. . . . Regretfully we admit tragic losses in today's action among a small holding force . . . a gallantry which allowed the major portion of our landing party to reach the Escambray Mountains.

Weeks after the Bay of Pigs disaster, Allen Dulles made his first public appearance on the NBC television program *Meet the Press*. "Mr. Dulles," the moderator asked, "in launching the Bay of Pigs invasion, you were obviously expecting a popular uprising to support it. Yet none occurred. How could you have been so wrong?"

"A popular uprising?" Dulles asked, looking puzzled as he took a puff from his pipe. "That's a popular misconception. But no, I wouldn't say we expected a popular uprising. We were expecting something else to happen in Cuba . . . something that didn't materialize."

FOUR

Operation Mongoose

*History tells us that there will surely be
a next time.*
— GEN. EDWARD G. LANSDALE

I

TRICIA Nixon had a message for her father the day after the Bay of Pigs. "JFK called," she said. "I knew it! It wouldn't be long before he would get into trouble and have to call on you for help." Nixon returned the call immediately.

"Dick," the President said, "could you drop by to see me?"

Nixon sat on a sofa near the fireplace in the Oval Office; Kennedy was in his rocking chair. He described his melancholy meeting with the hierarchs of the Cuban Revolutionary Council; some had lost relatives and friends on the battlefield. "Last night they were really mad at us," JFK said. "But today they have calmed down a lot and, believe it or not, they are ready to go out and fight again if we will give them the word and the support."

Kennedy was in a black mood. He got up from his rocker and paced back and forth, loosing in navy blue language a blistering indictment of his advisers: the CIA; the Joint Chiefs; members of his own staff. "I was assured by every son of a bitch I checked with— all the military experts and the CIA—that the plan would succeed," he said.

After venting his Irish, Kennedy asked, "What would you do now in Cuba?"

The man who had been the Cuba Project's action officer in the Eisenhower White House replied unhesitatingly. "I would find a proper legal cover and go in. There are several justifications that could be used, like protection of American citizens living in Cuba and defending our base at Guantánamo."[1]

Kennedy slowly shook his head. If the United States grabbed Cuba, Khrushchev might grab Berlin, he said. Kennedy turned philosophical. "It really is true that foreign affairs is the only important issue for a President to handle, isn't it?" he asked rhetorically. "I mean, who gives a shit if the minimum wage is $1.15 or $1.25, in comparison to something like this?"

Nixon told this story in his 1978 *Memoirs*. He neglected to mention the similarity to his memorable remark on the famous Watergate White House tapes when the President said, "Who gives a shit about the Italian lira."

"You blew it!" Joseph P. Kennedy, Sr., greeted his son when he arrived at the family compound in West Palm Beach. Castro had cost the old man money. The patriarch had taken a sizable loss when the Coca-Cola franchise he and Irish tenor Morton Downey owned in Cuba went the way of the revolution. Now Castro was strutting around the Bay of Pigs battlefield, showing foreign correspondents how his forces had humiliated the Yankee-backed invaders. Joe Kennedy was mad as hell. As far as he was concerned, his son had put his trust in the wrong hands. "I know that outfit," he said of the CIA, "and I wouldn't pay them a hundred bucks a week."[2]

As father talked turkey to son in Palm Beach, the CIA's $100-a-week men were busy doing what Allen Dulles, with his talent for euphemism, called damage control. A C-46 took off from Happy Valley and headed out over the Caribbean. A hundred miles from the coast, the plane gently banked, and its crew slid out scores of boxes designed to burst open in the air. A white cloud of paper — David Phillips's leaflets bearing the slogan, "Cubans, you will be free!" — floated toward the sea.

At Base Trax, CIA agents dug a large hole, dumped all the records of Brigade 2506 into it, and bulldozed it over. Guatemalan soldiers and laborers demolished the camp, carting away all the debris, even the cement foundations of the barracks. Then the road into the camp was bulldozed. As the jungle took hold, Base Trax would cease to exist.

In Miami, CIA agents hastily flown down from Washington badgered the families and friends of brigade members into silence about the agency's role. They invoked the sacred themes of national security and Cuban liberation. The CIA men boarded a commercial vessel on the Miami River that had been slated for duty in the invasion but was not ready on time; with acetylene torches, they cut away the deck gun mounts.

In Washington, the logs of the two United Fruit freighters that had hauled supplies for the invasion arrived at Quarters Eye. Sometime later, according to former United Fruit executive Thomas McCann, the logs were returned to the company "encased in sealing wax. As far as I know they are still in the company vaults, the official record of our participation in that fiasco permanently safe from public view."[3]

In Birmingham, Alex Carlson, the lawyer fronting for the Double-Chek Corporation, had the unpleasant task of keeping the lid on the deaths of Americans in the invasion. He visited the widows of Pete Ray, Riley Shamburger, Leo Baker, and Wade Gray, telling them that their husbands had vanished on a C-46 cargo flight in Central America. "He said my husband was dead and to start life anew," Mrs. Gray recalled. "He said they had spotted one of the plane's engines floating in the water. I didn't think engines floated."[4]

The widows resented any implications that their husbands were rank mercenaries, but all they could get out of authorities in Washington was a runaround. Soon, however, checks totaling $6,000 a year began arriving in the mail. At first they came from a Miami Springs bank and were signed by Carlson, but then they were sent by the Bankers Trust Company of New York drawn on a trust fund set up by persons unknown.[5]

CIA Inspector General Lyman Kirkpatrick rolled his wheelchair through the corridors of Quarters Eye, conducting the internal probe his duties required when an operation badly backfired. His report, which has never been released, reverberated through the agency. It saddled the "black operators" with the blame and pointed the cloak-and-dagger finger directly at Allen Dulles. These operators, Kirkpatrick said, "chose to operate outside the organizational structure of both the CIA and the intelligence system."

Kirkpatrick concluded that the entire Bay of Pigs operation was wacko from the start. After interviews with more than 300 CIA men who had worked on the Cuba Project, he found that no one had "seriously considered" whether the possibility of overthrowing Castro was anything other than exile moonshine. "All intelligence reports coming from allied sources indicated quite clearly that he was thoroughly in command of Cuba and was supported by most of the people who remained on the island.

"If there was a resistance to Fidel Castro," said the CIA inspector general, "it was mostly in Miami."

This was contrary to all precepts of damage control. Dulles called in Kirkpatrick and got him to write a toned-down version of his report. Kirkpatrick did a rewrite which did to Dulles what Teddy Roosevelt had done to San Juan Hill. Loyal Dulles spear carriers managed to bury the report in the agency archives, and it has never been declassified. Kirkpatrick later gave an indication to the authors of the tone of this suppressed treatise: "Allen and John Foster Dulles were the two biggest spooks in the United States," he said.[6]

In a windowless room in the bowels of the Pentagon, Bobby Kennedy jotted furiously on a note pad as a sorry parade of witnesses told of the slaughter at the Bay of Pigs. There was Roberto San Román, Pepe's brother, who had escaped in a rowboat and still showed signs of his long exposure at sea before being rescued. There were Grayston Lynch and William Robertson, the gung-ho CIA paramilitaries who had been the first ashore and the last to give up. There were Jake Esterline, the staff officer in charge of the Cuba Project, Dean Rusk, McGeorge Bundy, and a conga line of Pentagon brass.

RFK was presiding over a secret inquest by the Cuba Study

Group, an *ad hoc* coroner's jury assembled by his brother. The study group was supposed to find out how to do it right. Even at this early stage—the hearings lasted most of the month of May—the Kennedys were determined to settle the score with Castro. "Both Jack and Bobby were deeply ashamed after the Bay of Pigs, and they were quite obsessed with the problem of Cuba," former CIA Deputy Director of Intelligence Ray S. Cline has said. "They were a couple of Irishmen who felt they had muffed it . . . and, being good fighting Irishmen, they vented their wrath in all ways that they could."[7]

General Edward Lansdale, who was to lead the new phase of the Cuba Project, described the Kennedys as emotionally overwhelmed with Cuba. "Bobby felt even more strongly about it than Jack," he said. "He was protective of his brother, and he felt his brother had been insulted at the Bay of Pigs. He felt the insult needed to be redressed rather quickly."[8]

The Kennedys were able to avoid the exigencies of a public probe because the Bay of Pigs was a bipartisan disaster. On May 1 former President Eisenhower declared himself in opposition to any "witch-hunting" investigation. "The last thing you want to have is a full investigation and lay all of this out on the record," he said.

General Maxwell Taylor, the uncertain trumpeter whose advocacy of "flexible response" had put him in Eisenhower's doghouse, was brought back to chair the Cuba Study Group. Allen Dulles and Arleigh Burke served with RFK on the panel, with the CIA's Colonel J. C. King as chief staff officer. Colonel Fletcher Prouty, the Pentagon focal point officer with the CIA and an ardent CIA hater, saw it as "a CYA operation." Howard Hunt had the job of answering staff inquiries for the CIA. He thought the game plan was "to whitewash the New Frontier by heaping guilt on the CIA."[9]

RFK seemed shocked by evidence of CIA duplicity developed at the closed-door hearings. McGeorge Bundy testified that Dulles and Bissell had led the White House to believe that the invasion would precipitate a popular uprising. "Success in this operation was always understood to be dependent upon an internal Cuban reaction," Bundy said. Yet it was learned that an agency Special National Intelligence Estimate only four months earlier had forecast nothing "likely to bring about a critical shift of popular opinion away from Castro."

The CIA had also misled the White House on the state of readiness of the Cuban armed forces and their will to fight (RFK scribbled in his note pad: " . . . never would have tried this operation if [we] knew that Cuban forces were as good as they were and would fight."[10]). Most disturbing of all were revelations that the CIA had controverted higher orders. Despite the President's instructions that no Americans be used, for example, Lynch and Robertson were the first to land. And the CIA apparently was convinced JFK would change his mind when the chips were down. San Román and other survivors testified that CIA advisers in Guatemala promised U.S. military support as needed.

Not until the brigade was released almost two years later did the charge surface that the agency had had a rump plan for circumventing the President. While the brigade was still at Base Trax, Colonel Frank assertedly took aside its commanders and confided that "forces in the administration" were trying to cancel the invasion. If that should happen, the brigade was to take its American advisers prisoner and continue preparations. Frank would tell them when and how to get to Nicaragua and would hand them "the whole plan."[11]

Through all this the seal remained unbroken on the CIA's biggest secret. Allen Dulles sat through the hearings without even a vague allusion to the CIA-Mafia assassination plot, which would have removed Castro before the Bay of Pigs.

The Cuba Study Group looked forward to a militaristic future. Brigade survivor A. L. Estrada has recalled that the day after he and several comrades testified, they were taken to the White House to meet the President. Bobby Kennedy was there, and the CIA men known as Rip and Gray — William Robertson and Grayston Lynch. It was all very upbeat. "RFK asked if I wanted to work against Castro again," Estrada said.

General Taylor wrote the Cuba Study Group's report, portions of which are still classified. "It is recommended that the Cuban situation be reappraised in the light of all presently known factors," he said, "and new guidance be provided for political, military, economic and propaganda action against Castro."[12]

Taylor proposed a radical reorganization of the government to fight the Cold War on all fronts. "We are in a life and death struggle," he wrote. The jingoistic general asked the President to consider proclaiming a national emergency, to review treaties restraining "the full use of our resources in the Cold War," and to reappraise the adequacy of his "emergency powers."

It was hard-line stuff. Bobby Kennedy, whom an associate described as a "piano-wire hawk," enthusiastically endorsed it. John Kennedy took a middle road. He did not reorganize the government. But he reorganized the Secret War.

The President revamped the Cuba Project through a flurry of National Security Action memorandums. No. 55 instructed the Joint Chiefs to "know the military and paramilitary forces and resources available" and take stock of their readiness, adequacy, and room for improvement. "I look to the Chiefs to contribute dynamic and imaginative leadership in contributing to the success of the military and paramilitary aspects of the Cold War programs," he declared.

No. 57 dealt with the CIA. Kennedy reiterated the principle that clandestine operations should be secret and deniable; he observed critically that the Bay of Pigs was neither. He decreed that any future operation that grew to a size requiring logistical support from the military should come under the overall command of the Pentagon, one of the recommendations of the Taylor Report.

Angry as he was with CIA duplicity, Kennedy needed the agency to service his ambitious plans for counterinsurgency operations around the world. He moved to strengthen it while simultaneously bringing it under control. He told Arthur Schlesinger, "It's a hell of a way to learn things, but I have learned one thing from this business—that is, that we will have to deal with the CIA."

To crack the whip on the CIA, the President assigned the man he trusted the most, his brother. It was a time of heavy burdens on the Department of Justice—civil rights turmoil in the South was increasing in intensity, and the drive against organized crime was barely in first gear. But the CIA was Robert Kennedy's top priority;

the daily grind at Justice was handed off to Byron "Whizzer" White, the former football ace.

The White House tantalized the exiles with hints of a new assault on Castro. On May 4 Cuban Revolutionary Council President José Miró Cardona emerged, smiling, from a meeting with JFK. He would later say that the President had personally "formalized a pact which called for a new invasion." Additional meetings with Kennedy led Miró to announce that the United States would supply money and military experts to train and equip exile forces, organize sabotage inside Cuba, and encourage guerrilla units so that they would be strong enough to help "when the big strike comes."[13]

Meanwhile, in Ciudad Trujillo, a plot the CIA had on a back burner was about to boil over. It was called EMOTH. The CIA had the same murderous plans for the right-wing dictator of the Dominican Republic as it had for Castro. The rationale for eliminating Generalissimo Rafael Trujillo was that Trujillo's bloodily repressive regime was paving the way for Castroism in the country, the way Batista had done in Cuba.

It was a moment of excruciating irony for the CIA. An assassination scheme it now wanted to fail was about to succeed.

The Dominican conspirators planned to kill Rafael Trujillo in the apartment of his mistress. They asked the CIA for machine guns. On April 7, Richard Bissell approved shipping the weapons via diplomatic pouch. His rationale was a model of bureaucratese: "A determination had been made that the issuance of this equipment to the action group is desirable if for no other reason than to assure this important group's continued cooperation with and confidence in this Agency's determination to live up to its earlier commitments to the group."[14]

The Bay of Pigs disaster changed everything. In the prevailing climate the CIA could not risk another failure. The agency prevailed upon Henry Dearborn, the U.S. consul in Ciudad Trujillo, to try to dissuade the conspirators, but the plot had picked up momentum and could not be braked. The crunch was on. If the assassination attempt failed and the CIA was publicly implicated, it would be another Bay of Pigs. The ball was tossed to the White House.

The CIA informed the President that some weapons had already been turned over to the conspirators and that it was prepared, if authorized, to transfer machine guns and grenades "in the direct custody of our station in Ciudad Trujillo." The agency refrained from making any recommendations as to whether to proceed; it had, after all, told the President the Bay of Pigs would work. Kennedy ordered the agency to pull out of the conspiracy. "We must not run risk of U.S. association with political assassination since the U.S. as matter of general policy cannot condone assassination." Many file copies of this cable were kept.

The cable went out on May 29. On May 30, 1961, Trujillo's thirty-one-year rule ended while he was being chauffeured down the seaside highway en route to a rendezvous with his mistress. His car was overtaken and forced to a stop. He died fighting back.

Army and secret police loyalists clamped a news blackout on the capital as they searched for the conspirators. Henry Dearborn got wind of what had happened and cabled the State Department. The news was relayed to JFK, who was in Paris meeting with Charles de Gaulle. There Pierre Salinger casually mentioned the assassination during a press conference. It was the world's first notice that the dictator was dead.

Salinger's gaffe caused Excedrin headaches in Washington; the news from Paris implied that the United States had advance knowledge of the assassination. "If people think we did anything to Trujillo," fretted Dean Rusk, "they might look at this as a license to go after Kennedy."[15]

Ramfis Trujillo also happened to be in Paris. He reacted to the news of his father's death by chartering an Air France 707 on the family credit card to return home. Upon landing, he had all the known conspirators run down and executed. An air of liberal dismay hung over the White House. Richard Goodwin, the overeager presidential assistant who had boosted EMOTH, was twisted in knots by the fact that the old regime survived. "He danced around the White House, demanding that we get Allen Dulles on the line and call out the fleet," an aide to McGeorge Bundy recalled. "He was ready to send in the goddam Marines! Fortunately, cooler heads prevailed."[16]

Dearborn and Lorenzo "Wimpy" Berry, an American entrepreneur whose supermarket had been used as a weapons terminal, were secreted out of the Dominican Republic. If the younger Trujillo knew of the CIA connection, he saw no need to make a public issue of it. His father was gone, and the country was his.

II

It had been a typical Camelot bull session. The subject was Cuba. The President was in his rocker. Tad Szulc, the *New York Times* correspondent, and Richard Goodwin, speech writer and loyal camp follower to the brothers Kennedy, were with him in the Oval Office.

Then the President asked, "What would you think if I ordered Castro to be assassinated?"

Szulc said he was flabbergasted by Kennedy's suggestion. He mumbled something about opposing political killings as a matter of principle; in any event, he said, he doubted liquidating Castro would solve the problem.

Szulc recalled that Kennedy leaned back in his chair, smiled, and said he had been just testing because he was under considerable pressure from unnamed advisers in the intelligence community to have Castro killed. Kennedy said that he himself was violently opposed because the United States should never be a party to assassinations for moral reasons. "I'm glad you feel the same way," he declared.

Szulc later wondered if Kennedy was being coy. "I cannot say to what extent he knew, that November," he wrote, "about a scheme elaborated by Military Intelligence officers soon after the Bay of Pigs (and of which I was vaguely aware at the time) to kill Castro and his brother Raúl, the Deputy Premier and Defense Minister, using Cuban marksmen who were to be infiltrated into Cuba from the United States Naval base at Guantánamo on the island's southeastern coast."[17]

While details of the Guantánamo caper remain shrouded in the convenient mists of the Camelot assassination plots, enough facts have surfaced from a variety of sources to sketch it in outline. The double assassination was scheduled for the revolutionary holiday of the 26th of July, barely three months after the Bay of Pigs. On that day both Castros appeared in public. Fidel was in Havana, leading a celebration for visiting Soviet space hero Yuri Gagarin. Raúl was in Santiago, close to Guantánamo, speaking at ceremonies marking the eighth anniversary of the attack on the Moncada barracks.

Szulc's sources were correct. Military Intelligence was involved. It was ONI, the Office of Naval Intelligence. After the American Embassy in Havana was closed in January 1961, the sprawling Guantánamo naval base became doubly important as an intelligence post and clandestine staging area. The CIA collaborated closely with its naval hosts, but on this assassination plot ONI appears to have been in the driver's seat. The officer in charge was a Navy lieutenant commander, and one of the assassins had long been under ONI control. His name was Luis Balbuena, a thickset man called El Gordo ("the Fat One"). Balbuena had been a theatrical booking agent in Oriente Province before taking a job on the Guantánamo base. He had joined the 26th of July Movement in the struggle against Batista. He knew Fidel and Raúl personally. A Miami police detective who interviewed him in 1963 reported: "Early in 1959, he, with other top members of the revolution, started conspiring against the government. He was the contact between the United States Naval Intelligence and the Oriente underground."[18] Balbuena was an elected official of an anti-Castro council of Cubans employed at the Guantánamo base, which promoted counter-revolutionary activities.

A second marksman was Alonzo Gonzáles, about whom little is known other than that he was an Episcopalian priest who had designs on becoming bishop of Cuba once Castro was deposed. Gonzáles reportedly had been trained at the CIA "academy" in Virginia known as the Farm. Balbuena admitted to a U.S. Senate investigator that he had worked with Gonzáles out of Guantánamo in 1961 and confirmed that the ambitious priest was proficient with firearms. On all other details Balbuena invoked the seal of confession.[19]

Gonzáles slipped out of Guantánamo, heading for Havana. He

vanished without a trace. Balbuena told the Miami police that he "was involved in an attempt to assassinate Raúl Castro" which was "discovered by the Cuban Government," forcing him to take sanctuary inside the naval base (he was evacuated to Miami in 1962).

How the Cubans discovered the plot has never been learned, but they evidently knew a great deal. Two weeks after the 26th of July holiday passed without incident, Industry Minister Che Guevara reeled off a list of American aggressive acts against Cuba at the hemispheric nations' conference in Uruguay. Among them was the charge that the United States had mounted an assassination attempt against Raúl Castro (no mention was made of Fidel) from the Guantánamo base to take place on July 26. Guevara said the plot was for the killing to be followed by a mortar shelling of the base, giving the impression that enraged Cubans were taking revenge for Raúl's death at the hands of counterrevolutionaries. The shelling would give the United States a "clear-cut case" of Cuban aggression and provide a pretext for armed intervention—the old Guantánamo shell game.

This scenario was an ersatz version of the abortive *Santa Ana* mission during the Bay of Pigs. It also resembled a number of other things, including George Smathers's suggestion to JFK during their stroll in the Rose Garden that any assassination be coupled with a staged incident at Guantánamo to give an excuse for armed intervention. And it fit Richard Nixon's post-invasion counsel to the President that a "proper legal cover" such as "defending our base at Guantánamo" be found for "going in."

It was not the best of times for Dick Bissell. Over the summer the CIA had mounted sporadic raids against Castro. But it was hardly more than going through the motions. The Kennedy brothers hauled the chief of clandestine services on the carpet. An aide recalled that Bissell was "chewed out in the Cabinet Room of the White House by both the President and the Attorney General for, as he put it, sitting on his ass and not doing anything about getting rid of Castro and the Castro regime."[20]

Shortly after Bissell was dressed down, two separate assassination plots were hatched. One was directed by the CIA station in Miami, while the other seems to have been a largely indigenous effort, albeit with CIA knowledge.

The CIA's Miami-directed plot centered on a former Cuban Treasury Ministry employee, one Luis Toroella, who had been brought to Florida for training and by the time of the Bay of Pigs had infiltrated back to Santiago in an underground network with the code name Amblood. The CIA supplied the underground with stacks of cash, sufficient weapons, and a yacht. Amblood maintained contact with the agency through a letter drop in Quito, Ecuador. An Ecuadorian military intelligence officer cooperating with the CIA's Quito station rented several postal boxes in the names of Amblood members in Santiago, and letters with secret ink messages were mailed back and forth. The drop was linked with Miami by the U.S. diplomatic pouch. For urgent traffic, Toroella used the less secure means of direct radio communication with the Miami station.[21]

On September 24 the Cuban government announced that it had smashed the Amblood ring. What went wrong has never been determined. Twelve members were charged with planning to fire bazookas at Fidel Castro from a garage across the street from the Havana City Sports Stadium when he spoke at a rally. In addition to Toroella, who was subsequently executed, the list included Octavio Barroso of the Oriente section of Unidad, the underground coalition forged by the CIA, and former Oriente Governor Segundo Barges.[22]

Scarcely a month later a second plot was smashed. The delegated triggerman was Reynol Gonzáles (no relation to Alonzo Gonzáles of the Guantánamo plot), a member of Manuel Ray's underground; he was arrested on October 24 hiding on a suburban farm belonging to Ray's supporters. The mastermind behind the scheme was Antonio Veciana Blanch, an accountant who, according to the *U.S. News & World Report*, had begun "working with other accountants, embezzling government funds in Havana to finance an anti-Castro underground."[23] Weapons were found in an apartment rented by Veciana's mother near the Presidential Palace. Veciana and his mother were able to escape and make their way to Miami. He became the first chief of Alpha 66, one of the most militant and durable of the exile action groups. It would not be his last attempt on Castro's life.

At this point in time, what the Kennedy administration knew about and condoned of the geometrically expanding assassination plots was a question not dealt with by the Senate Intelligence Committee in its 1975 probe of assassination plots against foreign leaders. The panel thoroughly explored the CIA-Mafia assassination schemes. But it did not so much as hint that the Guantánamo, Amblood, and Veciana plots ever took place.

The oversight appears to have been deliberate. Although the committee heard Tad Szulc tell what John Kennedy had said about detesting assassination as a tool, no allusion was made to Szulc's information about the Guantánamo plot that had previously appeared in an *Esquire* magazine article. Che Guevara's accusation that the United States was behind an attempt on Raúl Castro was ignored, as were essential data on the Guantánamo plot, including the identity of Luis Balbuena and the current location of his ONI case officer. The ONI man was retired and living in Texas. (The authors of this book furnished this information to the committee.)

The committee's Democratic majority managed to preserve unsullied the reputation of a Democratic administration. Dick Bissell told the senators that he believed Allen Dulles had informed John Kennedy of the "underworld" plot "through some channel," although the language would have been sufficiently obtuse to allow the President to maintain "plausible deniability."[24] Kennedy whipped ahead with plans to get rid of Castro at PT-boat speed. He ordered an evaluation of the consequences of Castro's demise and the prospects for military intervention if it happened. According to the Senate Intelligence Committee's 1975 report:

> Two studies were prepared. National Security Action Memorandum 100 (NSAM 100) directed the State Department to assess the potential courses of action open to the United States should Castro be removed from the Cuban scene, and to prepare a contingency plan with the Department of Defense for military intervention in that event. . . . The focus of these studies was on the possible courses

of action open to the United States in a post–Castro Cuba, rather than on the means that might bring about Castro's removal. It does not appear, however, that assassination was excluded from the potential means by which Castro might be removed.[25]

The CIA's Board of National Estimates was called upon to prepare a forecast called "If Castro Were to Die" that concluded: "His loss now, by assassination or by natural causes, would have an unsettling effect, but would almost certainly not prove fatal to the regime." That meant, of course, that Castro's death would accomplish nothing unless action were taken to capitalize on it. The military contingency plan was thorough. Fletcher Knebel described it in *Look* magazine:

> In October, 1961, President Kennedy, still bearing his scars from the [Bay of Pigs] disaster, secretly ordered the Joint Chiefs of Staff to prepare an invasion plan for Cuba — to be used if and when needed. This top secret plan took months to prepare, but when the strategists and computers had finished, with every plane, warship and assault unit tagged, it was calculated that the first troops could hit the Cuban beaches eight days after a "go" signal.[26]

It appears that among the partisans of Camelot a consensus had developed that the blame, if any, was to be laid at Bobby's bier. This theory surfaced in March of 1967, when Drew Pearson and Jack Anderson pointed an accusing finger at Bobby Kennedy as the man who gave the assassination nod:

> Top officials, queried by this column, agreed that a plot to assassinate Cuban dictator Fidel Castro was "considered" at the highest levels of the Central Intelligence Agency at the time Bobby was riding herd on the agency. . . . This much can be verified: . . . During this period, the CIA hatched a plot to knock off Castro. It would have been impossible for this to reach the high levels it did, say insiders, without being taken up with the younger Kennedy. Indeed, one source insists that Bobby, eager to avenge the Bay of Pigs fiasco, played a key role in the planning.

There was no documentation that RFK initiated assassination planning or even specifically okayed it. "Plausibly deniable" remained functional. Richard Helms, who later became CIA director, testified that "it was made abundantly clear to everybody involved in the operation that the desire was to get rid of the Castro regime and get rid of Castro . . . the point was that no limitations were put on this injunction."[27]

Ray Cline has pictured RFK as a man driven by demons: "Bobby was as emotional as he could be, and he always talked like he was the President, and he really was in a way. He was always bugging the Agency about the Cubans. I don't doubt that talk of assassinating Castro was part of Bobby's discussion with some Agency people."[28]

But even the zealous Bobby's role was to be tempered. "To the extent that Bobby was involved in anything," said Richard Goodwin, the Camelot apologist, taking refuge in allegory, "it would have been like Henry II asking rhetorically, 'Who will free me of this turbulent priest?' and then the zealots going out and doing it."[29]

III

It was, even by Georgetown standards, one helluva dinner party. It was the spring of 1960. The hosts were Senator and Mrs. John F. Kennedy. The guests included journalist Joseph Alsop, painter William Walton, some Georgetown socialites, and a man from the CIA. The guest of honor was John Kennedy's favorite author, Ian Fleming.

As coffee was being poured from silver spouts, Kennedy asked Fleming what his man James Bond might do if M. assigned him to get rid of Castro. Fleming had been in British intelligence and had drafted the paper that became the organizational structure for the wartime OSS. He was quick to answer. According to his biographer, John Pearson, Fleming thought he would have himself some fun. He said the United States was making utterly too much fuss over Castro—building him up into a world figure and that sort of thing. Senator Kennedy asked what approach he would take. "Ridicule, chiefly," said Fleming, who entranced the table with his proposals for giving Fidel the James Bond treatment.

Fleming, eyes atwinkle, said there were three things which really mattered to the Cubans—money, religion, and sex. Therefore, he suggested a triple whammy. First, the United States should send planes to scatter Cuban money over Havana, accompanying it with leaflets showing that it came with the compliments of the United States. Second, using the Guantánamo base, the United States should conjure up some religious manifestation, say a cross of sorts, in the sky which would induce the Cubans to look constantly skyward. And third, the United States should send planes over Cuba dropping pamphlets, with the compliments of the Soviet Union, to the effect that owing to American atom bomb tests the atmosphere over the island had become radioactive; that radioactivity is held longest in beards; and that radioactivity makes men impotent. As a consequence the Cubans would shave off their beards, and without bearded Cubans there would be no revolution.[30]

Fleming had great fun with this. He was staying at the house of British newsman Henry Brandon. The next day CIA Director Allen Dulles called Brandon to ask to speak to Fleming. Brandon said his guest had already left Washington. Dulles expressed great regret. He had heard about Fleming's terrific ideas for doing in Castro and was sorry he wouldn't be able to discuss them with him in person.

It is testimony to the resounding good sense exercised by the CIA during the Secret War that all three of Fleming's spoof ideas were in one form or another attempted or at least seriously considered. CIA scientists fooled around with developing a chemical that would dissolve Castro's beard and ruin his macho image, the CIA was involved in a plot to flood Cuba with counterfeit currency, and—according to testimony before the Senate Intelligence Committee—this suggestion came from one of America's most famous spooks who became a key actor in the Secret War:

> He had a wonderful plan for getting rid of Castro. This plan consisted of spreading the word that the Second Coming of Christ was imminent and that Christ was against Castro [who] was anti-Christ. And you would spread this word around Cuba, and then on whatever date it was, that there would be a manifestation of this thing. And

at that time—this is absolutely true—just over the horizon there would be an American submarine surface off Cuba and send up some starshells. And this would be the manifestation of the Second Coming and Castro would be overthrown. Well, some wag called this operation "Elimination by Illumination."[31]

The author of record of that bright idea was the Ugly American himself, Air Force Major General Edward G. Lansdale, who had directed the Philippines government's successful campaign against the Huk guerrillas and had guided the Diem regime in Vietnam. Along the way Lansdale inspired some contradictory character sketches. In *The Ugly American*, Eugene Burdick depicted him as sensitive to the problems of the masses and anxious to help; in *The Quiet American*, Graham Greene portrayed him as Alden Pyle, the culturally tunnel-visioned instigator of bloodshed and chaos.

To President John Kennedy, Lansdale was the right man at the right time. He was summoned to Camelot to revitalize the CIA's efforts against Cuba. He described his job as "putting the American genius to work" to destroy Fidel Castro. The general was liberal enough to realize that, as he put it, Castro "had aroused considerable affection for himself personally with the Cuban population." The Bay of Pigs invasion had solidified support for Castro. JFK's draconian move to turn the island into an economic leper colony had provoked the premier into expropriating all American capital in Cuba, enabling him to play Santa Claus. "Castro's bringing of Havana's poor into the Sears & Roebuck [sic] store to select the clothes and necessities they needed was the best political public relations gimmick since Boss Hague commandeered Christmas turkeys from the Teamsters to give to Jersey City voters," Lansdale wrote.

Lansdale's idea was that the Cuba Project "take a very different course" from the "harassment" operations of the past and try to crack the Castro regime from within. The Lenin of counterinsurgency suggested developing leadership elements among the exiles as "a very necessary political base" while putting together the "means to infiltrate Cuba successfully" and organize "cells and activities inside Cuba." The objective was to have "the people themselves overthrow the Castro regime rather than U.S.-engineered efforts from outside Cuba."[32] Cuba was to become another Vietnam, 1960s version. The bottom line in this strategy meant reversing Castro's popularity, although this was something Lansdale hadn't yet figured out just how to do. It was a task fit for *The Quiet American*.

Lansdale's quiet approach fit in with Kennedy's rock-and-hard-place predicament over the Berlin Wall; he had to avoid tweaking the Russian Bear's nose. As badly as he wanted Castro out of the way, he could not at that point be up front about it. On November 30, a memorandum to all concerned instructed that the Lansdale program "use our available assets . . . to help Cuba overthrow the Communist regime."[33] It was to be called, in Lansdale-like language, Operation Mongoose. The mongoose is a ferretlike mammal noted for its ferocity in killing poisonous snakes.

On November 28, two days before the Mongoose directive, Allen Dulles was chauffeured away from the CIA's spanking new headquarters on the banks of the Potomac River at Langley, Virginia, fired after eight years as director. There was special irony for Dulles in John Kennedy's words as he dedicated the huge mausoleum of a building that afternoon. "Your successes are unheralded," the President told the assembled CIA employees, "your failures are trumpeted." Dulles's most trumpeted failure had been the Bay of Pigs; the "something else" he had counted on hadn't happened.

Dulles had had signals that he was on the way out. His access to the Oval Office had been politely curtailed. He had not been invited to *ad hoc* meetings of the Special Group. Bobby Kennedy treated him almost deferentially while preparing him for slaughter. It had been handled in the classy Kennedy way. The President allowed a decent interval. On Dulles's last day JFK awarded him the National Security Medal. Dulles was given the status of a CIA consultant to carry out "historical research" and allowed to keep his bulletproof Cadillac limousine.

Kennedy manifested his displeasure with the agency by appointing a complete outsider. Replacing the legendary Dulles was John A. McCone, a Republican industrialist who had made a fortune in shipbuilding and, since 1958, had chaired the Atomic Energy Commission. By any standards this was no spook background. Dulles's ouster was only one straw in Kennedy's big broom. Charles Cabell, whose loyalty to the Camelot White House had become suspect, was supplanted by General Marshall "Pat" Carter. General Lyman L. Lemnitzer was sent to Paris to command NATO troops, and Maxwell Taylor took over as Joint Chiefs Chairman. The last to go was Richard Bissell, to a sinecure at the Institute for Defense Analysis, a military think tank.

Bissell's successor as chief of clandestine services was Richard M. Helms, a survivor type who had emerged unscratched from the invasion wreckage. ("Do you realize there isn't one piece of paper in this agency associating Dick Helms with the Bay of Pigs?" Deputy Director L. K. "Red" White once marveled to a colleague.) At age forty-eight, tall with thinning black hair, Helms had pushed his way up the CIA ladder by playing the role of gray-flannel bureaucrat to perfection. Helms's style was the unwritten word, the implicit suggestion, the dangling participle, the semantic evasion. He avoided making enemies by slowly starving an operation he didn't like rather than lopping it off. He was regarded as Mr. Cool, as in "ice."

Helms took over in February 1962. It was his responsibility to make Mongoose work.

No. 6312 Riviera Drive in Coral Gables was one of the expensive homes lining the quiet palm-fringed street a few blocks from the campus of the University of Miami. The Cubans coming and going at odd hours were assumed to be of the servant stock of Little Havana. The two-story tile-roofed house was protected by a stone wall and iron gate. A cupola crowned the roof. The backyard was on the Coral Gables Waterway, which fed into Biscayne Bay and the Gulf Stream. Pleasure boaters passing by had no reason to look twice at the innocent-appearing boat moored in the covered slip. The boat was actually a souped-up armed raider belonging to the CIA. No. 6312 Riviera Drive was a "naval base" used by the agency's ace Cuban boatmen, including Eugenio Martínez, a decade later a sailor in the Watergate navy.

Off the Tamiami Trail in the heart of the Everglades, a dirt road meandering north ended at a swamp. A dock was posted with a sign reading: WALOOS GLADES HUNTING CAMP. PRIVATE PROPERTY. NO TRESPASSING. Behind a curtain of trees was a clearing with two Quonset huts. Every so often a Bell H-13 helicopter with taped-over registration numbers would bring in a V.I.P. The "camp" was an agency operations base.

Among the living coral reefs off Elliott Key, part of the Biscayne National Monument, a gaggle of Cubans gathered around a ram-shackle house on a beach. The Cubans were members of a commando team, the structure their safe house. In a corner of the living room was a shrine of the Virgin of Cobre in memory of lost comrades. Once a week or so the men were boated to Miami for visits with their families.

These were a few of the many disguised facilities set up by the CIA throughout south Florida as Operation Mongoose was cranked up. Agents kept pouring in as the Miami station became the largest in the world. It operated on a budget of well over $500 million a year, employing between 600 and 700 American personnel. All major CIA stations abroad assigned at least one case officer full time to gathering intelligence, trying to turn the host country against Cuba, and encouraging the defection of Cuban officials. Reports from this far-flung network were funneled to the Miami station for correlation and action.

Eastern Airlines' midday Electra flight from Washington to Miami became known inside the CIA as the Miami Milk Run because as many as half the passengers might be on the agency payroll. The swarm of agents arriving for Mongoose, many accompanied by their families, gave the local real estate market a shot in the arm. The station now used the gibberish code designation JM/WAVE. It was relocated from Coral Gables to the abandoned Richmond Naval Air Station in the hinterlands south of Miami. During World War II Richmond had been a base for blimps hunting German submarines in the Straits of Florida. The huge hangars had been destroyed by a hurricane, and the bare foundations and jutting girders lent the impression of an air-age Stonehenge. The Navy had deeded the desolate site to the University of Miami for field research and future development, and it was shown on maps as the South Campus. In turn, the university obligingly gave the CIA squatter's rights. The colonnaded white frame headquarters building was refurbished and became the "home office" of Zenith Technical Enterprises, Inc., the dummy front that had been created for the invasion.

No effort was spared to give Zenith, which supposedly was engaged in electronics research, the touch of authenticity. Army Captain Bradley Earl Ayers, who was at JM/WAVE on detached duty, recalled:

> I saw that they had missed no detail in setting up the false front of Zenith Technical Enterprises. There were phony sales and production charts on the walls and business licenses from the state and federal governments. A notice to salesmen, pinned near the door, advised them of the calling hours for various departments. The crowning touch was a certificate of award from the United Givers' Fund to Zenith for outstanding participation in its annual fund drive.[34]

Zenith was listed in the white pages of the telephone directory.

The University Inn, close to the University of Miami campus, became the CIA's transient headquarters. Some senior agents, however, preferred other accommodations, such as the more uptown DuPont Plaza Hotel, at the mouth of the Miami River, the circular lines of which gave it a resemblance to the Watergate in Washington. A network of apartments and motel suites was rented for agents moving in for the duration. The CIA encouraged its personnel to "nest" together for security reasons. They tended to socialize together as well. Among the CIA watering holes of legend were the Stuft Shirt Lounge at the Holiday Inn on Brickell Avenue, the lounge in ITT's Three Ambassadors Hotel, the Waverley Inn, and the 27 Birds, which agents liked because it sounded like a code name.

The JM/WAVE station chief was Theodore Shackley, a promising young (thirty-four) protégé of future CIA Director William Colby. Tall, with a polished Boston accent, Shackley had been station chief in Laos and Saigon, the stamping grounds of General Lansdale, then was attached to the Berlin base (under William Harvey) during the crisis there. He was recalled to headquarters shortly after the Bay of Pigs to lead a team making a "vulnerability and feasibility study" of the Castro regime. In February 1962 Shackley arrived at JM/WAVE.

The deputy station chief was Gordon Campbell, a tall man with close-cropped silvering hair and a military bearing. Campbell oversaw the maritime branch which was vital to operations against the Cuban island. He lived appropriately enough on a yacht berthed at the Dinner Key Marina in south Miami. A big, vile-tempered New Mexico Indian named Dave ran the operations branch with a heavy hand. There were several other branches: personnel, which handled American employees; logistics, which purchased and allotted supplies and equipment; cover, which arranged false identities and fronts; real estate, which acquired properties the other branches needed; training; communications; and intelligence. The heart of the intelligence branch was a restricted "reading room" that stocked daily reports on Cuban activities, U-2 photos of Cuba taken almost daily, summaries of letters and reports smuggled from the underground in Cuba, and clippings from the U.S. and foreign press.

As it expanded, JM/WAVE began to resemble its parent bureaucracy in Langley. "I had envisioned it as a highly responsive, uncluttered organization," Bradley Ayers said, "but it now appeared to be a sprawling bureaucratic monster." The perks of rank allowed Ted Shackley and Gordon Campbell to drive black Cadillacs. A second echelon got Pontiacs, while the spy lumpen had to settle for Plymouths and Chevrolets. All told, JM/WAVE leased more than 100 cars and had a private gasoline station to service them.

The largest personnel group was the case officers, who controlled nearly 3,000 Cuban agents and subagents. Many of the Cubans were referred to the CIA by relatives or friends already on the payroll. The agency seemed to have an insatiable need for more. It recruited from the pool of refugees arriving in Florida at the rate of some 1,000 a month. The newcomers, who were processed through the CIA-run Opa-Locka detention center, filled vacancies for everything from small-boat pilot to mom-and-pop cooking and housekeeping team in a commando camp.

To provide cover employment and commercial disguise for operations, the CIA set up dummy corporations and proprietary companies in such proliferation that Dun & Bradstreet must have been hard put to keep tabs. In all there were fifty-five, ranging from the recondite Caribbean Research & Marketing on Okeechobee Road to travel agencies, boat repair shops, fishing firms, detective bureaus, gun stores, and real estate brokerages. In a few cases it was simply a matter of switching plaques on the front doors of cover companies that had been created for the invasion, but Radio Swan, the CIA propaganda station in the Caribbean, required a more elaborate transition. In September 1961 the main office of the shell Gibraltar Steamship Corporation, which listed Radio Swan as a subsidiary, was moved from New York to the Langford Building in downtown Miami. Curious newsmen noted that luggage being moved into the office suite was marked "George Wass," supposedly a Radio Swan official. Then Gibraltar Steamship disappeared from the earth, and the Vanguard Service Corporation, "consultants," came into being. Radio Swan also vanished, to reappear as the Vanguard subsidiary Radio Americas.[35]

The CIA was rather awkward about it. Vanguard retained Gibraltar's office suite and telephone number, although there was a changeover in staff and management. Well-known Florida businessman William H. West, Jr., became president, to be shortly succeeded by Roosevelt C. Houser, director of the large Miami National Bank. Manager Roger Butts described Radio Americas as "a privately owned commercial station operating on Swan Island" that was supported "by income from sponsors." But the station broadcast no commercials and was not even licensed by the FCC.

A new front, Paragon Air Service, was incorporated in Delaware for the stated purpose of engaging in air and sea commerce and research and development. Bradley Ayers, using the cover identity Daniel B. Williams, was one of those assigned to Paragon. He disclosed that its activities:

> . . . were international in scope and were channeled into South
> Florida and the Caribbean through a complicated network of other
> CIA paper corporations and false contractual relationships with ac-

tual business firms. The firm had a Miami office, phone number and
mailing address, bank accounts, lawyers, accountants and all the
other tangible characteristics of a legitimate business. The Paragon
Air Service phone actually rang in the cover branch [at JM/WAVE]
and was answered by one of the station's staff. My alias of D. B. Williams included an employment record, social security number, character references and credit record.

Ayers used his real and cover identities interchangeably. "To
remember who I was in any particular situation would take practice," he said.[36]

To transport commando and infiltration teams to Cuba, the CIA
acquired a fleet of specially modified boats that were based at the
Homestead Marina, not far from JM/WAVE, and other marinas
throughout the Florida Keys. The boats were registered to Ace Car-
tography, Inc. which was chartered in July 1962 as a "marine survey" firm. The Ace address given on the articles of incorporation
turned out to be the office of a Miami lawyer who was listed as vice-
president. However, the names of the registered agents required by
Florida law were more revealing. They were none other than William A. Robertson, Jr., and Grayston L. Lynch—"Rip" and
"Gray"—the first Yanks ashore at the Bay of Pigs.

Since Operation Mongoose called for continuous sabotage raids,
the CIA recruited exiles as frogmen with UDT (underwater demolition team) capabilities. The men were "employed" by a front called
Marine Engineering and Training, which was incorporated shortly
after Ace with an address belonging to a law firm in suburban
Homestead. Funding was channeled through the Federal Reserve
Bank in Atlanta. The CIA was tight with the taxpayers' money in
only one respect. The exiles were paid $275 a month during training
and $325 while on active duty.

Mounting a secret war from Florida required no–questions–asked
collaboration from many sectors of the local Establishment. Exile
commandos might find their paychecks drawn on the payroll accounts of local corporate offices and Miami department stores.[37]
Special checks were to be cashed, no questions asked, at the First
National Bank of Miami's main office on Biscayne Boulevard.

Other banks winked at transparently false information on loan applications. The privately endowed University of Miami was unstinting in its cooperation. University departments provided cover
for CIA operatives, and some military officers on duty with the CIA
were "attached" to a nonexistent Army support group supposedly
doing undersea and classified weapons research with the university.

The Miami newspapers remained as obliging as during the Bay of
Pigs preparations. A former JM/WAVE agent recalled:

> A paper like the Miami *Herald* would have one or two reporters
> with jurisdiction for Cuba, and we would give them access to the sta-
> tion. So we would feed them information and give them a career out
> of handouts. The guys learn not to hurt you. Only occasionally do
> you give them a big lie, and then only for a good reason. The paper
> was always willing to keep things quiet for us.[38]

At the smaller Miami *News* the editor, Bill Boggs, was a close friend
of the Kennedys, and the chief Latin American reporter, Hal Hendrix, was close to the CIA.[39]

The cooperation of state and federal authorities was also required
since laws were being broken on a wholesale scale. Incorporation
papers filed with the Florida secretary of state and in some instances
the Department of Conservation contained known false information. Income tax returns gave bogus sources of income. FAA regulations were violated by the filing of spurious flight plans and the
taping over of registration numbers. The transportation of explosives on Florida highways transgressed state law. Possession of illegal explosives and war matériel contravened the Munitions Act, and
acquisition of automatic weapons defied the Firearms Act. Every
time a boat left for Cuba the Neutrality Act was broken; every time
it returned Customs and Immigration laws were skirted.

The CIA quietly arranged for a suspension of the enforcement.
Police and sheriffs' departments from Miami to Key West quickly
released agency people stopped for anything from trespassing to
drunk driving. Customs, Immigration, Treasury, and FBI agents all
looked the other way. An elaborate recognition system and special

numbers to call were set up. Boat crews, for example, were given a password of the day for use if challenged by the Coast Guard.

Robert Plumlee, a pilot for the Dodge Corporation front, told the authors how he evaded detection by U.S. radar picket planes with the aid of CIA contacts in the military. When a mission to Cuba was scheduled, his Dodge handler would come by with a packet containing instructions, air charts, and the coordinates of the remote airfield in Cuba that was his destination. Plumlee, whose radio code name was Zapata, would hop over to Marathon Key or Loxahatchee and wait to take off at exactly the time his instructions stated. His course would take him through a temporary gap in the radar screen created when the giant Lockheed Constellation picket planes made U-turns at the ends of their runs. "Obviously Dodge was being fed the times by the military," Plumlee said.[40]

Frank Sturgis became one of many commuters to the Secret War. When his unlisted number rang, it was Joaquín Sanjenís, the Operation 40 commander, on the other end with an "If you choose not to accept this mission" type of assignment. Sturgis was being used in an intelligence phase of Operation Mongoose referred to as study flights. After Sanjenís's call he would drive to the airport, take off in his small plane, and fly a prescribed course that would deliberately penetrate Cuban airspace. Sturgis was a guinea pig to activate the coastal defense system that had just been installed by the Russians. Alerted by the drone of his engines and the blip on their radar screens, the Cubans would talk excitedly over the radio, start up tracking devices, and warm up night-fighting MiGs. The feared *quartre boches* — four-barreled antiaircraft guns aimed by radar — would point at the inky sky, and rocket crews would fix the intruder's position on target display boards.

The electronic signals given off by these frenetic preparations would be picked up by the USS *Oxford* or *Pocono*, spy ships that took turns lying off Cuba in international waters. When analyzed in Washington, the signals told much about the nature and effectiveness of the defenses. For acting as an airborne sitting duck — Sturgis says he was shot at several times — the pay was $600 a flight, with no insurance but double pay to the widow in case of death.[41]

Sturgis also took part in a Mongoose scheme called Operation Fantasma, after the Spanish for "phantom." He and other contract pilots dropped leaflets on Camagüey, Cienfuegos, and Matanzas in central Cuba exhorting the people to form "phantom cells" for sabotage against the regime. They were urged to carry matches at all times to be ready for sabotage opportunities, to burn cane fields, to take receivers off the hooks in telephone booths to tie up communications, and otherwise to harass the government. The pamphlet drops were backed up by broadcasts from Radio Americas on Swan Island.

One Fantasma flight ended in tragedy. On December 14, 1961, a leased Piper Apache took off from Fort Lauderdale Airport and headed east over the Gulf Stream. On board were the pilot, Robert Thompson, copilot Robert Swanner, and Sturgis. Flying low to avoid detection, the plane landed on Norman's Cay in the Bahamas, where Sturgis had established an advance base. The plane was loaded with propaganda leaflets, and Thompson and Swanner took off to drop them over Cuba. They never returned.

Three days after the Apache's disappearance, Sturgis called Thompson's wife and told her the plane had been lost at sea. Shortly before Christmas she received an unsigned telegram forwarding $500. The telegram said, "Merry Christmas." "I knew the money had been sent by Sturgis and the CIA because it was the exact amount my husband would have been paid for the trip if he had returned," she said. Thompson had confided to her that he was only one of a number of pilots hired for secret missions. According to Mrs. Thompson, Sturgis threatened to "tell all he knew about the CIA" if the government didn't come across with more money for the families of the lost men. "But all I ever got was that five hundred dollars," she said.[42]

Eugenio Martínez, the CIA boatman, was also a commuter. He drove from his Miami home to the base on Riviera Drive or one of the small-boat harbors staggered through the Keys where CIA craft were moored. An effusive man with intense dark eyes and flaring black hair, Martínez had owned a hospital, hotel, and furniture factory in his native Pinar del Río Province. He was consumed by a desire to do in Castro and became one of the CIA's most loyal and durable Cubans. In attempting to minimize the CIA connections to Watergate, Richard Helms downgraded Martínez by terming him a kind of tipster who "interviewed émigrés" and reported snatches of information for a retainer of $100 a month. Frank Sturgis was outraged by this characterization of the friend he refers to as Rolando. "Rolando made twelve hundred dollars a month, and if the Company paid him twelve thousand, it wouldn't have been enough. Rolando was never any kind of tipster. He was a *práctico*, a CIA boat pilot, who guided the clandestine inshore runs to Cuba, to land agents or to pick them up, to bring them back to Key West. There is no more dangerous work. And Rolando has ten years at it, more than anyone else. . . . In Miami, Rolando is a goddamn hero today. There is not a Cuban shoeshine boy who'd accept a quarter from him; he's just a giant to them. A *tipster!*"[43]

Martínez exemplified the *prácticos* who knew the shorelines of their native provinces like the backs of their hands. "I have personally carried out over three hundred fifty missions to Cuba for the CIA," Martínez asserted proudly after Watergate. "Some of the people I infiltrated were caught and tortured, some of them talked."[44] The infiltrators usually wore hoods so that the *prácticos*, if later caught, could not identify them. Martínez wanted to bring out his own parents, but the CIA turned thumbs down because he might be captured and jeopardize operations. He never saw them before they died.

On occasion the *prácticos* took their passengers directly from the Keys to Cuba, but more often it was done in stages. A larger mother ship would tow the fast intermediate boat piloted by the *práctico* to within a mile or two of the coast. From there the *práctico* would guide his boat close to the beach, then launch black rubber rafts with muffled electric motors for the final leg. Sometimes decoy boats went in first to draw off any Cuban patrol craft in the vicinity.

The workhorse of the intermediate fleet was the V-20, a twenty-foot boat with a V-shaped hull powered by twin 100-horsepower Graymarine engines that cruised at 35 mph and could skip over shallow coral reefs. The double-thick fiberglass could withstand the poundings of the open sea as well as jabs from coral outcroppings.

Armor plate protected the fuel tanks and occupants. The gun mounts and towing shackles were concealed so that the V-20 looked like an ordinary fishing boat. The fleet also included crew boats designed to shuttle workmen to offshore oil platforms, Boston Whalers, and Swift boats.

When the *prácticos* landed a commando party, they stayed in contact by walkie-talkie radio so that they could make the pickup when the raid was over. They carried their own rifles to provide cover, if necessary, and occasionally went onshore. They had a supply of Cuban pesos and false papers in case they were cut off, and they were instructed to say they were on a marine survey project if captured. The most hazardous missions were the exfiltrations — picking up teams that had been landed some time before. There was always the possibility that the team had been captured and forced to reveal the time and place of the pickup.

Most of Eugenio Martínez's fifty-odd missions before the Bay of Pigs were to deliver infiltration teams to work with the underground. As Mongoose began, the tempo of sabotage raids against shore installations picked up. In December 1961, Martínez landed a commando team for a ten-day operation. They blew up a railroad bridge and, in a scene out of *The Bridge on the River Kwai*, watched as a train tumbled off the severed tracks. After torching a sugar warehouse, they were pursued by militia. They reached their rubber raft, but the electric motor wouldn't start. Their radio distress signal, "Pittsburgh, Pittsburgh," was heard by Martínez and Rip Robertson, however, as they waited offshore. In the best John Wayne tradition Robertson piled onto another raft, putted to the beach, and brought his men back.[43]

A few miles south of JM/WAVE a dirt road led from Quail Roost Drive through a stand of pine to a nondescript pastel blue house. It seemed like just another house in that sparsely settled area, but it was actually a school for Cuban agent recruits being taught Tradecraft. The chief instructor was called Bruno, a veteran of the Central European underground during the Nazi occupation. The training was tedious, made doubly so by Bruno's heavily accented English, which had to be translated into Spanish, and by the lack of technical background among the exiled bank clerks, waiters, and musicians who made up the class.

The Quail Roost school was only one of many concealed training facilities spotted around south Florida that gave courses in everything from clandestine communications to guerrilla warfare. The burgeoning secret army the graduates joined posed a formidable logistical challenge. Near JM/WAVE headquarters on the South Campus was a paramilitary supermarket—a large warehouse that stocked everything imaginable from Castro military uniforms to caskets. The old Navy bunkers housed tons of munitions. A case officer planning a mission could make out a shopping list of weapons from a fifty-four-page illustrated catalogue showing Czech snub-nosed machine guns (of the type used by Castro's militia), Russian submachine guns, tear gas pistols, mortars, rockets, and almost every military rifle and carbine manufactured in the world. The items had stock numbers and units for easy ordering. There were no prices.

Operation Mongoose did not get off to an auspicious start. The CIA crash-trained remnants of Brigade 2506 in commando tactics at a base near Key West and set up a mission to demolish a railroad yard and bridge on Cuba's north coast. The commandos, supervised by Grayston Lynch, were to land at night so that the demolition would be attributed to resident partisans in keeping with the Mongoose scenario. But their boat was spotted by a Cuban patrol craft, and the mission had to be aborted. "We couldn't fire on them because we had orders to land in Cuba, blow the bridge and attack the railroad yard," Roberto San Román explained. "We had to attack that and make it appear like an inside raid, from Cubans inside."[46]

A far more audacious plan was undertaken: the demolition of the huge Matahambre copper mines complex in Pinar del Río. Disabling the mines would constitute a severe blow to Cuba's shaky economy. "They gave us good training," San Román said, "with scale models of the shafts and the way they took the minerals up from the mines. And we had big targets and special demolition equipment and all that. We were in that training for two weeks, using rubber rafts, big ships and small ships, and time clocks for the demolition. And then after all that work they put us in a ship that was good for nothing. At sea, the battery went dead, one engine went out, and the ship began taking water and the radio failed." Grayston Lynch took off in a catamaran that had been towed along, to seek aid. He was picked up by a freighter and signaled the Coast Guard to rescue the drifting commandos.[47]

This would not do. The Kennedys increased the heat on Mongoose. Bobby Kennedy and Maxwell Taylor were added to the Special Group, which was renamed Special Group Augmented (SGA) and devoted almost exclusively to Cuba. According to notes taken by a CIA aide at an SGA meeting on January 19, 1962, RFK crisply declared that "a solution to the Cuban problem today carried top priority in U.S. Gov't. No time, money, effort—or manpower is to be spared. Yesterday the President had indicated to him that the final chapter had not been written—it's got to be done and will be done."[48]

While the White House tightened the economic embargo on Cuba, CIA agents in Europe pressured European shippers to turn down Cuban consignments. A special technical staff at CIA headquarters devised techniques for everything from blocking Cuban credits abroad to contaminating Cuban sugar shipments. In Frankfurt, Germany, a ball bearings manufacturer was persuaded to send off-center bearings to Cuba; in England Leyland buses on order by Cuba were sabotaged on the docks.

The Kennedys did not consider this sufficient. The pressure for more spectacular results was on Lansdale, who was in almost daily contact with the attorney general. He passed the pressure on to an interagency group formulating plans for approval by the SGA, saying that "it is our job to put the American genius to work on this project, quickly and effectively. This demands a change from the business as usual and a hard facing of the fact that we are in a combat situation—where we have been given full command."

Lansdale hinted that "we might uncork the touchdown play independently of the institutional program we are spurring." Although he later denied this referred to assassination, assassination was very much a topic of discussion among the Standing Group. Early in Mongoose, Lansdale had proposed a "Basic Action Plan" to kill "the cadre of the regime, including key leaders," as well as intelligence officials and Russian and Czech technicians, only to see it tabled.[49] As frustrations over the Mongoose lack of results grew, Robert McNamara offhandedly suggested, "Shouldn't we consider the elimination or assassination of Castro?" He was sharply rebuked by CIA director John McCone, a devout Catholic. "The subject you have just brought up, I think it is highly improper," McCone said.[50]

IV

Big Jim O'Connell crouched behind a bush across the street from the lot on which the enclosed U-Haul trailer was parked. Johnny Roselli was next to him. It was April 1962 in Miami. As the morning dragged on, the sun got hotter, but they had to make sure that the trailer was picked up by the right people. It contained $5,000 worth of explosives, detonators, rifles, handguns, radios, and boat radar.

The pickup was supposed to be made by Tony Varona or one of his men. Roselli, still using the by now threadbare fiction that he was acting for Wall Street interests, had gotten Varona to agree to renew his assassination effort against Castro in exchange for the load of equipment. He had given the Cuban leader the keys earlier. The trailer had been rented under assumed names by JM/WAVE chief Ted Shackley and William Harvey, who was now in charge of Cuban Task Force W and had come down from Washington with O'Connell to help get Operation Mongoose moving.

The sweating O'Connell kept glancing at his watch. Finally, a car drove slowly onto the lot, and a Cuban got out and looked warily around. Roselli tapped the CIA man on the shoulder and nodded okay. The Cuban hitched up the trailer and drove away.[51]

It was a bootleg operation. Bill Harvey was already champing at his bit. The Special Group had clamped tight controls on Mongoose, tabling Lansdale's master plan, which included the use of "gangster elements" for attacks on "key leaders." Harvey rebelled at the restrictions. He complained to Director McCone about the requirement for advance SGA approval of "major operations going beyond the collection of intelligence" and the fact that applications had to be spelled out in "excruciating detail" even to such things as "the gradients on the beach, and the composition of the sand on the beach in many cases."[52]

Harvey was delighted, then, when he received what he termed "explicit orders" from Richard Helms to revive the Roselli project without seeking SGA approval. When questioned by the Senate Intelligence Committee in 1975, Helms conceded that he had not been instructed to do it, but then again he had not been told not to. He said that he believed he was acting within the parameters of Mongoose and would not expect any high administration official to "sign off" on assassination by putting it in writing. Helms didn't even cut in John McCone on the secret. "It was a Mafia connection," he explained, "and Mr. McCone was relatively new to the organization, and this was, you know, not a very savory effort."[53]

After his Miami trip Harvey decided that Maheu and Giancana were "untrustworthy" and "surplus" and cut them off from the operation. His lack of regard for the pair stemmed from the infamous abortive bugging episode in Las Vegas.

On April 21 Harvey returned to Miami with four poison pills fabricated by the Technical Services Division, telling Roselli they "would work anywhere at any time with anything." Roselli passed the pills to Tony Varona, reporting back that the hit squad had targeted not only Fidel but also Raúl Castro and Che Guevara. Harvey approved, saying "everything is all right, what they want to do."[54]

No one who was the object of Bobby Kennedy's wrath quickly forgot it. "If you have seen Mr. Kennedy's eyes get steely and his jaw set and his voice get low and precise," former CIA General Counsel Lawrence Houston recalled, "you get a definite feeling of unhappiness." Houston had accompanied Colonel Sheffield Edwards, one of the originators of the Castro death plots, to the office of the attorney general in May, after Bobby had been tipped off about the CIA-Mafia collusion. Edwards sheepishly gave a "full briefing," including the fact that Maheu had been hired to "approach Giancana with a proposition of paying $150,000 to hire some gunmen to go into Cuba and to kill Castro."[55] Kennedy was hopping mad that he had not been told.

The CIA-Mafia capers were developing complications out of

Peyton Place. Around the time of the Bay of Pigs, Edwards had put a damper on the FBI investigation of the Las Vegas bugging of Sam Giancana's girlfriend on the grounds that it might not only expose an "intelligence operation" connected with the invasion but jeopardize future plans that might yet "pay off." J. Edgar Hoover spitefully sent a memorandum to Kennedy reporting on Edwards's intercession and the fact that the CIA was using Maheu as a "cutout" in dealing with Giancana, who was helping in "clandestine efforts against the Castro government" of an unspecified nature. Edwards had not disclosed the purpose of the Las Vegas bugging.

The Hoover memo presented a problem. Kennedy was revving up his nationwide drive on organized crime, and Sam Giancana was high on his wanted list. Now it turned out that the mobster had been working with a federal agency, a situation which implied protection from prosecution for anything short of treason or first-degree murder. But the Hoover memo was written in the past tense, suggesting that the CIA-Mafia alliance had been discontinued. Kennedy wrote on its margin: "I hope this will be followed up vigorously."[56]

The bureau complied, and its tight surveillance of Giancana turned up a sexual snag of tabloid dimensions. A woman named Judith Campbell was making repeated calls to the White House from the mobster's home phone in Chicago. The calls, it developed, were to the President himself. The shapely Miss Campbell had met JFK through Frank Sinatra and had by her own admission been trysting with him for some months. What made the relationship doubly distressing was the fact that the President's playmate was continuing to see her old Mafia friends Giancana and Roselli. The potential for disaster was unlimited.

In February 1962, J. Edgar Hoover alerted Bobby Kennedy and presidential aide Kenneth O'Donnell to the hot rock. A month later the FBI director arranged a private luncheon with JFK. There the matter was presumably discussed. According to the Senate Intelligence Committee's 1975 report, "the last telephone contact between the White House and the President's friend occurred a few hours after the luncheon."

If that took care of Campbell, there remained the considerable problem of Giancana—if prosecuted, he could be expected to tell what he knew about the President's mistress. There ensued some fancy footwork seemingly designed to make the CIA a foil in covering up the mess.

The day after his lunch with JFK, Hoover fired off a memorandum to Edwards advising that the Justice Department wanted to know whether the CIA "would or would not object to the initiation of criminal prosecutions" for bugging against Maheu and the man who actually made the installation. Giancana was not mentioned. Edwards's reply was predictable. The CIA would object because, as Hoover reported back, "prosecution of Maheu undoubtedly would lead to exposure of most sensitive information relating to the abortive Cuban invasion in April, 1961, and would result in most damaging embarrassment to the U.S. Government."[57]

Armed with this "national security" objection, the Justice Department advised the CIA that it envisioned "no major difficulty in stopping action for prosecution." Naturally none developed. It was at this point that Bobby Kennedy hauled Edwards on the carpet to explain how the CIA had got mixed up with the mob in the first place and in the process was informed of the assassination plotting. Although Bill Harvey had given the poison pills to Roselli only two weeks before, Edwards told Kennedy that the assassination project had been terminated. RFK's rage was confined to his having been left in the dark about Giancana. He did not preach about the immorality of assassinations, and he did not forbid further collusion with the Mafia. He simply ordered that he be the first to know if the CIA again took up with the mob. "I want you to let me know about these things," Kennedy is quoted as saying, by Edwards.[58]

Edwards realized that he had painted himself into a corner and could not now admit to the attorney general that he had lied about the project's being terminated. Upon his return to Langley he called Harvey and gave him a selective briefing on the session. But to protect himself he wrote an internal memorandum stating, "On this date Mr. Harvey called me and indicated that he was dropping any plans for the use of Subject [Roselli] for the future." Harvey found out about the memo when questioned by the Senate Intelligence Committee in 1975, and he was furious. He declared that it "was not true, and Colonel Edwards knew it was not true"; the falsification was intended to show that Edwards was "no longer chargeable" should the operation backfire.[59]

Only days later Harvey received his first report from Roselli on the operation's progress: The pills and guns had been safely smuggled into Cuba. In June the mobster said that a three-man assassination team had been dispatched, and in September that a second team was ready to slip into Havana and attempt to penetrate Castro's bodyguard. The "medicine," meaning the pills, was still "safe" in Cuba.

The CIA could only watch and wait. Colonel Edwards could only pray that RFK would not discover his lie. And the Kennedys could only hope that Sam Giancana would keep his big mouth shut.

V

The Punta del Este daily, *El Día*, had an interesting item that had readers letting their soft-boiled eggs get cold on a February morning in 1962: "Ambassador Morrison has turned in his expense account for the day: Breakfast, $1.50; Taxi in the morning, $2; Lunch, $2.50; Afternoon taxis, $3; Dinner with the foreign minister of Haiti, $5,000,000."

The ambassador was the United States Ambassador to the Organization of American States, DeLesseps S. Morrison. The rather dear dinner was actually a pledge to Haiti to build an airport in Port-au-Prince sufficient to bring Haiti into the jet age. The pledge was, in fact, a bribe, in return for Haiti's voting to oust Cuba from the OAS. DeLesseps Morrison was the Kennedy administration's point man for the not inconsiderable task of cutting off Cuba from the rest of the hemisphere. This involved both a diplomatic offensive and some skulduggery that were carried out in coordination with the Secret War.

Morrison was the ideal man to lead the Kennedy administration's diplomatic offensive. A handsome reform mayor of New Orleans, Chep Morrison was a stereotype New Frontiersman in style and politics. A. J. Liebling once described him as "a mélange of Jimmy Walker for looks and manner, Fiorello La Guardia for energy and probity, and Big Bad Bob Moses, the builder, for getting things done." His great-granduncle was Ferdinand de Lesseps, the French engineer who built the Suez Canal and tried to build the Panama Canal. A dashing widower, Morrison was frequently seen in nightclubs with ladies of the dazzle of Zsa Zsa Gabor. His politics were Kennedy politics: On domestic issues he was a liberal, one of the original voices of the New South, but when it came to communism, Morrison could have been mistaken for a John Bircher.

Although Morrison carried the title of Ambassador to the Organization of American States, he was in fact a roving JFK troubleshooter. After the Trujillo assassination he became JFK's Johnny-on-the-spot in Ciudad Trujillo to make sure that Trujillo's son kept communist fingers out of the power-sharing pie. Ambassador Morrison waterskied, drank and danced aboard the Trujillo family yacht *Angelita*. He was not told that *el jefe*'s body was stored in the refrigerator compartment belowdecks for fear of a Mussolini type of desecration.

In August 1961, Morrison led the U.S. delegation to the Inter-American Economic and Social Conference at the Uruguayan seaside resort of Punta del Este. The main item of discussion was the Alliance for Progress that JFK had promised in his inaugural address "to assist free men and free governments in casting off the chains of poverty." One billion dollars in economic aid was allotted for the first year, a lure the underdeveloped countries were expected to find irresistible. In dangling such a solid gold carrot the United States hoped to reverse a widespread feeling in Latin America that, as Adlai Stevenson put it after a reconnaissance trip in June, "The Cuban peasant has acquired his place in the sun."

Among the Americans in the delegation was Richard N. Goodwin, the Kennedy speech writer who had become the White House "expert" on Latin America. Morrison could take Goodwin or leave him, but not necessarily in that order. He delighted in repeating an anecdote about Goodwin: Shortly after coming to the White House, Goodwin approached a newspaperman and said, "I'm going to be appointed to a high Latin American post. Can you suggest some good books I ought to read?"[60]

To Morrison's dismay his young colleague displayed an intellectual curiosity about Che Guevara, the leader of the Cuban delegation who, Morrison cattily observed, came "dressed like a school principal."

"I'd like to pick that fellow's brains and find out what makes him tick," Goodwin remarked upon spotting Che surrounded by admirers in the lobby of the conference hall.

"Dick, all I can say is, I'm steering clear of him," Morrison said reprovingly. "We just shouldn't have anything to do with that bunch."

"Well, I don't know," mused Goodwin, chewing on his cigar. "I'd still like to know what goes on behind that beard."

Guevara gave him the chance. During a plenary session he sent over a box of Cuban cigars inlaid with the national seal. "It had a handwritten card in it from Che," Goodwin recalled. "It said in Spanish: 'Since I have no greeting card, I have to write. Since speaking to an enemy is difficult, I extend my hand.' "[61]

Later, at an open house hosted by a Brazilian delegate, Che showed up and beckoned Goodwin into a private room. Guevara smiled. "Shall this meeting be conducted as between enemies meeting on neutral territory, or as between two private individuals who wish to discuss a common problem?" he asked.

"As between enemies," Goodwin replied. "I must also remind you that I am not authorized to speak in the name of President Kennedy or in the name of the American people."[62]

Che cheerfully asked Goodwin the thank to President for the Bay of Pigs. Beforehand, he said, Castro had had only a tenuous grip on the country, which was plagued with economic woes and internal rivalry. The invasion had solidified the premier's hold; he was the hero who had rebuffed the most powerful nation in the world. Goodwin thought he should get in a dig of his own. He asked Guevara to have Castro seize the Guantánamo naval base to give Kennedy an excuse for using America's military might openly. Guevara grinned. Fidel would never be so stupid, he said.

Che expressed a willingness to negotiate with the United States without preconditions, but Goodwin doubted that the Kennedy administration would agree. Guevara suggested that a simple exchange of hijacked airplanes might open the door. He declared that Cuba had no political or military alliances with anyone and would make none if the United States promised not to launch a second invasion. After an hour the meeting broke up.

Morrison blamed the rump meeting, which he denounced as "an Alfred Hitchcock goings-on," for nearly wrecking his design for "ousting Cuba by the O.A.S. from the inter-American society." Che subsequently met secretly with President Arturo Frondizi of Argentina, repeating his pitch for coexistence. But word leaked out, provoking an uproar. Defending himself against military and conservative critics, Frondizi argued, "If the United States could meet with Major Guevara, how could I refuse to see him?"

The Punta del Este conference ended with the OAS nations accepting the Alliance for Progress. As he signed for the United States, Douglas Dillon, the stuffy Wall-Streeter serving as secretary of the treasury, warned that none of the money would go to Cuba so long as she was "under the control of a foreign power — namely the Soviet Union."

When Goodwin briefed John Kennedy on his trip, he brought along Che's gift box of cigars. "He took one out and started puffing on it," Goodwin recounted. "Then he looked at me and said, 'You should have smoked the first one.' "[63]

The Cuban consul in Buenos Aires, career diplomat Vitalio de la Torre, resigned unexpectedly after having held his post through the Prío and Batista regimes. He took eighty-two documents from the Cuban Embassy safe and turned them over to an emissary of the Cuban Revolutionary Council in Miami. The documents purported to detail a master plan devised in Havana for the overthrow of the Frondizi government by means of infiltration of business and politics and the training of guerrillas.

The CRC held onto the documents, planning to use them to maximum propaganda advantage during Frondizi's state visit to the United States. The week before the Argentine chief of state left, however, *La Nación* of Buenos Aires ran a long article accompanied by photocopies of the documents.

The article whipped up a storm of protest against Cuba, which claimed that the documents had been forged by Cuban exiles working in collusion with the CIA. That is exactly what had happened.

The forgery was the opening shot in a campaign aimed at "proving" that Castro was "exporting" the revolution by subverting OAS nations. The goal was to help Morrison get Cuba kicked out of the OAS.

The Cuban exile magazine *Avance* inadvertently told too much. It reported that de la Torre had gone into asylum rather than comply with instructions from Havana to meet with Che Guevara at an upcoming Punta del Este conference. De la Torre was said to have gone to the consulate the day he quit and taken the documents, which he gave to the CRC's Tony Varona, who just happened to be staying in a Buenos Aires hotel. The real tipoff was *Avance*'s boast that de la Torre had been collaborating with Cuban exile groups in Argentina for more than a year. If the consul had been a double agent for that long, his defection with the damning documents on the eve of a crucial conference hardly seemed coincidental.

The argument quickly escalated into an international *affaire d'honneur*. The U.S. State Department announced that it had exhaustively questioned de la Torre and was satisfied that the documents were genuine. Argentina, which had been trying to steer a neutral course since the Bay of Pigs, was skeptical. It wanted to examine the documents scientifically. The CRC sent photocopies but refused to make the originals available. Argentina insisted on the originals in order to make a conclusive examination. The CRC finally handed over what it said was a pertinent group of thirty-three documents.

Argentine documents experts were amazed at the crudity of the forgery. Only one of the thirty-three matched the photocopies previously sent, and that one had a forged signature and did not even relate to affairs of state. Tony Varona lamely explained that the CRC had not released all the documents to Argentina because it lacked faith in the Foreign Ministry and looked unfavorably on the continued diplomatic relations between Buenos Aires and Havana.

At the same time Cuba produced its own evidence of forgery. On October 9, Undersecretary of Foreign Affairs Carlos Olivares, whose "signature" appeared on many of the documents, met with the chiefs of a number of foreign diplomatic missions in Havana to point out that it was not he, but the head of the Foreign Ministry, who normally signed correspondence. And, Olivares said, when Foreign Minister Raúl Roa or he signed a document, a special wax seal would be impressed on their signatures. In addition, he pointed out, the registration numbers were out of sequence, as the ministry's general registration book demonstrated.

Argentina closed its books on the affair. There was a familiar ring to it all, like a similar fast shuffle in Peru the previous year when an anti-Castro group "stole" a letter from the Cuban Embassy in Lima "proving" that Havana was fomenting a revolt. (It was this phony letter that William Pawley exploited to draw a commitment of Peruvian marines for the Bay of Pigs invasion. It has since been speculated that E. Howard Hunt had a hand in manufacturing the fake letter — one of his CIA specialties.)

To U.S. Ambassador Morrison, however, the suspect Argentine documents were as real as gold teeth. On October 13, Peru, acting for the United States, proposed that the OAS foreign ministers meet to consider expelling Cuba because of its subversive actions. Morrison addressed a letter to the OAS secretary-general in support of the Peruvian position, attaching two exhibits to "prove" his case. The exhibits were the bogus documents.

The conference began in the Uruguayan resort on January 30, 1962. It was clear from the start that Morrison would gain no easy victory. He was palpably upset when the Brazilian delegate "began by talking 'coexistence,'" putting the analogy "Why do we not consider Cuba to us as Finland is to the Soviet?" Mexico and Argentina — with Brazil, the three countries representing two-thirds of the people of Latin America — felt the same way. Morrison, who had been selling democracy, found himself having to woo such repressive regimes as Paraguay, Nicaragua, and Haiti to get the necessary two-thirds majority to oust Cuba.

That was when Morrison had his $5 million dinner with the foreign minister of Haiti. Democratic Haiti cast the deciding vote that ousted Cuba.

It was an emotional moment for Chep Morrison. Dean Rusk gave the closing speech replete with such lines as "Wherever Communism goes hunger follows." Tears welled up in Morrison's eyes.

"I confess I was never prouder to be an American," he said.

VI

At precisely ten-thirty on the night of August 24, 1962, two low-riding motorboats carrying the most unruly stepchildren of the CIA, the Cuban Student Directorate (DRE), slipped under the radar screen guarding Havana Bay and past two Czech-built patrol craft. Their target was the Hotel Icar near the water's edge in suburban Miramar. The DRE underground in Cuba had reported that every Friday evening newly arrived Russian, Czech, Polish, and Chinese advisers and technicians met in the empty Blanquita Theater nearby, then walked over to the Icar for dinner and drinks. Often they were joined by Fidel Castro and high-ranking Cuban officials. One of the DRE boats was armed with a 20 mm cannon; the other, with a heavy machine gun. If all went well, Castro would die in the shelling and gunning. All did not go well.

"It all went smooth until we got close enough," said José Basulto, a gunner on the DRE boat *Juanin*. "Then one of our extra gas tanks, made of plastic, began to leak and gas ran all over the deck. We didn't know what to do. The gas was right under the cannon, and I was going to shoot it. We were afraid the shots might spark and cause an explosion. But there was Cuba—and we were too deep in the thing to back out."

As they drew into position on the flat waters, the raiders could make out uniforms moving back and forth in front of the Icar's picture windows. They opened fire. A Czech physician strolling on the hotel lawn saw the tracer bullets coming. "Their marksmanship was poor and they were pretty far out," he told newsmen. "But soon pandemonium ensued. Guests in nightgowns raced through the hotel. Panic seemed more dangerous than the effects of the raid." The Icar was pockmarked with shell holes, and the lobby left a shambles, but there were no serious casualties.[64]

After five minutes the boats fled. The Cuban jets which pursued them were hampered by poor visibility, and the boats made it to their base on Marathon Key in Florida. Castro denounced the United States and accused it of complicity in an attempt on his life. The State Department replied that the incident was a "spur of the moment" private act carried out without government knowledge.

In fact, the raid had been carefully planned and approved by the JM/WAVE station. The DRE had a long history of CIA connections. During the revolution its members, mostly students from the University of Havana, had been backed by former President Carlos Prío and fought against Batista in the Escambray Mountains as a second front that hoped to reach Havana before Castro. In preparation for the Bay of Pigs, CIA-trained DRE infiltration teams were landed in Cuba but left virtually stranded; seventy-four men were captured when promised airdrops failed to materialize. "It never got us the supplies it promised and never did things it was supposed to do," one DRE leader complained of the CIA.

Although the DRE was sore at the CIA, it couldn't keep its hand out of the agency's cookie jar. A CIA internal memorandum of the time described the group as an *enfant terrible* of vagrant ways whose leaders appeared as "oracles" because of their adroitness in wangling money.[65] However, the DRE had a viable underground, and an underground was vital to Mongoose. The CIA instructed the group's trainees in Tradecraft at the La Moderne Motel, in Miami, and in demolition, by blowing up old trucks near where the Palmetto Expressway was being constructed and the blasts would go unnoticed. They were then infiltrated into Cuba by CIA boats.

Although a military flop, the Icar raid provided the DRE with the opportunity to call a press conference. Pudgy, baby-faced Juan Salvat, a DRE founder who had led the bold action, and the two boat skippers gave graphic accounts of their derring-do that ended up in *The New York Times*. The DRE heros were summoned to Washington to an audience with Bobby Kennedy and Dick Helms, the master of the plausibly deniable, who "told them they were doing a great job but wasting their time in such independent actions."[66] The publicity brought mailbags full donations — the total reached some $200,000 — and the support of the ever-scheming William Pawley. The former ambassador envisioned the DRE as a sort of waterborne Flying Tigers, speeding in and out of Cuba on intelligence-gathering missions. He and a friend, Justin H. McCarthy, vice-president of the St. Regis Paper company in Jacksonville, persuaded some of their well-heeled acquaintances each to sponsor a boat and

crew, much the way Catholic schoolchildren used to sponsor foreign orphans whom they called "pagan babies."

One of those who signed up enthusiastically was Clare Boothe
Luce, the wife of *Time-Life* publisher Henry Luce and an ambassador
to Italy under Eisenhower. The anticommunist blonde took a
maternal interest in the three-man crew she "adopted," referring to
them as "my young Cubans." She brought them to New York three
times to mother them.

Clare Boothe Luce's adopted Cubans were about to trigger an epochal confrontation between the two superpowers over Cuba.

In the early fall the DRE underground in Cuba began sending
back a flurry of urgent messages: The Russians had some fifteen bal-
listics missile bases completed or under construction. Submarine
pens were being built on the Isle of Pines and at Mariel Bay, where
eight Soviet missile-firing subs were positioned. These reports were
passed on to Washington but, since U-2 overflights had not detected the activity, were largely ignored.

They were not ignored in high Republican circles in New York,
however. On October 10, 1962, Republican Senator Kenneth
Keating of New York, one of the recipients of the DRE's underground intelligence, announced that he was convinced that Soviet
offensive missile sites were in place in Cuba. The Kennedy administration was put on the defensive. Four days later a U-2 piloted
by Major Rudolph Anderson, Jr., a veteran of photo reconnaissance
during the Korean War, circled over Cuba at a height of thirteen
miles, his cameras whirring. As soon as he landed at Laughlin Air
Force Base in Texas, the film magazines were put on a plane for
Washington.

As photo interpreters began poring over Anderson's film, Rip
Robertson was briefing Eugenio Martínez and his boat crew at a
base at Summerland Key near Key West. Once again the target was
the Matahambre copper mining complex in Pinar del Río. If the giant towers supporting a long cable car system that delivered the ore
to the port of Santa Lucía could be destroyed, production would be
halted for a full year. Martínez and his men were impressed with the

special urgency of the mission. "You do it," said Robertson, who on such occasions spoke in a growl, "or don't bother to come back alive."

The next morning, as John Kennedy was being told that the photo interpreters had identified a Russian offensive missile site in Anderson's film, Martínez, his crew, and eight commandos left Summerland Key on the *Explorer II*, a 150-foot CIA "mother ship." They arrived off Santa Lucía after dark. Martínez piloted the commandos to the beach in his own boat, which had been towed. The commandos crept up on the tower bases to plant C-4 demolition charges. They were discovered by a militia patrol and retreated under fire; two didn't make it back to the boat. Night after night Martínez returned close to shore, blinking an infrared light, hoping with diminishing hope to make contact with the missing men.

At dusk on October 22 Martínez was once again laying off the beach, waiting for dark, when his radio operator tuned to a Miami station and learned that President Kennedy was about to make a speech to the nation. Martínez and his crew listened as Kennedy declared a blockade of Cuba and demanded that Premier Khrushchev remove the missiles to end this "provocative threat to world peace." Martínez and his men were jubilant. They were sure that an invasion of Cuba was at hand. When he got back to Summerland Key, Martínez was told by a CIA officer that an invasion was, in fact, imminent. The agent asked if Martínez would volunteer to parachute into his home province of Pinar del Río in advance of the American troops.[67] He volunteered.

U.S. armed forces were already on an invasion alert. Earlier in the month, when Senator Keating made his charges, JFK had quipped at a press conference, "I'm not for invading Cuba—at this time," prompting laughter. The President's deeds belied his words. Even then amphibious and airborne divisions were being deployed in the Canal Zone and southern United States, and the Atlantic Fleet was preparing for "exercises" in the Caribbean. On the day of the famous U-2 overflight, leaders of the Cuban Revolutionary Council were meeting with representatives from the Pentagon and State Department. According to the exiles' Miró Cardona, they requested "the massive enlistment of all Cubans of military age," even those newly arrived "who ought to enlist before registering as refugees."

In Bill Harvey's mind, there was no doubt that the missiles would have to be removed by force. He sent agent teams into Cuba to be ready to support U.S. military operations. When Bobby Kennedy heard about this, there was a terrible scene; Kennedy felt the CIA's unauthorized move could upset the delicate negotiations with Moscow. As Harvey later delicately phrased it before the Senate Intelligence Committee, there was a "confrontation" during which the attorney general "took a great deal of exception." This left Harvey in permanent dutch with the Kennedys. A CIA colleague said that Harvey "earned another black mark as not being fully under control."[68]

In the Missile Crisis end game, Khrushchev withdrew the missiles, and Kennedy quietly agreed, among other concessions, to halt hostile actions against Cuba. Castro took Kennedy at his word and realigned his defenses, positioning them to protect strategic targets rather than rebuff an invasion. Castro seemed satisfied that any future threat would be internal or from exiles based outside the United States.

But JFK had no intention of living up to the nonaggression pact. He found a technical excuse to get out of it. On January 11, 1963, Dean Rusk, testifying behind closed doors to the Senate Foreign Relations Committee, called the pledge a "strictly contingent commitment" that depended upon on-site inspection for missiles. Since Castro had refused, Rusk contended, the pledge was null and void.

Operation Mongoose was terminated, but only because it had been too much of a Mr. Nice Guy approach in Bobby Kennedy's view. At a Special Group Augmented meeting on the eve of the Missile Crisis, RFK had voiced disappointment that there had been no tangible successes—even the two raids on the Matahambre mines had been aborted—and vowed to pay "more personal attention" to the operations. This he quickly did. The SGA was replaced by an interagency Cuban Coordinating Committee charged with conceiving covert actions.

The importance of this new effort was underscored by the creation of a Standing Committee on Cuba within the National Security Council to determine future operations in the Secret War.[69] The President's brother himself would chair it. As General Lansdale said, Bobby Kennedy wanted to see "boom and bang" on the island of Cuba.

FIVE

The Secret of the Brothers Kennedy

> *Everyone in my family forgives—*
> *except Bobby.*
> —JOSEPH KENNEDY, SR.[1]

I

THE long black Cadillac pulled onto a remote pier in the port of Palm Beach as an early dusk turned the blue Florida waterways charcoal gray. There would be no moon that night, and all day the sun seemed to have shown no enthusiasm for its job. Gordon Campbell got out of the car and walked up the gently swaying gangplank onto the waiting ship. A tall man of military bearing, Campbell was in charge of the CIA's naval operations in the Caribbean.[2] He carried a soft leather briefcase.

Captain Alejandro Brooks watched him from the open bridge of the *Rex*. Normally a sailor as at peace with himself as with the sea, tonight Captain Brooks admitted to being slightly edgy. The vans which brought his crew of forty Cuban exiles had arrived hours before. Campbell was late with their sailing orders. The crew stood about the deck chattering in Spanish. Twice Brooks had to caution them to hold it down. The *Rex* was berthed within walking distance of the Kennedy family's Palm Beach home. Just two months before, the President had become furious when he learned that the CIA raider ship had been docked in West Palm Beach while he was there vacationing.

Captain Brooks did not relish the idea of the *Rex* sitting around port war-ready. Campbell was barely off the gangplank when he ordered his men to cast off. The blue and white flag of Nicaragua fluttered from the mast of the CIA ship as it left the lights of West Palm Beach winking in its wake and headed toward open sea.

The 174-foot *Rex* was the flagship of the CIA's secret Caribbean navy. She was an ex-U.S. Navy patrol craft of early 1940s vintage, formerly engaged in the business of subchasing. The CIA had rescued her from the limbo of the Navy's mothballed fleet at Glen Cove and painted her a classy dark blue. She was reconditioned with oversized searchlights, elaborate electronic gear that towered noticeably amidships, and a large seagoing crane on the aft deck capable of raising and lowering twenty-foot speedboats. The *Rex*'s 3,600-horsepower diesel engines gave her at flank speed a respectable twenty knots.

It cost the CIA a half million dollars a year to keep the *Rex* and its phantom crew afloat in the Caribbean. The CIA's navy included a sister ship to the *Rex*, the *Leda*, plus another four similar ships of the line, and a dozen smaller vessels, all well armed. The *Rex*'s chain of ownership was a case study in the corporate contortions the agency went through to disguise its pirate fleet. The *Rex* was registered out of Bluefields, on the Caribbean coast of Nicaragua, but its owner of record was the Belcher Oil Company, a Miami firm which fueled cruise ships. Belcher's books showed it acquiring the ship from the Somoza-owned Paragon Company, a poor relation to Paragon Air Service, Inc., a CIA dummy corporation. Belcher in turn leased the *Rex* to Collins Radio International of Dallas for "electronic and oceanographic research." Collins was a division of Collins Radio of Cedar Rapids, Iowa, a major defense contractor that more than once provided cover for CIA operations. The *Rex*'s dockage fees were paid by neither Belcher Oil nor Collins Radio, but by a third outfit called Sea Key Shipping Company, which operated out of a post office box. When she left port, the *Rex* gave as a destination Caicos Island in the outer Bahamas; she returned to port only "from the high seas." Normal customs and immigration inspections were waived for the *Rex*. She came and went mysteriously from West Palm Beach, only a ship that passed in the night.

The Cuban seamen of the Rex were paid $300 a month. Their checks were written on the account of a commercial fisheries company. Most of the crew had experience in the Cuban navy or merchant marine. They had been recruited by a team of former Batista naval men working for the CIA. Political trustworthiness was as much a job requirement as seamanship, and the crew was subjected to polygraph tests designed to ferret out any creeping Castro sentiments. The CIA could not afford any mutinies on its own *Bounty*.

At sea between West Palm Beach and Miami, the Cuban crew brought up the guns from belowdecks and secured the *Rex*'s heavy artillery—two 40 mm naval cannon, a .57 recoilless rifle, two 20 mm cannon, and two .50-caliber machine guns—in their topside mounts. The oceanographic research vessel was now a man-of-war.

Captain Brooks stood on the bridge under the black canopy of the Caribbean night. He opened the sealed orders that his landlubbing CIA commander had taken from his briefcase and handed to the Cuban with a flip salute. He used a flashlight to read them. What he read did nothing to ease the nervousness he had felt that afternoon. The *Rex*'s normal run was to stand off a mile and a half from the Cuban coast and dispatch landing parties in launches. Tonight, October 21, 1963, the *Rex* had a special mission which would bring it a dangerous half mile from the Cuban shore, well within the red zone of Castro's coastal defenses.

Off Elliot Key, an insignificant speck in the Caribbean below Miami, the *Rex* throttled back its twin screws. It had a date at sea. The captain strained to make out the rafts that were but a darker dark on the water. Suddenly there were two of them, stubby fingers extending from the hand of the night. The rafts were of black rubber; the men in them were dressed in black; they wore black stockings over their faces. They boarded the *Rex* in silence.

There were twelve of them. They were members of the Commandos Mambises, the elite of the CIA's anti-Castro commandos. They took their name from the determined guerrillas who had fought in Cuba's war of independence against Spain. Their emblem was the Lone Star of Cuba. They were the Green Berets of the Secret War.

The Commandos Mambises numbered fewer than fifty, mostly

men without families to miss them. Their leader was Major Manuel Villafana, a Cuban General Patton known for his spit-and-polish sternness, who had commanded the Bay of Pigs air force. Major Villafana insisted that the CIA pay his men little; he wanted them motivated by hate, not money.

The Mambises' target was a half mile off to port when Captain Brooks ordered the *Rex* engines stopped in choppy seas. Cuba lay like a long brown cigar on the dim horizon. He looked at the luminous dial of his CIA-issue Rolex; it was four minutes before midnight. As his eyes searched the night, he gradually made out the alligator's tail of Pinar del Río Province at the western end of the island. The Cape Corrientes light, normally flashing its warning, was dark tonight. This added to the captain's sense of things amiss. The tropical night was sea damp. He shook his head and barked out orders.

Two fiberglass speedboats slid down special high-speed davits mounted on the afterdeck and splashed into the water. Their 100-horsepower inboard motors coughed to life, the noise muffled by exhaust deflectors. The double-bottomed boats had been specially designed for the CIA's amphibious operations and were known, with more affection than logic, as Moppies. They carried two .30-caliber Browning machine guns and a radio to communicate with their mother ship. The steering columns were located in the rear. At the wheels were *Rex* quartermasters.

The Moppies' engines idled as the stocking-masked commandos climbed down cargo nets from the *Rex*. Backpacks stuffed with C-4 plastic explosives were carefully handed down. The Moppies sped off with a faint hum and left the *Rex*, its running lights out and the no-smoking lamp on, a shadow in the sea.

The Moppies stopped at the mouth of a high-banked river. The commandos inflated black rubber rafts equipped with silent-running outboard motors for the last leg of the journey upriver. Ahead was a rendezvous point with two Mambises who had been infiltrated a week earlier. The rafts slowed in the river, and the Mambises signaled shore with an infrared blinker. After a waitful minute the answer came back. It was in the wrong code — a trap. The commandos opened fire at the riverbank with M-3 grease guns as they frantically wheeled the rafts around and headed back toward the Moppies at the river's mouth. The shore instantly lit up red and blue as machine guns on both banks opened up on the fleeing rafts. One raft was torn apart by tracer bullets, spilling the dead and the dying into the water. Before the other raft could reach the sea, the Moppies were speeding back toward the *Rex* with Cuban patrol boats in pursuit. The abandoned commandos turned toward shore where Castro's militia awaited them.[3]

In the lead Moppie, the steering wheel had been shot away. Quartermaster Luis Montero Carranzana held the steering column in a death grip. He was suddenly framed in the searchlight of a Russian P-6 patrol boat, and for him the Secret War was over. The other Moppie headed for deep sea and the spot in the night sky where the *Rex* had been. The Moppie pilot kept speeding until he reached international waters, where he stopped a merchant ship by firing his machine gun across its bow and was rescued. The *Rex* herself had vanished.

When Captain Brooks saw the firefight erupt, his stomach fell. He sensed a setup. He immediately ordered flank speed. His quartermasters in the Moppies and the commandos in their rafts would have to fend for themselves; he was following the first rule of the sea, which was survival, and the edict of the CIA, which was to sacrifice all else to avoid the capture of the *Rex* and its cargo of secrets.

Brooks first made a feint toward the open sea, then doubled back and began hugging the coastline, hoping to be close enough to shore to avoid being picked up on coastal radar. He ran in the dark with his lights off.

Captain Brooks's premonition paid off. Minutes after the firefight began a pair of Cuban helicopters were over the scene. They made a beeline for the mile-and-a-half zone where the *Rex* usually waited for the commandos to return and dropped clusters of flares, illuminating a vast expanse of sea. What happened next was recounted by Pepe, the gunner's mate on the *Rex*. "As we cleared the head I saw the running lights of a freighter," Pepe said. "I knew right away what was going to happen. The freighter ran right into the light of the flares. The Cubans thought it was us. They opened up on her."

The ship was the 32,500-ton *J. Louis*, flying the Liberian flag and hauling a cargo of bauxite from Jamaica to Corpus Christi, Texas. The time was 12:40 A.M. Five Cuban MiG-21s equipped for night fighting began strafing and rocket-launching runs on the *J. Louis.* Her bewildered skipper, Captain Gerhard Krause, later estimated that the jets made fourteen to twenty passes. The attack continued for more than an hour. Large-caliber bullets chewed holes in the deck and hull, and fires on the forecastle and superstructure took three hours to put out. Miraculously none of the crew was injured.

When the attack began, Captain Krause radioed an international SOS call: Unarmed freighter under MiG attack off coast of Cuba. Some 200 miles to the north, at Key West, U.S. Navy pilots scrambled for their F-4 Phantom jets and took off for the scene of the attack.

Only six weeks before, in early September, the Soviet Union had issued a warning that it would "not tolerate" further raids on Cuba by exiles "armed and supplied with North American weapons." Moscow made it clear that it knew the CIA was breaching the Missile Crisis agreement which stated that the United States would refrain from sponsoring further military adventures against Cuba.

Now, because of a situation of the CIA's making, American and Cuban jets were minutes from combat.

The U.S. Phantoms were called back to base just before reaching Cuba, leaving the *J. Louis* to be strafed at will by Castro's jets. It is clear that the CIA initiated the recall order, but why remains unknown. The agency's command post for Cuban operations on the South Campus of the University of Miami—disguised as the electronic research firm called Zenith Technical Enterprises—had a huge rhombic antenna that constantly scanned the Caribbean. The CIA controllers may have assumed from the confusing jumble of radio traffic that it was the *Rex* under attack—the *Rex* herself was maintaining radio silence to avoid detection—and under the unwritten rules of clandestine warfare she was considered expendable. Or, more cynically, the CIA controllers may have realized that the Cuban jets had the wrong ship but wanted the attack to continue so that the *Rex* could escape.

While the MiGs were preoccupied with the *J. Louis,* the *Rex* slunk out of Cuban waters. Once the Castro command realized its mistake two gunboats were sent in pursuit. Outgunned by the Cuban vessels, Captain Brooks broke radio silence and asked the Zenith command post for instructions. "Do what you have to do," was the noncommittal reply.

Brooks decided to make a run for Mexico's Yucatán Peninsula, some seventy miles distant. He made it, slipping inside Mexican territorial waters off Cozumel Island. The gunboats honored the boundary, playing cat and mouse with the *Rex* for two days. When they finally withdrew, the *Rex* headed for Key West, detouring to take in tow a gray, unmarked Catalina amphibian that had been forced down with engine trouble while on a CIA mission. It was business as usual in the Secret War.

The morning after the Caribbean almost exploded into war, it developed that the shot-up *J. Louis* flew the Liberian flag as a matter of tax convenience. The ship was actually owned by an American corporation belonging to the man of megabucks, billionaire Daniel Ludwig. This information was seized upon with uncharacteristic alacrity by the folks at Foggy Bottom. At noon in Washington, a State Department spokesman said that "we are investigating the facts in the case to see whether a U.S. protest will be made on the basis of this violation and the U.S. ownership of this vessel."

Two days later, the portrayal of the United States as the aggrieved party achieved a state of high brass when State Department press officer Robert J. McCloskey, rejecting a call by Fidel Castro for an end to the American economic blockade of Cuba, cited the *J. Louis* incident as the reason. McCloskey said that the United States had no choice because of Cuba's recent "aggressive course."

On August 18, 1963, in the Guatemala City version of Fleet Street, Rafael Martínez Pupo, a perspiring bank executive, made the rounds of the foreign news services burdened with a heavy pile of press releases.

The papers he handed out with a flutter bordering on panache bore the Lone Star emblem of the Commandos Mambises, an organization of ferocious Cuban exile freedom fighters which that very day sprang into being via the fine pudgy hand of Señor Pupo.

The press handout trumpeted the "victory" of the Mambises in a sneak attack on the Cuban port of Casilda, where an 8,000-gallon oil tank had been set afire.

Señor Pupo put off the routine inquiries of journalists for more important matters. He rushed off to telephone Salvador Lew in Miami, a journalist with the reputation of an exile propagandist, who had flacked for Juanita Castro, Fidel's disaffected sister. Lew, no stranger to the scoop, rushed to put the news out over WMIE, then the CIA's favorite radio station in Miami, which broadcast on a frequency close to the heartbeat of Little Havana.

As he handed out his releases boasting of the Mambises' first attack, Pupo predicted that the commandos would shortly attack the port city of Santa Lucía in Pinar del Río. He seemed to be in the know.

Even as Salvador Lew was singing the praises to Little Havana of this new, fiercely independent commando organization, the Mambies were creeping ashore and placing demolition charges at the Matahambre copper mine, linked to Santa Lucía by a cable car system. They were discovered, and the commando team's leader, a former Batista army lieutenant, was captured and later executed, but enough plastic explosives went off to rock the mine and allow Señor Pupo, in Guatemala City, to claim it as a charge heard around the world. "The war of liberation continues. Commandos Mambises have struck again," he said. These sentiments were shortly shouted from the rooftops of Little Havana by reporter Lew. The Mambises were hailed as politically independent and self-supporting Cuban patriots who had taken up arms because the Kennedy administration had turned the other cheek to Castro.

Lew denies knowing that the Commandos Mambises were CIA. "I assumed the sponsors were well-to-do Cubans," he told the authors. Jay Mallin, the ex-*Time* correspondent in Havana and Miami, acknowledges that "the Mambises were a CIA operation all the way. There was no way for the press to get to them for a story — Salvador Lew simply gave a handout."

The exile community, which is nothing but suspicious, immediately began asking questions about these brave Mambises. They didn't have an office in Miami, the Rome of the anti-Castro church.

They didn't seem to have an office anywhere, not even for the faith-ful to send donations. There was none of the standard exile fare — the frenetic, boasting press conferences after a raid, the shoot-for-the moon promises, the leaders strutting about Little Havana with palm leaves thrown at their feet, the constant hustling for money to finance future raids. The only Mambises person ever to surface was the aforementioned Señor Pupo, a Cuban businessman who had made a bundle in food and electronic firms in pre-Castro Cuba. Pupo was all sweetness but could shed little light on the Mambises; he claimed that there were Mambises "cells" all over the United States and Latin America, that they had 1,000 men under arms in the mountains of Cuba, and that the Mambises' military base was on Navassa Island, an uninhabited rock off Haiti. In fact, the Mambises were quartered in CIA safe houses in southern Florida.

The Commandos Mambises were a wholly owned creation of the CIA, and a crash creation at that. They were trained at a CIA am-phibious base near New Orleans. They were floated as a trial bal-loon to test world opinion about exile raids ostensibly carried out with no American support. If the Mambises got a good press, the CIA had more acts to follow.[4]

The creation of this elite commando unit can be traced to discus-sions of the Standing Group on Cuba in the spring of 1963. Accord-ing to the Standing Group minutes, everyone had agreed with Robert Kennedy that "the United States must do something against Castro, even though we do not believe our actions would bring him down." In less diplomatic words, the Standing Group was antsy.

Their imperative to "do something" was authorized by President Kennedy on June 19 — a greatly escalated program of sabotage aimed at petroleum facilities, railroad and highway transportation, and electric power and communications facilities in Cuba. This led to the CIA's launching its Caribbean secret navy and the creation of the Commandos Mambises. A measure of the White House green light was that for the first time the CIA was allowed to violate the sanctum sanctorum and target previously off-limits installations that had been owned by American companies.[3] It was a major esca-lation of the Secret War.

II

There was unusual activity at television station CMQ in Havana. Fidel Castro was having a news conference, American style. He did most of the talking, and it was all about the CIA ship *Rex*.

Two days before, on October 28, the *Rex* had returned to her home port of West Palm Beach — after first checking to make sure the President was not visiting the nearby Kennedy family home — from the Caribbean sea chase after the *J. Louis* incident. This was what Castro, no stranger to drama, had been waiting for. He announced that Cuba had captured four men from the *Rex*, and he exposed her and her sister ship, the *Leda*, as CIA pirate craft. He told the world where the *Rex* was docked in West Palm Beach and described the CIA flagship down to her distinguishing electronic gear amidships and her war paint of patriotic blue.

Castro knew how to milk a story. He followed his first press conference with a second and put these prisoners of the Secret War before the television cameras in Havana.

At the White House, Press Secretary Pierre Salinger was not in a talkative mood. "We have nothing to say," he said. Castro's captives had a lot to say. Luis Montero Carranzana stated that he was the *Rex*'s quartermaster and had been piloting one of the fiberglass launches when the firefight erupted. He had been on a number of CIA raids, he said, including the Mambises' copper mine raid and a yacht mission that had landed a dozen infiltrators. "I landed many times in Cuba," Montero admitted. "I delivered packages there. We anchored five or six miles from the Cuban coast and went ashore in two launches. We would leave six men and twenty-five or thirty packages there. I did not know the mission of these men. Then we returned to the ship. Before daybreak we returned to Key West or Miami." Montero said he was at first paid $250 a month, which was later raised to $275.[6]

Also starring on Havana television that day was Dr. Clemente Inclan Werner, in earlier days a well-known Cuban yachtsman. He said that he had been smuggling arms for the Christian Democrats when the CIA recruited him into its Commandos Mambises fighting force. He had been trained in firearms and explosives and the fine arts of invisible inks at a CIA school for guerrillas on a suburban Miami estate. Inclan drew a monthly salary of $400, which represented a raise, he noted with some pride, of $100 over the CIA minimum wage.[7]

The four CIA foot soldiers went next to court, where they were convicted and sentenced to thirty years. After the *Rex* incident and the embarrassment of Castro's press conference, the Commandos Mambises, of blown cover, disappeared as fast as they had appeared. Castro had taken the air out of the CIA's trial balloon.

The Havana television show focused for a brief if not too shining moment the attention of the competitive American press on the CIA ships. Newspersons came to the port of West Palm Beach to stare at the *Rex*. "It comes and goes at various intervals. We don't ask any questions, and they don't volunteer any information," port operations director J. Sonny Jaudon said. J. A. Belcher of the Belcher Oil Company, the nominal owner of the *Rex*, could only say damned-if-I-know about his mystery ship. "I don't know if it had any connection with the CIA, but I don't see how it could," he said.[8]

At Port Everglades, where Castro said the CIA ship *Leda* docked, reporters had no trouble finding her, an ungainly orange and green ex-patrol craft with a pair of fiberglass launches sitting amidships, a proliferation of antennas and a construction crane mounted on the aft deck, and a Nicaraguan flag at her mast. The *Leda* was registered out of Greytown, Nicaragua, to a firm called Lake Cay Company, Inc., said to be engaged in "oceanographic surveys." Her captain was Gaspar Brooks, a brother of the *Rex* skipper. A spokesman for the city of Port Everglades complained that port security teams were not allowed on board for routine safety checks and that men carrying baggage "leave and arrive like cruise line customers" but were never stopped by Customs, even though "we know they leave the country." "They could be carrying a million dollars' worth of narcotics and we'd never know it," said the petulant city official. A *Leda* crewman shouted over the rail at newsmen, "Don't take pictures of the ship. You'll just be helping Khrushchev."[9]

The pre-Watergate investigative inclinations of the American free press lasted about as long as a British summer. The CIA's secret navy had for all practical purposes been exposed, and the story was there for the taking, but there were few takers. The press never caught on to the size and purpose of the CIA's fleet which, before the Soviet buildup of Castro's navy, was the most powerful in the Caribbean.

One reporter who tried to track down the CIA's navy was Edna Buchanan of the Miami Beach *Daily Sun*. She found the CIA ship *Villaro* in Fort Pierce. "She was a funny ship," a friend of a *Villaro* crewman told Buchanan. "She changed colors all the time. Sometimes the hull would be blue with a green deck. Other times it was gray with an orange deck."

Buchanan found another CIA ship, *Explorer II*, berthed in full view of motorists at a pier off the MacArthur Causeway in Miami Harbor. The low, sleek vessel was painted black and gray, her tripod mast bristled with radar and electronic gear, and her engines were constantly idling. She stood out like a sore thumb of cliché among the peeling tramps and brightly hued cruise ships. "She doesn't look like it, but she's the fastest thing in the water," a coast guardsman told Buchanan.

The reporter learned that *Explorer II*'s Spanish-speaking crew numbered more than two dozen, much larger than that needed for civilian use. She was registered out of Honduras, and Coast Guard records listed the owner as Exploration, Inc., with a Miami Shores address. "There is no telephone listing for the firm," Buchanan wrote, "and what's more, the address is not in Miami Shores." Canvassing the waterfront, Buchanan found out that the ship "slipped out of the harbor two or three times a month, returning in several days as quietly as she departed."

One night Buchanan went down to the ship and questioned the man on deck watch. "He replied he didn't know who owned the ship and just shook his head when asked the name of his employer." Returning in daylight with a camera, she found herself being photographed in return by a crewman. "The camera-wielding crewman claimed association with Florida Atlantic University in Boca Raton," she said. "In heavily-accented English, he said the *Explorer* is 'an oceanographic ship,' gathering samples for the college. Asked what they do, he explained that they 'test water salinity and gather samples of sea life.'"

The pier owner who collected the ship's dockage fees was tight-lipped. "We handle her for an agent in Jacksonville," he said. "That's all I want to say about it." In Jacksonville the trail led to the Southeastern Shipping Corporation, the business of which, in papers filed with state regulatory agencies, was stated succinctly as "research." It was the standard cover for the Navy nobody knew. For her efforts, Buchanan was rewarded by her editors with a question mark. CIA SHIP? was the headline they tagged on her article.[10]

The smaller vessels of the CIA fleet included the heavy-duty, fifty-foot Swift boats the Navy employed in Vietnam. They were used for everything from landing frogmen off Cuba to dumping huge wads of foil to foul up Cuban coastal radar. One of the CIA Swift boats was registered to a firm called Ace Marine Survey, the president of which was a New Orleans public relations man who did work for such CIA-sponsored groups there as Friends of Democratic Cuba. Anyone checking Ace Marine Survey's Miami address found it to be smack in the middle of the Miami River. This odd situation so fascinated a local newspaper columnist that he dialed the number listed for the company in the telephone directory. The conversation, which may be apocryphal but was a longstanding source of amusement in soldier-of-fortune circles, began when the Miami columnist told the secretary who answered that she was underwater and asked, "What is your address?"

SECRETARY: Why do you want to know?
COLUMNIST: Well, where are you located?
SECRETARY: I don't know.
COLUMNIST: Does anyone there know where you are located?
SECRETARY: Just a minute, I'll check. (Pause) No one here knows.
COLUMNIST: How did you get to work?
SECRETARY: Somebody brings me.

III

Three skiers maneuvered slowly — one awkwardly — down the gentler slopes of the New Hampshire mountain. Bobby and Ethel Kennedy were on one of their weekend snow outings. They had brought along a man who had never seen snow before.

It was January 1963. Only a few weeks before, Manuel Artime, the CIA's "Golden Boy" of Brigade 2506, had been in a tropical dungeon in Modelo Prison on the Isle of Pines. Artime owed his freedom to his skiing host, who had personally raised the final $1 million ransom through Richard Cardinal Cushing, the Kennedy family priest.

The talk around the ski resort fireplace that weekend was dominated by new ways to deal with "that guy with the beard," as Kennedy frequently referred to Castro. But underlying RFK's genuine sympathy for the exiles was the slight edge of extortion, for Artime knew things about the invasion that were better left unsaid.

Artime returned to Miami from his snow frolic with a special portfolio from Robert Kennedy rehabilitating him as an exile leader. He was restored on an economic level as well. Before the weekend he had been broke and living off a girlfriend in a Little Havana house called Casa Rosa because of its pink color, a hue the right-leaning Artime disliked intensely. With Bobby's juice, Artime found himself on a CIA retainer of $1,500 a month to revive his Movement for the Recovery of the Revolution (MRR). Before long the MRR was receiving a steady $250,000 a month to launch an ambitious operation code-named the Second Naval Guerrilla.

The objective: to attack Cuban shipping and mount commando raids on shore installations. The CIA would supply the funding and logistical support, intelligence data, and guidance. Artime would function independently but submit each operation to the CIA for approval.

It was like old times in Little Havana. The MRR battle flag, a gold trident on blue, hung outside a newly opened headquarters. General Edward Lansdale flew down for a personal inspection. Recruits banged on the door, and Bay of Pigs veterans were sought out as war fever again spread through the exile colony. A group holding maneuvers in a field proudly told quizzical Miami police that they were "training for the next invasion of Cuba."

Since the Missile Crisis the United States was off limits for major military activity, so in the summer of 1963 Artime went shopping for a Latin American country that would allow him a military base. He didn't have to travel any farther than Managua, his first stop.

Luis Somoza was only too happy to buy into a second chance. When Artime hinted that he might need a second base in another country, the helpful Nicaraguan put in a call to President Francisco J. Orlich of Costa Rica, his neighbor to the south. He explained that the United States wished to support a fresh anti-Castro operation removed from its own territory. Orlich did not feel in a position to refuse. Only a few months before President Kennedy had honored him with a visit during which he committed additional Alliance for Progress aid while stressing the need "to halt the flow of agents, money, arms and propaganda from Cuba to Central America."[11]

Two jungle camps were set up in Costa Rica on the property of Colonel Vico Starki Jiménez, a friend of Orlich's brother and leader of a small right-wing party. A naval base was erected at Monkey Point in Nicaragua, from which Brigade 2506 had embarked two years earlier for the Bay of Pigs. Infusion of money arrived through devious channels. According to Miami *Herald* reporter Al Burt:

> An American would call the office [in Little Havana] and say that a certain amount of money had been deposited in a Miami bank under a certain name. The MRR would then draw on it. In Costa Rica, an official said the checks would arrive in the mail, drawn on the accounts of legitimate American firms, usually from New York City banks. One official claimed to have received a check for $167,784 in a plain white envelope bearing a U.S. cancellation but no return address. He endorsed it, as arranged, to a New York shipping firm in payment for two World War II torpedo boats. His records show that the check was issued on November 19, 1963, and they reveal the check number, the bank and the American firm. He said other checks had come in different amounts; one for $450,000 was used to purchase modern military equipment.[12]

The CIA largess enabled the MRR to purchase the finest quality, from the newest German rebreathers for frogmen to name-brand laundry soap. Equipment manufactured in the United States was "sanitized" to hide its source; identifying marks on parachute canopies were cut out, and blank panels sewn in. Most of the arms were bought in West Germany, wrapped in German newspapers, and brought across the Atlantic by barge. If the MRR campaign boomeranged, Castro would have no hard evidence to indict the United States.

The Second Naval Guerrilla "navy" was similarly neutered. Two 180-foot attack cargo ships of World War II vintage, the *Joanne* and *Santa María*, fitted with 20 mm naval cannon, .50-caliber machine guns, and recoilless rifles, were registered to a dummy company called Maritime Bam, Ltd., the president of which was a Cuban exile businessman who doubled as MRR purchasing agent. They flew the Liberian flag but carried an assortment of national banners that could be hoisted as the occasion demanded. The CIA allowed the MRR to borrow the *Tejana III*, the speedy ex-subchaser used on runs to Cuba before the Bay of Pigs. The fleet's smaller boats included two prototype Swift boats.

Upon viewing the fleet assembled at Monkey Point, General Somoza was encouraged to announce that "in November strong blows will begin against Cuban Prime Minister Fidel Castro by groups we are training." On November 15, 1963, the first contingent of MRR commandos, trained on the Farm in Virginia and Isolation Tropic in North Carolina, sailed from Norfolk on board the *Joanne*. Ordinarily an exile could travel outside the United States only with the discretionary permission of immigration authorities; the expeditionary force had been exempted. Some 300 men were under arms in the Costa Rican camps (in Miami MRR "social workers" paid their salaries, including child allowances, to their wives in cash). Their commander was the redoubtable Pepe San Román, who had become an unofficial military advisor to Bobby Kennedy.

Some six months earlier, Pepe San Román had been at Miami International Airport to meet a very special flight from Havana. The airliner door opened, and sixty of Brigade 2506's most seriously wounded men hobbled down the steps. A band struck up "The Colonel Bogey March." Twenty thousand spectators crowded the runway in an emotional, tearful welcome.

The last man down the steps was Enrique "Harry" Ruíz-Williams, a survivor of the invaders' Heavy Gun Battalion. He fell into the arms of his former commander, Pepe San Román, now a commando in the Secret War. When the *embrazos* and reminiscences were over, San Román went to a telephone and called Robert Kennedy. He said, "I want you to meet this guy who can tell you what the hell is going on out there."[13]

Several days later Williams and San Román flew to Washington to meet with the attorney general. "I was really nervous to see him," Williams said, "the number two man in the country. And when I walked into that office, here was this young man without a coat and his sleeves rolled up and tie unknotted." The two hit it off immediately.

Harry Williams was a Kennedy kind of man, tough and liberal and ferociously anticommunist. Burly, round-faced, and handsome, he combined the geniality of a Lions Club toastmaster with a tough-minded singleness of purpose. The venality of the Batista regime disgusted him—particularly the overnight riches acquired by a Havanan he had once played football with. "We used to call him *cafe y leche*—coffee and milk—because he never had a cent. I went to Colombia for two years, and when I came back, this guy had a big restaurant. He paid my meals, he paid my drinks, and he said, 'Will you come with me?' We went out. He had a big Cadillac with a chauffeur, and he showed me two apartment houses he owned. And I asked, 'Well, Diego, what did you do to own this?' And he said, 'Well, I sat down next to the chauffeur of Alemán.'" José Alemán was the Batista official who arrived in Miami with suitcases full of embezzled millions.

Williams was a geologist by profession, American-trained, a graduate of the Colorado School of Mines. He lived in Oriente Province, where he came in contact with the rebel units of Raúl Castro and Che Guevara. He gave them food, dynamite, trucks, and tractors. Before the victory Williams left Cuba. He returned after Batista fled but within a few months decided that communists were calling the shots in the new government. He decided that the simplest solution was to get rid of Castro.

At the Bay of Pigs, even as the outcome of the invasion became inevitable, Williams was determined to keep fighting. "I want you to go to the front and make sure of your direction of fire," he told a subordinate, "because we are going to put in the history of Cuba how many men we kill today." The words were hardly out of his mouth when a shell exploded at his side. His body was riddled with shrapnel, but "*Un bicho malo nunca muere* ["A bad bull never dies"]," he told Pepe San Román. As the brigade scattered, Williams and other wounded were left in a seaside cottage. The next day Fidel Castro himself came inside, and Williams reached for a pistol under his mattress. Castro saw the move and remonstrated gently, "What are you trying to do, kill me?"

"That's what I came here for," Williams shot back. "We've been trying to do that for three days." Castro ordered the wounded evacuated to a hospital.

Williams made it clear to Bobby Kennedy that his overriding concern was the return of Brigade 2506, and he was put in touch with New York attorney James Donovan and RFK aide John Nolan, who were negotiating with Cuban representatives. But Williams grew impatient with the protracted process and suspicious of Kennedy's intentions. Several times he was invited to Hickory Hill, the Kennedys' Virginia estate, but politely excused himself. It wasn't until after the brigade was ransomed that he finally accepted.

"Why haven't you come?" Ethel Kennedy teased him. "Don't you like us or something?"

Williams replied, "I didn't know whether I was going to be a friend of your husband or not."[14]

The uninjured members of the brigade arrived in Miami on Christmas Eve, 1962. A welcoming ceremony was scheduled for the Orange Bowl four days later. John Kennedy was invited but was uncertain whether to accept. One of his "Irish Mafia," Kenneth O'Donnell, warned, "Don't go there. After what you've been through with Castro, you can't make an appearance in the Orange Bowl and pay a tribute to those rebels. It will look as if you're planning to back them in another invasion of Cuba."

"You're absolutely right," JFK concurred. "I shouldn't do it."[15]

But he did. When Pepe San Román presented him with the brigade's battle flag, Kennedy responded, "I can assure you that this flag will be returned to this brigade in a free Havana." A great roar went up, followed by wild cheering by the brigade. They thought the President had made a promise.

The Kennedy administration's promises to the exiles were compromised by a secret agenda. Jack Kennedy would return the flag to the brigade in Havana, but it would be a brigade of his choosing, not theirs; the Kennedys were not going to lose the second battle of Cuba because they preferred being Mr. Nice Guys. They were not about to restamp the entire baggage of the failed invasion. They would pick their own people, Kennedy people, and the second act of the Cuban drama would be directed from the White House, not Langley, not Miami. This was how the Kennedys saw it; but in their patrician manner, they didn't tell it that way. They continued to wave before all the exiles the flag of a free Cuba while simultaneously cutting away many exile groups, and conversely anointing others to participate in the secret agenda. As it developed, this would lead to the most bitter of consequences.

Harry Williams got the full Kennedy treatment. Bobby Kennedy flashed his charming beaver-toothed smile and told him that he had been chosen to lead the new exile force in the next invasion of Cuba. Almost fifteen years later, when we interviewed him, Williams remembered RFK's exact words: "We've selected you to be, let's say, the man we trust the most in the exiles, but at the same time I want to make it clear that we're going to be calling the shots." Williams asked what that meant. Kennedy replied that the interests of the United States and of the exiles might not always be the same; there were other secret agendas affecting the secret agenda. But their goals were the same — the elimination of Castro. When the President determined it was the right moment, they would strike. Meanwhile, their job was to be prepared. Bobby told Williams not to worry. "We're going to go," he said.[16]

Kennedy arranged for Williams to deal directly with Cyrus Vance, then undersecretary of the army, in working out details for the enlistment of volunteers from the brigade. "We had at least three or four big meetings at Bobby's office," Williams said, "with leaders of the brigade and Vance and two or three others. Joe Califano, who was working with McNamara, was there too." Nearly half the returned brigade members joined the Army and were shipped to

Fort Jackson, South Carolina. Three hundred who were considered officer material were sent to the command school at Fort Benning. One was Felipe de Diego, whose Operation 40 experience helped him as an intelligence officer.

With RFK playing the Godfather, the CIA had to accept Williams even if it didn't control him. "I had the backing of Bobby," Williams said, "and they listened to me whether they liked it or not. And they liked it enough. I told my things to Bobby. And Bobby was the one that made this thing go. He'd call these people, and his secretary would tell me, 'Someone's going to see you.' "

The CIA agents finally assigned to Williams on a permanent basis were Howard Hunt and James McCord, the future Watergaters. "I was confused," Williams remembered. "Both of them said to call me Don Eduardo. Both Hunt and McCord." Hunt became Williams's link to the Langley headquarters, while McCord liaisoned with brigade veterans at Fort Jackson. Beginning in early 1963 Williams had dozens of meetings and countless telephone discussions with Hunt and McCord. The meetings were in Washington or New York, away from the rumors of Miami. Usually the CIA odd couple would pick him up at his hotel and take him to lunch or would come to his room late at night. "It's funny how these professional intelligence people work," Williams observed of Hunt. "He never opened up to me. He knew I liked my martinis, and he'd have a martini with me. But I never trusted him, and he never trusted me."[17]

The plan that Williams finally devised was to launch an amphibious landing on Oriente Province from a base in the Dominican Republic. Although Trujillo Fils had been pressured into exile by the United States, the country remained in the hospitable hands of the Trujillo clan's puppet president, Juan Balaguer. The choice of Oriente Province offered obvious strategic advantages—a mountainous terrain, paucity of highways, and great distance from Havana. It would be the most difficult of all for Castro to defend. And the supply lifeline from the Dominican Republic would be comparatively short. He reasoned the pitfalls of the Bay of Pigs could thus be avoided.

During our interview Harry Williams thrust a beefy finger at a map of the Dominican Republic on the wall of his geological survey office in Fort Lauderdale as he pointed out the base that he had intended to use. It was near Montecristi in the isolated northwest corner of the country and had been set up by an old counterrevolutionary friend of Williams, Eloy Menoyo, whose Guerrilla Second Front of the Escambray was at that time conducting joint raids on Cuba with a new action group called Alpha 66.

IV

His CIA cover name was Maurice Bishop. He was in his mid-forties, six feet two inches, 200 pounds, dark hair, with deep lines across a high forehead and sunspots under blue eyes. He was soft-spoken and fancied Miami-style sportswear. He was fluent in French and carried a bogus Belgian passport. In 1963 he was the case officer for Alpha 66. Bishop tended to act impulsively in furtherance of his political convictions, which were main-line Ayn Rand. He had only an impolite gesture for U.S. foreign policy. He directed his exile troops in a private war against the Russians in Cuba that came close to precipitating a U.S.-Soviet military showdown.

While attached to the Havana station in 1960, Bishop had recruited the lean, stern counterrevolutionary accountant, Antonio Veciana, who instigated the abortive attempt on Castro's life in October 1961. After Veciana fled to Miami, Bishop was back in touch. Under the CIA man's guidance Veciana organized Alpha 66. The name was taken from the first letter of the Greek alphabet, signifying a new beginning, and the number of charter members. It was the kind of intellectual touch Bishop liked.

Eloy Menoyo had helped Veciana put Alpha 66 together. Menoyo's defection from the revolution was more colorful than most. In January 1961, Castro assigned him to board the Portuguese luxury liner *Santa Maria*, which had been hijacked by revolutionaries, and proceed to Portuguese Angola to start an insurrection. Instead, he took off for Florida in an open boat. He was detained for months because the CIA suspected his intentions. Stubbornly independent, Menoyo retained the Second Front name for his action group, and the coalition was often referred to as Second Front/ Alpha 66.

Although maintaining ties to the CIA, Alpha 66 considered itself autonomous and self-sufficient. Its nucleus was composed of the Cuban professional class — lawyers, doctors, and accountants. The accountants were invaluable to the fund-raising effort since they knew which exiles had large deposits in the banks outside Cuba. A membership drive produced some sixty chapters throughout the United States and Latin America which raised money, staged social events, and funded scholarships to send the sons of counterrevolutionary heroes to Notre Dame.

The long-range objective was to infiltrate and disrupt the Cuban military and political establishments, starting a groundswell that would hopefully lead to a domestic uprising. But as the months passed without tangible results, Alpha 66 found itself in competition for public recognition and support. Other action groups were mounting hit-and-run raids on Cuba and greatly magnifying the results in press communiqués. The CIA looked tolerantly on these dramatics since it could pass off raids by its own teams as the work of uncontrollable exiles (at times the situation became ludicrous when two or more groups claimed credit for a CIA raid). Alpha 66 decided to up the ante by zapping the Russians.

The first raid was on September 10, 1962. Former Havana businessman Tony Cuesta piloted a motor launch through predawn darkness toward the port of Caibarién on the Cuban north coast where there had been reports of Russian military construction. The anxious Cuesta and his crew opened up on the first target they saw, the *San Pascuel*, an old steamer grounded on a concrete base and used for molasses storage. Then they raked the British freighter *Newlane* and, as custom helicopters chased them away, took a parting shot at the coastal tramp *San Blas*.

Havana radio angrily branded the scattershot raiders as "criminals armed and paid by the U.S." Alpha 66 sharpened its aim on October 10, when its commandos went ashore at Isabela de Sagua, some 150 miles east of Havana, and killed twenty persons, including several Russians.[18] Then came the Missile Crisis.

JFK's promise to Khrushchev to leave Cuba alone had been kept secret from the exiles, but Maurice Bishop knew about it. What Bishop did not know was that Kennedy intended to renege on his promise. He misinterpreted the post-Mongoose lull as evidence nothing would be done. He decided to force the President's hand. "Bishop believed that Kennedy and Khrushchev had made a secret pact to do nothing about Cuba," Antonio Veciana revealed not long ago. "He kept saying Kennedy would have to be forced to make a decision, and the only way was to put him up against the wall."[19]

Bishop deliberately targeted Russian ships, hoping to antagonize the Russians into another confrontation with the United States. The next strike came on March 18, 1963, at Isabela de Sagua. Two launches carrying Alpha 66 and Second Front commandos fired on the anchored Russian freighter *Lvov*, inflicting heavy damage. The commandos then went ashore and attacked a Soviet infantry camp, wounding twelve soldiers.[20] Then they held a press conference in Washington to brag about it.

Although the exploit reaped a windfall of contributions from heartened exiles, the Russian reaction was a disappointingly mild diplomatic protest. Another raid was scheduled, this time with Tony Cuesta leading a squad of Commandos L (for liberation), a spin-off group from Alpha 66. To ensure dramatic national coverage, a correspondent for *Life* magazine, which had drawn an editorial bead on Castro, was asked along. He was Andrew St. George, who had switched to covering the counterrevolutionaries.

U.S. Coast Guard patrols had been tightened after the *Lvov* incident, and stealth was required. One night the forty-three-foot yacht *Alisan* slipped her moorings at a Miami marina and sailed out into the Gulf Stream, where she took in tow a speedboat named *Phoenix*. The *Alisan* proceeded to the small Caribbean island of Anguilla, where a 20 mm Lahti cannon and guns had been cached. For eight days Cuesta and his commandos remained poised on Anguilla, waiting for the weather to turn propitious, while St. George snapped pictures.

On the afternoon of March 27 Cuesta suddenly announced, "*Bueno vamos.*" About eleven that night the *Phoenix* saw the lights of Caibarién. Just then a Cuban patrol boat closed in, its searchlight stabbing randomly into the darkness. But it left as swiftly as it had come. As he groped his way into the harbor, Cuesta spotted the Levantine silhouette of the Russian merchantman *Baku*. "*Ahora!*" he shouted.

Cuesta slammed the throttle forward, and the *Phoenix* raced toward the quarry. As the distance narrowed, armorer Ramón Font opened up with the Lahti cannon. Ten shells crashed into the command bridge and side of the *Baku*. The speedboat swung around, its arc taking it within inches of the freighter. As the commandos fired rifles to keep Russian sailors back from the rail, Font lit the fuse on a limpet mine lashed to the stern. But as he tried to dump it overboard so that its magnet would clamp onto the *Baku*'s hull, the lashings snarled. It seemed an eternity as he feverishly undid them.

The *Phoenix* was barely away before the *Baku* was rent by a muffled explosion and a geyser shot up that reached above the funnels. "The ship was all alight, and as we fired we could hear the Russian sailors running and shouting," Cuesta recounted. "We had a homemade mine of fifty pounds of TNT, which we placed against the hull. We were only one hundred yards away when the explosion came."[21]

With a gaping hole in her side the *Baku* settled to the shallow bottom, ruining 10,000 bags of sugar.

This time the Kremlin bellowed in outrage, charging on March 27 that the United States was "offering Cuban counterrevolutionaries its territories and material needs," causing a "dangerous aggravation" of the situation in the Caribbean and the world. *Pravda* was even more pejorative, calling it an attack by "CIA bandits hiding behind the skirts of Cuban malcontents who had deserted their country to embrace capitalism."

Pravda, which is often wrong, this time was right.

The results of the provocations were the opposite of what Bishop had intended. JFK immediately issued conciliatory statements aimed at assuring the Soviets the hands–off agreement was still in force. For domestic consumption he warned that the raids, if continued, "will bring reprisals, possibly on American ships. We will then be expected to take a military action to protect our ships. It may bring counteraction. I think that when these issues of war and peace hang in the balance the United States government and authorities should . . . have a position of some control on this matter."[22]

Kennedy ordered a crackdown to prevent the exiles from tormenting the Russian Bear any further. Upon returning to Miami, the *Alisan* was confiscated, and the commandos as well as their leaders were served with papers restricting them to Dade County. Coast Guard air and sea patrols were intensified, and the FBI, Customs, and other federal agencies were instructed to actively seek out violations of the Neutrality Act.

The crackdown was necessarily indiscriminate, applying equally to actions aimed solely at Castro. First the Bay of Pigs, then the Missile Crisis, now this. José Miró Cardona of the CRC charged that Kennedy had switched to a policy of "peaceful coexistence" with Cuba. He flew to Washington to plead with Bobby Kennedy to have the crackdown revoked, but returned empty-handed. He resigned from the CRC, accusing JFK of "breaking promises and agreements" for a second invasion.[23]

The Kennedys took Miró Cardona's outburst as a splendid opportunity to cancel subsidies to the CRC, which, with Harry Williams now on deck, they found an unnecessary bother. The White House had its own Cubans, and its own secret plans for dealing with Castro — the rest of the exiles, in the words of one CIA man, "were told to stuff it," but they weren't told why.

The mood of the more militant exiles turned increasingly bitter. Many began to hate Jack Kennedy almost as much as Castro, and some wanted to kill them both.

V

Kennedy's crackdown was especially vexing to the unmannered soldiers of fortune who came to Miami to get some of the action against Castro. The lot of them might have been picked by central casting for a cold war *Hogan's Heroes:* Gerry Hemming, the tall, dashing leader of something called the Intercontinental Penetration Force, code name Interpen; Little Joe Garman, a rail-thin, six-foot-four gunslinger with a hair-trigger temper; "Skinny Ralph" and "Fat Ralph," a pair of merry pranksters with a penchant for things paramilitary; Robert K. Brown, a sometime Special Forces captain who published guerrilla warfare manuals from a mountain redoubt in Colorado; a likable one-armed Canadian named Bill Dempsey; handsome Martin Francis Xavier Casey, unofficial historian of the anti-Castro action groups.

These were some of the adventurers who lived in a big beige clapboard house at 1925 SW Fourth Street in the heart of Little Havana near the Orange Bowl. A faded red and white sign proclaimed "Glen Haven — Room with Meals," but the place was known around Miami as Nelli Hamilton's boarding house. Nelli, a stout and hearty septuagenarian widow, cosseted her violence-prone "boys" and laughed along with them when they called themselves Knights of the Boardinghouse or Soldiers of Misfortune because of their chivalry in helping losing causes.

Nelli had only a few house rules: no swearing, drinking, or guns at the table. She didn't mind if someone trooped through the living room toting a Coke six-pack filled with live grenades, but she raised a fuss if he hadn't wiped his feet. Nelli cooked on a six-burner black iron stove, and the fifty-odd boarders ate in shifts. Like Mary Worth in the comic strip, she was always around when her big lugs needed motherly advice. She supplied a nice box lunch on request.

In addition to the adventurers, Nelli's clientele included pensioners and blue-collar workers (one was a welder at the Miami Shipyards who frequently was summoned to make repairs on CIA boats at sea). There were also mental patients from the South Florida State Hospital for whom Nelli's was a kind of halfway house. Martin Casey made friends with a man who sat in a rocking chair for hours on end, staring at the television set while dipping his fingers in a jar of peanut butter. One patient became so distraught when his case worker insisted he get a job that he hanged himself. But most responded to Nelli's therapy. As Interpen instructor Howard Davis put it, "The insane ones at Nelli's had more common sense than some of the adventurers."[24]

Two weeks before the Bay of Pigs, Fat Ralph and five other of Nelli's boys decided to steal a forty-foot vessel named the *Polo* to pull a raid on Cuba. The Dirty Half Dozen sneaked onto the *Polo*, which was moored in a rectangular basin near the Julia Tuttle

Causeway, overpowered the watchman, and bound him with his own underwear. They loaded guns borrowed from Frank Sturgis. With admirable foresight they had brought along a man named "Rip" who had skippered oil company tugs on Lake Maracaibo in Venezuela. Rip was a man not unfamiliar with panache: tattooed around his neck was a loop of dashes with the legend "Cut on dotted line."

With a toot of the whistle—Rip was a man of habit—the *Polo* churned out into the basin. But it veered, struck a bank, and bounced off. For some time it crisscrossed the basin, hitting banks, bouncing off. Rip hadn't known that the *Polo*'s pneumatic steering system took time to build up pressure. Finally, he gained steerageway and headed out of the basin. But by now a police launch had been called and was in pursuit. A couple of the boys dived in and escaped by swimming; the rest were arrested.

But not convicted. At the trial the *Polo*'s listed owner, Captain Henry Linder, refused to name the real owner, and the judge dismissed charges. In fact, the *Polo* belonged to the CIA. It had made supply runs to the underground in Cuba from a base on Big Pine Key. The stolen vessel was ticketed for air-sea rescue duty in the invasion. The unwanted publicity spoiled that plan.

Nelli's was home to some memorable characters. There was the Professor, a dipsomaniac teacher out of the Ivy League who plotted to blow up a Yugoslav tramp steamer hauling phosphates between Cuba and Mexico. There was a midget named Pete who loved to hang around the adventurers and made an arresting sight as he marched off on the heels of the towering Hemming and Garman. One day FBI agents showed up to apprehend a fugitive in one of the backyard cottages Nelli rented out. Just then Hemming and Garman marched by with their midget and a squad in close-order drill, "Hup—two—three—four!" The G-men were so taken with the spectacle that the fugitive was able to slip out a rear window and escape.

Some of Nelli's "boys" were tough customers. One was linked to the Canadian Mafia, another was a big-time gambling layoff man who sold stolen guns and explosives to exiles. Another of Nelli's boys ripped off the leader of an exile group for more than $1,000 by delivering a packing crate filled with concrete blocks and grass instead of the agreed-upon arms and ammunition. The exiles complained to the Miami police, who consulted with customs agents, and quietly arranged for the money to be returned. "No further action," the police reports said, "with sanction of U.S. Customs agents."

At times Nelli's seemed more like a barracks than a boarding-house. Guns were broken down and cleaned on the back lawn, and parachutes were laid out on the street in front for packing. Hemming would hold muster for his Interpen instructors before setting out for the training site on No Name Key, not far from Key West, where trainees would lunge at one another with wooden knives and simulate hand-to-hand combat by day, at night trading off sleeping on the floor and crawling on their bellies through the mangrove thickets on "patrols."[25]

Good right-wingers all, Hemming and his crew shied away from CIA funds—with government money goes government control—and got support where they could find it. Hemming staged one of the world's more unusual fund-raisers—a paramilitary fashion show of sorts—at the gaudy Fontainebleau Hotel in Miami Beach. A husky soldier of fortune, Gerry Patrick Hemming blushingly modeled a guerrilla warfare outfit of camouflage suit, combat boots, and Aussie bush hat. Among the guests, according to Hemming, were Fontainebleau president Ben Novack, ousted Venezuelan dictator Marcos Pérez Jiménez, Howard Hughes's business associate C. Osmet Moody, ex-CIA men on the Hughes payroll, and several mobsters.

The show was a modest success. Novack, who prided himself as a civic leader, chipped in. So did the roly-poly, balding Pérez Jiménez, who yearned to regain power and figured having a private army on call might be useful. Other pledges were made.[26]

The action groups being trained by Interpen either divorced themselves entirely from the CIA or accepted its money while insisting on independence.

Gerry Hemming and Interpen were a case study in how such arrangements worked. At six feet six, Hemming was an Errol Flynn-like figure on the streets of Little Havana. He had done a four-year hitch in the Marine Corps, qualifying as a parachutist and underwater swimmer, before entering the U.S. Naval Academy Preparatory School. In 1958 Castro's revolution fired his imagination, and he joined the rebel army. He became a paratroop instructor and platoon leader, switching to the Air Force after the victory. His flying career came to an ignominious end when he ground-looped a Sea Fury.

Hemming soured on the revolution in 1960 and left Cuba. "I spent long hours typing out reports for the CIA," he said, "and made myself available for reinfiltration into Cuba." But the agency snubbed him, so he formed his own instruction corps. Interpen was a kind of Dirty Dozen times two—Americans, Cubans, Irish, French, Hungarians, Swedes, and Canadians, all with military specialties. Howard Davis, a pilot who had flown arms to Raúl Castro, was Hemming's right-hand man. Perhaps the most impressive credentials belonged to Robert K. Brown, a tough little man with a crew cut who had been a Golden Gloves boxer and judo instructor in Colorado. A first lieutenant in the Army Reserve, Brown was a graduate of the counterintelligence school at Fort Holabird, Maryland, and a former member of the Fifth Army pistol team. Brown's idea of civilian clothes was a black raincoat. He preferred battle fatigues at all times. It was his firm belief that the CIA was supremely inept.

Hemming had ranged as far as Texas trying to rustle up support for Interpen. He pitched oilmen Clint Murchison and Nelson Bunker Hunt and radio stations owner Gordon McLendon, among others, and received some donations. But some prospects thought he was going about it the wrong way—that "snuffing" Castro would be more businesslike and less costly. When the subject of assassination was raised in a small group Hemming was lecturing in the Texas Club in Dallas, an oilman piped up, "Screw Castro, let's get his boss!"

"Who's that?" another asked.

"Smilin' Jack," was the answer, meaning John Kennedy.[27]

When Hemming drilled one dry hole after another in Texas, he crossed the oilmen off his list. "They wanted nothing less than a Normandy invasion for their money," he complained.

One group trained by Interpen was the 30th of November Movement, named after the date of a 1956 uprising against Batista. 30th of November had its roots in the Cuban labor movement and shunned the CRC as too aristocratic. Although unwilling to accept CIA control, it took the agency's money. Hemming has a copy, for example, of a 30th of November letter dated December 31, 1961, addressed to its CIA case officer, "Mr. Charles," requesting 30,000 pesos "to increase the effectiveness and security of the personnel that are presently in operation in Cuba." The Funds were promptly remitted.

Most of Interpen's raw material came from Triple A, the action group formed by Carlos Prío's former education minister, Aureliano Sánchez Arango. A week after the Bay of Pigs Sánchez had yanked Triple A out of the CRC because it "was under complete subordination to a U.S. agency" — the CIA. Sánchez rejected the invasion strategy and advocated a long-range program of underground and guerrilla activity. Since the testy Sánchez would have nothing to do with the CIA, Hemming says the agency funneled money to Triple A through the Howard Hughes organization.

The group was also backed by dispossessed Havana casino operators, among them Mike McLaney of the Nacional. McLaney was not the type to take eviction lying down, and Fidel Castro was high on his list of priorities. The gambling entrepreneur, a fan of Billy Mitchell's, had lined up private planes to drop bombs on Cuba. Coincidentally or not, the original plans for the Bay of Pigs called for fire bomb air raids on the Esso, Shell, and Texaco refineries near Havana. But company officials, hoping to regain them intact after the invasion, pressured the CIA into canceling the raids. "Later, Mike McLaney . . . sent the CIA a detailed plan for knocking out the three refineries," columnist Jack Anderson wrote. "But instead of getting his plan approved, McLaney got an urgent phone call warning him not to attempt such a thing under any circumstances."[28]

McLaney's contact man with the exiles was Sam Benton, who had been his lieutenant at the Nacional. Tall, with horn-rim glasses perched on a sparrowish face, Benton was an adroit gofer. In 1960, when McLaney sued Baltimore Colts owner Carroll Rosenbloom, Benton assumed the role of private detective replete with pearl-handled revolver. Rosenbloom had been a part of McLaney's syndicate that purchased the Nacional, but they had a falling out over an option McLaney claimed to buy into American Totalizer, a system for computing pari-mutuel odds at racetracks. Benton caused a sensational turn in the case when he produced affidavits from three witnesses who alleged that Rosenbloom habitually bet on games in violation of National Football League rules, once even laying $55,000 against his own team.[29]

Benton was something of a commission broker to the exiles. "Sam would never get near anything that might explode," McLaney told the authors. "He lined up actions, arranged to fund and supply them, and took a percentage cut off the top." He was also a bit of a con artist. He set up Cuban Refugee Relief, Inc., but before long police were looking into the fact that 90 percent of the money contributed was eaten up by administrative overhead, notably Benton's salary. Aureliano Sánchez, whom Benton listed as president, told Miami police he had "complete confidence" in Benton but knew little about Cuban Refugee Relief "since his political activities come first and he is always out of Miami."[30]

One action Benton lined up for Triple A was a scheme, hatched a month after the Bay of Pigs, to shell and sink a Cuban ship docked in Montreal to pick up aircraft parts. But an attorney for Triple A and Interpen, Charles R. Ashman, had a better idea. The previous September he had made news by slapping a writ of attachment on the plane that brought Fidel Castro and his party to New York after securing a $429,000 judgment against the Cuban government for an advertising firm that had promoted tourism. Why not wait until the ship was off Cape Hatteras, North Carolina, on its return voyage? Triple A could attack and beach it, and Ashman could attach a lien for the unsatisfied portion of his judgment. Everybody would profit.[31] But the plan collapsed when his CIA contact decided Benton talked too much and cut him off.

Interpen made the papers following an unsolicited announcement by Senator George Smathers, an irrepressible booster of anti-Castro raiders, that Cuban exiles were training in Florida for a second invasion. This prompted Dom Bonafede, the national security-conscious Latin American expert of the Miami *Herald*, to write that he knew all along that Interpen was involved but, "feeling that the story is within the sensitive area of national policy, withheld publication until after the matter was aired in Washington." Bonafede said that Hemming insisted for the record that Interpen was giving a civil defense course.

Before the Missile Crisis the feds looked bemusedly on Interpen, attempting to stop only boats actually headed for Cuba. "When you're good enough to get past us in a free country," one customs agent told Hemming, "then you've got a chance of coming back."[32]

When Kennedy ordered tighter surveillance, however, Interpen's days of license were numbered. This was suggested to Hemming when two Navy pilots from Key West stopped by Nelli Hamilton's. They flew F-4 Phantom jets on low-level photo reconnaissance runs over Cuba, they said, and suddenly had been instructed to make detours over No Name Key and take pictures. They were curious and, upon asking around, found out about Interpen. They had dropped by the boardinghouse to see if there was anything they could do to help.

On the night of December 4, 1962, as the United Press reported it, "United States customs officers captured a giant, bearded soldier of fortune and his band of twelve battle-garbed guerrilla fighters . . . just as they were about to invade Cuba in a rented boat." The last straw apparently had come two days earlier, when Hemming appeared on a Miami radio program, presumably monitored in Havana, to boast about Interpen's exploits. The wire service said the federal agents moved in when they heard the boat's engines start and nabbed Little Joe Garman, Ed Collins, and Bill Dempsey, the one-armed Canadian, along with Hemming and the others. The group was charged with violating the Neutrality Act by "an attempt to form an expedition to invade a foreign country."

Charles Ashman, their ever-inventive attorney, adroitly used truth as a defense, arguing that his Interpen clients were victims of selective prosecution since they had been singled out for prosecu-

tion while other commando units under CIA control went unmolested. The charges against Nelli Hamilton's boys were quietly
dropped.

VI

*I never understood the inner
compulsions of Stalinism until
I went to work for* Life.
  — ANDREW ST. GEORGE

Henry Robinson Luce, Lord High Admiral of the free world's
greatest fleet of publications, believed fervently in God, flag, and
Time, Inc., although not necessarily in that order. His blonde wife,
Clare Boothe Luce, the former ambassador to Italy, was the princess
regent of the respectable right wing. As a pair, Mr. and Mrs. Luce
were face cards at any party. As one, they put down their silver forks
on the dessert china imprinted with the blue of the presidential seal,
and walked out of the White House lunch. Their host, John Fitzgerald Kennedy, had reason to be distressed at this unceremonious
departure. He had arranged this special lunch in the spring of 1963
to convince the bellicose Lucepress to tone down its coverage of the
exile raids and leave Cuba to the devices of the President. The luncheon instead turned out to be the Bay of Pigs of Kennedy's press relations.

Henry Luce believed that a morally slanted press was a responsible press. The manner in which the Lucepress carried out this pre-
cept led the cartoonist Herbert Lawrence Block, known more
familiarly as Herblock, to observe that "it is Mr. Luce's unique contribution to American journalism that he placed into the hands of the
people yesterday's newspaper and today's garbage homogenized
into one neat package." *Life*, the flagship picture book of the Luce
fleet, afforded photojournalism some of its finest moments, while
the text accompanying the pictures that were worth thousands of
words was slanted with an ideological warp sufficient to stir Caxton
in his grave.

Lucepress executives were so anxious to do the bidding of their
patriarch that their editorial commitment overspilled the printed

pages of their publications, and they became spear carriers for the CIA. An instructive example of this interlocking of the free press and the espionage establishment is *Life*'s perennial publisher, C. D. Jackson. At a time shortly after the Dallas events of November 22, 1963, when the agency urgently desired to establish certain parameters of free speech for Lee Harvey Oswald's wife, Marina, Mrs. Oswald received a $25,000 advance for a book never to be published. The advance came from a New York publisher but was actually arranged by Jackson and *Life*'s Edward K. Thompson, through their Dallas representative, one Isaac Don Levine, the dean of American anticommunist writers.[33]

Jackson was president of the CIA's Free Europe Committee in the 1950s and was also special assistant to President Eisenhower for psychological warfare working on anticommunist propaganda for Eastern Europe. (In this capacity he worked with the same Isaac Don Levine, who was then with the CIA's Liberation Committee.)

Drew Pearson wrote in his *Diaries 1949–1959*, a book chock-full of the raw stuff of the fifties:

> *Life* magazine is always pulling chestnuts out of the fire for the CIA; and I recall that C. D. Jackson of the Life-Time empire was the man who arranged for the CIA to finance the Freedom Balloons. C. D. Jackson, Harold Stassen and the other boys who went with me to Germany spent money like money while I paid my own way. I always was suspicious that a lot of dough was coming from unexplained quarters and didn't learn until sometime later that the CIA was footing the bill.[34]

Reinhold Niebuhr, the theologian who shared Luce's Protestant faith, although not its temporal application, has remarked the dangers of the tendency to claim God as an ally for our partisan values as a source of political and religious fanaticism. Niebuhr's gospel is applicable to the Lucepress position on Cuba, which hardened into phobia. From the morning after the Bay of Pigs Luce's publications pushed for a new invasion of Cuba. *Fortune* took temporary leave of its strictly business senses to run a long CIA apologia blaming the Bay of Pigs on JFK's timidity. Clare Boothe Luce, herself no slouch with a pen, wrote that Cuba was an issue "not only of American prestige but of American survival."

In the spring of 1963 *Life* began a one-magazine campaign to congeal American jingoism behind the military adventures of the Cuban exiles. One blood-and-guts cover memorialized with a tilt toward hagiography the men who had fought in the Bay of Pigs. Another fighting *Life* front page heralded Andrew St. George's Caribbean theater-of-war report on the Commandos L attack on the Russian freighter *Baku*. Publicity of this sort swelled the non-CIA-controlled exiles. It was against this background that Kennedy invited the Luces to lunch at the White House. Luce said later that he would never have gone had not Joe Kennedy been such a good friend of his; he accepted the invitation in respect of the father, not the son.

Kennedy exercised all his considerable charm to convince the Luces that their publications should curtail their coverage of the exile commandos. The President did not confide in the beetle-browed king of the weeklies that he had his own plans for military action against Cuba; JFK wanted his Secret War kept secret.

Luce took the opposing view; that the exiles needed transfusions of the ink of the free press to encourage them in their resolve to overthrow Castro. (The talk around the water cooler at *Life* was that Luce had been persuaded by an Italian fascist friend—a man of his social circle—that Castro could be toppled if his opposition didn't become discouraged.)

The luncheon conversation became heated. At one point the nasty nine-letter word "warmonger" was used. This led to Mr. and Mrs. Luce's leaving before they had touched their desserts.

Luce went directly from the White House to the High Arctic of Time-Life's corporate headquarters in New York, where he convened an extraordinary meeting of all his editorial brass. If the United States of America was being chicken, Time, Inc., was declaring war on Cuba. The founder said that despite a corporate austerity program then in effect, they were going all out to assist the exiles in military actions against Cuba. Contact was to be made with principal exile groups to arrange for reporters and photographers to go along on raids. Time, Inc., would provide logistical and financial assistance where necessary, but he did not want the company ripped off the way the CIA had been.[35]

With this directive, Luce, the great editorial innovator, invented a new form of journalism for which he is yet to be credited in standard histories of the printed word. The Founder was taking his gremlins beyond the familiar world of checkbook journalism into the nether reaches of paramilitary journalism.

Life's feuding editorial duchies — the national desk, Miami bureau, and others — took the master's fiat as a competitive call. They constantly tried to upstage one another, spying, usurping credit, and striving to get the most dramatic pictures of the commandos wreaking havoc. Andrew St. George, who went along on most of the raids as *Life*'s unofficial chief war correspondent for the Caribbean theater, estimated that the magazine spent close to a quarter of a million dollars during 1963–1964, a sizable sum in the pioneer era of paramilitary journalism. The Hungarian said that he himself was paid some $50,000 in expenses as *Life*'s main contact with exile groups such as Alpha 66.

The front-line command post was *Life*'s regional bureau office in the DuPont Plaza Hotel in Miami, a magnet which quickly attracted hell-bent-for-action types like Gerry Hemming and Eddie Bayo, who belonged to Commandos L. St. George used the hotel's bar as a watering hole for his exile contacts. "They drank brand-name brands," he said. At first his financial orders were strictly beer budget: "You will give these people money in very small amounts — buy them fried chicken, beer, things like that. Help out as you can, but do not finance the raids as such." Apparently *Life*'s legal department was familiar with the Neutrality Act.

But the expenditures soon became more substantial. *Life* purchased ship-to-shore radios for Alpha 66 and paid commandos for exclusive stories — money often plowed back into the raids. The magazine became so deeply involved that it provided life insurance for commandos and correspondents. To make a claim, the next of kin had to fill out forms referred to by *Life* staffers as "widow papers."

While Luce was launching his private war, St. George was already getting shot at, having boats sunk from under him, and washing ashore on Caribbean isles. When he covered the October 1962 Alpha 66 raid that killed Russians on the eve of the Missile Crisis, it was nearly his final assignment. His boat was sunk, and he had to hide in Cuba as the crisis deepened. Finally, he stole a rickety sailboat and put out to sea. It took him so long to reach a friendly island that *Life* had already given his wife the "widow papers" to fill out.[36]

The Lucepress's paramilitary operations were, of course, top secret and alluded to by those involved by OSS types of code names such as the "Greek Project." In the early summer of 1963, *Life* became involved in a plot to kidnap two Russian officers from Cuba. This scheme was the product of a trinity of conspiratorial interests—frustrated exiles, Luce's increasingly rabid anticommunism, and a CIA cabal—bent on inflicting severe political damage on John F. Kennedy by showing him up as either a dupe of the Soviets or a supreme commander oblivious of a new missile threat in Cuba.

It was code-named Operation Red Cross. It was to lead to one of the most bizarre episodes of the Secret War.

On a June morning in 1963 the sixty-five-foot yacht *Flying Tiger II* left a private dock on exclusive Sunset Island in Miami's Biscayne Bay. A small boat bobbed in her wake at the end of a towline. At the helm was a captain employed by her owner, former U.S. Ambassador William Pawley, a yachtsman of some repute. But this was no leisure cruise. The *Flying Tiger* was on a mission to kidnap two Russian military officers from a Cuban missile site and bring them back to the United States—but not to turn them over to the government. The plan was to debrief them privately at the Gettysburg farm of Pawley's old friend Dwight Eisenhower, then to call in the press and embarrass JFK by displaying the Russkis as living proof that Soviet missiles were still on Cuba.

On board the *Flying Tiger*, as she slipped into the Straits of Florida and swung south, were Rip Robertson and two other CIA paramilitaries, Richard K. Billings, of *Life* magazine, and John V. Martino, a Mafia-connected technician who had once installed security devices in the Havana casinos and later became a co-conspirator with Cuban exiles. Their course would take them to a rendezvous at an atoll off the northeast coast of Cuba, with a seaplane carrying Pawley and the commando squad that would pull off the kidnapping.

The story of the *Flying Tiger*'s secret mission began earlier in the year when a flamboyant guerrilla named Eduardo Pérez, better known as Eddie Bayo, showed a well-handled letter around exile circles. It supposedly had been written by an underground cell in Cuba and smuggled out. It claimed that two Soviet Army colonels stationed in Cuba knew where the Russians had hidden offensive missiles in violation of the Missile Crisis settlement. The officers wanted to defect and gain asylum in the United States.[37]

No one in the exile movement questioned Pérez's credentials. A naturalized American of Cuban origin, he was given the war name Eddie Bayo because in attitude and daring he closely resembled the famous guerrilla war tactician, General Alberto Bayo, who trained Castro's volunteers before they set sail from Mexico to invade Cuba. Eddie Bayo fought under Raúl Castro against Batista. His tenacity in battle was such that he was awarded a medal for bravery that previously had been given only posthumously. After turning against the Castro regime, Bayo became a crew member of the storied CIA gunrunner *Tejana III*. He reportedly was involved in the July 1961 double assassination plot against Fidel and Raúl Castro that came out of the Guantánamo naval base. Later he joined Alpha 66 and participated in raids against the Russians.

Howard Davis, the Interpen instructor, took Bayo's information to New York financier Theodore Racoosin, a man well connected with the White House. Within the week Racoosin was in Miami, telling Davis that a "high official" of the Kennedy administration was interested in getting the two Russians out of Cuba. Davis introduced the financier to Bayo, who now claimed that the Russians were with his underground unit hiding out in the mountains. Racoosin seemed satisfied with the story, but a week after returning to New York he called Davis to say that his contacts in Washington had been unable to find any intelligence reports to support it. He suggested that an intelligence agent accompany Bayo into Cuba to meet with the defectors. But Bayo refused on the grounds his group no longer trusted the CIA. He insisted that he be given a boat, weapons, and support, so that he could go alone.

At this point Racoosin and his White House contact had second thoughts. Bayo might be pulling a con job to obtain money and equipment. Worse still, the story might be a plant, a baiting of the trap. The deal was off. But Racoosin told Davis that his friend in the White House would like Davis to organize meetings of anti-Castro leaders in order to find out what the CIA was doing. The President, it was said, didn't trust the agency and felt he was receiving bad information.[38]

It was through these show–and–tell meetings about the CIA that the matter of the Russian missile officers would pass from the hands of Kennedy's friends to those of his foes.

The first meeting was held in the office of Miami *News* editor Bill Boggs, a confidant of the Kennedys who was their local eyes and ears on the activities of the CIA. Racoosin was there. So were Hal Hendrix, the *News*'s Latin America specialist who was close to the CIA, and Jay Mallin, the old Havana hand for *Time* magazine. Davis had managed to round up a cross section of the anti-Castro movement: Gerry Hemming; members of the action group Student Revolutionary Directorate, which was under CIA supervision; Eddie Bayo; and John Martino. CIA foul-ups were discussed, but the question of the Russian missile officers was not brought up.

A second meeting was held a few weeks later in the office of Jack Gore, editor of the Fort Lauderdale *News*. Racoosin was there, along with Davis, Hemming, and Bayo. This time Frank Sturgis and a sidekick in his International Anti-Communist Brigade were invited. Sturgis was unhappy with the way things were going. After the *Baku* incident he had planned his own attack on a Russian ship, but British marines and Bahamian police had pounced on his men as they assembled on Norman's Cay. The Bahamian authorities, Sturgis was certain, had been tipped off by the FBI.

It was this meeting that brought William Pawley into the picture. The aging millionaire was working on his memoirs with author Nathaniel Weyl, the right-wing ghostwriter whose books in his own name included *Red Star over China* and *Red Star over Cuba*. At the same time the prolific Weyl was commissioned to ghostwrite John Martino's account of his three years in a Cuban prison entitled *I Was Castro's Prisoner*. Through Weyl, Martino arranged for two ex-CIA agents on Pawley's payroll to attend. And through Weyl's good offices he invited two Florida conservative leaders, Congressman William Kramer and Mrs. John H. Perry, wife of the publisher of the Palm Beach *Post-Times*.

Once again the discussion concentrated on the shortcomings of the CIA. When it was over, the participants broke up into small groups. Martino had Bayo show Kramer and Mrs. Perry his report from the underground and tell how he proposed to bring out the Russian officers. Hemming, who was listening, advised caution. "The Russians might have made up some remark about wanting to see the night life of Miami that was overinterpreted," he said. "And it might be an elaborate trap." Hemming noted that the report had been sent in the open mail via Mexico and Spain and that any area where Russians were stationed would be under extremely tight security.[39]

But Bayo's tantalizing story apparently struck a responsive chord with someone who heard it. A short time later Pawley received a phone call from Washington that would set in motion Operation Red Cross.

Pawley's caller was Senator James O. Eastland, chairman of the Senate Internal Security Subcommittee, before which the ambassador had testified in 1959 about the danger of a communist takeover in Cuba. A man named John Martino had been recommended to him, Eastland said, and had briefed him on the Russian officers project. The powerful Mississippi Democrat was obviously impressed. He suggested that what Martino needed was the kind of support Pawley could provide. Eastland was apparently unaware of Martino's Mafia connections.

Pawley was no stranger to secret missions. He had carried out "secret conversations" with Franco so that the United States could put military bases in Spain. At the CIA's request, he made an eleventh-hour visit to Batista late in 1958 to ask the tyrant to resign in favor of a junta backed by the United States in order to head off the imminent Castro takeover of the government; Batista told the founder of the Flying Tigers to go take a flying leap. Pawley told the authors that he also had an eerily similar, heretofore undisclosed, two-minutes-to-midnight meeting with Trujillo a short time before the Dominican dictator was assassinated in a CIA-backed plot. This visit was also at CIA request. He diplomatically suggested that Trujillo abdicate before events overtook him; Trujillo said a furious no. (Accompanying Pawley on his visit to Trujillo was a Miami acquaintance, one Bebe Rebozo, who later was to become famous as Richard Nixon's close friend.) Pawley however was leery of the proposed vigilante project. But he agreed to see Bayo and his Cubans and size up the situation.

The session went reasonably well. Pawley asked tough questions and got satisfactory answers. He wanted details, for instance, of the area around Baracoa in eastern Oriente, where the Russians were stationed—he knew Baracoa from his days as a youth in Guantánamo. Bayo and his men gave answers indicating that they were, in fact, natives of the area.

Pawley called Eastland back and told him it was a high-risk operation that he would have to discuss with Lieutenant General Pat Carter, the CIA deputy director. If he decided to go ahead, he would use his yacht *Flying Tiger* to tow the Cubans' small boat to the Baracoa area. Pawley made an appointment for Eastland to see Carter and, as he revealed later, "arrange for me to bring my boat back into my dock at Sunset Island without having to go through customs or immigration should we be successful in bringing out the defectors."[40]

In the end Pawley sat on his better judgment and decided to go ahead because, he said, of the project's "great importance to the United States." His first shock came when he took a look at Bayo's boat—"a piece of junk," he described it. Out of his own pocket he bought a twenty-two-foot speedboat and two large rubber rafts.

Then Pawley called the CIA. "I consulted Carter," Pawley said, "and he told me he could not become involved, that the CIA could not do anything directly but that he would try to fulfill my request and find me three good men—an armaments expert, a good navigator, and a good radio operator." The three who reported for duty

were the ever-ready Rip Robertson and paramilitaries known only
as Ken and Mike. "I had an excellent radio on board," Pawley recounted. "But I wanted to be in constant touch with the CIA office
in Miami or with the Coast Guard, which could rescue us if anything happened."

William Pawley fumed as John Martino and Eddie Bayo stood
shamefully before him the day before the scheduled departure.
"They told me they had accepted $15,000 from *Life* magazine,"
Pawley said, "with which they had bought the military equipment
that they needed for the voyage and that *Life* was to send along a
reporter and a photographer. As far as I was concerned, that blew
the deal. I couldn't conceive of the U.S. government letting me go
ahead under those circumstances."

Dick Billings appealed to Pawley, who finally agreed to speak to
Life managing editor George P. Hunt. Hunt flew down from New
York. He promised that all film would be turned over to Pawley,
and *Life* would guarantee that no story would be written without
his consent. The promise was put in writing. Pawley called Senator
Eastland and informed him of *Life*'s proposal. Eastland thought it
was all right to go ahead.[41]

The *Flying Tiger* left on schedule with Billings and the three CIA
men on board. Three days later, only hours before the *Flying Tiger*
was due at the rendezvous point, Pawley took off in a Catalina PBY
flying boat chartered from the Aircraft Ferry Company of Fort
Lauderdale, which frequently rented planes to the CIA. Also on
board was British free-lance photographer Terrence Spencer, who
had been hired by *Life*, as well as Martino and Bayo and nine of his
commandos. The only reason Pawley had rented the plane was his
strong distrust of the Cubans, who he feared might hijack the *Flying
Tiger* to Cuba. "I frisked every one of those guys as they got on
board," Pawley said. "At this point I had no assurance of any kind
what type of men I was dealing with—whether they were anti-
Castro or pro-Castro." While the plane was in the air, all the passengers were locked into a center compartment.

When the Catalina arrived at the atoll, however, the *Flying Tiger*
wasn't there. She arrived seven hours later—the CIA navigator had
lost his bearings in the murky weather. Pawley unlocked his state-

room where weapons obtained from the CIA were stored. Rip Robertson gave Bayo and his man a crash course in their use.

Zero hour for Operation Red Cross came on the late afternoon of June 8. A Lahti antitank gun of proven effectiveness against Cuban patrol boats was mounted on the *Flying Tiger*'s foredeck, and she crept toward Baracoa while the three CIA men kept machine guns trained on Bayo, his commandos, and Martino. At nine that night the yacht stopped at a point ten miles off the Oriente city, which, Pawley remembered, was "lit up like a church." The speedboat was loaded with weapons and equipment, and the commandos piled in. Pawley pleaded with Bayo to take only three men to avoid over-loading, or at least to take along rubber rafts, but to no avail. As he stepped into the boat, Bayo asked Pawley for his watch, saying, "I'll be back with it the day after tomorrow."

As Bayo and his men motored off, the *Flying Tiger* turned and headed back toward the atoll. There the *Flying Tiger* tried to establish radio contact with Bayo, but there was ominous silence. When the two days had passed and Bayo's party had not reached the atoll, Pawley radioed Miami and rehired the Catalina to search for them. For five days the plane scoured the waters and shoreline between Baracoa and the atoll, but there was no sign of the missing men. Pawley sadly ordered the *Flying Tiger* to set sail. He returned to Miami without his watch. He never got it back.

Life went without its scoop, and Pawley locked Spencer's photos in the bottom drawer of his desk. Everyone involved had been sworn to secrecy, and it was not until nearly a year later that CIA Director John McCone learned about the ill-fated expedition when families of the missing men asked the State Department for news of their fate. The sons of Luis Cantin, who had gone to war wearing a beat-up fedora, badgered Pawley for indemnification. Eventually the family of Alfredo Mir received a settlement from *Life*.[43]

At this stage of the constant assassination plotting, versatile John V. Martino was acting as a contact man for Johnny Roselli and the Mafia in renewed efforts to find Cubans capable of assassinating Castro. Tony Varona had failed to deliver the poison goods. Although he kept telling Roselli that the CIA's deadly gelatin capsules were still safe in Cuba, his three-man team repeatedly balked at leaving on the grounds that "conditions" were not right. Bill Harvey concluded that Varona was stalling and instructed Roselli to cut him loose.[43]

Roselli was at the time living it up in a luxurious Key Biscayne motel. According to CIA sources, Roselli and Martino were big pals, hosting barbecue cookouts together and racing around in speedboats. The idea of the pills had been dropped in favor of guns. In 1971 Roselli told columnist Jack Anderson that he obtained scoped rifles from Mafia sources, but the CIA insisted on substituting "sanitized" Belgian FAL assault rifles, of the type used by the Cuban Army, and communist ammunition so that if the assassination team were nabbed, it could not be proved it had come from the United States.

The sniper teams recruited by Roselli were based at secluded Point Mary on upper Key Largo. Bradley Ayers, the Army paramilitary specialist on detached duty with the CIA, recalls that during an orientation tour in the spring of 1963 Rip Robertson took him by boat to Point Mary for an overnight stay. The exile leader was a tall Cuban named Julio who, in perfect English, boasted that his teams operated independently, without direct supervision by a case officer. "But from time to time," Ayers wrote in his paramilitary memoirs, "a man called 'Colonel' John Roselli, who worked out of CIA headquarters in Washington, used the team for raids and other clandestine operations. Roselli, like Robertson, was one of the few Americans authorized to actually go on commando missions into Cuba." Ayers at the time had no idea that the daring "Colonel" Roselli of the CIA was actually a Mafia don.[44]

The nature of the "other" operations was revealed to Ayers early the next morning, when he was jolted out of his sleep by the crack of a rifle. "It's just our sharpshooter doing his daily marksmanship practice," Julio explained. "He shoots the sea ravens." To Ayers' amazement the sniper brought down three of the birds at 500 yards. Julio said that the man was rehearsing "for the day when he could center the crosshairs of his telescopic sight on Fidel Castro."

On his first mission Roselli had ridden one of a pair of Swift V-

20S carrying a sniper team to Cuba, but a patrol craft intercepted it and ripped out the bottom with machine-gun fire. The mobster jumped overboard and was rescued by the second boat, which outran the Cubans and made it back. To prevent such interruptions in the future, the CIA gave Roselli special radios tuned to Cuban security channels.

On March 13, a three-man team that had been infiltrated came within an eyelash of success. They had set up a sniper's nest on the grounds of the University of Havana and were set to pick off Castro as he climbed the front steps for a scheduled appearance. But just before the premier arrived, security police discovered the nest and arrested the team.[45]

Roselli at least was having fun. Ayers recalls that about this time he and his wife had as a dinner guest an army friend also working with the CIA, a major named "Wes." He got an unexpected earful. "Wes had been drinking before he got to the house that night," Ayers relates. He and John Roselli, the dapper American agent in charge of the continuing attempts to assassinate Fidel Castro, had been on a weekend binge together. They'd become close friends as they worked together, and with Roselli a bachelor and Wes without his family in Miami, their drinking friendship was a natural extension of their duty relationship." Wes told Ayers that "still more attempts to eliminate Castro were being devised."[46] The lonely army man never knew that his good-time buddy was in fact a mobster.

Roselli told Jack Anderson that he tried twice more with sniper teams, but Castro seemed to lead a charmed existence. Bob Plumlee, the CIA pilot, told the authors that sometime in May he flew Roselli several times to out-of-the-way Bimini Island in the Bahamas for parleys with, among others, ex-Cuban President Carlos Prío, veteran Miami CIA officer Bob Rogers, and Colonel King's deputy, Bill Carr. The Bimini meetings had to do with the sailing of a second private yacht and, according to Plumlee, yet another attempt to kill Castro.

Inside of a week of the *Flying Tiger*'s departure, the *Thor*, owned by Miami industrialist Alton Sweeting, a friend of Carlos Prío, who in 1958 had landed guerrillas from the yacht to back the ex-president's luckless bid to regain power, left Marathon Key with Sweeting at the helm and took up a heading toward Oriente Province. On board was a youthful CIA paramilitary named "Cowboy" who operated out of the Guantánamo base and a squad of Second Front/Alpha 66 commandos.

Also aboard was Bob Plumlee, who had been told by his Dodge case officer, Bob Rogers, that he was going along in case an airplane was "available" in Cuba to fly people out. He was told that the purpose of the mission was to land the commandos so that they could photograph Russian offensive missile sites. But Plumlee noticed a large quantity of explosives on the boat, and overheard talk that the commandos were going to Havana to blow up Castro.

The *Thor* put the commandos ashore not far from Baracoa, where Bayo had disappeared, then returned to Marathon Key. Two weeks later Bob Rogers assigned Plumlee to a "bring out" mission. Plumlee and a copilot took off in a DC-3 registered to an obscure outfit called Regina Airlines and, following a map supplied by Rogers, found a remote airstrip in Cuba. Five men were waiting, one of whom Plumlee recognized as an Alpha 66 commando from the *Thor*. Plumlee dropped them off on South Bimini Island, where they boarded the yacht *Windjammer II* and were taken to Miami. The CIA had apparently found the idea of using private yachts irresistible.

VII

During World War II the Germans counterfeited tons of Bank of England notes with which they planned to wreck the British economy. Hostilities ended before the notes could be put in circulation. Marío Garcia Kohly, a first-class extremist, was confident that he could undermine the Cuban economy with same technique.

The short, wiry Kohly had bulldozed his way into the anti-Castro picture through the good offices of Richard Nixon. In October 1960 he had a memorable round of golf. The foursome was Vice President Nixon, Deputy CIA Director General Charles Cabell, Kohly, and Ed Kendricks, Kohly's CIA case officer. They talked politics down the fairways of the Burning Tree Golf and Country Club, Ike's favorite golf course.

The game had been arranged by Kohly's attorney, Marshall Diggs, through the intercession of the ultramontane former senator from Maine, Owen Brewster, a longtime Nixon ally. Kohly considered it a presidential game. He fully expected that Nixon would be the next President of the United States, and he saw himself as the next president of Cuba. He had organized a De Facto Government of Cuba in Exile, which, Kohly told Nixon, had the multitudes as followers. Nixon listened as Kohly outlined his own invasion plan called Operation Lake.[47]

The Vice President was sufficiently impressed to ask the CIA to cooperate with Kohly. At age fifty-nine, Kohly had a checkered career behind him. His father had served as ambassador to Spain during the presidency of his good friend Carlos Prío. Kohly himself had contested Fulgencio Batista for a seat in Congress, and when Batista took power, Kohly wound up in jail for inflammatory speech making. Then Kohly reflexively opposed Fidel Castro as well. He told Nixon that Castro had put a $1 million price tag on his head; this was largely Kohly's inflationary view of his own worth.

The CIA had previously dismissed Kohly as a blowhard whose only deep commitment was to himself. But with Nixon's intercession the agency felt compelled to hold a round of meetings with him. As a result, Kohly said he "had reason to believe that because of his large and well-organized underground in Cuba" and his status among the exiles, the agency would install him as number one among the exile leadership. It never happened. Kohly was unmanageable, a CIA no-no; besides, his Operation Lake was at cross purposes with the CIA's original Trinidad Plan for the invasion. Kohly bitterly complained that the CIA had "picked his brains" on Operation Lake and on mobilizing guerrilla units, invasion forces, and underground subversion before requesting that he merge with the FRD (Democratic Revolutionary Front), the agency's government-in-exile.[48]

There is considerable doubt that the CIA seriously intended to bring Kohly into the FRD, and the invitation—if it was, in fact, extended—may have been a ploy to stall him. To Kohly this was outrageous. In his view FRD honchos such as Miró Cardona and Sánchez Arango, a former Prío Cabinet member, were "left-of-

center Castroites." Kohly contended that when he balked, the CIA
tried to buy him off with a $500,000 bribe.

From that point on Kohly was an unguided missile. He pestered
everyone he could think of with access to the Kennedy administration and finally gained the ear of Richard Cardinal Cushing of Boston, a close friend of the Kennedy clan. Kohly told Cushing that the
CIA's invasion would fail because communists and sympathizers
dominated the high command. The prelate is said to have conveyed
the warning to JFK and tried to dissuade him from going ahead.

After the Bay of Pigs Kohly rented a large townhouse on Thirty-
second Street in the Georgetown section of Washington next door
to Allen Dulles. This provided a pretentious setting for his efforts
to weld a new coalition. This time he called it the United Organizations for the Liberation of Cuba. For a man with Kohly's illusions
of grandeur, the counterfeit currency scheme seemed just the dramatic stroke to bring him to power in Cuba.

The little man with the big ideas was becoming a big bother to the
Kennedy administration. He had injected himself into the brigade
prisoner issue, and JFK was irritated by Kohly's boasts that he was
backed by the Pope of Rome via Cardinal Cushing in Boston. He
had McGeorge Bundy write the prelate that Mario Kohly was
definitely not his administration's choice for anything. However,
someone high up in the CIA thought Kohly was A-OK.[49]

The counterfeit currency project was the brainchild of a twenty-
six-year old engineering whiz named Robert D. Morrow, who was
employed by a CIA proprietary, Comcor, Inc., to design jamming
and coding devices. As Morrow tells it, he was assigned to help the
Kohly organization under Comcor cover. Since Kohly was out of
favor with the Kennedys, the CIA channeled money to him through
the National Bank of Mexico and a numbered account in the Island
Bank on Bimini in the Bahamas. Morrow recalled hopping over to
Bimini on one occasion to pick up $320,000 that was ready and
waiting.

Morrow figured that by printing large batches of bogus pesos
they could not only "blow the Cuban economy off the face of the
map" but enable Kohly's underground in Cuba to buy arms and

supplies. Kohly thought it was a capital idea. His CIA case officer, Ed Kendricks, checked and reported that although federal laws would be violated, "clearance" had been obtained to proceed. A few months later Morrow proudly showed Kohly a flawless-looking batch of ten-peso notes he said had been run off on plates made with the assistance of engravers at the U.S. Bureau of Engraving and Printing.[50]

Shortly after, Morrow and Kendricks were called in by General Charles Cabell, the lame-duck CIA deputy director who, just prior to the 1960 election, had attended the conference between Kohly and Richard Nixon on the Burning Tree golf links. Cabell, according to Morrow, confided that the CIA was locked in a "feud" with the White House, so that it was necessary to act independently at times.

The general gave Morrow and Kendrick a carbon copy of a hand-written memo by the President which he said had been passed on by one of the Secret Service bodyguards. Morrow claims to have remembered almost its exact words:

Memorandum to Attorney General:

If possible, try to apprehend all Cuban and American personnel currently engaged in manufacturing bogus Cuban currency. As you know, in its efforts to overthrow the Castro regime, the CIA has disregarded our direct orders and placed us in a politically embarrassing position. The names of all parties involved in the conspiracy should be in the agency's files.

Also you might consider leaking to the Cuban authorities that a massive counterfeiting scheme may be launched against them that could jeopardize the Cuban economy.

Cabell said that he had sufficient forewarning to thwart the arrests, but that the same morning word was received from an agent in Havana that Castro had ordered new currency printed in Czechoslovakia. (On August 6, 1961, the Cuban government did, in fact, order all pesos to be exchanged at par for new ones, saying the measure was to remove inflationary pressures from the "hundreds of millions of pesos" held outside Cuba.) They would have to start over. "The job has to be done to perfection in order to fool the Banco Nacional de Cuba's new Russian currency validators," Cabell said. "Then the printing operation begins. My guess is it'll be September of 1963 before we'll have enough currency printed for a sizable operation."

"What if the president or attorney general finds out?" Morrow asked.

"Who's going to tell them?" Cabell replied. "We want Cuba's economy broken before they discover what hit them. Then we deal with Fidel on our terms. . . . "

According to Morrow, the counterfeiting operation was moved to a bungalow in Baltimore already being used for electronic research and was financed through phony CIA contracts. But the *Washington Observer*, a rightist periodical that took up Kohly's cause, reported that in the spring of 1963 Morrow told Kohly that he wanted to go ahead without CIA assistance. "Morrow said his wife could engrave the plates for the new Cuban money," the *Observer* claimed, "but he needed $15,000 for expenses." Kohly got the money from Louis Berlanti, a wealthy Miami contractor who had had properties seized in Cuba.

At this point the government apparently decided to set a trap. A Maryland attorney who professed a desire to help Kohly's movement counseled him that the manufacture of bogus pesos was legal as long as they were to be used exclusively to undermine Castro. He even volunteered to put Kohly in touch with a New York printer who would run off the bills. In June 1963 Kohly and Morrow went to New York to meet with the printer, William Martin. As they left in a cab, Morrow remarked, "He's the damnedest printer I ever saw. I suppose you noticed he was packing a weapon?"

The intrigue thickened on the evening of August 16, when Louis Berlanti and his son Fred took off from Miami in their blue and white Beech Bonanza, filing a flight plan for St. Petersburg. They disappeared. A few days later the Berlantis' bodies were found floating in Lake Okeechobee north of Miami, and some bits of wreckage were retrieved. The condition of the bodies suggested a violent explosion, but no residues were detected in the debris. The cause of the crash was never determined.

Naturally speculation arose that it was sabotage. The Kohly camp was divided between those who theorized a Castro agent had planted a time bomb on the plane and those who suspected a Kennedy agent had done it to cut off their funds. Then the *Washington Observer* injected a sensational note by contending that Berlanti "had been authorized by Generalissimo Rafael Trujillo, the late Dominican dictator, to withdraw $53 million of Dominican funds from a New York bank. Berlanti had $30 million with him when his plane disappeared. The New York law firm of former Vice President Richard Nixon, representing the Trujillo family, is trying to locate and recover the missing millions."

On October 2 the trap was sprung. Morrow had finally finished some plates in three-peso denominations and sent them by courier to Kohly in New York. Kohly arranged to meet William Martin in a hotel room, but as soon as he handed over the plates, Martin announced that he was a Secret Service agent and Kohly was under arrest. At the same time Secret Service agents in Baltimore picked up Morrow and his wife. The three were charged with conspiracy to counterfeit the currency of a foreign government. Kohly bragged to reporters that he had planned to smuggle $50 million worth of the pesos into Cuba.[51]

The Morrows pleaded nolo contendere and received suspended sentences. Kohly pleaded innocent and went to trial. He was convicted and sentenced to two years but jumped appeal bond and continued his private war underground. After nine months he surrendered, then nervily applied for a reduction in sentence. He had a powerful friend in court in Richard Nixon, who wrote on March 9, 1965, to Judge Edward Weinfeld that Kohly, who was of "good repute," and his exiles had "been encouraged and aided by the United States in efforts to overthrow the Cuban Government, and such efforts, in the nature of things, have been covert and sometimes extralegal." The future law-and-order President urged the judge to take these "unique circumstances" into account.

Kohly served only nine months before being paroled by Lyndon Johnson on the condition he desist from anti-Castro activity.

VIII

Paulino Sierra Martínez, a Chicago lawyer proficient in tongues, materialized in Miami in the spring of 1963. The exile movement was dispirited and fragmented by Kennedy's crackdown. The tall, impeccably tailored Sierra invited, one by one, exile leaders to his splendid hotel suite and offered them support for their cause. He said that he represented "wealthy American interests"—he made vague allusions to a Lawyers' Corporation and American bankers—that could furnish money, lots of it, to the exile movement. All they had to do was unify behind a provisional government of Cuba with Carlos Prío as president—and himself, Paulino Sierra Martínez, as secretary-general.

Sierra was an unknown quantity to the Miami exiles. During the Batista regime he had been a high-level civil servant and aide to a Cuban senator. In 1960 he emigrated to Miami, where he taught judo and translated Spanish, French, Italian, and English for a living. The industrious Sierra moved to Chicago, where he passed the Illinois Bar, joined the legal counsel's office of the Union Tank Car Company, a major rail carrier, and founded the Cuban Bar Association, exile division.

Sierra brought with him to Miami an American entertainer from Dallas named William Trull, who frequently performed before Cuban audiences. He later said he felt the Chicago Cuban lawyer was using him to put over his plan. When the FBI became interested in their activities, Sierra and Trull gave conflicting versions of how they had met. Sierra insisted Trull had called him on March 10 after reading a *Chicago Tribune* article about Sierra's influence in Cuban exile affairs in Illinois. When Sierra mentioned his plan for a provisional government, he said the entertainer dropped the names of his good friends the Cleberg family, owners of the huge King ranch, and other Texas millionaires as prospective sponsors. The Clebergs had run an experimental breeding station in Cuba until Castro came along and confiscated 7,600 head of the topics-thriving Santa Gertrudis cattle, and the top management of the King Ranch was permeated with Cuban exiles.

Trull had another story. He said that Sierra initiated the contact and wired him the air fare to come to Miami and push the plan to the exiles. Trull said that when he raised the possibility of Texas financial sponsorship for the provisional government, Sierra scoffed and bragged that "representatives of the Las Vegas and Cleveland gambling interests" had offered him up to $14 million in backing in exchange for a 50 percent interest in gambling concessions in Cuba. All Sierra had to do was organize a successful ouster of Castro.[52]

The day after the *Tribune* article appeared, a man from Los Angeles approached Cesar Blanco, president of the Cuban Bar Association founded by Sierra, and asked how much money would be needed to work out a program to free Cuba. The man disclosed that a "Nevada group" would help out since the U.S. government was "powerless." He even offered Blanco the post of police chief in Cuba. A contemporaneous CIA report, possibly based on information from Blanco, said that the offer was made by "gamblers from the West" and that Sierra talked about $10 million in seed money in return for casino rights.[53]

Sierra was back in Miami in May with bigger and better promises. He told exile leaders Chicago backers were willing to spend $30 million. He tossed out the names of such corporate giants as United Fruit, Esso, Standard Oil, Du Pont, and United States Steel as examples of the polish of his sponsors' brass. Sierra said several high-ranking Navy and Army officers would arrange for arms for training bases for a Cuban invasion in a Latin American country. In reporting on his talks with the exile leaders, the Miami *News* headlined: GAMBLERS POP OUT OF EXILE GRAB BAG.[54]

In June the Chicago office of the FBI interviewed Sierra. It could find no evidence that Sierra had a viable organization. The FBI concluded that he was talking up a "con job" and closed its file. The move was premature. Sierra was just getting started.

Other interests besides the mob saw the efficacy of contingency planning for Cuba. Shortly after his interview with the FBI, Sierra sat in the Chicago Loop office of J. W. Van Gorkam, the executive vice-president of the Union Tank Car Company. With Van Gorkam was his superior, William Browder, the firm's counsel. Their discussion had little to do with the legal affairs of the company except as they might pertain to future business in a capitalist Cuba minus Castro. The Cuban lawyer reported that his Junta of the Government of Cuba in Exile (JGCE), as he now called it, was rapidly taking shape. Van Gorkam and Browder agreed that if the JGCE could attract the right people for Cabinet posts, it might gain financing from corporate sources and the approval of the U.S. government.

The executives were willing to commit the company to the effort to overthrow the government of Cuba. They said Sierra could continue to draw his corporate salary while organizing the junta and could bill Union Tank Car for personal and travel expenses. Browder later told the FBI that although he did not know who Sierra's financial backers were, he insisted on keeping JGCE funds under his control to avoid any possible charges of misappropriation or mismanagement. Browder refused to divulge the amount of money that thus came under his control except to say that it was "considerable."[55]

Sierra hastened to Miami to begin the Tinker Toy process of constructing his exile government. He secured a final commitment from Carlos Prío and obtained the cooperation of José "Pepin" Bosch of the Bacardi rum firm. He stacked up signed pledges from a variety of action groups, among them the 30th of November, the Second Front/Alpha 66 combine, Commandos L, and the increasingly violent MIRR (Insurrectional Movement for the Recovery of the Revolution) under Dr. Orlando Bosch.

Sierra went to Nicaragua to beseech General Luis Somoza for the use of a military base, then on to Colombia to negotiate for the isle of Andrés off the Caribbean coast, and finally he made a loop of eastern cities to meet with potential supporters. The travel slips added up to slightly more than $11,000.

Sierra next saw to stocking his armory. He ordered guns from Rich Lauchli, the Minutemen bigwig, whose Illinois shop was considered the Abercrombie & Fitch of the paramilitary right. The guns were picked up by Steve Wilson, an Interpen instructor and denizen of Nelli Hamiliton's boardinghouse. He went on a $7,000 weapons shopping spree in Detroit and sent for Dennis Harber, another of

Nelli's boys, to help him get his purchases to Miami. Sierra even ordered a two-man submarine from a California company.

Sierra's introduction to the boys from Interpen was through the provisional government's "minister of internal affairs," Carlos Rodríguez Quesada, who had been in contact with Gerry Hemming for some time. Sierra then offered Little Joe Garman, another of Nelli Hamilton's worthies, $11,000 to lead a raid on Oriente Province as part of his grand design of garnering publicity through noisy hit-and-run raids before mounting an all-out war.[56]

During his many Miami comings and goings, Sierra confided to trusted Cubans that despite the smoke screen about big American corporations, his main backing was coming from the gambling syndicate eager to reopen in Havana. It was, on the face of it, a prudent investment for the mob. The mob-CIA assassination attempts were still in progress, and if Castro were killed and his regime fell, there would be a power vacuum that Sierra's JGCE might fill. Sierra's choice of Carlos Prío as head of state could hardly have been objected to by the mob. Prío was a close friend—"bosom buddy," one source said—of Joseph "Sad Joe" Merola, a lieutenant of Gabriel "Kelly" Mannarino, who had sold the Sans Souci Casino in Havana to Santos Trafficante. Before Batista was defeated, Prío had relayed word to Mannarino that Castro would be willing to accept a smaller bite of gaming profits than the greedy Batista (the Cuban government has denied any such agreement). This welcome news prompted Merola and several Mannarino underlings to smuggle stolen guns to Castro's forces, and the casino owners bought "Fidelista bonds" to hedge their bets.[57]

By the fall of 1963 Sierra was spinning his wheels so fast that they almost flew apart. Money was going down the drain with nothing to show for it. The JGCE's minister of external relations, Manuel Lozano Pino, angrily resigned because of what he termed profligate spending as well as the inclusion of such left-wing help as Second Front/Alpha 66. A "military coordinator" sacked by Sierra, Gilberto Rodríguez Fernando, called Van Gorkam and Browder at Union Tank Car and complained bitterly about their employee's style of revolutionary leadership.

Sierra was called on the carpet in Chicago. Browder, surveying the accounts, accused him of squandering some $50,000. He ordered Sierra to turn over all monies and supplies in his possession to Second Front/Alpha 66. Sierra's star had burned out in the revolutionary government's firmament, yet he remained at the center of intrigue in Miami. "Although he has been somewhat ubiquitous among Cuban exile leaders in Miami since March 1963," a CIA memo written two days before President Kennedy's assassination said, "he remains somewhat of a mystery man in terms of his means of support, and indeed, his long range objectives. Perhaps his mysterious backers are providing him with sufficient funds to keep the pot boiling for the present."[58]

IX

The V-20 sped through the darkness to a rendezvous with a mother ship lying at anchor some seven miles off Islamorada in the Florida Keys. "Our Cuban operator expertly turned the craft and came about on the lee side, then maneuvered it beneath the overhanging hull of the looming vessel," recounted U.S. Army Captain Bradley Ayers. "We were surrounded by blackness. Silently, a line was thrown from the deck above us and a cargo net was dropped over the side. We clambered up it and over the cold, slippery rail of the converted World War II minesweeper."

The ship's diesels throbbed to life, propelling a commando team toward Cuba on a mission that had been approved by the Special Group in Washington only that morning. To the north the lights of Miami glowed, and the running lights of a large tanker could be seen in the Gulf Stream shipping lane. "It seemed unreal," Ayers said, "as if I were standing on the edge of the world."

This was a shakedown cruise for the CIA's secret navy. It was June 1963, only days after John Kennedy had okayed the sharp escalation of the Secret War and before the *Rex, Leda,* and other CIA ships were fitted and seaworthy for Caribbean duty. The minesweeper was an improvisation. She flew the Costa Rican flag and was registered as a commercial salvage vessel. She was armed with 40 mm cannons fore and aft and two .50-caliber machine guns. Her wheelhouse was crammed with the latest navigation and communications equipment.

The minesweeper headed for a dropoff point three miles off the northwest coast of Cuba near Bahía Honda, not far from Havana. The commandos were a veteran unit, a remnant of a larger group under the aegis of the Cuban Revolutionary Council that Rip Robertson had led on an unsuccessful strike against the Matahambre copper mine shortly after the Bay of Pigs. They were to go ashore on their rubber rafts and bury four containers at a prearranged site for later retrieval by agents inside Cuba. They would return to the minesweeper the following midnight.

The Bahía Honda area was heavily patrolled, but the mine-sweeper's captain was thoroughly familiar with the routines of Cuban Komar-class patrol boats and even knew the names of some of their captains and crew. "His information on the frequently changed routes and schedules of the coastal patrols was less than twenty-four hours old. He also knew the exact locations of the powerful coastal searchlight and gun placements in the area the team would be infiltrating," said Captain Ayers, who had been trans-ferred from his job as executive officer of the Army Ranger Training Camp at Eglin Air Force Base to work with the CIA on an under-cover basis to train Cuba exiles for the new military fronts being opened in the Secret War.[59]

During the day of waiting for the commandos' return, it was planned that the minesweeper would wander around in interna-tional waters, pretending to be engaged in a sea-bottom survey. For a touch of realism, the ship would trail sampling probes from booms.

As they chugged toward Cuba, Ayers noticed a smaller vessel trailing behind flashing blinker signals. It was a fast seventy-five-foot Louisiana crew boat, originally built to shuttle workers to off-shore oil rigs, and was registered to a dummy petroleum company chartered in Delaware. Supposedly the boat was doing offshore oil research and mapping. Its real role was to decoy Cuban patrol boats away from the minesweeper during the dropoff and recovery oper-ations.

At first all went well. The decoy boat, its lights ablaze and engines running noisily, ran in circles just outside Cuban territorial limits, while a few miles away the minesweeper prepared to disembark the commandos. "All illumination on board the ship had now been extinguished," Ayers said, "and there was only stifling heat and the eerie redness of the blackout lights." The commandos donned dark work clothes and baseball or watch caps.

> Two men carried light packs, one containing rations and the other containing a small, specially developed long-range radio transceiver. With the receiver, they could talk with the mother ship and, under optimum conditions, with CIA reception stations at various locations throughout the Caribbean. The team leader wore a .45-caliber pistol in a shoulder holster, while each of the other men carried a standard M-3 .45-caliber submachine gun and four clips of ammunition. All labels and identifying marks had been removed from the equipment.[60]

In a special kit that included Cuban money was "a special capsule containing a painless, rapidly acting lethal poison."[61] The CIA encouraged suicide as an alternative to capture.

The commandos were landed without incident. The next day the minesweeper and smaller boat went into their "research" pantomime. At midnight the commandos had not returned. Ayers and his crew waited anxiously. Two hours later the commandos' rafts had belatedly reached the rendezvous zone only 1,000 yards off the coast when an onshore spotlight caught them in its beam and heavy machine-gun fire raked the water. One raft made it to the minesweeper. The other was hit and sunk. The minesweeper crew plucked several survivors from the sea before escaping into a rainsquall.

Her captain radioed JM/WAVE for permission to transfer the rescued commandos and Ayers to the smaller crew boat, which flew an American flag. He then took off for Costa Rica at flank speed.

Despite heavy casualties, the mission had been accomplished. After the decoy boat arrived safely at Stock Island, the CIA leaked details of the action to the Cuban Revolutionary Council in Miami—with predictable results. The CRC, limping along without subsidies after being cut off by the Kennedy administration, seized the opportunity to claim credit for the action as a successful arms drop and took a swipe at the President for banning raids.

The exiles kept in the dark never had a clue that Kennedy was running two tracks on them. The next day *The New York Times* reported that the CRC's boastful announcement had set off Caribbean jitters on Wall Street and caused the market to drop.[62] If the administration couldn't control the reckless militarism of these Cubans, somebody might start a war.

Bradley Ayers introduced himself by his cover name of Dan Williams of Paragon Air Service to the tall Cuban called Martínez (no relation to Eugenio Martínez) who answered the door to the dilapidated wooden building of a fish-packing company on the Tampa waterfront. Martínez invited him upstairs to an apartment overlooking the harbor, and Ayers handed over the battered suitcase as he had been instructed by JM/WAVE. As Martínez opened the suitcase and took out stacks of papers and bundles of money, the army captain gazed at the boats moored below. He suddenly recognized them for what they were—CIA V-20 strike boats carefully disguised as fishing craft. The fish-packing company doubled as a surreptitious naval base.

"Would you like to stay for a Cuban supper?" Martínez smiled. "It says here in these papers that you are authorized to accompany us on a little fishing expedition tomorrow night, if you still want to."

Ayers smiled back. He had thought he was merely in Tampa for a stopover on a military flight to his former command, Eglin Air Force Base in north Florida, where he was supposed to evaluate a new high-performance airplane. Now he realized those orders were a subterfuge to get him out of Miami without knowing his actual destination. The minesweeper mission three weeks earlier had convinced the CIA that it was too dangerous to have a mother ship move as close to shore as required to launch the rubber rafts and that it might have better luck with the fast V-20s, which could outrun Cuban patrols and had sufficient range to return to the Florida Keys by themselves.

Ayers was leading an instruction team giving exiles a crash course in running the boats, while the Navy sent in a UDT training detachment to work with him molding Cubans into frogmen. The instructional base was an old mansion on Linderman Key known as Pirate's Lair that had been bequeathed to the University of Miami, which in turn lent it to the CIA. The labyrinth of narrow canals in the mangroves provided ideal hiding places for the V-20s.

Ayers, the paramilitary perfectionist, wasn't satisfied with the state of the training. He wanted to go along on a V-20 raid against Cuba to observe trainees under fire. The American Army captain kept pestering the JM/WAVE brass for permission to go into combat with the Cubans. This was not something the agency would approve up front as it was contrary to all procedures and a highly risky card in the game of "plausibly deniable." But the CIA found a sneaky way to give him his wish. Martínez waved him to the table. Soup was on.

Martínez was one of those singular chameleons of the Secret War, an ordinary businessman who changed into an extraordinary fighter. Ayers observed that Martínez took fish orders while at the same time preparing for the mission: "He struck me as very practical, shrewd and profit-oriented."

They left Tampa in two large trawlers owned by the fish company, carrying the same commando team sometimes used by Johnny Roselli and towing four V-20s. "In keeping with our cover as a commercial fishing operation," Ayers said, "the big nets were hauled aboard twice each day by the booms and groaning winches, and hundreds of pounds of fish, including eels, rays, octopuses, sharks and other strange-looking sea creatures were dumped into the storage lockers."

The trawlers fished their way east along the Cuban littoral to a point twelve miles off Isabela de Sagua. That night the commandos piled into three of the V-20s, and Ayers and Martínez, wearing a gaudy Hawaiian shirt and Bermuda shorts, into the fourth. "With wide collar flapping and spindly legs atop tennis shoes, he was a comical sight in our situation," Ayers said. "Hell, he looked like a drunken millionaire on a midnight cruise off Miami Beach."

The miniature armada swept past a surprised Komar patrol boat on vigil at the harbor entrance, but two of the V-20s struck coral reefs in rapid succession, flinging their occupants into the water. Luckily the rugged boats continued to run, and the raid was carried out. The next day Fidel Castro took time out from feting visiting American college students who had defied a State Department ban on travel to Cuba to announce that a boatload of exile raiders had been captured by gunboats following a sea fight.[63] This was Martínez's raid. The other three V-20s—including the one with the American Army captain—had escaped after damaging a railroad bridge and telephone lines.

The raid demonstrated the utility of the V-20s. They had survived high-speed impact with jagged coral, outpaced Cuban patrol boats, and still managed the long run back to Florida. Still, there were problems. Towing the boats in choppy seas might damage the hulls, and transferring men and equipment in even moderate swells was a tricky, time-consuming task. This problem was solved with the launching of CIA mother ships like the *Rex* and *Leda* that could carry the V-20s on board and lower them to the sea fully loaded via high-speed davits.

The CIA's navy was shaping up in a way that would do *Jane's Fighting Ships* proud. CIA ships at sea stopped at the aptly named Stock Island, where the agency maintained a massive warehouse. The fleet of V-20s and similar small, fast craft expanded, and the agency set up a repair shop off SW 117th Street in South Miami which was busy twenty-four hours a day. "In a matter of hours," Ayers said, "they could convert standard, commercially manufactured boats of various design into rugged fighting or infiltration craft. When the modifications were completed, the boats were painted or rigged to look like common fishing or pleasure craft."[64]

The size and complexity of the program now exceeded Ayers's most optimistic expectations. "The manpower, equipment, and facilities involved—not to mention the many square miles used for training—would have represented a major undertaking at any military facility," he said. "The amazing thing was that we were doing all of this in virtual secrecy amid a very active civilian community."

The CIA's navy was combat-ready in the summer of 1963.

JM/WAVE was abuzz with rumors that big things were in the offing. They were.

X

Johnny Roselli and Bill Harvey consoled each other over drinks. The mobster's "hits" had missed; he was giving up. The CIA man was also a burnt out case—he had been dumped as chief of the Cuban Task Force for his Missile Crisis hijinks. Both men indulged themselves in saying nasty things about Bobby Kennedy. Kennedy's drive on organized crime was now focusing on Sam Giancana and his underlings, including Roselli; the FBI surveillance of Roselli was as tight as a non-Sanforized shirt, and, unbeknownst to Roselli or Harvey, they were being watched.

When the FBI's report of the CIA man and the mobster drinking together was filed, Sam Papich, the bureau's liaison with the CIA, tipped off Harvey that J. Edgar Hoover would soon have to know that the agency was holding hands with the Mafia. Harvey played it cool. He asked Papich to let him know if Hoover was going to tell John McCone. Then he got Dick Helms to agree that McCone should remain in the dark unless the FBI chief intended to enlighten him.

Hoover did not inform McCone—at least not directly. The wise old bureaucratic owl had long resented the very existence of the CIA, the functions of which he had once hoped to assume, and missed no opportunity to embarrass it in public. Information was leaked to Chicago *Sun-Times* reporter Sandy Smith, a "good contact" of the bureau. On August 16 Smith, citing "Justice Department sources," revealed Sam Giancana's link with the CIA. Apparently unaware of the assassination aspect, Smith wrote that Giancana hadn't done any actual spying but pretended to go along with the CIA "in the hope that the Justice Department's drive to put him behind bars might be slowed—or at least affected—by his ruse of cooperation with another government agency."

The story kicked up a fuss, not only because of the unsavory collaboration but also because of the claim that the mobster was making a fool of the CIA. McCone summoned Helms for an explanation. The freshman CIA director was in for another shock. Helms produced the only copy of the May 1962 memorandum from Colonel Edwards to RFK that falsely implied the assassination project had been discontinued sometime before, and McCone learned for the first time that his agency had been involved in a murder compact with the mob. "Well," said McCone, thinking that the ongoing assassination project had been dropped before he took over, "this did not happen during my tenure."[65]

Helms did not correct him. Nor did he add that a separate project to kill Castro had been inaugurated after McCone became director.

James Donovan, the New York lawyer who had negotiated the brigade's release, and RFK aide John Nolan squinted in the bright Caribbean sunlight as they watched the bearded skin diver swim toward their yacht, a fish stuck on his spear gun. The diver was Fidel Castro, sport fishing off Varadero Beach east of Havana, where the premier kept a vacation retreat. A Russian-built patrol boat moved slowly back and forth, guarding against intruders.

It was early April 1963, and Donovan and Nolan had resumed the shuttle diplomacy on behalf of twenty-four Americans, including three CIA contract employees caught bugging the New China News Agency in 1960, still in Cuban jails. Nolan knew that the CIA was "running a kind of program" against Castro—intelligence reports alluding to commando raids often crossed his desk, and Harry Williams would drop by whenever he was in Washington to meet with CIA agents.[66] But neither Nolan nor Donovan had the faintest notion that the agency intended to use them as dupes in a fantastic scheme to assassinate their host.

The scheme was the brainstorm of Desmond FitzGerald, who had just succeeded Bill Harvey as chief of the Cuban Task Force W. If Dick Helms was the Lone Ranger of the CIA, Des Fitz, as he was called, was its Great Gatsby. He had gone to Harvard Law and served with the OSS in China in World War II. Not long after joining a proper law firm and marrying socially prominent Marietta Tree (they were later divorced), he was proselytized by the CIA and became head of clandestine services in the Far East during the 1950s. Des Fitz was an anomaly among his faceless cloak-and-dagger colleagues, batting tennis balls on East Hampton courts and serving as an untiring presence at society parties.

FitzGerald was clearly cut from the Camelot cloth, and he was a natural choice to take over the Cuba Project as the Kennedys put the pressure on. In the Orient he had a reputation for decisive action, and he did not dally now. He decided that Castro should be assassinated. But first there had to be a plan to bypass the premier's tight security. The CIA had learned quite a bit about Cuban security procedures from Donovan and Nolan in the course of providing them with logistical support for their secret trips. Castro rarely adhered to a schedule and frequently did the unexpected. He was always accompanied by his personal aide, Dr. René Vallejo, a Harvard-educated physician. When Castro left a building, guards materialized from all sides. In his jeep he had an AK-47 automatic weapon mounted on the dashboard and an array of guns on the floor. A second jeep with guards followed his closely. On the highway the vehicles hopscotched each other.

Obviously the security was designed to thwart shooting attacks. FitzGerald proposed rigging an exotic-looking seashell with an explosive device and leaving it on Varadero Beach so that it could be detonated remotely when Castro swam by, but the Technical Services Division rejected the idea as impractical. Then FitzGerald's classical mind turned to Greeks bearing gifts, with Donovan and Nolan in the role of unwitting Hellenes. A skin diver's wet suit was dusted inside with a fungus that would produce a chronic skin disease, and the breathing apparatus was contaminated with tubercle bacillus, in plain language tuberculosis germs. The gear would be slipped to Donovan, who would present it to Castro as a gift. The plan had to be abandoned when, as the Senate Intelligence Committee put it in 1975, "Donovan gave Castro a different diving suit on his own initiative."

The failure of the wet suit scheme did not deter FitzGerald. In several months he could come up with one equally as bizarre.

On September 7 Fidel Castro attended a party at the Brazilian Embassy in Havana. He drew aside Daniel Harker of the Associated

Press and warned against "terrorist plans to eliminate Cuban leaders." His eyes flashing, the premier declared: "United States leaders should think that if they assist in terrorist plans to eliminate Cuban leaders, they themselves will not be safe."

Harker's dispatch quoting Castro threw the CIA brain trust at Langley into a tizzy. Only that day a report had arrived from the Brazil station describing a secret meeting in São Paulo with Rolando Cubela, a Castro official who was a CIA agent. Cubela said that he was prepared to attempt an "inside job" on Castro's life as a necessary first step in a coup. Was Castro's caveat at the Brazilian Embassy a signal that he knew of the São Paulo meeting? Was Cubela a double agent?

Major Rolando Cubela had expected to become one of the bright young stars of the revolutionary government after leading his Student Revolutionary Directorate troops into Havana after Batista's fall. But his patron, Carlos Prío, had been cast aside, and he himself was shunted from one middling post to another, winding up as the Cuban delegate to the International Federation of Students. Humiliation gnawed at his enormous ego. By 1961 he was ready to defect.

The CIA had a better idea. With his access to Castro he could be a valuable source within the regime. Also, he might be able to organize a coup, in which case he would be a big man in the new government. Cubela was persuaded. He was given the code name Amlash.

The agency lost contact with Cubela after the Missile Crisis but sought him out again after the June 1963 decision to escalate the Secret War. In a follow-up to the São Paulo meeting, his case officer told him that his assassination-coup proposal was being considered at the "highest level."

It was, but only within a select circle at Langley. Dick Helms was all for it, as was Desmond FitzGerald. John McCone was not consulted. But stiff opposition was voiced by FitzGerald's counterintelligence chief, who considered Cubela a security risk because of his heavy drinking and bragging.

There was already a leak. A Miami FBI informant reported that Cubela was meeting with the CIA and even cited a date and place. The information apparently originated with an exile who was a lifelong friend of Cubela's. Even though the FBI was "friendly," it was a serious security breach. As the 1976 Senate Intelligence Committee report pointed out, Cubela's friend was involved "with anti-Castro exiles and underworld figures who were operating [a] guerrilla training camp in New Orleans."[67] There was no telling how far the news had spread—and to whom.

Since the FBI neglected to advise the CIA that it had a problem, Helms and FitzGerald sent word to Cubela that all systems were go. But the Cuban traitor, perhaps leery of CIA promises, insisted on meeting Bobby Kennedy personally. That meeting was out of the question because only a month before, the CIA had assured Attorney General Kennedy that all assassination plans were defunct. But Helms had a solution: Des Fitz would go, posing as Kennedy's "personal representative." There was no need to ask Kennedy; he had already said to pull out all the stops.

They met on October 29 in Paris, where the Cuban was tending to IFS business, and FitzGerald blandly assured Cubela that the attorney general had committed the U.S. government to the project. Cubela asked that an arms cache, including grenades and a high-powered rifle, be dropped inside Cuba. Then, almost as an afterthought, he asked that a technical means be devised for killing Castro that would not cost him his own life.

Two weeks later the CIA received feedback on the session from an attaché at the Cuban Embassy in Madrid named José Luis González Gallarreta, an agent in place for the CIA. González, code name Amwhip, had been added to the project as a contact. According to González, Cubela "could not understand why he was denied certain small pieces of equipment which permitted a final solution to the problem, while, on the other hand, the U.S. government gave such equipment and money to exile groups for their ineffective excursions."[68]

From FitzGerald's standpoint, it was a legitimate complaint. He instructed the Technical Services Division to invent such a device.

XI

Something big was in the works. Bradley Ayers could sense it at JM/WAVE. He tried to guess what was up as he rode along the Tamiami Trail deep into the Everglades. The CIA Cuban at the wheel wasn't talking. The agency seemed to be going to elaborate precautions to keep him in the dark. His instructions had been only to go to the Kendall Flying School at the Tamiami Airport. He was to wait until a car with a certain license plate drove up. That was his Cuban driver. In two hours on the road he hadn't said a word.

The late-afternoon shadows were closing in on the trees when the driver pulled off the highway onto a dirt road bordering a canal. An airboat was waiting. For the next half hour Ayers skimmed over saw grass. The plane landed at a run-down dock with a sign: WALOOS GLADES HUNTING CAMP. PRIVATE PROPERTY. NO TRESPASSING.

There was a clearing with two small Quonset huts. Two helicopters sat in the shadows. One was a military Bell H-13 with its registration numbers taped over; the other, a civilian model with the name of a West Palm Beach air service on the tail boom. Two men emerged from a Quonset into the flickering light of a campfire. One was Gordon Campbell, the JM/WAVE assistant CIA station chief in Miami. The other was the attorney general of the United States.[69]

Ayers had met RFK once before, at a JM/WAVE cocktail party at a posh Key Biscayne home just after the stepped-up program had been authorized in June. Kennedy had apparently hopped over from the family compound in West Palm Beach to inspect preparations at the Everglades camp. He grasped Ayers's hand and wished him good luck on his mission. Ayers didn't yet know what it was. Then the younger Kennedy got in the civilian helicopter and flew off.

Campbell waved Ayers into a Quonset, which was brightly lit with Coleman lanterns. There were charts, maps, and papers on a table. "We just got the green light from upstairs to go ahead on some missions we've been planning for some time," Campbell said. Permission had been granted to use two-man submarines to attack Cuban ships in harbor, and some of Ayers's UDT men were to participate.[70] This was not as James Bondish as it may seem. In World War II the Japanese had used midget submarines at Pearl Harbor with some success, and later in the war a British midget sub had negotiated the defenses to Singapore Habor and blown up a large Japanese warship. Airborne commando raids also were on the board, Campbell said, and Rip Robertson's group was packing off for Eglin AFB for training. Ayers was to whip into shape a twelve-man commando team to strike at a major oil refinery by mid-December.

The refinery strike was one of thirteen operations, including hits on an electric power plant and sugar mill, that had been okayed by the Special Group on October 24. All were to be carried out by the end of January. On the drawing boards at Langley were "progressively stronger" attacks to last through 1965.

Ayers's refinery raid was to kick off the program. The CIA wanted a winner. After Ayers had been drilling his commandos for two weeks, Campbell summoned him from the Everglades for a drink aboard the CIA executive's yacht. "I want you to understand that the Agency cannot allow this mission to fail," Campbell told Ayers. "Everybody from the President and Special Group on down has his eyes on this one. This is the first important target they've given us the go-ahead on, after months of selling and arguing on our part. If we can hit Castro a couple of good blows like this, he'll fall right on his ass . . . and that's what the President wants."[71]

Campbell mixed highballs, and they drank over blueprints of the refinery obtained from the former American owners. Campbell brought out snapshots of the target recently smuggled from Cuba and U-2 photos of the area on the south-central coast. The plan was more complex and ambitious than previous hit-and-run raids. Mother ships would approach to within a mile of the target, then drop off three V-20s. Under cover of darkness one commando unit would land, creep up on a long pier supporting a pipeline used for unloading tankers, and garrote the guards from behind. With an infrared blinker they would signal the other two V-20s to come and tie up to the pier. Then the commandos would lay down a mortar barrage on the brightly lit cracking towers and storage tanks, setting off a monstrous explosion. As they withdrew, they would attach time-delay demolition charges to the pier and pipeline.[72]

It was a commando raid straight out of World War II textbooks. The down-to-the-last-bullet details were approved by Bobby Kennedy, who never forgot that he had been left out of the Bay of Pigs planning until it was too late. There is, of course, a certain incongruity to the picture of the attorney general of the United States, counselor to the President and shaper of administration policies, mucking about in the swamps and poring over battle charts by the light of Coleman lanterns. But this was the existential Robert Kennedy, who, as former Undersecretary of State George Ball expressed it, was "fascinated by all that covert stuff, counterinsurgency and all the garbage that went with it."[73] It was the same Robert Kennedy who, in his war on organized crime, liked to ride around the streets of New York in FBI cars. He was as determined to precipitate Castro's demise as was the mob, and it was entirely in character that he wanted to get a feel of the action and to personally spur on the troops.

But for Jack Kennedy, the raids would provide some political options in the upcoming 1964 reelection campaign. History was repeating itself in its usual droll way. In 1960 JFK had seized the offensive on Cuba while Nixon, privy to the pending invasion, had to sit on his hands. Now Nixon, the emeritus Republican leader, and nominee Barry Goldwater were stalking the land, using against Kennedy such buzz words as "Soviet beachhead" and "Castro's exportation of the revolution." Cuba would definitely be a major issue, and the raids could considerably strengthen Kennedy's political hand.

The program was just about at the go. The CIA's navy was operating in the Caribbean. Manuel Artime's Second Naval Guerrilla was nearing readiness in Central America. And Harry Williams was shuttling between Miami and Washington, finalizing details of his vanguard assault force, based in the Dominican Republic, which could be unleashed once the stepped-up raids helped conditions inside Cuba deteriorate to the point where the regime lost control.

Meanwhile, a clandestine operation from which the CIA was deliberately excluded was being conducted from the White House. It was an alternate solution to the Cuban problem, what its originator, McGeorge Bundy, called a "separate track." It was one of many tracks the secretive Kennedy brothers—trusting neither the exiles nor the CIA—were running in the fall of 1963.

The separate-track idea had first been broached the previous April, when Bundy submitted a memorandum to the National Security Council Standing Group on Cuba offering "possible new directions" for American policy, among them moving "in the direction of a gradual development of some form of accommodation with Castro." In early June the Special Group also agreed it would be a "useful endeavor" to probe "various possibilities of establishing channels of communication to Castro." But two weeks later the President authorized the intensified sabotage effort, and there the matter rested.[74]

Then, in September, the Guinean ambassador to Havana told William Attwood, Kennedy's special adviser for African affairs at the United Nations, that Castro was unhappy with Cuba's Soviet satellite status and was looking for a way out. The report coincided with hints Attwood had received from other sources that Castro was growing restive under Soviet pressures and was ready to make "substantial concessions" to achieve an accommodation with the United States. In addition, there was the CIA report—later proved false—of a rift between Castro and Che Guevara, who was said to regard Fidel as "dangerously unreliable" from an ideological standpoint. Attwood thought this plausible since he himself had interviewed Castro as a journalist in 1959 and judged him "too emotional to be a disciplined Communist."[75]

It was the first American overture Castro had made since being rebuffed by Nixon in 1959. Attwood suggested to Adlai Stevenson and W. Averell Harriman, the assistant secretary of state, that discreet contact be made with the Cuban Mission at the UN to determine "if in fact Castro did want to talk on our terms." JFK, who was simultaneously approached by Stevenson, approved of Attwood's conferring with Dr. Carlos Lechuga, the Cuban chief of mission, as long as it was clear "we were not soliciting discussions."[76]

The course was perilous for both Kennedy and Castro. The militant exiles and their conservative American allies would be outraged if they got wind of it, and Castro could expect stiff, if not violent, opposition from his left flank.

The negotiations were held in the strictest secrecy on both sides. Acting as intermediary was ABC newswoman Lisa Howard, who had interviewed Castro the previous May and was trusted by him.[77] Sometime later when Robert Kennedy was in New York running for Kenneth Keating's seat in the Senate, Lisa Howard openly campaigned against Bobby and for Keating. Friends said she had learned from Cuban sources that all the while she was talking peace to Castro for the Kennedys, the morally flexible brothers were indulging in invasion and assassination plans against him. She later died, a reported suicide.

While Attwood and Lechuga talked at the UN, Howard and Dr. René Vallejo, Castro's personal aide and confidant, were in touch by long-distance telephone. The discussions went smoothly, to the point where Vallejo told Howard that Castro would like Attwood to come to Cuba. An unmarked Cuban plane would fetch him at Key West and fly him to Varadero Beach, where talks could be held in seclusion. On November 18 Attwood, acting on the President's instructions, phoned Vallejo to propose that preliminary negotiations be held at the UN after an agenda was worked out. Vallejo agreed.[78]

Everything was now building toward a climax. Bundy told Attwood that the President wanted to see him about the next move "after a brief trip to Dallas."[79]

It was November 21, 1963.

SIX

The Mystery of 544 Camp Street

*I now fully realize that only the powers
of the Presidency will reveal the secrets of
my bother's death.*
                        —ROBERT KENNEDY,
                              June 3, 1968,
                  two days before he was shot

I

IT is not to detract from the reputation of New Orleans as the fun spot of the Southern Rim to suggest that to many of the loyal readers of the New Orleans *Times-Picayune* the news in the summer of 1963 was largely devoid of good cheer. The paper was full of stories about John F. Kennedy's new wave of civil rights policies, which were not greeted with universal approbation in the parish city, and dispatches about the progress of arms control negotiations in Washington and Moscow, two capitals that remained in little more favor in the modern South than in the preceding century.

There was, however, in the first edition of the *Times-Picayune* of the first day of August of that year a local item of international implications that seemed on first reading to be good news. CACHE OF MATERIAL FOR BOMBS SEIZED, the headline read. The FBI in its preliminary announcements of the arms raid said that the contraband grabbed was part of the bureau's ongoing investigation of a plot "to carry out a military operation against a country with which the United States is at peace." The joy diminished considerably when it became evident several editions later that the country in question was Cuba.

The previous day FBI agents had raided a pink cottage in a sparsely settled resort area north of nearby Lake Pontchartrain and confiscated more than a ton of dynamite, twenty 100-pound aerial bomb casings, bomb fuses and striker assemblies, a 50-pound container of Nuodex, and all the stuffings to make napalm.

The New Orleans FBI chief, Harry G. Maynard, a square-jawed cop out of Dick Tracy who combed his black hair straight back and parted it down the middle, refused to comment beyond the bare facts of the raid. He would not speculate if the target country was Cuba. He declined to say if arrests were imminent. There was reason enough for that since the FBI had already thrown the alleged criminals back into the intelligence swamp of the CIA. They were not small fish.

Cuba became the target apparent when newsmen questioned the wife of the vacation cottage's owner, William Julius McLaney, a businessman, formerly in the business of gambling in Havana, Cuba. "If it weren't for that goddamn Castro," William McLaney had once said, "Caesar's Palace would have been built in Havana."[1] Mrs. McLaney said that she and her husband had lent their summer place to a Cuban newly arrived in New Orleans named José Juárez. She said that she personally did not know José Juárez. They had turned over their retreat as a "favor to friends" they had known in the good old days in Havana. As to the kinds of people Mr. Juárez might be associating with on their front porch, Mrs. McLaney said that her husband was "such a good-hearted guy that he didn't ask any questions."

The FBI had grabbed eleven men at the resort bomb site and then released them without charges. Among the Lake Pontchartrain Eleven released by the FBI was Sam Benton, a middleman between the gambling interests and the Cuban exiles whose belt was cinched on the mob side. Benton was a sort of impresario of revolution who specialized in finding funding, usually in the shade of the law, for exile enterprises, and who took a finder's fee off the top. Benton in the fifties had worked in the Havana casinos and described himself as a "commission broker in Latin American commodities"—which included goods not listed on any exchange. He was also described, in testimony before a Senate rackets committee, as "a dealer in counterfeit money, both domestic and foreign, [who] has been involved in dealing with stolen securities and other securities closely associated with . . . gamblers in Miami."

Another individual but briefly inconvenienced by the FBI's raid on the rural napalm factory was Rich Lauchli, a baby-faced tough guy, cofounder of the fanatical Minutemen and an Illinois arms purveyor who had previously supplied guns to the mob-financed, Chicago-based provisional government of Paulino Sierra for a Castro-less Cuba. Most of the others caught up in the FBI net were Cubans. Mrs. McLaney's mystery guest, Mr. Juárez, was not to be found.

As with so much of the Secret War, the Lake Pontchartrain raid was evidence that circles existed within circles. The most violent and rabidly rightist of exile elements, feeling that JFK had betrayed them, were turning to the mob and the radical paramilitary right wing for help in a war that was to turn against the government itself. While JFK was slapping these unauthorized exile operations down with his left hand, they were getting a little help from the CIA's right hand.

The Lake Ponchartrain plot was bigger than the FBI's Maynard had let on. The chain of events leading to the Lake Pontchartrain bust began in Miami on June 14, when a tipster told the FBI "that a group of Cuban exiles had a plan to bomb the Shell refinery in Cuba." The next day customs agents, apparently alerted by the FBI, arrived at an abandoned airfield south of Miami just as a twin-engine Beechcraft was about to be loaded with two 250-pound bombs, 300 sticks of dynamite, 55 gallons of napalm, and a supply of grenades and M-1 rifles. Benton was there, along with four of the five Cubans later nabbed at the McLaney cottage. They were briefly detained.

This raid also made the papers. The pilot had flown in from another state and was headed for a bomb run on the industrial complex in Cuba before flying on "to a friendly Central American country," the Miami *Herald* reported. An FBI follow-up report on October 3, 1963, from Miami to headquarters stated: "It was ascertained that Michael McLaney supplied the money and explosives for this operation." Mike McLaney, the former Havana casino operator who used Benton as his contact with the Cubans was William McLaney's brother and business partner.

Mike McLaney's faith in victory through air power had been frustrated. Shortly after the Bay of Pigs he had submitted a plan to the CIA to fire-bomb the Shell, Esso, and Texaco refineries. Top brass said no. This time McLaney was ignoring channels.

On July 19 the FBI's informant "advised there was another plan to bomb Cuba, using bomb casings and dynamite located on the outskirts of New Orleans, Louisiana." That tip sent the FBI to the McLaney cottage — a trip which in turn caused the hurried evacuation of another nearby exile training camp that the bureau evidently did not know about. The camp had been set up a year earlier by Gerry Hemming and Frank Sturgis at the request of the New Orleans branch of the Cuban Revolutionary Council.

At the time of the FBI raid Sturgis's training camp was occupied by the Christian Democratic Movement (MDC) under the guise of training security guards for a lumber mill in Guatemala. But the MDC military chief, Laureano Batista, later admitted to the New Orleans district attorney that the trainees actually were destined, with the approval of General Somoza, for the CIA-supported naval guerrilla base of Manuel Artime in Guatemala.

The camp was used by various groups of the exile far right — the DRE, 30th of November Movement, and MIRR — all of which huddled under the wing of Paulino Sierra's short-lived, mob-connected provisional government. In 1976 the Senate Intelligence Committee disclosed that the camp "was directed by the same individuals who were involved in procuring the dynamite the FBI seized," a reference to Rich Lauchli and Sam Benton and his Cubans, who had moved from the moribund Triple A to the growing MIRR of Dr. Orlando Bosch,[2] a fanatical ex-pediatrician so far to the right that he considered the Miami *Herald* a tropical edition of the *Daily Worker*. He had fought in the revolution but was one of the first to turn against Castro. In the pre-Bay of Pigs era, MIRR operatives were trained in sabotage by the CIA and infiltrated into the Escambray Mountains, where they were supplied by Sturgis's boat runs.

While other exile leaders sought the limelight, Bosch worked in the shadows and was particularly close to the murderous Operation

40. But he quickly became convinced that the CIA was using the exiles ineffectively. Bosch rebelled early in 1963, when the agency sliced one of his major infiltration operations down to one five-man crew. "We will do this if you send your mother with us," he told the case officer. He published an angry pamphlet, *The Tragedy of Cuba*, charging the Kennedy administration with betraying the exile cause. The House Select Committee on Assassinations reported that he sent a personal copy to President Kennedy.[3]

Bosch combined his operations with Frank Sturgis's International Anti-Communist Brigade, whose ranks included a swashbuckling commando named Alex Rorke. (Rorke was the son-in-law of Sherman Billingsley, an ex-Oklahoma bootlegger whose Stork Club in New York was frequented by such celebrities as J. Edgar Hoover and Joe DiMaggio.) In March Sturgis, Rorke, and the MIRR military chief, Major Evelio Duque, took off in Rorke's cabin cruiser, *Violynn III*, intent upon lining up a Soviet tanker in the sights of a deck cannon they had borrowed from the Minutemen. But someone had tipped off the FBI, who notified Bahamian authorities. *Violynn III* was impounded by British police upon arriving at Norman's Cay for refueling.

Bosch's collaboration with Sturgis resulted in eleven air strikes against Cuba, beginning on April 25, when Rorke dropped a spray of bombs on the Shell and Esso refineries near Havana. *The New York Times* termed this "the first bombing raid since the Bay of Pigs." But after the twin raids at the Florida airfield and Lake Pontchartrain, Bosch came to the conclusion that he would be better off out of range of a schizoid government that was doing in its own troops. He announced that the MIRR would thereafter launch its air raids with three twin-engine planes based in Central America, "where the host country approves." Ex-MIRR pilot Carl M. Davis has since identified the country as Guatemala, where an airstrip was hacked out of a half-million-acre jungle plantation owned by United Fruit.

Bosch's flight commander was a friend of Sturgis's who had done contract flying for the CIA. Sturgis's buddy lined up the pilots, paying them $2,000 a mission (he charged Bosch $4,000) and selected the targets: a MiG base at Santa Clara; oil storage tanks near Casilda; the huge Brazil sugar mill. Bosch had to furnish the planes as well, and it cost him dearly. No one seemed to know where the money came from. Some funding for Bosch came from Paulino Sierra's provisional government and its gambling-interest backers, but this wasn't enough to keep Bosch in the military manner to which he was becoming accustomed. Pilot Howard Davis, an Interpen instructor, says that Mike McLaney himself was "all flaps and no throttle" when it came to putting up money. For a time speculation centered on Carlos Prío, who had openly voiced support for Bosch.

It eventually became known that the major backer was H. L. Hunt of Dallas. Hunt, a millionaire who ate brown bag lunches, was the benefactor of countless right-wing causes. Tony Veciana, who was negotiating for Alpha 66 for the use of MIRR airplanes, remembers an incident when his CIA contact, Maurice Bishop, summoned him to Las Vegas. "We were in a hotel and Bishop left to do something," Veciana said. "In his briefcase I saw a memo with the plans we were doing, movements to contact, the activities of commando groups in Texas. The memo had the initials 'To HH.' There was a millionaire in Texas, very conservative. I thought, since Bishop was so right-wing himself, maybe he was in contact with the millionaire. Other times I think he works with Howard Hughes [who had not yet arrived in Las Vegas]."[4] During a 1968 trial of Bosch's group in Miami, a telephone tape transcript was introduced in which Bosch indicated that a Mr. Hunt—"the one of the wells"—was providing backing.

Orlando Bosch remained the mystery figure, the behind-the-scenes manipulator flitting in and out of the country on his errands that almost invariably were lethal. Many of Bosch's early associates, such as Alex Rorke, met violent or mysterious deaths. On September 30, Rorke took off from Fort Lauderdale airport in a blue and white twin Beechcraft and banked south. With him were pilot Geoffrey Sullivan and a Cuban exile. Rorke had filed a flight plan for Panama, although he had told his wife that he was going to Nicaragua to confer with General Somoza about an important export venture. There was later speculation that he was on a secret mission for Bosch.

A few hours later the Beechcraft refueled at Cozumel off Mexico's Yucatán Peninsula, took off again, then vanished, as in poof! Gone.

No one ever learned what happened to the Stork Club Kid, except that it was, for him, the end of the good times. Frank Sturgis heard a rumor that the craft had been shot down by Castro. Gerry Hemming is convinced that the Cuban passenger was a double agent who hijacked the plane to Cuba. There is the additional theory that the socially well-connected Rorke—who had once been an FBI employee—was the anonymous informer who repeatedly tipped the bureau about the *Violynn III* mission, the bombing run from the Florida airstrip, and the bomb cache at Lake Pontchartrain—all Bosch-directed plots. Bosch found out, the story goes, and sent Rorke on a flight to oblivion.

Among the mysteries of Lake Pontchartrain is why the FBI—otherwise diligently following JFK's orders to crack down on the Neutrality Act violators—would release the Lake Pontchartrain Eleven and attempt to cover up the fact that they had been detained in the first place. One answer lies in the Secret War connection between the McLaney summer cottage and the other nearby exile training camp, and a dingy office building on Camp Street in downtown New Orleans, where the right flank of the Cuba Project went bump in the night with creatures of various persuasions.

II

W. Guy Banister, a salty, snappish man with wavy gray hair, was the boss of the Chicago FBI office until his retirement in 1955. He was not the typical FBI clone. He wore a .357 Magnum revolver under his coat, said unmentionable things about headquarters ("The bureau and the field have been living in adultery for years"), and religiously defied J. Edgar Hoover's two-martini limit. When he retired, he became a New Orleans police official. He was sacked for shooting off his gun in a bar, and then he opened a private detective agency called Guy Banister & Associates at 544 Camp Street.

A onetime Banister associate described the business in a manner not easily categorized in the Yellow Pages: "Guy participated in every important anti-Communist South and Central American revolution which came along, acting as a key liaison man for the

U.S.-Government-sponsored anti-Communist activities in Latin America."[5]

During the Bay of Pigs mission, Banister collaborated with the New Orleans delegate to the Cuban Revolutionary Council, Sergio Arcacha Smith, an immaculate man with a pencil mustache who had served in the Batista diplomatic corps. Arcacha's office was located conveniently across the hall from Banister's in the 544 Camp Street building and was known as the Cuban Grand Central Station. Arcacha created the Crusade to Free Cuba in order to solicit donations in the Anglo community. With Banister as an incorporator, Arcacha also formed the Friends of Democratic Cuba with outwardly similar goals. Ronnie Caire, Arcacha's public relations coordinator at the time, has revealed that the Friends doubled as "an undercover operation in conjunction with the CIA and FBI which involved the shipment and transportation of individuals and supplies in and out of Cuba."[6]

The building at 544 Camp Street had figured in the planned diversionary strike and provocation during the Bay of Pigs. The munitions in the *Santa Ana*'s hold had been procured by Arcacha and Banister. A week earlier Arcacha and two CIA contract employees, David Ferrie and Gordon Novel, had picked them up at a Schlumberger Well Services Company bunker outside New Orleans. Novel later described the bunker as "a CIA staging point for munitions destined to be used as part of the abortive Bay of Pigs attack." The munitions were stored temporarily at Novel's and Ferrie's residences — and Banister's office. A close friend of Banister's recalled seeing numerous wooden crates stenciled "Schlumberger" in the office. "Five or six of the boxes were open," he said. "Inside were rifle grenades and land mines and some little missiles I had never seen before. When a friend warned Banister that possession of the munitions might bring trouble, Banister said that no, it was all right, that he had approval from somebody. He said the stuff would just be there overnight, that somebody was supposed to pick it up. He said a bunch of fellows connected with the Cuban deal asked to leave it there overnight."[7]

The *Santa Ana* mission failed when the rebel impostors got cold feet about attacking U.S. forces directly, which would have provided a pretext for full-scale American intervention. Banister's clandestine activities intensified after the Bay of Pigs. A frequent visitor to his Camp Street office was Colonel Orlando Piedra, the ex-chief of Batista's secret police, a highly feared man who may have been involved with Operation 40. Among their discussions were assassination plots against Castro. According to one exile who sat in on a conversation between Banister and Piedra, one of the plots under consideration involved "putting poison in the air-conditioning ducts in the Havana Presidential Palace and killing all occupants."[8]

Jerry Milton Brooks, a former Minuteman who was a political researcher for Banister during this period, says that the ex-FBI man became Louisiana coordinator for the Minutemen. Banister was also instrumental in the Anti-Communist League of the Caribbean, a pet project of Nicaragua's General Somoza, and was part of a global network of right-wing hard-liners. The Anti-communist League of the Caribbean was one of a global family that originated with the Asian People's ACL, a creature of the Nationalist Chinese, and included the pro-Batista ACL of Cuba and the Chicago-based ACL of America. Banister's associate, attorney Maurice B. Gatlin, Sr., of New Orleans, was counsel to the ACL of the Caribbean as well as a member of the steering committee of the umbrella World ACL, along with Richard Nixon's good friend Alfred Kohlberg of the China Lobby. The ACL affiliates engaged in propaganda and lobbying and collaborated with the intelligence branches of their respective governments.

Banister was also prone to racist comments. He published a smear sheet called the *Louisiana Intelligence Digest* that labeled the civil rights movement as communist-inspired and hurled imprecations at John Kennedy for his "pinko" support of blacks. The ex-Chicago FBI chief also had a network of young informants on the Tulane and Louisiana State campuses. Banister collected information on the left from every imaginable right-wing source, amassing what he proudly hailed as the largest file system of "anti-Communist intelligence" in the South. Jerry Brooks regularly couriered this data over to the New Orleans FBI office, which incorporated it into its files.[9]

Jerry Brooks said that Maurice Gatlin, who regarded him as a protégé, often bragged about his dual life. "I have pretty good connections," Gatlin asserted. "Stick with me—I'll give you a license to kill." One connection was the CIA, for which Gatlin said he was a "transporter," arranging the movement of people in and out of the country and delivering money abroad. "He showed me his passport," Brooks recalled. "It was filled with the stamps of airports all over the world." On one occasion Gatlin displayed a thick wad of bills, saying that he was going to Paris to give the money to a French Army clique preparing to assassinate Charles de Gaulle.[10]

During the summer of 1963 a clean-cut ex-Marine named Lee Harvey Oswald began passing out pro-Castro literature on the streets of downtown New Orleans. One batch of pamphlets was rubber-stamped with the return address "FPCC, 544 Camp St., New Orleans, La." It was the address of the small weather-beaten Newman Building at the corner of Camp and Lafayette streets. On the ground floor was Mancuso's Restaurant. On the second floor was the vacated office of the Cuban Revolutionary Council—Arcacha had departed for Texas the year before following a rhubarb over missing funds. Also on the second floor was Guy Banister & Associates. The security-minded Banister used a side-entrance address of 531 Lafayette Street.

For Oswald to receive left-wing mail at the right-wing Camp Street building would have been tantamount to Madalyn Murray O'Hair's having an office at the Vatican. The missing link between Oswald and the paramilitary right wing was David William Ferrie, the sometime CIA operative who had helped remove the munitions from the Schlumberger bunker and who was extremely close to Guy Banister. Former New Orleans DA Jim Garrison, no stranger to hyperbole, once called Ferrie "one of history's most important individuals." He was certainly one of its strangest. Ferrie was a moth to the light bulb of anticommunist causes. In 1950 he offered his services to the U.S. Air Force, saying, "There is nothing that I would enjoy better than blowing the hell out of every damn Russian, Communist, Red or what-have-you." An Eastern Airlines pilot, Ferrie became commander of the Falcon Squadron of the Civil Air Patrol. In 1956 a high school student named Lee Harvey Oswald came briefly under his wing; there is a formal photograph of Oswald in Ferrie's unit looking somber in his CAP uniform and cap.

Ferrie got into the anti-Castro action early. He flew fire bomb raids in 1959 in the pay of former Cuban Congressman Eladio "Yito" del Valle, who had piled up a small fortune smuggling cigarettes and contraband in partnership with Santos Trafficante, the well-known Mafia figure. Ferrie was psychologically devastated by the Bay of Pigs. In a speech before the Military Order of World Wars, he ranted on so bitterly about Kennedy's "double cross" of the invasion that members of the audience walked out. He was obsessed with how the CIA bungled the invasion and would sketch on a blackboard where the battle plans had gone sour for the benefit of his roommates. An Eastern colleague recalled Ferrie was convinced that "the communists" were out to get him.

But he had friends. Not long after the Bay of Pigs, Arcacha Smith wrote to Captain Eddie Rickenbacker, Eastern's chairman, praising Ferrie's work for the CRC in purging dissidents. Arcacha urged Rickenbacker to grant the pilot an extended leave with pay "so that the work at hand can be completed." This became unnecessary when Eastern fired Ferrie for being a homosexual. Guy Banister flew to Miami to put in a good word for him at the dismissal hearing.

Banister then took Ferrie into his firm. Ferrie's talents were catholic — medical dilettante, Greek scholar, sidewalk lawyer. One of Ferrie's clients was Carlos Marcello, the New Orleans Mafia chieftain. Marcello in 1961 had been deported to Guatemala by the Immigration and Naturalization Service. He slipped back into the United States in February 1962. The Little Man, as the short Marcello was called, was due to go on trial in December 1963, and Ferrie was assisting in the defense.

Ferrie was a hairless man who wore an ill-fitting red wig and pasted-on eyebrows. He religiously attended to his anti-Castro duties. He became an instructor at the Lake Pontchartrain camp when it opened. He told associates that he was training Cuban guerrillas and flying to Cuba and back with passengers, using the Florida Keys as an intermediate stop. And he confided to one of his CAP cadets that he was training five-member small-weapons units in "guerrilla warfare tactics under the auspices of the U.S. Marines for action in Cuba."

On August 5, only five days after the FBI raid on the Lake Pont-chartrain camp, Oswald showed up at a store run by Carlos Brin-guier, the local DRE representative who had helped in the evacuation of the Christian Democrat trainees from the lake. Displaying a Marine manual, Oswald told Bringuier he "had been in the Marine Corps and was willing to train Cubans to fight Castro." A friend of Bringuier's who heard the conversation recalled that Oswald boasted he knew "a few things about guerrilla warfare. . . . He said the thing he liked best of all was learning how to blow up the Huey P. Long Bridge."[11]

Bringuier could therefore hardly believe his eyes when he spotted Oswald on the street a few days later dispensing his pro-Castro literature. There was a heated exchange of words, then a scuffle. Both were jailed for disturbing the peace. Oswald put in a call to his uncle, Charles "Dutz" Murret, who had been his surrogate father in the formative years, seeking the $25 bail. Murret, who is described by the House Select Committee on Assassinations as an associate of "significant organized crime figures affiliated with the Marcello organization," wasn't home. But his daughter contacted family friend Emile Bruneau, a big-time gambler, who arranged for the bail to be posted.[12]

After the fight a Cuban Revolutionary Council public relations man named Manuel Gil set up the famous radio debate between Oswald and Bringuier in which Oswald declared on August 21 over WDSU, the local NBC affiliate, "I am a Marxist." Three months later those words would be rebroadcast, this time to the nation, after John Kennedy was shot.

The debate contributed to a well-established belief that Oswald was in fact a committed Marxist who had tried to infiltrate Bringuier's group. But information compiled by the authors and by the House Select Committee on Assassinations suggests it was all a charade. Guy Banister's widow has revealed that her husband's office storeroom contained a supply of the "Hands Off Cuba!" handbills that were distributed by Oswald. George Higgenbothan, one of Banister's collegiate undercover agents, recalled that when he kidded his boss about sharing a building with people papering the streets with leftist literature, Banister snapped, "Cool it—one of them is mine."[13]

The House Select Committee on Assassinations investigators discovered in 1979 that Jack Mancuso, proprietor of the restaurant below Banister's office, served Oswald as well as Banister—both were frequent customers. And Delphine Roberts, Banister's longtime secretary, told the House Select Committee that she "saw Oswald in Banister's office on several occasions, the first being when he was interviewed for a job during the summer of 1963." It seems less than coincidental, then, that Oswald landed a job at the Reily Coffee Company, a firm less than a block away. Reily Coffee was managed by another ex-FBI agent.[14]

At the coffee company Oswald distinguished himself only by his absences. He was let go in late July and immediately began his street evangelicalism, although he quickly discarded the 544 Camp Street address in favor of a postal box under a fictitious name. In late August he was seen waiting in line to register to vote in Clinton, Louisiana, during a registration drive by the Congress on Racial Equality (CORE) in the area. The six people who saw Oswald, including state legislator Reeves Morgan, a deputy sheriff, and a registrar of voters, noticed him because he drove up in a big black car. With him, the witnesses said, were David Ferrie and Clay Shaw, a New Orleans foreign trade official who had a long history of CIA connections.[15]

Any doubt that Oswald was setting up a left-wing Potemkin Village in New Orleans was dispelled by Delphine Roberts in her testimony before the House Select Committee on Assassinations and in her elaborations to British journalist Anthony Summers, author of *Conspiracy*.[16]

She knew that her boss received CIA funding and that he ran a network of young agents. When Lee Oswald showed up, filled out an "agent" form, and went into a long closed-door meeting with Banister, she gathered that the two had already known each other. Thereafter Oswald appeared frequently, using a vacant office. He accompanied David Ferrie to the training camp north of Lake Pontchartrain "to train with rifles." It therefore came as something of a

shock when Roberts spotted Oswald dispensing pro-Castro literature on the streets. "He's with us," Banister calmed her. "He's with
the office." Roberts understood. "I knew there were such things as
counterspies, spies and counterspies," she said, "and the importance
of such things."[17]

Oswald was now in the most dangerous of worlds. He was acting
out pro-Castro pantomimes under the command of a violently anti-
Castro cabal dominated by autonomous intelligence operatives and
mob elements.

In June 1963, a mysterious man named George de Mohrenschildt
arrived in Port-au-Prince, Haiti. His intimates called him the Baron.
The son of a czarist nobleman, he was variously rumored to have
spied for the French, Germans, Soviets, and Mexicans during World
War II. After the war he became widely known in White Russian
circles in America and widely mentioned in the society pages. In the
days before tennis players wore shorts he was seen on the courts at
the Long Island estate of Jack and Janet Bouvier, Jackie Kennedy's
parents. He was also seen, with unseemly rapidity for the day, in the
divorce courts. His fourth (and last) wife was Jeanne, well known
in her own right as a fashion designer and the daughter of a director
of the Nationalist Chinese railway system.

De Mohrenschildt's business was oil. In 1945 he became a co-
owner of the Cuban-Venezuelan Oil Trust Company, which he described as "a land development company to promote eventually a
large oil drilling campaign in Cuba." He was also government-
connected, as so often happens with transnational operators. In the
late 1950s he traveled to Yugoslavia and Ghana as a geological consultant for the CIA-funded International Cooperation Administration, charged with directing the oil flow from those countries away
from the Soviet Union and toward the West. In 1960 he gained an
audience in Mexico with Soviet First Deputy Premier Anastas
Mikoyan.

In 1962 de Mohrenschildt opened an office in Dallas and joined
the exclusive Dallas Petroleum Club. By this time he was on a first-
name basis with such Who's Whoers as William R. Grace of Grace

Lines, oilman John Mecom (owner of the New Orleans Saints of the National Football League), and Houston construction magnates George and Herman Brown, who had sponsored Lyndon Johnson's political career. Another of de Mohrenschildt's oil pipelines was George Bush. In a telephone register found after his death was the entry: "Bush, George H. W. (Poppy) 1412 W. Ohio also Zapata Petroleum Midland." Zapata Midland was the oil company Bush had cofounded in Midland, Texas, before establishing Zapata Off Shore in Houston in 1956.[18]

Up to now the charming White Russian had been only rubbing shoulders with the archangels of finance capital. Then an amazing thing occurred. He and his wife, Jeanne, became, as Marina Oswald would later express it, "our best friends in Dallas." The Baron hastened to look up the lowly Oswalds after they returned from their unsettling stay in the Soviet Union. The two couples became as thick as thieves. This unnatural relationship puzzled the Warren Commission, which finally wrote it off as just one more strange aspect of Oswald's strange existence. There was another explanation.

In April 1963, about the time that Lee Oswald left Dallas for New Orleans, de Mohrenschildt traveled to New York and Washington en route to Port-au-Prince, ostensibly preparing to undertake a $300,000 contract for geological surveys awarded by the Haitian government. Two years before, he and Jeanne had hiked through Central America, arriving in Guatemala just as the Cuban brigade shoved off for the Bay of Pigs, and upon his return he had submitted a written report with photographs to the CIA. The Haitian contract, the Baron told his social friends, had eventuated from a chance encounter with Haitian officials during that hike.

De Mohrenschildt may have been undertaking a contract of an entirely different kind. A clue surfaced in 1976, when a declassified CIA Office of Security file dated April 29, 1963 revealed: "[Deleted] Case Officer had requested an expedite check of George DE MOHRENSCHILDT for reasons unknown to Security." That terse sentence blended nicely with the concurrent disclosure of former CIA contract agent Herbert Atkin that de Mohrenschildt's real mission when he arrived in Port-au-Prince in June was to oversee a CIA approved plot to overthrow the dictator "Papa Doc"

Duvalier. "I knew de Mohrenschildt as Philip Harbin," said Atkin, now an oil company employee in Los Angeles. It was a chivalrous touch, typical of the Baron. Jeanne de Mohrenschildt had been born in Harbin, China.

The map of de Mohrenschildt's life was dotted with close links to both the CIA and Army Intelligence. He finally admitted the year of his death in 1977 that a CIA agent in Dallas had asked him to keep an eye on the Oswalds after their return from Russia. This at least would explain the puzzling intimacy between the shabby Oswalds and the dashing de Mohrenschildt. He was, in CIA lingo, Oswald's "baby sitter." He was also something of a clairvoyant. On November 22 de Mohrenschildt was having a drink in a Port-au-Prince hotel when he heard the news from Dallas. He asked immediately if the suspect's name were Lee Oswald. "It was subconscious," he later explained, "a sort of flash that came probably from knowing that Oswald had a gun."[19]

It was not unusual for the CIA to want to keep an eye on one of its own; Oswald had resided in the Soviet Union, and the agency wanted to make sure he had not been converted into a double agent by the KGB. For its part the KGB had also viewed Oswald with suspicion, according to post-Cold War disclosures made by ex-KGB officers to American television interviewers. Certainly Oswald's background was "funny." As a radar controller in the Marine Corps he was posted to the top-secret Atsugi Naval Station in Japan, home of the fleet of U-2 spy planes that were overflying the eastern territories of the Soviet Union and China. Somehow Oswald emerged from this stint fluent in Russian, which he put to use in staging a defection in Moscow in 1959. The KGB inevitably looked upon Oswald's wrist-slashing to escape deportation as a piece of CIA guerrilla theater, and kept a wary eye on him during his more than two-year stay in Minsk.[20]

After returning to the United States, Oswald had no trouble finding a job at a Dallas graphic arts firm that was flush with military contracts. His conversations with a co-worker, Dennis H. Ofstein, who also spoke Russian, suggest what his mission in the Soviet

Union had been. Oswald told Ofstein that all the time he was in Minsk he never saw a vapor trail, indicating that he had been on the lookout for the telltale contrails of Russian military aircraft. Ofstein recalled Oswald's remarking on the deployment of Soviet military units and said that according to Oswald "they didn't intermingle their armored divisions . . . the way we do in the United States. And they would have all their aircraft in one geographical location, and their tanks in another geographical location, and their infantry in another." Oswald also showed Ofstein a photograph of a block-like building. Ofstein said that Oswald told him that this was "some military headquarters and that the guards stationed there were armed with weapons and ammunition and had orders to shoot trespassers." Clearly Oswald was going out of his way to snoop on Soviet military alignments. How he most likely relayed this intelligence to the CIA station in the Moscow embassy is suggested by an entry in his address book: "microdots," which at that time were a common means of communication among espionage agents.[21]

Oswald may have sealed his doom in the summer of 1963 by strutting around the streets of New Orleans, proclaiming himself in favor of Castro and the Communist Party. He was now in the limelight as an agent of Fidel Castro, not Guy Banister. (When the assassination occurred Castro would reap the blame because of Oswald's pro-Cuba posturing. Perhaps there might then be a retaliatory invasion of Cuba launched from the Guantánamo naval base—long a wet dream of Cuba Project plotters.)

But during that pivotal summer of 1963 Oswald couldn't conceive of becoming a "patsy"—as he would cry out after his arrest for Kennedy's murder. He was focused on the idea that he would soon reap the reward of all good agents—a comfortable sinecure. Oswald told Adrian Alba, the owner of the garage next door to where he was working, that his application was about to be accepted "out there where the gold is"—the NASA Saturn missile plant in suburban Gentilly.

NASA of course didn't employ security risks. But tucked into its Gentilly facility was an active CIA station that provided a Kelly Girl service for operatives in between assignments.[22]

The Cuban Student Directorate was suspicious of Lee Harvey Oswald. Believing that he had tried to infiltrate them, they tried to manipulate him. One of Bringuier's aides was sent to penetrate Oswald's communist "cell." He came back with the impression that Oswald's Fair Play for Cuba chapter did not exist. The Directorate people thought Oswald was acting strangely for a loyal supporter of the Beard. He proffered his services as a potential assassin for Castro, bragging that he could shoot anyone; he mentioned John Connally as the target. The next thing the Directorate heard was that Oswald had come into some money and disappeared.

Oswald was, in fact, on his way to Mexico City. On September 25 he boarded a bus for the first leg of the long journey. That same evening there occurred a remarkable incident. Three men appeared unannounced at the Dallas doorstep of Sylvia Odio, a well-known Cuban exile and a backer of Manuel Ray's JURE, the social-democrat group that most exiles considered flamingly pink. The trio's Latin-looking spokesman called himself Leopoldo. He said it was a "war name." He introduced a dark companion with a stocky build as "Angelo." The third man, an Anglo who stood shyly in the background, he introduced "Leon Oswald."

The man called Leopoldo said that they had just come from New Orleans and were "leaving for a trip." He claimed that he and his friends were affiliated with JURE. As proof he gave Mrs. Odio current details about her parents who had been imprisoned on the Isle of Pines since 1961 for harboring one of Tony Veciana's would-be assassins. Leopoldo appealed for money "to buy arms for Cuba and to help overthrow the dictator Castro." Odio, unsure of the strangers, was noncommittal.

A day or so later, while Oswald was riding a bus through the Mexican interior and confiding to two Australian tourists that he was going to Cuba with the hope of meeting Castro in person, Leopoldo telephoned Sylvia Odio. He spoke glowingly of Leon, saying he was an American ex-Marine and a crack shot. "He is great, he is kind of nuts. He told us we don't have any guts, you Cubans, because President Kennedy should have been assassinated after the Bay of Pigs. . . . It is so easy to do. He has told us."[23]

Oswald arrived in Mexico City with a book by Lenin under his arm. He went directly to the Cuban Embassy and applied for a visa that would allow him to visit Cuba en route to the Soviet Union. He tried to ingratiate himself with the consular officials. He showed them newspaper clippings about his fight with Bringuier, a U.S. passport showing that he had lived in Russia, and forged documents naming him secretary of the New Orleans chapter of the FPCC. The Cubans checked at the Russian consulate and were told that there would be a four-month delay in processing visas. Oswald said he was in a big hurry. As a friend of the Cuban revolution he demanded an immediate Cuban visa. Oswald was told that was impossible. He would have to have the Soviet one first. He created such a fuss that Consul Eusebio Azcue was summoned. Azcue advised that "a person of his type was harming the Cuban Revolution rather than helping it" and kicked Oswald off the compound without his visa.

Oswald persisted, bouncing between the Russian and Cuban embassies. Neither relented. He had said that his wife was in New York—she wasn't—and would follow him to Russia, but it seems clear that from the start he intended to go no farther than Havana and was attempting to get around the Cuban visa policy, or was attempting something else. Mostly, he was attempting to be visible. Speculation over Oswald's curious actions in Mexico City has developed into a cottage industry. Not the least, and not the least supported, of the explanations is that Oswald—or it may have been Oswalds, plural, as there is a body of evidence, photographic and otherwise, that someone impersonating Oswald may have been visiting the embassies[24]—was polishing his left-wing brass in a way to implicate the Cuban revolution in the Dallas crime.

III

Edward I. Arthur was one kind of Dead End Kid, a part-Shawnee Indian orphan who had grown up in reform schools and graduated from jail. Ed Arthur was also a patriot. At fourteen he conned his way into the Army and got as far as jump school before his tender age was discovered. During the Missile Crisis, Arthur went to Miami and signed on as a weapons expert with Commandos L, the

MIRR ally, where he quickly developed a reputation as one tough Indian.

With his powerful build, black crew cut, and bluff manner, Arthur looked the part of an executioner. This may account for why Sam Benton, one of the mob's busiest schemers, singled him out for the job he had in mind. It was September, barely a month after Benton had been nabbed by the FBI at Lake Pontchartrain. Benton had met Arthur two weeks before through attorney Charles Ashman, the legal firebrand of the anti-Castro movement. He called Arthur at the Mayflower Hotel to say that he might have a lucrative assignment for him.

They drove toward Miami Beach. On exclusive Pine Tree Drive, Benton pulled into a winding driveway leading into a magnificent but deteriorating estate. He stopped under the weather-beaten porte-cochère and led Arthur into the impressive house. The sunken living room, with a commanding marble fireplace, looked out over a large expanse of lawn broken by a swimming pool and leading down to a boat slip with davits. The Fontainebleau Hotel stared down from across muddy Indian Creek.

A swarthy man was sitting on a couch as big as a bus stop. A too sharply dressed younger man lounged by the window in the classic "torpedo" pose. A beautiful blonde came in, wearing a dress that had been buttered on. Arthur thought he had walked into a George Raft movie. The phone rang, and the blonde picked it up. She said Chicago was on the line. The swarthy man took the phone. "Yeah, we've got him here now," he said. "Ninety grand. We'll see what we can do." He promised to call back and hung up.

The man on the couch had a business proposition. He wanted Ed Arthur to assassinate Fidel Castro. The pay would be $90,000. "We have access to an airplane and 500 pound bombs and other munitions," he said. "What about flying over the Presidential Palace and dropping bombs?"

Arthur argued that Castro moved around too much—the palace might be leveled without him in it. "I could do the trick with a scoped rifle from a hotel across the street," Arthur suggested. "It's more practical." The man nodded. He and Benton tried to impress Arthur by dropping names of Havana nightclubs the dispossessed owners of which they said were backing the effort—the Half Moon Club, the Tropicana. Arthur said he'd have to think about it. "I recognized those clubs as syndicate-owned," he said later. "I had no qualms about bumping off Castro, but I wanted no part of the syndicate."

On the drive back to the hotel Benton chatted like a parrot. He told Arthur he was missing a "wonderful opportunity" if he didn't accept the proposition. He said "the organization" had been double-crossed by Castro. He repeated the mob party line that Castro had promised the casinos could continue to operate for $12 million up front plus a percentage of the receipts, then shut them down after getting the money.

Benton rambled on. The assassination project had the approval of "certain well-connected people in Washington," he said. Pushing back his coat just enough to reveal a revolver, he mentioned that he had to go to New Orleans to see the Little Man. He repeated the name again, with reverence. Arthur had no doubt Benton was talking about Carlos Marcello.[25]

Arthur never did figure out why he was offered the uneven sum of $90,000. It was more like the mob to deal in round figures. A mob source said that Benton was a kind of "broker" who took a 10 percent slice off the top, which would account for the offer.

When the authors interviewed him, Arthur looked at a photograph of Mike McLaney and thought he recognized the tough-talking man who had propositioned him. At the time McLaney lived two blocks down the street from the mansion, which, we learned by following Arthur's detailed description, is at 4609 Pine Tree Drive, Miami Beach. It was purchased in 1960 by Marcos Pérez Jiménez, the ex-dictator of Venezuela who fled with a large chunk of the national treasury. Carlos Marcello, who was in the habit of visiting Venezuela during Pérez's reign, was rumored to be part owner of the Pine Tree Drive estate. Pérez was in tight with the casino crowd—his daughter married one of Meyer Lansky's casino managers—and he had given money to Interpen's Castro crusades. The stocky, balding Pérez kept a mistress at the mansion, familiar to readers of this volume as Frank Sturgis's beautiful spy, Maria Lorenz.

Pérez and Lorenz were gone by the time Ed Arthur visited the mansion. Only two months before, Bobby Kennedy had had Pérez extradited to Venezuela to face embezzlement charges. The mansion remained in his name for years. In 1974 the caretaker, an old Pérez retainer, remembered that McLaney had visited there frequently in "the old days."

Assassination was not a subject that McLaney, who now runs the Casino Internationale in Haiti, wished to discuss when we interviewed him. He was still smarting over charges made in the fall of 1973 before a Senate subcommittee that he tried to arrange the assassination of Bahamas Premier Lynden Pindling in 1968. The charges were leveled by a convicted peddler of stolen securities, Louis P. Mastriana, who claimed that FDR's son Elliott, then the mayor of Miami Beach, acted as a middleman. McLaney was mad at Pindling, Mastriana testified, for reneging on casino concessions after Meyer Lansky had invested $1 million in the premier's election campaign through McLaney. Mastriana said he was offered $100,000 to "whack" Pindling.

"If I was going to hit Pindling," McLaney asked rhetorically, "would I do it through a guy as dumb as Roosevelt?" He is equally incensed by suggestions of his organized crime connections. "Listen"—he wagged a thick finger—"I met Meyer Lansky once, and then for only thirty seconds." But all he would say about the Lake Pontchartrain episode was that "they were making some napalm there." McLaney did not see the wisdom of talking about other aspects of his campaign against Castro. "Have a drink," the gambler said. "They have long memories up in Washington and might not recognize that the statute of limitations has run out."

The two men stood under the flashing lights that said Carousel Club. It was tacky enough—the type of place where Dallas attorney Carroll Jarnagin hoped to find a job for one of his clients, an exotic dancer who used the stage name Robin Hood. Tall and blond, Jarnagin looked out of place as he and his out-of-work customer walked in and slid into a booth. A chess champion and student of such prodigious memory that he once scored 100 on a Southern Methodist

University chemistry exam involving complicated formulae, Jarnagin would recall his October 4, 1963, visit to Jack Ruby's club in precise detail.

The day following the assassination of JFK, Jarnagin wrote a letter to J. Edgar Hoover reporting on the alleged meeting between Ruby and Oswald. In the dimly lit club Jarnagin recalls he noticed a rumpled young man in a windbreaker appear in the lighted entrance and ask for Ruby. The attorney believes he recognized him as Lee Harvey Oswald. Oswald had arrived from Mexico City the previous night.

Jarnagin overheard the putative Oswald and Ruby talking in a nearby booth. Oswald said he had just gotten in from New Orleans. He needed money. "You'll get the money when the job is done," Ruby said, adding that if there was a slip-up "they" would want all their money back or feel double-crossed. The job, Jarnagin remembered, was to shoot Texas Governor John Connally, who, Ruby said, was not opening up the state to the rackets. "The boys in Chicago have no place to go, no place to really operate," Ruby complained. "They've clamped down the lid in Chicago, Cuba is closed."

Ruby knew what he was talking about. The lid was indeed on in Chicago. Bobby Kennedy's organized crime steamroller was in high gear — and Sam Giancana was directly in its path. Giancana felt bitter, believing that contributing to JFK's election had earned him protection (the Chicago mob automatically put its muscle behind candidates endorsed by Mayor Richard Daley's Democratic machine, and Giancana boasted to his and JFK's girlfriend, Judith Campbell, that he had put her boyfriend in the White House). That summer Giancana had filed a suit charging FBI agents with too much tailing — they followed him everywhere, cocktail lounges, church, his late wife's mausoleum, even the golf course. A federal judge ordered the surveillance relaxed, specifying that agents stay at least one foursome back on the links. Bobby Kennedy also was pushing a law through Congress that would jail anyone refusing to testify before a grand jury under immunity, and Sam Giancana, no stranger to the Fifth Amendment, was in line to be one of its first major applications.

According to Jarnagin, Oswald suggested that Bobby Kennedy ought to be hit. Ruby said no—the security in Washington was too tight; besides, his brother would stop at nothing to solve his death. It was Connally who had to go. When Oswald argued that killing the governor would also bring plenty of "heat," Ruby replied, "Not really, they'll think some crackpot or communist did it, and it will be written off as an unsolved crime."[26] There were other credible reports of an Oswald-Ruby link, including that of a garage owner, who said Oswald drove Ruby's car, and an auto repairman, who said Oswald brought Ruby's car in for repairs.

Jack Ruby was an alumnus of the Chicago mob, class of 1947, who retained his old-school ties. He was known to hang around with a rising young mafioso named Sam Giancana and with mob enforcers Lenny Patrick, who was a shirttail relative, and Dave Yaras. When Ruby opened a nightclub in Dallas after the war, it coincided with a major move by the Chicagoans into Texas rackets territory. Ruby became the fixer for payoffs to police, the man to see for a piece of the action. In deference to syndicate protocol, he made his peace with Joe Civello, who was aligned with Marcello and Trafficante in the Sunbelt Mafia.

When the syndicate turned Havana into a casino boomtown in the late 1950s, Ruby's old Chicago chum Dave Yaras was "credited" by the McClellan Senate Rackets Committee—Robert F. Kennedy, chief counsel—with playing a significant mob role in Havana as well as being implicated with the corruption-ridden Teamsters Local 320 in Miami. Ruby himself did not miss out on the action. One report had it that he had helped smuggle guns to Castro when the mob was hedging its bets. Ruby was especially close to a gambling supervisor named Lewis J. McWillie, whom he visited in Cuba in the summer of 1959. McWillie, who described Ruby as a "brother," had followed a lucrative trail to Havana, where he was employed by Norm "Roughhouse" Rothman at the Sans Souci. Later he was manager of Lansky's Tropicana. According to an FBI memo, "McWillie solidified his syndicate connections through his association in Havana, Cuba with Santos Trafficante; . . . Meyer and Jake

Lansky; Dino Cellini and others who were members of or associates of 'the syndicate.' "[27]

When the House Select Committee on Assassinations examined Ruby's long-distance telephone calls preceding the Kennedy assassination, it found that he had been in touch with such heavies as Robert "Barney" Baker, Jimmy Hoffa's muscle and bagman in Chicago; Irwin Weiner, a Chicago bondsman "well-known as a frontman for organized crime and the Teamsters"; Murray "Dusty" Miller, a Hoffa deputy and "associate of various underworld figures"; Nofio J. Pecora, a top lieutenant of Carlos Marcello's; and Dave Yaras's fellow hired gun, Lenny Patrick. Ruby wasn't the only mob type busy making phone calls on or about November 22. Baker called Yaras in Miami Beach on the eve of the assassination. The call lasted three minutes. No one knows what they talked about.[28]

In 1970 Ruby contact "Dusty" Miller went all-out for George Bush in his second campaign for the U.S. Senate seat from Texas. Miller's support was so extraordinary that the Nixon White House took notice. On October 13, 1970, political dirty-tricks specialist Charles W. Colson memoed chief of staff H. R. Haldeman that " 'Duster' [*sic*] Miller, who heads the Southern Region for the Teamsters, is actively backing George Bush with money and political support." Bush also received hefty contributions from the oil industry and more than $100,000 from a secret White House fund, but was beaten by Democrat Lloyd M. Bensten, Jr.

Sam Giancana was impatiently jiggling his ankle. The drawn-out Castro project had been a slow-burning failure, and his credits were being used up with the CIA, which had been helping him out in the importation of prostitutes from Marseilles. Johnny Roselli was to be given his walking papers. In October, shortly after Oswald returned from Mexico, Giancana called a summit meeting in Miami.

It was held at the secluded mansion on Pine Tree Drive. Giancana opened the table to discussion in the Mafia equivalent of democracy; no one disagreed with his verdict that Roselli be replaced, nor with his choice of a replacement, Charles Nicoletti, the Chicago mob's senior hit man. Nicoletti was an Al Capone protégé who had stuffed more bodies in trunks than anyone cared to count. When he was given a contract, the victim was considered as good as dead.[29]

But Fidel Castro wasn't the only enemy on the mobsters' minds that day. Like Giancana, Trafficante had become a prime target in Bobby Kennedy's war on crime. This only inflamed Trafficante's long-standing grudge against the Kennedys. A year earlier he had met in Miami's Scott Bryan Hotel with Miami businessman José Alemán, whose father, a former Batista official, became famous for taking millions from the Cuban treasury in suitcases. They discussed a $1.5 million Teamsters loan to Alemán that "had already been cleared by Jimmy Hoffa himself." Trafficante spoke harshly of the President: "Have you seen how his brother is hitting Hoffa, a man who is a worker, who is not a millionaire, a friend of the blue collars? He doesn't know that this kind of encounter is very delicate. Mark my word, this man Kennedy is in trouble, and he will get what is coming to him."

Alemán expressed the view that Kennedy would surely be reelected.

"No, José," Trafficante said softly, "he is going to be hit."[30]

IV

"At 12:23 on November 22, from his office on the 7th floor of the Mercantile Building, Haroldson Lafayette Hunt watched John Kennedy ride toward Dealey Plaza, where fate awaited him at 12:30. A few minutes later, escorted by six men in two cars, Hunt left the center of Dallas without even stopping by his house."[31] These words are written in *Farewell America*, a book produced by French intelligence. Ghosted by a veteran operative of the French SDECE, *Farewell America* purported to present then President Charles de Gaulle's views on Kennedy's assassination.

Farewell America went on to say that Hunt was taken from Dallas to a hideaway in Mexico where he was joined by General Edwin A. Walker, who had been drummed out of the Army for drumming right-wing propaganda into his troops. H. L. Hunt (the "one of the wells" funding Orlando Bosch's MIRR) and Walker stayed hunkered down in Mexico until Christmas under the watchful eyes of private guards and FBI agents.[32] However, *Farewell America* offered no proof of the Hunt-Walker hideaway. (There's an interesting sidenote to all this: one of H. L.'s sons, Nelson Bunker Hunt, had cosponsored a black-bordered screed against Kennedy, which was printed in a Dallas newspaper on November 22.)[33]

Farewell America also asserted that former "specialists" for the CIA's covert operations division were members of an assassination "team" at Dallas. (General Walker would later prove useful to the Warren Commission. It concluded that on the previous April 10 Oswald had taken a potshot at Walker, who was in the study of his home. The Commission saw this as establishing Oswald's "propensity" to kill, but even if true—the evidence is flimsy—all it proved was that Oswald couldn't hit a sitting target, much less a moving one.)

Within minutes of the assassination a man giving the name Jim Braden was detained by a deputy sheriff in the Dal-Tex Building on Dealey Plaza, next to the Texas School Book Depository where Oswald was employed. The deputy suspected there had been a sniper there. Braden, dressed in a topcoat and snap-brim hat, alibied that he had come to Dallas from Los Angeles on oil business, and had entered the building to look for a pay phone. He was released after producing a credit card and driver's license.

What the deputy didn't know was that "Jim Braden" was an alias of Eugene Hale Brading, an ex-con with a string of thirty-five arrests ranging from embezzlement to bookmaking. He had left Los Angeles two days earlier, and on November 21 had checked in as required with a federal probation officer who reported that Braden "advised [me] that he intended to see Lamar Hunt [another son of H. L. Hunt] and other oil speculators while here." According to Paul Rothermel, an ex-FBI agent who was chief of security for the Hunt Oil Company, Brading and three California associates did see both Lamar Hunt and Nelson Bunker Hunt the day before the assassination.[34]

Bradley Ayers was briefing his killer commando team at the CIA base on Elliott Key near Miami. A single-engine Cessna came over low. Ayers thought it was a press plane trying to find exile training bases. He ordered his men inside the house. But as the Cessna circled and came back, he recognized it as one of the CIA's. As it passed overhead, a white object was released directly over the old house. It was a roll of toilet paper, streaming out as it fell toward the ground. Taped inside the cardboard tube was a message in Gordon Campbell's printing:

> NOVEMBER 22, 1963
> PRESIDENT KENNEDY HAS BEEN SHOT BY AN ASSASSIN. SUSPEND ALL
> ACTIVITY. KEEP MEN ON ISLAND. COME ASHORE WITHOUT DELAY.

Ayers's mind shot back to a scene at the Point Mary safe house used by Johnny Roselli's team: "The crack of a rifle fired by an anti-Castro sniper shatters the quiet, and a cormorant, sitting on a mangrove root five hundred yards away, explodes in a burst of crimson and black, leaving only bits of feather to float on the blue water."[35]

French correspondent Jean Daniel was engaged in a marathon interview with Fidel Castro at the premier's villa. Three weeks earlier Bill Attwood had arranged for Daniel to interview John Kennedy, who indicated that peace with Cuba was uppermost on his mind. Kennedy had asked Daniel to report back to him after talking with Castro.

An aide interrupted with the news from Dallas.

"This is bad for Cuba," Castro said.

Then, upon hearing that Lyndon Johnson had been sworn in as President at the airport, Castro asked, "What authority does he exercise over the CIA?"[36]

David Ferrie was all smiles in the New Orleans federal courthouse. All his trips to Guatemala and conferences at Churchill Farms had just paid off. Carlos Marcello had been acquitted.

Ferrie and two young male companions piled into his Ford station wagon and drove like speed freaks through the worst rainstorm of the season, heading for Houston.

Harry Williams told the authors in an interview that on that day he was meeting in a CIA safe house in northwest Washington with Richard Helms, Howard Hunt, and several other CIA agents. It was, Williams would say, "the most important meeting I ever had on the problem of Cuba." Williams was buoyant. Plans for his invasion from the Dominican Republic were crystallizing. Manuel Artime was "ready with his things in Central America," and he and Williams were about ready "to do a whole thing together."

Williams and the CIA brass were about to go out for a late lunch when they heard that the President had been shot in Dallas.

It was evening in Paris. Desmond FitzGerald and a local CIA case officer met with Rolando Cubela, code name Amlash. The case officer assured Cubela that President Kennedy's speech in Miami four days earlier signaled that he supported a coup. Kennedy had branded the Castro government a "small band of conspirators" who formed a "barrier" that, once removed, would ensure American backing for progressive goals in Cuba. The case officer said that FitzGerald had had a hand in writing the speech, which was not true.

FitzGerald handed Cubela an ordinary-looking ball-point pen fitted with a hypodermic needle so fine that the victim would not feel its insertion. He recommended that Cubela use Blackleaf-40, a lethal poison that was commercially available.

Upon leaving the meeting, FitzGerald and the case officer learned that the President had been assassinated.[37]

In Washington, at Teamster headquarters, Harold Gibbons — Jimmy Hoffa's right-hand, and a liberal on Teamster terms — cut short his lunch when he heard the news from Dallas. Hoffa was out of town. Gibbons went back to the office, dismissed all employees for the day, ordered the flags at half-staff, and sent a message of condolence to Mrs. Kennedy.

When Hoffa heard about this he was furious. "He started scream-

252 DEADLY SECRETS

ing at me 'Why the hell did you do that for him?' and 'Who the hell was he?' " Gibbons said.[38]

Sylvia Odio and her sister, Annie Laurie Odio, were glued to the television set in their Dallas apartment as bulletins on the assassination came in. A suspect named Lee Harvey Oswald had been apprehended. When his picture was flashed on the screen, Sylvia fainted. She had recognized him as the silent third man, introduced as Leon Oswald, who had materialized on her doorstep two months earlier, the one Leopoldo later quoted as saying, "President Kennedy should have been assassinated after the Bay of Pigs."

Annie Laurie, who also had seen the trio, agreed that Oswald was a dead ringer for the man.

The NBC network scored a coup, thanks to its New Orleans affiliate WDSU. Early in the evening it played a tape of Oswald's voice professing admiration for Fidel Castro and declaring, "I am a Marxist!" The tape had been made during Oswald's August radio "debate" with Carlos Bringuier of the Revolutionary Student Directorate.

There was joy in the CIA's Tokyo station. "It was a scene of great excitement, confusion, and wild talk. The conservatives were obviously elated and there was talk of an invasion of Cuba," said Jim Wilcott, the Tokyo station financial officer in 1963. According to Wilcott, CIA hardliners "hated Jack Kennedy" because they felt he betrayed the agency over the Bay of Pigs. Agents were breaking out bottles and having drinks to Oswald. Tongues became loose, and there was a great deal of talk about Oswald's connections with the CIA. It was accepted as given that Oswald worked for the agency. This is what Wilcott says he learned:

> Oswald was originally under control of the Tokyo station's Soviet Russia Branch. He was trained at Atsugi Naval Air Station, the secret base for Tokyo CIA special operations. [Oswald's standard biography has him stationed with a Marine Corps unit at Atsugi from 1956 to 1958.] When Oswald returned from the USSR in June of 1962, he

was brought back to Japan for debriefing. They were having some kind of difficulty with Oswald. The Soviets were on to him right from the start. That apparently made him very angry and he became difficult to handle.

Wilcott told the authors that at first he found it difficult to accept that the man who was said to have shot the president worked for the CIA. "Then I heard about more and more employees who had been working on the Oswald project in the late 1950s." Part of Wilcott's job was to hand out cash for covert CIA operations. "When I expressed disbelief, they told me 'Well, Jim, so and so drew an advance from you for Oswald' or 'You gave out money for the Oswald project under such and such a crypto.' "[39]

Guy Banister was chain-drinking bourbons in the Katz & Jammer Bar, next door to the Newman Building. With him was one of his investigators, Jack S. Martin, a coreligious with David Ferrie in an offbeat reactionary sect called the Apostolic Orthodox Old Catholic Church. After a while the two went up to Banister's office. An argument erupted. Suddenly Banister whipped out his monogrammed revolver and savagely pistol-whipped Martin. Martin was rushed to Baptist Hospital and treated for head injuries. But he refused to press charges. He told the police that Banister was like a father to him, and they had simply argued over "politics and other things."[40]

In Tampa that evening Santos Trafficante was having dinner at the International Inn with his longtime attorney, Frank Ragano, a trusted mob associate. Trafficante was in a "euphoric" mood. "The SOB is dead," he exulted. "We'll get back into Cuba now."[41]

At a late-night press conference, Dallas District Attorney Henry Wade stated, "Oswald is a member of the Free Cuba Committee." He was immediately "corrected" by Jack Ruby, who had mingled with the reporters. "No," Ruby said, "he is a member of the Fair Play for Cuba Committee."

Ruby's specific labeling of Oswald as left wing suggested that he knew more about what was politically correct than might be expected from a simple nightclub proprietor. And from newsreel footage taken that night it is evident that Ruby had already begun to stalk Oswald, looking for his chance. He can be seen among the throng of reporters as he edged to within a couple of feet of the suspect. But just as Oswald exclaimed, "I emphatically deny these charges," Ruby was blocked off by one of the escorting detectives.

As dawn broke over Foggy Bottom the next day, the State Department was concerned that "some misguided anti-Castro group might capitalize on the present situation and undertake an unauthorized raid against Cuba" in the belief that the assassination heralded a change in U.S. policy. J. Edgar Hoover hastened to calm their fears by dispatching agent W. T. Forsyth to Miami, who reported that informants in the anti-Castro community there "know of no plans for unauthorized action against Cuba." In his memorandum to the State Department the FBI chief added: "The substance of the foregoing information was orally furnished to Mr. George Bush of the Central Intelligence Agency."[42]

At that time George Bush was head of the Houston-based Zapata Off Shore Company—an offshoot of Zapata Petroleum—which was engaged in drilling for oil in the Gulf of Mexico and the Caribbean. Zapata platforms were in place on the Cay Sal Bank, within thirty miles of the northern coast of Cuba.[43] Down the bank a short distance was Cay Sal Island, a tiny outcropping subleased by Howard Hughes from the Bahamian government. According to Gerry Patrick Hemming the TOOLCO (Hughes Tool Company) crates delivered to Cay Sal didn't always contain drilling bits; sometimes they contained arms and ammunition for the CIA–Mafia assassination teams using the island as a springboard to Cuba.[44] When asked in 1988 by reporter Joseph McBride about what role if any he had played with the CIA in 1963, Bush gave an ambiguous answer through a White House spokesman. For its part the CIA first said it could neither "confirm nor deny" Bush's agency affiliation at that time, then fed reporters a red herring in the form of George William

Bush, an obscure ex-CIA employee who was befuddled by the idea that he had ever had a high-level briefing on anything.[45]

On Saturday morning Secret Service agents, armed with Fair Play for Cuba literature of Oswald's bearing the address 544 Camp Street, went to the Newman Building to find out if the Dallas suspect "had occupied office space." They learned that "Cuban revolutionaries" had been tenants until recently. They talked to an exile accountant who revealed that "those Cubans were members of organizations known as 'Crusade to Free Cuba Committee' and 'Cuban Revolutionary Council.' " The accountant said that one Sergio Arcacha Smith was authorized to sign checks for both organizations, but he had moved to Texas. Guy Banister's office, where pro-Castro "Hands Off Cuba!" handbills of the type distributed by Oswald were stored, was closed.

The agents reported that they had been unable to find any trace of the Fair Play for Cuba Committee.[46]

In Dallas Deputy Sheriff Buddy Walthers typed up a "Supplementary Investigative Report" in which he advised the Secret Service that "for the past few weeks at a house at 3128 Harlendale some Cubans had been having meetings on the weekends and were possably [sic] connected with the 'Freedom for Cuba Party' of which Oswald was a member." Walthers's informant subsequently told him that "Oswald had been to this house before" and that the Cubans had suddenly moved out.

Jack Martin's head was still throbbing when he called Herman Kohlman, a contact in the New Orleans district attorney's office, and said he had information linking Guy Banister and David Ferrie to the assassination. Martin speculated that Oswald had been in Ferrie's Civil Air Patrol squadron and had been taught to shoot with a telescopic sight by the pilot. Ferrie's role in the conspiracy, Martin thought, was to fly escaping participants across the Texas border into Matamoros, Mexico.

Kohlman took the allegations seriously. DA investigators hit all of Ferrie's known haunts to bring him in for questioning. But no one knew where he was.

David Ferrie was standing by a pay phone in Winterland Skating Rink in Houston. The proprietor, Chuck Rolland, thought it all a bit odd. Ferrie had called from New Orleans the previous day, saying he wanted to ice skate and asking what hours the rink was open. But after driving all that way, he wasn't skating.

At 5:30 P.M., after standing by the phone for two hours, Ferrie received a call. Then he left.

New Orleans attorney Dean Andrews was lying on his bed in Hotel Dieu Hospital when he received a call from a man he knew as Clay Bertrand. A hip-talking Falstaffian figure, Andrews ran a kind of turnstile law practice in which he secured the release of gays caught in police dragnets in the French Quarter. The previous summer Bertrand, who had referred a number of clients to Andrews, had sent over one who was distinctly different: Lee Harvey Oswald. The ex-Marine wanted help with his "yellow paper" discharge and he wanted his Russian wife's immigration status set straight.

This time Bertrand wanted him to go to Dallas to defend Oswald. But before Andrews could get released from the hospital, Oswald was dead.

When Andrews reported the solicitation the FBI swarmed all over him. Andrews couldn't produce Bertrand and the pressure got to him. He decided they would never leave him alone. "You finally came to the conclusion that Clay Bertrand was a figment of your imagination?" asked Wesley Liebeler, staff attorney of the Warren Commission. "That's what the Feebees put on . . . You can tell when the steam is on," said Andrews. "They never leave. They are like cancer. Eternal."

A few months later Andrews bumped into Clay Bertrand, "a swinging cat," in Cosimo's bar in the French Quarter. Still clinging to the notion that the FBI would want to talk to him, Andrews tried

The intense political struggle between Carlos Prío and Fidel Castro was to be won by Castro, as evidenced here in his triumphant procession from Oriente Province to Havana. He was stopped by cheering crowds on his three-day journey. Castro's swift success alarmed U.S. intelligence and sent tremors through the diplomatic community in Havana. (*Andrew St. George*)

A recruiter for E. Howard Hunt works the streets of Miami's Little Havana in 1961. Hunt's talent for recruitment was to be employed once again when he assembled the Cubans for the Watergate burglary team. (*Andrew St. George*)

Gerry Patrick Hemming, the American leader of Interpen, which, after the Bay of Pigs, trained exile commandos for groups disaffected with the CIA. Hemming told the authors that a number of his wealthy potential Texas sponsors suggested killing JFK. (*Carl Davis*)

A paramilitary journalist of note, Andrew St. George tracked down Fidel Castro in April of 1957 and interviewed him at the rebel headquarters in Sierra Maestra. St. George was on assignment from Time-Life at a time when the young rebel leader was attracting worldwide attention. (*Andrew St. George*)

Nelli Hamilton, whose Miami boardinghouse was "home" to visiting Castro fighters during the mid-1960s. "Everybody's favorite granny" lived upstairs with her antimacassars, family snapshots, and a cache of guns under her bed, while the paramilitarists trained in her side yard. (*The Miami Herald*)

Commandos L supply vessel *Alisan* transferring arms and equipment to the speedboat *Phoenix* at dusk off the Cuban coast, March 1963. The resulting raid on the *Baku* precipitated a new episode in the diplomatic war between the U.S. and the Soviet Union following the Cuban missile crisis. (*Andrew St. George*)

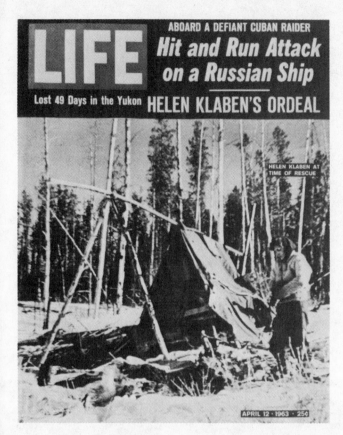

A *Life* cover from 1963, with an article inside on the sinking of the Soviet ship *Baku*. This was part of the Luce campaign to overthrow Castro and put pressure on JFK to take a hard line against communist Cuba. (*UPI*)

The legendary Eddie Bayo, who disappeared on the *Flying Tiger* kidnapping expedition (he stands at center, holding rope). Here, Bayo and members of Commandos L prepare the *Phoenix* for the *Baku* raid. (*Andrew St. George*)

William D. Pawley, former U.S. ambassador to Cuba, pictured here in Miami in 1961 with Cuban survivors of the Bay of Pigs fiasco. Pawley later became involved in a covert plot to kidnap Russian missile technicians from Cuba. He committed suicide in 1977, three years after the authors interviewed him. (*Wide World Photos*)

Former Cuban president Carlos Prío (on right with glasses) listening to Fidel Castro's inaugural speech, Havana, 1959. Seated with him (left to right): Raul Castro, Che Guevara, and Aleida March, a heroine of the revolution. Prío was rejected in his bid to become a leader in the new government. He went to Florida and became a significant figure in the counterrevolution. (*Andrew St. George*)

A group of Cuban exiles in Miami mourns a pilot killed in a raid on Cuba in 1963. The Little Havana community of Miami was extremely close-knit and rabid in its determination to overthrow Castro. (*Andrew St. George*)

Frank Sturgis, pictured here in 1977. A collaborator with Dr. Orlando Bosch in the air raids against Cuba, he was arrested for his part in the Watergate burglary. (*Wide World Photos*)

Mitchell L. WerBell III, shown here with his weapons collection. A fanatic, even among paramilitarists, he was arrested in 1967 with Rolando Masferrer for plotting to overthrow Haitian president François Duvalier following the breakup of CBS's Project Nassau. The authors interviewed him at his fortresslike home in Powder Springs, Georgia. (*Wide World Photos*)

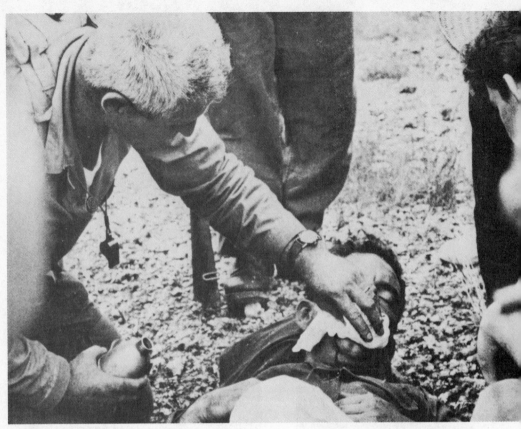

Julio Hormillo lies injured after a rifle misfired during the CBS filming of a Project Nassau training exercise. Hormillo lost an eye in the accident. He later sued CBS and settled out of court for $15,000. (*Andrew St. George*)

to "get a nickel in the phone and call the Feebees . . . but he saw me and spooked and ran."[47]

Before his probe broke into the news in early 1967, New Orleans DA Jim Garrison had lunch with Andrews, who had gone to Tulane law school with him. Garrison pressed Andrews for the true identity of Bertrand, but Andrews was having none of the old school tie. "If I answer that question you keep asking me, if I give you that name you keep trying to get, then it's goodbye Dean Andrews," he whined. "It's bon voyage, Deano. I mean like permanent."[48]

With Andrews scared to death, Garrison had to use other means to find out who was the man behind the Clay Bertrand mask. The DA's investigators fanned out into the French Quarter and came back with word that Clay Bertrand was a nom de bar for Clay Shaw, the prestigious director of the International Trade Mart. The identification was confirmed when Shaw was booked for conspiracy in the assassination. Asked if he used any other name, Shaw blurted out, "Clay Bertrand."[49]

But at the trial in early 1969 the judge refused to allow the booking officer to testify that Shaw had admitted being Bertrand, thus thwarting the prosecution's effort to establish a solid legal connection between Shaw and Oswald. Other witnesses who could also have testified about the connection were either dead or beyond the reach of the DA's office. And on the question of Shaw's CIA affiliation, which might have provided a motive, Garrison came up short.

At the time of the trial it was known that Shaw was on the board of directors of a Swiss-based firm called Permindex, which was a subsidiary of the Rome-based Centro Mondiale Commerciale. Ostensibly both were created to promote international trade. But in 1962 the Italian government kicked CMC out of the country as a CIA front, and the Swiss government dissolved Permindex when it was proven to be a conduit for funds for the Secret Army Organization, a cabal of right-wing French generals plotting to get rid of Charles de Gaulle. When French intelligence traced the money used to finance the generals' assassination attempt on de Gaulle that year, they found that $200,000 of it had been deposited in the Permindex account in the Bank de la Credit Internationale.[50]

The circumstances suggest that half of the money was delivered to Paris by Maurice Gatlin, who had told Jerry Brooks that he had $100,000 for the Secret Army Organization to assassinate de Gaulle. (De Gaulle narrowly escaped from a crossfire ambush set up by the generals.)

Clearly Gatlin, who boasted that his role as a CIA "transporter" gave him a license to kill, was chock full of deadly secrets. But Garrison never got to interview him. In 1964 he was pushed or jumped from the sixth floor of the El Panama Hotel in Panama City and was killed.[51]

Clay Shaw was acquitted. Jurors polled after the verdict said Garrison had proven a conspiracy, but hadn't plugged Shaw into it beyond reasonable doubt.

It was not until 1975 that compelling evidence of Shaw's CIA links surfaced. Victor Marchetti, who at the time of the Shaw trial was a staff assistant to then CIA Director Richard Helms, disclosed that Helms had acknowledged that Shaw was associated with the agency, and had instructed his top aides to "do all we can to help Shaw" during his trial. According to Marchetti, CIA General Counsel Lawrence Houston assured Helms that the agency was "on top of the situation."[52] In a 1979 civil deposition Helms himself reluctantly conceded that Shaw was one of the agency's own, but downgraded his position to "part-time contact."[53]

In Miami the Student Revolutionary Directorate put out an extra edition of its publication *Trinchera* reporting that Oswald had been in Miami during the Missile Crisis and again in March 1963. On the first occasion Oswald handed out literature paid for with a Fair Play for Cuba Committee check at an anti-Castro rally in Bayfront Park and thus "instigated a riot." *Trinchera* claimed that Oswald had come to Florida to try to infiltrate exile groups.

While David Ferrie was loitering by the phone at the ice rink in Houston, Eugene Hale Brading arrived in Houston on, he told his parole officer, more oil business. From Houston Brading flew to New Orleans, where his Empire Oil Company had a mailing address at the Père Marquette Building—Room 1701.[54] A few steps down the hall was Room 1706, which he had given parole authorities as his contact address. And across the hall was Room 1707, the office of C. Wray Gill, the attorney for Carlos Marcello. In recent weeks David Ferrie had been in and out of Room 1707 while working as an investigator for Gill in his defense of Marcello on Robert Kennedy's immigration prosecution.

Bobby Kennedy instinctively believed that there was more to his brother's assassination than Lee Harvey Oswald. But he was not in a position to turn the Justice Department loose to try to discover who was responsible. He was now a lame-duck attorney general, hated both by Hoover and Johnson.

Bobby did the next-best thing: He instructed Daniel P. Moynihan, then Assistant Secretary of Labor and a charter member of the Kennedy inner circle, to secretly investigate the possibility that Bobby's arch-enemy Jimmy Hoffa was behind the plot. (Kennedy thought that Hoffa might have bribed the Secret Service.) Moynihan assembled a small team of trusted Justice Department agents to discreetly carry out the inquiry, but in the end he was forced to report that no evidence of Hoffa's complicity could be found. However, his inquiry did conclude that Secret Service protection of John Kennedy in Dallas had been derelict, if not corrupt.

The rump investigation of the assassination disappeared into the Camelot mists until 1968, when the French intelligence magnum opus *Farewell America* materialized. The author of record, James Hepburn (Hervé Lamarr, a veteran French intelligence operative), confided to the authors that the book's detailed chapter on the breakdown of Secret Service protection was based on information supplied by "a Kennedy insider." A clue to which insider lay in a cryptic line in the book: "Only Daniel Patrick Moynihan, a former longshoreman, had some idea of such things."

When confronted with this information in 1968 by a reporter from *Ramparts* magazine, Moynihan, now the senior senator from New York, jumped as if a live grenade was rolling toward him. In CIA fashion he declared he would neither confirm nor deny his secret mission for Bobby Kennedy. After leaving the room to use the phone the suddenly unamiable Irishman returned and announced that he had nothing more to say.[55]

At 11:20 A.M. on Sunday Jack Ruby shouldered his way through a line of reporters in the basement of the Dallas jail and fatally shot Oswald as he was being led to an armored car for transfer.

That afternoon Seymour Ellison, a law partner of Melvin Belli in San Francisco, received a phone call from Las Vegas. Ellison, who had done legal work for Moe Dalitz of the Desert Inn, knew that the caller was connected with casino proprietors who had been ousted from Cuba. "Sy," the Las Vegas man said, "one of our guys just bumped off that son of a bitch that gunned down the President." He wanted Belli, who was in Riverside defending an associate of mobster Mickey Cohen in a murder trial, to take on the defense of Jack Ruby. It was to be understood that the client of record would be Jack's brother, Earl Ruby. Ellison called Belli, who was excited about taking the important case. The Las Vegas group sent a $25,000 retainer, but the promised big money down the line never materialized. Belli not only lost the Ruby trial but lost a considerable amount of his own money in expenses.[56]

On Monday Guy Banister received a telephone call from Ernest C. Wall, Jr., of the FBI, which had just been ordered to take over the assassination investigation by President Johnson. No introduction was needed. The Spanish-speaking Wall had long been a bureau liaison with anti-Castro groups, including the Friends of Democratic Cuba created by Banister and Arcacha Smith. His call apparently was prompted by the fact that Secret Service agents had come up with Arcacha's name in connection with the Newman Building.

Wall was simply going through the motions, if his report is any criterion. Consisting of one paragraph, it said Banister "advised that

SERGO [sic] ARCACHA SMITH of the Cuban Revolutionary Council, who was the head of that organization . . . some time ago, had told him on one occasion that he, SMITH, had an office in the building located at 544 Camp Street. Mr. BANISTER stated that he had seen a young Cuban man with SMITH on a number of occasions in the vicinity of 544 Camp Street, but could not recall the name of this young man."[57] End of report. Thus was the lid put on the mystery of 544 Camp Street.

Upon returning to New Orleans from his Houston trip, Ferrie surrendered to the DA's office. He insisted that the trip had been recreational, made on the "spur of the moment" in celebration of Carlos Marcello's court victory. Ferrie claimed that on Saturday he and his companions had ice skated in Houston and on Sunday had gone goose hunting near Galveston.

DA Jim Garrison found the story absurd. He ordered Ferrie booked as a "fugitive from Texas" and turned over to the FBI. The suspect was questioned by Ernest Wall, the same FBI agent who had phoned Guy Banister earlier, and was released. The FBI report noted that Ferrie had admitted being "publicly and privately" critical of Kennedy for withholding air cover at the Bay of Pigs and had used expressions like "He ought to be shot." The FBI said that he did not mean the threat literally.

In Chicago an FBI bug picked up a conversation between Sam Giancana and one of his lieutenants. The lieutenant remarked that Oswald was an "anarchist" and a "Marxist Communist." Giancana coolly replied, "He was a marksman who knew how to shoot."[58]

Now, for once in the whole sorry intelligence swamp mess in which Lee Harvey Oswald floated, things began to go click click. It was possible to see the sudden clockwork as cogs in the wheel of disinformation about Oswald calculated to direct angry suspicion about the President's death toward the left, in general, and Cuba, in particular. Oswald's watch-me activities in New Orleans and Mexico City — and the mysterious visitors of Mrs. Odio — had set the stage. Then in rapid sequence:

On Tuesday John Martino, the Mafia technician who had been on the *Flying Tiger* expedition, charged on a talk show over Miami radio station WQAM that Oswald had distributed Fair Play for Cuba Committee literature in Florida and had traveled to Cuba via Mexico in September.

Interviewed by FBI agent James O'Connor, Martino stated the information came from a Cuban source, who also said that Oswald "had made a telephone call to the Cuban Intelligence Service in Cuba from a private residence in Miami" and, in Houston, "tried to sell marijuana and handled the exchange of Cuban pesos for American dollars."

Pressed to divulge his source, Martino said that the Cuban was enroute from California to join the counterrevolution and could not be contacted. Martino never did produce the Cuban.[59]

That same day the Pompano Beach *Sun-Sentinel* attributed to Frank Sturgis the news that Oswald had been in telephone contact with Cuban intelligence and "had connections with the Cuban government in Mexico and New Orleans, Louisiana." The article was by-lined by James C. Buchanan, whose brother Jerry belonged to Sturgis's International Anti-Communist Brigade.

Agent O'Connor talked to Sturgis, who conceded he had made "offhand comments" to Buchanan but styled them "guesses, speculation and rumor."

In Dallas the Secret Service predictably intercepted a letter addressed to Oswald that had been mailed from Havana. Dated November 10 and signed by "Pedro Charles," the letter implied, as the Secret Service put it, that "Oswald had been paid by Charles to carry out an unidentified mission which involved accurate shooting." In Washington the Justice Department received a similar letter addressed to Robert Kennedy and signed by "Mario del Rosario Molina," who claimed Oswald "assassinated President Kennedy at the direction of Pedro Charles, a Cuban agent who has traveled in the United States under various aliases," and that Oswald "met with Charles in Miami several months ago and was paid $7,000 by Charles." Both letters were postmarked in Havana the day after the assassination.

Laboratory examination determined that the two letters were written on the same typewriter. They were dismissed as a crude attempt by persons unknown in Cuba to blame Castro.[60]

In Washington J. Edgar Hoover and Nicholas Katzenbach, who was minding the Justice Department store in the absence of Bobby Kennedy, were greatly concerned about the ripple effect the rumors of Oswald's foreign ties were generating. Hoover was desperate to avoid suspicion that the FBI had failed in its duty. Katzenbach and other senior government officials were fearful that implications of a foreign-directed conspiracy might provoke international tensions. The previous day he had memoed Bill Moyers, a special assistant to the new President:

> The public must be satisfied that Oswald was the assassin; that he did not have confederates who are still at large. . . . Speculation about Oswald's motivation ought to be cut off, and we should have some basis for rebutting thought that this was a Communist conspiracy or (as the Iron Curtain press is saying) a right-wing conspiracy to blame it on the Communists.

In discussing the situation, Hoover and Katzenbach agreed that it was imperative to convince the world quickly that Oswald had acted alone. Katzenbach told the FBI chief that the report LBJ had ordered him to prepare should "settle the dust, insofar as Oswald and his activities are concerned. . . . "[61]

It was a hot lead in the estimation of Maurice G. Martineau, acting special agent in charge of the Secret Service office in Chicago. A reliable informant, Thomas Mosley, had just told one of his agents that the day before the assassination, a Cuban exile with whom he had been negotiating the sale of machine guns boasted his group now had "plenty of money" and would make the buy "as soon as we take care of Kennedy." The exile, Homer Echevarría, had been outspokenly critical of the President.

In an urgent communication to headquarters, Martineau advised that he was undertaking a top-priority investigation. In subsequent

meetings surveilled by the Secret Service, Mosley found out that
Echeverría was affiliated with the 30th of November Movement
and that an associate named Juan Francisco Blanco Fernández was
military director of the DRE. From what Echeverría and Blanco disclosed, the arms deal was being financed by Paulino Sierra's provisional government with money obtained at least in part from
"hoodlum elements," who were "not restricted to Chicago."
(Sierra's operation cashed in its chips shortly after the assassination.
It was not to be heard of again.)

It was a significant development, and Martineau was prepared to
place an undercover agent inside the Echevarría group. It is possible
that an expanding investigation might have uncovered the Sierra
cabal's link to the Lake Pontchartrain camp and the Mafia and the
Castro assassination plots, which in turn would have opened a Pan-
dora's box of leads to Ruby and Oswald. But the FBI effectively
choked off the investigation. After LBJ ordered it to assume primary
jurisdiction in the JFK case, the bureau "made clear that it wanted
the Secret Service to terminate its investigation," as the House Select
Committee on Assassinations phrased it. The Secret Service complied, turning over its files to the FBI. The FBI did not pursue the
matter.[62]

On December 3 the UPI put a story on the wires that led off: "An
exhaustive FBI report now nearly ready for the White House will
indicate that Lee Harvey Oswald was the lone and unaided assassin
of President Kennedy, Government sources said today." The story,
carried in newspapers throughout the nation, was leaked to the UPI
on orders of J. Edgar Hoover.

On December 9, barely three weeks after the assassination,
Hoover handed President Johnson the FBI summary report con-
cluding that both Oswald and Ruby acted alone. Although the report was supposedly confidential, more details were leaked.

On December 16 the Warren Commission, conceived by LBJ as
a means of substantiating the FBI findings, sat down for its second

executive session. As the members bantered about such items as where their wives should park to pick them up, Congressman Gerald Ford dropped a little bomb. A wire service bureau chief he knew had called. "Jerry, I'm surprised that we got, and the other press services got, stories out the very same day." Ford knew what he was fishing for. "The minute he said that," the congressman said, "it led me to the belief that he was inferring that there had been a deliberate leak from some agency of the Federal Government, and now they wanted us to confirm by Commission action what had been leaked previously."

The commission realized it had been stuck with the FBI's conclusion. "I just don't find anything in that [FBI] report that has not been leaked to the press," Earl Warren complained.

"Anyone can look at it," General Counsel J. Lee Rankin chipped in, "and see that it just doesn't seem like they're looking for things that this Commission has to look for in order to get the answers that it wants and it's entitled to."

Allen Dulles puffed on his pipe. He proposed that all material on Oswald in the Soviet Union be forwarded to the CIA for evaluation, prompting a rejoinder from Senator Richard Russell: "I think you have more faith in them than I have. I think they'll doctor anything they hand to us."[63]

Dulles didn't react to the slur; in fact, he could afford a smile. Things were going his way. At the first session a week earlier he had handed his colleagues his manifesto: an obscure book advancing the notion that American assassinations were always committed by demented loners. And Dulles was as secure as only a CIA chief who had kept the secrets could be. There was nothing in writing in the CIA files that would link Oswald to the agency. Such contracts were written with ink that disappeared.

The ex–CIA chief might also have felt smug about his knowledge of the CIA-Mafia assassination plots against Castro. They had been hatched when he was director and he had been fully briefed, but he had no intention of briefing the Warren Commission. His silence insured that the existence of the hit squad targeted on Castro and then switched to Kennedy would not be exposed.[64]

On December 19, dual pairs of FBI agents took turns double-teaming a bank robbery suspect named Richard Case Nagell in the El Paso, Texas, hoosegow. A lanky man with a vertical scar on his forehead, Nagell was supremely uncooperative, so much so that the FBI report of the extended grilling session consisted of but one sentence: "For the record he would like to say that his association with OSWALD (meaning LEE HARVEY OSWALD) was purely social and that he had met him in Mexico City and in Texas."[65]

As a bank robber Nagell could have been out of *Ripley's Believe It Or Not*. On September 20 he had walked into the State National Bank in El Paso, pulled out a .45 automatic, and fired two shots into the ceiling. He never asked for a dime. He walked outside, sat down on the curb, and waited to be arrested. He did it, he would later say, for "the sole purpose of having myself arrested and detained by federal authorities." He wanted to be in the comforting arms of the law for his own protection—he said he had stumbled into "a domestic-formulated and domestic-sponsored conspiracy" to assassinate John Kennedy.

All of this could have been written off as a bit whacko were it not for Nagell's exemplary record—with the military and with the CIA. During the Korean War he had won a battlefield commission, then graduated from the army intelligence school at Fort Holabird, Maryland, at the top of his class. Upon leaving the Army, he was recruited by the CIA, which dispatched him to Mexico City during the Missile Crisis and thereafter assigned him to keep tabs on the more fanatical Cuban exiles there.

During his assignment in Mexico Nagell encountered Oswald, whom he knew only as Aleksei Hidell. Nagell claimed Oswald was being used by an anti-Castro cabal bent on assassinating Kennedy, a group who wanted the assassin branded a Castro agent so the United States might invade Cuba.

In early September Oswald, unaware that he was being set up, boasted to Nagell, "We will kill him before the month is out." Nagell frantically warned his CIA case officer, whom he identified as one Robert Graham, about the assassination plot. Nagell said Graham told him to "take care of" Oswald as a means of "stopping the clock"—but Nagell could not bring himself to murder. Instead, on

September 13, he sent off a registered letter to J. Edgar Hoover giving the FBI the details of the plot to kill Kennedy. A week later he strode purposefully into the El Paso bank. It was the first bank handy on his way out of Mexico.

When he heard that Kennedy had indeed been shot, Nagell handed a jailer a note asking to see the Secret Service on an urgent matter. An FBI agent showed up. Nagell, angered that the bureau had failed to heed his warning, refused to talk to him. He continued to stonewall the FBI. At his trial he would say only that the bizarre robbery attempt had provided a "temporary solution" to an "unbearable problem."[66]

The judge meted out the maximum sentence of ten years. This was a stiff rap for a war hero and first offender who didn't even try to take any money. Five years later an appellate court overturned Nagell's conviction on the grounds that there was no evidence of intent to rob.

The man who had shot a bank walked out of Leavenworth Penitentiary, carrying with him whatever secrets he knew about the assassination of John F. Kennedy.

On May 13 CIA Counterintelligence Chief James Angleton called FBI Domestic Intelligence Chief William C. Sullivan to suggest that the FBI, like the CIA, carefully rehearse the testimony of its top officials before the Warren Commission. Angleton said that "it would be well for both McCone and Hoover to be aware that the Commission might ask the same questions, wondering whether they would get different replies from the heads of the two agencies." Angleton gave Sullivan examples of what he believed McCone would be asked and the "replies that will be given":

Q.   Was Oswald ever an agent of the CIA?

A.   No.

Q.   Does the CIA have any evidence showing that a conspiracy existed to assassinate President Kennedy?

A.   No.[67]

In 1979 the House Select Committee on Assassinations concluded that there most probably had been a conspiracy and that the

FBI and CIA were derelict in not pursuing it. Hoover, the committee charged, had had "a personal predisposition that Oswald had been a lone assassin" and had wrapped up the investigation with unseemly haste. An FBI assistant director told the committee that conspiracy was an "ancillary matter." "We were in the position of standing on the corner with our pocket open, waiting for someone to drop information into it," he said.

The committee also found that after the Warren Report had been issued, the FBI steadfastly refused to explore fresh leads pointing to a conspiracy. It specifically noted that in 1967 the bureau had balked when given information by Earl Warren "regarding organized crime figure John Roselli's claim of personal knowledge relating to Cuban or underworld complicity" and "took repeated action to discredit the source" instead of investigating advice that "New Orleans Mafia leader Carlos Marcello had allegedly made a threat against the life of President Kennedy."[68]

The committee similarly rebuked the CIA for passivity, echoing 1976 criticism by the Senate Intelligence Committee. The Senate report stingingly observed:

> Even if CIA investigators did not know that the CIA was plotting to kill Castro, they certainly did know that the Agency had been operating a massive covert operation against Cuba since 1960. The conspiratorial atmosphere of violence, which developed over the course of three years of CIA and exile group operations, should have led CIA investigators to ask whether Lee Harvey Oswald and Jack Ruby, who were known to have at least touched the fringes of the Cuban community, were influenced by that atmosphere. Similarly, arguments that the CIA domestic jurisdiction was limited belie the fact. CIA's Cuban operations had created an enormous *domestic* apparatus, which the Agency used both to gather intelligence domestically and to run operations against Cuba.[69]

The Warren Commission, hamstrung by its dependency on the FBI and the evasiveness of the CIA, went about its business as best it could. Staffers assigned to probe Oswald's background could find no plausible motive for him to have shot Kennedy. Leads suggesting that he had Cuban backing were washing out; one, in which a Nicaraguan falsely claimed to have witnessed Oswald's being handed a thick wad of bills in the Cuban Embassy in Mexico City, was suspected as the handiwork of General Somoza.

Two staff attorneys, W. David Slausen and William Coleman, began thinking along opposite lines. In an internal memo they wrote:

> The evidence here could lead to anti-Castro involvement in the assassination on some sort of basis as this: Oswald could have become known to the Cubans as being strongly pro-Castro. He made no secret of his sympathies, so the anti-Castro Cubans must have realized that law enforcement authorities were also aware of Oswald's feelings and that, therefore, if he got into trouble, the public would also learn of them. . . . It is possible that some sort of deception was used to encourage Oswald to kill the President. . . . The motive of this would, of course, be the expectation that after the President was killed, Oswald would be caught or at least his identity ascertained, the law enforcement authorities and the public would blame the assassination on the Castro government and a call for its forceful overthrow would be irresistible.

Slausen and Coleman pressed for an investigation of this hypothesis. The most logical place to start would have been with Guy Banister, who was certainly capable of engineering such a scenario. But Banister was permanently unavailable, having been found dead in bed of an apparent heart attack with his monogrammed Magnum at his side. When gathering up his effects at the 544 Camp Street building, his widow, Mary Banister, reportedly found the large stack of Oswald's Fair Play for Cuba literature. No investigation was ever conducted along the lines Slausen and Coleman urged.

The CIA's Maurice Bishop had a delicate assignment for Carlos Veciana. He wanted Veciana to offer his cousin, a member of the Cuban intelligence service in Mexico City, a large sum of money to defect and say that it was he and his wife who met with Oswald in the Mexican capital. Veciana agreed but had difficulty making contact.[70]

By August the Warren Commission, under pressure from LBJ to get its report out in time for the November 1964 election, had concluded its deliberations and was in the process of preparing its final report. Major questions remained unanswered. One concerned the report of Sylvia Odio that in September three men claiming association with JURE had solicited her help, and that one had called back touting Oswald as a potential assassin of Castro or, in the alternative, Kennedy. Odio remained firm in her account, and she had checked out as a solid witness.

On August 23 Chief Counsel J. Lee Rankin wrote to J. Edgar Hoover requesting that an attempt he made to identify the three men. "It is a matter of some importance to the Commission," Rankin said, "that Mrs. Odio's allegation either be proved or disproved."

Rankin, a man not partial to hyperbole, was not understating the problem. Unless something popped up to explain Mrs. Odio's story, her strange visit was *prima facie* evidence of a conspiracy to set up Oswald.

The answer came out of the blue, as if in answer to a prayer. In vetting its files, the Dallas FBI reported that the previous October an agent had questioned Loran Hall and a William Seymour after the pair was stopped by police hauling a load of supplies and medicine to the Interpen encampment in the Florida Keys. At the time a notation was made: "Active in the anti-Castro movement . . . Committee to Free Cuba." (Although the bureau may not have made the correlation, the Committee to Free Cuba was headed by Eladio del Valle, the onetime smuggling partner of Santos Trafficante and the man who hired David Ferrie to drop fire bombs over Cuba. Loran Hall has said that he was present when Sam Giancana offered Eddie Bayo $30,000 to kill Castro in February 1963 and that Trafficante staked Bayo the expense money.)

When finally located in California on September 16, Hall volunteered that the previous September "he was in Dallas, soliciting aid in connection with anti-Castro activities. He said he had visited Mrs. Odio." Hall named Lawrence Howard, a Mexican-American Interpen instructor, and Bill Seymour, who "generally resembled" Oswald, as his companions.[71]

The Warren Commission, confronted with a press deadline, took refuge in geography. Comforted by the convenient Hall explanation, it wrote off the Odio incident by noting that Oswald had begun his journey to Mexico and probably did not have time to detour to Dallas.

Howard and Seymour subsequently denied to the FBI that they had been at Odio's, whereupon Hall recanted his story on the basis that he had confused dates and places.

The Odio file remained closed. Still open was the question of who had impersonated Oswald, setting him up as a potential assassin of Castro and Kennedy.

The Warren Report was unveiled to a salute of twenty-one publicity guns. Gerald Ford became its star salesman. His "inside account" was *Life*'s October 2 cover story on how the commission "pieced together the evidence" and "nailed rumors of a conspiracy."

Tony Veciana was having no luck in reaching his cousin in Cuban intelligence in Mexico City. He finally asked Maurice Bishop if the money offer still stood. "Bishop said there was no need to talk about that plan any longer," Veciana recalled.[72] He said Bishop told him to "forget the whole thing and not to comment or ask any questions about Lee Harvey Oswald."

In 1979 the House Select Committee on Assassinations, after spending $5.4 million to exhume the leads buried over ten years before by the Warren Commission, concluded that the President's murder was probably the product of a conspiracy. The most probable conspirators were mobsters and possibly anti-Castro Cubans.

But the committee said too many years had passed to be sure.

Sam Giancana knew more about Oswald's role in the assassination that he ever let on to his mob underlings. In May 1966 he told his younger brother, Chuck, that he was about to leave Mexico to internationalize his rackets operations with the CIA as his partner. The agency, he said, had been his partner on a number of deals over the years when there was mutual profit to be made. To emphasize how close the relationship was he brought his cigar to his lips and boasted, "We took care of Kennedy . . . together."

Giancana explained that Oswald was no Castro sympathizer but "CIA all the way," a co-opted Marine trained to speak Russian in order to infiltrate the Soviet Union. When the decision to knock off Kennedy was made in the spring of 1963 Oswald was instructed by his pro tem CIA handler, Guy Banister, to advertise himself "as a Commie nut." This made him, Giancana said, the perfect "fall guy" for the assassination.

The Mafia kingpin told his brother the plot went right to "the top of the CIA," numbering some of the agency's former and present leaders. He said major funding for the hit came from "millions in oil" — wealthy Texas oilmen he had known over the years.

Giancana added that both the CIA and the mob had supplied personnel for the hit, but there was no need to worry about J. Edgar Hoover's going all out for the truth. "He hated the Kennedys as much as anybody and he wasn't about to help Bobby find his brother's killers."

While Hoover was passively covering up, Giancana went on, the CIA was doing it actively. "If anybody knew too much, the CIA found out about it and took care of the problem." This was an allusion to the string of mysterious deaths of people who in one way or another were connected to the deadly secrets of Dealey Plaza.[73]

On June 4, 1968, eight years after his brother had squeaked by Richard Nixon to win the presidency, Bobby Kennedy pressed the flesh with the kitchen help as he moved through the pantry of the Ambassador Hotel in Los Angeles. He had just won the California Democratic primary, and was, in his own words, "On to Chicago!" He was on a roll, predicted by many to wrest the Democratic nomination from the Vietnam War-proponent Hubert Humphrey and soundly beat the charmless Nixon, who also continued to hawk the war.

As Bobby passed through a set of swinging doors he was accosted by a gunman. A flurry of shots was fired. He fell backward, mortally wounded.

Nixon, the consummate anticommunist who had inspired the early attempts to oust Castro, captured the White House by, some say, default. His destiny would be Watergate, his fate sealed in a reversal of fortune by the anti-Castro team that mounted the break-in. But the question nagged: Why was Bobby shot at the precise moment that he achieved the momentum to go all the way and stop the Vietnam War? And there was another, more veiled enigma: Why was Bobby shot at the precise moment that he was on the way to gaining the power he needed to investigate his brother's death? As a U.S. senator he was powerless. But from the White House he could unleash the Justice Department on a new investigation. There was every indication that if elected he would go for it.

Barely an hour after the news from Dallas broke, Bobby Kennedy was called by Haynes Johnson of the Washington *Evening Star*, who was on leave from the paper to write a book on the Bay of Pigs invasion. Johnson was in Harry Williams's room at the Ebbitt Hotel in Washington, the CIA's lodging of choice for visiting operatives precisely because it was so nondescript. Williams, who had just arrived from his penultimate meeting with CIA officials on "the problem of Cuba," was Johnson's prime source among the Bay of Pigs veterans. He was also Bobby's best-and-brightest choice to lead a renewed effort to get rid of Castro. As Bobby well knew, the CIA agenda had included assassination.

"One of your guys did it," Bobby told Johnson in a flat, unemotional voice.[74]

Apparently Bobby immediately assumed that the murder plots against Castro had boomeranged. According to *Farewell America* (whose author had access to a report on the assassination prepared by Daniel Patrick Moynihan), that night Secret Service Chief James Rowley told Bobby that his agency believed JFK had been the victim of a powerful organization. "Ten hours after the assassination," *Farewell America* asserted, "Rowley knew that there had been three gunmen, and perhaps four, at Dallas that day, and later on the telephone Jerry Behn [head of the White House detail] remarked to Forrest Sorrels [*head of the Dallas Secret Service*], 'It's a plot.' 'Of course,' was Sorrels's reply."[75]

As a lame-duck attorney general the best Bobby could do was have Patrick Moynihan conduct the closet inquiry focusing on Jimmy Hoffa as the button-pusher. As Hoffa gloated after the assassination, RFK was now "just another lawyer." Publicly Bobby took the stance that he believed in the Warren Report even though he hadn't read it, but privately he seethed. Journalist Tom Braden, who was close to Bobby, asked him, "Why don't you just go on a crusade to find out about the murder of your brother?"[76] Bobby just shook his head and said that it was too horrible to think about and that he decided to just accept what the Warren Commission said.

But his acceptance turned to determination once he hit the presidential trail. He had confided to campaign aide Richard Lubic, who was with him in the Ambassador Hotel pantry the night he was shot, that he would reopen the case once he was elected. On May 28, 1968, a week before he was shot, he disappeared for several hours in Oxnard, California, to check privately on a report that a telephone call warning of the assassination had originated there on the morning of November 22, 1963.[77]

When Bobby was gunned down it seemed like an open-and-shut case. A diminutive young man named Sirhan Sirhan was overpowered after allegedly firing all eight shots from his .22-caliber revolver. The following morning the shoot-from-the-lip mayor of Los Angeles, Sam Yorty, branded Sirhan a leftist who was "inflamed by contacts with the Communist Party" (the allegation turned out to be untrue). At the same time L.A. Chief of Detectives Robert Houghton announced that he was forming an elite Special Unit Senator (SUS) to run out all leads pointing in the direction of a conspiracy. He didn't want another Dallas with its lingering doubts. But the two detectives he named to head up the SUS conspiracy section were strange choices. One was Lieutenant Manuel Pena, who had gone on detached duty with the CIA in Latin America on several occasions. Pena had "retired" from the LAPD in November 1967, only to show up again in the Glass House (LAPD headquarters) a couple of months before the RFK shooting. The other was Sergeant

Enrique "Hank" Hernandez, who boasted of receiving a medal from the Venezulean government when it had been concerned with blocking Fidel Castro's "exportation" of the revolution. Both LAPD men had worked for the Office of Public Safety of the U.S. Agency for International Development, known to insiders as "the Department of Dirty Tricks" because it taught foreign intelligence agencies in Latin American nations such niceties as techniques of assassination.[78]

In view of the dual roles of Pena and Hernandez it would have been appropriate to ask whether it was the LAPD or the CIA that was controlling the investigation. But at that time perhaps only a few insiders knew that the cops had also been spooks. In any event they managed to put the damper on any flicker of conspiracy. They browbeat a key witness, Kennedy worker Sandy Serrano, insisting that she had invented her story of being brushed aside on a hotel stairway by a fleeing couple and of hearing the woman, clad in a polka-dot dress, boasting, "We shot him!" And they trashed the account of Oliver Owen, a fundamentalist preacher and horse trader. Owen said Sirhan had wanted to buy a lead pony from him and had asked that the horse be delivered to the rear of the Ambassador Hotel on election night, when he would have the money. (Sirhan had four $100 dollar bills on his person when arrested.) What made Owen's disclosure even more provocative was his description of the young couple accompanying Sirhan. But the SUS pair dismissed Owen as a publicity seeker — even though he hid from the press.[79]

Owen, who styled himself as "The Walking Bible" because he had memorized all the verses, was a mysterious figure in his own right. One of his religious followers, Gail Aiken, was the sister of Arthur Bremer, the gunman who would take George Wallace out of the 1972 presidential race when his candidacy was threatening to siphon off votes from Nixon.[80] Owen was also a member of the race track and prizefight crowd, and owned a piece of a boxer named "Irish Rip" O'Reilly.

The other piece of the fighter belonged to Edward Glenn, the proprietor of a dry-well venture called Midland Oil Company. Glenn knew Eugene Hale Brading (aka Jim Braden) who had been detained at Dealey Plaza minutes after the assassination but had ali-

bied that he was in town on oil business. According to Los Angeles
FBI agent Roger J. LaJeunnesse, Glenn and Brading would "pal
around together on occasion—from Miami to San Diego—with
stops in between like Dallas and New Orleans."[81] Tipped off by a
newsman that Brading had been at the scene of the crime in Dallas,
Chief Houghton dispatched SUS officer Manuel Gutierrez to interview Brading at his home near San Diego. This time Brading
claimed he was at the Century Plaza Hotel, a fifteen-minute drive
from the Ambassador, on the night RFK was shot.[82]

In his book *Special Unit Senator* Houghton details his agents' suspi-
cions of a man who could only be Brading, adding: "In addition to
his Mafia and oil contacts, he was friendly with 'far-right' industri-
alists and political leaders of that area," meaning Texas. But to
Houghton it was all historical coincidence.[83] Yet if the SUS had
been inclined to put it all together it might have found a vital link
(just as the FBI might have if it had traced Oswald back to 544 Camp
Street).

And there are other links. Sirhan had been an exercise boy at the
Santa Anita Race Track where he came in contact with a Henry R.
Ramistella, also known as Frank Donneroummas, who had a rap
sheet showing arrests in New York and Miami. When Donneroummas moved on to the nearby Granja Vista del Rio Ranch,
which bred and trained race horses, he brought Sirhan with him.
The ranch was partly owned by actor Desi Arnaz, the ex-husband
of Lucille Ball who came from a wealthy Cuban family and was
staunchly anti-Castro. After RFK was shot the police seized a notebook from Sirhan's home that was filled with fragmented, cryptic
phrases which a psychiatrist later testified were scrawled by Sirhan
while in a hypnotic trance. One entry recorded that he had found
a job at the ranch: "Dezi [*sic*] Arnaz's Res Sirhan $600 per month."
Another read: "Frank Donaruma [*sic*] pl please ple please pay to 5
please pay to the order of Sirhan Sirhan the amount of 5." This suggests that Sirhan was a hired gun.[84]

If so, he was not alone, and may have been there only as a distrac-
tion to draw attention away from the real killer. After the LAPD
closed the SUS shop and declared Sirhan the lone assassin, irrefuta-
ble evidence has come to light that, as was the case at Dealey Plaza,

there were more shots fired than the authorities admitted. The LAPD crime lab reported that it had accounted for all eight of the bullets from Sirhan's gun; but former FBI agent William A. Bailey, who had inspected the pantry right after RFK was shot, came forward and disclosed that two additional bullets had lodged in the jamb of the swinging doors. And attorney Vincent Bugliosi, the famed *Helter Skelter* author, obtained a statement from a police officer that he had located a bullet embedded in the door to the stage where RFK had delivered his victory speech. The count was now eleven, three more than Sirhan, who had no chance to reload, could have fired.[85] In 1982 Dr. Michael Hecker, one of the country's leading forensic acoustics experts—he analyzed the gap in the Nixon White House tape—determined that there were at least ten and possibly as many as twelve sounds of gunshots on the audio tapes made by reporters accompanying Bobby through the pantry.[86]

Not only was there a second gun, there is solid evidence that whoever fired it was the killer. No witness in the pantry saw Sirhan closer than a foot or two from RFK, and he was in front of the senator. The coroner's reported stated that according to the powder tattooing the shot that killed Kennedy was fired from the rear at a distance of one to three *inches*. This was point-blank, execution style.

544 Camp Street, Dealey Plaza, The Ambassador Hotel. They are of the same coinage. "This coin shows one of the Roman gods," Sam Giancana told his brother Chuck in illustrating the CIA-Mafia alliance. "This one has two faces, two sides. That's what we are, the Outfit (Mafia) and the CIA, two sides of the same coin."[87]

SEVEN
Across the Windward Passage

I

THE car was a hot rodder's dream, an old Chevy rigged for heavy-duty loads, painted battleship gray with zoot-suit sidewalls. As it hit the New Jersey Turnpike heading south for Miami, the Chevy was running easy, fast but legal. The driver, a swarthy man given to smoking Montecristos flown to him from Havana, was not about to get a traffic citation.

He could have been the villain in any B movie—dark, heavyset, wearing a droopy mustache stolen from Zapata and dark glasses for nighttime driving. At his hip was a half-empty bottle of Myers Jamaican rum. He took a slug, and the dark liquid sloshed on his war surplus shirt. He said "shit" in five languages.

Next to him in the death seat Carlos was trying to catch some badly needed sleep. "You're as jumpy as a flea, *muchacho.*"

"Do you blame me?" said Rolando Masferrer, drying his hand on his pant leg. "We aren't exactly loaded down with dirty laundry back there, are we?"

Masferrer's fears were well grounded. His "laundry" was guns, grenades, and ammunition—and interstate transportation was a lock-the-door-and-throw-away-the-key offense. But the Cuban

Masferrer was an old hand at gunrunning. He was also handy at revolution, and that was on his mind as he carefully guided the car through the night away from the lights of New York.

He glanced over at Carlos, whose dark eyes glittered with expectation, and suddenly removed his hands from the wheel, waving them wildly as he described in detail what he was planning for his next conquest — Papa Doc Duvalier, dictator of Haiti.

Masferrer puffed away at his cigar, filling the old car with pungent smoke. Clamping the stogie in his teeth, he set the bottle of rum between his legs and barked in heavily accented English, "This Papa Doc — wait until I get him — I'll crack his balls like hazelnuts — you watch, little one — I'll get him good!"

And Rolando Masferrer, one of the cast of crazy men who were reshaping the Secret War as it took a wacko turn rightward, drove on south.[1]

Squalor, disease, voodoo, violence, and goon squads. Haiti. The spectacularly beautiful piece of Caribbean real estate occupying the mountainous western third of the island of Hispaniola where steep mountains fall into deep green valleys soothed by the cool blues of the seas that wash her shores. The giant jaws of the northern and southern peninsulas close around the western Gulf of Gonâve. To the north is the Atlantic Ocean; to the south the Caribbean Sea; and across the eastern border, the Dominican Republic. The eastern tip of Cuba is but forty miles away — across the Windward Passage.

All the blessings of nature have never been enough to counteract the harsh poverty and superstition that rule Haiti's five million people. Haiti's only bargain was that forty-mile stretch of azure water which proved irresistible to action groups interested in spring-boarding across to Cuba during the Secret War in the Caribbean. Haiti beckoned all comers and for a time became the stage for a comic opera of border invasions, amphibious commando landings, assassination attempts, guerrilla infiltrations, and even palace bombings carried off by an odd lot of adventurers recruited from the best of the Bogart movies. Central casting, supported by the CIA, the FBI, the mob, and, on at least one occasion, the CBS television network, sent over leading men like Rolando Masferrer, a notorious hatchet man during the days of Cuban dictator Batista, who carried a paper sack under his arm that wasn't filled with the usual brown-bag fare. Masferrer stocked his sack with the things that made him happy: some good reading material, an assortment of his favorite cigars, and a loaded Colt .45. Others who would later be listed in the credits included Jay Humphrey, a six-foot four-inch pilot-muscleman who squeezed into cockpits for combat missions; Mitchell Livingston WerBell III, a very rich man who loved guns more than women; a priest with eclectic tastes; and a paramilitary journalist who was fond of popping out of closets wearing jungle fatigues.

Haiti seemed perfect for the series of ragtag invasion plots they would plan—each one in turn more bizarre and more under-nourished. Not only was the distance to Cuba minimal, but Oriente, the Cuban province closest to Haiti, was the most logical place to bring a counterrevolution. By 1962 Castro had ringed his island with a modern defense system. Yet most of his units were guarding the central and western sectors, leaving the Oriente wilderness relatively undefended. Should disaster loom, the Guantánamo naval base would offer sanctuary.

The only problem with Haiti was its frumpy dictator, Dr. François "Papa Doc" Duvalier, a feeble-sounding little Führer without a friend in the world. But when you're President for Life, Protector of the People, Maximum Chief of the Revolution, Apostle of National Unity, Electrifier of Souls, Grand Patron of Commerce and Industry, Benefactor of the Poor, and Haiti's absolute ruler, who needs friends? An observer of the Duvalier regime said in 1970, "he has shown himself a more durable despot than Hitler, more murderously cunning than Stalin, more feared than Mussolini, and a good bit richer than all three departed dictators put together."[2] Increasing the Duvalier bank balance was the bottom line for Papa Doc, and his greed first sent him to the U.S. government for empire-building bucks and later, when the Kennedy administration cut him off, found him making deals and shooting craps with the syndicate.

In the convoluted politics of the Caribbean, this choleric anticommunist also had reached an accommodation with the Cubans. He realized that the Windward Passage was narrow in both directions and that superior Cuban forces could overrun Haiti faster than the Wehrmacht had blitzed Poland. Not only were his own armed forces feeble, but he distrusted them to the extent that he kept the air force's propellers locked in the basement of the Presidential Palace. Nor could he count on aid from Washington. So it was a matter of survival. In 1971 Mike McLaney, a gaming operator who was running a casino in Port-au-Prince, told a reporter that Duvalier "once told me how he killed a whole boatload of Cubans who accidentally landed from the Windward Passage." They were trying to escape from Cuba. In his dry, whispery voice, the voodoo dictator, who dressed in a black suit and black homburg, boasted, "There were about twenty of them. I sent my Macoutes down there and they killed them all."[3]

It was the legendary vulnerability of Haiti that convinced the action groups that the country could be taken with a vest-pocket army. Contributing to the legend was a crazy-quilt expedition that in 1958 came close to cutting short Papa Doc's reign at one year. The instigator was an exiled Haitian Army captain named Alex Pasquet. At a Miami cocktail party Pasquet met Arthur T. Payne, a brawny deputy sheriff, and soon they agreed that taking Haiti was a cinch. Promised a high post in Pasquet's replacement government, Payne began fund raising with astonishing results. He "sold" gambling concessions in the new Haiti to Miami Beach hotelmen with syndicate connections and wheedled a large contribution from a wealthy contractor on the promise of construction awards. Smaller donors contributed thousands more.

The plan called for activating the underground opposition in Haiti and precipitating a rebellion. The brash Payne flew to Port-au-Prince posing as a tourist and made the rounds of names given to him by Pasquet. But the Tonton Macoutes, Papa Doc's private Gestapo, tailed him, and he was unceremoniously deported while his contacts were rounded up and executed.

Thereupon Payne and Pasquet decided to make an invasion. More money was required, and after it was all over, an investigation commissioned by Miami authorities found that an ants' pile of local interests had chipped in: bolita operators, mobsters, gunrunners, even

Bahamian politicians. Meyer Lansky reportedly backed the venture on the theory that a stable Haiti under a puppet president would lure tourists and make gambling feasible. Payne and Pasquet even found common cause with Fidel Castro's 26th of July Movement, which was trying to defeat Batista. Castro was still smarting from a Duvalier double cross. Shortly after Papa Doc was elected in September 1957, Fidel Castro, with the financial backing of Carlos Prío, paid $200,000 for the privilege of using Haiti as an operational base against Batista. But Batista upped the ante, dropping $1 million into Papa Doc's till with a pledge of $4 million more.

The master plan called for Pasquet and Payne to lead a landing party and the underground to rise, while a planeload of arms stood by at Miami. In late July the two leaders accompanied by four Americans and two Haitian exiles boarded a pebbled old fishing smack, the *Mollie C*, and set sail for Haiti. On the late afternoon of July 28 the mini-army landed north of Port-au-Prince and commandeered a truck. Within hours they had seized the Dessalines Barracks flanking the Presidential Palace.

In Miami, however, the first mishap occurred. The plane loaded with weapons and members of the 26th of July Movement was impounded by customs agents as it stood by in a remote corner of the airfield.

In Port-au-Prince things were going unbelievably well. The barracks soldiers were locked in the mess hall, and Payne had one of them telephone the palace. "Tell Duvalier that we hold the barracks and we'll attack at dawn unless he surrenders," the deputy sheriff ordered.[4]

Papa Doc, who had retired for the night, hastily pulled on his trousers, ready to flee. At this critical juncture one of the invaders ran out of cigarettes. "Go out and buy me a pack of Pall Malls," he instructed one of the captives.

The soldier bought the cigarettes and was returning when he changed his mind. He went to the palace and broke the news that only eight men were holding the barracks. Duvalier mustered his Macoutes and militia, who stormed the barracks. The hapless invaders, down to the last man, were chopped to pieces.

For the second half of the nineteenth century the United States did not recognize the black republic of Haiti. In 1915 the Marines were landed to seize the gold reserves, beginning an occupation that would last for nineteen years. Although Franklin Roosevelt pulled out the Leathernecks in 1934, Haiti had by then become an American vassal state. The mulatto elite that ran the country danced to the tune played at the U.S. Embassy.

This servile relationship was illustrated by a 1955 visit paid by then Vice President Richard Nixon in which he heaped praise on the puppet regime and took to the streets to press flesh with the people. Nixon stopped a woman riding a donkey bearing milk containers and conversed through a government interpreter. She demanded, "Tell this *cocoyé* [a term of derision] to let me go on my way." The translator told Nixon, "She is happy to meet the Vice President of the United States." All smiles, Nixon inquired about her family. She had no husband and three children, the woman said, which the translator presented as: "She is engaged." Placing his hand on the donkey's rump, Nixon asked, "What is the animal's name?" The woman retorted, "He must be crazy. Doesn't he know a donkey when he sees one?"

In the winter of 1956–57 Haiti, the poorest nation in this hemisphere, erupted in violence, and the president was deposed. The country reeled into chaos, with successive governments tumbling like bowling pins. Haiti's nervous neighbor on the east, Rafael Trujillo, decided to throw secret support behind a forty-nine-year-old country doctor named François Duvalier as the best bet to restore stability. The mild-mannered Duvalier, who had studied at the University of Michigan, easily won the September 1957 election.

One of his first moves was to have some of his most loyal aides fitted with weights and dumped in the Gulf of Gonâve, the Papa Doc version of starting with a clean slate. Another was to seek even more United States support. In 1958 Marine "advisers" arrived, and by the end of 1961 some $20 million in aid was in his coffers. In January 1962 Haiti in effect sold its vote in the Organization of American States to the United States for a $5 million price.

But the Kennedy administration was unable to stomach Papa Doc's chamber of horrors for long. Late in 1962 it dispatched a psychiatrist to Port-au-Prince and had the embassy arrange a private dinner with Papa Doc. The psychiatrist returned to Washington with the diagnosis, "Duvalier is a psychopath — there are unmistakable symptoms of paranoid megalomania. He is a very sick man."

At first the Kennedy administration tried to persuade Duvalier to clean up his act, but when the futility of reform became clear, a virtual ultimatum was delivered by Ambassador Raymond Thurston. As Duvalier later recounted it to a European journalist, "Ambassador Thurston appeared one evening to tell me plainly that I must go. He came and said that the country was in revolt and my enemies were about to seize power, but that the United States would save me personally provided, of course, that I gave no trouble and went quietly." This was the same type of unofficial "word" that had been given Batista and Trujillo, and the result was an even more emphatic no. Duvalier gave Thurston twenty-four hours to pack and leave.

The White House reacted by suspending aid and recalling the Marines and diplomatic mission. It had already cut off arms. Papa Doc seized the occasion to deliver a rambling speech soothsaying doom for John Kennedy. When Kennedy was struck down at Dallas on November 22, 1963, Duvalier planted the rumor that he had sent zombies to Texas.[5]

Under Lyndon Johnson relations with Haiti were repaired somewhat, although it was not until the Nixon administration took over that the old status quo was restored. The event was symbolized by the appearance of Nixon envoy Nelson Rockefeller in Port-au-Prince in 1969.

Economic and military aid ensued. In November 1970 Washington secretly lifted the arms ban and granted export licenses to a Miami firm, Aerotrade, Inc. A major stockholder in the company was Haitian Defense Minister Luckner Cabronne, who was once quoted as saying that "a good Duvalierist stands ready to kill his children or children to kill their parents." Despite these ravings, Cabronne had solid business instincts. He controlled the tourist resort at Ibo Beach, the country's taxi system, and Air Haiti. The Marines were again sent in, but this time they were superannuated ones on Aerotrade's payroll who were to serve as advisers. Weapons, munitions, and a half dozen patrol craft were also imported.

The concept of using Haiti as a dagger pointed at the heart of Cuba was nothing new, as we have seen. What was new was the idea of using Haiti without Duvalier. During the six-year hiatus between the severance of normal relations by JFK and their resumption by Nixon, that benighted nation was the target of some half dozen invasion plots in which the CIA was not a totally innocent party.

II

While the serio-comic-tragic Haiti invasions were cranking up, prior plots against the Cuban mainland, and Fidel Castro, were awkwardly cranking down. "Lyndon Johnson says he doesn't want to hear another thing about those goddam Cubans," Howard Hunt had told Harry Williams a few months after the JFK assassination. In bitter tones Hunt was explaining why Williams's Dominican-based assault project had been cancelled. It was in accord with Johnson's new policy on Cuba — in the Texas vernacular he was calling in the dogs, pissing on the fire and going home. Cuba had been a Bobby Kennedy project, and anything with Bobby's fingerprints on it LBJ wouldn't touch. In his memoirs H. R. Haldeman gave an illustration of the unspoken hostility that existed between the two men. Johnson called Bobby, trying to entrap him. But the tape of the conversation turned out unintelligible. Johnson later learned that Bobby always carried a scrambler in his pocket.

As LBJ built up his own war in Vietnam, the huge JM/WAVE station in Miami echoed with ghosts. But the CIA was not finished with Castro. Assets were shuffled and transferred, and agents sent into deep cover on the payrolls of other federal agencies such as the DEA. When finance officer James Wilcott, who had been transferred from Tokyo to JM/WAVE, took issue with the money manipulations, he was brusquely told, "You ask too many questions."

The CIA had never trusted Harry Williams, who besides bore the stigma of having been RFK's hand-picked leader. But the agency continued to take good care of its own Golden Boy, Manuel Artime, providing him funds in exchange for a promise that he would clear all missions in advance. But as time went by, Artime's Second Naval

Guerrilla based in Central America proved a spectacular flop. It needed a big score. On the evening of September 13, 1964, the opportunity seemed to present itself.

The MRR attack vessel *Santa Maria* was creeping through the Windward Passage, bent on shooting up a Cuban shore station, when a large moving blip appeared on her radar screen. In the darkness a Swift boat was launched to identify the vessel. Approaching from the rear at a quartering angle, the Swift boat trained its searchlight on the fantail and spotted the word "Sierra." It was the biggest prize of all—the *Sierra Maestra*, the pride of Castro's merchant fleet recently built in an East German yard.

The *Santa Maria* launched a second Swift boat, and for twenty minutes the two angry sea hornets poured a stream of fire from 57mm recoilless rifles and .50-caliber machine guns into the freighter. She went dead in the water, blazing fiercely. The crew abandoned ship.

The *Santa Maria* jubilantly radioed the news to the Central American bases. MRR troops celebrated as if it were New Year's Eve, and Artime prepared to fly to Panama to announce the victory. He was halted by an urgent message from the Somerset Corporation, a CIA front in Panama which coordinated the Second Naval Guerrilla. Intelligence data placed the *Sierra Maestra* in waters far from the action zone. A shaken Artime ordered that the Swift boats take a closer look at the name on the fantail of the abandoned ship. It read in full: "*Sierra Aranzazu*, Bilbao."

A ghastly mistake. The *Sierra Aranzazu* was a smaller Spanish motor vessel carrying a cargo of cork, toys and garlic to Cuba. Her captain, second mate and third engineer had all been killed, and seventeen sailors were injured.

Artime flatly denied that his MRR was guilty of this maritime outrage, suggesting that Castro himself had done it to discredit the MRR. He flew to Madrid, purportedly at the CIA's prompting, to repeat his fib personally to Generalissimo Francisco Franco, who didn't believe a word of it.

From this point on it was all downward for the MRR. More blunders and a financial scandal forced Artime to pack up and leave Central America. The CIA had spent an estimated $10 million in cash subsidies in addition to logistical support. Some $2 million in un-vouchered funds had disappeared, but no one was prosecuted. But the agency had yet another assignment for its tarnished Golden Boy. They gave him a new code name for his new duty. Now he was B-1.

In the fall of 1964 Rolando Cubela urgently requested the CIA to furnish him with a silencer for a Belgian FAL rifle to be used to assassinate Fidel Castro. According to an agency memorandum, "Amlash was told and fully understands that the United States government cannot become involved to any degree in the 'first step' of his plan. If he needs support, he realizes he will have to get it elsewhere. FYI: This is where B-1 could fit in nicely in giving any support he would request."

When Desmond FitzGerald read the memo, he concurred that B-1, Manuel Artime, was just the man. Artime had an amphibious capability that could provide backup muscle for Cubela's coup. More important, Artime was to act as a "cutout" so that the assassination plot could not come home to the CIA. For one thing, Cubela was not considered wholly trustworthy. For another, neither John McCone nor the LBJ White House knew about the plot, and Fitz-Gerald did not feel disposed to tell them.

This operation had to be more "plausibly deniable" than usual. FitzGerald instructed his special affairs staff to bring Cubela and Artime together in such a way that "neither of them knew that the contact had been engineered by the CIA." In the case of Artime, this instruction was so much horse feathers. The arrangements were made by James Noel, the former Havana station chief who had helped Artime escape to Miami, and E. Howard Hunt, Artime's CIA political officer for the Bay of Pigs. But the motions were gone through. In his autobiography *Undercover*, Hunt writes that he had to resign from the CIA and become a "contract agent" in order to undertake a "delicate but hardly time-consuming political action assignment" in Madrid. At the time of the assassination "arrangements," James Noel was the CIA head of station in Madrid.

The Madrid meetings between Artime and Cubela were held in MRR safe house in the Torre de Madrid apartments. The safe house had been used in operations sabotaging ships under construction in Spanish yards for the Cuban merchant fleet. Artime was to supply Cubela with a silencer for the FAL rifle and bombs to conceal in a suitcase or lamp or other object that could be placed next to Castro. The plan called for the MRR to step up its raids on Cuba one month before the assassination date to "prepare the public and raise the morale and resistance spirit of the people." Within forty-eight hours of the assassination an MRR expeditionary force of 750 men would land.

Never a slouch as a salesman, Artime boasted to Cubela of the tremendous support he commanded from the CIA, certain Latin American countries, and the Organization of American States. He promised that after he landed in Cuba and a junta in which he and Cubela shared power was formed, the United States and the OAS would back them, and at least five countries would recognize the new government.[6]

It was an ambitious plan that, despite Artime's exaggerations, had a reasonable chance for success. The CIA channeled $100,000 into the project through Jim Noel. One of Artime's men flew to Miami, picked up a hand-crafted silencer and "small, highly concentrated explosives" from JM/WAVE, and turned them over to Cubela in Madrid. Cubela stuffed them in his diplomatic pouch and returned to Havana, where he remained in contact with the MRR through José González, the embassy attaché code-named Amwhip. In Havana Cubela began putting together his cabal, starting with Major Ramón Guin, also a CIA agent in place.

Once the stage was set, some of the actors began behaving strangely. Information came to the CIA that one of Cubela's widening circle of conspirators was in clandestine contact with Cuban intelligence. A security interrogation of González was even more unsettling: He was deemed to have lied, and it began to be feared that he and perhaps Cubela himself were in touch with Cuban intelligence. Then Cubela's "lifelong friend," the exile who had transported explosives to the McLaney property at Lake Pontchartrain in 1963, walked into the Immigration and Naturalization Service office in New York and began talking. He knew about the projected assassination and coup and the CIA involvement.

In July 1965 the CIA, afraid that Cubela was baiting a trap, cut off all contact with him. For months there was strained silence. Then, on February 28, 1966, security police in Havana arrested Cubela, Major Guin, and five others for plotting to kill Castro. During the trial a prosecution witness named Juan Feliafel took the stand to tell an incredible tale of double agentry. As a member of Cuban intelligence he had been instructed in 1963 to go to Miami, pose as an exile, and infiltrate the anti-Castro movement. Shamming his way through three CIA lie detector tests, Feliafel was trained in demolition and clandestine operations near Miami and sent on seventeen missions to Cuba. The eighteenth proved crucial. Feliafel had learned of the Amlash plot through the sheerest coincidence: His brother Anís had become chief of intelligence for the MRR. When his launch was challenged by a Cuban patrol boat, Feliafel took advantage of the commotion to dive into the water and swim to shore. Four days later Cubela, Guin, and the others were arrested.

The defendants were convicted, and Cubela, in an outburst of histrionics, cried, "To the wall! To be executed! That is what I want! It is deserved!" But Castro personally intervened, declaring that it was more important to eliminate the vices that created traitors than to liquidate the traitors themselves. The sentence was twenty-five years. Castro sent Cubela books to read in prison.

It was a show-stopping climax to a dramatic trial that received world press attention. When he read about it in *The New York Times*, Dean Rusk demanded to know what the CIA's role might have been. Dick Helms sent him a soothing memo stating that contact with Cubela had been confined to "the express purpose" of intelligence gathering. "The Agency was not involved with Cubela in a plot to assassinate Fidel Castro," Helms wrote, "nor did it ever encourage him to attempt such an act."

III

When Papa Doc showed no signs of cleaning up his act despite repeated proddings, the brothers Kennedy handed the problem to the CIA. At the time, however, the agency was concentrating on the sabotage program against Cuba and provided the Haitian Coalition in New York with only token training and equipment. What the Haitians needed was moxie and money. They got the first from a flamboyant exile politician named Raul Dagnais. And they got the second from the Canadian branch of the Society of Jesus.

It was a wintry day in early 1963 in Montreal as Raul Dagnais began plotting the downfall of a tropical dictator. The previous visitors to his suite had been mostly Jesuits in mufti, men with their own special motive for bringing Haiti into a more Christian era. In 1958 the Canadian Jesuits had persuaded Duvalier to allow them to open a mission in the heavily Roman Catholic country, but before long Papa Doc had installed voodooism as the state religion and given the Black Robes all manner of trouble. It was not a situation that the Jesuits, who from their earliest days had a reputation for meddling in the affairs of various states to the extent that their head was known as the Black Pope, were inclined to accept. So when Dagnais renewed his acquaintances from the mission days, his plea for funds fell on attentive ears. Whether the Jesuits tapped a Vatican font or private resources is unknown, but the sum that Dagnais could build his budget on went into six figures.

This day the visitor to Dagnais's suite was Robert Emmett Johnson, a paramilitary journalist and mercenary schemer who had once been on Trujillo's payroll. The two quickly agreed on terms for Johnson to coordinate the project and just as quickly came up with a plan to make it lights-out for Papa Doc. Dagnais had already recruited an official in Duvalier's retinue, while Johnson knew a French Foreign Legion veteran named Marc Krausse who was an expert on do-it-yourself bombing. Krausse would go to Port-au-Prince to teach the official how to rig an explosive device that would go off when Papa Doc flipped on the light switch in his bedroom. Krausse was purchasing the necessary components when the official sent word that he would like to bow out gracefully.[7]

Dagnais and Johnson turned to more conventional plans, consulting with General Léon Cantave, a white-fringed ex-chief of staff of the Haitian Army who headed the Haitian Coalition. Cantave impetuously called for a seaborne commando raid on Port-au-Prince with Johnson stepping ashore first, but the American balked. "Like an old Errol Flynn movie, we were to pour ashore, guns blazing, and assault Papa Doc's palace," Johnson recalled. "I told them I wasn't Errol Flynn."[8]

The upshot was that Cantave would hole up in the thick Dominican forest near the frontier with Haiti and attack when the situation was auspicious. Since the two countries were natural enemies, the Dominican commanders in the area were more than willing for Cantave to pitch his tents. In the meantime, Bob Johnson had nightmares over the unpreparedness of the green Haitian volunteers and consulted with Gerry Hemming and Howard Davis of Interpen, who turned him over to Eddie Bayo. Johnson and Bayo drew up a formal agreement that, once Haiti was freed, the Cubans could use it as a base to attack Castro. The deal was consummated when Johnson picked up bills in the thousands of dollars that Bayo owed on arms and equipment, and Bayo reciprocated by crash-drilling the Haitians.

By early August (a month after Bayo vanished on the *Flying Tiger* mission) the Haitian Coalition treasury was so depleted by profligate spending that Cantave was forced to move prematurely. He led a force ashore near Cap Haïtien, expecting air support from Alex Rorke (it was a month later that Rorke flew off to oblivion). But Rorke's borrowed B-25 sat punchless on the ground at Little Inagua Island, the promised bombs and ordinance not having arrived. Cantave's commandos were soundly thrashed and fled across the frontier to sanctuary in the Dominican Republic.

Papa Doc imagined a vast conspiracy and unleashed his Tonton Macoutes to wreak vengeance on anyone even rumored to have aided Cantave. Severed heads were impaled on pikes in the capital, and entire families were slaughtered in the countryside. It was a grisly last straw for the Kennedy administration, which sent Ambassador Raymond Thurston over to the palace with his ultimatum, which was resoundingly rejected.

When Papa Doc reacted to the Kennedy maneuvers, hinting that he might seek a bipartite agreement with Castro, the CIA had a chance to dangle the specter of communism coming to Haiti, a theme beamed incessantly from the Radio Americas transmitter on

Swan Island. With the specific authorization of JFK, the agency trained more than 100 Haitian Coalition exiles at the Green Beret center at Fort Bragg and a base next to the Army intelligence head-quarters in Maryland. The Haitians were formed into thirteen-man units modeled on Special Forces "A" teams and sent to Cantave's Dominican camp, which was being supplied by night airdrops from unmarked U.S. Navy planes.

Then came Dallas. Deliverance from John Kennedy was no guar-antee of the future for Papa Doc. Duvalier instructed his consular officers in the United States to hire private detectives to spy on his opposition. Apparently the sleuths came up with something. In February 1964 Papa Doc expelled eighteen Canadian Jesuits on charges of subversive activities and closed down their mission.

IV

Tall and movie-star handsome, Carl Davis was itching for action. Davis had flown for Dr. Bosch's MIRR, was a denizen of Nelli Hamilton's boardinghouse, and had seen brief service with the CIA contingent in the Congo in 1964. His disgust over indiscriminate attacks on civilians in the Congo had given way to barely sup-pressed excitement over a new project that would bother no one's conscience: elimination of the bloody tyrant François "Papa Doc" Duvalier. It was May 1968, and Davis's period of enforced idleness in San Francisco was coming to an end. "I'm leaving for Miami to-night," he confided over an early-morning cup of coffee. "Watch the papers next week for something on Haiti."[9]

A week later, on May 21, the Miami *Herald* bannered: HAITI CLAIMS MYSTERY B-25 DROPPED TWO BOMBS ON CITY. That afternoon the *News* headlined: HAITI CALLS ON U.N. TO HALT BOMBING. The next morning the *Herald* proclaimed: HAITIAN ARMY CRUSHES EXILE INVA-SION FORCE, printing a map with bomb bursts to show where fighting was still going on. One day later the *Herald* reported, "Reliable reports indicated the Haitian army garrison at Cap Haï-tien, whose loyalty to Duvalier was believed questionable, offered no resistance to the invaders. Cap Haïtien, a center of anti-Duvalier unrest, reportedly welcomed the invaders. Port-au-Prince, where one person was reported killed and several others injured in the bombing attack Monday, was calm Wednesday."

But by the end of the week the dispatches had petered out, and Papa Doc was still in power. A week later a dejected Davis returned to San Francisco with a firsthand account. The invasion had been mounted by paratroopers of Jeune Haiti ("Young Haiti"), a CIA-backed exile group composed mostly of university students from Harlem. For years the Haitian Coalition, to which Jeune Haiti belonged, had been in league with anti-Castro factions who had been promised that a free Haiti could be used as a base for incursions across the Windward Passage into Cuba's back door. Davis said he was in line to become air marshal in the New Haitian government.

The architect of the invasion was Jay W. Humphrey, a six-foot-four combat veteran of the Korean War who had earned the title "Mr. Washington State" in body-building contests. Humphrey, a pilot, had been recruited by the CIA for the Bay of Pigs and was on the standby list when the beachhead collapsed. When a plain Chevy with two men in business suits had driven up to his Florida home recently, he knew he was about to be drafted again.

Humphrey moved to Freeport in the Bahamas to muster the invasion away from the vigilance of American authorities. It was virtually axiomatic that Haiti, with only a vest-pocket army, was there for the taking, a belief fostered by the 1958 expedition that came very close to succeeding.

Humphrey was planning on more than bluff this time. From an advance base on remote Little Inagua Island in the Bahamas, where the two resident Englishmen were soused with whiskey courtesy of the invaders, two B-25s carrying the Jeune Haiti paratroops took off for Port-au-Prince. They intended to bomb the Presidential Palace to rubble, entombing Papa Doc under tons of masonry, then to swing north to Cap Haïtien and discharge the paratroops. "With that bastard Duvalier bombed to death," Davis said, "the Haitian Army would be demoralized."[10]

The two B-25s, piloted by Humphrey and Davis, flew low in tandem over the Port-au-Prince docks and drew a bead on the white, triple-domed palace. In each bomb bay were nested aerial bombs containing 1,000 pounds of high-velocity plastic explosive. But as the planes began their runs, a four-barrel Oerlikon antiaircraft gun no one knew would be there opened up. The startled pilots took evasive action, but it caused the bombs to miss. Spectacular craters were left on the palace lawn, but Papa Doc escaped with only a ringing in the ears.

The B-25s banked and headed for Cap Haïtien, where they landed safely. One of Duvalier's army commanders who was in on the plot came out to greet them, but someone panicked and shot him. Then a gunboat unexpectedly appeared offshore and began shelling the airfield. The paratroops managed to take control of the airport and a nearby radio station, from which they broadcast appeals for an uprising, but their commander got cold feet as the shells exploded and ran back to the planes. Humphrey's engines wouldn't start, so his B-25 was abandoned. It later was put on display as a war trophy at the François Duvalier International Airport in Port-au-Prince.

Although the Haitian Army needed to offer only token resistance, a crack 400-man tactical force that had been trained by a U.S. Marine mission years before routed the paratroops and chased them into the hills. They were pursued by the Tonton Macoutes, who murdered them to the last man.

An epitaph was written by American journalist Geraldine Carro, who lost her fiancé, Max Armand, in the battle. In a *True* magazine article, Carrow told how the CIA took Armand and some thirty other Jeune Haiti volunteers from New York to Maryland in covered trucks and gave them eight weeks of Special Forces training before sending them to Haiti. When things went awry, Carro said, "the CIA guys—the people who trained and equipped the boys—were terrifically bitter, and said someone was pulling strings behind their backs to destroy the expedition. The only thing they could do was chip in, just like an office collection, and pay for a Requiem Mass, a memorial service for the dead. It was right here in New York, on 14th Street. I went too. All the CIA guys and families and girls of the dead boys were there; the aisle was a river of tears."[11]

That damn ack-ack gun guarding the palace, that damn gunboat that materialized at Cap Haïtien—if it hadn't been for them, Carl

Davis fumed, Papa Doc might have been dead and Haiti liberated. Where had they come from? Duvalier had been under an American arms embargo, and his military forces were so pitiful they were considered a pushover—if they even chose to fight.

Actually, the war equipment had been a gift from the Mafia, which had its own methods of procurement. It was a simple matter of protecting one's investments. Upon being expelled from Cuba, the casino operators had sought other havens in the Caribbean: the Bahamas, Puerto Rico, Venezuela—and Haiti. But Papa Doc was despised and vulnerable, and it was only good business to insure his longevity. So the Mafia had gone shopping.[12]

Despite the cutoff in American aid, Papa Doc was not edging toward the poorhouse. In fact, he was sitting on more piles of cash than ever before. The money mill had begun to grind in 1961, when a glib New Yorker named David Iacovetti spread before Duvalier's covetous eyes plans for a hip-pocket version of the Irish Sweepstakes. It would be called the Republic of Haiti Welfare Fund Sweepstakes, an ennobling name conjuring up visions of food for the mouths of the poor. Tickets would be sold through an already-established network of outlets in the northeastern United States, and winners determined by the results of prestigious horse races such as the Kentucky Derby.

It was an offer more charitable souls than Duvalier would have found difficult to refuse. Whether or not he knew or even cared that Iacovetti represented the Carlo Gambino Mafia family of New York and that the outlets were mob-owned, Papa Doc grabbed at the chance. All told, the Republic of Haiti Welfare Fund Sweepstakes raked in $6 million, and the bucks from Haiti's share stopped at his desk. It might be said in consolation that even if Papa Doc got richer from the scheme, Haiti's poor didn't get any poorer. They couldn't.

So began a partnership between Duvalier and the Mafia that would well serve both sides. Haiti, despite its dizzying mountains, verdant valleys, and quaint native customs, was a tourist backwater skipped by the majority of cruise ships. The squalor was too stark; Papa Doc's reputation, too soiled. It may have occurred to the

Mafia, however, that high-rolling gamblers flown in on junkets might not be so squeamish, especially if they never ventured away from the casinos. In 1963 Joseph "Joe Bananas" Bonanno, another New York godfather in the four-family combine, made the initial move by obtaining a casino concession from Duvalier.

The investment paid almost immediate dividends when, later that year, Bonanno became entangled in an internecine dispute known as the Banana War and decided it was advantageous to his health to disappear. For two years he sunned himself in the bosom of the Protector of the People, another of Papa Doc's honorific titles, while the press wrote him off as dead and his enemies wished it were true.

As the Mafia gambling investment in Haiti grew, so did its stake in protecting Papa Doc. With the lesson of Castro still fresh, the mobsters began a quiet lend-lease program of their own. As New England mafioso Vincent Teresa described it:

> When Papa Doc needed guns and the U.S. government wouldn't provide them—in fact, the feds secretly tried to overthrow Papa Doc—Dave [Iacovetti] arranged to have machine guns and rifles and all kinds of ammunition smuggled to Haiti from his sources in the U.S. Dave made a lot of money on that deal, and Papa Doc was able to turn his army into one of the best-equipped forces in the Caribbean.[13]

That was a slight exaggeration, but Papa Doc was at least acquiring enough firepower to give him a shot at remaining President for Life. According to Andrew St. George, naval craft were procured in a typically devious way, by a shadowy European named Max Intrattor, who had been a money mover for the casino operators in pre-Castro Havana. With the instinct of a homing pigeon, Intrattor went to Rome, where the purchase of surplus American subchasers and PT boats could be arranged with a minimum of official curiosity. The boats were converted to Haitian specifications in Italian shipyards, then sailed through a maze. "They were first routed to Belgium," a federal source told St. George, "then to Montreal, then to a lot of dummy Bahamian consignees—no Haitian government had ever used that sort of quadruple shuffle before."[14]

By the time American authorities had figured out the boat deal Papa Doc had what passed for an air force. One of Joe Bonanno's lieutenants in Port-au-Prince paid a Palm Beach pilot handsomely to buy two propeller-driven T-28s from private dealers, crate them, and smuggle them into Haiti. Then the lieutenant paid a Miami armorer to install gun mounts, cannon, automated bomb bays, and rocket struts. Thus fitted, the planes were ideal for pouncing on the Haitian Coalition commandos.

Upon returning to Miami, however, the armorer was grabbed by customs agents, who used him as a cooperative witness in preparing indictments against several mafiosi. But the case was ordered dropped for "reasons of national security." It turned out that the armorer also did contract jobs for the CIA, and putting him on the stand might compromise his work.

It was ironic that the CIA had been forced to come to the rescue of its old ally, the Mafia, for the two were now pitted against each other in the matter of Haiti. And voodoo antics aside, Papa Doc was a tough adversary. "He was worse than any crime boss I ever met," Vincent Teresa said, "and I've met more than a few." With the Mafia now behind him, Papa Doc was more than just a petty Caribbean tyrant.

Now for the first time, Papa Doc was displaying a sense of humor that was not macabre. A college professor named Raymond Joseph, who had become a political leader of the Haitian Coalition, was taping regular programs at the studios of WRUL in New York after being fed glimpses of Papa Doc's daily life by palace informants. Joseph became a Haitian Hedda Hopper, regaling his listeners with tales of the old boy's strange libidos, tiffs with his wife, Simone, and regal plans for the future of his obese son, Jean-Claude. The only thing Papa Doc could have liked about the programs was the lack of commercials.

As usual he sent out his Tonton Macoutes, but instead of hacking the guilty, they sneaked into the WRUL studios and substituted tapes in a shipment ready for Swan Island. A few evenings later the CIA had reason to rue the day it pioneered automated programming. Radio Americas burst forth with paeans of praise for Papa

Doc as the Apostle of National Unity and Electrifier of Souls. It was some time before someone could get there to turn it off.

For a while it appeared that hostilities between Papa Doc and Uncle Sam might end in truce. LBJ did not consider Haiti one of the hot spots of the world, and he never did, as he was wont to express it, "lift up the cow's tail and look the situation straight in the face." Some of his reluctance may have been attributable to the fact that one of his seminal political backers, oil Croesus Clint Murchison of Dallas, owned vast working ranches in Haiti and was on excellent terms with Papa Doc. Johnson effectively scrapped the Kennedy hard line by appointing Benson E. L. Timmons III as the new ambassador. The tame Georgian went out of his way to appease Duvalier, appearing with him in public and seeing to it that U.S. Navy personnel were given shore leave in Port-au-Prince.

But LBJ apparently neglected to interdict the CIA, which in 1966 did its own *danse macabre* with a top-rank American pianist named Robert Pritchard. It seemed that Pritchard, out of a perverse empathy for the black nation, had become a boon companion of Papa Doc's but had fallen from grace by giving a forbidden public concert. At first the CIA tried to exploit the situation by inveighing Pritchard to report on palace intrigue, but it soon had a bizarre plan to terminate Papa Doc with prejudice. There appeared on Pritchard's doorstep a CIA-paid agent carrying a small cage in which was a mouselike creature. The agent inserted a tiny potion into the cage, and the creature was immediately paralyzed. Would Pritchard, as a service to his country, slip the same potion into Papa Doc's dish on one of their convivial occasions? Pritchard would not. In fact, he was so indignant at the attempt at artistic perversion that he notified Papa Doc as well as a U.S. Embassy political officer.[15]

"Wouldn't anything be better than this situation?" the political officer retorted in frustration. Papa Doc was riding high. He had rebuffed some nuisance raids, a feat he recognized for himself by adopting the title Supreme Chief of the Armed Forces. But the Haitian Coalition was still confident it could unhorse him. The Canadian Jesuits may have gone on retreat, but a new sponsor had materialized. It was CBS television news, which promised to take no commercial breaks.

V

One day in the spring of 1966 Andrew St. George plumped himself down in a naugahyde chair in the CBS production headquarters, a midtown Manhattan skyscraper. The man sitting behind the desk, ample and bespectacled, was Jay McMullen, producer of such television documentaries as *The Silent Spring of Rachel Carson, Biography of a Bookie Joint*, and *Hoffa and the Teamsters*. The charming Hungarian, who had done assignments for McMullen in the past, animatedly told of the latest adventure in progress—a planned invasion of Haiti by Cuban and Haitian exiles.

The commander in chief was to be Rolando "El Tigre" Masferrer, touted by St. George as a Loyalist veteran of the Spanish Civil War who had swung to the right, battled Castro, and now was in New York as "one of the most successful weapons dealers specializing in exile supplies." McMullen, fascinated with St. George's tales of pistol politics in the Caribbean, agreed that it might make an interesting documentary on "international intrigue" and how arms were smuggled in the United States.

Thus was born Project Nassau, as the network code named it. It would not turn out to be the best of moments for CBS's unblinking eye, and McMullen was not destined to win another award. In fact, the documentary never aired. Instead, CBS was hit with lawsuits by a Cuban exile who lost an eye during the filming of a training exercise and a Port-au-Prince hotel owner who claimed a false invasion report by CBS ruined his tourist business. CBS production headquarters was also the address on a flock of subpoenas from a congressional committee probing the propriety of a news organization's helping overthrow governments.

All these traumas might have been avoided if McMullen had bothered to delve into the background of Rolando Masferrer, a blend of Renaissance man and unconscionable rogue. Masferrer affected silk scarves, wrote poetry, painted, and patronized classical music. In his youth he was a militant communist, and he returned from the Spanish Civil War with a limp and the nickname El Cojo—"the Lame One."

Not long afterward Masferrer again volunteered, this time for the romantically named Caribbean Legion, financed by prominent Caribbean democrats to mount filibustering expeditions against dictatorships. Under his command was another young crusader, Fidel Castro. "I blame myself as the man who gave him his rudimentary training in military affairs," Masferrer lamented years later. "He was in charge of a platoon of men and behaved very discreetly."[16]

It was during the Batista regime that the idealistic Lame One metamorphosed into the dreaded El Tigre ("The Tiger"). He became a bullyboy, baiting his communist ex-colleagues, won a Senate seat from his native Santiago in Oriente, and formed a private army called Los Tigres that whipped the local politicians and press into line. When Castro landed in Oriente in 1956 to begin his revolution, Masferrer sent Los Tigres into the hills to try to hunt down his old comrade-in-arms.

When Castro triumphed, Masferrer fled for his life to Florida, where he found his reputation had preceded him. Rumors abounded that he had amassed as much as $17 million through crookery, and he said, "someone even printed a story that Gina Lollobrigida came all the way from Italy to see me, which unfortunately wasn't true." Masferrer said the true figure was $30,000, which he quickly spent on his personal counterrevolution. Ten of his raiders, including three American youths, were captured and shot.

Masferrer spent Bay of Pigs week in bed, the victim of his own notoriety. By direction of the White House he was confined in Miami's Jackson Memorial Hospital with a "No Visitors" sign on the door, the "possible coronary" diagnosis nothing more than a sham. The feds continued to hound him, and when he took a job writing for the New York-based *El Tiempo*, a journal subsidized by Batista's son Rubén and Nicaraguan strong man Anastasio Somoza, he was ordered restricted to Manhattan. But the Tiger violated the order almost daily, helicoptering to the Shiloh Hunting Club in New Jersey, where the nucleus of his invasion army was encamped.

Still, the other principals in the venture seemed solid enough. Slated to be the next president of Haiti was Father Jean-Baptiste Georges, a former education minister active in the Haitian Coalition. Adding a touch of professional steel was an international arms dealer named Mitchell Livingston WerBell III, who St. George

boasted "was in frequent touch with the CIA." WerBell was a colorful character, a connoisseur of fine whiskey, bon vivant of stagger-
ing stamina, and showman *extraordinaire*. He was known to drag a
potential customer from a hotel bar to the lobby, where he demonstrated a gun by firing into the phone book. Once, in the Georgetown Inn in Washington, he impressed Israeli officers with how
quiet his expensive silencer was by shooting through the window
at garbage cans below.

He also impressed McMullen when the producer flew down to
the WerBell estate in the piney woods of Powder Springs, Georgia,
near Atlanta. The place was guarded by a fence, German shepherds,
and a paramilitary detail in blazers and berets. The commodious den
was a virtual heraldry museum, exuding the kind of Teutonic
efficiency that made for successful revolutions. Perhaps most of all
McMullen was impressed with WerBell's putative CIA connections
which, since it could hardly be expected that the U.S. government
would type up a letter of marque, promised to immunize the project
from the criminal provisions of the Neutrality Act. Oh, yes, Wer-
Bell confirmed, he had been in the OSS and was a member in good
standing of the intelligence Old Boy Network. He even confided
that he "had a base in the Dominican Republic from which the CIA
operated boats, some going from there to Cuba." As proof, WerBell
showed his guest snapshots of himself, the boats, and Dominican
generals. One was General Antonio Imbert, who had participated
in the Trujillo assassination and was described by WerBell as "very
sympathetic to any anti-Communist activity."[17]

If it crossed McMullen's mind that Papa Doc was not exactly a
practicing Marxist, he didn't mention it. The producer was hooked.
He committed CBS to underwrite expenses—the amount would
reach nearly $200,000—in return for exclusive filming rights. With
the money and prestige of CBS behind him, Masferrer began putting the arm on Little Havana exiles for contributions to the "Tiger's
Invasion Fund," convincing them that Haiti was merely a stepping-
stone to Cuba. His total take has been variously estimated from
$100,000 to several million dollars, some given through hope, some
through fear. "You couldn't be neutral about him," an acquaintance

said. "Masferrer was either a saint or a gangster, and even those close to him feared him more than they liked him."

In June McMullen took a camera crew to Miami to begin filming. In what would become a familiar ritual, McMullen stood off to the side while St. George bargained with Masferrer; then the producer peeled off the agreed-upon cash, and St. George handed it to Masferrer. Some lively footage was put into the can:

> MCMULLEN: How long have you been involved in, I gather, gathering arms and getting back to Haiti to the underground?
> HAITIAN: Two years.
> MCMULLEN: Would you tell us what you hope will be accomplished by this shipment?
> HAITIAN: To kill the head man of Haiti.
> MCMULLEN: Who is President Duvalier?
> HAITIAN: Who is President Duvalier.
> MCMULLEN: That's what you hope?
> HAITIAN: That's what I hope, yeah. The first bullet should hit him.

McMullen then turned his microphone in the direction of Wer-Bell, who was standing over the arms shipment.

> WERBELL: We have enough here to completely arm a full-scale airborne platoon. In total rounds, including the bazooka and rockets and the mortar ammunition, I'd say there's about 50,000 rounds going out in total. The actual dollar and cents value I'd say would be around, oh, about $35,000.
> MCMULLEN: By 6:45 P.M. the truck was loaded. We were told that the truck would drive to a secret docking area north of Miami where the weapons would be reloaded into this motor boat.

One of the cameramen, James R. Wilson, was sufficiently shaken by the scenes to notify the CIA. He was referred to the FBI, which turned him over to Stanley Schacter, a senior customs officer in Miami long familiar with the anti-Castro plottings. Wilson promised to keep Schacter current in return for anonymity but didn't know that McMullen, apprehensive over possible Neutrality Act repercussions, had already briefed the customs man. McMullen later took the position that if the government was informed of what was going on and lodged no objection, "my assumption was that there was no objection."[18]

The filming was interrupted when McMullen had to go to Houston to cover a space shot, and when he returned, he was warned by a Masferrer aide, "Get out of Miami. Things are hot now, and we're going to cool it for a while." So McMullen decided to shoot some footage at the Shiloh base in the scenic Delaware Water Gap area, then trail Masferrer to Miami, documenting how the arms smuggling worked. But as Masferrer sped away with a load of arms, the CBS crew took a wrong turn, and McMullen and St. George spent the night looking for them.

McMullen was upset, feeling that the chance for continuity had been blown. But St. George had an idea. He put in a call to Mitch WerBell in Powder Springs, and before long the CBS crew was winging to Georgia. Paid a $1,500 bonus, WerBell put on a synthetic show. "The way we staged it," he later recounted, "was I borrowed . . . twenty or twenty-five old Enfield rifles—they went out in the First World War if you all recall—and we put them in one of the houses on my farm and then drove the boat up there, and while everybody was cranking away on the cameras, loaded these arms in the boat."[19]

Before flying off to Miami to catch up with Masferrer, McMullen hired Atlanta *Journal* reporter Tom Dunkin, who had done considerable coverage of the anti-Castro groups, to photograph WerBell's boat as it was trailered to Florida—the Enfields had been returned to their owner. En route Dunkin aimed his camera at such mileposts as an Entering Florida sign and a toll booth on the Sunshine Turnpike. In Miami McMullen interviewed Tony Rojas, Masferrer's brother-in-law, who pretended to have been the driver on the trip. "I'm with an army for reaching Haiti," Rojas declared as the cameras rolled. "The government of Haiti are like communist, too. They kill babies, sacrifice, no respect for the law, no respect nothing."[20]

Project Nassau was ready for its climactic scenes. McMullen set up field headquarters at the Ocean Reef Club on Key Largo, the locale of the Humphrey Bogart movie, and leased a sixty-five-foot two-masted schooner named the *Poor Richard* to serve as the mother ship in a sequence showing how arms were smuggled out of the country. But before the *Poor Richard* could cast off, creditors slapped a lien on her, and she was tied up indefinitely.

It was only the first in a series of misadventures that would have brought a sneer to Bogart's lips. The next episode, as McMullen billed it on his voice-over, was "the training of some Cubans scheduled to participate in the invasion of Haiti." McMullen was led to believe that he was filming at a secret site, but it actually was an open area south of Miami used by gun buffs from miles around. Masferrer arranged for a former marine drill instructor to take charge to lend authenticity. The sound track recorded the instructor yelling "Fire!" and the bursts of gunfire — then frantic voices in Spanish. The cool voice of the instructor cut in. "Knock it off — shut up. Now this happened for two reasons. Number one, you had dirty ammo or a dirty rifle. Second, this is what is known as a hang fire. This thing did not fire immediately, and it blew back."

Writhing on the ground with an eye spouting blood was trainee Julio Hormilla. He lost the eye and sued CBS for $1 million. His attorney, Richard F. Burns, a young New Yorker who had opened shop in Little Havana, took the ingenious position that for all practical purposes Hormilla had been a film extra hired by CBS, with other actors and extras, to play a role. His complaint charged that after the accident CBS employees prevented medical aid "until the cameraman could photograph the plaintiff in his agony and thereby add realism to their television production."

In the wake of the accident McMullen heard a distressing rumor that Masferrer was trying to strike a deal with Papa Doc to chuck the invasion in return for $200,000 and had put out feelers through the Haitian consul general in Miami, Eugène Maximilien. McMullen sent WerBell, wired for sound, over to the consulate for an earnest talk with Maximilien. The consul suggested that they step out into the garden in case the telephone was bugged. "Max," WerBell wryly replied, "the last thing in the world we have to worry about is being too near the telephone." WerBell repeated Masferrer's supposed offer to see what the reaction would be. Masferrer flew off

to Port-au-Prince to confer with his master. "Why do you want to
throw me out?" Duvalier relayed back. "I will give you a base
[against Cuba]."[21]

Masferrer later denied making any such offer and countercharged
that Maximilien had volunteered to support the invasion in return
for a post in Europe. Only WerBell knows. He refused to turn over
the tape to CBS, explaining that it might cost Maximilien his life.

By this time McMullen was having second thoughts about Project Nassau. He was in a perverse mood in October when Masferrer
and Father Georges showed up at CBS headquarters and presented
him with the news that "We are not talking about smuggling any-
more. We are not talking about getting arms into Haiti. We are going to hit them with an invasion."

McMullen was inclined to cut his losses and store his film in the
CBS archives. The argument that changed his mind came from an
unlikely quarter: Stanley Schacter and his partner, Wallace Shanley.
The customs officers acknowledged that in some respects
McMullen had been hoodwinked, but they urged him to stay in to
prevent the guns from being taken underground. "This isn't just a
ragtag operation," Schacter and Shanley insisted. "It is heavily
financed. They really are going to have an invasion." As McMullen
recalled the conversation, "They intimated to me that there was a
much bigger story there: that there was Mafia money involved because they had been promised gambling rights in the Haitian casinos
if the invasion were a success. So we stayed in."[22]

It would, of course, have been typical of the Mafia to hedge its
bets, as it had with Castro. In any case, McMullen laid another
$1,500 on WerBell's palm to sound out his Dominican generals on
whether, as WerBell subsequently expressed it, their government
"would be receptive to the possibility of the combined Cuban and
Haitian anti-communist groups operating from the Dominican
Republic." For his trip to Santo Domingo WerBell was to sail the
Poor Richard so that CBS could film an arms shipment by sea. Having
paid off the lien on the *Poor Richard*, McMullen was hedging his own
bets.[23]

While WerBell was navigating the Gulf Stream, McMullen took
his cameras over to Nelli Hamilton's boardinghouse, where, he ex-

plained in his narration, "the expedition's American contingent" was billeted. "They called themselves adventurers—men looking for a cause and some excitement," the producer intoned. "Some of them had never heard a shot fired in anger." One of the Americans said that he heard about the expedition through the grapevine. "Are you worried about this at all?" McMullen asked.

"It doesn't faze me a bit," was the reply. "I've never fought, but, well, in God we trust. If He wants me to live, I live. If He wants me to die, I die."

WerBell and his crew then packed their gear and took off for New York, where they filmed a council of war between Father Georges, Colonel René J. Leon, a former executive officer to General Cantave, and Cuban exile Father Diego Madrigal:

McMULLEN: Father Georges, do you think that the assassination of President Duvalier at the time an invasion attempt is made would quicken the whole process of taking over?
FATHER GEORGES: No doubt about it, of course.
McMULLEN: . . . Colonel Leon, in your plan to invade Haiti, have you considered the possibility of bombing the palace and eliminating . . . ?
COLONEL LEON: That would be perfect—perfect target, you know, for the invasion.
McMULLEN: What do you think of that, Father Madrigal? Do you think a bomb on the palace would help this plan?
FATHER MADRIGAL: Yes, I think so. Yeah, sure.
McMULLEN: Would it be difficult to bomb the palace, Colonel?
COLONEL LEON: It would be easy.

It was McMullen's impression that the invasion was at hand, so CBS sent correspondent Bert Quint to Port-au-Prince to report firsthand. Quint arrived to find the capital in the grip of invasion jitters. Then, on November 19, Quint scored an international scoop by flashing the news that a 300-man force had landed near Cap Haïtien and captured the city. Richard Burns, whose law partner Edwin Marger happened to own the King Christophe Hotel in Cap Haïtien, received a call from Marger ordering more turkeys sent down for the holidays. "Forget the turkeys," Burns screeched, "you've been invaded."[24]

It had been a horrible mistake—there was no landing. McMullen's woes multiplied on Thanksgiving Day, when WerBell returned, showed off his tan, reported the Dominicans would not provide a base, and left for Powder Springs. Finally convinced that the whole thing was one big turkey, the producer left to break the bad news at CBS headquarters. Masferrer, as brazen as ever, trailed after him, detailed an invasion plan, and asked for $30,000 more. This time McMullen didn't reach for his wallet.

Some insiders in Miami considered Masferrer the only problem and decided to do something about it. Jay Mallin, the CIA-connected former *Time* journalist, invited Father Georges out to his Coral Gables apartment—Mallin's several books on military affairs were prominently displayed—and tried to persuade him that The Tiger should be caged for lack of military expertise and replaced with Captain Robert K. Brown, the Special Forces reservist and Interpen instructor. As he finished his pitch, the bedroom door burst open and Brown rushed out in combat fatigues with a fistful of charts. Kneeling on the floor, Brown spread out the charts and began expounding on the proper way to invade. Father Georges was so unnerved by the performance that he rushed out the door and ran straight to Masferrer, who decided he must move fast. The Tiger rounded up a half dozen of his "American contingent" at Nelli Hamilton's, including Marty Casey and Joe Garman. They took over uninhabited Coco Plum Island in the Keys, using an old concrete blockhouse guarded by a .50-caliber machine gun as a command post. The arsenal was brought in: 151 rifles, 23 machine guns, 9 mortars, 2 rocket launchers, an assortment of other weapons, and plenty of ammunition. Howard Davis was appointed air marshal for the B-25, B-26, and venerable DC-3 that Masferrer had access to. One hundred Cubans and Haitians were summoned to active duty. It was not, by Caribbean standards, too shabby a force.

With what was left in the treasury Masferrer bought a diesel shrimp boat for an amphibious assault. "As long as things moved according to some timetable and with fair dispatch," Howard Davis said, "it looked as if the government was going to let us go. Then things got so fouled up I couldn't believe it. When the boat didn't arrive on schedule everything fell apart."[25] The boat had run aground, and had to be pulled free by the Coast Guard. During the delay customs agents began staking out Coco Plum Island.

On the day after New Year's 1967 the party was over. The customs men sprung a raid. Howard Davis was approaching Coco Plum by car when he saw the blue dome lights of the customs vehicles and made a hurried U-turn. Some of the would-be invaders managed to flee into the brush. Marty Casey made it to the highway and boarded a bus, but when the driver didn't ask for his fare, he realized it belonged to the Immigration Service. Apparently Customs was under instructions simply to disperse the group and let it go at that; the officer in charge told the prisoners they could drop their arms and go home. But Masferrer insisted that he could not forfeit all the arms and ammunition out of justice to his sponsors. So, after the officer in charge made several long-distance phone calls, the seventy-four men who remained were taken into custody.

The group was indicted for conspiring to violate the Neutrality and Munitions and Control acts, but the press derisively labeled it the "Bay of Piglets" and questioned whether Masferrer had had any intention of setting out to sea. Masferrer has steadfastly denied that it all was burlesque for profit. In a 1974 interview with the authors, he contended that at the outset, Fathers Georges and Madrigal visited the White House office of William G. Bowdler to seek official approval. Bowdler, a State Department career man, was LBJ's Latin America expert on the National Security Council. According to Masferrer, Bowdler gave the padres a discreet okay on two conditions: that the preparations be extremely low profile and that Masferrer's role be as inconspicuous as possible.

Neither of these conditions was honored, although Masferrer did try to disguise himself as "Pancho" before the CBS cameras. But the claim that there had been tacit government sanction was given credence when the charges against WerBell were suddenly dropped. The U.S. attorney said he had acted after consulting with the Justice Department but gave a "no comment" when asked by reporters whether WerBell's links with the CIA were the reason (it has recently been revealed that Justice had long had a policy of allowing the CIA to veto criminal prosecution on grounds of national security). Masferrer, Father Georges, Casey, and others were convicted and sent to jail.

Masferrer had plenty of time to think about how near he missed in the Marion, Illinois, penitentiary. When the customs men swooped down, he claimed, the shrimp boat was almost ready to shove off with Haitian and American commandos and link up at sea with five other boats carrying Cubans. The mini task force was to sail straight into Port-au-Prince Harbor and seize the high ground: the Ministry of the Treasury Building, which dominates the palace, and the Dessalines Barracks. From this vantage point the commandos could surround the barracks, pour in bazooka and mortar fire, toss tear gas grenades, and subdue the 110-man garrison within an hour. Masferrer said he had no intention of trying to take over all Haiti militarily; toppling Duvalier in the capital would suffice.

Project Nassau was leaving some nasty hangovers at CBS headquarters. Richard Burns tenaciously pursued the Hormilla lawsuit (CBS settled out of court for a modest sum), and his law partner Ed Marger filed suit, complaining that Quint's "false reporting" had wrecked his tourist trade (the suit was eventually dismissed). Burns was not finished. He wrote to Congress protesting that CBS had pulled "one of the greatest hoaxes played by an allegedly responsible news media on the American public."

In late 1969 the House Interstate and Foreign Commerce Committee, which oversaw the licensing of broadcasters by the FCC, put CBS through the wringer on the issues of manufactured news and aiding and abetting illegal acts. McMullen neatly riposted that WerBell's CIA ties had implied government sanction, for which there was precedent in that "the Bay of Pigs was an illegal act." But the sharpest exchange was between WerBell and Torbert H. Mac-Donald, a conservative from Massachusetts. WerBell was righteously explaining that he was an "anti-Communist and right-winger" who had joined Project Nassau because "any activity that any American can give to a group that is attempting to kill the boil and cancer of Communism in the Western Hemisphere deserves every effort" when MacDonald cut him short. "Rather than trying to overthrow him," MacDonald lectured the witness on such a staunch anticommunist as Papa Doc, "I should think you would uphold him if your entire feeling was to strike a blow for liberty against Communism."[26]

The committee hearings ended with CBS acutely embarrassed but otherwise unharmed. Even before they had begun, however, Papa Doc had survived two more attempts to curtail his Presidency for Life. The first was the CIA-backed Jeune Haiti action, which adopted the idea of bombing Duvalier in his palace but was aborted by the Mafia's antiaircraft gun. The second, called Operation Gold-flow, was undertaken without the CIA. But it had a familiar cast of characters, *sans* Masferrer, and brought together in ecumenical accord, if only for a moment, the Canadian Jesuits and the Israeli government.

VI

Howard Davis and Edmund Kolby, a Purple Heart veteran of the Special Forces, dropped into the gold-rush-era offices of celebrated San Francisco attorney Melvin Belli. It was early 1969, and the pair was trying to raise funds for an invasion of Haiti by offering equities in the post-Duvalier economy. Although Davis and Kolby found no takers in the Belli firm, they did come up with a recruit. One of Belli's partners mentioned the unusual approach to Carl Davis, who had sworn off such ventures after the disastrous Jeune Haiti affair a year earlier. Davis suddenly got that old feeling and dialed the hotel number the visitors from Miami had left.

They met at the Hippo Restaurant on Van Ness Avenue, where, amid curling smoke from the barbecue pit, the newest fate of Papa Doc was discussed. When the coffee-stained battle maps were laid out, Carl Davis was sold. Howard Davis and Kolby left to continue their fund-raising tour, saying they'd be in touch.

Three weeks later they called. Carl Davis left immediately for Miami, but a few days later he was back in San Francisco convinced that this effort, like its predecessors, was jinxed. The group had a camp deep in the Everglades, he said, but one of the Haitians had been accidentally shot and killed. The fatality prompted the sheriff's office to raid the camp and detain a dozen men, among them Kolby and Bill Dempsey, the one-armed Canadian from Nelli Hamilton's boardinghouse.

In a way it was a shame that Davis bailed out, for he was to miss perhaps the best-endowed operation of all. The Everglades camp boasted such amenities as a simulated village that the commandos could practice bush-whacking, a fleet of all-terrain vehicles, and jump towers for paratroop training. A rented hangar at the Miami airport served as the air operations center and parachute rigging port. It housed a Beech Silvair and a huge Lockheed Constellation leased from Fort Lauderdale aircraft broker Ed Cantrell, who had been led to believe it was to be used to haul cargo around the Caribbean.

The logistical abundance was due principally to the generosity of the Canadian Jesuits whose mission in Haiti had been shut down by Papa Doc. They funneled the money to a Haitian car-wash owner in New York acting as banker. He parceled it out as needed to the operations group in Miami commanded by Colonel René Léon, a former executive officer to General Cantave, who was ticketed to be the next president of Haiti. The lesson of Project Nassau had been learned. Jay Mallin went to Washington to secure a promise of benign neglect from his CIA and State contacts and came back with a code name as well. It was Operation Goldflow.

Soon the phone lines between the Haitian leadership in New York and the Miami base were humming with cryptic Goldflow talk. "How's Connie?" someone in New York might ask about the Lockheed airplane. As preparations progressed, a staging base was set up on South Caicos Island in the Turks and Caicos chain, a Jamaican dependency that was considered politically "cool." Howard Davis shuttled back and forth in the Silvair, transporting arms, supplies, and personnel, including Kolby, Dempsey, "Fat Ralph," and Marty Casey, who had finished serving time on the ill-fated Masferrer caper. When D-Day arrived the assault force would jump off from Little Inagua Island not far from Cap Haïtien.

The prospects for success seemed to glow even brighter when, improbably, Israel came into the picture. A Miami stockbroker with

Israeli connections learned about the operation and imagined a deal that would give Tel Aviv a Caribbean ally with a vote in the United Nations. The stockbroker talked with the right people in the Israeli Embassy in Washington, with the result that a military attaché flew to New York to huddle with his colleague and Haiti's "future president," Colonel Léon. They came up with a plan in which Haitian recruits would be flown in blacked-out planes to the Sinai Desert and afforded intensive commando training by Israeli experts. The first signals that were sent back from Tel Aviv sounded favorable, but in the end the Israelis backed off. Moshe Dayan, the political general, may have been chary of the potential backlash.[27]

"Happy to take care of your gambling needs!" read Pan American and Trans Caribbean airline ads promoting travel to Haiti. Shortly after the demise of Project Nassau, Dave Iacovetti had introduced a New England Mafia gambling impresario to Papa Doc. The gambling expert proposed that a swank casino be installed in the El Rancho Hotel high in the hills overlooking Port-au-Prince. Duvalier had agreed, provided his Tonton Macoutes oversaw the take to ensure that he got his cut.

The El Rancho and a cluster of other casinos were soon in full swing with milling throngs of well-heeled junketeers flown in by arrangement of the Esquire Sportsman's Club, a Mafia front in Boston. According to Vinnie Teresa, "The mob from all over the country ran its junkets into Haiti." The boys were taking no chances on erratic turns of the wheels of fortune. In early 1969 federal agents in Miami impounded two planeloads of dice and roulette tables that could be electronically manipulated in favor of the house. They were, of course, consigned to Port-au-Prince.

The Mafia's beneficial interest in Papa Doc's good health was rising with each landing of junket planes from the mainland. And once again that solitary ack-ack gun on the palace lawn was to prove worth its weight in gold.

Goldflow was drying up. Urgent requisitions from Miami were piling up on the desk of the New York banker, who was feeling grievously slighted in his own ambitions for a top niche in the new

Haiti. Although Colonel Léon suspected the worst—the sulky banker was diverting the money to his own account—he was helpless without a direct pipeline to the Jesuit wellhead in Montreal. Alternate money sources had to be found, Léon told his fretting subordinates, and the most expeditious way was, in effect, to advertise. They would make a strike against Papa Doc, one so noisy and dramatic that it would be bound to attract press coverage—and contributors.

Léon flew to South Caicos to improvise the raid. He sent some of the Americans to Grand Turk Island to purchase a suitable boat, but while they were gone, a police sergeant showed up, discovered the buried arms, and gave Léon twenty-four hours to get off the island. "One of our Haitians had been romancing the local girls," Howard Davis said he found out later. "I think this aroused the sergeant's displeasure." There was no time for boats. While Léon was contemplating what to do next, a solution plopped out of the sky. The Constellation was unexpectedly landing from Miami, laden with fifty drums of JP-4 jet fuel and other supplies. As pilot Lawrence "Jim" Carlin and copilot Howard Davis clambered down the ladder in their orange flight suits, it occurred to Léon that he had his transportation.

"All those months of preparation were about to go down the drain," Davis later said. "We had to do something rash." There was one slight problem. Although the squat, balding Carlin, once a pilot for the Du Pont family of Wilmington and Palm Beach, was a part of the operation, the flight engineer, William Dernbach, and the mechanic, Marvin Simpson, were not. They were employed by the Connie's lessor and had no inkling of what was going on. During the 700-mile flight from Miami, Dernbach later said, "Davis told me the jet fuel was for some generating plant at Caicos, and Carlin told me we were going on to San Juan with cargo for a dress manufacturer."[28]

Dernbach and Simpson were indispensable members of the flight crew and had to be taken along. They might have wondered about all the whispering behind their backs, why the fuel drums were left on board, why the plane's registration numbers were altered with black tape. But they said nothing.

That night Jay Mallin in Miami was alerted to stand by for a press release the next morning. At 7:00 A.M. on June 4, 1969, Jim Carlin lifted the Constellation off the runway and backtracked to Great Exuma Island in the Bahamas for refueling. Then he took a compass heading for Port-au-Prince. In the aft cabin Léon, Kolby, Dempsey, Casey, and Fat Ralph lashed flares with striker fuses to the jet fuel drums and arranged them near the cargo door. Simpson pitched in without saying a word. As the Haitian coast came into view, Carlin pointed to Colonel Léon and casually remarked to Dernbach, "This is the next president of Haiti." It was Dernbach's first clue that he wasn't on a cargo flight.

Swooping in from the west over the Gulf of Gonâve, the watery grave of countless victims of Papa Doc, Carlin descended to 500 feet and depressurized the cabin. The cargo door was opened, and Casey hooked a chain tether to his belt to prevent his falling out. As they neared the city, Carlin throttled back to 120 knots with approach flaps lowered, and the gull-winged plane seemed suspended in the air. The first target was the Dessalines Barracks. As they swept over, the muscular Casey shoved out the 200-pound drums as fast as he could.

The Constellation made a 180-degree turn and came back over the city, this time dropping a litter of drums in the direction of the military airfield. Over the harbor it doubled back again, pointed straight at the palace. "We were so low I could see an officer firing his .45 automatic at us," Casey recounted.[29] There was more small-arms fire as the drums cartwheeled down, and the Haitian commandos instinctively flattened themselves on the cabin floor, increasing their chance of being hit.

Then it happened. A delayed-action shell from the Mafia's antiaircraft gun tore through the flight-deck floor and lodged in Dernbach's briefcase before exploding. The flight engineer was knocked senseless against his instrument panel, but the air charts crammed into the briefcase had damped the explosive force enough to prevent disaster. Jim Carlin stared straight ahead, his knuckles white with a death grip on the wheel. "You all right?" Davis asked from his copilot's seat. When Carlin didn't answer, Davis felt him to make sure he was still alive.[30]

Marty Casey was still pushing drums out the door. Davis saw that they were coming up on a crowded slum area and, with the intercom disabled, yelled back frantically, "No! No!"

But Casey thought he yelled, "Go! Go!" and increased the tempo of his exertions. He realized his mistake when he saw a shack erupt in flames.[31]

Then he saw smoke filling the flight deck. He grabbed a fire extinguisher and ran forward but was brought up short by the tether and flopped on the deck like a hooked fish. The fire was quickly put out, and a damage assessment made. The navigational gear was knocked out, and the wing tanks were emitting thin streamers of fuel. But the plane was airworthy.

"Papa Doc may be dead," one of the Haitians ventured.

"Port-au-Prince should be in flames by now," another added.

Colonel Léon instructed that they drop the remaining fifteen drums on Cap Haïtien, then land at the airport, where he and his seven commandos would disembark. "I think he had a deal with someone there to surrender the garrison," Davis said later.[32]

When the Constellation arrived over the airport, however, military trucks and rolled tarpaulins were staggered along the runways to prevent a landing. Carlin and Davis were forced to fly on by dead reckoning. They tried to find Inagua Island, but it was obscured by thunderstorms. They kept a northwesterly heading. By four in the afternoon the fuel gauges had dipped perilously low, and Carlin ordered everyone to assume the eggshell position for ditching. "Let's see who we can raise on the radio," he told Davis. "Let them know we're ditching, so they can look for us."[33]

Davis made contact with a station that came in loud and clear and crisply informed him that his plane was on the radar screen of the U.S. Air Force missile tracking installation on Grand Bahama Island a few miles away. Davis told the Air Force officers who greeted the plane on landing that they had simply lost their way and run low on fuel. They were opening a business on Caicos Island to rent scuba diving gear to tourists, he said, and to provide a search and rescue service. It was a cover story Davis had concocted at the start, but the officers swallowed it. Apologetically they said that only jet fuel was available. Davis would have to wait overnight and arrange for regular aviation gasoline to be trucked out from Freeport in the morning.

It was a costly delay. The next morning the Air Force commander himself came out to the Constellation. He had heard the news of a fiery raid on Port-au-Prince in which six slum dwellers were killed. He noticed the bullet holes. He summoned the Bahamian police, who politely invited all the vistors downtown. Davis hung on to his cover story, but the police had only to talk to Marvin Simpson to learn the truth.

Simpson, Dernbach, and six of the Haitians were freed. But the police bundled the six Americans, Colonel Léon, and his aide-de-camp onto an Eastern Airlines flight to Miami, where the FBI was waiting. In December 1969 the Port-au-Prince Eight were tried and convicted of violating the Neutrality Act and sent off to the federal detention center at Eglin Air Force Base. Papa Doc was still President for Life.

Howard Davis remains bitter that they were even prosecuted. "Attorney General John Mitchell personally forced the prosecution," he says. "They had damn little evidence that we had conspired in the United States and could have let it go. Yet he forced it."[34]

If Mitchell did force it, as seems likely, he was acting in accord with yet another flip-flop in American policy that took place after Richard Nixon entered the White House. One month after the raid on Port-au-Prince, Nixon envoy Nelson Rockefeller went out of his way to pay Papa Doc a visit, present him with a letter of greeting from the White House, and appear à deux with the dictator on the palace balcony to the cheers of a multitude herded onto the grounds by Tonton Macoutes. This unseemly display of affection was followed by an administration renunciation of the Alliance for Progress as a failure and unmistakable signs that Nixon intended to leave social reform to others and consort with existing anticommunist governments, however opprobrious they might be. Economic and military aid to Haiti was restored.

With the turn of events, Papa Doc was acting like a man with a new lease on life. His rake-offs from the casinos were swelling to the point where he was having difficulty keeping track of the numbers on his Swiss bank accounts. But he was nothing if not greedy. He called in Vinnie Teresa and asked him to take over the hotels that had been shut during the tourist slump with a mind to converting them into casinos. Teresa diplomatically declined on the grounds that he would be taking away business from his New England associates. Actually Duvalier was ignorant of Mafia protocol: One didn't step on another's turf and live to count the proceeds. To make amends, Teresa offered Papa Doc a gift of a brand-new Cadillac—a stolen Cadillac, of course. "Vincent"—Papa Doc laughed—"don't worry about that. Once it gets to my island, it's safe."

EIGHT
The Old Boy Network

I

JIMMY Breslin, the streetwise journalist, was having breakfast with Johnny Roselli at the Watergate Hotel after the gangster had testified before the Senate Select Committee on Intelligence Operations. The talk turned to the distasteful subject of cutting deals. The silver-haired mafioso told the journalist that he was so mad at his lawyer for bringing up his patriotic services to the CIA in court in a futile attempt to reduce Roselli's sentence for card cheating that he wouldn't even tell Breslin this louse of a lawyer's first name. "The lawyer should not have tried to use that to get me out," said the strong and silent Roselli. Breslin thereafter wrote eloquently about how the mobster had "showed class" by keeping his silence these many years about his CIA connection.

Breslin was conned. The flag of the patriotic gangster that was unfurled in court on Roselli's behalf was part of a well-oiled system functioning to make life easier for Roselli and others. The proof offered to the court that Roselli was really a George Washington in the rough was in the form of columns on Roselli's CIA exploits by Jack Anderson, the famous muckraker. How that story got to Anderson is a story in itself, one about the legendary Old Boy Network in which the interests of the intelligence establishment, organized crime, and megabuck corporations overlap in concentric self-serving circles.

The story of the use of Anderson's widely read column in the gangster's behalf begins in 1967, when Howard Hughes took over the ninth floor of the Desert Inn and began playing monopoly with the Las Vegas strip, and quickly moves to Washington and New Orleans.

When Hughes wanted all of the Desert Inn, Robert Maheu, his Old Boy alter ego, tapped Roselli as a friendly intermediary with the owners, the old Cleveland Mayfield Road Gang, headed by Moe Dalitz. Maheu, of course, had known Roselli socially since they both worked with the CIA to assassinate Castro.

At Roselli's prompting Dalitz retained Maheu's old FBI colleague, Ed Morgan, as legal counsel. When escrow closed on the Desert Inn, the first of many Hughes acquisitions, Morgan received a $150,000 finder's fee and promptly wrote out a $50,000 check to Roselli.

Maheu and Morgan were as close as salt and pepper sets. When Maheu opened his "management consultants" firm in Washington in the 1950s, Morgan insisted that he take office space in the same building as his own office. Morgan was one of the unique breed of capital lawyers as highly regarded for their power brokering as for their forensic skills. His clients numbered blue-chip corporations, the teamsters, and, not least, the Society of Former Special Agents of the FBI. When Howard Hughes decided he wanted to buy some television stations, Maheu contacted Morgan to represent Hughes before the FCC.

Maheu got Morgan to represent Roselli in his many-splendored problems with the Immigration and Naturalization Service, which wanted to buy Roselli a one-way ticket to the old homestead in Esteria, Italy. Roselli complained to Morgan that it didn't seem fair for the government for which he had risked his life to turn on him now. He disclosed his role in the Castro assassination plots and added a sensational twist. He said that he subsequently learned from "sources close to Castro," that the premier had found out about the plots and decided "if that was the way President Kennedy wanted it, he too could engage in the same tactics." So, Roselli said, Castro dispatched assassination teams to the United States to gun for Kennedy. There was a nice Latin touch: The teams were said to be composed of the would-be assassins Roselli had dispatched who were captured by Castro.[1] The story was like a pulp plot in one of Howard Hunt's spy novels. (Roselli later told his Mafia buddy, Jimmy (The Weasel) Fratianno, according to Ovid Demaris's 1981 biography of Fratianno, that he had made up the Castro-revenge yarn and lied to Morgan so that the lawyer would curry favors for him with the feds. Roselli rather indelicately described the whole story as "bullshit.")

Morgan took the startling allegation straight to Drew Pearson and his then associate, Jack Anderson, whom he counseled on FCC matters. Old Boys do business with everyone. In turn, the conscientious Pearson took it to his good friend Earl Warren, who thought it substantial enough to warrant FBI investigation. Morgan told the FBI that his source was "clients" who had participated in the plots as fringe members of organized crime, but he would not identify them: attorney-client privilege. The bureau did not pursue the matter.

On March 3, 1967, Pearson and Anderson published the story. They attributed it to "sources whose credentials are beyond question" but who were nameless. The columnists conjectured that Bobby Kennedy might have been "tormented by more than natural grief" after the assassination by "the terrible thought that the CIA plot, which he must have at least condoned, put into motion forces that may have brought about his brother's martyrdom."

RFK was furious, telling aides he had once learned of a CIA-Mafia plot but had stopped it. LBJ ordered the CIA to explain. Dick Helms briefed Johnson but omitted any mention of the Amlash plot that had played itself out during his administration. Johnson later told a journalist, "We were running a goddamn Murder, Inc. in the Caribbean."

Morgan took Roselli's story directly to Pearson and Anderson, so it seems clear that his intent was to have it shouted from the mountaintops. There were several conceivable Old-Boy type motives: (a) It would help Roselli pressure the government by threatening to reveal more. (b) It might for various reasons influence Jimmy Hoffa's pending Supreme Court appeal, which Professor Peter Dale Scott, a conspiracy expert, has observed was "a cause preoccupying not only Giancana and Trafficante but also Jack Anderson's close friend and officemate I. Irving Davidson," a Teamsters lobbyist.[2] (c) The Castro-did-it "scoop" would undercut the theory of New Orleans District Attorney Jim Garrison that the CIA and its anti-Castroite troops were prime suspects in the Kennedy case. (d) All of the above.

At this point the flamboyant Garrison was in the headlines. He didn't believe the story of the strange Dave Ferrie, Oswald's former flying squadron mentor, that after JFK was shot, he had rushed off to Houston to go ice skating. The DA's investigators were focusing on Ferrie's past CIA connections. Garrison's probe threatened to expose the CIA–Mafia collaboration using militant Cuban exiles to go after Castro, even if it couldn't be tied into the Kennedy assassination.

Garrison's prosecution was shot out from under him. On Washington's Birthday 1967, only days after the DA with typical understatement had termed him "one of history's most important individuals," Ferrie was found dead in his apartment: a mysterious death. On the same day, in Miami, Eladio del Valle, a smuggling partner of Santos Trafficante who had paid Ferrie $1,500 a mission to fire bomb Cuba, was shot and hacked to death and left sprawled in his Cadillac even as Garrison's men were looking for him.

The CIA was squirming. Its various fronts and its Mafia alliance might come unglued because of Garrison. Former agency executive Victor Marchetti recalls attending several high-level meetings during which Dick Helms expressed alarm over the DA's conspiracy charge against Clay Shaw, an official of the New Orleans International Trade Mart. Marchetti said that Helms identified Shaw as a CIA "contact," and Ferrie as a contract agent at the time of the Kennedy assassination. Helms warned that these ties had to be kept secret and that Shaw would "receive all the help the CIA could give him."

When Garrison couldn't deliver the conspiracy goods, the national media rat-packed him. Leading the pack was James Phelan, who wrote an attack on Garrison in *The Saturday Evening Post* and was NBC's principal "talking head" in a television documentary that was slanted 180 degrees. Phelan, an incurable Howard Hughes buff (it was his purloined manuscript that enabled Clifford Irving to fake a Hughes autobiography), was a confidant of Old Boy Bob Maheu, and other Old Boy fine hands can be discerned in various Garrison hatchet jobs.

By 1971 Roselli was in dire straits—he had been convicted on the Friars Club rap, and the Immigration and Naturalization authorities were breathing down his neck. Agency sources say that Morgan warned the CIA that his client might feel obliged to blow the whistle on the assassination plots. At any rate the agency approached the Immigration and Naturalization Service, as the Senate Intelligence Committee later put it, to "forestall public disclosure of Roselli's past operational activity with the CIA" that might occur if the deportation was pressed.

Roselli was never deported, although INS proceedings often seem to take forever. It is known that Morgan produced the mobster for Jack Anderson and his associate, Les Whitten (Pearson was now dead), to interview. This time the purpose was clear: Roselli's name would appear in the column in the hope that his heroism would sway the judge to leniency. Roselli provided an oil spill of details, including the meetings in Miami with Bill Harvey and Big Jim O'Connell. However, true to the code of the Mafia, he did not implicate Giancana or Trafficante.

Whitten tried to get substantiation for the story by calling Harvey, who was then retired from the CIA. "I'd like to help, but I can't," Harvey said. However he branded Roselli's Friars Club conviction a "bum rap" and disclosed that he had gone to bat at the Justice Department for Roselli. Why would Justice have it in for Roselli if it really was a bum rap? Whitten asked.

"This is a long story," Harvey replied. "I don't think it ought to be printed."[4]

II

Public relations covers a multitude of modern sins. The International News Service in the fiercely independent fifties accommodated Generalissimo Rafael Trujillo, an image-conscious *jefe*, by sending stories out over its wires about what a nice place the Dominican Republic was; for pretending such a fiction was hard-news fact, the ink-stained palms of the INS toilers were crossed with perfumed cash by Trujillo's public relations person. When the China Lobby funneled money to the liberal *New Leader* magazine to run a pro Chiang Kai-shek article, the funnel was the public relations firm in the employ of the Taiwan government. A New York public relations man on the payroll of Ngo Dinh Diem helped plant glossy features in American popular magazines — most notably *Look, The Saturday Evening Post,* and *Life,* the sunken and lately refloated *Niña, Pinta,* and *Santa Maria* of the mass-circulation slicks — misinforming the reading public that Vietnam was, among numerous superlatives, America's "miracle of democracy" in Southeast Asia. The PR man, one Harold Oram, was in the course of his professional duties registered as a foreign agent of the Republic of South Vietnam.

Such activities on the part of big-league image manufacturers may be deplorable. But they are fair game under the First Amendment to the Constitution, which bars the government from interfering with the press but thereafter reasonably expects that the watchmen of the Fourth Estate will purchase their own garlic cloves to ward off other evil spirits attempting to bend the iron integrity of journalism. That the press has been so sorely used has been an object of some concern to the ethics committees of the various societies of professional journalists, but there has been little such viewing with alarm of the other and perhaps less venial categories of sin for which public relations provides convenient cover. The Central Intelligence Agency has come to employ American public relations firms for far more subtle tasks than the manipulation of the media — a sleight of hand in which the record would indicate the CIA is in need of but little outside assistance.

Former CIA Director Richard Helms used to treat the lords and ladies of the Washington press establishment to lunch in the director's private dining room and send them home happy with Madeira and stuffed with nasty bits of intelligence about rival services, particularly the hated Pentagon. The CIA has traditionally had a good press, which, for most of its purposes, meant no press at all. Helms with few exceptions artfully utilized the press to tickle the noses of rival superagencies while keeping the CIA rather remarkably out of the indiscriminating spotlight of investigative reporting. Even when the agency did get into hot water, as in the 1975 flap over domestic spying, it exhibited a remarkable ability to recoup by showing a little leg to the press and allowing a glimpse of its James Bondian side — after a January of unusually cold winter criticism the CIA enjoyed a March thaw of warm media attention and praise for its heralded Howard Hughes-Russian-mystery-submarine raising caper, a long-standing "secret" that the agency held for release until the most convenient time, orchestrating the press with an experienced conductor's arm, all the while pleading with the press not to break the story, the way Brer Rabbit pleaded not to be thrown in the briar patch.

It is unlikely that one will find an internationally connected public relations firm afloat without a distinguished Old Boy or two on board to add to the polish of the brass. The good gray Old Boys seem to nest comfortably in the Quetzalcoatl feathers of public relations. The successful elasticity of the profession is in no small way aided by the fact that despite "public relations" being more or less a household term, hardly anyone, including some college majors in the field, can tell you exactly what public relations is. This thriving ambiguity is to many public relations' greatest asset. Its cheerful anonymity proved of special appeal to Old Boys, and the CIA was not far behind. The agency, using mostly Old Boys become PR boys, increasingly turned to the oleo world of public relations for cover for its commercial fronts, spies, and assassins and as a conduit for funds for dirty-trick operations at home and abroad.

The prototype, if not the pioneer firm, in the Old Boy-public relations-CIA network was an impressive bucket shop begun by Robert A. Maheu back in the early fifties. To hear him tell it, wild horses couldn't drag Bob Maheu away from the bureau during and shortly after World War II, when the FBI was in the counterespionage game in a big way. Maheu's under-cover assignments with the bureau ranged from working with German espionage agents to having an administrative go at "setting up a counterintelligence network to try to get all the agencies to cooperate."[5] But a few years after the war — after J. Edgar Hoover had bid the wrong trump in his play to make the FBI the nation's law enforcement-intelligence monolith, and lost the trick to the C.I.A. — Special Agent Maheu found himself dusting the Tupperware in a New England FBI field office. He retired early. "I had difficulty in finding a Communist in the State of Maine. And chasing draft dodgers and car thieves was not commensurate with where the action was."[6]

The action was with the Old Boys of the OSS both in and out of government — in Wall Street law firms and in the duckling Central Intelligence Agency — who were carrying their World War II intrigue and derring-do into the Cold War. The heavy thud of the Iron Curtain's descending was a blessing for these activist-minded intelligence operatives who had returned to civilian life with the sweet taste of espionage still in their mouths and yearning for more. They were to be saved the deadly dull business of writing their memoirs because the new war into the front ranks of which the Old Boys slithered was to be one without end.

Bob Maheu did not formally return to the government after his retirement from intelligence work with the FBI, although it was not a retirement in the sense of sitting on the porch at Tara. Maheu never really left the intelligence complex, which expanded, after the war, into a sort of intelligence-industrial complex. Old Boys continued to serve in their country's clandestine services while serving other and corporate masters; there was rarely a conflict of interest, and more often than not a confluence of interest existed. And some of the Old Boys, like Bob Maheu, launched businesses that were a virtual duplication in the private sector, a fifth dimension involving profit, of their government intelligence trade. Some of these Old Boys began detective services; others got into "consulting," a field even more amorphous than public relations (the late Howard Gussage once defined a consultant as a person who borrows your watch and then charges you to tell you what time it is). Still others were strictly involved in public relations. Bob Maheu's company was unusual in that it was all three in one.

Robert A. Maheu Associates began as an investigative agency in Washington in the early fifties. Almost immediately, as Old Boy luck would have it, Maheu was off to Italy with the great attorney Edward Bennett Williams to investigate one of the more bizarre murder cases of the postwar period. The story of Bob Maheu's first big case is on its own terms fascinating but is also of interest as the precursor of the currents of espionage and politics running deep and silent through Maheu's FBI-OSS-CIA-connected civilian career.

Maheu's client was former OSS Lieutenant Aldo Icardi, who had been convicted after the war, *in absentia,* by an Italian court of the murder of his OSS commanding officer while behind enemy lines on a top-secret mission in northern Italy in 1944. The Icardi case was a real cloak-and-dagger murder mystery, a classic of the fifties' men's-adventure-magazine genre. The victim was Major William Holohan, in civilian life a Securities and Exchange Commission attorney, who had been handpicked by OSS General William "Wild Bill" Donovan to head a team parachuting into the German-held mountains near Milan with a reputed $100 million[7] in gold to distribute among the feuding Italian partisans in an ill-fated effort to bring the war against the Hun to a speedier close. Icardi, a University of Pittsburgh kid from the wrong side of the Ivy League tracks, went along as a translator since the Harvard-educated Holohan knew no Italian. Holohan and the gold subsequently disappeared. While the major was sorely missed, everyone more or less forgot about what happened to him amid the busy-work of winding up the Italian campaign.

The mystery of the missing major remained dormant until 1950. Then a body, said to be the major's, was recovered in lamentable condition from Lake Orta after some guilt-ridden former Italian partisans belatedly confessed to a dark plot to put the major in a watery grave. An Italian court subsequently put the murder case into the squawk-box arena of fifties' anticommunism by charging that the left-leaning Lieutenant Icardi had poisoned and shot Major Holohan and dumped him in the lake because the major, a good Catholic, had been favoring the Christian Democratic guerrillas with his gold at the expense of Icardi's ideological favorites, the red Garibaldini.[8]

Congressional investigations immediately took off in the Cold War-charged atmosphere of Washington. By the time Williams and Maheu joined the frenzy on the side of the beleaguered OSS veteran, the lawmakers had worked themselves into a pother of perjury charges and extradition hearings. However, the investigation by Williams and Maheu eventually resolved the case, although not to everyone's satisfaction, on the side of Icardi's innocence, by turning the tables with an evidentiary thesis that the Italian communists had killed the unfortunate major and taken his gold, then attempted to make further postwar capital out of the foul deed by framing an American spy, and an Italian to boot.

Maheu's extensive contacts with the OSS Old Boys during the Icardi to-do got him further wired into the intelligence community. It is a matter of some speculation as to when Maheu began working for the CIA; one of the speculators who puts the date on the early side is R. Harris Smith, a former CIA man who wrote a history of the OSS in which he describes Maheu in the context of the Icardi investigation as having "alleged CIA connections."[9] At any rate, Maheu, by his own admission, was doing "contract work" for the CIA in the fifties. He branched out from detective work and hung out shingles of management consulting and public relations. In Washington such a rubric combination is normally a euphemism for lobbying, but Bob Maheu was up to more than that, practicing the full range of the Old Boy scale, and one catches occasional glimpses of him scurrying through the fifties like Glinda the sorceress — now assisting financier Robert Young in his epic proxy fight for control of the New York Central railroad; now using his Old Boy contacts to help staff congressional committees in need of investigators; now deep into international oil intrigue, sabotaging the biggest deal of Aristotle Onassis's life, which would have given the Greek grandee a tanker monopoly on the transportation of Saudi Arabian oil.

The Onassis sabotage provides a scale of the heights at which Maheu operated. His client was Stavros Niarchos, always Avis to Onassis's Hertz, who hired Maheu to sink a scheme of Goldfinger proportions whereby the rival Onassis, working with Hjalmar Schacht — a high roller with several blank spaces in his résumé, such as the years when he served as Adolf Hitler's financial adviser — had bribed the lascivious King Saud to give Onassis the exclusive right to transport oil from Saudi territory. This would have crippled the tanker business of Onassis's competitors, foremost among them Niarchos, and would have left the American oil companies with a most unwelcome Hobson's choice as to the method and cost of shipping their oil. Considering the CIA's history as a private police to protect the well-being of American oil companies, the goals of Maheu's client and of the CIA were the same in fighting Onassis.

Maheu bugged Onassis's Rome hotel suite and fashioned what he overheard into a nasty story that he published in a CIA-owned newspaper. The ensuing controversy sank the contract. Maheu has allowed that he first cleared his plan of action with the State Department and "another intelligence agency."[10] His use of the word "another" in this context is interesting, leaving the impression that Maheu thinks of himself and the other Old Boys as a coequal intelligence service all their own. He should be in a position to know.

Things were going along rather splendidly for Robert Maheu's Old Boy public relations firm—"The business of America is business," Calvin Coolidge once said, and the business of Old Boys was to arrange little government favors for their clients while on occasion doing unmentionable favors for the government—when, in 1960, one of Maheu's clients decided that he liked his connections so much that he wanted all of them. The client was used to getting what he wanted, and he got it.

Whatever defamatory things Howard Hughes may have said about Bob Maheu after their eventual falling-out, it would appear upon dispassionate analysis that the billionaire received his money's worth during the decade that the premier Old Boy was in his employ.

Sometime before, Howard Hughes had learned the hard way that politics—at least in the traditional sense of being conservative or liberal—had unfortunately not much to do with profitable relationships with the federal bureaucracy. Hughes was hardly a pinko billionaire—he strove to cancel bookings of *Limelight* into his RKO theaters because of Charlie Chaplin's scandalous flirtation with Bolshevism. But for a man of vaulting patriotism, Hughes's relations with Washington had always been at best unsatisfactory, and often stormy. The Civil Aeronautics Board blocked Hughes's acquisition of Northeast Airlines and was against him during the

Rabelaisian legal free-for-all over control of Trans World Airlines, a battle that kept process servers working overtime during the early sixties. Hughes's luck with the military was not much better—his woes went back to the mid-thirties, when he had talked himself blue in the face trying to sell the government on his visionary plane designs. This was in the days when the Army was in charge of aviation, before the Army Air Corps grew up and moved away from home and became the Air Force. Hughes at that time was a daredevil-handsome hero pilot, celebrated for breaking world speed records in planes of his own revolutionary design. But he couldn't sell them to the military for money or even for love—when the frustrated Hughes offered to spend his own money building a prototype plane, the Army remained noncommittal. The billionaire's well-known obsession with secrecy and security stemmed from his conviction that disloyal employees had taken his designs for the distinctive pursuit craft later known as the P-38 to his archrival Lockheed, which ended up building it; Hughes believed—it was a belief not unsupported by the facts—that Lockheed got the job by plying generals with liquor and the end products of concupiscence. When World War II began, Hughes discovered that the plans for his record-breaking H-I monoplane—which the Army had likewise refused to build—had somehow got into the hands of the Japanese. Hughes's design became with few modifications the Japanese Zero. No wonder the capitalist was mad. He had designed both sides' planes without making a buck.

Howard Hughes was compulsive about hygiene, secrecy, and communism, but he was also, it turns out, a bit of a junkie about public relations. During his lengthy career Hughes kept trying different public relations men the way a chain smoker tries cures to break the habit. After observing his rivals provide the military with the best booze and blondes, Hughes hired the Expense Account King, Los Angeles public relations man Johnny Meyer, to wine and dine the brass in the manner to which they had become accustomed. That helped some, but not enough. Hughes kept the effervescent Meyer on his payroll while continuing to hire other top public relations people and paying them their Sunday prices. Carl Byoir, the PR heavy, was at Hughes's side during the 1947 High Noon showdown in the U.S. Senate over a most-favored-airline bill that would have squeezed Hughes's TWA out of the international air market by anointing Pan American as the United States flag-carrier airline around the world.

Hughes hired the legendary Russell Birdwell, the flack for *Gone with the Wind,* to ballyhoo *The Outlaw,* the forties' classic in which movieman Hughes single-handedly elevated the female breast to the revered position in this society that totems have in further-advanced civilizations. Birdwell's aggressive promotion of Jane Russell's mammaries grossed out certain segments of public opinion. The puritans of Pasadena shielded their eyes with handkerchiefs, as from a blinding eclipse of the sun, when a skywriting plane hired by Birdwell painted the words "The Outlaw" in the sky, proceeded to draw two huge orbs side by side, and then placed a large dot in the center of each. But the fuss made the less-than-artful western big box office, even though Hughes yielded to the blue-noses and left the critical mass of Miss Russell's chest on the cutting-room floor.

Despite such successes Hughes continued to search for the perfect PR man with the determination of Ponce de León seeking the Fountain of Youth. When Hughes developed a fetish about privacy, he kept on hiring publicity and PR people to keep his affairs *out* of the press. For all this, it would seem that it wasn't until Howard Hughes encountered Robert Maheu — that is, Robert A. Maheu Associates, Public Relations, Investigations, Management Consulting, of Washington, D.C. — that the billionaire began to see what public relations could *really* do for him. This was something Bob Maheu showed him.

Hughes's Washington vexations amount to a "before" picture of the ninety-eight-pound weakling who has sand kicked in his face by the muscular beach bully — to be compared to the "after" picture, as the billionaire's fortunes increased in Washington under the Maheu-Old Boy practice of public relations.

As public relations people Old Boys are appreciably more expensive than the run of the litter; ex-FBI Old Boys with hot CIA connections would seem to be especially dear, since Robert Maheu turned out to be one of Howard Hughes's more expensive purchases. Maheu's firm began doing work for Hughes in the late fifties; in 1960 Maheu fired all his other clients and went to work exclusively for Hughes at a whoopee salary of $500,000 a year. Even by Hughes's damn-the-torpedoes spending habits, this was something extraordinary; Noah Dietrich, Hughes's faithful second-in-command for three decades, was paid a princely $75,000 a year.

For that sort of money Old Boy Maheu didn't loaf around on the job. During the decade that Maheu was in Hughes's employ the billionaire's relations with Washington changed dramatically for the better. The period of Maheu's ascendancy was also, coincidentally or not, the flowering of Hughes's relationship with the CIA.

When Charles Colson, the former Lord High Executioner of the Nixon White House, told Watergate investigators in 1974 that Howard Hughes had "close organizational ties with the CIA"[11] (and, by implication, with Watergate), few among the Washington press corps had a clue to what he was talking about; some, uncharitably, simply didn't believe him — this in the period of Colson's well-publicized conversion to Christ.

As it turned out, Colson knew whereof he was hinting. However, the regal beagles of the Washington press corps were not about to accept a handout from a man who said he would run over his own grandmother to reelect Richard Nixon. They turned up their noses at the bone Colson threw them in the form of the name Global Marine, Inc. — thereby depriving the reading public, for a matter of some months, of the Mandrake-the-Magician story of the Hughes-CIA Russian-submarine-raising event which belatedly broke the media sound barriers in the spring of 1975 (Global Marine was the company operating the spy ship for Hughes).

The billionaire's linkage to the CIA goes far deeper than the celebrated submarine caper. It affords an instructive example of the workings of the intelligence-industrial complex. It is, in large part, and as one might suppose, similar to the mutual back scratching of lazy giants. The benefits — both fringe and direct — are substantial on both sides. The CIA, for its part, could never have managed to hide its full-scale covert war against Castro, supported as it was by massive domestic operations, without the zealous cooperation of businessmen-patriots of the stripe of Howard Hughes, who had their own Caribbean islands to let. Hughes, on the other hand, had ready access to a CIA cornucopia of privileges—guiding hands through governmental red tape, economic intelligence, protection from interference by other government agencies attempting to perform their statutory duties, and even hidden government financing for major projects. Of these benefits, Hughes took his fill.

The flirtation between the Hughes organization and the CIA took place in the late fifties, and in the prenuptial negotiations as well as the marriage rites, Old Boy Robert Maheu served in various Cupid capacities, including that of best man. The honor of being father of the bride went to CIA clandestine services director Richard Bissell—the accomplished, forward-looking spy with a mad scientist's gleam in his eye, who during the fifties pushed the agency toward technical espionage in a big way. The conventional wisdom is that the CIA shifted to the more secure perimeters of outer space for its spying after the embarrassing incident when a U-2 spy plane piloted by Francis Gary Powers was downed over Russia. (It must be remembered, however, that things are not always what they seem with the CIA. At least one intelligence community veteran, L. Fletcher Prouty, a former air force intelligence officer, has speculated that someone in the CIA deliberately planned the spy plane crash to ruin the forthcoming Eisenhower-Khrushchev summit meeting.) But the fact is that Bissell was eyeing the heavens long before Powers's 1960 crash. Bissell proved prescient. In the early sixties there was a technological explosion in the intelligence trade. Cloaks and daggers were out, and computers were in. The CIA, by having pioneered successful spy-in-the-sky electronic reconnaissance satellites, maintained the edge over the rival Pentagon intelligence agencies.

The Hughes Aircraft Corporation became a major supplier of the CIA's spy satellite needs. The visionary engineer-billionaire seemed to be whistling the same tune as the CIA's scientist-spooks, and together they made some beautiful music. During the same period Hughes Aircraft also became a prime contractor for NASA, the space monolith based in Hughes's hometown of Houston.

Retired military, ex-CIA scientists, and Old Boy types flocked to the Hughes organization, and soon there was as much national security shoptalk around the Hughes plant in Culver City as in a charabanc of generals. For example, A. D. "Bud" Wheelon resigned as a CIA deputy director for science and technology to become president of Hughes Aircraft. Ed Nigro, a Pentagon three-star general, resigned early, at age 48, to go to work managing Hughes in Las Vegas. "I felt I could come out here and still serve my country," Nigro told reporters.

Hughes was never too bashful to ask. He wrote a memo to Maheu floating the idea that Nigro might use his Pentagon influence "to keep the Vietnam war going" so that Hughes Aircraft could sell more helicopters. (There is no evidence Nigro did any such thing.) Hughes also told Maheu to pay off federal officials to stop underground nuclear tests in Nevada. That didn't work either, although Richard Nixon did offer to send Henry Kissinger to hold the billionaire's hand when the bomb went off.

In general, however, the change in Hughes's traditionally rancorous relations with Washington was short of miraculous; gone were the days when Hughes had to put up his own money to build prototype planes just to force the government to deal with him. Soon the government would be secretly financing one of his pet projects, the *Glomar Explorer,* to the amount of several hundred million dollars. The Hughes–CIA marriage was, in many ways, one which could be said to have been made in heaven. The eccentric billionaire's bacteriophobia and his penchant for ultrasecrecy meshed perfectly with the CIA's security-conscious anal retentiveness. Soon the Hughes organization was servicing the CIA on a worldwide basis, becoming the largest private contractor employed by this agency. No job was too big or too small. Hughes Aircraft and the Hughes Tool Company were used as a "paymaster-type front" for undercover agents wherever they might be. Payments would usually be made in cash, Hughes-person to CIA-person, but at times checks were drawn for CIA personnel on Hughes payroll accounts. Hughes would be reimbursed to the penny and mill by the CIA.

Cay Sal is a barren, scrub-covered outcropping in the Bahamas archipelago surrounded by inhospitable coral reefs. It is off the tourist paths and commercially valueless. In the Secret War against Castro, however, the island was a priceless piece of real estate: It was only thirty miles off the northern coast of Cuba, it had an airstrip, and it belonged to Howard Hughes.

Under the corporate cover Cay Sal, Ltd., the tax-exempt Hughes Medical Institute subleased the island in 1956 from Miami dredging and construction tycoon Clarence B. Moody, who held a long-term lease from the Bahamian government. The property was managed for Hughes by Moody's son Osmet. There was a resident caretaker on the island, and a customs officer in Her Majesty's service who, for a bottle of whiskey, would gladly look the other way.

This voluntary astigmatism was important, for the Hughes organization made Cay Sal available to the CIA. "You didn't go near Cay Sal unless it was cleared, either by Moody or the agency," said Gerry Patrick Hemming, the Secret War paramilitarist. The penchant for privacy was necessitated by the fact that the island was being used in a manner seriously breaching British neutrality. Hemming saw crates stenciled TOOLCO (Hughes Tool Company) destined for Cay Sal that were filled with arms and military supplies. Dom Bonafede observed in the Miami *Herald* of August 25, 1963: "Since Castro's elevation to power in 1959, the Cay Sal Bank has served a dual purpose as a rendezvous and arms storehouse for exile raiders and, for anti-Castro refugees, the first stop to freedom, a gateway similar to the Berlin Wall to anti-Communist East Germans." The guerrillas were instructed that, if discovered, they should say they were rehearsing for a Hughes movie.

The covert action planners of the CIA looked upon the Hughes organization in somewhat the way an outlaw does a hideout: Clyde Barrow hunkering down in J. J. Hunsinger's father's house; the agency had to keep its domestic operations in the shade, and the Hughes empire cast a large shadow. While thus serving his country right or wrong, Hughes received extraordinary financial rewards of a magnitude that would easily dwarf the modest stipend attached to the Valley Forge Freedom Medal awarded to less secretive patriots.

The few facts which, however indiscreetly, have surfaced about this corporate *liaison dangereuse* tend to support the impression that the billionaire and the espionage agency did not link hands entirely in a burst of patriotic frenzy. Hughes earned a piddling $547 million from selling TWA, while his combined income from secret non-competitive CIA contracts was $6 billion. Congressional probers were enamored of a rumor, widely circulated in the intelligence community, that the CIA had persuaded the IRS to head off tax investigations presumably to protect some CIA cover within the Hughes organization. This is the unwritten "CIA exemption" for cooperating businessmen. Another wealthy American businessman who has enjoyed a covert relationship with the CIA is New York City's J. M. Kaplan, whose prestigious charitable Kaplan Fund was in the early sixties a CIA conduit to transmit funds to domestic and overseas groups. The IRS had moved to strip the Kaplan foundation of its tax-exempt status for wholesale abuses of the laws governing charitable foundations, abuses which the IRS charged included Kaplan's use of the foundation's tax-free funds to acquire voting stock in companies he wished to take over. But the CIA intervened to protect its conduit, and the IRS action was stalled. When former Congressman Wright Patman attempted to investigate the IRS's failure to pursue the Kaplan case, the CIA again stepped in, and Patman abruptly halted his investigation.[12]

The CIA, ever-protective about Hughes's *Glomar Explorer*, also reportedly put pressure on the Securities and Exchange Commission during an SEC investigation of Global Marine, Inc., the Hughes-connected firm which operated the ship. The SEC apparently was concerned that Global Marine was not telling all to the public about the financing of its ocean-mining expeditions. One of the items the firm neglected to state in its stock prospectus was that the CIA had invested between $300 and $400 million to build the ocean-mining ship. The firm's stock was sold to the public at $68 a share, and conceivably such information might have affected the market.[13]

A little-noticed hearing of the National Labor Relations Board in March 1975 disclosed that the *Glomar Explorer* had made an unscheduled stop at Valparaiso, Chile, during the height of the CIA-backed coup that felled the Allende government in 1973.

The unexpected revelation of the CIA ship's mysterious visit to

Chile was made during testimony in a National Labor Relations Board hearing on a labor complaint involving the *Glomar Explorer*. According to seamen who were on board, the vessel stayed in Valparaiso Harbor for twelve hours; it was the only ship that the incoming military regime, which took control of the Chilean government, allowed to leave in the aftermath of the coup.

The *Glomar Explorer* made its unexplained visit during the course of its maiden voyage from Port Chester, Pennsylvania, where it was built, to Long Beach, California. An official of Global Marine, Inc., identified as Thomas Williams, boarded the ship when it docked in Valparaiso and held a lengthy closed-door meeting with the ship's "mining personnel."

It was unknown why a Hughes official would be in Chile at the precise time of the coup, but in the course of the NLRB testimony the "mining personnel" were revealed as an elite crew — presumably CIA agents — who stayed apart from the other crew and ran the ship, with authority over even the captain.

The benefits that Howard Hughes reaped from his Old Boy–CIA connections were enormous, but it is not the first time the CIA has helped large American corporations achieve windfall profits. Witness the oil companies, for whom the CIA has toadied and schlepped inexhaustibly. The marriage of the billionaire and the CIA has worked so well because both partners have had such keen mutual interests and the same likes and dislikes.

III

Robert Maheu, ex of the FBI, CIA, and Howard Hughes, walks tall among Old Boys, less decorously referred to in some law enforcement circles as the FBI Mafia. That description is imprecise since the Old Boy lineup, although top-heavy with ex-FBI types, includes row upon row of former CIA agents, Justice Department officials, and IRS investigators — even some retired Canadian Royal Mounties.

The Old Boy network in its clubby, discreet manner has afforded the CIA a powerful extracurricular arm in mounting covert operations overseas and at home, where the ever-ready Old Boys have afforded the agency a better than arm's length posture in its extra-legal domestic activities. The CIA's deployment of the Old Boy network while camouflaging the agency's at-home operations has at the same time greatly complicated the task of tracing just where a CIA operation ends and private knavery begins. The Old Boys tend to mix covert intelligence activities both legal and illegal with the ordinary pursuit of private gain. The Secret War is perhaps the ultimate example of such a mixture.

Old Boys are pervasive, if not ubiquitous. One of them introduced Richard Nixon to Bebe Rebozo. The Old Boy responsible for that fateful handshake was Richard Danner, who left the FBI in the late forties to become the city manager of Miami Beach in the heyday of mob rule. Danner was once involved in a bizarre midnight summit meeting in a Miami Beach gravel pit between rival gangsters competing for control of the local constabulary. Danner is a fascinating individual because his fate over a quarter century has been almost that of a deus ex machina in bringing the political and private fortunes of Richard Nixon into the orbit of many of the main actors in the Secret War.

After introducing Nixon to Rebozo, Danner accompanied the young senator on a 1952 rest and recreation trip to Havana a short time after Batista's return to power. Along for the ride was Dana Smith, the steward of Nixon's celebrated secret campaign slush fund which provoked the Checkers speech of that banner election year. Smith suffered a losing streak at the Havana gaming tables and generally had a falling-out with Lady Luck. He ended up writing a bad $4,200 check to the Sans Souci Casino, which was under the management of Norman "Roughhouse" Rothman, who took extreme umbrage. Senator Nixon eventually had to write a letter pressuring the State Department to pressure the gambler to let Smith off the hook.[14]

Consistent with the clubby Old Boy tradition, Danner was later hired by Bob Maheu to work for Howard Hughes. The billionaire kept Danner busy handing out his largess, but the ex-FBI man found time, as so many Old Boys do, to do a little moonlighting—General Motors, for instance, hired him to coordinate its spying on Ralph Nader.

It was Richard Danner who delivered the mysterious $100,000 in $100 bills to his old friend Bebe Rebozo as a Hughes postelection 1968 "campaign contribution" to Nixon. This was at a time when Hughes's controversial acquisition of the California airline Air West was awaiting Nixon's approval and when Hughes needed a Justice Department easing of antitrust proceedings barring him from adding to his collection of Las Vegas casinos. (Hughes got both wishes.) Watergate investigators have theorized that it was White House fears that the opposition might have evidence of the suspicious Hughes $100,000 which motivated the break-in at the Democratic National Committee.

Richard Danner was again in the news in January 1974, when he visited President Nixon and Bebe Rebozo at Camp David. A White House spokesman described the meeting as strictly social. He said the three discussed old times.

Old Boys never seem to die, and their companies don't seem to fade away either. Around the dawn of the fifties, when Richard Danner was busily managing the crime-soaked sun spot of Miami Beach, another ex-FBI agent, one William Roman, was making whoopee in the practice of law. Among Roman's clients was Keyes Realty of Miami, the gold-plated firm which was fortunate enough to be the broker for Southern Florida real estate into which was invested (via legitimate fronts) many of the the hundreds upon hundreds of millions of dollars that syndicate figures and fleeing Cuban government officials hauled out of Batista's Cuba in suitcases and cardboard boxes. Despite the nature of its laurels, President Nixon picked Keyes Realty to broker the deal establishing the Florida White House on Key Biscayne. And—to keep this Old Boy firm perfectly contemporary—Watergate burglar Eugenio Martínez was employed as a vice-president of Keyes Realty. In 1971 Martínez helped set up another Miami real estate company, Ameritas, which was located in the Keyes building. Ameritas was distinguished among Miami real estate firms as the one selected to be the corporate cover for the burglars in the Watergate break-in. (Martínez's boss at Ameritas was Bernard Barker, later another Watergate convict. Barker was financed in many of his real estate ventures by

Bebe Rebozo, silent partner to Richard Nixon. Rebozo in turn had extensive business dealing with Keyes Realty, and a Keyes officer was a director of Rebozo's Key Biscayne Bank.)

One more example which also comes full circle from Caribbean wheeler-dealing to Watergate is that of Robert Peloquin, an Old Boy still relatively tender in years. Peloquin is either a white knight or a black sheep among the Old Boys, depending upon whom you talk to. He was a top Justice Department organized crime buster during the sixties, but he resigned to go into the gambling business as an officer of the spanking new casino on Paradise Island, Huntington Hartford's former dream spot in the Bahamas.

Before he left the Justice Department, Peloquin was issuing storm warnings that the tropical storm called Meyer Lansky was about to blow into the Bahamas in a big way. He concluded a January 18, 1966, memo that was positively forbidding about the future of the Paradise casino by stating, "The atmosphere seems ripe for a Lansky skim."

Once he traded in his government business suits for tropical worsteds, Peloquin assumed a more cheerful view of things. In a matter of months he was able to assure the world that he had made Paradise Island safe from the syndicate. This assurance did not sit too well with some organized crime watchers, who pointed out, somewhat grumpily, that Eddie Cellini, a Lansky draft choice of many years standing, was the casino manager.[15] Peloquin nonetheless prevailed in his opinion that the island was as clean as a missionary's toothbrush, and Richard M. Nixon, along with other beautiful people, attended the January 1968 gala opening of the casino.

Peloquin went on to bigger and better Old Boy things. In 1970 he formed a private detective firm, Intertel, which subsequently employed a gaggle of ex-FBI, -Bureau of Customs, -IRS, and -Interpol agents to protect susceptible businesses from the dry rot of organized crime. Intertel agents spirited Howard Hughes out of Vegas in the dead of night, without as much as a hello or a good-bye. To illustrate the all-round coziness of the Old Boy situation, Intertel came to police all the Hughes Las Vegas gambling properties—among them the Silver Slipper, which was managed by Richard Danner.

The Silver Slipper was no ordinary casino, and Danner no ordinary manager. It was the only card in the billionaire's deck of gambling properties that was not organized as a corporation; Hughes possessed it, chips and all, personally — a quirk of some importance as it allowed Hughes to avoid the nettlesome laws governing political gifts by corporations, and this fact got an impressive number of corporate nabobs in deep water in the aftermath of Watergate. When Hughes wished to make a discreet political contribution, Danner simply walked into the Silver Slipper counting rooms and scooped up a pile of $100 bills — the preferred denomination for cash political gifts — and put the loot in his attaché case, since Old Boys do not walk around carrying bags in the literal sense. The $100,000 delivered by Danner to Bebe Rebozo for the convenience of Richard Nixon came straight from the Silver Slipper.[16]

NINE

Nixon's Vendetta

. . . the problem is it tracks
back to the Bay of Pigs.

—RICHARD NIXON,
the presidential tapes

I

IN 1969, the freshman administration of Richard M. Nixon took several actions that showed the Mafia patriots of the Secret War that their government had not forgotten them. Shortly after the Inaugural Ball, the long-standing deportation proceedings against Johnny Roselli were dropped. Government lawyers explained in court, without going into specifics, that the Mafia soldier had performed, "valuable services to the national security."[1]

Nixon then fired Robert Morgenthau, the United States Attorney for New York City, who had been sending investigators as far afield as Switzerland gathering information to indict syndicate grandees and their businessmen-fellow travelers. The crusading U.S. Attorney was hot on the trail of the Switzerland-to-Miami bank account axis and the offshore funds that were the bricks and mortar of the mob's laundry. This ill-gotten cash was then turned into clean dollars to funnel into Southern Rim real estate deals and other gold-plated investment opportunities to which the men of the syndicate were partial. A typical laundry operation was to take the skim from a casino in the Bahamas and route the cash via mob courier to a cooperating bank in Switzerland, which transferred it, often by way of several additional cleaning stations, to a mob-controlled bank in Miami where the money would be "borrowed" and invested in real estate. Thus a mob type could show the IRS a legitimate source for his funds, while deducting the interest from his income tax.

Morgenthau was not only indicting, and convicting, gangsters and some of their respectable business-type associates, but he was working with Wright Patman, the intractable Texan who headed the House Banking and Currency Committee, on legislation that would allow federal investigators to follow the path of mob funds through the sinuosities of the international financial structure. The Nixon administration opposed the legislation, Treasury Department officials who had favored it had a change of mind, and the bill was watered down over Patman's protests to the point where it no longer represented a serious threat to the mob's international rinse and spin dry cycle.[2] Despite the fact that a special Republican task force had recommended to the administration that Democrat Morgenthau be kept in his job on the grounds that he was one of the best prosecutors in the nation, he was fired by Attorney General John Mitchell. Mitchell said Republicans needed the patronage.[3]

The new administration's good will toward the syndicate seraphim knew almost no bounds. The pressure from Washington eased off on Sam Giancana, who at one point in the difficult years previous had to get a court order limiting the number of feds who could tail him on the golf course. Charges against some mob types evaporated, and Gabriel "Kelly" Mannarino, a prominent Eastern Seaboard mafioso, was blessed with a surprise witness for the defense during a New York federal court trial where he was charged, along with other mafiosi, in a union kickback scheme. The surprise character witness for Mannarino was a CIA official. FBI men at the trial, appearing as witnesses for the prosecution, were so shocked that they tried to hustle the CIA man out of the courtroom. (Mannarino was acquitted.)

The Mannarino incident can be taken not only as a measure of the length of Richard Nixon's arm but also of his memory. Back in 1952, "Kelly" Mannarino was the owner of the Sans Souci casino in Havana, where then-Senator Richard Nixon had gone to gamble with Dana C. Smith, who was shortly to achieve fame as the manager of Vice President Nixon's celebrated Checkers-era slush fund that precursed the loose stashes of cash in safes, desk drawers, brief cases, and paper bags of the Committee to Re-Elect the President in the Watergate year of 1972. It was at the Sans Souci that Smith wrote the previously mentioned rubber check for his gambling losses for which Senator Nixon officially asked the State Department to intercede to keep Mannarino from collecting. In one of those serendipitous instances so characteristic of Nixon's career, "Kelly" Mannarino's brother Sam was one of the mob types who helped Roselli and Giancana plan their hit attempts on Castro in 1960 when Nixon was White House overseer of the military attempt that would have freed Havana's casinos from the revolution's puritan grasp.

Cuba — syndicate-dominated, pre-Castro Cuba — and the type of entrepreneurial sporting gentlemen in silk suits and pinky rings that those quick to judgment might call shady characters have haunted the lives of Nixon, his friends, and business associates like dark stars. All of these dark stars were to collide in the Watergate firmament, and would bring Nixon's own chief of staff, in the final bunker-type weeks of the Watergate White House, to order a secret investigation of his boss's ties to organized crime.

> SECRET RICH MAN'S TRUST FUND KEEPS NIXON
> IN STYLE FAR BEYOND HIS SALARY
>
> —headline, New York Post, September 18, 1952

In Cuba, the darkest star was Meyer Lansky, whose incredibly profitable crooked relationship with Fulgenico Batista would make both men worth hundreds of millions, and make hundreds of others worth tens of millions — money that was laundered through a maze of banks and law firms into real estate deals that would build much of Greater Miami and ultimately involve Richard Nixon and his closest friend in a web of dirty money that would make Nixon a millionaire while in the White House and cause the Secret Service to warn the chief executive about the unsavory character of the company he was keeping.[4]

The Lansky-Batista axis began in the 1930s when Lansky contracted with the sergeant-dictator to supply raw molasses for his bootlegging operations, an arrangement that continued through World War II during the booze shortage in the United States.

The two got along like cheese and bread, and their friendship even survived a difficult moment in 1944 when Lansky went to Cuba as President Roosevelt's secret emissary to inform the pudgy dictator that FDR thought he was too much on the pink side and wished him to step aside as the island's chief honcho. Batista had legalized the Communist party in 1938, and the grateful reds backed him for president in 1940. FDR feared the communists would gain too much influence in the government if Batista won a second term.[5] This was another example of the limits of what is described in some history books as the noninterventionist, "Good Neighbor" policy of FDR, which had its baptism of hypocrisy in 1933 when U.S. Ambassador to Cuba Sumner Welles put Batista into power in the first place by pushing and shoving Cuba like a pinball freak playing a machine with the tilt mechanism broken. In tapping Lansky to give the bad news to his dictator friend, FDR was continuing in the tradition he had pioneered of utilizing the mob in both political and national security matters.[6] Not only did Lucky Luciano get a fifty-year sentence reduced to Ping-Pong time for helping keep the wartime peace on the East Coast docks, but the entire Sicilian Mafia was drafted to aid in the invasion of Sicily and the subsequent Allied occupation of the island. (It is a little-known fact of military history that General George Patton's extraordinary race through western Sicily to Palermo was made possible by the Sicilian Mafia leader, one Don Calogero Vizzini, riding with Patton's advancing troops and giving the Mafia version of a papal blessing to the American effort.[7]) The CIA continued to cut deals with the Mafia, utilizing it in the cold war to break up left-wing dock strikes in Marseilles and during the war in Southeast Asia to keep its ragtag "secret armies" in Laos and Vietnam in line; the Mafia is particularly good at devil's bargains, and the CIA ended up indirectly financing the Corsican Mafia's huge opium lift from Southeast Asia—often aboard planes of the CIA owned Air America—which eventually ended up as street heroin in the United States.[8]

Meyer Lansky, never one not to collect, also got his pound of government flesh. In return for his mission to Batista for Roosevelt, longtime Lansky-watcher Hank Messick believes that Lansky received immunity from federal prosecution.[9] It would seem the case. Although Lansky's personal fortune has been estimated at $200 to $300 million, all undeclared, and he has been widely recognized for decades as the boss of organized crime in the United States, it was not until the late 1960s that the IRS did anything about bringing tax evasion charges against him, and then Lansky beat the rap.[10]

Batista settled into comfortable exile in a Daytona Beach mansion, up the coast from Lansky's Florida turf in Broward County where the sheriff was so accommodating he sent deputies to ride shotgun on the swag from Lansky's rug joints. Lansky found time while building the Florida Gold Coast to operate a casino in the Hotel Nacional and the racetrack in Havana. But it was in the early fifties, after Lansky arranged Batista's return to Cuba through a quarter-million dollar bribe to the then president, Carlos Prío,[11] that Havana began to really fulfill the syndicate empire builder's dream of a Las Vegas in the Caribbean. Alongside the rocketing casino trade, fueled by mob-organized junkets from the mainland, the satellite rackets—prostitution, narcotics, and wholesale abortions—spun in profitable orbit. Cuba's government officials and favorbrokers got a piece of everything, twice: once from the syndicate, once again from the government treasury, where the cashflow of the poverty-ridden island was diverted into gold-lined pockets. Batista's brother-in-law, Robert Ferrandez Y. Miranda, was sports director of the Cuban government. He tooled around Havana in a golf cart emptying the slot machines.

Havana in the fifties became the capital city of organized crime, an anything-goes Disneyland run by the mob and a major conduit for the narcotics flowing into the United States. Washington's attitude toward such corruption and crime strutting its stuff but ninety miles from the mainland ranged from a curious unconcern to boys-will-be-boys approval. Batista kept the mob in the driver's seat, and Washington kept Batista in power through economic and military aid. In Washington two of Batista's most devoted supporters were Florida Senator "Georgeous George" Smathers and his good friend

Senator and later Vice President Richard Nixon. Miami-born of a wealthy family, Smathers had a natural inclination toward Havana and the shower of wealth it rained on southern Florida, to borrow Thomas Macaulay's descriptive phrase about Britain's plunder from India. On the other hand, Nixon, a wrong-side-of-the-tracks kid from California, held the condominium and Naugahyde sleaze of Miami and the open sesame–open city of Havana in a sort of promised-land awe.

Nixon even dreamed of Havana. According to his biographer, Earl Mazo, as early as 1940 "during a brief trip to Cuba he spent a bit of his vacation time exploring the possibilities of establishing law or business connections in Havana." Mazo is hard put to explain the young California Quaker's fascination for the Caribbean open city, but is quick to point out that although as a kid Nixon worked as a barker for a shady wheel-of-chance operation, "Nixon barked for the *legal* front of the concession, where the prizes were hams and sides of bacon, which was a 'come on' for a back room featuring poker and dice [italics added]."[12]

II

At 11:35 A.M. on December 15, 1971, the radio in the Miami riverside offices of the Bahamas Line blared out a distress call from one of the company's ships. It was Captain José Villa of the 1,400-ton *Johnny Express*. He was being pursued by a Cuban Navy gunboat and was turning north to elude it. The *Johnny Express* was en route back to Miami after discharging cargo at Port-au-Prince. Her position was not far from Little Inagua Island in the lower Bahamas.

At 12:55 Captain Villa, a Cuban exile, reported that the gunboat was closing in. At 1:00 he said he had been ordered to heave to. "Don't stop," Bahamas Line official Francisco Blanco radioed. "You are in international waters."

At 1:31 Villa, his voice urgent, reported the *Johnny Express* under fire and himself wounded. Nine minutes later he screamed, "They are shooting at us from close range."

At 2:00 Blanco, after hurried consultation with other company officials, advised Villa to try to beach his ship. "We are going to keep going until they sink us," the captain defiantly replied. Then radio contact was lost. Finally, at 2:20, Villa came back on the air, saying the gunboat was firing at his radio mast. He begged for help. Ten minutes later he began his final transmission: "The deck is covered with blood. I am dying, Chico. Tell the Coast Guard to come quickly. Tell them there are dead and wounded here."[13]

The gunboat rammed and boarded the *Johnny Express* and took her in tow to a Cuban port. Villa and two wounded crewmen were rushed to a hospital. Although it appeared to be an outrageous act of piracy, the initial reaction from the White House was strangely subdued. Press Secretary Ron Ziegler deplored the attack as "a violation of international practice" but said that since the *Johnny Express* flew the Panamanian flag, it was a matter for Panama to deal with. In fact, a sister ship of the *Johnny Express* had been bloodlessly seized by the Cubans twelve days earlier, with scarcely a whisper of protest.

The uncommon quiet in the federal city was necessitated by the fact that the barrage of accusations being laid down by Havana Radio to justify the seizure was essentially true. The Cubans charged that the *Johnny Express* was owned by CIA front men, had landed "agents, arms, and explosives" in Cuba for the CIA on three occasions in 1968 and 1969, and had been used as a mother ship two months earlier to launch and retrieve a fast motorboat that had raked the seaside town of Boca de Sama with machine-gun fire, killing and wounding civilians.[14] That night Miami television station WTVJ broadcast an editorial, "James Bond May Be Needed," which asserted that the *Johnny Express* might have been more than an innocent noncombatant. The station showed a Coast Guard "intelligence photo" of the ship with what "appeared to be a 20-foot inboard boat with a fast hull design sitting on the cargo deck."

The *Johnny Express* was operated by the brothers Santiago and Teofilo Babun, the American success stories of a large family that had left Lebanon a generation earlier. Others of the Babuns had settled in Haiti, where they became influential in governmental affairs. Still others had gone across the Windward Passage to Oriente Province, where they prospered in commerce. Santiago and Teofilo belonged to the Oriente branch of the family, all of whom hop-scotched to Miami when Castro took power. Santiago plotted with the CIA before fleeing to the Gold Coast. When his son Santiago, Jr., joined Brigade 2506, the proud father prepared his own contribution—a 173-foot vessel that he fitted with guns at his own expense. His generosity was cruelly thwarted when the invasion occurred before the work was completed.

In 1964 Santiago's cousin, Rudolph Babun, the Haitian consul in Miami, was implicated in the smuggling of T-28 airplanes to Haiti and was forced to leave the United States. In 1968, the year that Havana Radio claimed the *Johnny Express* was first used to drop off arms and agents in Cuba, Santiago, Jr., and Teofilo were arrested by Miami police after a huge cache of explosives was found in the shipping company's yards.[15] The Babun family was clearly not unfamiliar with devices military.

If Washington was playing down the incident because of the potential CIA angle, Richard Nixon at his Florida White House on Key Biscayne was playing it up. He had Captain Villa's wife and three children brought to the compound and was photographed with a comforting arm around her shoulder while branding the seizure an "unconscionable act" and demanding Villa's immediate release. Perhaps taking a cue from the Commander in Chief, the Pentagon and State Department warned Cuba that all measures allowed by international law would be taken to prevent a recurrence, and air and sea patrols would be doubled. Havana Radio answered that gunboats would not hesitate to capture any vessel believed engaged in "counterrevolutionary activities." Both sides talked as if the stretch of water between Cuba and the Bahamas were a Torpedo Alley.

The record of history is unclear as to what Richard Nixon, standing with his arm around Isabel Villa, told the poor woman to comfort her. Nor is it known whether he told her the truth behind her husband's fate or the story of his own role in it. If he did, she got an earful. For Nixon was rekindling the Secret War from the dead coals of the Kennedys.

And yet Nixon's revisionist toasting of communist leaders in the faraway great halls of Moscow and Peking was marked by the absence of even a tip of the hat to the communist in neighboring Havana. The signal was clear enough to the CIA and the Miami exiles. The Secret War was to take some new shots. Some of them were Dr. Strangelove dirty.

During 1969 and 1970 the CIA deployed futuristic weather modification technology to ravage Cuba's sugar crop and undermine the economy. Planes from the China Lake Naval Weapons Center in the California desert, where hi tech was developed, overflew the island, seeding rain clouds with crystals that precipitated torrential rains over nonagricultural areas and left the cane fields arid (the downpours caused killer flash floods in some areas).[16]

In March 1970 a U.S. intelligence officer passed a vial of African swine fever virus to a terrorist group. The vial was taken by fishing trawler to Navassa Island, which had been used in the past by the CIA as an advance base, and was smuggled into Cuba. Six weeks later Cuba suffered the first outbreak of the swine fever in the Western Hemisphere; pig herds were decimated, causing a serious shortage of pork, the nation's dietary staple. The United Nations Food and Agricultural Organization called it the "most alarming event" of the year and futilely tried to track down "how the disease had been transmitted."[17]

The Nixon administration saw a renewed series of CIA-supported attempts on Castro's life. Gerry Patrick Hemming's exile group was involved in a triple assassination play when Castro was the guest of Salvador Allende in Chile in October 1971. Castro was to be shot with a trick gun inside a camera upon his arrival in Santiago. The camera-gun plot was confirmed by Tony Veciana, who said he was instructed by his case officer, Maurice Bishop, to organize the shoot. "It was very similar to the assassination of Kennedy," Veciana stated, "because the person Bishop assigned to kill Castro was going to get planted with papers to make it appear he was a Moscow Castro agent who turned traitor, and then he himself would be killed." The forged papers were supplied by a former Batista security agent named Luis Posada Carriles, who had enlisted for the Bay of Pigs and later was afforded intelligence training at

Fort Jackson. By 1971 Posada had become a high-ranking official of the Venezuelan security service, DISIP.[18]

The assassination attempt misfired, by the merest chance. "We had TV cameras with machine guns mounted inside to kill Castro during his speech," Veciana said, "but one agent had an appendicitis attack and we had to rush him to the hospital. The other agent said he wouldn't do it alone." The plotters had a backup plan to kill Castro when he toured a mountain copper mine near Antofagasta in Chile's north country. This only failed because of Castro's nine-lives type luck. The premier was driven up a narrow winding road to the mine site. Halfway up a disabled car blocked the road, forcing Castro's vehicle to a stop. There were 400 pounds of dynamite in the car, wired to an electric detonator. The plunger was pushed, but the dynamite failed to explode.

There was yet a third attempt when Castro stopped off in Peru on his way home from Chile. It was planned for the moment when Castro appeared in the door of his Ilyushin jet upon landing at the Lima airport for a state dinner with President Juan Velasco Alvarado. A Beechcraft Baron with a 20 mm cannon behind its door was positioned on an apron where it could blast away at Castro and then make a quick getaway. However, the Ilyushin unexpectedly pulled into a special security area, blocking it from the Beechcraft. The pilot perhaps understandably refused to taxi to another position because it would blow his chances at escape.[19]

By Gerry Hemming's account, the fall of 1970 saw a scheme so fantastic that it seemed to plagiarize the pulp novels. It began when the exile crews of Florida fishing boats decided to suspend hostilities long enough to make a quick buck. In a kind of floating commodities exchange, they swapped staples with their Cuban counterparts — coffee and flour, in short supply in Cuba, for lobsters and fish that brought a premium price on the American market. The bootlegging became so lucrative that a Cuban P-4 patrol boat began escorting the Florida boats in and out of the small port of Cayo Bahia de Cádiz to expedite the trading.

The crew of one fishing boat, the *Linda,* became friendly with Fidel's P-4 crewmen, who eventually talked about going to the

United States. A plan was proposed in which the P-4 would escort the *Linda* out of port and keep going all the way to Key Biscayne — at a time when Nixon was in residence in his compound — and, with its Cuban markings plainly visible, open fire on *chez Nixon*. It was meant to be a provocation sufficient to touch off an invasion of Cuba; if Nixon were killed or injured, that would be too bad, but also more provocative: a perfect specimen of the Caribbean plot mentality. "What do you think Spiro Agnew would have done about six hours later," Hemming said, "thinking it was a Castro operation?"[20]

The plan had reached the stage at which two planes had been acquired to fly the conspirators out of the country when it was aborted by an insider's tip to the Secret Service for the usual reward. A few days later the *Linda* was tied up on the Miami River, the crew aboard put under house arrest, when Nixon floated by on Bebe Rebozo's houseboat, the *Coco Lobo*. Unaware that he had been deemed expendable by the unhappy Cubans glaring out of the portholes at him, the President yelled greetings while Rebozo obligingly pulled the *Coco Lobo* over so his friend could shake some Cuban hands. Hemming was nervous because the crew was drunk and automatic carbines were on their bunks, but they didn't give Nixon the time of day.

III

In Little Havana crowds milled along Flagler Street, forming knots in front of fruit and vegetable stands, talking animatedly in sidewalk cantinas over Spanish cider and tiny cups of thick Cuban coffee. News travels fast in Little Havana, and the talk of the town was Howard Hunt. He was back.

Howard Hunt came home to Miami on the eve of the tenth anniversary of the Bay of Pigs on April 17, 1971. A memorial to the fallen members of Brigade 2506 was dedicated in Little Havana. That day Hunt went to the home of his old bagman, Bernard Barker. He left a note pinned to the door: "If you are the same Barker I once knew, contact me. Howard." There was his room number at a Miami Beach hotel.

Barker was one of the few Cubans who knew Hunt as other than
"Eduardo." They reminisced over lunch. Barker had been in Manuel
Artime's MRR, then gone into real estate. Hunt, too, had remained
close to Artime, who was godfather to one of his children. Hunt, after the Bay of Pigs, had ghostwritten Allen Dulles's book *The Craft
of Intelligence.* When Dulles fell out of the CIA, Hunt fell out of favor.
In 1963 the U.S. ambassador in Madrid vetoed his appointment as
assistant chief of station there because of his reputation as an in-
triguer, and he was forced to resort to a journalistic cover for his part
in the Artime-Cubela-Amlash assassination plot.

Hunt retired from the CIA to the agency-connected Robert R.
Mullen Company, a Washington public relations firm with clients
of the solvency of General Foods and the Hughes Tool Company.
Like Bob Maheu's Old Curiosity Shop of a decade before, Mullen
employed Old Boys who also did odd jobs for the CIA. The White
House wanted Hunt for a special assignment, and the Mullen
management readily granted him leave.

Hunt came on deck as chief spook of the White House Special Investigative Unit, aka the Plumbers. Even in this prepuberty state of
the 1972 campaign the White House was a greenhouse of paranoia.
When Hunt reported for duty, the first file handed him bore the
name Daniel Ellsberg, the Johnny Appleseed of the Pentagon
Papers. Armed with spy paraphernalia provided by an accommodating CIA, Hunt cased the Beverly Hills office of Ellsberg's
psychiatrist, rooting for the clinical details of a whistleblower.

Bernie Barker's heart of loyalty beat double time when Hunt
asked him to assist in a "national security" matter under a "superstructure" organization "above both the FBI and CIA."[21] The operation, Hunt said, would reactivate 120 CIA veterans. Barker's yes
was automatic. He even thought there were two salesmen-burglars
in his real estate firm who would jump at the chance. Jump they did.

Barker's firm, Ameritas, was a subsidiary of the Florida-famous
Keyes Realty, the solid-gold brokerage company which had been so
fortunate to be the major investment funnel for the hundreds of millions of dollars that syndicate figures and freebooting Cuban politicians hauled out of Batista's Cuba. Keyes had also been instrumental
in Richard Nixon's balance sheet.

The facts of Nixon's mainland investments were first revealed in 1971 by a *Newsday* investigative team. (Participating reporters received tit-for-tat from the Nixon White House in the form of IRS harassment.) In 1962, Nixon began buying into Fisher's Island, Inc., which had been formed by Rebozo and Smathers to acquire the island in Biscayne Bay from Lindsay Hopkins, Jr., a director of the CIA dummy Zenith Technical Enterprises, which provided cover for the JM/WAVE station. By 1968 Nixon had accumulated 185,891 shares at a reported bargain price of $1 each. A year later he sold back the stock to Fisher's Island, Inc., at $2 a share, doubling his money. At that time he was the only stockholder to have made a profit. This was seen by some students of Nixon lore as a way for his rich, Cuban-connected friends to give their man easy money.

The Fisher's Island windfall was followed by a series of maneuvers that left Nixon the holder of Key Biscayne property of suspect genealogy. The property was carved out of the southern half of Key Biscayne which, over twenty years before, had been held in a trust composed of Keyes Realty; Agustín Batista, the Christian Democratic Movement patriarch; and others.

In 1948 control of the property passed into the hands of Wallace Groves, an amiable scoundrel who fronted for Meyer Lansky. Three years later, when Groves suddenly decamped for the Bahamas to lay the groundwork for Lansky's expansion into gambling there, the property was vested in the name of Elena Santeiro Alemán, which is to say nothing much had changed. Her father had been Lucky Luciano's lawyer in Havana, and she was the wife of Jose Alemán, an official under both Batista and Prío, who, upon setting foot on Florida soil, had smiled when the customs men gasped at the bundles of "personal" money in his baggage. She was also the mother of José Alemán, Jr., a lifelong friend of Rolando Cubela's and the man who, in negotiating a teamster loan in 1962, quoted Santos Trafficante as saying Kennedy was going to be hit.

In 1960 Elena Alemán sold the property for $12 million in promissory notes to Arthur A. Dessler, a Jimmy Hoffa associate. Dessler and Lou Poller, another Hoffa buddy and teamsters front man, used the real estate to gain control of the Miami National Bank (Poller and Miami National were named in the 1971 indictment of

Meyer Lansky for skimming). Then Dessler defaulted on the promissory notes. Alemán took back the property and tore the notes up. Net result: The teamsters had a "laundry" bank.

In 1963 Elena Alemán put the property in trust with the Miami Beach First National Bank, owned by the George Smathers family. At the same time she obtained from the bank a multimillion-dollar loan, for which she put up as collateral securities held by the Ansan and Mohawk corporations, the holding companies created in the late 1940s by her husband and ex-Batista Cabinet Minister Anselmo S. Alliegro to invest the funny money coming out of Havana. In 1965 she deeded the southern tip of the property to the state of Florida for the Cape Florida park. She made $8 million on the sale. The rest was sold through the Smathers bank for "$10 and other valuable consideration"—to Arthur Dessler.

One year later Dessler sold the property to the Cape Florida Development Corporation, which was formed by Bebe Rebozo and Donald Berg, a Key Biscayne boniface who fraternized with Lansky gaming manager Lou Chesler on one hand and Dick Nixon on the other (the Secret Service later cringed every time Berg and Nixon got together). In 1967 Rebozo brought Nixon to Key Biscayne to pose for publicity pictures with him and Berg to promote the lagging development. In gratitude Nixon was allowed to buy two lots at greatly discounted prices.

Rebozo showcased Nixon again in January 1968 at the gala opening in the Bahamas of the Paradise Island casino. The casino was the pride of James Crosby, president of its owner, Resorts International, and a friend of Rebozo's. Resorts International gratefully kept a modest account at Rebozo's Key Biscayne Bank (where Nixon had savings account No. 1), and Rebozo felt free to call on Crosby for advice on some IBM stock he had taken as security for a $195,000 loan, stock which turned up on the FBI's "hot sheet" as stolen by the Carlo Gambino Mafia family. Crosby donated $100,000 to Nixon's 1968 campaign and provided a company yacht for Nixon's pleasure at the Miami Beach convention.

It was also in 1968 that Rebozo pocketed a $200,000 profit on a Little Havana shopping center called El Centro Commercial Cubano in a virtually risk-free deal. Through George Smathers's senatorial clout, he had secured an $80,000 loan from the Small Business Administration, plus a $2.4 million rent guarantee on the basis that the center would be occupied by businesses run by low-income Cuban immigrants. When it opened, millionaire Rebozo was running a laundromat and wealthy Manuel Artime had a grocery store. Rebozo had awarded the construction contract to mobster Big Al Polizzi, but that might have been nothing more than helping an ex-con go straight.[22]

When Nixon decided he needed a Florida White House after the 1968 election, he bought George Smathers's home on Bay Lane in Key Biscayne as well as the next-door residence of a Cuban exile family. Keyes Realty handled the transactions, and most of the mortgage money came from the Smathers's bank. When the presidential compound was ready, Bebe Rebozo moved in.

Over the Labor Day weekend of 1971 Hunt and G. Gordon Liddy stood lookout while the three Cubans from Miami broke into Dr. Lewis Fielding's Beverly Hills office, photographing everything with Ellsberg's name on it. But the swag was disappointing; there was nothing that might sully Ellsberg's reputation to be leaked. A "get all the dirt" number on Senator Ted Kennedy, who conceivably might be drafted as the Democratic candidate, was no more successful. According to Frank Sturgis, who had joined the team, they were given the names of four girls in Washington who supposedly had romantic interludes with Kennedy and interviewed them under the pretext of Democratic party research on the senator. The questioning was deliberately hostile to Kennedy. As Sturgis explained it: "The idea was to tap their phone wires and listen in afterward to see who they called to report our visit, what they said in the first blush of anxiety. Well, we pulled off the interviews all right, but we could never find the right pair of phone numbers to tap."[23]

About this time Hunt checked in with Manuel Artime, who had become rich through importing meat and machinery from Nicaragua in conjunction with Anastasio Somoza. Artime later told a Watergate investigator that Hunt said "something had to be taken care of in Panama"—after Nixon's reelection—and wanted Artime to join the team. According to Artime, the mission concerned

Panamanian officials who helped smuggle drugs into the United States. But the Watergate investigation unearthed evidence that the actual mission was the assassination of Panamanian ruler Omar Torrijos Herrera.[24]

As the 1972 election year began, Hunt's group was moved over to the Committee to Re-elect the President, reuniting him with Jim McCord, who had worked with the ex-Combatientes at Fort Jackson and was now CREEP's security director. One of the first jobs planned under the CREEP aegis was a burglary of the office of Hank Greenspun, publisher of the Las Vegas *Sun,* to obtain "blackmail-type" material on Senator Edmund Muskie, then the Democratic front-runner. Hunt believed they might kill two birds with one stone, since Greenspun possessed a thick batch of Howard Hughes's internal documents. But Hughes relayed word that he didn't give a damn about the documents because they presumably had already been copied. Muskie went into a tailspin, and there was no need to discredit him.

In March at Key Biscayne, John Mitchell, who had resigned as attorney general to take over CREEP, approved a wide-ranging espionage and dirty tricks campaign against the Democrats that was code named Gemstone. The Democratic hierarchy's suites in the Fontainebleau Hotel in Miami Beach would be bugged during their convention in July. An executive of Smathers's Miami Beach First National Bank reserved a block of rooms for a "friend" named Edward Hamilton, an alias used by both Hunt and Sturgis. During this same period Hunt and Barker visited Carlos Prío at his Miami Beach home. What the Gemstone operatives wanted is unclear, although after Watergate Prío claimed that Hunt had asked for help in "public relations" in Haiti and elsewhere in Latin America. In any event Prío became head of Cuban-Americans for Nixon-Agnew, and during the Republican convention in August he rode in a gold Cadillac, directing a goon squad that roughed up antiwar demonstrators.[25]

Before that, on May Day, J. Edgar Hoover suddenly died, and word came down that there might be a protest demonstration at the anticommunist hero's funeral. Barker hurriedly rounded up a gang to fly to Washington to prevent the protest. The crew that signed on included Frank Sturgis and his sidekick Pablo Hernández, who had already signed on with the Miami police to act as a provocateur at the conventions by selling automatic weapons to demonstrating Vietnam Veterans Against the War (the vets had no interest in the weapons). De Diego went, and so did baby-faced Hiram González, a 30th of November activist who in 1962 had walked out of a Cuban prison dressed in drag. Another was Angel Ferrer, McCord's former contact with the Fort Jackson ex-Combatientes who was now on the Torriente Plan council.

Two weeks later a young man named Arthur H. Bremer sporting a twisted grin gunned down Alabama Governor George Wallace, wounding him severely enough to take him out of the presidential race. Wallace was posing a serious threat to the "Southern Strategy" that had been credited with Nixon's narrow win in 1968. The polls showed that if Wallace were to run as a third-party candidate in November, he would siphon off enough votes from Nixon to create a virtual deadlock between the President and either Hubert Humphrey or George McGovern, who were then running neck and neck for the Democratic nomination.

Charles Colson instructed Hunt to fly at once to Milwaukee, Bremer's hometown, and plant evidence in his apartment that he was associated with the left. Hunt balked on the ground that the FBI would already have sealed off the apartment. When this intriguing bit of information surfaced after Watergate, Colson claimed that he told Hunt to clean up evidence, not to plant any. Colson said when Nixon heard of the shooting, he became agitated and "voiced immediate concern that the assassin [*sic*] might have ties to the Republican Party, or even worse, the President's re-election committee."[26]

The explanation is fascinating not for what it settles but what it raises about Nixon's qualms about his Gemstone operatives going too far. The all-encompassing "Bay of Pigs thing" was to haunt him. It might not have been a false fear. Bremer's older sister, Gail Aiken, and brother, William, lived in Miami. (As mentioned earlier, in 1968 Aiken, then living in Los Angeles, was exceedingly close to Oliver Owen, a fundamentalist preacher. Owen had had an association with Sirhan Sirhan prior to the RFK assassination, which had the effect of clearing Nixon's path to the White House.) Two months

before the Wallace shooting William Bremer was indicted in a
$36,000 swindle (he was subsequently convicted) that had all the
earmarks of an organized crime caper. (William Bremer was represented by Ellis Rubin, a respectable, if offbeat, attorney, who later
represented the Miami Four in the Watergate break-in.)

The beat was picking up. Sturgis's friend Jack Anderson wrote
that Sturgis and Martínez might have been implicated in the May 13
break-in of the Chilean Embassy. On May 22 Hunt assembled his
Miami team in the Hamilton Manger Hotel in Washington under
the guise of an Ameritas sales meeting. There were Barker, Martínez, Sturgis, and de Diego (who registered under the name José
Piedra, a brother-in-law who had been shot down over the Bay of
Pigs), as well as a new addition, Virgilio González, the professional
locksmith who was a loyal follower of Carlos Prío's. Hunt told
them that if they helped the White House now, "it would be a decisive factor at a later date for obtaining help in the liberation of
Cuba."[27] He briefed them on the target: the Democratic National
Headquarters in the Watergate complex. He said they would be
looking for evidence that Fidel Castro had secretly contributed $1
million to McGovern. Hunt knew this challenge would pump up
the Cubans for the mission.

By this time McGovern had the nomination within his grasp, and
although Castro was a convenient buzz word, Hunt was actually
seeking documentation that might link McGovern to the domestic
radicals against the war. According to Sturgis, Hunt also instructed
them to zero in on DNC chairman Lawrence O'Brien's office and
look for "anything on Howard Hughes." For the past two years
O'Brien had been doing public relations work for Hughes, and the
White House was frantic to know what O'Brien might know about
a sizable "gift" Hughes had given Nixon. The possibility had been
enhanced the previous Thanksgiving when the preposterous
Hughes vacated Las Vegas by night and flew to the Paradise Island
Hotel in the Bahamas, leaving Bob Maheu first sacked and soon em-
bittered. Maheu and O'Brien were old friends. Maheu got O'Brien
the Hughes PR account (which, when O'Brien took over as DNC
chairman, had shifted to the CIA's Mullen agency). Maheu was a

walking encyclopedia of Hughes contributions to Nixon via Rebozo and others.

If money talks, then Howard Hughes, from his Desert Inn penthouse, was one of the world's great ventriloquists. He once sent Bob Maheu to Lyndon Johnson's ranch to offer $1 million to call off nuclear testing in the Nevada desert, which Hughes felt was scaring off the casino trade and irradiating his drinking water. Maheu, unable to bring himself to proffer such a bribe to the President of the United States, asked instead if there was anything that Hughes, a great admirer, might do. Johnson suggested a donation to the LBJ Library project, noting that there was a $25,000 limit. When Maheu reported back to Hughes, the billionaire scoffed, "Hell, I couldn't control the son of a bitch with $25,000."[28]

Over the years Hughes had laid millions on politicians of every stripe on the condition that they were either in office or had a reasonable chance to win their elections (an apparent exception was John Kennedy). In the 1968 campaign he honored both candidates with $100,000. "I want you to see Nixon as my special confidential emissary," Hughes memoed Maheu. "I feel there is a really valid possibility of a Republican victory this year." Maheu didn't see Nixon personally but gave the money to Rebozo (Humphrey got his personally, in a limo in front of the Century Plaza Hotel in Los Angeles).

A year after Nixon settled into the White House he received another $100,000 from Hughes, which, since there were no campaign debts to clear up, was suspiciously in the category of gratuity.

Even by Hughes's standards, $100,000 wasn't nickel-slots money. Its passage into Rebozo's hands came at a time when Hughes's controversial acquisition of Air West was awaiting the Nixon administration's approval and when he needed Justice Department easing of an antitrust action barring him from adding to his collection of Nevada casinos. Hughes got everything he wanted.

IV

"One of the things we were looking for in the Democratic National Committee's files, and in some other Washington file cabinets, too,"

Frank Sturgis said,"was a thick secret memorandum from the Castro government, addressed confidentially to the Democrats' platform committee." The 150-page memo Sturgis was looking for reportedly detailed CIA covert operations against Cuba over a long span. "It said that the Castro government suspected the CIA did not tell the whole truth about these operations even to American political leaders; therefore, the Cubans were providing an itemized list of all such 'abuses.' The complaints were especially bitter about various attempts to assassinate the Castro brothers."[29]

The Democrats were exceedingly unlikely to make a campaign issue of assassination plots that could be traced back to Camelot. The Watergate White House would more logically be concerned about the possibility of a later entry on such a list — the 1971 assassination attempts against Castro in Chile. This was a bombshell that the Democrats might be tempted to explode. What makes this conjecture all the more intriguing is the Chilean connection. Sturgis said that the search for the memo extended "to some other . . . file cabinets" — a veiled reference to the still-unsolved break-ins at the Chilean Embassy and Cuban United Nations Mission in New York in early May.

At this time Nixon's covert campaign to overthrow Salvador Allende's government was well under way.

Playing a key role in the campaign against Allende was the multinational goliath International Telephone & Telegraph Company, which had close ties to both the CIA and the White House. ITT had secretly offered to put up $400,000 for the Republican convention to be held in San Diego and for Nixon to rest his head at the company's Sheraton Harbor Island Hotel; somebody called it "renting the President." Nixon by most accounts was all for the deal, and San Diego was given the coveted nod. In a perhaps noncoincidence, the Justice Department gave ITT a favorable settlement of a major antitrust case.

In February 1972 Jack Anderson printed excerpts from an ITT internal memo written by lobbyist Dita Beard that exposed this squirrelly deal. The walls began to melt, and the White House in-house Mafia was sent out on damage control. Gordon Liddy whisked the shellshocked Mrs. Beard via magic carpet to a Denver hospital, and Howard Hunt flew to her bedside, disguised with pancake makeup and an ill-fitting wig provided by the CIA.

The bubbling ITT scandal, the Chilean skulduggery, the Castro assassination plots, Howard Hughes—these were some of the suspected genies somewhere in a bottle at Democratic headquarters that had to stay corked.

The story of Watergate is told and retold like *Rashomon,* and each time the shades of truth change as with the seasons. On June 16 Sturgis, Barker, Martínez, and González flew to Washington for another crack at the DNC offices in the Watergate complex. The first try in early May had been unsuccessful; over the Memorial Day weekend they managed to get in and photograph documents while McCord installed bug transmitters. But McCord had set the power level so low to avoid detection that the transmissions were only marginally intelligible.

No one had the feeling they were going to the well once too often, and if by some chance they were caught, they had been told not to worry; "fail-safe" arrangements had been made to quietly retrieve them. When they got off the plane at National Airport, Sturgis bumped into Jack Anderson, to whom he had been feeding information for years, but said he happened to be in town on "private business." When they entered the lobby of the Howard Johnson motel across from the Watergate, Sturgis spotted his movie idol Burt Lancaster and impulsively asked for his autograph.[30]

The bugs in the DNC offices were being monitored in the Howard Johnson by Alfred Baldwin, an ex-FBI man whose name McCord had picked out of the roster of the Society of Former Special Agents of the FBI. Ordinarily McCord, now employed by the Nixon campaign, would not have accompanied the visitors, but he went along to turn up the volume on his transmitters. The team was busily snapping photos of documents when a security guard noticed tape on door locks and called the police.

Sturgis recalls that he had hardly been booked at the police station when an attorney named Douglas Caddy arrived and told him, "Olympus is watching over you." Sturgis assumed that it was a shibboleth that the fail-safe mechanism was in operation, even though he didn't know that Caddy was close to Howard Hunt and once had had office space in the Mullen agency. But if there was a plan to usher the Miami Four through the judicial turnstile with a minimum of fuss, dismissing them as anti-Castro zealots carried away by the million-dollar rumor, it was spoiled by McCord's name on the police blotter. The press immediately tied him to CREEP.

Nixon was in Key Biscayne when the break-in news hit the papers, although not the front pages. Press Secretary Ron Ziegler issued his famous statement that it was nothing more than "a third-rate burglary." Then the police began sniffing along the White House trail. In Barker's pocket they had found an address book with the initials "H.H." and the inscription "W. House," along with a check signed by an E. Howard Hunt. And Hunt, who was hiding in the home of a CIA attorney in Los Angeles, relayed a message to the White House that had novelist Hunt's melodramatic ring: "The writer has a play to sell."

When the Watergate temple walls began to fall on Nixon, it was the Cuban connection that he feared would pull the roof down around his head. The President rushed from Florida to huddle with his self-styled "son of a bitch" Bob Haldeman in the Oval Office and belabored the problem:

> We protected Helms from one hell of a lot of things. . . . Of course, this Hunt, that will uncover a lot of things. You open that scab there's a hell of a lot of things . . . say, "Look the problem is that this will open the whole, the whole Bay of Pigs thing" . . . very bad to have this fellow Hunt, ah, he knows too damned much, if he was involved — you happen to know that? If it gets out that this is all involved, the Cuba thing, it would be a fiasco. It would make the CIA look bad, it's going to make Hunt look bad, and it is very likely to blow the whole Bay of Pigs thing which we think would be very unfortunate — both for the CIA and for the country, at this time, and for American foreign policy . . . the problem is it tracks back to the Bay of Pigs."[31]

The whole Bay of Pigs thing. Nixon's entire life was coming back to haunt him. The mob. The real estate. The cash. The CIA. The deals.

When Jack Anderson published his columns on Johnny Roselli and the CIA plots in 1971, two things immediately occurred. Chuck Colson discussed with Hunt the feasibility of drugging Anderson, perhaps fatally, and White House aides instructed Helms to turn over a copy of the CIA's 1967 in-house investigation on the CIA-Mafia plots. At first Helms refused, but he finally acceded to Nixon's personal order and turned over a partial report.

Although Gerry Hemming and other paramilitaries in the know insist that the attempts on Castro's life in Chile were set up by a White House squad, the Cuban government says it has evidence that the CIA "participated directly." The probability is that both views are correct. Alpha 66's Tony Veciana was brought into the plot by his longtime CIA case officer, Maurice Bishop. Veciana guessed that the "To HH" he saw on one of Bishop's memos reporting on exile actions in 1963 meant H. L. Hunt or Howard Hughes. But it just as easily could have been Howard Hunt.

It was about the time of the Chile attempts that Hunt propositioned Artime to join an operation directed against Panama that embraced the assassination of Omar Torrijos. Hunt could assume that Artime would have no qualms about such messy business, since they both had participated in the Amlash plot against Castro.

Nixon had other reasons for jitters over the "Cuba thing." There was his friend and his Key Biscayne boarder, Bebe Rebozo. Rebozo was the key to the gingerbread house of real estate transactions that sat in the deep woods of funny Cuban money. A respectable interpretation of the irrationality of the famous "Saturday night massacre" has Nixon firing Special Prosecutor Archibald Cox because the agent of Camelot was pursuing the Rebozo angle like a dog into the marrow of the bone.

Jeb Stuart Magruder told the Senate Watergate Committee, "I don't think there was ever any discussion that there would not be a cover-up." One hot rock was the $89,000 in cash that had been channeled to Barker to help finance the Gemstone operations. Barker told Sturgis that the money came from Chilean "investors" opposed to Allende, but Watergate investigators concluded that it was the product of illegal corporate contributions made in the United States. In any case, the $89,000 was sent to a Mexico City attorney for laundering, reaching Barker without a ring around the collar. After the break-in the White House instructed the CIA to try to get the FBI to lay off this aspect of its investigation on grounds it would expose an agency conduit and imperil "national security."

Nixon was more than willing to ensure the silence of Hunt, the man who "knows too damned much," by buying all rights to his "play." Throughout the 1972 campaign tens of thousands of dollars in hush money were shoveled to Hunt. For a time the lid stayed on. When Hunt's wife, Dorothy, died in a Chicago plane crash after the election, her purse was full of $100 Watergate bills.

After the constitutional crunch of 1974, when the Supreme Court forced Nixon to give up his tapes, one of the most incriminating passages the hangmen of impeachment in Congress weighed was Nixon's obsessive concern with silencing Hunt about the Bay of Pigs. The end came quickly. As Nixon plunged deeper into melancholia, the ever adjustable White House chief of staff, General Alexander Haig, who had more or less taken charge of the affairs of state, ordered the Army's Criminal Investigation Command to probe Nixon's possible ties to organized crime, specifically Mafia leaders in narcotics trafficking. The probe was abbreviated when Nixon resigned. The CIC chief investigator, Russell L. Bintliff, told the Washington Star on December 5, 1976, that he had turned up "strong indications of a history of Nixon connections with money from organized crime."

"Gentlemen," the beleaguered Nixon told a group of editors as he was being fitted for the shroud of resignation, "your President is not a crook." The editors were meeting at the Florida Disneyland. It was, all things considered, an appropriate place for Richard M. Nixon to make that statement.

TEN
A Murderous Legacy

I

ON a June morning in 1972, the week after the Watergate break-in, Joaquín Sanjenís left his modest import-export office in Miami's Cuban *barrio* and drove down SW Eighth Street to the Anthony Abrams Chevrolet Agency. José Joaquín Sanjenís Perdomo was a plain man of undifferentiated features, which was, in his profession, an asset: He was a professional spy. His personality suited his work in that neither encouraged close personal relationships. His was a lonely life, sweetened by habitual cups of thick Cuban coffee; he looked forward to his forthcoming retirement, although he would not live long enough to enjoy it. It is testimony to the importance his employers gave to his carefully nurtured anonymity that when he died, of natural causes, in 1974, his family was not notified until after the funeral. Joaquín Sanjenís was, for over ten years, the head of the CIA's supersecret Operation 40 in Miami.[1]

The wear of a decade of living in shadows showed on the spy's face that morning as he drove into the automobile agency's service entrance. Sanjenís had launched scores of ships and planes on clandestine raids against Cuba and had sent hundreds of men on missions from which there had been no return. He was able to offer only the most mute of patriotic explanations to the bereaved families. There were no official missing-in-action reports in the Secret War against Cuba. It was Joaquín Sanjenís's job to keep his troops, as himself, faceless.

The Anthony Abrams Chevrolet Agency was a familiar rendez-vous. That morning Sanjenís was meeting an old friend, Félix Gutiérrez, a comrade-in-arms, comrade-in-espionage. Gutiérrez was Sanjenís's chief deputy in Operation 40. He had been an officer in the hated SIM, the secret police of former Cuban dictator Fulgencio Batista, and was among the first to flee the island when Castro came to power.

Sanjenís and Gutiérrez were veterans of the Bay of Pigs. They joined Operation 40 prior to the invasion. It began as a phalanx of right-wing cutthroats who were to follow in the path of the invading brigade and murder any middle-of-the-road leaders in towns and villages who might object to a restoration of the Batista status quo. Operation 40 had another political function—to purge the Cuban exile ranks of the anti-Castro left, the exponents of *Fidelismo sin Fidel*. Operation 40 agents spied on their comrades for the CIA. They were the thought police of the Cuban invasion. After the Bay of Pigs, the CIA kept Operation 40 intact in Miami, and Sanjenís and Gutiérrez became noncoms in the agency's new Secret War. They continued to inform on their fellow Cuban exiles, and played out the dirtiest hands in the CIA's deck.

On a normal day the two old soldiers would have indulged in reminiscences of battles past. But today the boss of Operation 40 was uncharacteristically nervous. It was less than a week since the bungled break-in at Watergate. Already it seemed events not wholly within his control were conspiring to threaten the vaulted security of Operation 40. Joaquín Sanjenís had sufficient cause for worry. Among the not-so-common burglars arrested in the Watergate office complex were varsity-letter graduates of his school for domestic commandos—and other past and present members of Operation 40 were involved in clandestine political activities which, if uncovered, could unmask the CIA's contraband multimillion-dollar paramilitary assets in Miami.

Sanjenís and his deputy hurriedly discussed certain steps they would take to guard against such an undesirable eventuality. The existence of Operation 40 was to be hidden whatever the cost—in money or in men sacrificed. For among its secrets were some of the most explosive of the Cold War—the CIA's interface with the Mafia, the plots to assassinate Castro, and the CIA's role in the capture and execution of Che Guevara.

The pilot of the twin-engine Beechcraft Model 18 watched the glowing dials on the instrument panel as he droned along a few thousand feet over the black roof of the Bolivian jungle. In minutes it would be time to make a ninety-degree turn to the right. He was flying in a grid pattern. The pilot worked for Mark Hurd Aerial Surveys, Inc., an American firm. His job was to take daylight photographs of the terrain through which a proposed highway across the Andes Mountains would run. But now it was night; the camera in the plane's belly was pointed down at jungle darkness. What he was really doing was looking for Che Guevara.

It was early October 1967. The CIA had been hunting Che in several countries. Che and his band of revolutionaries were thought to be organizing an insurgency movement somewhere in the heart of South America. The latest intelligence reports had them moving by night through the thick Bolivian jungle. Finding them on foot had proved impossible. The CIA resorted to a newly developed film that could "see" at night.

The first clue that Che had left Cuba had come in April 1965, when his name was omitted from a new list of Cuban Communist party functionaries and his replacement was named as minister of industry. He could no longer be found in his usual haunts. Soon the rumors began. The ruling junta in the Dominican Republic claimed that he had been killed in the first days of fighting in the 1965 insurrection, implying that Castro was behind it. Another report had it that Castro himself had ordered his liquidation. There was even wishful speculation that he had sold out to Western intelligence and was being exhaustively debriefed.

Finally, in October, Castro announced that Che had relinquished his Cuban posts and citizenship to "press the struggle against imperialism" in a new field. In fact, Che was in the Congo helping in the losing civil war against the Mobutu regime, which, ironically, pitted him against the CIA Cubans from Miami. Then he slipped back to Havana and obtained Castro's blessing for a guerrilla experiment in Bolivia that, if successful, could mean two, three, many Vietnams in South America.

The CIA was determined to see that he failed. In what was supposed to appear as an all-Bolivian operation, a squad of Green Berets was brought in from the Panama Canal Zone to drill Bolivian Rangers in counterinsurgency, and a "Che Team" of two Cubans from Operation 40 in Miami was flown in to monitor the hunt. The team leader was a car salesman at Anthony Abrams Chevrolet when not on CIA assignment.[2] There was immediate friction, owing in large measure to resentment of the Green Berets to the idea of taking orders from Cubans.

The tensions were hardly lessened by the superior attitude of the Operation 40 duo. By 1967 Joaquín Sanjenís had expanded the group to the point where it received more than $2 million a year from the CIA, in addition to extensive logistical support. The Sanjenís group had been busy both on the sabotage run to Cuba and on the domestic front — organizing the picketing of the British consulate in Miami to protest the sale of English buses to Cuba; boycotting Shell gasoline and Scotch whiskey; picketing the French consulate to protest the sale of locomotives to Cuba; picketing the Mexican consulate in New York to protest that country's relations with Cuba; and attempting to prevent a Japanese ship from unloading her cargo in Miami. Violence was not a proscribed activity. "There was never a problem," one participant said. "We were detained once or twice, but each time someone would call the Miami police, and we would be immediately released with no charges."

Operation 40 was also running a kind of Cuban Cointelpro. "It began like a counterintelligence operation," the participant said, "but it soon became domestic snooping plain and simple. As far as I know, they haven't discovered a single Castro spy here, but they sure made many detailed reports, including gossip about personal lives of all prominent Cubans, if anything, usurping the functions of the FBI." Another Cuban recalled, "It was like a small secret army, and some of its members were making personal threats and demanding personal favors."[3]

For months Che and his band eluded the CIA stalkers, prompting Fidel Castro to taunt, "If the yanquis are so anxious to find Che why don't they send up a U-2 to take a picture of him?" Castro thought he was kidding. The CIA knew otherwise.

The U-2 at 68,000 feet took photos clearly showing a golf ball on the green of a golf course. But Che's band was harder to spot than a golf ball on a green — during daylight hours they were shielded by the dense jungle growth. The agency had encountered similar difficulties tracking down Vietcong units in Vietnam jungles. So the CIA master tinkerers developed a capability, using infrared photography, to register heat rays rather than light. Infrared photos pick up heat emissions — from underground, concealed or disguised installations, even buried piping systems. Each heat source — an engine, a radio, a boiler, an oven — can be identified by slight color differentials on the film. This was called, in state-of-the-art language, the heat signature.

Shortly before the hunt for Che, this breakthrough in space-age technology was being fine-tuned by the University of Michigan Infrared Physics Laboratory at Willow Run under a government contract to perfect the new "infrared optical imaging and signal processing techniques" for counterinsurgency application. The idea was to see if the film would register the heat from a human body.[4] Che Guevara was the first target. From intelligence data the CIA knew that Che transmitted at night on a shortwave radio and cooked at night with a Dien Bien Phu oven developed by the Vietcong; neither gave off any light, but both gave off heat. And when the fugitives were on the move, their closely spaced bodies created a warm pocket in the cool night air.

The CIA formed a special aerial survey detachment to track the Che band by their heat emissions. Each night a high-flying plane from Howard Air Force Base in the Canal Zone soared high over the jungle vastness, its cameras unreeling. Far below a Mark Hurd Beechcraft lumbered along, its single camera pointed at the ground from what was, in the military version, the bomb bay. The Minneapolis-based Mark Hurd firm had done aerial surveys in practically every corner of the globe, a job not normally attempted at night; its clients numbered oil, construction, and utility companies, foreign governments, and the United States agencies. The road survey contract in Bolivia had been let by the Agency for International Development, often used by the CIA as a cover.[5] Some CIA watchers claimed that if you knew about Mark Hurd contracts around the world, you could predict where the next trouble spot would be.

Mark Hurd pilots flew out of meadows and small airstrips that had been built by oil exploration firms. Radio transmitters packed in on mules served as navigational beacons for flying the grid patterns. The operation was kept on a need-to-know basis. Once, a detachment of U.S. Ranger-supervised Bolivian soldiers became curious about a large stockpile of fuel cans in a meadow. They noted that the Beechcraft being refueled did not have current Bolivian in-transit stickers and tried to arrest the crew. "We just sat on our equipment," the Mark Hurd pilot recalled. "Apparently one agency knew we were there, and another didn't."

The exposed film was rushed daily to California, to Mark Hurd's main air base at the Santa Barbara airport. Each developed roll, called a heat print, was tacked into position on a huge board standing in a screened-off area of the company's hangar. As the prints accumulated, they formed a picture called a mosaic — in this case an eerie, multicolored trail made by the body heat of a group moving through the jungle. The heat signatures of the radio and oven confirmed that it was Che's band. Their route through the back-country could now be plotted.[6]

In the diary he kept of his doomed Bolivian campaign, Che noted in an entry dated September 10, 1967, that airplanes had been "flying all over the Zone." He didn't know what was hunting him.

The Operation 40 team from Miami entered Bolivia under the names Felix Ramos and Eduardo Gonzales. The rites of passage were simple for they had a sponsor in a high place — Antonio Arguedas Mendietta, the Bolivian Minister of the Interior and chief of intelligence who was also working for the CIA. One of the Interior Minister's duties for the agency was to "infiltrate agents, principally Cuban exiles, into the Bolivian intelligence services and into left-wing groups."[7] Arguedas did his job well. "Bolivia is filled with CIA agents," he said.

Che Guevara was big game for the CIA. To make sure he would be caught in their high-tech snare, the agency established a Special Operations Group in Bolivia with safehouses in La Paz and the oil town of Camiri. SOG/Bolivia coordinated the work of its aerial snoops with the 8th Special Forces Group which was training the uncoordinated Bolivian army to take on Che's guerrilleros.[8] But Che's fall was due as much to his incautious haste to repeat the Sierra Maestra in the Andes and to the perfidy of the Bolivian Communist party as to the American big-game hunters. The fact that Che's men did not speak the language did not endear them to the natives they had come to serve. And despite the prevailing American wisdom that Castro is Moscow's puppet, the conservative Kremlin leadership was opposed to exporting the Cuban revolution to Latin America; when Castro would not heel, Moscow ordered its toadies in the Bolivian C.P. to sabotage Che's revolutionary efforts in the hills.[9] They even dispatched a beautiful KGB agent known as Tania to spy on Che, a job complicated when she fell in love with him; she was killed in a cross fire with Bolivian troops a month before Che died.

Che's trackers ambushed him and his men on October 8, 1967, in a canyon near the hamlet of La Higuera. Che was hit in the leg. Ramos, the Operation 40 agent, was with the Bolivian ambushers. He immediately began photographing the contents of the wounded man's knapsack.[10] Although the Bolivian government announced that Che had been killed in the firefight, he was taken to La Higuera and locked in the schoolhouse. The next day the Bolivian military brass, including a rear admiral of the armed forces of that landlocked nation, arrived by helicopter to view their prize. With them, according to eyewitnesses, was the CIA agent known as Gonzales. That afternoon Che Guevara was machine-gunned to death in the schoolhouse by a Bolivian Ranger. His body was strapped to a helicopter and flown to the larger town of Vallegrande where the two Operation 40 agents supervised the embalming process. A Reuters dispatch from Vallegrande mentioned that a CIA agent was present but this information did not appear in American newspapers.[11] It was later disclosed that the embalmers had cut off Che's hands before he was cremated, to prove that he was dead.[12]

The CIA had finally succeeded in an assassination attempt.

II

Some of the best bombers
in the world live in Miami.

— CAPTAIN THOMAS BRODIE,
Dade County bomb squad

The Castro revolution brought Cuban doctors, lawyers, bankers, and publishers to Miami. It also brought the biggest crooks in Cuba. The story of the building of Little Havana in Miami by Cuba's fleeing middle class is well known; they did not see the revolution as something in their middle-class interests. Not so well known is the fact that virtually all Havana's criminal class — Cuban gangsters, hit men, drug traffickers, Batista remittance men and shakedown artists and pimps — also migrated to Miami; they did not see the revolution as something in their interest. This was a considerable number of crooks, as pre-revolution Havana was the empress city of organized crime, free port for the mob where in the late 1940s Lucky Luciano established the Cuban Connection in the world narcotics trade.

The Cuban Connection was moved wholesale to Miami, which became the drug-smuggling capital of the United States. In 1980, *Forbes* magazine discovered to its surprise that "these days drugs are generally conceded to be Florida's biggest business." The respected business journal reported that Miami bankers "talk about customers pulling up at their doors with suitcases filled with money — in the $20, $50, and $100 denominations that are the drug trafficker's favorite currency. The banks are disinclined to turn them away, not with interest rates at record levels. But they can hardly fail to suspect where the money comes from, even if they do report to the Treasury, as they're required to, all cash transactions in excess of $10,000. Once these funds are on deposit, it's fairly easy to transfer them by wire or check to offshore banks — in the Bahamas, Cayman Islands, Panama, or Switzerland — beyond the reach of the

IRS. How much stays in Florida is anybody's guess, and government narcotics officers guess maybe $7 billion. Certainly, among the thirty-seven Federal Reserve bank units, Miami was almost alone in having a sizable currency surplus last year—$3.9 billion, versus $2.4 billion in 1978—and most of that surplus was in $20 bills."[13] *Forbes* was philosophical about the massive amounts of dirty money propping up the Florida economy: "If war is the logical extension of diplomacy, as von Clausewitz maintained, organized crime is the logical extension of business. It is sharp practice turned murderous, tax avoidance made systematic, competition followed to its logical conclusion."

The "Cuban Mafia" that federal narcs say is the rotten core of the big Miami narcotics apple—marijuana and high-grade cocaine smuggled by plane and boat from Colombia, Ecuador, and Peru—utilizes the routes' contacts, and techniques for transporting Caribbean contraband that were developed by the CIA during the Secret War. In many cases the CIA and the Mafia share the same bad apples. In 1970, a plane belonging to Operation 40 piloted by a henchman of Joaquín Sanjenís crashed in Southern California with several kilos of cocaine and heroin aboard. Shortly thereafter, another Operation 40 man, Juan Restoy, a former legislator under Batista, was caught with the Bay of Pigs veteran Alonso Pujol in a federal narcotics sweep in Miami. The bust was hailed at the time by Attorney General John Mitchell as nailing "a nationwide ring of wholesalers handling about 30 percent of all heroin sales and 75 to 80 percent of all cocaine sales in the United States." Mitchell neglected to say the ring existed compliments of the CIA, but when Restoy subsequently broke out of jail and was killed in a shoot-out, Little Havana buzzed with a rumor that he had been set up and executed by a CIA assassination squad to prevent his testifying about agency involvement in the narcotics traffic. Considering the well-known literature—such as Alfred W. McCoy's *The Politics of Heroin in Southeast Asia*—about CIA participation in dope smuggling in Asia's Golden Triangle, the rumor was not without precedent.

In any case the publicity generated by the California crash convinced the CIA that Operation 40 had become a liability, and it was phased out. Sanjenís retired in 1972 after being secretly awarded a medal. As so often happens in the covert world, Operation 40 had an afterlife of its own. "While many Cubans here believe that with the closing of the Sangenis [*sic*] office the files on the persons under surveillance were sent to Washington," *The New York Times* reported on January 4, 1975, under a Miami dateline, "several informants assert that a copy of the files was made and is still in this area and that it is being used for blackmail purposes."

The Operation 40 drug smuggling appears to have been part of a much larger network stemming from the CIA-Mafia alliance to assassinate Castro. A joint federal-state task force reported that in 1974 four Cubans from Miami met secretly in Las Vegas with Anthony "The Ant" Spilotro, a big man in the Chicago Mafia family whom the feds claim oversees the mob's Vegas operations from a jewelry store and is known to jangle loose diamonds in his pocket the way lesser hoods jangle keys. Three of the Cubans were former associates of Dr. Fernando Penabaz, a prominent Havana lawyer who fled the island, took part in the Bay of Pigs, and wrote a bitterly anti-Castro book with the purple title *Red Is the Island*. Dr. Penabaz was caught up in the 1970 Miami drug sweep and is serving a twenty-year sentence in the Atlanta penitentiary for smuggling nine and a half pounds of cocaine. The fourth Cuban was said to be a partner of the late Juan Restoy.

The task force report said the four Cubans were part of the smuggling network of Santos Trafficante, Jr., the Florida Mafia boss who had collaborated with the CIA on the Castro assassination plots. Spilotro reportedly gave the Cuban quartet $500,000 to "seed" a Vegas cocaine ring to peddle nose powder to "the high rollers."[14] All four were Bay of Pigs veterans and subsequent Secret War noncoms whose CIA training and experience left them well qualified to handle the smuggling end of the operation. "The CIA not only taught these individuals how to use weapons," the task force's report asserted, "but made them experts in smuggling men and material from place to place under Castro's nose. This training seems to be applied here." One of the disgruntled investigators said the CIA had given the Cubans vital Latin American contacts and familiarized them with "every port and inlet into this country."[15]

The man calling himself Rafael lives on a luxurious cabin cruiser in Miami and has a numbered bank account overseas. He is reputed to have a sizable income from "Cuban investments." An indication of the nature of Rafael's "investments" is the fact that every so often he takes the cabin cruiser at least thirty miles out to sea and dumps overboard an automatic pistol with a handmade silencer. Rafael is a professional hit man whose skills were honed by the CIA. After each murder, his CIA training taught him to get rid of the evidence in the ocean.

Outraged when Castro confiscated his father's Havana business, Rafael volunteered for the CIA's expedition force and was infiltrated into Cuba before the Bay of Pigs. After the invasion disaster, he managed to make his way back to Miami but could find only menial jobs. "My old contacts from the CIA days set me up in my present profession," he says. "The others are taking chances by loansharking, running bolita, bookmaking, or labor racketeering. I know nothing about these things. I only know how to kill."

Rafael's most remunerative client is the Mafia, to which he was introduced by the Cuban Old Boys. Having handled some forty jobs at $20,000 each, he is definitely in the luxury-boat bracket. "In the United States, I kill criminals for other criminals," he says. "In South America, I kill political figures for other political figures. I work only for the conservative elements of society in South America. I kill only communists and communist sympathizers."[16]

The politics of the hit men are reflective of the far-right world view of the Cuban Mafia, which hails from decidedly nonpinko stock. Many of the Cuban narcotics traffickers were government officials or army officers in the mob-entwined Batista regime. The CIA enlisted them in its Secret War and trained them in sabotage, high-quality explosives, and automatic arms and bazookas. In the CIA ranks they mingled with nice, middle-class, anticommunist kids who learned that playing with fire can be fun and thereafter found it difficult to give up their acquired cloak-and-dagger habits. Some lasting relationships developed.

During the Secret War, almost any exile with a CIA safe-conduct pass had access to the best powder and shot of the United States Army, including C-3 and C-4 explosives. The CIA had made

Miami a paramilitary munitions dump. When it decided to phase out the Secret War, it took away the fuses but left the powder. Michael Townley, the confessed assassin who blew up former Chilean diplomat Orlando Letelier on Embassy Row in Washington, D.C., described how the agency made it easy for the likes of him: "The one thing I found out in Miami . . . in the early seventies, late sixties . . . [was that] due to all the stuff that they had obtained from the CIA . . . you could buy plastic explosives on any street just like you'd buy candy — weapons, explosives, detonators, anything that you wanted — and it was exceedingly cheap."[17] Rolando Masferrer told the authors: "You can buy anything you want in Miami if you have the money, with the exception of the atomic bomb — probably."

The murderous legacy of the Secret War has evolved during the 1970s into a hemisphere-wide network of right-wing terrorists — a sort of Cuban exile PLO operating with apparent impunity in the United States — composed of veterans of CIA training who continue to function using their former agency's assets on behalf of CIA-axis clients among police and intelligence organizations in Latin American nations. The enlistment of the lethal services of the agency's former paramilitarists is not inconsistent with what Thomas Powers, Richard Helms's biographer, has called the CIA's history of "the funding and technical guidance of police organizations that tortured and killed local opponents."[18]

Cuban-exile terrorism by the end of the decade had spun a murderous web linking Cuban exiles with elements of the American CIA, the Chilean gestapo known as the DINA, the Venezuelan secret police, the Korean CIA, and European paramilitsry fascist groups. This pattern began in 1968, when the CIA mothballed its remaining Caribbean paramilitary bases that had been running at half steam since LBJ's ascension to the White House. The MIRR of Orlando Bosch, the berserk former baby doctor, melted into the alphabet soup of the past as a new terrorist coalition called Cuban Power began to make its presence felt. On May 31 a Japanese freighter docked at Tampa and a British merchantman under way off Key West were badly damaged by explosions. The next day in Miami a man identifying himself as Ernesto called a press conference to warn that "other ships are going to explode." Although Ernesto wore a sack over his head in the manner of a Mafia defector at a Senate hearing, he was identified as Bosch.

The former baby doctor prescribed large doses of terror for anyone trading with the enemy. In Los Angeles the Mexico Tourist Department and Air France offices and three businesses were bombed in succession. In New York the diplomatic and tourist offices of six countries doing business with Cuba were hit, and a time bomb was found in the Rockefeller Center office of Air France. The bombers, like the religious lunatic on the train in *On the Twentieth Century,* always stuck red, white, and blue "Cuban Power" stickers all over the scene of their carnage.

Fingerprints left on a glossy sticker in Los Angeles led to the arrest and conviction of two Miami exiles, Héctor M. Cornillot y Llano, Jr., and Juan García Cárdenas (whose wife, Inez García, became a *cause célèbre* of the women's liberation movement in 1974, when she went on trial for fatally shooting a rapist). Cornillot was a Bay of Pigs veteran later schooled in demolition by the CIA. "Many of the Cubans who were sent on this invasion never actually went," an FBI agent testified before the grand jury that indicted the pair. "We found they went to small islands near Cuba where they buried all of these weapons, knowing they could go back later and sell them."[19]

Bosch was thwarted in an attempt to hijack and torch the *26 de Julio,* pride of the Cuban merchant fleet, in the Straits of Florida when a boatload of his commandos were intercepted by the Coast Guard. But he did succeed in bombing British, Japanese, Canadian, and Spanish vessels with limpet mines. On September 16 Bosch and a Cuban Power team took aim with a 57 mm recoilless rifle at the Polish freighter *Polancia* docked across Government Cut in Miami Harbor. But the FBI had been tipped off by an informant inside Cuban Power, Ricardo "The Monkey" Morales Navarrete, a chubby-cheeked former CIA volunteer in the Congo. Morales supplied Bosch with shells the FBI had altered so that they would not go off on impact. But when Bosch opened fire on the *Polancia,* a Coast Guard patrol boat happened along in Government Cut and one of the whizzing shells narrowly missed decapitating a young sailor. Bosch and eight others were convicted. The pediatrician was sent to the Marion, Illinois, penitentiary, where he ended up playing gin with Rolando Masferrer.

While Orlando Bosch was in prison, Cuban Power split in two. One faction went into narcotics peddling and shaking down Little Havana businessmen for money for the "liberation of the fatherland" under threat of being bombed. Others joined the National Cuban Liberation Front (FNLC), which reportedly had in mind assassinating Senators Jacob Javits and Claiborne Pell when they journeyed to Cuba in early 1974. The FNLC claimed "credit" for a series of explosions of package bombs mailed to Cuban embassies (employees who opened the bombs in Lima and Madrid were seriously injured). On March 20, 1974, two Miami men inserting a bomb in a hollowed-out book being prepared for mailing were badly injured when the device went off prematurely. One was Humberto López, Jr., the founder of the FNLC, who had received demolition training from the CIA and accompanied Bernie Barker's goon squad to Washington for the funeral of J. Edgar Hoover. From his hospital bed López issued a "combat," message calling on exiles "to close ranks to continue fighting until we cross the last foxhole."

It developed that Orlando Bosch had powerful friends at court. He was released from prison in the fall of 1972 after serving only four years of his ten-year sentence. Interceding on his behalf were Florida politicians with an eye to the big exile vote, including the mayor of Miami, Maurice Ferre, and Florida's Republican governer, Claude Kirk. "When I think of free men seeking a homeland," Kirk told a Latin Chamber of Commerce meeting, "I must neccessarily think of Dr. Bosch."

Bosch posed as the "pillar of the community" that Kirk had extolled him as, but all the time he was plotting to regain to regain control of the exile terrorist troops. In early 1974 Bosch disclosed that he had formed a new group, Cuban Action, and was negotiating a merger with the FNLC. Cuban Action was raising funds, he said, by selling bonds in Little Havana redeemable after the death of Castro, with a $3 million bounty set aside for whoever could do the deed. In the meantime, Bosch declared, he was going underground in Latin America "to direct the internationalization of the war."

First there was a little unfinished business at home. A week after the newspaper interview, Ricardo Morales Navarrete, the FBI informer who had been instrumental in sending Bosch to prison, turned the ignition of his car and was nearly killed in an explosion that ripped away the floorboards. The previous week, exile leader José de la Torriente, a founder of FNLC who had fallen from favor with the militants, was sitting in the living room of his Coral Gables home when someone poked the snout of a gun through the window and blew him away. Thus began a new bloodline of violence in the exile community—the snuffing of fellow Cubans who disagreed politically with Bosch or otherwise displeased the butcher. Little Havana took on aspects of an armed camp, with residents carrying handguns in their belts and automatic weapons in their cars.

At the same time Bosch's promise of an "internationalization of the war" was becoming a reality as bombs went off in Cuban government establishments in Canada, Mexico, Peru, France, Jamaica, and Spain. Concerned with the potential impact on foreign relations, the Justice Department sent a special investigating team to Miami. All the people it questioned suddenly developed lockjaw. Meanwhile, more bombs rocked the Cuban Embassy in London and Consulate in Mérida, Mexico.

In November 1974 Bosch was arrested in Venezuela after brazenly announcing that he had perpetrated a bombing of the Cuban Embassy. Although the FBI had been searching for him as a parole violator, the Justice Department refused to extradite on the grounds he was an undesirable alien better off left outside the country. Within days Bosch was back on the streets in Caracas, his release pressured by Cuban exiles close to President Carlos Andrés Pérez. One was Orlando García, the president's CIA-trained security adviser. Another was Luis Posada Carriles, of the Venezuelan secret police. Posada provided cover jobs with Venezuelan television for the trigger men in the 1972 assassination attempt on Castro in Chile.

Bosch hopped across the Andes to Chile, where he was welcomed by the right-wing military junta that had overthrown Allende and was put up in a government guesthouse. According to Miami newsman Oscar Iborra, who interviewed him there, the dour doctor had a Venezuelan chief of staff and a dozen Chilean bodyguards. "Bosch had a book on the life of Yasir Arafat with him and an impressive stack of cash on the table," Iborra said. "He told me he had all the money, friends, and protection he is going to need to defeat Castro."[20] The Cuban exile version of the PLO was in its gestation period.

Bosch remained ensconced in Chile through most of 1975 while the murder rate shot up in Miami. On February 21, three days after announcing he intended to return to Cuba to challenge Castro to an election, liberal leader Luciano Nieves was gunned down in a hospital parking lot after visiting his sick son. On October 31, Halloween, Rolando Masferrer started up his 1968 Ford Torino and was blown to bits. A premailed communiqué signed "Zero" declared the right-winger had been executed because of his "systematic work in the destruction of the anti-Communist struggle."

By early 1976 Bosch was on the move again, entering Costa Rica on a bogus passport. Through an informant Miami Police Lieutenant Thomas Lynch, a specialist on terrorism, picked up word that Bosch was planning the bombing assassination of Secretary of State Henry Kissinger when he visited Costa Rica in March. The apparent motive was Kissinger's earlier overtures to improve relations with Cuba. Costa Rican authorities were notified, and four days before Kissinger's arrival Bosch was tossed into jail. "We offered to send him back," Foreign Minister Gonzalo Facio Segreda said of his contact with the U.S. State Department, "but the reply was that they were not interested."[21]

In Miami the murders continued with an almost occultish fascination for holidays. On April 13, only days after police received a message that another exile leader would die during Easter week, Ramón Donestevez, a liberal who had sailed to Cuba several times trying to gain the release of political prisoners, was found shot through the head in his boatyard office. On the eve of May Day Emilio Milian, news director of radio station WQBA, who had editorialized against terrorism, lost both legs when his car exploded in the station parking lot. The Miami police sent an urgent request to CIA headquarters for a list of all exiles trained in bomb making, as well as, if possible, an accounting of C-3 and C-4 plastic explosives left behind when the agency closed shop. The CIA did not respond.

> I wasn't going to church every day. We
> were conspiring there. Planning bombings and
> killings. . . . People were coming in and out.
> I was plotting with them. . . . It was a great
> meeting. Everything was planned there. . . .[22]
> —DR. ORLANDO BOSCH

The Little Havana rumor mill was working overtime in the summer of 1976 with word of an extraordinary summit meeting of exile leaders being held in the Dominican Republic resort town of Bonao. The gathering represented the fulfillment of every black wish of Orlando Bosch. The Bonao conference was to Cuban terrorism what the Apalachin conference was to the Mafia.

The formal occasion was the organization of a terrorist umbrella group called the Commando of United Revolutionary Organizations, known as CORU. The new group greatly increased the capacity for murder and mischief of all concerned. It merged Bosch's Cuban Action and the FNLC with two other exile organizations which had no compunctions about slaughter. One was the Cuban Nationalist Movement, a crypto-fascist movement action group which looked fondly upon the Italy of Mussolini and the Germany of Hitler. The Lone Rangers of the CNM were the Novo brothers, Guillermo and Rivero, Cuban exiles who interpreted the right to bear arms guaranteed in the constitution of the United States as a right to bear bazookas. Guillermo Novo shot a bazooka across the East River at the United Nations Building when Che Guevara was speaking there in 1964, and his brother was arrested in an attempted bazooka attack on the Cuban exhibition at the 1967 Montreal World's Fair. The CNM was involved in the 1975 assassination of Rolando Masferrer in Miami, and was also linked with an Italian fascist organization in the 1975 shooting of an exiled Chilean anti-fascist in Rome.[23]

The CNM and the Novo brothers, together with a second exile group, Brigade 2506 (another paramilitary group in operation since the mid-1960s, which also joined up with Bosch's CORU), appear to be the two major groups—in addition to the scarlet pimpernel himself, Orlando Bosch, who was active in forging Cuban exile ties to the right-wing international terrorist network. All of them, for instance, had links with the Chilean DINA, which was organized with the agency's support as a sort of Chilean Adam's rib of the CIA. Brigade 2506 members were Bay of Pigs veterans who never stopped fighting the agency's battles. They fought in the Congo and in Vietnam, and in 1975 organized a recruiting station in Miami for Cuban volunteers to fight with the CIA-backed UNITA in the Angolan war. One Brigade 2506 member died fighting for Somoza in the last days of the dictator's rule in Nicaragua. The former head of the Brigade, Roberto Carballo, visited General Pinochet in Chile and also was reported by Dade County police intelligence to be on the personal retainer to the exiled dictator Somoza in Paraguay.[24] Cabrillo sat at the head table at the Bonao conference where it was decided that the CORU would be modeled after their idol, the PLO. The Cubans lost little time in getting down to their father's business.

Inside a six-week span the Cuban United Nations Mission in New York was bombed; a bomb exploded in a van carrying luggage to a Cubana airliner in Kingston, Jamaica; the office of British West Indies Airlines in Barbados was bombed; the Air Panama office and Cuban Embassy in Bogotá, Colombia, were attacked; a Soviet ship off Cuba was shelled; two Cuban officials in Argentina were kidnapped and never seen again; the Cubana office in Panama was bombed; and a Cuban fisheries technician in Mérida, Mexico, was killed during an attempt to kidnap the Cuban consul there. Later, on a CBS documentary, Brigade 2506 member A. L. Estrada blandly assured an interviewer that CORU was only "trying to eliminate a communist in Mexico. We learned from them [CIA]."[25]

Terrorism was cloaked in legitimacy, a fact brought home over Labor Day 1976, when Brigade 2506 held its first congress. At the time the brigade monthly *Girón* had just published CORU "war communiques" boasting of recent terrorist acts and announcing that its commandos would soon attack airplanes in flight. The keynote speaker was Anastasio Somoza, who had recently hosted the fugitive Bosch in Nicaragua as CORU was being assembled. U.S. Congressman Claude Pepper spoke. A featured guest was Miami Mayor Maurice Ferre, who had helped secure Bosch's release from prison.

III

The raspy-voiced anonymous caller asked Isabel Letelier, "Are you the wife of Orlando Letelier?" When she answered yes, he said, "No, you are his widow." Orlando Letelier had been Salvador Allende's ambassador to the United States. In exile in Washington, he was a symbol of opposition to the military junta ruling Chile. On September 21, 1976, Letelier and two American companions, Ronni and Michael Moffitt, were driving along Embassy Row when a radio-triggered bomb blew apart their car. Letelier and Ronni Moffitt were killed, Michael Moffitt miraculously survived.

The case was cracked when investigators learned that a longtime American resident of Chile, Michael V. Townley, had arrived in Miami a month before and contacted Cuban exiles associated with CORU. Townley, it developed, was an agent for the brutal Chilean secret police, DINA.[26] Charged with conspiracy to murder, he began to supply information indicating that DINA had instigated the plot with the idea of using the Cubans to carry it out. Eventually warrants were issued for Cuban Nationalist Movement leader Ignacio Novo, CNM member Virgilio Paz, and José Suárez, all of New Jersey, and Guillermo Novo, Ignacio's brother, and Alvin Ross Díaz of Miami. Ignacio Novo's rap sheet showed that he had been charged in the 1965 bazooka attack on the United Nations and was currently on parole for a 1975 plot to bomb Cuban facilities in Montreal. When arrested in Miami, Ross and Guillermo Novo were in possession of a pound of cocaine, and in Ross's address book was a listing for Major Pedro Díaz Lanz, Frank Sturgis's buddy who once had been in Bosch's MIRR. (Guillermo Novo and Ross were brought to trial on the murder. They were first convicted, then acquitted on a retrial. Paz and Suarez remain fugitives.)

Two days after the Letelier murder Orlando Bosch flew from Nicaragua to Caracas, where, after passing through immigration on a forged Costa Rican passport, he was met by Luis Posada and Orlando García. By this time Posada had left DISIP to form a private detective agency called Commercial Industrial Investigations that had intimate ties with the secret police. Bosch was welcomed like a visiting dignitary. Garcia took him to meet President Pérez, and he was feted at a $1,000-a-plate dinner attended by high government offlcials and Cuban exiles.[27]

Two weeks after the festivities, on October 6, Cubana Airlines Flight 455, with seventy-three persons aboard including the Cuban national fencing team, left Trinidad, stopped at Barbados, and took off again for Cuba. The plane blew apart in the air, killing all on board. In Miami calls to the media claimed credit on behalf of CORU and El Condor, an FNLC satellite.

At a mass funeral for the Cuban victims, attended in Havana by a million people, Fidel Castro renounced a 1973 skyjacking treaty with the United States because, he alleged, the CIA had been directly involved. He also contended that a double agent inside the CIA had intercepted a message to an agent in Havana that indicated yet another attempt on his life was in the works and a detailed itinerary of his forthcoming trip to Angola was being sought.

A fuming Henry Kissinger categorically denied any American role in the airplane sabotage and warned that Cuba would be held "strictly accountable" for any rise in air piracy. As it turned out, however, Castro was not entirely off base in blaming the CIA, for the mass murder was charged to agency Latin alumni. Two men who had deplaned in Barbados, Freddy Lugo and Ricardo Losano, were interrogated after joking about the bombing in a taxicab. The two were employed by Luis Posada in his detective firm and confessed that Posada and Bosch had supplied them with two bombs, which they planted on the Cubana aircraft. When police in Caracas raided Posada's fortresslike residence, they found "equipment and plans," including a map of Washington, D.C., that suggested a tie-in between the Cubana sabotage snd the Letelier assassination (murder charges were eventually droppcd for "lack of evidence").

The CIA hand in the terrorist destruction of the Cubana airliner materialized two weeks later when a Cuban double agent named Ignacio Rodriguez-Mena met with his CIA handler in Madrid. Ike Mena, as he was known, was a Cubana official. He had missed boarding the doomed flight only because his wife was late arriving at the airport. Now in a rage, he alleged the agency had to have been somehow complicit. The CIA man soothingly claimed that he personally hadn't participated, hadn't known about it. But then, in an apparent attempt to ensure Mena's future collaboration with the agency, he declared: "For your peace of mind I assure you, and headquarters told me to assure you, that from now on we will take special precautions so that you, and your wife and family, will not be aboard any aircraft that may be subject to an attack like that."

Mena was visibly shaken by the tacit admission.

"Yes, it's true," the handler went on. "We trained these people in explosives. We even gave them the explosives they used."

Mena went ballistic, slapping the CIA man around and calling him and his colleagues criminals and murderers.[28]

For decades the agency had forestalled exposure of its clandestine apparatus and the illegalities it committed by shuffling fronts, covers, and personnel like a deck of cards. Funding from the CIA's huge unaudited budget was routed through puzzle boxes to conceal its source, and purchases were made and contract agents paid in the guise of commercial enterprise. But when the Secret War was cut back during the Johnson administration, contract agents were rarely needed for full-time service. So the CIA set up a kind of undercover Kelly Girl service, placing the agents on the payrolls of the Drug Enforcement Administration and other federal agencies on the proviso they would be available as needed. It found other ways of continuing Secret War operations with no one the wiser.

The first thing the agency did was to set up a financial proprietary for funding operations that took full advantage of the Bahamas' stringent secrecy laws. It was called the Castle Bank & Trust, Ltd., and was based in Nassau. The Castle Bank was hardly a friendly neighborhood emporium offering prizes for deposits of $500 or more; it served a far more select clientele. On the list of 308 account holders that surfaced years later were such names as actor Tony Curtis; members of the rock group Creedence Clearwater Revival; *Playboy* publisher Hugh Hefner; his *Penthouse* counterpart Robert Guccione; the Pritzker family of Chicago, who were involved with the Teamsters' pension fund and Hyatt Hotels; and Moe Dalitz and two of his old Desert Inn partners.[29]

Many of the depositors were simply enjoying the advantages of an offshore bank, and had no idea that it was a Langley subsidiary. The Castle Bank had been chartered around 1965, and its president and founder, Paul L. E. Helliwell, was known only as a Miami lawyer who was the local Thai consul. But he was the same Paul Helliwell who had been a CIA recruiter and paymaster for the Bay of Pigs, a rough-and-tumble operator whose OSS colleagues in China recalled that he bought information with "three sticky brown bars" of opium.[30]

The saga of the Castle Bank is one more illustration of how the CIA and the mob commingled assets to their mutual advantage. For many years the bank was one of the agency's best-kept secrets, surviving even a searching Internal Revenue Service probe into the use of offshore banks in the Caribbean for tax evasion purposes. By 1972 the probe, called Project Haven, had zeroed in on the bank, but investigators were frustrated by the wall of secrecy surrounding it. The following year, however, an IRS undercover agent blackbagged a bank officer's briefcase, coming up with the list of account holders and other eye-catching documents indicating a quarter billion dollars in assets. The investigators whistled in anticipation of the biggest tax-dodge strike in history.

But their jubilation was short-lived. Richard Nixon's IRS commissioner, Donald Alexander, pulled the plug on the investigation on grounds that his underlings had committed an illegal search. Although several investigators were unimpressed with Alexander's sudden emergence as a civil libertarian and resigned in disgust, it was commonly assumed that the controversial decision was a political move to protect friends of the administration.

It was not until April 18, 1980, when *The Wall Street Journal* ran a story headed "Big Tax Investigation Was Quietly Scuttled by Intelligence Agency," that the Castle Bank was stripped of its cover. The story, under the byline of organized crime specialist Jim Drinkhall, said that Project Haven was terminated primarily because the bank was "the conduit for millions of dollars earmarked by the CIA for the funding of clandestine operations against Cuba and for other covert intelligence operations directed at countries in Latin America and the Far East." A federal attorney told the *Journal* he first learned of the connection when CIA attorney John J. Greaney asked the Justice Department "to keep out of certain accounts at Castle because they were run by the agency." Another government official close to the case was quoted: "The CIA convinced Justice that exposure of Castle and, of necessity, other Helliwell dealings, would compromise very sensitive and very significant intelligence operations."

An ex-federal official interviewed by the *Journal* revealed that Helliwell and the Castle Bank were "deeply involved" between 1964 and 1975 in financing covert forays against Cuba by CIA operatives using Andros Island, the largest in the Bahamas chain. A former member of the Helliwell law firm was quoted as saying that in the late 1960s, when "the CIA had arranged to transfer a huge amount of money through Castle," his boss "put the whole office on a security alert like it was some kind of war operation."

It is entirely possible that funds deployed through the Castle Bank were spent on such sensitive operations as the 1965 Amlash plot to assassinate Castro and the 1971 scheme to bump off Castro in Chile. In any case the cost to American taxpayers ran considerably higher than the operational price tag. The shutdown of Project Haven knocked the props out from under 488 pending IRS tax cases in which the deficiencies totaled in the hundreds of millions of dollars.

The Project Haven dismantling, coupled with the Watergate backlash, severely crimped Helliwell's operations. The new CIA directors, James Schlesinger and his successor William Colby, handed out pink slips by the scores in the covert action section, and congressional committees began poking into hitherto sacrosanct nooks and crannies demanding, among other reforms, stricter accountability and supervision for clandestine operations. The CIA coffers were not empty, but the crush was on. According to Gerry Hemming, "these contract guys panicked and started setting up some new proprietary companies to fund Latin American operations. They might've looked for financial support through narcotics, too. But primarily the proprietaries could supply enough funding to keep things going and buried from the scrutiny of Schlesinger and Colby until things quieted down."[30]

One company apparently used in this shell game was Intercontinental Diversified Corporation, which was founded by Wallace Groves and claimed as vice president, general counsel, and director Paul Helliwell's senior law partner, Mary Jane Melrose. Intercontinental was a Bahamian holding company with ventures in real estate, utilities, and harbor management that until recently was listed on the New York Stock Exchange (Groves has sold his equity, and the firm is being reorganized with the Bahamian government as a part-owner). In November 1974 two Intercontinental officials were given the same CIA clearance that Groves had received years earlier.

In 1978 Intercontinental came under the scrutinizing eye of the Securities and Exchange Commission after more than $3 million turned up missing. Nearly that amount was recovered from a Canadian bank, but then another $1.3 million remained accounted for. A substantial portion of that sum was found to have been channeled through the Castle Bank. The *Journal* reported that a former CIA official had made the "astonishing statement" that almost $5 million of Intercontinental funds were siphoned off for the agency's use "because we had friends there." No indictments were ever returned.

Where this money went no one knows. The CIA spent it on something "off the books."

This same pattern was repeated in the case of the Miami-based Bell Mortgage Corporation, whose role came to light only after its machinations ended up in the courts. Bell was founded in 1969 by Cuban exile Andres Castro, and for a time it prospered legitimately. The downfall began in 1973, when Andres Castro was approached, Hemming says, by contacts who said "the CIA was looking for patriotic citizens to help as fronts for laundering money and financing operations. They told him a lot of banks were running scared because of Watergate, so funds were frozen in Florida and other places."

Castro, no slouch as a patriot, did everything asked of him. He allowed two contract agents, Guillermo Iglesias, a Bay of Pigs veteran, and Antonio Yglesias, also a brigade member, who had been an engineering officer in Artime's Second Naval Guerrilla and a control agent for the CIA's exiles in their dealings with the IRS, to settle into Bell's office with a free hand. The pair supplied Castro with sophisticated communications gear, gave him training in codes, and prevailed upon him to buy an executive jet. They flew him to Managua and introduced him to Anastasio Somoza, who reportedly confirmed that the money was to be used in a CIA operation involving Chile, Panama, and Costa Rica (Hemming identifies the targets as Allende of Chile and Torrijós of Panama). Castro later maintained that Bell raised more than $3 million through counterfeit mortgages and inflated real estate appraisals, most of which was channeled to paper corporations Iglesias and Yglesias had him create in Miami and Latin American countries.[31]

How many other Bell Mortgages generated funds on the sly is anybody's guess. But the covert operators and terrorists had no continuing need for another commodity—the capability to wage irregular warfare. That had been donated to them years before by the CIA. "You can knock them off the payroll," a former agency case officer said, "but you can't take back what you taught them."

On January 7, 1977, Juan Peruyero, the outspoken past president of Brigade 2506, was walking out of his house to go to work when two gunmen riding in a gold Cadillac shot him to death. Although the crime was not solved, it appears that Peruyero was the victim of a rift in Brigade 2506 over continued membership in CORU after the Cubana bombing. The shooting ended a three-year bombing and murder binge that reached more than 100 attacks, with 80 percent of the cases unsolved.

Long ago the CIA cast its bread upon the waters of the Gulf Stream. Now it is coming back in the form of death and destruction. Every time the United States even looks benignly toward Cuba, every time an exile steps out of line, more will come back.

IV

In Union City, New Jersey, which has become an exile Havana on the Hudson, Eulalio Negrin was a vocal advocate of normalization of relations with Castro. In October 1979 he began getting phone calls in the middle of the night. There would be no sound except the metallic ticking of an alarm clock. Negrin knew his time was running out: He prepared a will and bought a casket. On Sunday morning, November 25, as he was getting into his car with his twelve-year-old son, three ski-masked men drove up and raked him with automatic weapons fire. Negrin was D.O.A. at the hospital.

The assassination capped nearly a decade of terror in the New Jersey–New York area in which the toll reached over one hundred bombings and killings. As the momentum picked up federal authorities sidelined themselves with the excuse that it was all a local matter. Then, on December 11, barely two weeks after the Negrin murder, a powerful blast funneled through the three-story Soviet mission to the United Nations on East 67th Street in New York, blowing out windows and injuring several diplomatic personnel and a policeman standing outside. On January 13, 1980, the Aeroflot office on Fifth Avenue was wrecked by an explosion, and again Russian nationals were casualties. "It took the Russian bombing to rattle a few cages around here," a New York police official told *Village Voice* reporter Jeff Stein. "Omega 7 blew up the Cuban mission three times lately and nobody made a peep. With the Russians, though, it's a whole new ball game."[33]

It's a ball game the FBI found difficult to win. Omega 7 has claimed credit for episodes of violence dating back to 1975 as well as the Negrin assassination and the Russian bombings. An offshoot of Orlando Bosch's CORU, Omega 7 is a drug-financed wing of the Cuban Nationalist Movement. As with the CORU in Miami, the alliance enjoyed political and financial sustenance from the pillars of the community. (Julia Valdivia, then mayor of Union City, was outspoken in her support of the CNM.)

Typical of the CNM leaders was Felipe Rivero of Miami, one of the CIA's Bay of Pigs stepchildren who originated a "war throughout the roads of the world" designed to attack Cuban outposts and diplomatic personnel around the globe. According to grand jury transcripts, Rivero was one of DINA's first contacts in the plot to kill Letelier.[34]

The Omega 7 actions rattled the North. Following its attacks on Russian facilities, Omega 7 retargeted the Cubans. In March 1980 a bomb was discovered attached to the car of Raul Roa, the Cuban ambassador to the United Nations. On September 11, 1980, the seventh anniversary of the Chilean military coup that doomed Allendé, Felix García Rodriquez, an attaché with the Cuban mission to the United Nations, was shot and killed from ambush as he drove through the streets of New York. Minutes later an anonymous caller notified the Associated Press, adding: "He's a communist. The next will be Raul Roa." A second caller told UPI that Omega 7 was responsible. "We intend to continue to eliminate all these traitors from the face of the earth," he warned.

The CNM and its northern affiliate, Omega 7, were the precursors of the narcoterrorism of the late 1970s and 1980s when many of the anti-Castro Cubans trained by the CIA became involved in drugs-for-guns operations, profits from which helped fund the Contras. And Omega 7, which was intimately connected with Latin American death squads, participated in Contra training programs.

The nature and dimension of the terrorist network spawned by the Secret War has now emerged. It is hemispheric in scope, with tentacles reaching around the world. It links Cuban exile extremists with the secret police of Venezuela and Chile, and is countenanced and abetted by influential political figures in the United States and Latin America. In its capacity for violence it may even surpass the Red Brigade in Italy, the Baader-Meinhoff gang in West Germany, the Red Army in Japan, and the Palestinian terrorists. But it has received nowhere near the international press and law enforcement attention that was lavished on those left-wing groups.

The CIA's involvement in the drugs-for-guns Cuban terrorist groups was kept just below the water line. A police investigator working on a narcotics case told Jeff Stein that after he had linked Cuban exile suspects with a company in Miami called Zodiac, "which turned out to be a CIA front," he dropped the investigation. A New York police official confided that the invisible CIA hand stymied investigations. "You get just so far on a case and suddenly the dust is blown away," he said. "Case closed. You ask the CIA to help, and they say they aren't really interested. You get the message."[35]

EPILOGUE
The Dogs of War

THE dog of war had not been well. He walked slowly to the weapons room, leaning on his swagger stick. Outside in the Georgia dusk behind his private lake, men in red berets and combat fatigues were firing silenced submachine gun pistols on the testing range; the crickets were making more noise. He greeted his guests with an imperial nod, and there was a ghost of a smile in his bloodspeckled eyes. His guest were tough men, murderers many, generals some, soldiers of fortune all. They were afraid of nothing in the world except, perhaps, their host, who could see they were ill at ease, and this pleased him. He had summoned them for a Last Meeting, and only he knew the agenda. Mitchell Livingston WerBell III, the master armorer of the CIA, was getting ready to die.

The floor was carpeted in wall-to-wall white bearskin; the walls were festooned with the paraphernalia of death—unsheathed swords, bayonets, daggers, throwing knives, blowpipes that spit curare-tipped darts, .45 automatics, .38 specials, accurized sniper rifles with night scopes, lightweight submachine gun pistols that shoot twenty rounds per second of special subsonic .380 ammunition. All the guns were equipped with silencers—long black snouts

---

like muzzles on anteaters. The silencer was Mitch WerBell's trade-
mark; his sound-suppressed machine guns were quieter than an
IBM Selectric. Click-click-click-phhhhhft! and a man is a ham-
burger. Professor J. David Truby, a military historian who writes
dissertations on weaponry, called the silencer designer "a creative
genius." A pulp adventure magazine once dubbed WerBell "The
Wizard of Whispering Death." Those who laughed at that phrase
were those who didn't know him.

A red light flashed in the weapons room, indicating that the electronic main gate had opened to the sixty-acre estate. Fenced in like
a military reservation, the grounds were policed by attack dogs, and
surveillance cameras and nasty anti-intrusion devices were secreted
in the underbrush. It was no place for a Scout troop to wander off
course. Above WerBell's desk was an elaborate communications
system plugging directly into the Georgia Highway Patrol and the
police department in nearby Powder Springs (the former home of
his submachine gun factory). There were intercoms connecting him
to the firing range, the bomb-testing range, the hand-to-hand combat training area, and the kitchen, where there was a ready supply
of his favorite dish—steak tartare—aka raw meat.

On WerBell's desk was a solid silver canister of single-malt scotch
from the Isle of Islay; he sipped it neat as he talked, the way other
men might sip water. He called the meeting to order with a wave
of his swagger stick. A well-known Texas millionaire smuggler and
a Thai general seated next to each other on a leopard couch ducked
involuntarily. (A swagger stick in WerBell's hands is like a sword
in Merlin's. The man has created cigars that shoot a single bullet, at-
tache cases with built-in submachine guns, and a shoulder holster
rocket pistol which shoots a miniature .50 caliber missile that can
zap an entire roomful of people.) Handguns lay all over the weapons
room like clothes at an orgy. The ones with pink rubber bands
around the handles are loaded, WerBell said. Most of the guns had
pink rubber bands around the handles. The darts and arrows lying
on the coffee tables were dipped in curare. WerBell cautioned his
guests: if they had any open cuts on their hands they should be wary.

The men sitting in the room had gone a few miles with the man
who owned the arsenal surrounding them. Some used to run with

him from Florida on speedboat raids against Cuba to land teams of assassins and saboteurs. (Mitch would take his sons along for the ride on these raids, the way some fathers take their kids to the ball-park.)[1] Others had fought and drank and whored with him in Manila and Saigon and Bangkok and other strange places where flying fishes play. Some knew him from the daring days of the old OSS — the WWII spooky Adam from whose rib evolved the Eve of the CIA and all the forbidden fruit that came with it. Others were clients, men in mufti and brassy medals, civilians in polyester and Foster Grants that hid slow unblinking eyes. They were an uncommon lot of adventurers: ex-CIA officers who choose to remain out in the cold, experts in assassination and torture, incurable paramilitary plotters, Middle Eastern arms buyers, honchos of Latin American intelligence services, wealthy homicidal schizoids. What they had in common, besides Mitch WerBell, was a vested interest in controlled mayhem; all felt comfortable in the company of dictators. The Americans among them were habitual violators of the Neutrality Act, the Firearms Act, the Munitions Act, the IRS, the FAA, Customs and Immigration regulations, and the laws of the common-weal ranging from breaking and entering to assault and battery to wrongful death.

A combat helicopter roared low over the house, bringing in the hired guns of some degenerate industrialist to be whipped into a private army by WerBell's paramilitary instructors — at a fee of $2000 per man for five days training; when they left, they would be certified as qualified killers. WerBell spoke over the clatter of the chopper and announced that he was talking about his limited tenure on this earth. Mitch had the Big C, just like his buddy John Wayne (in one of his last flicks, *McQ,* a shoot-'em-up about an ex-cop's unnatural affair with a machine gun, the Duke had insisted that his friend Mitch's brand-name weapon be given star billing.) WerBell took a sip of scotch. "The docs have already been at me with the knife," he said. But there was not a manjack among the assembled assassins who had the nerve to ask the most macho man in the world if the rumors were true that the doctors had cut off his balls.

The bleak news brought forth in the group a feeling of a certain nostalgia. There was the expectation of a Last Will and Testament, and of a night that would be spent retelling old stories of secret wars. Among Mitch's close friends, there arose the warming thought that a sharing of the wealth might be on the agenda. There was an abundance of the filthy stuff to go around— WerBell had headed half a dozen companies devoted to the clandestine sciences, raised $7 million on Wall Street to underwrite the manufacture of his deadly submachine gun pistols, owned a bomb-testing range and a private boot camp, and generally deported himself like a Caliph of Baghdad, flying around the world in a private Lockheed Jetstar in the company of his pet wolfhound, Fritz, and a series of stunning blondes who were the raw stuff of Calvin Klein jeans ads.

But WerBell had other ideas. He sat ramrod straight at his desk, displaying the spare toughness of the bad guy in a Sergio Leone Italian western, and proceeded to tell each and every one of them off— complaining about fees not split, risks not taken, women not shared, betrayals he knew they had contemplated but didn't have the guts to carry out. He had made them what they were today and they were all a bunch of worm-bellied ingrates who deserved to have tarantulas put in the cradles of their grandchildren.

Just because he was going to die didn't mean they were going to get away with murder. Each person in that room owed him something, Mitch said. He began to call the roll: a sword cane here, several submachine guns there, a rare Beretta .38 Espeziale here, a disguised belt buckle-knife there, and who the hell had his samurai suicide gun—the 8 mm. Nambu that some geek in the room had palmed. Each of them had a part of his precious arsenal, and before he died he wanted everything back, even the bullets. If he was going to meet his maker, he wanted to be armed with every weapon at his command.

"Why, that cheap son of a bitch," Andrew St. George, the paramilitary journalist, said later on. "He actually thought he's mean enough to take it with him."

On the week before Christmas of 1983, Mitchell Livingston WerBell III went through the narrow door through which he had previously pushed so many others. That Last Meeting had taken place in 1980. The day after his guests left Powder Springs he received the Last Rites; then he beat the Big Casino out of another three years. Mitch was a fatalist—he believed what Sam the Gonoph said—"All life is six-to-five against"—and he ignored his disease and continued at the business of his father, the war god Mars. He killed the pain with shots of scotch and soothed his martial breast by putting on the regimental kilts and playing the pipes; he would sometimes play alone outdoors at night, like a dog baying at the moon.

Mitch WerBell was a charter member of the intelligence Old Boy Network. He had been a secret agent with the OSS during World War II; thereafter he was always on the spot on the griddle where the Cold War was heating up. He was a player in the CIA's secret cross-border war against China in the 1950s through the 1960s; he went to Vietnam as a weapons adviser with the simulated rank of Brigadier General; and he did the prep work for the 1965 invasion of the Dominican Republic. He frequently worked with the CIA and infrequently worked against them. While the agency was fumbling the ball on its attempts to assassinate Fidel Castro, the ever-gung-ho WerBell initiated his own assassination plots. His wild nocturnal speedboat rides to Cuba were scenes out of some paramilitary *Strangelove* movie—Mitch playing the pipes under a moonless Caribbean sky, the Confederate flag flapping from the rear of the boat. (Sometime later, the U.S. government hypocritically indicted WerBell for his anti-Castro plots while ignoring its own.)

The last decade of WerBell's life was filled with sufficient adventures and misadventures for the lifetimes of ten men. In 1973 WerBell began a "New Country Project" for a group of capitalist revolutionaries on Abaco Island in the Bahamas who wanted to shed the bondage of Nassau. The secessionists believed that the black population of the tourist islands was turning whites off and that sparsely settled Abaco, with a lower profile of blacks, could become a haven for investment money in gambling casinos, resorts, and housing restricted to the wealthy. The new currency would be called the rand, not in emulation of South Africa's medium of exchange but in honor of Ayn Rand, the dowager empress of rugged egoism.

WerBell sounded out his contacts in the high Arctic of the CIA and the State Department. He got the word that there would be no great American objection, provided there was no violence. WerBell was confident there would not be. He proceeded to sign up Soldier of Fortune-supreme Robert K. Brown to recruit a dozen Vietnam vets as the nucleus of an Abacoan standing army strong enough to dissuade Bahamian Premier Lyndon Pindling from invading with his own puny armed services. The date for seccession was set for New Year's Day 1975.

However, three months before liberty day WerBell was indicted in Atlanta, and the plan had to be canceled. That indictment, later dropped, stemmed from his aggressive marketing of his silencer-equipped Ingram machine gun, which starred in the movie *Killer Force*. (There are some interesting connections here. WerBell was manufacturing the Ingram under the name Defense Services, Inc., and marketing it through an outfit called Parabellum, which was headed by Anselmo Alliegro, Jr., an heir to the shadowy Ansan millions. Parabellum employed Gerry Hemming and Rolandito Masferrer, nephew of the dreaded El Tigre Rolando Masferrer. When Anastasio Somoza's dictatorship in Nicaragua was collapsing in 1979, Cuban veterans of the Secret War rallied to his cause. Some engaged in combat against the insurgent Sandinista guerrillas; others acted as instructors with the elite National Guard, which had enabled the Somoza family to remain in power over the decades. One of the instructors was WerBell's partner in arms dealing, Anselmo Alliegro, Jr. In September 1980 Somoza, in exile in Paraguay, met a violent end. There were many flowers but few tears at his funeral.)

In 1973 WerBell was busy with other projects as well. Early that year he was approached by Martí Figueres, the son of outgoing Costa Rican president Pepe Figueres, who wanted to buy WerBell's entire stock of 2,000 silenced Ingrams. Figueres was acting on behalf of Robert Vesco, the freebooting fugitive American financier who had sacked Bernie Cornfeld's financial empire. The feds were after Vesco for seeking to influence an SEC investigation of an illegal $200,000 cash contribution he made to the infamous 1972 Nixon campaign. He fled to Costa Rica, where he surrounded himself with right-wing Cuban bodyguards. Vesco was welcomed with open arms by Pepe Figueres, who displayed an unabiding affection for fugitive rich men. But the incoming president, Daniel

Oduber, had made it perfectly clear that Vesco would not find the climate equally salubrious during his administration. Vesco watchers speculated that Vesco wanted the large supply of Ingrams to seize Costa Rica from Oduber.[2]

The deal offered fringe benefits to WerBell. He could manufacture his Ingrams in Costa Rica, free from nettlesome U.S. export license restrictions. There were fringe benefits to Vesco too—an armed-to-the-teeth home base from which to indulge his most megalomaniac plans, which included some sort of supercapitalist nation-state tax haven, not a little dabbling in the lucrative international drug market, a private army, and a gambling empire all his own. (Vesco had recently been in negotiations with Resorts International president James Crosby to buy the Paradise Island casino in the Bahamas.) Here history began to swing in a nepotistic Nixonian circle, for Vesco had the same cozy relationship with Nixon's brother Ed as Howard Hughes had had with Don Nixon; there is also to be considered the claim of banker Allan Butler that Nixon and Bebe Rebozo were silent partners in the toll bridge linking Paradise Island with Nassau. The deal was close to closing when it was scotched by the SEC indictment of Vesco. It does not, however, appear that the Nixon administration really wanted Vesco back in the United States to stand trial with all the potentially embarrassing consequences. Although the Justice Department submitted extradition papers to Costa Rica, they were made out, said the Vesco-hating Daniel Oduber, "in such a form that it seemed aimed toward making the extradition fail."[3]

But the indictment that really pissed off WerBell was a 1973 rap against his company Defense Services and his son Mitch IV, for allegedly attempting to sell the Ingrams to a federal undercover agent. A shaky case, it was eventually laughed out of court. However, at that time Senator Henry Jackson's Permanent Subcommittee on Investigations was hot on the trail of Vesco and the illegal arms business, and the indictments against WerBell were returned on the very day Jackson's panel issued a subpoena for WerBell's appearance. The Nixon administration's timing suggested that the idea behind the indictments was to clamp a silencer on WerBell's mouth; WerBell himself figured it to be a gag order, because it effectively prevented him from testifying before Jackson's subcommittee. (There was no love lost between Vesco and WerBell either. Although WerBell was usually comfortable in the company of wealthy right-wingers, the two of them got along like wet cats in the rain. During one of their heated business discussions WerBell literally spit in Vesco's face. The best thing that he had to say about Vesco was that he was "a fat-faced fucking crook.")

The Jackson subcommittee had hoped that WerBell might shed some light into the dark holes it had come across in its investigation. There were the startling rumors that Vesco himself was some sort of overprivileged CIA operative; such loose talk was strengthened by the later admission of Vesco collaborator Pepe Figueres that he had also collaborated wholeheartedly with the agency for years. ("This is a savage world," Figueres said. "I have no illusions.") There was additionally the stunning coincidence that both Santos Trafficante and Orlando Bosch had taken up temporary residence in Costa Rica at the time of Vesco's paramilitary intrigues. And the Jackson subcommittee was eager to trace the spider web of Wer-Bell's entanglements with his old friend Colonel Lucien "Black Luigi" Conein, the legendary CIA operative. In 1972 Conein had been appointed by Nixon to the Drug Enforcement Agency's Special Operations Group to set up an international network to smash the drug trade, and he proselytized a group of Cubans who had fought against Castro into a unit code-named Deacon 1. It was said that Conein's methodology included plots to assassinate key international drug figures. What made this all the more dicey was that Howard Hunt had originally brought Conein into the White House in 1970—and it was Hunt who reportedly tried to enlist Manuel Artime in a plot to snuff Omar Torrijos of Panama after the 1972 elections.[4])

In the end, Mitch WerBell didn't supply any answers to Jackson's subcommittee. "From now on, call me Mitch the Fifth," he told Andrew St. George after the indictment was scrapped.

Mitch beat the indictment with a "graymail" defense, meaning that various agencies of the government were so entangled in the affairs of Mitch WerBell that it would have to expose itself to convict him. Mitch thereafter dropped out of the arms business. He said there were too many untrustworthy youngsters getting into government and mucking up the works of the Old Boy system. WerBell's exit from the field was greeted with relief by the managers of many of the leading hostelries of the U.S.; they had grown weary of puttying up the bullet holes left in their finest suites after Mitch had demonstrated the silent Ingram submachine gun pistol to a prospective purchaser.

Then Mitch got into security and counter-terrorism, the boom businesses of the late 1970s and early 1980s. His Sonics Inc. put corporate he-men through counter-revolutionary basic training at his Powder Springs estate. He was working right up until the end. His last assignment was directing security for Larry Flynt. The month before he died, he was arrested while accompanying Flynt to a federal court hearing in Los Angeles. Mitch (of course) was charged with carrying a weapon. The publisher of *Penthouse,* rival girlie slick to Flynt's lower grade *Hustler,* later charged that Flynt had paid WerBell $1 million to put together a hit team to off him.[6]

Mitch WerBell was a man with the courtly manners and geopolitical perspective of another century—he couldn't understand why everyone couldn't be a Romanov. Mitch's anticommunism was of the golden eagle variety. He believed firmly in the forcible suppression of error and was fond of quoting the provision of Mussolini's penal code which said that "Terms of imprisonment are always deserved."

Mitch WerBell's life was an Errol Flynn movie with Max Steiner music in the background. He was at once the most stylish and the craziest man the authors have ever known. He wasn't beyond dusting someone with pneumonia powder, but he was so damn charming that you couldn't help but like the old devil. Whatever he was, Mitch WerBell was a good one; he was the genuine item. He was never, as Whistler said of mauve, pink trying to be purple.

When Nelli Hamilton died, her clapboard boardinghouse was razed to make way for ticky-tacky apartments. Her paramilitary pigeons found other nests. In 1970, after being released from jail for his part in the bombing of Port-au-Prince, Marty Casey met a young woman named Judy Dowis at a Miami beach party and listened sympathetically to her story of a brother unjustly imprisoned in Mexico City. The brother, Joel Kaplan, had been convicted in 1961 of the murder of a business partner. Judy insisted that he had been framed for dark and devious reasons having to do with the CIA. Their uncle was J. M. Kaplan of New York, the sugar baron who, during the 1960s, had allowed the agency to use his Kaplan Foundation as a conduit for funds to anticommunist groups in the Caribbean and had received IRS most-favored-nation status in return.[7]

His sense of outrage fired by this seeming miscarriage of justice, Casey mustered out Nelli's boys. The job: Bust Kaplan out of a Mexican jail. Bill Dempsey, the one-armed Canadian, went to Mexico City and hatched a plan for Kaplan to "fall ill" and be taken out of the prison in an ambulance, but the driver he hired got drunk and babbled to officials. Then a scheme by Carl Davis to smuggle Kaplan out in a laundry truck went awry. But in the end Casey came up with a winning connection, an aerial smuggler from Texas named Vic Stadter. On August 18, 1971, Stadter's helicopter landed in the exercise yard of Santa Maria Acatitla Prison and ten seconds later took Joel Kaplan to freedom.[8]

Nelli's boys started getting a little pudgy around the middle and most settled down. Casey and Gerry Hemming married Cuban girls and had families. Howard Davis began flying commercially out of Tamiami Airport. Bill Dempsey went back to Canada and Little Joe Garmen went to Kentucky. Carl Davis did well in real estate in California's Napa Valley. He insisted that he didn't miss the action, but every once in a while the phone would ring and off he'd go. As a girlfriend once said, "It's the only time his eyes light up."

Sam Benton was released from prison on the $50 million securities scam in 1974, just in time to break bread with the Miami Four at a party marking the second anniversary of the Watergate break-in. He died two years later, of natural causes.

Mike McLaney moved from Haiti to the exclusive Jockey Club in North Miami, in an apartment decorated with Haitian paintings that brood on the walls. He promoted Haitian tourism and continued to run the Casino Internationale in Port-au-Prince. One of his casino employees was Lewis McWillie, Jack Ruby's close friend.

Prior to WerBell's aborted Abacoan venture, Bob Brown did a tour of duty in Vietnam as a Green Berets team commander. "Basically I agreed with what we were trying to do there," he said. He was severely wounded by shrapnel and returned to Boulder, Colorado, to launch Paladin Press, a paramilitary mail-order house selling everything from guerrilla warfare manuals (the IRA's as well as Mao's) to commando knives and folding rifle stocks.[9] In 1971, shortly after Papa Doc died, Brown was called to Montreal by Andrew St. George, who had maintained contact with the anti-Duvalier Haitians. The Haitians wanted Brown to muster an assassination squad to hit young Jean-Claude Duvalier, the new President for Life, and his top three aides, but this was downgraded to a kidnapping when someone suggested that Jean-Claude's doting mother, Simone, was the only person who knew how to get Papa Doc's millions out of Swiss banks. The plan never got off the ground.[10]

Brown is now the publisher of *Soldier of Fortune* magazine, a process color slick of blood-and-guts anticommunist adventures which showcases the last word in weaponry, touts the armed forces of South Africa, and serves as a clearinghouse for "mercs" (one mercenary who answered a help-wanted-in-Angola ad, Daniel Gearhart, was captured and executed in 1976). Veterans of the Secret War against Castro repeatedly pop up in the magazine's pages. Jay Mallin, the former Lucepress journalist, was a contributing editor on terrorism and Latin America. One issue featured the memoirs of Ed Arthur, the Commandos L adviser who had been propositioned to kill Castro. (Arthur did a hitch in Vietnam and was badly wounded.) Another issue featured a color picture of Mitch WerBell wearing combat fatigues, demonstrating his revolutionary Ingram M-10 machine gun.

Unlike Mitch WerBell, Johnny Roselli talked too much. After serving his time on the Friars Club rap, he had retired to the comfort of Miami Beach. In May 1975 Roselli was subpoenaed before the Senate Intelligence Committee for closed-door questioning on the

Castro assassination plots and, declared Chairman Frank Church, "gave us a good deal of detail." Sam Giancana was also on the committee's list' but on the night of June 19, only days before his scheduled appearance, someone gained entrance to his Chicago home and shot him point-blank in the head. The murder weapon, a .22 Duramatic automatic pistol with silencer, was later found snagged in brush on a bank of the Des Plaines River. Police traced the last recorded sale of the gun to a Miami dealer in 1965. The murder went unsolved.

On August 7, 1976, Roselli's body was found stuffed into a chain-weighted oil drum in Dumbfoundling Bay near Miami. He had disappeared ten days earlier, just before the Church committee released its report on the John Kennedy assassination that incorporated Roselli's claim—which the House Assassinations Committee would later debunk in favor of a Mafia-did-it theory—that the CIA-Mafia attempts on Castro had boomeranged on the President. Roselli's murderer or murderers remain unidentified.

On March 29, 1977, Charles Nicoletti, the Mafia enforcer under Giancana who had replaced Roselli as head of the mob's Castro project, was executed gangland style in Chicago. At the time the House Assassinations Committee was trying to find Nicoletti for questioning about a possible link between the Castro plots and Kennedy's death. The UPI dispatch reporting Nicoletti's demise said that he had broken with the mob after Giancana's death because he felt the CIA "was taking over the operation . . . The CIA-syndicate deal reportedly called for at least tacit CIA cooperation in smuggling prostitutes from Marseilles, France, into the United States to staff mob-operated brothels in Las Vegas and other cities. . . ."[11] This particular twist was so bizarre that House assassinations investigators thought it was planted to steer attention away from the Mafia-Kennedy angle.

The House Select Committee's report, released in 1979, which concluded that there probably had been a conspiracy in the JFK assassination, blamed the FBI and CIA for depriving the Warren Commission of information that would have brought it to the same conclusion fifteen years before. The committee noted that individuals such as Santos Trafficante and Carlos Marcello possessed the motive, means, and opportunity and might have acted together. It stated that "for organized crime to have been involved in the assassination, it must have had access to Oswald or Ruby or both." The evidence showed that "Oswald did, in fact, have organized crime associations" and that Ruby was "known to organized crime elements."

When the committee's chief counsel, G. Robert Blakey, was asked by newsmen who he thought were the maniacs responsible, he replied, "I think the mob did it.[12] It was left for Roselli to posthumously defend his beloved Mafia against such charges. According to a 1981 biography of mob hit man Jimmy Fratianno, Roselli thought the mob-killed-Kennedy theories fabulously funny: "You know, we're supposed to be idiots, right? We hire a psycho like Oswald to kill the President and then we get a blabbermouth, two-bit punk like Ruby to shut him up. We wouldn't trust those jerks to hit a fucking dog."

John Martino — the Mafia handyman who helped former Ambassador Pawley launch the ill-fated *Flying Tiger* expedition to Cuba — palled around with Johnny Roselli on Castro assassination maneuvers, then was a cog in the Oswald disinformation machinery that began whirring immediately after President Kennedy's assassination, and later prospered as a businessman in Miami, although the nature of his business remained vague. He traveled frequently in Latin America, and at one point was reported to be selling bulletproof vests. In 1975 he had a revealing conversation with a Texas business associate, Fred Claasen. Martino said that he had been a CIA contract agent, and knew about the conspiracy to murder President Kennedy:

> The anti-Castro people put Oswald together. Oswald didn't know who he was working for — he was just ignorant of who was really putting him together.

Martino said that the shooting of officer Tippit in the Texas Theater was not according to the plan:

Oswald was to meet his contact at the Texas Theater. They were to meet Oswald in the theater, and get him out of the country, then eliminate him. Oswald made a mistake. . . . There was no way we could get to him. They had Ruby kill him.

Martino's revelations did not become known until 1978, when *Dallas Morning News* reporter Earl Golz published an interview with Claasen about the 1975 Martino conversation. Martino died shortly after his talk with Claasen. The House Assassination Committee dispatched an investigator to talk to his widow. She said that "the government" had picked up her husband's body. Among Martino's private papers was evidence of a long relationship with Santos Trafficante.

The 1971 camera-gun plot on Castro's life in Chile proved to be Tony Veciana's final performance for his CIA director, Maurice Bishop. "After this," Veciana said, "a lot of differences began to come up. So many lives being lost, and nowhere." On July 24, 1973, the Alpha 66 founder was arrested by DEA agents on narcotics dealing charges. He claimed "a set-up because of my previous activities." Two days later, he said, Bishop paid him more than $150,000 for his thirteen unfulfilled years of service to the CIA. He served seventeen months in the Atlanta penitentiary.[13]

When the Senate Intelligence Committee quizzed Veciana in 1976 about his work under Bishop, Senate investigators took him secretly to a meeting of the CIA's Association of Retired Intelligence Officers on the theory that he might point out as the pseudoanonymous Bishop the person of David Atlee Phillips, the former Havana deep cover agent who, with Howard Hunt, ran the propaganda shop during the Bay of Pigs. Veciana refused to say. A year later the House Assassinations Committee became engrossed with Veciana's contention that in August 1963 he was in Dallas with Bishop during a brief meeting with Lee Harvey Oswald. The committee interviewed two ex-CIA agents who verified that a Maurice Bishop had reported to Langley around that time; neither knew Bishop's true name. So convinced was the committee that Bishop was of crucial importance that it circulated an artist's composite sketch of him to the news media, the way police do with rapists. No one stepped forward to identify him.

The final Assassinations Committee report in July of 1979 contained a section on Veciana's disclosures about his mysterious mentor, Bishop. Three months after it was published Veciana was driving his pickup truck home from his Miami marine supply store when a 1971 Buick station wagon pulled alongside and four .45-caliber slugs ripped into the cab. The shots only grazed the lucky Veciana, and he was out of the hospital in two days. A police spokesman said that among motives, "We are looking into possible political circumstances."

George de Mohrenschildt, the man believed to be Oswald's CIA babysitter, paced back and forth in his Dallas apartment in June 1976 as he talked with journalist Dick Russell about the infamous young man he had befriended. "They made a moron out of him," the White Russian said, "but he was really smart as hell. Ahead of his time, really, a kind of hippie of those days. In fact, he was the most honest man I knew. And I will tell you this — I am sure he did *not* shoot the President."

The posthumous exoneration conflicted with de Mohrenschildt's statement years before that when he heard the news of the Dallas shooting, he immediately believed that Oswald had done it. De Mohrenschildt was a man of many contradictions. The House Assassinations Committee wanted to pin him down since he obviously knew much more than he had ever divulged. There was a report that he had told an interviewer early in 1977 that American intelligence had been involved in a conspiracy to kill President Kennedy. But now de Mohrenschildt was making himself scarce.

On March 29, 1977, House investigator Gaeton Fonzi rang the bell at de Mohrenschildt's daughter's home in Palm Beach. There was no answer, so Fonzi left his calling card. But the Baron was there. That evening he was killed by a shotgun blast to the head. The police said it was suicide.

It later was discovered that de Mohrenschildt and his wife had been working on a book about Oswald titled *I'm a Patsy*.[14]

Carlos Prío hoped eternal for a return to the glorious days of his Garden of Eden at his La Chata farm. "As unreal as it seems," a Miami journalist said of the increasingly elder statesman, "he's still jockeying to maintain political viability in case something happens in Cuba to spring him back into the realm of power."[15] In 1974 Prío had assembled a coalition of old-line businessmen, educators, and military officers called Belligerent Cubans that promised to "campaign against Castro" in league "with elements within Cuba and without CIA help." Spokesmen warned that if worse came to worst, they would mount a PLO type of "urban guerrilla action" inside Cuba to terrorize the Castro regime. But Belligerent Cubans turned out to be more pussycat than tiger, and Prío reportedly went on the Zero death list.

April 5, 1977, was a black day to anti-Castro Cubans. That day the University of South Dakota basketball team symbolized a watershed thaw in U.S.-Cuban relations by playing in Havana. That day, also, Carlos Prío was found shot to death in his Miami Beach home. The House Assassination Committee had also been seeking to interview him. It was a week after de Mohrenschildt's death. The police said it was again suicide.

When Frank Sturgis, Eugenio Martínez, Virgilio González, and Bernie Barker unexpectedly pleaded guilty to the Watergate break-in, Judge John Sirica was dismayed because the move foreclosed questioning at a trial that might reveal who sponsored them, and why. Sturgis was shipped off to a federal detention center, where he found himself facing unrelated charges stemming from a long-forgotten 1968 incident. The charges were filed just before the five-year statute of limitations expired. This led Sturgis to suspect the Nixon White House of dredging them up because Special Prosecutor Archibald Cox had told Judge Sirica that Sturgis was cooperating in the Watergate investigation.

The charges resulted from the caper that was Sturgis's last campaign in the Secret War. It began when Joaquín Sanjenís of Operation 40 introduced him to a Colonel Francisco Quesada, who wanted Sturgis to take on a daring operation out of an old "Mission Impossible" script. "We were going to hijack a Soviet freighter off

Cuba. We were going to sail it to the Venezuelan coast and hold it and the crew hostage for the return of the *Pueblo* and its crew," Sturgis said. The electronic spy ship USS *Pueblo* had been seized by North Korea in January 1968 (the crew was released a year later).

Sturgis chose to accept. He said he assumed that since Sanjenís was involved, the operation was either sponsored by the CIA or had its sanction. Following Quesada's instructions, he placed a newspaper ad for volunteers to fight communism in Latin America. With a promise of $1,800-a-month pay, he recruited what he affectionately called "my Dirty Dozen." He called them, somewhat pretentiously, the Secret Army Organization. He instructed his team to lease cars in Florida and rendezvous in Mexico. There Sturgis rented a fishing smack and put out to sea with the Dirty Dozen aboard to link up with a gunboat he had been informed would assist in the hijacking. A storm blew the smack onto a reef off British Honduras, and the armed marauders were jailed in Belize. Sturgis placed a distress call to his old friend, former Senator George Smathers, who, according to Sturgis, said, "Why didn't you ask me along?" They were quickly released.

As it later turned out, several of the Dirty Dozen had sold their leased cars for cash in Mexico. This was the no-no of which Sturgis was so belatedly accused. The trial was held in October 1974. Sturgis's attorney, the flamboyant Ellis Rubin, tried to subpoena CIA files — and the White House tapes. "The Mexican thing was really a CIA operation," Rubin said, "and Sturgis was acting in that capacity." The trial ended in a hung jury, and Sturgis was not retried.[17] He returned to Eglin AFB to complete his Watergate sentence. There he received a season's greetings card from old buddy Norm "Roughhouse" Rothman that said, "Merry Christmas — and welcome to the club." Rothman was resting in the Atlanta penitentiary after being convicted of being a member of a ring that in 1969 stole $4 million worth of IBM and Burroughs Corporation stock from the vaults of Wall Street brokerage houses.

Upon being released, Sturgis took up the quiet life of a salesman, but he could not seem to be left in peace by the Klingons of the Secret War. In 1976 Maria Lorenz, Castro's ex-mistress and Sturgis's beautiful spy, came back into his life like a party crasher. Rupert

Murdoch's supermarket tabloid *The Star* arranged a reunion for Frank and Maria in New York, where she was living with her daughter by the deported Venezuelan dictator Marcos Pérez Jiménez, the erstwhile master of the Miami Beach mansion on Pine Tree Drive where Castro assassination plots were hatched. In the *Star* article, Lorenz claimed for the first time that when she returned to Castro's lair in 1960, she had two poison capsules supplied by Sturgis hidden in a cold cream jar. (She said they dissolved before she could administer them to Fidel.) Sturgis volunteered the Johnny Roselli line that Castro was behind the Kennedy assassination, using Jack Ruby as one of his agents.[18]

The tabloid's pages were the last place that Frank and Maria would be pictured together smiling. A year later she called the New York cops to complain that Sturgis was trying to coerce her out of testifying before the House Select Committee on Assassinations. No faded rose, Maria had a whale of a tale to tell. This time she claimed to have been present at a meeting in September 1963 at Orlando Bosch's Miami home that was attended by Lee Harvey Oswald. She said that at the time she knew Oswald, whom she had met earlier at an Operation 40 safe house, as Ozzie. Also present were Sturgis and his close amigo, Major Pedro Díaz Lanz. The discussion concerned a trip to Dallas.

About November 15, Lorenz went on, she rode to Dallas in a two-car caravan with Bosch, Sturgis, Díaz Lanz, Gerry Hemming, the "Novo brothers" (possibly Ignacio and Guillermo Novo of the Cuban Nationalist Movement), and Oswald. There were several rifles and scopes in the motel rooms, and Jack Ruby came by. Lorenz said she returned to Miami around November 19 or 20.[19]

The New York police arrested Sturgis on Lorenz's complaint, but the charges were dropped for lack of evidence. Sturgis's lawyer maintained that the lady had lured him to New York as a publicity stunt to promote a book she was writing about her CIA activities. The House Select Committee on Assassinations later reported that it could find no substantiation for her tale of going to Dallas.

Not long after getting out of jail on their Watergate sentences, Sturgis, Martínez, and Gonzáles gathered in a suite high in the Eden Roc Hotel overlooking the tinsel of the Miami Beach strip. "If circumstances repeated themselves," they were asked, "would you do it again?"

"Yes," they said in unison.[20]

On April 20, 1976, the CIA agent who had orchestrated the hunt for Che Guevara in Bolivia, retired. The brief ceremony, during which he was awarded the Intelligence Star for Valor, was held in his Miami home. He had refused to accept it from Director George Bush at Langley because he considered Bush a political appointee who was wet behind the ears when it came to covert actions.

Upon retiring Ramos resumed using his true name, Felix I. Rodriguez, which had been mothballed during his years of agency service. Rodriguez, who resembles Desi Arnaz, had belonged to the landed gentry in pre-revolutionary Cuba, and he carried a personal grudge against Castro. In 1961 while training with Brigade 2506 before the Bay of Pigs invasion, he volunteered to assassinate Fidel. He said that the CIA presented him with "a beautiful German bolt action rifle with a powerful telescopic sight, all neatly packaged in a custom-made carrying case." The weapon had been presighted for a location where Castro made frequent appearances. But after several abortive attempts to infiltrate Cuba, the mission was abandoned.[21]

Rodriguez went on to a number of assignments under his JM/WAVE case officer, Thomas Clines. During the October 1962 Missile Crisis he was poised to parachute into Cuba to plant a beacon pointing to a Russian missile site, but the crisis passed. He became communications officer in Nicaragua for Manuel Artime's Second Naval Guerrilla, which was conducting hit-and-run raids to soften up Cuba for a second invasion. He went on to lead helicopter assault teams in Vietnam.

But by his own account Rodriguez's most magnificent moment came when he lifted off in a helicopter from La Higuera, Bolivia, on October 9, 1967, with Che Guevara's body lashed to the right skid. "On my wrist was his steel Rolex GMT Master with its red-and-blue bezel," he recounted. "In my breast pocket, wrapped in paper from my loose-leaf notebook, was the partially smoked tobacco from his last pipe."[22]

It was the Secret Warrior's dream come true. But after becoming a CIA pensioner Rodriguez still couldn't shake the anticommunist demons that drove him. Even before he was officially disconnected from the CIA he flirted with trouble. It should have been a red flag that Tom Clines, who was still on active duty manning the Cuba Desk at Langley, was offering him a private deal. Rodriguez accepted and rode herd on a shipment of arms consigned to the Christian militia, the CIA's favorite faction in war-torn Lebanon.

Whether Rodriguez knew it or not his paycheck came from Edwin P. Wilson, yet another JM/WAVE alumnus now doing a long stretch in federal prison for illegal arms sales to Libya. Both Clines and Theodore Shackley, who had been station chief at JM/WAVE during the heady sixties, continued dealing with the corrupt Wilson and wound up with blighted careers. It was a particularly bad tumble for Shackley, who wore bottom-bottle glasses and was dubbed the Blond Ghost because his past was largely blank. Insiders had touted the Blond Ghost to succeed the Chief Spook, George Bush, as director.[23]

With the election of Ronald Reagan in 1980 it was bombs away again. Rodriguez drew up a paramilitary battle plan aimed at decimating the Salvadoran insurgent units that were becoming increasingly successful against government regulars. In his memoirs Rodriguez speaks deferentially, almost obsequiously, about the tinhorn Salvadoran generals he convinced to go along with his plan, turning a blind side to the fact that they moonlighted with death squads and were the guns for hire of the ruling extremist oligarchy. In Washington Rodriguez took his proposal to Donald Gregg, who had been his CIA boss in Vietnam and who had become George Bush's national security adviser. Gregg arranged a fireside chat with Bush, whom Rodriguez had earlier spurned, and the two became pen pals. In the end Rodriguez's plan, which featured *Apocalyse Now*-style helicopter gunship raids, went operational.

Inexorably Rodriguez was drawn into Oliver North's resupply network to the Nicaraguan Contras, which used funds diverted from secret arms sales to Iran. Also inexorably he wound up testifying before Congressional committees when the lid blew off and exposed the ring of former military and agency brass who had charged more bucks for the bang. On the stand Rodriguez denied briefing Bush on the weapons smuggling, and indignantly rejected accusations that he had solicited millions in drug money to finance the Contras.[24]

But Rodriguez had his star-shell moment when the independent counsel probing the Iran–Contra affair asked, "Did you participate in Operation Mongoose to kill Castro with an exploding cigar?"

"No, sir, I did not," he responded. "But I did volunteer to kill that son of a bitch in 1961 with a telescopic rifle."[25]

Late in the 1970s, a Brigade 2506 boat was ready to slip out of the Florida Keys for an assault on Cuba when federal agents closed in and arrested A. L. Estrada and several cohorts. The men were charged with possession of illegal arms. At their trial Grayston Lynch, retired from the CIA and living in Tampa, testified that the CIA's Cuban exiles were never told to stop fighting. A jury returned a verdict of not guilty.

"Miami is not a base—it's a warehouse," Estrada declared on the courthouse steps. "The war is not over."[26]

In January 1981 General Alexander Haig made it ringingly clear to the Senate Foreign Relations Committee considering his nomination as Secretary of State that the Reagan administration intended to adopt a tough-as-nails policy against Cuba. Never so much as hinted at during the round of hearings was the jingoistic general's dirty duty in the Secret War in 1964–65, during the Lyndon Johnson era. At the time, Haig was a lieutenant colonel posted to Joseph Califano, a holdover from the Kennedy administration who oversaw the Defense Department liaison with the Cuban exiles (Califano was Haig's lawyer during the confirmation hearings). According to a story by Joe Trento in the Wilmington (Delaware) *News-Journal* on January 10, 1981, Haig kept exile leaders informed of the continuing efforts to assassinate Castro and coordinated information about the progress of the plots between the Defense Department, the White House, and the CIA.

A Marine officer who worked with Haig and currently is a top official of the Defense Intelligence Agency told the *News-Journal*: "Califano and Haig worked hand in hand in keeping the nationalists from the Cuban Brigade happy. They even checked out potential members for the hit teams with older members of the Cuban Brigade." Haig tried to dissuade the exiles from carrying out unauthorized raids by telling them Castro was as good as dead.

This was confirmed by Ricardo Canette, a founder of the violent Cuban Nationalist Movement who turned government witness. "Haig kept promising us things. We kept pressing the government," Canette said. "One of the ways they satisfied us was by giving us a role in the support teams to hit Castro. We were allowed to participate in the shipment of weapons in March 1964 into Cuba for a hit."

When Haig hoisted the battle flags before the Senate panel, exile groups in Miami cheered. The long thaw in the Cold War against Castro was over, and, they were sure, the hot war would start again.

In 1987 the cherub-cheeked former CIA Director William Casey, a World War II intelligence operative who had struck it rich in banking, made an award presentation. Casey had never lost his passion for off-the-books, shoot-from-the-hip clandestine operations, which Ronald Reagan undoubtedly sensed when he appointed him top spook in 1981. If anyone could wage a cool "hot war," it was Casey. Vintage Casey stuff was the diversion of Iranian arms-for-hostages funds to the Contras, the mining of Nicaraguan harbors, and the terrorist speedboat assaults on seaside Nicaraguan villages.

The awards ceremony was held in Room 503 of the Anthony House Hotel in Washington, a secure location in keeping with the CIA practice of Carmelite privacy on such occasions. The medals were touched by their recipients only briefly, to be returned to a CIA vault. This time the man of honor was a rotund, bespectacled Cuban named Eduardo Leal Estrada, who held a strategic position with the Cuban telecommunications entity EMTELCUBA. Over the years Leal had fed invaluable information to the CIA on the island's communication system, in particular transmissions concerning Fidel Castro and what frequencies they were on. So that Leal didn't go away empty-handed, the agency's assistant director of operations took him aside and confided that a $10,000 bonus had been deposited in his U.S. bank account.[27]

Leal never collected the $10,000, nor for that matter the nearly $200,000 that had been placed in his account for services rendered as a CIA agent-in-place in Havana. On July 6, 1987, Cuban television launched an eleven-part series called "The CIA War Against Cuba," in which no less than twenty-seven double agents who had infiltrated the agency came in from the cold and told their stories. Leal was among them. Most had survived at least one CIA lie detector test, and they averaged fifteen years of agency "service." Some were recruited while abroad, others by the active CIA spy nest operating out of the U.S. Interests Section in Havana.

From what the double agents said it was clear that the campaign against Cuba, which had been in remission during the Carter years, resumed full force as soon as Ronald Reagan and old CIA hand George Bush set foot inside the White House. Casey set up shop at Langley, and Alexander Haig, who had played a liaison role in CIA assassination attempts during the Johnson administration, became ensconced in Foggy Bottom.

Short of a second invasion under Casey it was the same agency playbook: plots on the lives of Cuba's leaders, schemes to sabotage its economy and means of production, terrorist exile raids on its shores. The murder plots were particularly troubling since they defied the congressional ban on attempts to kill foreign leaders that followed the 1967 exposure of the CIA-Mafia collaborations. Evidence that the Reagan administration wouldn't scruple to violate the ban became public in 1986 when American planes bombed the residence of Libyan strongman Muammar Qaddafi intending to kill him but winding up killing his young daughter and wounding two sons.

One of the double agents, Mauro Casagrandi, was an Italian businessman residing in Cuba as the representative of Cogis, one of the first European firms to breach the U.S. economic blockade. Yet the CIA figured that because Casagrandi had spent several years in the United States on a Bank of America scholarship, he would readily become a spy. What the agency didn't know was that during his stay in the United States he had wandered the country, witnessing the abject poverty of the Navajo Indian reservation and the inner city ghettos. He saw none of this in Cuba.

On December 11, 1975, Casagrandi was propositioned by the CIA in Madrid. Upon returning to Havana he went straight to Cuban security. From then on he played a double role, feeding his agency handlers sanitized intelligence—everything from Cuban troop movements to Angola to defend against the apartheid South African incursion to the state of the Castros. Casagrandi realized that the CIA was fixated with Fidel. His handler asked what would happen inside the country if Fidel and his brother Raúl were to "disappear." According to Casagrandi, the CIA wanted to use him in an assassination scheme both to provide "information, and in some actual role."

Ike-Mena, the double agent who had narrowly missed being aboard the bombed Cubana airliner, believed that he had become the target of CIA suasions because he played professional baseball in the United States on farm teams for the Washington Senators and Milwaukee Braves. How could someone who had rubbed shoulders with Mickey Mantle and Joe Dimaggio not prefer the American way of life? The CIA told him that arrangements had been made for him to become a professional umpire once he had made his last out as a spy.

So convinced was the CIA that Mena was one of the good guys that they "recruited" his wife, Mercedes Herrero, also a Cubana airlines official. The Menas soon became aware that murder was on the CIA's mind. The agency wanted floor plans of Herrero's office because Castro had to pass through it on the way to his plane. "They wanted any particulars about Fidel that could aid them in assassinating him," she said. In October 1986 when Castro visited Zimbabwe for a conference of nonaligned nations, the CIA was desperate to know "what license the plane carried, what route it was to take, time of departure, what stops it would make, what technical equipment it carried."

Double agent Juan Luis Acosta Guzmán and his wife related an even more specific story about the CIA's plotting to eliminate Castro. Acosta, a ruggedly handsome Catholic with family in the

United States, had been a natural target for recruitment because he roamed the seas as a tuna boat captain. From the start it was obvious that the agency propositioned him for one purpose: the ongoing dream of killing Castro with toxins. "They thought they could produce a sickness in Fidel that would kill him slowly, not leaving a trace," he said. In April 1985 in the Canary Islands his CIA handler broached the subject again: "Look, we are most interested in eliminating Fidel. We win ninety percent of the battle against Cuba by eliminating him." What the agency had in mind was for Acosta to insinuate his way onto a boat taking Castro out to indulge in his sport of skin diving. A dose of the CIA laboratory's newest lethal chemical tossed on the water while Castro was in it would cause a delayed-action death.

Cuban diplomat Israel Hernández Marquez, who had been "recruited" in 1977, also testified about the CIA's obsession with killing Castro. In 1983 he was asked to find out if the Cuban president intended to fly to Europe for a congress of nonaligned nations on Cubana or Aeroflot, the Soviet civilian airline. When it turned out to be neither of the above — Castro stayed home — Hernandez's handler divulged that the CIA had paid the Mafia $3 million to knock off Castro. But it wasn't money down the drain — the "investment" would be used for another attempt.

Other double agents who furnished the CIA with disinformation on everything from Cuban banking abroad to the susceptibility of crops to certain types of bacteria were dunned for information on Castro's habits and movements. Alberto Puig, a sports director, was instructed by his agency handler "to find out the exact location of the shelters built for the top leaders of the country." Antonio García Urquiola, a captain with Mambisa Shipping Lines, met with CIA contacts in ports around the world. He said that Langley told him they "knew that Fidel generally moved around the city in three cars," but needed precise data on which car he was in and the times and locations of his movements.

Then in early 1987 the CIA committed an overt act by telling García in Mexico to buy a speedboat to be used in an assassination plan. Upon his return to Havana García received a confirming message to "buy a vessel of the type discussed at the last meeting. With pesos I will give you new radio and probably other device which technicians showed you May eight five."

On February 28, 1987, a CIA agent working out of the U.S. Interests Section made a dead drop of pesos and equipment for García at the corner of 63rd and 100th streets in the Marianao district of Havana. The agent had no way of knowing he was being secretly filmed for Cuban security's version of "Candid Camera."

When the drop was shown on Havana television on July 10, 1987, the CIA agent wasn't smiling.

Richard Nixon's code for deadly secrets was "the Bay of Pigs," a frequent reference on the Watergate tapes. No less an authority on the man than Bob Haldeman, Nixon's former White House gatekeeper, wrote in his book, *The Ends of Power,* that "In all of those Nixon references to the Bay of Pigs, he was actually referring to the Kennedy assassination." Nixon may have felt the need to cover up Watergate because an investigation would have exposed CIA misdeeds. Such an investigation would have divulged the deadliest secret of the twentieth century—the governmental entanglements with organized crime, the mob-CIA plots to kill Fidel Castro, and the great backfire when the mob and the CIA plotters turned on President Kennedy and murdered him in Dallas.

The plotters had their reasons. Far right elements in the ofttimes liberal CIA were furious that Kennedy had not provided air cover when the Bay of Pigs invasion plans began to unravel, in their view dooming the operation. They were angry that JFK did not take the missile crisis as the opportunity to invade Cuba, and fearful that he would pull out of Vietnam in his second term as president. The mob—which had long enjoyed a profitable association with the president's father (who made his fortune on bootleg booze)—had a quite legitimate claim to having been responsible for Kennedy's hairbreadth defeat of Nixon in 1960 (the famous Chicago vote count), and felt betrayed by Bobby Kennedy's demonic pursuit of the Mafia's elder statesmen. Nothing angers the mob more than ingratitude. The anti-Castro Cubans trained and employed by the CIA, who the agency allowed to prosper as major criminals and terrorists, hated JFK because they believed he was seeking peace with Castro. As readers of this history know, this was not Kennedy's firm intention, but he was running a double track policy toward Cuba — as he was toward Vietnam.

The early 1990s saw a burst of Kennedy revisionism, and renewed questioning of the orthodox explanations of the Kennedy assassination, prompted by Oliver Stone's great agitprop movie *JFK*. The movie has readdressed the question of whether Kennedy was set in his counterinsurgency ways on Vietnam or if, as John M. Newman argues in his 1991 *JFK and Vietnam: Deception, Intrigue and the Struggle for Power,* he really planned to leave but for political purposes tried to also make it look like he would stay.[28] The authors believe both Kennedy brothers were men of murderous determination and would not have left Vietnam, or Cuba, alone — but if one takes the revisionists at the best of their argument, Kennedy was running two tracks on Vietnam, and his assassins killed him because they thought he would pull out. In this context, the assassination of John F. Kennedy is one of the greatest ironies, and greatest tragedies, of American history.

As the thirtieth anniversary of the JFK assassination nears, a few players left alive who have knowledge of what actually happened are surfacing. Each new revelation confirms the authors' thesis when we began this book back in the 1970s — that JFK was killed by the CIA-mob Castro assassination plotters run amok. In January of 1992 a particularly poignant revelation was made by attorney Frank Ragano, the longtime confidant and lawyer for both Jimmy Hoffa and Carlos Marcello. Ragano was interviewed by Jack Newfield in the New York *Post.*

Ragano is a man given great respect by Mafia expert Nick Pileggi who says the lawyer was the messenger for many years between Hoffa and Marcello — making unnecessary, dangerous face-to-face meetings. Pileggi says Ragano is a man who really knows the secrets.[29]

Ragano said that early in 1963 he carried a message from Hoffa to Marcello and Santos Trafficante. Hoffa's instructions were: "Tell Marcello and Trafficante that they had to kill the president. This has to be done."

Two weeks after the assassination, Ragano met in New Orleans with Carlos Marcello, who he said looked like the proverbial cat that swallowed the canary. The mobster was a happy camper. "Jimmy owes me and he owes me big," Marcello told the lawyer.

Ragano also told Newfield about his death-bed visit in Tampa in 1987 to the dying Castro assassination plotter for the CIA, Santos Trafficante. The fading don rambled on philosophically about the epochal events of his criminal life.

He had only one regret: the assassination of the president. Killing Jack Kennedy had been a mistake, Trafficante told the lawyer, because it had brought too much pain on Jackie and the rest of the Kennedy family — for that matter, on the entire nation.

"We should have killed Bobby," said the dying don.

NOTES AND SOURCES

INTRODUCTION: GEORGE BUSH'S DEADLY SECRETS

1. "Apaches Want Geronimo's Skull Back: Bush's Father Took It, Leader Claims," *Austin American Statesman,* October 20, 1988.

2. "14 Million in Medical Aid Funneled to Central America," *The Washington Post,* December 27, 1984.

3. Letter from Senator Prescott Bush to White House aide C. D. Jackson, March 26, 1953. Bush described Mallon as "a very old and dear friend" and classmate. "I might say that Neil Mallon is well known to Allen Dulles, and has tried to be helpful to him in the CIA, especially in the procurement of individuals to serve in that important agency."

When Henry Neil Mallon died on March 2, 1983, the office of Vice President Bush issued a statement, carried by the Associated Press: "He gave me my first job and, when I started my first business, he was at my side sharing his vast experience. One of our sons, Neil Mallon Bush, was named for this wonderful man . . ."

4. George Bush with Victor Gold, *Looking Forward* (New York: Doubleday, 1987), p. 167.

5. Authors' interview with Peggy Adler Robohm, Madison, Connecticut, February 1989. Robohm has made an extensive study of Skull and Bones' secret rosters.

6. "Coming in from the Cold, Going Out to the Bush Campaign," *The Washington Post,* March 1, 1980.

7. Daniel Schorr, *Clearing the Air* (Boston: Houghton-Mifflin Co., 1977), p. 147.

8. John Kelly, "Agent in Place: The CIA Investigation that George Bush Blocked," *Los Angeles Weekly,* December 16, 1988; Scott Armstrong and Peter Kornbluh, "On Trial: North and Our System," *The New York Times,* February 27, 1989. See also, Scott Armstrong, et al., "Bush's Year at the CIA," *Mother Jones,* October, 1988.

---

9. Memorandum by Deputy Assistant Attorney General, Criminal Division, U.S. Department of Justice, Robert L. Keuch, October 14, 1976.

10. Letters by CIA Director George Bush to Richard Helms and John McCone, October 13, 1976.

11. Letter by John McCone to George Bush, November 18, 1976. McCone wrote Bush that parts of a memorandum by a CIA official he had been asked to read aloud to the criminal grand jury "contradicted [the official's] own as well as several others' sworn testimony before the Church committee."

12. Memorandum For The President, by White House Counsel Phillip Buchen, October 22, 1976.

13. Joe Conason, "Company Man: Bush Got Help in 1980 from CIA Agents," *Village Voice,* October 25, 1988, p. 21; "Two Ex-Officials Trade Claims of Lying, Spying," Los Angeles *Times,* July 8, 1983.

14. *The New York Times,* July 7, 1983. For a general reference to the theft of Carter's briefing book and other dirty tricks in the 1980 campaign see Jody Powell, *The Other Side of the Story* (New York: Morrow, 1984), pp. 274–89.

15. Pete Brewton, "D.C. Bank Swept Up in Intrigue, Funds Channeled to North Account," Houston *Post,* June 10, 1990.

16. *Ibid.*

17. "Agent in Place: The CIA Investigation that George Bush Blocked," *Los Angeles Weekly,* December 16, 1988.

18. John Ranelagh, *The Agency: The Rise and Decline of the CIA* (New York: Simon & Schuster, 1987), pp. 545, 644. Turner fired 820 "cowboys," reducing the ranks of covert operatives to 400 from approximately 1200.

19. "U.S. Declines to Probe Afghan Drug Trade," *The Washington Post,* May 13, 1990.

20. Lawrence Lifschultz, "Bush, Drugs, and Pakistan: Inside the Kingdom of Heroin," *The Nation,* November 14, 1988.

21. *The Nation ibid.;* and authors' interview with Jack Blum, chief counsel to the Kerry Subcommittee on Terrorism, Narcotics, and International Operations, U.S. Senate. New York City, 1989.

22. John Cummings, "Miami Confidential," *Inquiry,* August 3, 1981; and "NBC Nightly News" interview with Richard Gregorie, February 22, 1989. Gregorie led the war on drugs for eight years in the U.S. Attorney's Office in Miami, but resigned in disgust in January 1989 stating that opposition from Washington made it almost impossible to pursue key cocaine bosses. "I am finding the higher we go, the further I investigate matters involving Panama, high level corruption in Colombia, in Honduras, in the Bahamas, they are concerned that we are going to cause a problem in the foreign policy areas and that is more important than stopping the dope problem," Gregorie said. "We are not being allowed to win this war."

23. Michael Defeo, et al., "Lucien Conein and DEA Office of Intelligence" and "CIA Training of DEA Personnel," Report to the Attorney General, June 13, 1975.

24. John Kelly, *Op. cit.,* and authors' interview with CIA researcher John Hill, March 3, 1990.

25. Peter Dale Scott and Jonathan Marshall, *Cocaine Politics,* (Berkeley: University of California Press, 1991), p. 28.

26. Authors' interview with Jack Blum, October 17, 1989.

27. Jonathan Kwitny, "The Mexian Connection: A Look at an Old George Bush Venture," *Barron's,* September 19, 1988.

28. *Ibid.*

29. Richard Ryan, "The Mistress Question," *Los Angeles Weekly,* October 14, 1988.

30. Tim Wheeler, "The Bush File: The Coverup," *People's Daily World,* July 14, 1988; and Theodore Draper, *A Very Thin Line* (New York: Hill and Wang, 1991), pp. 82–83.

31. *New Republic,* July 23, 1990.

32. Holly Sklar, *Washington's War on Nicaragua* (Boston: South End Press, 1988), p. 289. See also Peter Dale Scott, "Northwards With North: Bush, Counterterrorism, and the Continuation of Secret Power," *Social Justice,* XVI 2, Summer 1989.

33. Theodore Draper, *Op. cit.,* p. 578. Brooks was the first to call North's operation a "government within the government."

34. Scott and Marshall, pp. 159–61.

35. Authors' interview with Peter Dale Scott, November 27, 1989.

36. "Shooting Deepens Mystery of Itinerant Spy," Miami *Herald,* May 13, 1990.

37. *Drugs, Law Enforcement, and Foreign Policy,* Report from the Kerry Senate Subcommittee on Terrorism, Narcotics and International Operations, pp. 75–78; see also Penny Lernoux, *In Banks We Trust* (New York: Doubleday, 1984), pp. 144–68.

38. See Chapter 9 in this book, pp. 293–94.

39. The National Security Archive, *The Chronology: The Documented Day-by-Day Account of the Secret Military Assistance to Iran and the Contras* (New York: Warner Books, 1987), pp. 69, 152–53, 171, 338.

40. "Gregg, Rodriguez, and 'Contradictions': Ambassador-Designate's Statements Key Concerning Bush's Knowledge of North Operation," *The Washington Post,* May 22, 1989. See also "Bush Staff Got Calls About Contra Plane," *The New York Times,* December 16, 1986, and *The Washington Post,* November 1, 1986.

41. "Inquiry Sought in CIA's Alleged Use of Drug Ranch," *The Washington Post,* July 6, 1990.

42. "Lawyers Say Government Refused to Prosecute Drug Smuggler," *Los Angeles Times,* August 19, 1988; see also Scott and Marshall, p. 41.

43. Hearing Record of the Kerry Senate Subcommittee onTerrorism, Narcotics and International Operations, U.S. Senate, Washington, D.C., April 13, 1989, Vol. 1: The Contras, U.S. Government Funds and Drug-Linked Firms, p. 118. Honduran drug trafficker Juan Ramon Matta Ballesteros's SETCO Air was paid $185,924.25 by the U.S. State Department for air transport services for "humanitarian assistance" to the Contras. The most complete account of Contra terrorism is in Reed Brody, *Contra Terror in Nicaragua: Report of a Fact-finding Mission, September 1984–January 1985* (Boston: South End Press, 1985). See also Christopher Dickey, *With the Contras* (New York: Simon & Schuster, 1985), and Tony Avirgan and Martha Honey, *La Penca: On Trial in Costa Rica* (San Pedro, Costa Rica: Editorial Porvenir, 1987).

44. "U.S. Ties to Cuba in a Warming Trend," *The New York Times,* October 4, 1987.

45. White House Press Release, May 22, 1989.

46. Jane Franklin, *The Cuban Revolution and the United States: A Chronologial History* (Melbourne: Ocean Press, published in association with the Center for Cuban Studies, 1992), pp. 233–54.

47. Lynn Geldof, *Cubans: Voices of Change* (New York: St. Martin's Press, 1992), p. 34.

48. "Miami Mystery," *The Wall Street Journal,* August 9, 1988.

49. "HMO Czar Charmed VIPs," Miami *Herald,* December 20, 1987.

50. *Ibid.*

51. "Jeb Bush's Firm Got $75,000 from IMC," Miami *Herald,* March 4, 1988.

52. *Op. cit.,* Miami *Herald,* December 20, 1987.

53. *Op. cit., The Wall Street Journal,* August 9, 1988.

54. *Ibid.*

55. *Ibid.*

56. *Ibid.*

57. "Cuban Linked to Terror Bombings Is Freed by Government in Miami," *The New York Times,* July 18, 1990.

58. Franklin, p. 223, 250; *The New York Times, ibid.*

59. *The New York Times, ibid.*

60. Lernoux, p. 152.

61. The story of the Nugan Hand Bank is told in Jonathan Kwitny's *The Crimes of Patriots: A True Tale of Dope, Dirty Money, and The CIA* (New York: W. W. Norton, 1987). For a synopsis see Lernoux, pp. 63–76.

62. Cummings, *Inquiry.*

63. Lernoux, p. 153; Scott and Marshall, pp. 30–31.

64. John Dinges and Saul Landau, *Assassination on Embassy Row* (New York: Pantheon, 1980), p. 251.

65. *Ibid.,* pp. 181–86.

66. The coverup of the Letelier assassination is unraveled in the Dinges and Landau book, and in Taylor Branch and Eugene M. Propper, *Labyrinth* (New York: Viking, 1982), and Donald Freed with Fred Landis, *Death in Washington* (Westport, Conn.: Lawrence Hill, 1980).

67. Armstrong, et al., *Mother Jones.*

68. Freed, p. 153.

69. Dinges and Landau, p. 269.

70. Freed, p. 155.

71. Dinges and Landau, p. 264.

72. Scott and Marshall, p. 27.

73. *Ibid.,* p. 200. The five founders of CORU who later joined the Contras were Frank Castro, Luis Posada Carriles, Jose Dionisio Suarez, Armando Lopez Estrada, and Juan Perez Franco.

74. "U.S. in New Bid to Oust Noriega," Los Angeles *Times,* November 16, 1989.

PROLOGUE: A SWIM FOR HAVANA

1. See, generally, Hugh Thomas, *Cuba: The Pursuit of Freedom* (New York: Harper & Row, 1971); and Philip W. Bonsal, *Cuba, Castro, and the United States* (Pittsburgh: University of Pittsburgh Press, 1971), pp. 285–286.

2. This account by a former Auténtico, Eduardo Suárez-Rivas, *Un Pueblo Crucificado* (Coral Gables, Fla.: Service Offset Printers, 1964). The charge is repeated in Fulgencio Batista's memoirs *Cuba Betrayed* (New York: Vantage Press, 1962). See also Bonsal's "Cuban American Relations and the Dynamics of Cuban Politics" section. Hugh Thomas says only that Prío was "extraordinarily attracted by the idea of money," and that his brothers "were both interested in the good life as well."

3. Bonsal, *op. cit.,* p. 281.

4. Hank Messick, *Lansky* (New York: Berkley Publishing Corp., 1971), p. 153.

5. This was the famous Cayo Confites expedition of 1947, an exemplar of Caribbean intrigue. Juan Bosch, who for a brief and shining period in the 1960s headed the Dominican Republic, was involved. So was the dreaded Rolando Masferrer, who was to become a Batista enforcer and Castro's sworn enemy. Whether Castro actually made his legendary swim carrying his machine gun is less than certain; accounts differ. Masferrer, in an interview with the authors, said Castro actually escaped by land. However, Hugh Thomas in *Cuba* (p. 812) cites Bosch as confirming the swimming exploit.

6. Castro spent two years on the Isle of Pines—the island that was the inspiration for Robert Louis Stevenson's *Treasure Island,* later of less happy memory as the site of a political prison used by both the Batista and Castro regimes. Castro was freed by Batista in a general amnesty on May 15, 1955; shortly thereafter he made his way to Mexico to plan his return to Cuba.

7. Authors' interview of Carlos Prío Socarrás, Miami, April 12,1974.

8. *Ibid.*

CHAPTER I: "PLAUSIBLY DENIABLE"

1. An excellent study of U.S. Ambassador to Cuba Sumner Welles's manipulations—which were sort of the granddaddy of CIA "destabilization" tactics—during the last year of the Machado rule is by Luis E. Aguilar, *Cuba 1933: Prologue to Revolution* (Ithaca, N.Y.: Cornell Univ. Press, 1972).

2. See, for example, Ladislas Farago, *The Broken Seal* (New York: Random House, 1967), p. 55. Stimson believed in the old-fashioned credo, "The way to make men trustworthy is to trust them."

3. Editors, *Ramparts* magazine, March 1967.

4. Senate Intelligence Committee, Senate Report 94–755, April 23, 1976, Book II, pp. 98–104 and p. 107; see also Morton H. Halperin, *et al., The Lawless State* (New York: Penguin, 1976), p. 3. The CIA's antidissident Operation CHAOS logged over 300,000 names of individuals and organizations. The agency's two decades of letter-opening, between 1953 and 1973, produced according to Halperin a computerized index of nearly one and a half million names.

5. *Ibid.* CIA documents on California Peace and Freedom Party in authors' possession; see also Los Angeles *Herald-Examiner,* March 9, 1979.

6. *Ibid.*

7. Senate Intelligence Committee, Book VI, p. 265. "It's like trying to nail Jell-O to a wall," said then Senator Walter Mondale of the CIA's "plausibly deniable" strategy.

8. For example, Robert Amory, Jr., the deputy director in charge of the overt side of the CIA house, learned about the Bay of Pigs invasion over the radio.

9. Thomas Powers, "Inside the Department of Dirty Tricks," *The Atlantic,* August 1979, p. 46.

10. John Pearson, *The Life of Ian Fleming* (New York: McGraw-Hill, 1966), p. 322.

11. Peter Dale Scott, *Crime and Cover-Up* (Los Angeles: Westworks, 1977), p. 29; *Time,* April 19, 1976.

CHAPTER 2: THE GANGSTER AS JAMES BOND

1. David C. Martin, *Wilderness of Mirrors* (New York: Harper & Row, 1980), p. 121. For Roselli's criminal background see, for example, Ed Reid, *The Grim Reapers* (Chicago: Henry Regnery, 1969), pp. 294–95. The story of his involvement with the CIA in assassination plots against Castro was compiled from a number of sources, primarily former Los Angeles Assistant U.S. Attorney David Nissen, who prosecuted Roselli (telephone interview, June 24, 1974); columnists Jack Anderson and Les Whitten, who furnished notes of their 1971 interview of Roselli; and Senate Select Committee to Study Governmental Operations with Respect to Intelligence Activities, *Alleged Assassination Plots Involving Foreign Leaders,* Senate Report No. 94–465, November 20, 1975, hereafter referred to as Senate Assassination Plots Report (Harvey's note to himself appears on p. 183 of that report), and additional sources.

2. Robert A. Maheu, deposition, *Maheu v. Howard Robard Hughes et al.,* U.S. District Court, Los Angeles.

3. *Ibid.*

4. *Ibid.*

5. *The Washington Post,* June 9, 1975.

6. Senate Assassination Plots Report, p. 72.

7. Leonard Mosley, *Dulles* (New York: The Dial Press, 1978), pp. 485–86.

8. Senate Assassination Plots Report, p. 72.

9. David Wise and Thomas B. Ross, *The Espionage Establishment* (New York: Random House, 1970), p. 130.

10. David Atlee Phillips, *The Night Watch* (New York: Atheneum, 1977), p. 91.

11. Robert Sam Anson, *They've Killed the President* (New York: Bantam Books, 1975), p. 297.

12. *CBS Morning News,* July 28, 1975; cited in Anson, *op. cit.,*p. 297.

13. Jack Anderson, "Merry-Go-Round," San Francisco *Chronicle,* January 4, 1978.

14. Senate Assassination Plots Report, p. 46.

15. *Ibid.,* p. 13.

16. *Ibid.,* p. 74.

17. Authors' interview of William Pawley, Miami, November 27, 1963.

18. *CBS Reports.* "The CIA's Secret Army," June 10, 1977.

19. Rufo López-Fresquet, *My Fourteen Months with Castro* (Cleveland: World, 1966), p. 110.

20. Senate Assassination Plots Report, p. 92.

21. *Ibid.*

22. Interview with Richard M. Bissell, *CBS Reports, op. cit.*

23. Senate Assassination Plots Report, p. 74.

24. *Ibid.*

25. Howard Kohn, "The Hughes-Nixon-Lansky Connection," *Rolling Stone,* May 20, 1976.

26. Senate Assassination Plots Report, pp. 76–77.

27. *Ibid.,* pp. 79–80.

28. *Ibid.,* p. 80.

29. *Ibid.,* pp. 76–77.

30. Authors' interview of Andrew St. George, New York, April 23, 1974.

31. San Diego *Union,* interview of Herbert Klein, March 25, 1962.

32. E. Howard Hunt, *Give Us This Day* (New York: Arlington House, 1973), p. 38.

33. Senate Assassination Plots Report, p. 93.

34. *Ibid.*

35. Authors' interview of William Pawley.

36. Wise and Ross, *op. cit.,* p. 13.

37. Paul Meskil, "In Havana, Rooms Under the Pool," New York *Daily News,* June 20, 1975.

38. Paul Meskil, "CIA's Mata Hari Stole Castro's Secrets," New York *Daily News* as reprinted in the San Francisco *Chronicle,* April 20, 1975.

39. Authors' interview of Frank Sturgis, Miami, April 11, 1974.

40. Meskil, "CIA's Mata Hari."

41. Phillips, *op. cit.,* pp. 97–98.

42. Andrew St. George, "Confessions of a Watergate Burglar," *True,* August 1974.

43. Hunt, *op. cit.* pp. 62–65, 73.

44. Authors' interview of Lyman Kirkpatrick, Providence, Rhode Island, April 26,1974. Kirkpatrick contracted polio while on CIA assignment in the Middle East in 1950 and after his confinement to a wheelchair was named Inspector General.

45. José Torres, "The Dilemma of White Skin," *Village Voice,* August 27, 1980.

46. Lyman K. Kirkpatrick, *The Real CIA* (New York: Macmillan, 1968), pp. 168–69.

47. *Ibid.,* p. 175.

48. Authors' interviews of Andrew St. George, New York City, April 23, 1974, March 6, 1975.

49. *Ibid.*

CHAPTER 3: "THE FISH IS RED"

1. Drew Pearson, "Merry-Go-Round," San Francisco *Chronicle,* May 10, 1961.

2. Thomas P. McCann, *An American Company: The Tragedy of United Fruit* (New York: Crown, 1976), pp. 93–94.

3. Albert C. Persons, *Bay of Pigs* (Birmingham, Alabama: The Kingston Press, 1968), p. 4.

4. *Ibid.,* p. 29.

5. Authors' interview of W. Robert Plumlee, San Francisco, January 19, 1976.

6. Hunt, *op. cit.,* p. 62.

7. Authors' interview of Victor Marchetti, Washington, D.C., November 24, 1973.

8. Taylor Branch and George Criles III, "The Kennedy Vendetta," *Harper's* magazine, August 1975.

9. Persons, *op. cit.,* p. 31.

10. York (Pennsylvania) *Gazette and Daily,* November 25, 1960.

11. For an account of the U.S. press role in Vietnam, see Warren Hinckle, *If You Have a Lemon, Make Lemonade* (New York: Putnam, 1974), pp. 145–65.

12. There is a full discussion of the shameful treatment of Hilton in an article by David Horowitz, *Ramparts,* October 1969.

13. Victor Bernstein and Jesse Gordon, "The Press And The Bay of Pigs," *Columbia University Forum,* Fall 1967, quoting Clifton Daniel's 1966 speech before the World Press Institute. Bernstein and Gordon's essay is an excellent study of the American press's less-than-glorious Bay of Pigs performance. Bernstein was managing editor of *The Nation* in 1961 when the establishment media ignored its story about the forming invasion.

14. *Editor and Publisher,* February 2, 1963.

15. *The Washington Post,* April 27, 1961.

16. *Washington Monthly,* April 1973.

17. Senate Assassination Plots Report, pp. 123–24.

18. Messick, *op. cit.,* p. 189.

19. Smathers tape in the John F. Kennedy Library, made available in 1970.

20. Senate Assassination Plots Report, p. 186.

21. Roy Norton, "The CIA's Worldwide Kill Squads," *Saga,* June 1970.

22. L. Fletcher Prouty, "The Betrayal of JFK Kept Fidel Castro in Power," *Gallery,* August 1976.

23. Jay Mallin, "The Call to Arms That Never Came," Miami *Herald Sunday Magazine.* March 10, 1974.

24. Authors' interview of Gerry Patrick Hemming, Miami, November 28, 1973. See also Mallin, *op. cit.,* and Andrew St. George, "The Untold Story Behind the Bay of Pigs Disaster," *Parade,* April 12, 1964.

25. Senate Assassination Plots Report, pp. 81–82.

26. *Ibid.,* p. 81.

27. Hunt, *op. cit.,* p. 84.

28. *Ibid.*

29. Authors' telephone interview of staff investigator Michael Ewing, House Select Committee on Assassinations, November 10, 1978.

30. Senate Assassination Plots Report, p. 80.

31. Hunt, *op. cit.,* pp. 160–61.

32. Senate Assassination Plots Report, p. 82.

33. Hunt, *op. cit.,,* pp. 184–85.

34. Frank Mankiewicz, *Perfectly Clear* (New York: Popular Library, 1973), p. 153.

35. Denny Walsh in the *Sacramento Bee.* June 1, 1975. Walsh, a specialist on organized crime, cited a former CIA employee as his source.

36. Kohn, *op. cit.*

37. *Time,* June 16, 1975.

38. Senate Assassination Plots Report, p. 97.

39. Paul Grabowicz and Joel Kotlin, "The CIA Puts Its Money Where Its Friends Are," *New Times* November 27, 1978.

40. Haynes Johnson, *The Bay of Pigs* (New York: Norton, 1964), p. 69.

41. Authors' interview of James Wilcott, Concord, California, February 1979, and Wilcott testimony before House Select Committee on Assassinations, March 26, 1978.

42. Persons, *op. cit.,* p. 45.

43. Hunt, *op. cit.,* pp. 188–89.

44. Johnson, *op. cit.,* p. 85.

45. Persons, *op. cit.,* pp. 47–48.

46. The Cuban Government, material furnished to the authors, January 1979.

47. Johnson, *op. cit.,* p. 85.

48. Persons, *op. cit.,* p. 49.

49. Anthony Sampson, *The Sovereign State of ITT* (New York: Fawcett Crest, 1974), pp. 256, 271, 274–76.

50. Hunt, *op. cit.,* pp. 196–200.

51. Haynes Johnson, *The Bay of Pigs* (New York: Dell, 1964), p. 97. For Howard Hunt's version of the broadcast, see Hunt's *Give Us This Day,* p. 201.

52. Hunt, *op. cit.,* p. 189.

53. Phillips. *op. cit.,* p. 108.

54. Robert F. Kennedy memorandum dictated June 1, 1961. The memorandum was among RFK papers obtained by Arthur M. Schlesinger, Jr., and published in *Robert Kennedy and His Times* (Boston: Houghton Mifflin, 1978), p. 445.

55. Persons, *op. cit.,* pp. 56–58.

56. Wise and Ross, *op. cit.,* p. 71.

57. Robert F. Kennedy memorandum, *op. cit.*

CHAPTER 4: OPERATION MONGOOSE

1.. Richard M. Nixon, *Memoirs* (New York: Grosset & Dunlap, 1978), pp. 234–35.

2. Authors' interview of FBI agent assigned to Cuba Desk, New York, April 23, 1974.

3. McCann, *op. cit.,* p. 94.

4. David Wise and Thomas B. Ross, *The Invisible Government* (New York: Random House, 1964), p. 183.

5. *Ibid.*

6. Authors' interview of Lyman B. Kirkpatrick, Jr., Providence, Rhode Island, April 26, 1974

7. Branch and Criles, *op. cit.*

8. *Ibid.*

9. Hunt, *op. cit.,* p. 213.

10. Schlesinger, Jr., *op. cit.,* p. 324.

11. Johnson, *op. cit.,* p. 75.

12. Senate Assassination Plots Report, p. 135.

13. *U.S. News & World Report,* "A Refugee Leader Blames U.S. For 'Broken Promise'," April 29, 1963.

14. Senate Assassination Plots Report, p. 202.

15. *The New York Times,* "Kennedy's Fears of Foreign Assassinations," July 23, 1975.

16. Bo Burlingham, "The Other Tricky Dick," *Esquire,* November 1975.

17. Tad Szulc, "Cuba on Our Mind," *Esquire,* February 1974. Szulc wrote the article from notes he had taken during the discussion with JFK. Richard Goodwin, who sat in, vouched for the accuracy of Szulc's report.

18. Report of Officer G. M. Zenoz, Intelligence Unit, Miami Police Department, April 3, 1963. Zenoz questioned Balbuena in connection with a bombing.

19. Interview of Luis Balbuena, April 24, 1968, by Gordon Home, Senate Subcommittee on Administrative Practice and Procedure, conducted in Miami.

20. Senate Assassination Plots Report, p. 141.

21. Philip Agee, *Inside the Company: CIA Diary* (London: Penguin Books, 1975), pp. 123, 168, 196.

22. *The Times* (London), *The New York Times,* and *El Tiempo,* September 25, 1961.

23. *U.S. News & World Report,* October 29, 1962.

24. Senate Assassination Plots Report, pp. 117–18.

25. *Ibid.,* p. 136.

26. Fletcher Knebel, "Washington in Crisis," *Look,* December 18, 1962.

27. Senate Assassination Plots Report, p. 140.

28. Branch and Criles, *op. cit.*

29. Burlingham, *op. cit.*

30. Pearson, *op. cit.,* pp. 321–23.

31. Senate Assassination Plots Report, p. 142.

32. *Ibid.,* p. 140.

33. *Ibid.,* p. 139.

34. Bradley Earl Ayers. *The War That Never Was* (Indianapolis: Bobbs-Merrill, 1976), p. 26.

35. Wise and Ross, *The Invisible Government,* pp. 334–35.

36. Ayers, *op. cit.,* p. 29.

37. Interview of Fernando Fernández by Bernard Fensterwald, Jr., Miami, 1968.

38. Branch and Criles, *op. cit.*

39. For Hendrix's relationship with the CIA, see Sampson, *op. cit.,*p. 256. Hendrix later went to work for ITT and was a key figure in that company's collaboration with the CIA in the campaign to dislodge Salvador Allende in Chile.

40. Authors' interview of W. Robert Plumlee.

41. Authors' interview of Frank Sturgis.

42. Fort Lauderdale *News,* June 16, 1963.

43. Andrew St. George, "Confessions of a Watergate Burglar."

44. *Ibid.*

45. Branch and Criles, *op. cit.*

46. Johnson, *op. cit.,* pp. 261–62.

47. *Ibid.*

48. Senate Assassination Plots Report, p. 141.

49. *Ibid.,* p. 144.

50. *Ibid.,* pp. 164–65.

51. *Ibid.,* p. 84.

52. *Ibid.,* pp. 143–44.

53. *Ibid.,* p. 83.

54. *Ibid.,* p. 84.

55. *Ibid.,* pp. 132–33.

56. *Ibid.,* p. 128.

57. *Ibid.,* p. 131.

58. *Ibid.,* pp. 132–33.

59. *Ibid.,* p. 134.

60. Karl Meyer and Tad Szulc, *The Cuban Invasion* (New York: Praeger, 1963), p. 57.

61. *The New York Times,* July 23, 1975.
62. *Ibid.*
63. *Ibid.*
64. *The New York Times*, August 27 and 30, 1962.
65. CIA dispatch 12395, November 8, 1963.
66. House Select Committee on Assassinations, final report, 1979. Vol. 9, p. 82.
67. Branch and Criles, *op. cit.*
68. Senate Assassination Plots Report, p. 148.
69. *Ibid.,* p. 170.

CHAPTER 5: THE SECRET OF THE BROTHERS KENNEDY

1. Teamster leader Harold Gibbons recounting a conversation with Joseph Kennedy, Sr. Steven Brill, *The Teamsters* (New York: Pocket Books, 1979), p. 30.

2. Campbell worked under the cover of Marine Engineering and Training Corporation of Homestead, Florida; the 1962 incorporation papers gave its business as "offshore surveys." In addition to being an operational cover, MET was used for recruitment and training of CIA seagoing commandos. Cuban frogmen used in CIA infiltrations were signed up by the company and sent north for advanced underwater demolition training at a secret base called Isolation Tropic, located at an old Navy seaplane port on the Pasquolank River near Elizabeth City, North Carolina.

3. Authors' interview of "Pepe," a former gunner's mate on the *Rex,* Miami, December 3, 1973

4. Authors' interview of Robert K. Brown, Washington, November 24, 1973; authors' interview of Gerry Hemming; authors' interview of Martin F. X. Casey, Miami, November 29, 1973; authors' interview of Jay Mallin, Miami, April 11, 1974.

5. Senate Assassination Plots Report, pp. 172–73.

6. *The New York Times,* November 7, 1963.

7. *Ibid.*

8. *The New York Times*, November 1, 1963.

9. Fort Lauderdale *News,* November 1, 1963.

10. Miami Beach *Daily Sun,* March 1, 1967.

11. *Cuba, The U.S. & Russia 1960–63* (New York: Facts on File, 1964), p. 122.

12. Al Burt, "The Mirage of Havana," *The Nation,* January 25, 1965.

13. Authors' interview of Harry Williams, Fort Lauderdale, November 28, 1973.

14. *Ibid.*

15. Kenneth P. O'Donnell and David F. Powers, *"Johnny, We Hardly Knew Ye"* (Boston: Little Brown, 1970), pp. 276–77.

16. Authors' interview of Harry Williams.

17. *Ibid.*

18. *Cuba, The U.S. & Russia 1960–63*, p. 107.

19. Richard Russell, "Three Witnesses," *New Times,* June 24, 1977.

20. *Cuba, The U.S. & Russia 1960–63*, pp. 126–27.

21. *Life,* April 12, 1963.

22. *Cuba, The U.S. & Russia 1960–63*, p. 126.

23. *Ibid.,* p. 131.

24. Authors' interview of Martin Casey; authors' interview of Howard K. Davis, Miami, February 23, 1974.

25. Harold H. Martin, " 'Help Us Fight!' Cry the Angry Exiles," *Saturday Evening Post,* June 8, 1963.

26. Authors' interview of Gerry Patrick Hemming.

27. *Ibid.*

28. Jack Anderson, "Merry-Go-Round," San Francisco *Chronicle,* May 4, 1963.

29. Miami *Herald,* March 3, 1963. Rosenberg later bought the Los Angeles Rams.

30. Report of officer G. M. Zenoz, Intelligence Unit, Miami Police Department, March 3, 1963.

31. Ashman later wrote two thin muckraking books, *Kissinger: The Adventures of Super-kraut* and *The Best Judges Money Can Buy.* In 1974 he reportedly was subsidized by Vice President Rockefeller to write a hostile biography of John B. Connally, who was Richard Nixon's first choice to succeed Spiro Agnew.

32. Authors' interview of Gerry Patrick Hemming.

33. U.S. National Archives Warren Commission conference with Isaac Don Levine, May 28, 1964, p. 2.

34. Drew Pearson, *Diaries 1949–1959* (New York: Holt, Rinehart & Winston, 1974), pp. 461–62.

35. Authors' interview of Andrew St. George.

36. *Ibid.*

37. Authors' interviews of Gerry Patrick Hemming and Howard K. Davis. Also Robert K. Brown and Miguel Acoca, "The Bayo-Pawley Affair," *Soldier of Fortune,* February 1976.

38. *Ibid.*

39. *Ibid.*

40. Interview of William D. Pawley, Miami *Herald,* January 8, 1976.

41. *Ibid.*

42. Authors' interview of William D. Pawley; also Hemming.

There was more to come, a twist as bizarre as the *Flying Tiger* story itself. In January 1976 the authors published the first account of the *Flying Tiger* affair in movie producer Francis Ford Coppola's short-lived experimental weekly, *City of San Francisco.* The wire services picked up the story. In Phoenix and Los Angeles two men, neither known to the other, read the news accounts of the authors' story. Both contacted us, anxious to add what they knew. One was Bob Plumlee, the CIA contract pilot under Dodge Corporation cover. The other was Loren E. Hall, once an Interpen instructor who had worked with Eddie Bayo. The information each gave us separately fit together perfectly. It concerned the ongoing plans to assassinate Fidel Castro. It provided an entirely different interpretation of the purpose of the *Flying Tiger* mission.

First, Hall's story. Swarthy, tough-talking Loren "Skip" Hall soldiered in the revolution, but not long after victory he found himself behind bars in Havana after choosing the wrong side in a political dispute. Among his fellow Americans in the prison were Santos Trafficante and John Martino, who had got caught installing security devices in Trafficante's Deauville casino. When Martino was finally released in late 1962, Hall was already working with Interpen. It was a reunion with a purpose—the demise of Fidel Castro. And the man who just might pull it off was the macho Alpha 66 commando Eddie Bayo.

Loren Hall called to say that William Pawley had been conned—that Bayo's real intent on the "kidnap" mission was to collect the balance of a $30,000 Mafia bounty on Castro. When Hall read the wire service story of our account of the *Flying Tiger* affair, he said he almost dropped his coffee. It said that Bayo told Pawley that *Life* was coming along because the magazine had given him $15,000 for equipment, but that former *Life* executive George Hunt, who confirmed our story of *Life*'s involvement in the *Flying Tiger* plot, flatly denied that Bayo had been handed so much as a dime from the picture book. Hunt was right, Hall insisted; he said the $15,000 had come, instead, from the Mafia.

Hall claimed that in February 1963 he sat in on a meeting between Martino and Bayo and two of his Cubans during which Sam Giancana showed up and offered a $30,000 prize for killing Castro. After further negotiations with Trafficante, Bayo was paid a $15,000 advance.

A good chunk of the money was used to buy explosives and the components for electronic devices to detonate them from a distance, Hall said. Bayo planned to "blow all to hell" the Presidential Palace while Castro was in it, and the Ministry of Agriculture Building for good measure. Martino, the electronics expert, rigged the devices.

Loren Hall also provided a conclusion of sorts to the saga of Eddie Bayo. He said that Bayo's brother-in-law, Luis Castillo, eventually received word from a source in Cuba that the Bayo group had been ambushed by Cuban militia after landing from the *Flying Tiger*. Bayo and two others slipped away and got to Havana but were captured there and put in La Cabaña prison. The report seemed credible because Castillo had once been a guard at La Cabaña.

Hall said that he and several of the Interpen Cubans decided to break Bayo out of La Cabaña and blow up Castro while they were there. This mission of mercy and vengeance came to an inglorious end in October, when customs agents stopped Hall near the Interpen base at No Name Key and seized his trailer full of munitions.

43. Senate Assassination Plots Report, p. 84.

44. Ayers, *op. cit.,* pp. 36–38.

45. Information supplied by the Cuban government, January 1978.

46. Ayers, *op. cit.,* p. 95.

47. Robert D. Morrow, *Betrayal* (Chicago: Henry Regnery Co., 1976), pp. xiii–xiv.

48. 1971 memorandum of interview of Kohly in Washington, D.C., by Bernard Fensterwald, Jr.

49. Morrow, *op. cit.,* p. 80.

50. *Washington Observer,* October 1, 1966.

51. *The New York Times,* October 3, 1963.

52. House Select Committee on Assassinations, final report, *op. cit.,* p. 98.

53. *Ibid.,* p. 100.

54. Miami *News,* May 6, 1963.

55. House Select Committee on Assassinations, *op. cit.,* p. 101.

56. *Ibid.,* p. 100.

57. Miami *Herald,* February 4, 1960.

58. House Select Committee on Assassinations, *op. cit.,* p. 101.

59. Ayers,m *op. cit.,* p. 57.

60. *Ibid.*

61. *Ibid.*

62. *The New York Times,* June 21 and 22, 1963.

63. *Ibid.,* July 1, 1963.

64. Bradley Earl Ayers, *The War That Never Was* (Canoga Park, California: Major Books, 1979), pp. 182–83.

65. Senate Assassination Plots Report, pp. 107–08.

66. Authors' interview of John V. Nolan, Washington, D.C., April 4, 1974.

67. Senate Assassination Plots Report, pp. 17 and 19.

68. *Ibid.,* p. 18.

69. Ayers, *op. cit.,* pp. 196–97.

70. *Ibid.,* pp. 197–98.

71. *Ibid.,* pp. 218–19.

72. *Ibid.,* pp. 220–21.

73. Branch and Criles, *op. cit.*

74. James Wechsler, "JFK and Castro: Lost History?" New York *Post,* March 9, 1967.

75. William Attwood, *The Reds and the Blacks* (New York: Harper & Row, 1967), p. 142.

76. *Ibid.*

77. Senate Assassination Plots Report, pp. 173–74.

78. Attwood, *op. cit.,* pp. 143–44.
79. *Ibid.,* p. 144.

CHAPTER 6: THE MYSTERY OF 544 CAMP STREET

1. William McLaney made the remark to New Orleans District Attorney Jim Garrison in 1967, according to Garrison in an interview with the authors at the time.
2. Senate Select Committee to Study Governmental Operations with Respect to Intelligence Activities: "Final Report of the Investigation of the Assassination of President John F. Kennedy: Performance of the Intelligence Agencies." Released May 26, 1976.
3. House Select Committee on Assassinations, final report, *op. cit.,* p. 90.
4. Russell, *op. cit.*
5. New Orleans *States-Item,* May 5, 1967.
6. Interview of Ronnie Caire, New Orleans District Attorney's Office, February 28, 1967.
7. New Orleans *States-Item,* April 25, 1967.
8. Interview of Ricardo Davis, New Orleans District Attorney's Office, February 28, 1967.
9. Authors' telephone interview of Jerry Milton Brooks, January 16, 1969.
10. *Ibid.*
11. Warren Commission Hearings, Vol. 10, pp. 77, 85.
12. House Select Committee on Assassinations, *op. cit.,,* p. 209.
13. Interviews of Mrs. Mary Banister, New Orleans District Attorney's Office, April 29–30, 1967, and George Higgenbothan, April 12 and 16–17, 1967.
14. House Select Committee on Assassinations, *op. cit.,* pp. 175 and 703.
15. *Ibid.,* pp. 170–71.
16. Anthony Summers, *Conspiracy* (New York: McGraw-Hill, 1980), pp. 323–26.
17. *Ibid.* Also p. 333.
18. Mark Lane, *Plausible Denial* (New York: Thunder's Mouth Press, 1991), p. 332.
19. Dallas *Times-Herald,* December 11, 1966. For the DRE and Oswald, see House Select Committee on Assassinations, *op. cit.,* Vol. 9, pp. 83–84.
20. Warren Commission Hearings, Vol. 10, p. 202.
21. Warren Commission Hearings, Vol. 10, pp. 202–08, 226.
22. The CIA's practice of providing interim employment for its agents and assets is well known. It also helps those who assist its pet causes. See Peter Dale Scott, Paul L. Hoch, and Russell Stetler, editors, *The Assassinations: Dallas and Beyond* (New York: Random House, 1976) p. 287.
23. Warren Commission Report, pp. 321–34.
24. Richard H. Popkin, *The Second Oswald* (New York: Avon Books, 1966). For an extended discussion of the evidence on two Oswalds in Mexico City that has developed since Popkin's thesis, see Summers, *op. cit.,* pp. 372–85.
25. Authors' interview of Edward I. Arthur, Cardington, Ohio, March 13, 1974.
26. Authors' interview of Carroll Jarnagin, Dallas, September 21, 1966; Warren Commission Exhibit 2821.
27. FBI memorandum to the Warren Commission, March 26, 1964.
28. House Select Committee on Assassinations, *op. cit.,* p. 188; Warren Commission hearings, Vol. 25, pp. 294–95.
29. Miami *Herald,* April 1, 1977.
30. *The Washington Post,* May 16, 1976. Trafficante denied that he had ever said anything to that effect. Alemán later said that he believed Trafficante was referring to Kennedy losing the election, not the assassination.

31. James Hepburn, *Farewell America* (Vadux, Liechtenstein: Frontiers Publishing Company, 1968), pp. 251–52.

32. The authors' investigations convinced them that *Farewell America* had the disappearing-ink imprimatur of the French government all the way up to then President Charles de Gaulle. The story began in early 1968 when New Orleans DA Jim Garrison was asked by a caller representing a new European publishing house if he would be interested in seeing a manuscript on the JFK assassination. Would a rabbit like a carrot? The manuscript was a stunner. It presented the thesis that a committee composed of the CIA, the FBI, the Mafia, the American oil industry, and other powerful enemies of Kennedy had planned and executed the assassination. We concluded that the breadth of knowledge the book contained about these varied interests meant that it could not have been the work of a single author.

In conjunction with Garrison the authors of *Deadly Secrets* (then at *Ramparts* magazine) sent Steve Jaffe, a volunteer investigator, to Europe to track down the book's genealogy. The complex trail led to Paris and a veteran French intelligence officer named Hervé Lamarr. He confessed to being the author of record; he had used the nom de plume out of a flaming love for the actress Audrey Hepburn. The 'James,' he said was a take-off on *J'aime*, meaning "I love." A nice French touch, but his next one was even more impressive. Lamarr took Jaffe by the hand to the Elysée Palace and into the office of Andre Ducret, chief of the French Secret Service. Ducret disappeared for a few minutes into the adjoining office of the President and returned with de Gaulle's personal card on which he had inscribed in French, "I am very moved by the confidence you have expressed in me."

The nicely couched words confirmed that *Farewell America* was produced by the French government. From the start de Gaulle had intuitively rejected the Oswald-as-lone-nut theory. "*Vous me blaguez*," he told an American journalist. "Cowboys and Indians." In 1962 he himself had been the near-victim of a crossfire ambush staged by colonialist generals.

Clearly one intent of *Farewell America* was to promote the presidential candidacy of Robert Kennedy, but when he was assassinated in Los Angeles that project died with him. Before slipping back into the intelligence shadows, Lamarr gave the authors a film that had been made to promote the American edition of the book. The promo film incorporated the Zapruder film, which *Life* magazine had never allowed to be shown.

How had the French copped it? Richard Lubic, at the time a staffer on *Life*'s sister publication *Time*, told the authors that early in 1968 the film was missing for several days from its vault in the magazine's New York headquarters. Although the New York police gave it their best Kojack try, no suspect was ever identified. Obviously an inside job.

33. David E. Scheim, *Contract on America* (New York: Shapolsky Publishers, Inc., 1988), p. 188.

34. Warren Commission Hearings, Vol. 24, Commission Exhibit 2003, p. 202; and Peter Noyes, *Legacy of Doubt* (New York: Pinnacle Books, 1973), pp. 19–23. Noyes's investigation of the Braden angle began in 1967 when William Turner (coauthor of this book) gave him information that Braden had changed his name only two months before the assassination and used a business front called Empire Oil Company. When Turner tracked down the address of Empire Oil in Beverly Hills, a receptionist told him that Braden traveled most of the time and only stopped by to pick up mail.

Noyes discovered that two of the associates with Braden on November 21, 1963, when he visited the offices of the Hunt Oil Company, ran something called the Sunbeam Oil Company in Florida. According to the Crime Commission of Greater Miami, "The Sunbeam Oil Company has offices in Miami Beach. It appears that this is a pure 'front' for con-men schemes."

35. Ayers, *op. cit.*, pp. 235–36.

36. Jean Daniel, "When Castro Heard the News," *New Republic*, December 7, 1963.

37. Senate Assassination Plots Report, pp. 88–89, and Senate Select Committee to Study

Governmental Operations with Respect to Intelligence Activities, "Final Report: Performance of the Intelligence Agencies," pp. 1920. Dan E. Moleda, *The Hoffa Wars* (New York: Grosset & Dunlap, 1978), p. 161.

38. Steven Brill, *The Teamsters* (New York: Simon & Schuster, 1978), p. 374.

39. Authors' interview of James Wilcott.

40. Report of Lt. Francis Martello, New Orleans Police Department, November 25, 1963.

41. Ragano first told his story to columnist Jack Newfield of the New York *Post*, who printed it on January 14, 1992.

42. Joseph McBride, "The Man Who Wasn't There, 'George Bush,' CIA Operative," *The Nation*, July 16–23, 1988.

43. *Fortune*, April 1958.

44. Authors' interview of Gerry Patrick Hemming.

45. McBride, *op. cit.*

46. Warren Commission Report, Exhibits 1414, 3119.

47. Warren Commission Hearings, Vol. IX, p. 235ff. See also William W. Turner, "The Inquest," *Ramparts*, June 1967.

48. Jim Garrison, *On the Trail of the Assassins* (New York: Sheridan Square Press, 1988), pp. 79–83.

49. *Ibid.*, p. 251.

50. William W. Turner, "The Garrison Commission," *Ramparts*, January 1968.

51. *Ibid.*

52. Interview of Victor Marchetti, October 7, 1975, by Bernard J. Fensterwald, Jr., Committee to Investigate Assassinations.

53. Deposition May 17, 1979, Alexandria, Virginia; case of E. Howard Hunt vs. Alan J. Weberman, et al.

54. Peter Noyes, *op. cit.*, p. 67.

55. Warren Hinckle, *If You Have a Lemon, Make Lemonade* (New York: G. P. Putnam's Sons, 1973), pp. 263–64. See also Steve Jaffe's memo re his and William Turner's interviews with Lamarr in Paris, May 1968. Lamarr specifically named Moynihan.

56. Authors' interview of Seymour Ellison, San Rafael, California, March 28, 1980.

57. Warren Commission Document 683.

58. *The Final Assassinations Report* (New York: Bantam Books, 1979), p. 204.

59. Warren Commission Documents 59 and 961.

60. Warren Commission Exhibit 2763.

61. Warren Commission Document 395.

62. House Select Committee on Assassinations, *op. cit.*, pp. 158–59, 302–03.

63. Transcript of executive sessions, unpaginated.

64. CIA internal memorandum, September 15, 1976, obtained under the Freedom of Information Act. The memorandum, requested by then CIA Director George Bush, concerned the then recent Jack Anderson scoop that the CIA and the mob had teamed up to assassinate Castro. The story had been given to Anderson by attorney Edward P. Morgan, who was trying to thwart the deportation of his client, Johnny Roselli, by picturing him as an American patriot. (See Chapter 8.) Morgan, an ex-FBI agent, later told the House Select Committee on Assassinations that he still couldn't understand "how the CIA could have let the Warren Commission go down that road" without telling them of the anti-Castro plots. Morgan regretted that the assassination was never investigated as a straight homicide instead of as a political event.

65. Warren Commission Document 197.

66. Handwritten testimony of Richard C. Nagell dated September 19, 1966; statement of Nagell dated January 28, 1970; *Overseas Family* June 20, 1969.

67. Senate Select Committee to Study Governmental Operations, *op. cit.,* p. 315.

68. *The Final Assassinations Report, op. cit.*, p. 315.

69. Senate Select Committee to Study Governmental Operations, *op. cit.*, p. 59.

70. Russell, *op. cit.* See also Summers, op. cit., pp. 356–61. Summers traces how the House Assassinations Committee failed to pursue Veciana's startling revelations.

71. FBI interview report dated September 23, 1964, at Johnsondale, California.

72. Russell, *op. cit.*

73. Sam and Chuck Giancana, *Double Cross* (New York: Warner Books, 1992) pp. 326–35.

74. Haynes Johnson, "One Day's Events Shattered America's Hopes and Certainties," *The Washington Post*, November 20, 1983.

75. Hepburn, *op. cit.*, p. 301.

76. Schiem, *op. cit.*, p. 274.

77. Authors' telephone interview of Richard Lubic, March 18, 1968.

78. William W. Turner and Jonn G. Christian, *The Assassination of Robert F. Kennedy: A Searching Look at the Conspiracy and Cover-up* (New York: Random House, 1978), p. 64–66.

79. *Ibid.*, pp. 36–38, 50.

80. *Ibid.*, p. 265.

81. *Ibid.*, pp. 140–41.

82. Peter Noyes, *op. cit.*, p. 72.

83. Robert Houghton, *Special Unit Senator* (New York: Random House, 1970), p. 158.

84. Turner and Christian, *op. cit.*, p. 220; Scheim, *op. cit.,*, pp. 275–76.

85. Turner and Christian, *op. cit.*, pp. 316, 345–56.

86. Declaration of Michael H. L. Hecker, Ph.D., December 15, 1982, in possession of the authors.

87. Giancana, *op. cit.*

CHAPTER 7: ACROSS THE WINDWARD PASSAGE

1. Authors' interview of Andrew St. George.

2. *Ibid.*

3. Mike Wales, *Ed Arthur's Glory No More* (Westerville, Ohio: Dakar Publishing, 1975), p. 66.

4. Robert Emmett Johnson, "I Stuck Pins in a Voodoo Dictator," *True*, April 1968.

5. Andrew St. George, "The Mafia vs. the CIA," *True*, April 1970.

6. This account of the Artime-Cubela negotiations has been compiled from the Senate Assassination Plots Report, p. 178; *The New York Times*, March 6, 1966; and Havana government dispatches.

7. Johnson, *op. cit.*

8. *Ibid.*

9. Authors' interview of Carl Davis.

10. *Ibid.*

11. St. George, "The Mafia vs. the CIA."

12. *Ibid.*

13. Vincent Teresa and Thomas Renner, *My Life in the Mafia* (New York: Doubleday, 1974), p. 223.

14. St. George, "The Mafia vs. the CIA."

15. Jack Anderson with Les Whitten, "Merry-Go-Round," San Francisco *Chronicle*, April 7, 1975. The column was based on secret testimony before the Rockefeller Commission.

16. Authors' interview of Rolando Masferrer, Miami, December 5, 1973.

17. Hearings before the Special Subcommittee on Investigations, Committee on Interstate and Foreign Commerce, House of Representatives, "Network News Documentary Practices—CBS 'Project Nassau.' " Serial No. 91–55.

18. *Ibid.*, pp. 177–78.

19. *Ibid.*, p. 91.

20. *Ibid.*, p. 418, 471.

21. *Ibid.*, pp. 116–18.

22. *Ibid.*, p. 39.

23. *Ibid.*, p. 121.

24. Authors' interview of Richard Burns, Miami, December 1, 1973.

25. Robert K. Brown, "The Plot Against Papa Doc," *National Review,* January 24, 1967.

26. Special Subcommittee on Investigations, *op. cit.*, pp. 111–13.

27. The Israeli episode, as well as other details of Goldflow, were obtained in interviews with Colonel Léon in New York, March 12, 1974, and with Howard Davis and Martin Casey.

28. Miami *Herald*, December 10, 1969.

29. Authors' interview of Martin Casey.

30. Authors' interview of Howard Davis.

31. Authors' interview of Martin Casey.

32. Authors' interview of Howard Davis.

33. *Ibid.*

34. *Ibid.*

CHAPTER 8: THE OLD BOY NETWORK

1. Senate Intelligence Committee, "The Investigation of the Assassination of President John F. Kennedy," *op. cit.*, pp. 80–84.

2. Scott, *op. cit.*, p. 27.

3. Authors' interview of Victor Marchetti.

4. Les Whitten interview notes, undated.

5. Maheu deposition, *Maheu vs. Hughes.*

6. *Ibid.*

7. Edward Bennett Williams, *One Man's Freedom* (New York: Atheneum, 1962). Williams devoted an entire chapter to the Icardi case in his book.

8. *Ibid.*

9. R. Harris Smith, *OSS, The Secret History of America's First Central Intelligence Agency* (Berkeley: University of California Press, 1972), p. 369 n.

10. Maheu deposition, *Maheu vs. Hughes.* Testifying before the Senate Intelligence Committee in 1975, Maheu identified the CIA in connection with the anti-Onassis plot. See Senate Assassination Plots Report, p. 74 n.

11. *The New York Times*, March 26, 1975.

12. See "Tax Exempt Foundations, Their Impact on Small Business," hearings before Subcommittee No. 1 on Foundations, Select Committee on Small Business, House of Representatives, Eighty-eighth Congress, Second Session, August 31, 1964.

13. Jack Anderson, "Merry-Go-Round," San Francisco *Chronicle*, October 17, 1974.

14. See, for example, Messick, *op. cit.* Rothman sued Smith in Los Angeles Superior Court but dropped the suit after Nixon put the heat on.

15. *Life*, February 3, 1967; Reid, *op. cit.*, p. 119.

16. Jack Anderson, "Merry-Go-Round," San Francisco *Chronicle*, October 17, 1974.

CHAPTER 9: NIXON'S VENDETTA

1. Authors' interview of David Nissen.

2. *The New York Times*, November 30, 1969.

3. *The New York Times,* December 23, 1969.

4. Lucien K. Truscott IV, *Village Voice,* August 30, 1973.

5. Hank Messick, *Lansky* (New York: Berkeley, 1971), p. 123.

6. *Ibid.,* p. 67.

7. Alfred W. McCoy, *The Politics of Heroin in Southeast Asia* (New York: Harper & Row, 1972), p. 34.

8. *Ibid.,* pp. 44, 263–64.

9. Messick, *op. cit.,* p. 124.

10. *Ibid.*

11. Dennis Eisenberg, Uri Dan, and Eli Landau, *Meyer Lansky* (New York: Paddington Press, 1979), p. 294. See also Messick.

12. Earl Mazo, *Richard Nixon* (New York: Harper & Row, 1959), p. 15.

13. Miami *Herald,* December 16, 1971.

14. Miami *Herald,* October 15, 1971.

15. Miami *Herald,* December 17, 1971.

16. Authors' interview of participant in the China Lake project, Ridgecrest, California, September 27, 1975.

17. *Newsday,* January 6, 1977.

18. Russell, *op. cit.;* Jack Anderson, "Merry-Go-Round," San Francisco *Chronicle,* January 20, 1977.

19. Authors' interview of Gerry Patrick Hemming.

20. Authors' interview of Gerry Patrick Hemming; *Argosy* interview of Hemming, April 1976.

21. Authors' interview of Frank Sturgis.

22. Lucien K. Truscott IV, *op. cit.*

23. St. George, "Confessions of a Watergate Burglar."

24. Miami *Herald,* August 17, 1973; San Francisco *Chronicle,* June 6, 1974 and November 26, 1975.

25. Miami *Herald,* August 23, 1973.

26. *The Washington Post,* June 21, 1973.

27. Frank Mankiewicz, *Perfectly Clear* (New York: Times Books, 1973).

28. James Phelan, *Howard Hughes: The Hidden Years* (New York: Random House, 1976), p. 75.

29. St. George, *op. cit.*

30. Authors' interview of Frank Sturgis.

31. From the Nixon White House tapes. See, for example, Scott, *op. cit.,* p. 59.

CHAPTER 10: A MURDEROUS LEGACY

1. Authors' interview of Frank Sturgis.

2. Authors' interview of Andrew St. George.

3. Authors' interview of Carl Davis; *The New York Times,* January 4, 1975.

4. Authors' interview of Andrew St. George.

5. "Word from Hurd," internal publication of Mark Hurd Aerial Surveys, Inc., October 1968; authors' interview of Carl Davis.

6. Authors' interview of Carl Davis.

7. Authors' interview of Michele Ray, San Francisco, November 1967. See also Warren Hinckle, *If You Have a Lemon, Make Lemonade* (New York: G. P. Putnam's Sons, 1973), p. 279.

8. *Ibid.*

9. Hinckle, *op. cit.,* p. 284.

10. Authors' interview of St. George.

11. Authors' interview of Michele Ray.

12. *Ibid.*

13. James Cook, "The Invisible Enterprise," *Forbes,* September 29, 1980.

14. Reno (Nevada) *Evening Gazette,* January 8, 1975.

15. *Ibid.*

16. M. P. Fleischer, "Confessions of a Cuban Hit Man," *Tropic,* December 2, 1973.

17. *The Washington Post,* May 6, 1978.

18. Powers, *op. cit.*

19. Los Angeles *Times,* December 31, 1968.

20. Dick Russell, "Little Havana's Reign of Terror," *New Times,* October 29, 1976.

21. *The Washington Post,* November 22, 1976.

22. Jeff Stein, "Inside Omega 7," *The Village Voice,* March 10, 1980.

23. *Ibid.*

24. *Ibid.*

25. *CBS Reports,* "The CIA's Secret Army."

26. *The Washington Post,* May 6, 1978.

27. *The New York Times,* October 24, 1976.

28. Ron Ridenour, *Backfire: The CIA's Biggest Burn* (Havana: Jose Martí Publishing House, 1991), pp. 60–61. Mena recounted his contacts with CIA when he surfaced in 1987 as a double agent, actually working for the Cuban security service.

29. Jim Drinkhall, "IRS vs. CIA," *The Wall Street Journal,* April 18, 1980.

30. *Ibid.*

31. Interview of Gerry Patrick Hemming in *Argosy,* April 1976.

32. San Francisco *Examiner,* April 6, 1975; Wilmington (Delaware) *News Journal,* February 7, 1976. The *News Journal* reported that in 1976 Andrés Castro pleaded guilty to federal fraud charges and was sentenced to seven years. Iglesias and Yglesias disappeared and were believed out of the country. The CIA denied any part in the fraud.

33. Jeff Stein, *op. cit.*

34. *Ibid.*

35. *Ibid.*

EPILOGUE: THE DOGS OF WAR

1. Authors' interview of Mitch WerBell, Powder Springs, Georgia, 1976; authors' interview of Andrew St. George.

2. Michael Dorman, *Vesco: The Infernal Money Making Machine* (New York: Berkley Medallion, 1975), pp. 1–9.

3. *Ibid.,* p. 10.

4. Conein had a staff of nineteen, fourteen of whom were former CIA employees, according to the Defeo Report. Authored by a Justice Department employee and never released, the report raised questions about assassination plots against foreign leaders suspected of drug trafficking, and of CIA domestic operations conducted under DEA cover.

During the 1980s Vesco was reported living in obscurity in Cuba. During a *Washington Post* interview with Fidel Castro on February 3, 1985, Castro was asked about the status of the fugitive financier. He said that Vesco had come to Cuba for medical assistance, and that he had no business or economic ties of any kind with Cuba. Vesco is "simply treated as a human being," Castro said.

5. Criminal indictment No. CR 74–471A, U.S. District Court, Northern District of Georgia, Atlanta.

6. New York *Post,* October 27, 1988.

7. Eliot Asinof, Warren Hinckle, and William Turner, *The Ten Second Jailbreak* (New York: Holt, Rinehart & Winston, 1973), pp. 61–63.

8. *Ibid.* The full story of the Kaplan escape is told in this book.

9. Authors' interview of Robert K. Brown.

10. *Ibid.*

11. As published in the Miami *Herald*, March 30, 1977. The UPI dispatch was datelined Chicago.

12. *The New York Times,* June 4, 1979.

13. Russell, "Three Witnesses."

14. *Ibid.*

15. Richard Russell, "Little Havana's Reign of Terror," *New Times,* October 29, 1976.

16. Authors' interview of Frank Sturgis.

17. Miami *Herald*, September 14 and October 20, 1973.

18. *The Star*, September 7, 1976.

19. House Select Committee on Assassinations, *op. cit.*, Vol. 9, p. 93; New York *Daily News,* September 19, 1977.

20. Authors' interview of Sturgis, Martínez and González, Miami Beach, April 12, 1974.

21. Felix I. Rodriguez and John Weisman, *Shadow Warrior: The CIA Hero of a Hundred Unknown Battles* (New York: Simon & Schuster, 1989), p. 67.

22. *Ibid.*, pp. 9–10.

23. Peter Maas, *Manhunt: The Incredible Pursuit of a CIA Agent Turned Terrorist* (New York: Jove Books, 1987), p. 30.

24. Rodriguez, *op. cit.*, pp. 250–58.

25. *Ibid.*, p. 67.

26. *CBS Reports,* update "The CIA's Secret Army," January 24, 1978.

27. Ron Ridenour, *Backfire* (Havana, Cuba: José Marti Publishing House, 1991). To avoid repetitive footnotes it is here noted that the stories of these double agents are all contained in this source. Ridenour also disclosed that the double agents were equipped by the CIA with "microphones and cameras hidden in N50 Pentel pens, in cigarette lighters, briefcases with false compartments, even teddy bears." One couple was also provided with an RS-804 espionage communications set costing $250,000.

28. John M. Newman, *JFK and Vietnam: Deception, Intrigue and the Struggle for Power* (New York: Warner Books, 1992).

29. Authors' interview with Nick Pileggi, May 23, 1992.

BIBLIOGRAPHIC
NOTES

WE have made liberal use of the Senate Intelligence Committee's 1975 report concerning assassination plots against foreign heads of state, a document that has been widely cited as an example of responsiveness to the people's right to know. It would be remiss not to point out that that report issued under the chairmanship of Senator Frank Church, is as distinguished by what it omits as by what it includes. It contains not even a passing reference to the Guantánamo-based plots against both Fidel and Raul Castro shortly after the Bay of Pigs, even though the authors supplied documented information to the committee. It fails to mention the attempts on the life of François Duvalier which took place during the Johnson administration. Not a hint is given of the triple plot against Fidel Castro when he visited Chile during the Nixon tenure. One must suspect a bipartisan effort to confine the report to plots that had already been exposed.

Nevertheless the report is a prime source on those areas it did explore. So is a companion committee report released in 1976 titled "The Investigation of the Assassination of President John F. Kennedy: Performance of the Intelligence Agencies," which contains valuable information about Lee Harvey Oswald and Cuban exiles in the weeks leading up to the assassination (a certain amount of deciphering is required since, for example, the well-known Manuel Artime is disguised as "B-1," which may suggest he had a habit of gulping vitamins). The most ground-breaking of the congressional reports is that of the House Select Committee on Assassinations, which concluded its work in 1979. The volumes of the report define for the first time Oswald's link to the Mafia, and the longstanding connection of Jack Ruby with organized crime, and explore in some depth the tributaries leading to such militant exile groups as Orlando Bosch's MIRR, 30th of November, and Student Revolutionary Directorate. Bantam Books published a paperback edition of the report proper that is called, perhaps presciently, *The Final Assassinations Report* (1979).

Of the deluge of books on the JFK assassination, the authors have found these the most useful:

Hugh Thomas's thick volume *Cuba: The Pursuit of Freedom* (Harper & Row, 1971) is a standard source on prerevolutionary days and the budding counterrevolution, although care must be taken to weed out its errors. Ex-ambassador Philip Bonsal's *Cuba, Castro and the United States* (University of Pittsburgh Press, 1971) provides insights into the transitional period in Havana. The Bay of Pigs invasion has been chronicled by Haynes Johnson in *The Bay of Pigs* (Norton, 1963), Karl Meyer and Tad Szulc in *The Cuban Invasion* (Praeger, 1963) and Peter Wyden in *Bay of Pigs* (Simon & Schuster, 1979).

The only books dealing directly with post-Bay of Pigs secret operations are the first-hand accounts of Bradley Ayers in *The War That Never Was* (Bobbs-Merrill, 1976) and Edward Arthur in *Ed Arthur's Glory No More* written by Mike Wales (Dakar Publishing, Westerville, Ohio, 1975), although journalists George Criles III and Taylor Branch wrote a lengthy article on the subject, "The Kennedy Vendetta," in *Harper's* magazine (August 1975). A basic source for the story of CBS News's participation in the Haiti raids on President François Duvalier is the report of the Special Subcommittee on Investigations, Committee on Interstate and Foreign Commerce, House of Representatives, "Network News Documentary Practices — CBS 'Project Nassau' " Serial No. 91–55. The tangled financial dealings involving Richard Nixon, Bebe Rebozo, and Cuban exile money were first exposed in the short-lived *Sundance* magazine and deftly unraveled by Bob Green and his *Newsday* team in 1972.

Books on the CIA and secret operations that are on certain levels superior to the general literature on the subject are: William Blum, *The CIA: A Forgetten History: U.S. Global Intervention Since World War II* (London, Zed Books, 1986). This is the best general survey of CIA activities published to date, infinitely superior to the more famous *The Invisible Government*, which is an establishment-tainted, permissable-fact-soaked sop to the apologia that the CIA is an out of control rogue elephant rather than a mean instrument of U.S. policy.

Steven Emerson, *Secret Warriors: Inside the Covert Military Operations of the Reagan Era* (New York: Putnam, 1988) and John Prados, *Keepers of the Keys: A History of the N.S.C. from Truman to Bush* (New York: William Morrow, 1991), are cautious but in some areas interesting approaches to the elusive ways a democracy does things undemocratically.

Two fine books on the banks-business aspects of the CIA that began with the Secret War are Penny Lernoux's, *In Banks We Trust* (New York: Doubleday, 1984) and Jonathan Kwitny's, *The Crimes of Patriots* (New York: Norton, 1987). Also excellent reading on the more craven aspects of U.S. foreign policy are Kwitny's classic *Endless Enemies: The Making of an Unfriendly World* (New York: Congdon & Weed, 1984) and R. T. Taylor's, *Hot Money and the Politics of Debt* (New York: Simon and Schuster, 1987), the most sophisticated survey of the comingling of politics and dollars-in-flight.

The Secret War fed the development of narcoterrorism worldwide. On the 1970s–1980s interconnections of the CIA, anti-Castro Cubans, Latin America death squads, drug barons, and international fascism, highly recommended are Jonathan Marshall's *Drug Wars: Corruption, Counterinsurgency & Covert Operations in the Third World* (Berkeley: Cohan & Cohen, 1991), and Peter Dale Scott and Jonathan Marshall's *Cocaine Politics: Drugs, Armies and the CIA in Central America* (Berkeley: University of California Press, 1991). Earlier books that give the big picture of this whole sorry situation are Peter Dale Scott's hard-to-find *The War Conspiracy* (New York:

Bobbs Merrill, 1972) and Heinrick Kruger's *The Great Heroin Coup: Drugs, Intelligence, and International Fascism* (Boston: South End Press, 1980). Essential reading is the landmark *The Politics of Heroin in Southeast Asia* by Alfred W. McCoy (New York: Harper and Row, 1972).

A valued addition to the literature of U.S.–Cuba relations is Jane Franklin's *The Cuban Revolution and the United States: A Chronological History* (Melbourne: Ocean Press, 1992; published in association with the Center for Cuban Studies, 124 West 23rd St., New York, NY 10011).

On the topic of the Secret War against Castro, Felix I. Rodriquez has checked in from the cold on his role as a CIA contract agent and written with John Weisman, *Shadow Warrior: The CIA Hero of a Hundred Unknown Battles* (New York: Simon and Schuster, 1989). Rodriquez was involved in the Bay of Pigs and ongoing operations, hunted down Che Guevara in Bolivia under the nom de guerre Felix Ramos [see Chapter Ten], and in the Iran–Contra scandal. Not unexpectedly Rodriquez's account is selective and one-sided. Of special interest, however, is his description of being on an oral contract with the CIA without a scrap of documentation either at Langley or in his wallet.

From the other side of the ideological divide, a more interesting work is Edgar Chamorro's *Packing the Contras: A Case of CIA Disinformation* (New York: Institute for Media Analysis, 1987). A former contra leader tells how the CIA created them from ground zero, in a virtual rerun of scenarios used by the CIA in the Secret War against Cuba.

The following selected published materials the authors have also found useful:

Attwood, William, *The Reds and the Blacks.* New York: Harper & Row, 1967.

Brown, Robert K., "Phantom Navy of the CIA." *Sea Classics.* May 1975.

Burt, Al, "The Mirage of Havana." *The Nation.* January 25, 1965.

Christic Institute Declaration of Plaintiff's Consul, U.S. District

Court, Miami, Florida, March 31, 1988, *Inside the Shadow Government*. Washington, DC: Christic Institute, 1988.

Dinges, John and Saul Landau, *Assassination on Embassy Row*. New York; Viking, 1982.

Draper, Theodore, *A Very Thin Line*. New York: Hill and Wang, 1991.

Fensterwald, Bernard, Jr., and Michael Ewing. *Coincidence or Conspiracy?* New York: Zebra Books, 1977.

Garrison, Jim, *On the Trail of the Assassins: My Investigation and Prosecution of the Murder of President Kennedy*. New York: Sheridan Square Press, 1988. Garrison focuses on the CIA as the moving force.

Groden, Robert J. and Harrison Edward Livingston, *High Treason: The Assassination of President Kennedy and the New Evidence of Conspiracy*. New York: Berkeley Books, 1989. A wide-ranging book surveying many new angles of assassination research.

Hougan, Jim, *Spooks*. New York: William Morrow, 1978.

Houghton, Robert A., *Special Unit Senator*. New York: Random House, 1970.

Hunt, E. Howard, *Give Us This Day*. New York: Arlington House, 1973.

Johnson, Robert Emmett, "I Stuck Pins in a Voodoo Dictator." *True*. April 1968.

Kwitny, Jonathan, *Endless Enemies*. New York: Congdon and Weed, 1984.

Lane, Mark, *Plausible Denial: Was the CIA Involved in the Assassination of JFK?* New York: Thunder's Mouth Press, 1991.

Lopez-Fresquet, Rufo, *My Fourteen Months With Castro*. Cleveland: World, 1966.

Maas, Peter, *Manhunt*. New York: Random House, 1986.

Maheu, Robert A., deposition, *Maheu v. Howard Robard Hughes*. U.S. District Court, Los Angeles.

Mallin, Jay, "The Call To Arms That Never Came." Miami *Herald Sunday Magazine,* March 10, 1974.

Marrs, Jim, *Crossfire: The Plot That Killed Kennedy*. New York: Carroll and Graf Publishers, Inc., 1989. A thick volume that touches all the bases.

Marshall, Jonathan, Peter Dale Scott and Jane Hunter, *The Iran Contra Connection: Secret Teams and Covert Operations in the Reagan Era.* Boston: South End Press, 1987.

Melanson, Philip H., *The Robert F. Kennedy Assassination.* New York: Shapolsky Publishers, 1991.

———, *Spy Saga.* New York: Praeger, 1990.

Morrow, Robert D., *Betrayal.* Chicago: Henry Regnery, 1976.

Mosley, Leonard, *Dulles.* New York: Dial, 1977.

The National Security Archive, Laurence Chang, Glenn Baker, et al., editors, *The Chronology: Documented Day-by-Day Account of the Secret Military Assistance to Iran and the Contras.* New York: Warner Books, 1987.

Nixon, Richard M., *Memoirs.* New York: Grosset & Dunlap, 1978.

Peck, Winslow, "Death on Embassy Row," *Counterspy,* December 1976.

Persons, Albert, *Bay of Pigs,* monograph. Birmingham, Alabama: The Kingsport Press, 1968.

Phelan, James, *Howard Hughes: The Hidden Years.* New York: Random House, 1976.

Prados, John, *The President's Secret Wars.* New York: William Morrow, 1986.

Prouty, L. Fletcher, "The Betrayal of JFK Kept Fidel Castro in Power." *Gallery.* August 1976.

Ranelagh, John, *The Agency.* New York: Simon and Schuster, 1986.

Reid, Ed, *The Grim Reapers.* Chicago: Regnery, 1969.

Rodriguez, Felix I., *Shadow Warrior.* New York: Simon and Schuster, 1989.

Russell, Dick, "Three Witnesses." *New Times.* June 24, 1977.

St. George, Andrew, "Confessions of a Watergate Burglar." *True.* August 1973.

Sampson, Anthony, *The Sovereign State of ITT.* New York: Fawcett Crest, 1974.

Scheim, David E., *Contract on America.* Silver Spring, Md.: Argyle Press, 1983.

Schlesinger, Arthur, Jr., *Robert Kennedy and His Times.* Boston: Houghton Mifflin, 1978.

Scott, Peter Dale, Paul L. Hoch, and Russell Stetler, editors, *The Assassinations: Dallas and Beyond*. New York: Random House, 1976.

——, and Jonathan Marshall, *Cocaine Politics*. Berkeley: University of California Press, 1991.

——, *Crime and Cover-Up*. Los Angeles: Westworks, 1977.

Sklar, Holly, *Washington's War on Nicaragua*. Boston: South End Press, 1988.

Teresa, Vincent, and Renner, Thomas, *My Life in the Mafia*. New York: Doubleday, 1974.

Wise, David, and Ross, Thomas B., *The Invisible Government*. New York: Random House, 1964, and *The Espionage Establishment*. New York: Random House, 1970.

ABOUT THE AUTHORS

WARREN Hinckle III is the recipient of the Thomas Paine and H. L. Mencken Awards. Warren Hinckle was the editor of *Ramparts* magazine during its famous muckraking years in the 1960s. He was co-editor of *Scanlan's,* the magazine Richard Nixon hated most, editor of filmmaker Francis Ford Coppola's experimental *City of San Francisco* weekly in the 1970s, a columnist for the San Francisco *Chronicle*, and columnist and associate editor of the San Francisco *Examiner*. He is the author of seven books, including the highly acclaimed autobiography *If You Have A Lemon, Make Lemonade.* He edited *War News,* a national newspaper opposing the 1991 Gulf War, and is now editor and publisher of *Argonaut,* a literary and political journal. He lives in San Francisco and New York City with his wife, the author Susan Cheever, and their two children.

William Turner is a former ten-year veteran of the FBI and an expert on the paramilitary right in the United States. His most recent book is *The Assassination of Robert Kennedy,* written with John G. Christian. Hinckle and Turner are the co-authors of *The Ten-Second Jail Break,* which was made into the motion picture *Breakout* starring Charles Bronson.

INDEX